AF674646

Coming to Grips
with
Rural Child Work

COMING TO GRIPS WITH RURAL CHILD WORK

Edited by

NIRA RAMACHANDRAN
LIONEL MASSÜN

Foreword by

SHRI K.C. PANT
DEPUTY CHAIRMAN
PLANNING COMMISSION
GOVERNMENT OF INDIA

INSTITUTE FOR HUMAN DEVELOPMENT
&
UNITED NATIONS WORLD FOOD PROGRAMME
NEW DELHI

Published by

INSTITUTE FOR HUMAN DEVELOPMENT
IAMR Building, 3rd Floor, I.P. Estate,
Mahatma Gandhi Marg, New Delhi-110 002
Phones: 3358166, 3321610 / Fax: (011) 3319909
E-mail: ihd@vsnl.com / website: www.ihdindia.com

Distributed by

MANOHAR PUBLISHERS AND DISTRIBUTORS
4753/23, Ansari Road, Daryaganj, New Delhi
Phones: 3262796, 3289100 / Fax: (011) 3265126
E-mail: manbooks@vsnl.com / website: manbooks.com

First Published 2002
ISBN 81-900948-6-6

Laser Typesetting

Institute for Human Development
IAMR Building, I.P. Estate, Mahatma Gandhi Marg, New Delhi-110 002

Printed at

D.K. Fine Arts Press, Delhi-52

Contents

Foreword

One of the major dimensions of human development is the welfare of our children — the citizens of tomorrow. Participation by children in work is, therefore, a critical problem that confronts development planning in our country.

Indian policy makers and planners have all along been concerned with the issue of child labour. In 1954 an inquiry "Child Labour in India" conducted by the Labour Bureau of the Ministry of Labour had concluded that... "*at present, in the factory industries, child labour is not a serious problem... but there may be children below the minimum age for employment*". The National Commission on Labour (1966-69) in their recommendations had observed: "*The employment of children is indeed more of an economic problem than anything else. Nevertheless, we consider denial of opportunity to children for their development and education to be an issue of serious nature.*" In 1974, the National Policy on Children postulated, as one of its objectives, that no child under the age of 14 years shall be permitted to be engaged in a hazardous occupation and to be made to undertake heavy work. But we are still far from the goal. The Committee on Child Labour headed by Gurupadaswamy in its 1979 report recognised a distinction between 'child labour' and 'the exploitation of child labour'; though both are problems, they are of different orders.

Noting the emerging dimension of child labour, and the ineffectiveness of the existing labour legislations to deal with the problem, the Child Labour (Prohibition and Regulation) Act was enacted in 1986. It laid down procedures for deciding the employments, occupations or processes in which the employment of children should be banned. The Act bans the employment of children, below 14 years, in specified occupations and processes, and enhances penalties for violation. To implement the 1986 Act, the government adopted a 'National Policy on Child Labour' in 1987. The policy aims at action on a wide front covering the economic aspects of child work, education, health, nutrition, integrated child development, and seeks the involvement of state governments and NGOs in tackling the problem of child labour. A "National Project on Child Labour" was formulated to suitably rehabilitate the children withdrawn from employment. The National Authority for the Elimination of Child Labour (NAECL) was constituted on 26th September, 1994 under the Chairmanship of the Labour Minister to lay down policies, and to monitor and conduct the implementation of projects on child labour.

Every country faces the problem of working children at a particular stage of its demographic transition. The dimension of the problem of today is much more manageable than what confronted the country in the early 1980s. We are experiencing a decline in birth rates. At the same time, however, and fortunately so, with improvement in health services and disease control measures, child mortality rates in the zero to five years age group have also fallen sharply. Therefore, dependency rates of the young on the adult workers will decline at a much slower pace than the decline in birth rates. We can not, therefore, be complacent about the need to control the incidence of child work.

This volume, based on revised papers presented in the consultative workshop on "Food Insecurity and Child Work in Rural India" jointly organised by the Institute for Human Development and the World Food Programme, provides useful information on the status of the problem. Basic conceptual issues have been posed for examination in the food security framework. For example, whether food assistance could effectively reduce child work, and if so what sort of intervention is required. The causes of child labour, the gender dimension of child labour, inter-regional variations — in particular, the contrast between rural north and rural south India have been explored. In this process, a number of location-specific projects have been reviewed. Since these projects were initiated by funding organisations with a variety of orientations — governments at the centre and the states, ILO, UNDP and NGOs, the cross comparison of experiences and perceptions makes a study of the volume highly rewarding. Moreover, it imparts a good insight into the functioning of many government led major initiatives on nutrition (ICDS), education (mid-day meals) and food security (PDS).

This workshop focused on food insecurity as a determinant of child work in rural India and hence this volume has been organised in a perspective of "food security".

However, the question remains as to whether treatment of the problem at this stage of our development in a food security perspective alone can lead us to meaningful suggestions on the initiatives that should be taken to reduce the incidence of child work. Eventually, it is the "labour perspective" in which the policy, programmes and project level efforts have to be framed as the problem relates to work and employment. It is only in such a perspective that we can shift the larger problem of working children into its meaningful components. There is some analysis in the volume on the occupational profile of the working children. And this readily leads to the conclusion that the bulk of the 11 million working children are in agriculture related occupations. Therefore, a study of the rural labour market, land and labour productivity, shift from self-employed farmers to agricultural labour, and migration of labour to the urban informal sector, is also needed to understand the causes underlying the problem of child work.

While a comparison of the time trends in child labour across states and across rural and urban areas shows average decline in the incidence of working children, it also throws up some very disturbing trends. Child worker participation in the age group 10-14 decreased from 140 per thousand in 1993-94 to 93 in 1999-2000 in urban areas, and from 56 to 43 in rural areas. The performance of states, which were already well-off has improved even more. However, there are certain states, where the incidence of children at work increased. For example, in rural areas of Gujarat, the child worker participation rate increased from 84 in 1993-94 to 115 and from 33 to 36 in its urban areas. Urban Delhi as also rural Delhi, and urban Bihar, also show an increase in child work participation during this period. In Punjab, child labour participation has remained practically static, in contrast to the substantial decline at the all-India level. The problem of child labour in such states has to be explored further in the context of level of organisation of the labour market. By and large, the institutions for welfare of unorganised labour and some form of social security, howsoever small, are just not in place in many states, in particular for the immigrant labour households.

Mid-day meals at schools, nutrition through specialised centres or through the public distribution system make a dent on the problem of informal sector immigrants. Therefore, besides the food security perspective, other lines of exploration of the dimension of child labour have also to be explored. While a number of national level initiatives have been analysed in the volume, the National Child Labour Project, which was initiated in 1994, also needs to be evaluated. Food security framework has to be supplemented by labour security framework to understand the behavior of the labour market at locations where the incidence of child work is recording an increase.

The reasons as to why only a very few states are formulating the projects to eradicate child labour need to be examined, because national level efforts can deliver results only up to a point. Otherwise, our attention may remain oriented towards only those locations, which have been deliberately highlighted in the perspective of international trade, like Mirzapur and Sivakasi.

Parental poverty is the main cause of child labour. The family needs security other than food alone, particularly in urban areas. Hence, one has to explore the problem in a broader "social security" framework.

Out of approximately 200 million children in the age group 6 - 14 years, only 120 million are in schools, and net attendance at the primary level is only 66 per cent of enrolment. This is completely unacceptable and therefore the 10th Plan will aim at a radical transformation in this situation. A specific human development target that will be monitored during the 10th Plan, is:

"All Children in School by 2003; All Children to Complete five Years of Schooling by 2007".

The Sarva Shiksha Abhiyan, which has been launched to achieve this objective, is a strong reiteration of the country's resolve to give the highest priority to achieve this goal during the Plan period. Moreover, education has to include a strong element of 'skill development' if the family is to get some economic benefit from sending the child to school. Elementary education as a fundamental right is under the active consideration of the government.

K.C. Pant

New Delhi
October 22, 2001

Deputy Chairman
Planning Commission
India

Preface

India's economy has been progressing noticeably in the course of the last two decades. Poverty levels have been considerably reduced and agricultural production has witnessed a breakthrough. The flip side of this success is the static rate of malnutrition and persistence of child labour. Millions of children continue to be deprived of an enabling environment of adequate food, health care and schooling. Many more lose their childhood and land up in the streets, factories, teashops, or farms. India's aspiration to achieve higher growth is possible only if investments are made in the human capital. No country can move forward with half of its children undernourished, stunted, anaemic and illiterate.

Who are the most affected? Evidently, these problems are exaggerated in food insecure families. Food security is a complex problem and is influenced by food availability, vulnerability to natural disasters, access to food, and utilisation of food by the body. These three dimensions are influenced by a number of factors such as food production, poverty, livelihood access, nutritional status, health and rural infrastructure, and literacy.

Food being a basic need, poor families spend more than 70 per cent of their total income on food and yet are not able to obtain nutritionally adequate food for their families. Poor families tend to make trade-offs in order to meet their daily requirements of food and other necessities by keeping children at home or taking them out of school in order to help with time-consuming tasks involved in fulfilling food needs. They are sometimes hazardous both physically and mentally. All this unfortunately happens to the child who is not privileged to be nurtured. Girls are the worst victims of neglect and their roles are invisible.

What could be an effective strategy for addressing this problem? The obvious answer is to get children back to an environment, which provides them with good nutrition and health care and opportunities for early childhood education. There are strong links between food security and school enrolment and consequently education and child labour. This confirms the double dividend that can be reaped from free compulsory universal primary education both in the short and long terms. If it is true that the 110 million children who are not in school today are engaged in some form of child work, then education is an obvious solution. Needless to say, education helps children develop their abilities to the fullest and opens up wider avenues. It is a proven approach for reducing the incidence of child labour.

Interactions of malnourished children with their environments make children less likely to seek out, utilise and respond to available opportunities for learning. The Integrated Child Development Services (ICDS) and school feeding could provide the dual advantage of helping the concentration of children besides encouraging them to be in school. The complex nature of the problem suggests the need for a strategic combination of interventions to get the best results.

While food insecurity and malnutrition emerge as important determinants of low enrolment rates, high dropout ratios and child work, the complex inter-relationships between other explanatory variables such as adult illiteracy, lack of awareness, high dependence on agriculture, family size, social constraints, etc., do not allow for simple solutions to the issue. Addressing child labour through a holistic approach has received very little attention.

In order to understand the complexity of the issue and identify appropriate food based strategies; a workshop was jointly organised by the Institute for Human Development (IHD) and the World Food Programme (WFP). The three day consultative workshop on "Food Insecurity and Child Work in Rural India" analysed the role of food insecurity as a determinant of child work in the poorer districts of rural India and identified appropriate guidelines, criteria and mechanisms for a better programming of WFP's activities aimed at assisting governmental efforts to address the issue of child work. The workshop also identified areas for further research and in depth analysis on the role of food insecurity in rural child work.

Although, this was an entirely new way of looking at child labour, expert presentations from different parts of the country clearly pointed out the correlation between food security and child labour. It could be concluded that areas where child work exists are also areas where poverty, female illiteracy and undernutrition are high. The results of the analysis indicate the importance of food security and human development variables for reducing child labour. Both national and international experiences suggest that well designed school feeding programmes combined with health interventions and other school improvements involving the community and family can help increase retention and active learning capacity.

The workshop concluded that if food assistance has to be targeted against child work, more research is required to understand the coping mechanisms of the poorest segments of the population against food insecurity, as well as the sociological, cultural and psychological dimensions which affect school enrolment, dropout and attendance. After undertaking a fullfledged exercise of mapping the overlap of child labour and food insecurity, WFP will be glad to share with the Government of India the worldwide experiences accumulated in this field, particularly, prevailing models and approaches for the use of surplus food stocks to enhance female literacy and attendance in schools, in consonance with the suggestions made by the Prime Minister of India in his inaugural address to the Consultation on 'Towards Hunger Free India' in April 2001. This publication is just the first step towards examining the options of food assistance for preventing child work. We realise that we have a long way to go. WFP will work in close coordination with the Government of India and other major stakeholders such as ILO and UNICEF. The IHD is also deeply committed to the cause of eradicating child work and promoting schooling and has carried out a number of studies and conducted workshops/seminars in this key area either on its own or in partnership with other institutions including international organisations like WFP, UNDP, ILO, etc.

Participation by all agencies including government officials, international organisations, NGOs and academicians and social activists was promising. Our sincere thanks to all, who made this endeavour a great success.

Alakh N. Sharma
Director
Institute for Human Development
New Delhi

Pedro Medrano
Country Director
World Food Programme
of the United Nations
New Delhi

Editors' Preface and Acknowledgements

In March 2001, the Institute for Human Development and the World Food Programme of the United Nations jointly organised a consultative workshop on 'Food Insecurity and Child Work'. While the linkages between poverty and child work are universally accepted, the notion of food insecurity as a contributory factor to the incidence of child work has not been fully explored. As such, policies dealing with the problem of child work, while utilising food based interventions in the form of school feeding, take-home rations for school-going children or support in the form of food for families of child workers, have never tacitly acknowledged the role of food as a measure to tackle the issue. The workshop was organised with the objective of exploring the links between food insecurity, child work and schooling with a view to identifying criteria and mechanisms for a better programming of WFP's activities as well as for gathering orientations for further research in the area. The enthusiastic response from paper presenters as well as the participants of the workshop emboldened us, as workshop coordinators, to publish the papers presented at the workshop for wider dissemination and further action. The project was actively supported by both Institutions, the WFP sponsoring the book and the IHD undertaking its publication. All the papers have been extensively revised keeping in view the discussions following each presentation and the suggestions of the participants. Two papers, which were not presented at the workshop, but were invited later are those by Dr. Sudha Deshpande and Ms. Ute Meir, as we felt that the addition would make the book more complete.

As such, we would like to acknowledge our gratitude to all participants of the March workshop for their contribution to the book. We are grateful to Shri. K.C. Pant, Deputy Chairman, Planning Commission, for consenting to write the Foreword. Mr. Pedro Medrano, WFP Representative and Country Director, has contributed both as author and by intensively reviewing certain chapters of the book. Prof. Alakh N. Sharma must be thanked for shouldering the burden of publication. We are grateful to all the authors for bearing with us and revising their papers, some through several drafts, so that we could achieve the desired quality of publication. We acknowledge our debt to Ms. Carla Barbiero, First Secretary and Director, Office of Social Development, USAID for initial discussions on the theme. Profs. D.P. Chaudhri and Amitava Mukherjee contributed greatly in summarising the discussions of the workshop.

The tedious job of copy editing and proof reading has been very ably carried out by a team comprising of Mr. Rajesh Shanker, Mrs. Dipika Sen, Dr. A.N. Thakur and Mrs. Mita Majumdar. Messrs. Dhiraj Kumar and Neeraj Kumar have very patiently incorporated the changes made in a series of drafts. Mr. Dilip Dhawan has designed the cover. Finally, all omissions, of course, remain ours.

Nira Ramachandran
Lionel Massün

1

Introducing the Concept

NIRA RAMACHANDRAN

The rural areas of India are home to large numbers of children who remain outside the portals of school, either earning a small wage to supplement the family income as workers in fields, quarries, brick-kilns, cottage industries or petty businesses, or, what is even more common, as unseen hands—unpaid and unacknowledged—that facilitate the work of adult men and women. These large numbers of children are denied their right to childhood in all its connotations—the freedom to play, to learn and to develop to their fullest potential and, as such, must be classed as child workers, whether or not they are formally recognised as child labour. The tendency to ignore work engaged in by children in their own homes and with their own families stems from the belief that even poor parents can effectively protect their children from excessive drudgery when the latter work under their supervision. Thus, work undertaken under parental supervision is conceived as part of the household's moral economy and is an essential part of socialisation (Nieuwenhuys, 1999).

It is in this context that both international and country concerns remain focused on a small segment, of these deprived children—the child labourer. The continued prevalence of child labour in India, as in other developing countries, is, no doubt, a matter of great concern. Despite concerted efforts by the government, non-government organisations and international agencies, the phenomenon of child labour persists across the country. Conventional approaches to the issue centre on legal action, provision of non-formal education and vocational training to the child worker, introduction of adult education programmes and awareness campaigns, as well as provision of support to vulnerable families in child labour-prone areas. The NGO initiative has largely focused on weaning children away from work and into formal schooling through bridge courses and transit camps. While these efforts are certainly laudable and have succeeded in making a dent in the institution of child labour in specific micro situations, what perhaps, is needed now is a wider perspective and a broader strategy which could bring in sweeping changes across the country. At the outset, it needs to be recognised that rehabilitating child labourers in isolation from the millions of other out-of-school children, who are not formally identified as workers, cannot succeed. The narrow focus on child labour must broaden to encompass all children who are denied their right to childhood. If all such 'deprived children' are to be brought into the mainstream and allowed to develop to the fullest of their capacities, one must first seek the reasons for their not being in school, irrespective of whether they qualify for the tag of child labour.

A review of child labour eradication efforts in the country reveals that a two-pronged approach comprising of anti-poverty strategy and the universalisation of education underlies both government and international efforts. An essential part of both these strategies is food-based interventions. The utilisation of food-based interventions implicitly acknowledges the significant role that food security plays in the prevention of child labour. The success of the Tamil Nadu Mid-day Meal Programme as an incentive to school enrolment and retention is often quoted as a telling example of the benefits accruing from such intervention. NGO experience has also revealed that the food component of child labour rehabilitation packages overrides all other incentives. While food is the most basic of all needs and knows no regional boundaries, the role of food insecurity in the incidence of child labour or the importance of food assistance in its eradication have not been extensively researched or formally stated.

This chapter seeks to identify the factors, which deprive this group of children of their normal childhood and in doing so highlights the importance of food security as an explanatory variable, as also the possible basis of a common countrywide approach to the issue. The attempt is exploratory in nature and, it is hoped, will indicate directions for short-term interventions as well as policy formulation.

I. WHO ARE THE FOOD INSECURE?

Food insecurity may be defined as, the "present or potential inability to consume adequate, balanced diet, complete in all the nutrients essential for a healthy and productive existence, either temporarily or for long periods of time. Food insecurity has a time dimension: it may be present or potential. A state producing sufficient food per capita at present may not be able to produce the same per capita production in future, due to land degradation or lack of incentive price. A person consuming inadequate calories has food insecurity at present, if he is faced with uncertain income flows, he has potential food insecurity. In poor societies, food insecurity and livelihood insecurity go together. Further, potential food insecurity is related not only to existing malnutrition, but also to poor sanitation and health conditions. The likelihood of a person falling ill or consuming a diet, which is unbalanced, has potential food insecurity. Thus, potential food insecurity can occur either due to potential lack of availability or potential lack of livelihood or potential threat of disease and lack of absorption of food. Food insecurity may be chronic or transitory. Chronic food insecurity refers to a situation of persons consistently consuming diets inadequate in calories and essential nutrients. This often happens due to the inability to 'access' food either by production, purchase, gift or aid. Transitory food insecurity is a temporary shortfall in food availability and consumption. A fall in income, increase in food prices, shortage of production, a temporary shortfall due to floods, droughts, and other natural calamities, etc., lead to temporary food insecurity" (WFP). Defined as such, food insecurity, either chronic or seasonal, remains a condition in which over 200 million people in India still exist. The threat of potential food insecurity affects many more people. Spitz addresses the seasonality aspect of food insecurity and child work in Chapter 3.

On the food production front, the country, pursuing a focused agricultural policy of self-sufficiency in food, has achieved a breakthrough in production, resulting in its emergence as a surplus food (essentially, cereals) producing economy. However, despite the known commitment of every government, cutting across political affiliations, to ensure food security, coupled with the existence of some of the largest food assistance programmes in the world (the public distribution system (PDS), the integrated child development scheme (ICDS), the mid-day meal scheme (MDMS), food for work (FFW), etc.) and backed by huge subsidies, the realisation of a hunger-free society still remains a distant goal. Its repercussions lie not only in undernourishment, ill-health and a diminished ability to work and to learn, but a denial of access, in terms of purchasing power, to subsidised food, health care and education programmes instituted for these very target groups. What is perhaps of greater significance is that children from such households become from early childhood, paid or unpaid workers, some of whom are engaged in hazardous occupations, while all are denied the right to schooling, thus perpetuating the poverty syndrome.

It is being increasingly recognised that a food security approach to development planning can be more effective than the conventional one, as food security indicators such as amount consumed or nutritional status reflect geographical, intra-household and inter-temporal variations in the accessibility of food, better than the standard per capita income estimates. Also, as poor people spend a high proportion of their income on food, using food security yardsticks would lessen the risk of overlooking the needs of the poor. (Dearden and Cassidy, 1990).

The National Sample Surveys (NSS 46th round, 1990-91) revealed that chronic food inadequacy affected as many as 11 per cent of rural and 3 per cent of urban households in the country. Region-wise, some of the worst affected states are Orissa with 37 per cent of its rural households facing food shortages, followed by Bihar (26 per cent) and West Bengal (19 per cent). While urban households in the same states also face the problem of food scarcity, in all cases, it is in the rural areas that the problem is more acute. Vulnerability Analysis Mapping carried out by the WFP (2000) used four aspects of food security, i.e., 'food availability', 'food access', 'food utilisation' and 'vulnerability' to identify the most vulnerable states in the country and at a more disaggregated level, the most vulnerable districts within them. The states identified as 'most vulnerable' were Bihar, Jharkhand, Madhya Pradesh, Chhatisgarh, Gujarat, Orissa, Rajasthan and Uttar Pradesh (WFP, 2000) (Daly and Dash, Chapter 2).

In terms of caste and class distinctions, it is the agricultural labourer in rural areas and the casual labourer in urban areas who spend the largest proportion of their income on food (67 per cent and 64 per cent, respectively) and are thus most susceptible to even a day's loss of income. Both in urban and rural areas, social class contrasts persist even within occupational classes, with the Scheduled Tribes expending the largest proportion of their income on food both in rural and urban areas (69 per cent and 66 per cent, respectively) (Ramachandran, 1995).

As has been often stated, in India, hunger is not a result of lack of food, but of lack of entitlement or in other words, purchasing power. Apart from the backward states of the country, with a large proportion of the population below the poverty line, where chronic food shortages prevail, even households not normally deprived of food are rendered vulnerable in regions prone to natural disasters like droughts, floods and cyclones. A case in point is the coastal belt of Orissa where the current drought has reinforced the deprivation existing in the wake of the recent cyclone. In Bangladesh, which is prone to frequent natural disasters because of its location in the cyclone belt, the majority of working children are migrants forced into the cities for survival in the aftermath of disaster (Krishna, 1996).

Hunger, insufficient food or seasonal food distress, strongly affect the lives and social behaviour of families hovering on the edge of the poverty line. A study undertaken in two Himalayan villages of Uttaranchal reveals that seasonal food distress is patently evident even in regions, which are not classified as food distress areas. In these remote mountain villages, characterised by marginal landholdings and low productivity, the two major crops of wheat and rice provide food for about 10 months. Paddy is harvested in October and lasts till about May, when the wheat crop is ready for harvesting, while wheat supplies provide food for only about two months. The months of August and September are critical for the region, as not only do the foodgrain stocks run out, but this period also coincides with the monsoons and the consequent landslides and the cutting-off of the region from the plains denying it access to outside food supplies. While government initiatives in the form of stocking three months supplies of PDS foodgrain in local godowns have greatly helped towards ensuring the availability of food in the region, this period remains critical for landless labourers and marginal farmers. This is because the source of income of these vulnerable groups, which is derived from agriculture or other manual work like construction, also stops during the monsoons (Ramachandran, 2000). Similar situations exist in several states of the country (see Part III for studies on Bihar, Jharkhand, Rajasthan, Madhya Pradesh and Orissa.)

Not only actual food distress, but even the threat of future food shortages can become a powerful instrument in shaping the behavioural patterns of those affected by it. Self Employed Women's Association (SEWA), an organisation focusing its activities on the general empowerment of women, goes so far as to state in one of its documents that 'for poor women the process of liberation begins when they are able to feed their children and other dependents through productive work' (Jhabvala, 1991). Food insecure people devise their own coping mechanisms, the most basic of which is to have as many hands to work and earn as possible, thus furnishing a kind of insurance against future hunger. The direct result is large families and the induction of children into the labour force. Chaudhri and Wilson (Chapter 6) trace the relationship between nutritional poverty and large families.

Government estimates place the number of working children in the country at 11.3 million (Census of India, 1991). However, other estimates place the number of child workers much higher. A recent study, using both Census and NSS data estimates the number of working children (full-time workers alone) in the country as 12.7 million in 1991. If estimated figures for marginal child labour (using 1981 proportions) are added to these, total child labour in the country stands at 23.2 million as against 14.5 million in 1961, an increase of 160 per cent (Chaudhri, 1996).

The rural areas account for nearly 91 per cent of the total child labour in the country. Taking the country as a whole, about 4 per cent of the rural workforce comprises of children below the age of 15. However, there are large-scale inter-regional variations in the incidence of child labour. It varies between 0.45 per cent in Kerala to 6.25 per cent in Andhra Pradesh. In Assam, Madhya Pradesh, Maharashtra, Meghalaya, Orissa, and Rajasthan, the proportion of child workers is also above the national average. Even within the child labour endemic states, there are pockets of concentration, where industries heavily dependent on child labour are located.

Genderwise, while the absolute number of male child workers working as cultivators has declined, the number of full-time male child agricultural labourers has increased, a trend that is also evident in the case of girl child workers. Thus, it would be erroneous to conclude that the problem has been solved in the agricultural sector and is now concentrated in manufacturing and trade and commerce. Though the major part of NGO efforts and international concerns about child employment focuses on non-agricultural sectors, in terms of sheer numbers alone, the significance of the agricultural sector is enormous. In 1991, for instance the number of full-time child agricultural labourers was 3.1 million, while those in manufacturing (both rural and urban) totalled only about 0.5 million.

II. CHILD LABOUR, CHILD WORK AND DEPRIVED CHILDREN

A child in the age group 5-14, who undertakes paid work is defined as a child labourer. Even a cursory glance at the statistics reveals that of the 230 million children in the age group 5-14, only around 61 per cent attend school. So that the remaining 39 per cent or a total of 90 million children in the school-going age group are out of school. Of these, if only 11.3 million, are recorded as child workers, the remaining 79 million, 'nowhere' children make the issue, assume alarming proportions. There are two complementary points of view regarding these unaccounted for children: one view is that in the rural situation, a child who does not go to school is a working child. Collection of water, fuel, maintenance of the house and taking care of younger siblings, all constitute an important element of his or her life. While these activities do not necessarily fall under the definition of hazardous activities, inasmuch as they interfere with the normal development of the child and the child's ability to reach his/her true potential, they constitute exploitation of the child. In the context of rural India, therefore, a non-working, non-school-going child simply does not exist. (Sinha, 1996). As Schildkrout (1980) puts it 'any activity done by children which either contributes to production, gives adults free time, facilitates the work of others or substitutes for the employment of others, can be termed child work'. Hirway's paper, (Chapter 5), seeks to delve further into the issue using Time Use data to make a detailed analysis of how children spend their day.

> The varied terminology used to describe child work in the book is as follows: Child Labour: children in the age group, 5-14 who are engaged in paid work; Child Main Workers: Children in the same age group whose main occupation is reported as 'work'; Child Marginal Workers; Children aged 5-14 whose secondary occupation is reported as 'work'. Their primary occupation may well be schooling; 'Nowhere' Children: Children in the school-going age group who are neither at school nor at work. Terms specific to particular papers are explained in the papers themselves.

The other viewpoint looks at the continuing phenomenon of child labour from the supply side (Chaudhri, 2000). Sources of supply of child labour do not arise directly from an increase in the child population, but from a large pool of 'nowhere' children augmented by dropouts from school who also join this category. Estimates of 'out of the school' children in 2000 are recorded at 72.63 million or 30 per cent of the school-going population aged 5-14 years. While there has been a significant decrease in the proportion of out of school children—from 50 to 30 per cent—in the decade 1991-2000, a large number of children are still out of school, particularly in the states of Bihar, Jharkhand, Madhya Pradesh, Chhatisgarh, Orissa, Rajasthan and Uttar Pradesh. This becomes particularly significant when one takes into account the fact that these states together account for nearly 51 per cent of the total child population. (Zutshi, 2001). Thus, the issue is not one of main and marginal child workers alone, but more correctly, one that concerns all children of school-going age who are out of school-children who are denied their right to childhood and the opportunity to acquire skills and lead a better quality of life as adults. In the broader context of deprived children, therefore, the importance of schooling becomes paramount.

III. THE SPECIAL PROBLEM OF THE GIRL CHILD WORKER

While the incidence of child labour has shown a steady decline at the national level, an analysis of the trend for the rural girl child worker brings out the growing rates of girl child work participation in rural areas. While it may be argued that this trend can be attributed to definitional differences between Censuses, the fact remains that the upward trend in the incidence of child labour can be seen only in the case of girl child workers and only those living in rural areas.

An analysis of Census data from 1971 to 1991 (Table 1) clearly reflects the increase in girl child work participation rates in 13 of the 21 states for which data was available. In some of the backward states like Orissa, Rajasthan and Uttar Pradesh, girl child participation rates have doubled between 1981 and 1991. What is even more disturbing is the one hundred per cent increase in these rates in developed states like Punjab and Gujarat. States like Bihar and Gujarat, which recorded a fall in rural girl child work participation between the seventies and the eighties, have again recorded an upward trend in the 1991 Census. In absolute terms, the number of girl child workers has increased from 2.8 million to 3.5 million since 1971. Over 80 per cent of these girls are still caught up in the agricultural sector, mostly as full-time agricultural labourers. Ignoring their plight is socially inappropriate and an economic disaster because of its serious implications for the pace of demographic transition. (Chaudhri, op. cit.).

Table 1
Rural Girl Child Work Participation Rate, 1971-1991

State	Year		
	1971	1981	1991
Andhra Pradesh	5.22	12.92	13.58
Bihar	3.18	2.58	3.26
Gujarat	5.19	4.37	7.81
Haryana	1.13	1.9	2.24
Himachal Pradesh	9.4	6.66	5.90
Jammu & Kashmir	1.59	3.12	N.A.
Karnataka	6.53	8.76	11.34
Kerala	1.76	1.11	0.54
Madhya Pradesh	7.64	9.49	10.66
Maharashtra	7.59	9.89	9.86
Manipur	6.5	6.9	5.34
Meghalaya	10.35	10.23	N.A.
Nagaland	12.84	9.86	N.A.
Orissa	2.34	3.7	6.03
Punjab	0.17	0.46	1.01
Rajasthan	4.92	4.98	9.75
Sikkim	30.37	12.65	N.A.
Tamil Nadu	5.48	8.51	6.63
Tripura	1.19	2.00	N.A.
Uttar Pradesh	2.56	1.58	2.87
West Bengal	1.08	1.34	2.42

Source: Censuses of India, 1971, 1981 and 1991.

Another important aspect is the gender-based division of labour in rural India. Like adult labour, child labour is unevenly distributed with the more time consuming, arduous and low-skill tasks reserved for the female worker. According to a recent survey of 15 villages in Bihar, very few tasks are gender-neutral, only six out of 58 activities being performed by both boys and girls. Boys' activities in agriculture are restricted to ploughing and carrying paddy seedlings, both being highly seasonal activities. The major share of agriculture-related work is done by girls. In silk production, boys learn the more valuable skills—collecting wild cocoons is 66 per cent of the value added and weaving is 20 per cent, both done by boys. Spinning, which accounts for only 14 per cent of the value added, is done by girls. The above analysis clearly indicates that general trends in the reduction of child labour, do not hold true for the girl child. In fact, the work undertaken by the girl child worker has been grossly underestimated (Sohoni, 1994) As a consequence, therefore, current policies directed at rehabilitating the child worker may not suffice to address the problem of the girl child, which may require special attention. Deshpande's paper (Chapter 4) focuses on the girl child worker and the specific problems faced by her. Underlining the attitude to the girl child in India, Nieuwenhuys (1999) writes that "work undertaken by girls is often not perceived as child work for the simple reason that girls childhood is so short".

IV. CAUSAL FACTORS AND CORRELATES

The underlying cause of child labour is undoubtedly poverty, but poverty alone is not a sufficient explanatory factor. Other socio-economic factors like food insecurity, adult literacy in general, and female literacy, in particular, fertility rates, family size, adult wage rates, diversification of the rural economy and female labour participation rates to name a few, all have a role to play. Dev and Ravi (Chapter 9), examine relationships between child work, schooling and other socio-economic factors at various levels from state to district level in the southern region of the country, while Leclercq (Chapter 8) attempts the same for the north Indian states. The links between household income, food and nutrition security with the activity status of children are analysed in Gumber and Gupta's paper. (see Chapter 7).

Food insecurity has emerged as an explanatory variable in the last few years as a result of the experiences of both government and non-government agencies involved in providing food assistance to school-going children. The Tamil Nadu Mid-day Meal experience coupled with the provision of effective schooling facilities which has been successfully implemented over two decades, is a case in point. The impact of the scheme can be seen in the high enrolment rates (86 per cent) in the state, as also the minimal gender differences in retention rates. The success of the experience led the central government to introduce a mid-day meals programme in several states. A similar spurt in school enrolment and attendance has been witnessed in almost all the states where the programme has been successfully implemented. The Tamil Nadu intervention was in the form of providing a hot meal cooked and served to the children in school. This pattern has been, perhaps, somewhat less successfully, followed in other states like

Orissa and Gujarat. However, in the case of states, where the logistics of serving a hot meal could not be met, food assistance in the form of 3 kg. of rice or wheat per child distributed on the basis of 80 per cent attendance have.also contributed to achieving the same purpose. Two papers, one by Meir (Chapter 17) and the other by Kaul (Chapter 16), review various food-based interventions aimed at increasing school enrolment and retention in India and other developing countries.

It has been seen that the assurance of a daily meal for the child in the form of school lunch or adequate foodgrain tends to outweigh other considerations, which force the family to set their children to work. Another side benefit of food aid is derived from the positive impact of a full meal on the attention span and consequently, the cognitive development of a child who habitually excessive space functions on an empty stomach. Hunger contributes to a child's distractibility, inattentiveness to environmental stimuli and adaptive behaviours of passivity and inactivity. These effects are more apparent when the child who is hungry is also malnourished. The response to hunger directly impinges upon the development of a child's active learning capacity. Exploratory activity is likely to be shunned rather than sought after by the hungry child (Levinger, 1996).

Education, as has been noted, has both a direct and an indirect impact on child labour. In so far as children in school are kept away from the labour market, the relationship is obvious. A survey of 500 households with child workers in Karachi, (PILER and SEBCOM, 1990) revealed that 58 per cent of the children covered were working to supplement the family income, while 23.4 per cent were working because they did not want to go to school (given the extreme inadequacy and irrelevance of education in ordinary schools).

However, the role of education in creating awareness among parents of the need to send their children to school as against work for their children is equally important. This is particularly so in the case of women. A recent study analysing the relationship between female literacy and the incidence of child labour at the district level in rural areas, revealed that a significant negative relationship exists between the two variables. The elasticity coefficient of 0.595 implies that an increase in female literacy by one per cent would reduce the incidence of child labour by 0.59 per cent (Haque, 2000). Leclercq's study of the north Indian states in Chapter 8, brings out the importance of parental education, particularly that of the mother in the enrolment decision.

The same study brings out the close links between female labour participation and child labour. In homes where the mother works, older children are often kept away from school to help with the housework and look after younger siblings. This is particularly so, in the case of girls. In a home-based industry, the children are actually involved in the mother's work, particularly if the employment is on a piece rate contract basis. An NGO initiative in Uttar Pradesh focuses on providing worksheds with proper facilities at the village level for women piece rate workers in order to process the involvement of children in their mother's work.[1]

It is well known that low wage rates of adult male workers tend to force women and children to enter the workforce in an attempt to supplement the family income. A study on child labour in Sivakasi, the centre of the match and fireworks industry of Tamil Nadu, reveals that 17 per cent of the households get more than half of their income from child work, 40 per cent get one-third to half their income, while in the remaining households, children contribute about 20-30 per cent of the family income. (Gupta and Voll, 1999). In the hybrid cottonseed cultivation of the Telangana and Rayalseema regions of Andhra Pradesh where nearly 2.5 lakh girl children an employed, nearly 30 per cent of the household's income is contributed by their children (Venkateswarulu, undated).

The low wage rates paid to child workers further depress the market wage rate thus perpetuating the cycle of poverty and child labour. In the hybrid cottonseed cultivation areas of Andhra Pradesh, referred to above, child workers are paid about 70 per cent of the adult female and 45 per cent of the adult male wage rates. Haque's study (Haque, 2000) underlines this relationship with the top 20 districts having a high incidence of poverty and child labour also recording low wage rates for adult labour, and the reverse picture emerging in districts which have relatively higher wage rates (Kerala and parts of Punjab). The implication would be that policies aimed at the reduction of child labour would need to go into the issue of fixing adult wage rates at levels high enough to maintain the whole family.

The relationship between family size and the incidence of child workers is a part of the complex of poverty, food shortages and the effort to eke out a livelihood. Child labour eradication efforts must necessarily reinforce population control measures in rural areas. The paper by Chaudhri and Wilson (Chapter 6), as mentioned earlier, emphasises the relationship between nutritional poverty, family size and educational deprivation.

The diversification of the rural economy may also play a role by providing job opportunities and higher wage rates for adults, which in turn, obviates the need for children to contribute to the family income.

The perpetuation of child labour has often been attributed to socio-cultural factors. However, irrespective of socio-cultural differences, child labour has been a part of strenuous social and economic evolutionary phases, with all their immanent contradictions, in moving towards a fully industrialised and modern society (Voll, 1999). Child labour, therefore, is more a manifestation of the culture of poverty, rather than the reflection of a socio-cultural value system.

V. THE FOOD BASED APPROACH

Underlying the explanatory factors discussed above runs the common thread of food insecurity and lack of education. Regardless as to whether one seeks an explanation for child labour in low wage rates, female work participation, an undiversified rural economy, farm productivity, level of technology or family size, it essentially lies in the inability to access sufficient food for the family. Other basic needs like shelter, health care and education do not have the same immediacy. On the other hand, the importance of education both in terms of keeping children in school and away from work and in reinforcing the parent's determination to provide their children with education cannot be underplayed. With this in mind, the role of food aid in reducing the incidence of child labour on the one hand, and increasing school enrolment and retention, on the other, can be reviewed.

A series of papers on food-based interventions in Part IV (Kannan, Sharma, Mehtta and Medrano, Gupta and Gumber, and Joseph) provide an insight into the impact of existing food interventions on household food security and child deprivation. While Kannan cites the availability of a total package of food-based interventions as the reason behind Kerala's success with its schooling, health and nutrition programmes. Gupta et al. review the nutrition and pre-school education package provided through the ICDS as a means of escape from the vicious cycle of poverty, malnutrition, illiteracy and child work. Sharma, Mehtta and Medrano present an innovative scheme (the grain bank) of ensuring household food security for the poorest groups which cannot even access the existing PDS system, while Joseph details the ILO-IPEC project in Markapur District of Andhra Pradesh, where school, feeding programmes have had marked impact on reducing child labour in the limestone quarries.

VI. THE CASE FOR FOOD BASED INTERVENTIONS

The foregoing analysis has brought out the complex interrelationships between a host of factors which underlie child labour, prevent even non-working children from going to school and eventually draw them into the labour market, thus perpetuating the vicious cycle of poverty and child work. Underlying these complex linkages are the twin parameters of food insecurity and lack of basic education. In this background, it becomes important to review international and country experience of food-based interventions aimed at bringing children into schools and retaining them there.

Several research studies have attempted to assess the impact of school feeding programmes on enrolment and retention rates. The techniques adopted vary from comparative studies of similar schools with and without a school feeding programme, measuring changes in enrolment and attendance when a school feeding programme is interrupted or terminated, and assessing changes in enrolment and retention after the introduction of a school feeding programme. Methodologies vary from simple comparisons to sophisticated regression analysis permitting the assessment of the relative importance of each variable including school feeding as an explanatory factor.[2]

The Tamil Nadu Mid-day Meal Programme evaluation in 1984 (Babu and Hallam, 1989) used household surveys, school records and ICDS registers to assess changes in the level of the children's education resulting from the introduction of the scheme. The study found a highly significant increase in school enrolment and retention due to school nutrition. The impact of the programme clearly extended to middle school level, but the results suggested that a stronger incentive was needed to support high school education which involves a higher opportunity cost. The income transfer effect was found to be most significant amongst agricultural labour households (i.e., those marked by low income, food insecurity, and relatively higher opportunity cost associated with sending children to school).

A free mid-day meal scheme for all school children in Sri Lanka also showed encouraging results. A survey of 50 rural schools revealed that attendance in schools increased by 54 per cent because of the mid-day meal. Attracted by the scheme, even those children who had dropped out returned to school (Vishwa Yuvak Kendra, 1991).

A similar study in Morocco (Ministry of Education, 1995) covering 1600 households assessed the influence of the availability of a school canteen on child enrolment and retention It showed that the likelihood of children aged, 7-12 years enrolling in a primary school was significantly higher, if at least one of the schools in the catchment area was equipped with a full-scale canteen. The findings also indicated that the functioning of a full-scale canteen was a positive factor for retention, the implication being that a full-scale canteen provides more and better food and thus higher income transfer. This was particularly true for the girl child who is more likely to be kept from school to help with domestic chores or to earn money.

The United States Bureau for Food for Peace and Voluntary Assistance in a review of US bilateral food aid programmes (PL 480 Title II) spanning the periods 1980-85, came to the conclusion that several studies presented evidence of improved enrolment and attendance due to school feeding. A study from Tamil Nadu found a positive association between school feeding and enrolment as well as retention, especially for girls and scheduled caste children, and particularly, in those areas which were poor, but not too poor. These findings are substantiated by Levinger's (1986) review of studies on the educational effects of school feeding programmes in developing countries. She concludes that school feeding programmes (SFPs) do probably make a difference in enrolment and attendance if their design takes into account the environment in which they operate. SFPs should be targeted to the poor, but not too poor, stable, rural areas where enrolment and attendance are relatively low. In areas where poverty and the need for child labour are particularly high, the financial value of school meals needs to be very significant to offset the opportunity costs of schooling. This focus on borderline communities in economic and educational terms is based on the outcome of several studies from countries such as Kenya, the Philippines, Columbia and Guatemala.

An evaluation of the PL 480 Title II Programme in the Dominican Republic in 1982 revealed that the abrupt interruption of a school lunch programme due to non-availability of donated commodities resulted in the dropping out of about one-quarter of the enrolled children. This happened despite the fact that the programme had been successfully run for a period of 17 years starting in 1962. The decline in girl's enrolment was more drastic than that of boys, and the decline in enrolment was found to be highest in the higher grades.

VII. SCHOOL FEEDING AND LEARNING ACHIEVEMENT

Apart from the positive impact on enrolment and attendance, School feeding programmes have also been seen to have considerable impact on learning capacity. A study comparing test scores in French and Mathematics at the beginning and end of the school year for children in grades II and V was undertaken for primary students in Benin (Jarousse and Mingat, 1991). Results of the study revealed that learning achievement was much higher in schools that had a school canteen. This relationship remained significant even when controlling for all other variables. Similar results were obtained by the authors in Burkina Faso and Togo. The possible explanation for such a positive relationship could lie in the improved nutrition levels of the children or the fact that they attended school more regularly.

A similar study aimed at evaluating the school lunch programme in Orissa, (Roy and Rath, 1970) compared the academic performance of boys participating in the school feeding programme with those who did not participate. Examination scores revealed no significant difference between the two groups. Levinger, however, points out that the study did not provide sufficient control for the socio-economic status of the test group. As SFP schools had more children from households of a lower socio-economic status (SC and STs), it could be argued that the SFPs actually helped to bridge the gap the between better-off non-SFP schools and SFP schools of a lower status.

A review of existing research in this area (Pollit, 1990) cites studies from North America and Jamaica where various tests were administered to assess the cognitive functions of two sets of school children—one group who were given breakfast, the other who were not. Results revealed that temporary hunger caused children to be more easily distracted and become inattentive in class. Children with a previous history of undernourishment were particularly vulnerable to the adverse effects of missing breakfast and scored lower in most cognitive tests.

While the results of research on the relationship between school feeding, nutritional status, cognitive function and learning achievement is not always conclusive, there is significant evidence that short-term hunger affects children's cognitive function and the effects of missing breakfast, particularly, on the already undernourished children who may have to walk a long way to school, should not be taken lightly.

Clearly, food interventions must be designed with a specific objective in mind. A snack to offset short-term hunger, may not be a financially adequate incentive to promote enrolment and attendance. A better alternative in such cases may be take-home rations. A careful case by case assessment of needs should, therefore, precede the decision on objectives and possible interventions. In the Indian situation, food-based interventions could be targeted at the child in school or in households prone to child labour. In the case of such a household-based approach, food assistance must compensate for the opportunity cost of the child's labour. It must also necessarily be linked with withdrawing the child from work and sending her to school. This would necessitate an effective monitoring system.

On the other hand, the case for SFPs seems more conclusive as a single programme would achieve two objectives—one, bringing the child to school and out of the labour pool, and two, impacting positively on the child's learning achievement. The choice of approach could vary from region to region. Part III contains a collection of state level papers outlining state-specific food security and child work scenarios, as well as identifying determinants of child work specific to each region, with a view to providing policy guidelines. The states selected for analyses are among the most backward and food insecure, with high proportions of child workers, as well as out of school children, i.e., Rajasthan, Bihar, Jharkhand, Orissa and Madhya Pradesh. The state of Andhra Pradesh, though ranking much higher on the development scale, has also been studied as it holds the dubious record of having the highest incidence of child labour in the country.

The foregoing conclusions do significantly strengthen the case for food-based interventions as incentives for school enrolment and retention and, under certain conditions, as an assurance of more effective learning. However, the case for targeting the source of child labour by ensuring food security at the household level, remains at best, a tenuous one. The above review, however, does raise a number of key issues, the answers to which need further investigation. These are:

(i) Could food assistance effectively reduce child work?

(ii) If so, should food-based interventions be targeted at the school child or at the family?

(iii) Would a special food intervention targeted at the girl child worker help to reverse the growing trend of girl child work participation?

(iv) Could the assurance of food assistance during seasonal food distress periods/disasters break the food insecurity-child work cycle?

(v) Could food credit schemes be thought of on the lines of the existing micro-credit schemes?

VIII. OUTLINE OF THE BOOK

In keeping with the above questions, the book has been organised in four parts, each of which contain a set of papers dealing with a specific theme. Chapter I, as seen, introduces the concept. That poverty, seasonal food distress and vulnerability to hunger due to recurrent natural calamities alter the lifestyles and coping mechanisms of affected families with adverse consequences on the freedom and the education of their children is well known. What is, perhaps, not so evident, is that the availability of timely support in the form of food can become the turning point of the decision to enroll the child in school as against work, to ensure regular attendance of already enrolled children and to eventually break the vulnerable household-child labour syndrome.

Part I explores the concept across space, in terms of seasonality (time) and through the gender lens. Four papers deal with different aspects. Daly, Bhattacharyya and Dash bring out the spatial spread of child labour in the country. Beginning with macro aspects dealing with food security and targeted population, the paper maps food insecurity and child work across the states. In doing so, it provides explanations for child work in different regions and the existing linkages between food security, school drop-out and child work, with a view to exploring possible interventions. The seasonality factor that is evident in income, expenditure and related economic patterns in rural India and its impact on school attendance and drop out rates of children is analysed in P. Spitz's paper. The alarming increase in girl-child work participation rates from the seventies to the nineties, despite a decline in the overall incidence of child labour at national level, necessitates a clear focus on the status and determinants of gender discrimination in child work. Sudha Deshpande studies this issue in detail. How do children spend their time? An attempt to analyse the time-use pattern of children in sample states of the country is made by Indira Hirway .

Part II seeks to explore the determinants of child work with a view to establishing links between child work, schooling and food insecurity. This section contains four papers, two dealing with the issue at the national level (D.P. Chaudhri and E. Wilson and A. Gumber and D.B. Gupta), the other two focussing on the north and the south Indian states, respectively (M. Dev and C. Ravi and F. Leclercq). Expected relationships like the links between nutritional poverty, educational poverty, family size and child work are established, as also the visible gender bias against the rural girl child. However, what also seems to emerge is the fact that poverty is not a major determinant of child work or low enrolment ratios. Parental education and awareness, particularly female education status seems to play a dominant role.

Regional disparities across the country remain sharp. As such, no single policy measure is likely to suffice throughout the country. Part III contains a set of six papers covering six child labour-prone states of the country (Andhra Pradesh, Bihar, Jharkhand, Rajasthan, Madhya Pradesh and Orissa). Each state paper uses primary data to construct a profile of child workers in the state and seeks to analyse the region-specific determinants of child work and school enrolment ratios. The papers also attempt to assess whether at the household level, food security has a major role to play in the decision to keep children out of school and introduce them into the labour force. A comparative study by Nangia and Khan provides further insights using National Family Health Survey (NFHS II) data to compare the states of Andhra Pradesh, Madhya Pradesh and Orissa.

Linking nutritional and educational poverty with the persistence of child work leads naturally to the question of the means to off-set the impact of these determinants. School feeding or food assistance to vulnerable families may serve two goals: the immediate one of bringing and retaining more children in school and out of the labour pool, and the long term one of educating an entire generation, that would be unlikely to leave their own children undernourished and uneducated. Part IV is a collection of six papers dealing with this theme. Existing food-based interventions aimed at improving nutrition levels of children as well as school enrolment, retention and attendance are reviewed. The interventions range from food credit targetted at vulnerable households to the ICDS (Integrated Child Development Services) programme aimed at the pre-schooler, the Mid-day Meals Scheme for primary school children and total food security (the Kerala Experience) through a combination of these programmes. A case study of Markapur district in Andhra Pradesh presents the experiment (ILO-IPEC) of using school feeding to tackle the child labour problem in the limestone quarries of the region.

The last chapter seeks to answer the questions raised in the introduction through a review of the preceding chapters, also incorporating the highlights of the discussions at the workshop.

Notes

1. Manju Gupta, STEP Foundation, Personal Communication.
2. This section draws heavily from the document entitled 'The Operational Guidelines for WFP Assistance to Education'

References

Babu, S.C. and J.A. Hallam (1989), "Socio-Economic Impacts of School Feeding Programmes", *Food Policy,* February, pp. 58-66.

Chaudhri, D.P. (1996), *A Dynamic Profile of Child Labour in India, 1951-1991,* Child Labour Action and Support Project, ILO, New Delhi.

—— (2000), "Sources of Supply of Child Labour and the State: Explorations of Historical and Contemporary Evidence with Focus on States and Districts of India," Paper presented at the National Seminar on Child Labour: Realities and Policy Dimensions, National Institute of Labour, Noida, Dec. 5-7.

Dearden, P.J. and E.M. Cassidy (1990), "Food Security: An ODA View," *IDS Bulletin,* Vol. 21. No. 3, Institute of Development Studies, Sussex.

Gupta, M. and K. Voll (1999), "Child Labour in India: An Exemplary Case Study" in Klaus Voll (ed.) *Against Child Labour,* Mosaic Books, New Delhi.

Haque, T. (2000), "Socio-economic Causes and Impact of Child Labour: In Agriculture and Other Rural Sub-sectors in India," Paper presented at the *National Seminar on Child Labour: Realities and Policy Dimensions,* National Institute of Labour, Noida, and Institute for Human Development, New Delhi, Dec. 5-7.

Jarousse, J.P. and Alain Mingat (1991), cited in WFP, (1995) *Operational Guidelines for WFP Assistance to Education,* SCP 15/INF/3, 15th Session, SCP, Rome.

Jhabvala, Renana (1991), *SEWA—Progress Report.* July, Dec.

Krishna, Sumi (1996), *Restoring Childhood - Learning, Labour and Gender in South Asia,* Konark Publishers Pvt. Ltd., New Delhi.

Levinger, Beryl (1986), *School Feeding Programmes in Developing Countries—An Analysis of Actual and Potential Impact.* USAID, Washington D. C.

—— (1996), *Nutrition, Health and Education for All,* Education Development Center, Inc.

Ministry of Education, Morocco, Document cited in WFP (1995), *Operational Guidelines for WFP Assistance to Education,* SCP 15/INF/3, 15 th Session, SCP, Rome.

Nieuwenhuys, O. (1999), *Children's Lifeworlds: Gender, Welfare and Labour in the Developing World,* Social Science Press, New Delhi.

PILER and SEBCOM (1990), *Child Labour and Family Life in Karachi,* Pakistan Institute for Labour Education and Research and Socio-Economic and Business Consultants.

Pollit, Ernesto (1990), *Malnutrition and Infection in the Classroom*, UNESCO, Paris.

Ramachandran, Nira (1995), "How Sustainable is Our Food Security?", *The Administrator*, Special Issue on Sustainable Development, Vol. 60, No. 2, April-June, pp. 131-156.

—— (2000), *Review and Field Testing of Guidelines for Formulating and Implementing National Plans of Action for Nutrition*, Prepared for Nutrition Planning Assessment and Evaluation Service, Food and Nutrition Division, FAO, Rome.

Roy and Rath (1970), cited in : Levinger, Beryl (1989), "Malnutrition, School Feeding and Educational Performance," *Notes-Comments*, No. 186. Unit for Cooperation with UNICEF and WFP, UNESCO, Paris.

Schildkrout, E (1980) "Children's Work Reconsidered", *International Social Sciences Journal*, Vol. 32, No. 3, pp. 479-90, quoted in Nieuwenhuys O. (1999), *Children's Lifeworlds: Gender, Welfare and Labour in the Developing World*, Social Science Press, New Delhi.

Sinha, Shanta (1996), "Child Labour and Education Policy in India," *The Administrator*, Special Issue on Child Labour and Education, Vol. 61, No. 3, July- September.

Sohoni, N.K. (1994), *Status of Girls in Development Strategies*, Hari-Anand Publications, New Delhi.

USAID (1985), *PL 480 Evaluations, (1980-1985): The Lessons of Experience*, United States Agency for International Development, Washington D.C.

Venkateswarulu, D. (undated), "Girl Child Bonded Labour in Hybrid Cottonseed Production—A Study on Telangana and Rayalsaeema Regions of Andhra Pradesh," (mimeo).

Vishwa Yuvak Kendra (1991), *Future Strategies for Universalising Girls Education in South Asia*, New Delhi.

Voll, K. (1999) (ed.), *Against Child Labour*, Mosaic Books, New Delhi.

World Food Programme (2000), *Country Strategy Outline—India*, New Delhi.

Zutshi, B. (2001), *A Situational Analysis of Education for Street and Working Children in India*, UNESCO, New Delhi.

PART I

Profiling the Issue: Space, Time and Gender Dimensions

2

Food Security and Child Work in Rural India

G. DALY, D. BHATTACHARYYA AND B.P. DASH

I. INTRODUCTION

During the last two decades, there have been significant developments in the production of foodgrains in India. The average growth rate has been recorded at 3.2 per cent per annum[1], during this period, which is higher than the rate of growth in population (over 2 per cent per annum). Despite the progress achieved in the production of foodgrains, food insecurity has remained as one of the major concerns in India. The country has about 208 million undernourished people (FAO, 2000), a large percentage among this are children, adolescent girls and women belonging to Scheduled Tribes and Scheduled Castes.

The high level of undernourishment has resulted in higher maternal mortality increased numbers of underweight births, and higher susceptibility of infants and young children to diseases and death. This, in turn, reflects in the high incidence of stunting and wasting among the children, particularly in the rural areas and partially explains the low level of attendance in schools in such areas. About 40 per cent of the boys and 60 per cent of the girls are not enrolled in any school at the primary level and about 40 per cent of the children at the primary level, have dropped out of school. (NCERT, 1998). Children, who leave school, either get engaged in paid work activities which are often hazardous in nature or engage in household chores which restrict their physical and mental growth.

Child work is a complex phenomenon. The issue starts from the lack of unanimity on a clear definition of child work. The multiplicity of definitions has resulted in a wide range of estimates for the number of child workers in India, ranging from 11 million to over 100 million. This variation could also be attributed to different methods of surveys by different database agencies and difficulties in identifying child workers in unorganised sectors, particularly in the rural areas.

The main factors that force children to work are the high rate of population growth, lopsided economic development of different regions, unequal resource ownership, large scale unemployment, poverty, increasing disparity in wealth, cut backs in governmental social and educational budgets, etc. (UNICEF, 1999). A close review of these factors however, reveals that indicators of malnourishment like underweight, wasting and stunting, etc., strongly affect the capability of the children to concentrate on their studies. As a result, the majority of the children in these categories drop out at an early age. Household food insecurity is considered to be a major deterrent to the enrolment of children at the primary and secondary level.

In the light of the above issues, the present paper analyses the concept of food insecurity, levels of food insecurity across states and examines the link between the spatial incidence of food insecurity and child work. The paper is based on secondary data and suggests possible policy interventions for reducing the level of child work and food insecurity.

The paper has been divided into five sections that followed this introductory section. Section II presents the different dimensions of food insecurity and highlights the relative food insecurity positions of the states and their levels of vulnerability. Section III presents the trends and patterns in the level and incidence of child work across the states and identifies the areas, which are highly prone/vulnerable to child work. Section IV attempts to analyse the link between the incidence of child work and food insecurity. These sections also analyse the educational indicators, which might have a direct or indirect bearing on the incidence of child work. The last section, i.e., Section V, provides an analysis of the possible policy interventions to reduce the incidence of poverty and child work simultaneously.

II. FOOD INSECURITY IN RURAL INDIA

Food insecurity exists when all people, at all times, do not have physical and economic access to an adequate amount of, safe and nutritious food to meet their dietary needs and food preferences for an active and healthy life (FAO, 1999). Food insecurity has multiple dimensions that relate to demographic, nutritional, economic and social issues.

In the light of the above definition, WFP Delhi and MSSRF, Chennai jointly brought out an atlas of food insecurity in rural India. The atlas captures the levels of food insecurity in rural areas under the four major dimensions of food insecurity, viz., problem of Availability, Access to Food, Utilisation of food and Vulnerability to natural disasters. While the first three dimensions are interrelated phenomena, the fourth dimension of vulnerability acts as an exogenous factor, which directly affects all these three dimensions of food security.

Major Dimensions of Food Insecurity

The first major dimension of food insecurity, *Food Availability,* is a function of agricultural production (food crops, cash crops and livestock) and net food imports. It has different implications for national, sub-national and household level food security. *Food Access,* the second dimension, refers to the ability of households to secure food in the market place. It needs to be mentioned here that household purchasing power is the key to access. *Food Utilisation* refers to the nutritional security of all household members. How food is utilised individually is influenced by cultural factors (such as diet preferences and caring practices), physiological factors (how well food is absorbed by the body depend on quality of water and sanitation, health care and knowledge of nutrition) and, finally, distributional factors (intra-household distribution and control over food and other resources). The fourth dimension, *Vulnerability,* refers to a range of external factors that expose people to food insecurity across the other three dimensions. The concept diagram given below (Figure 1), shows the basic links.

Figure 1
Linkage between Dimensions of Food Insecurity

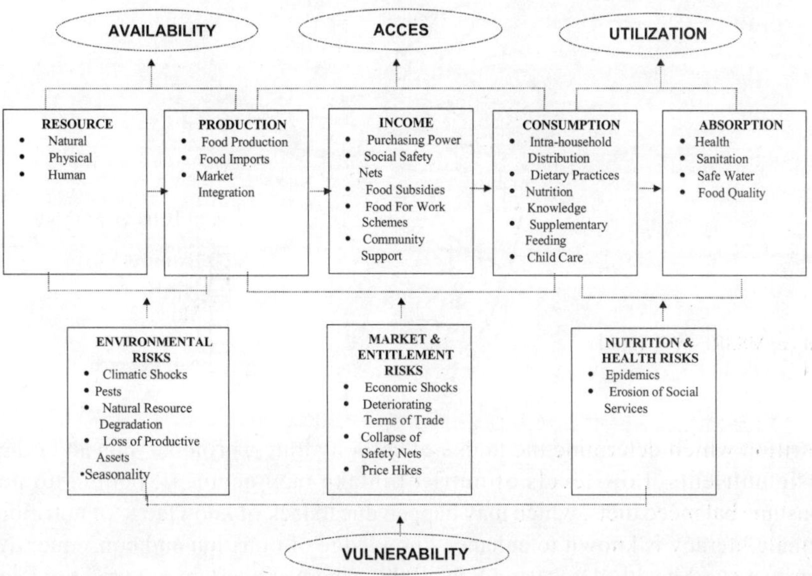

Food availability may be hampered by low levels of production or inadequate inflow of food into vulnerable geographical locations. Low production levels may be due to limitations, relating to markets, credit, technology and the natural resource base. It may also be due to lack of price incentives to production. Environmental sustainability is equally important for long-term assured production. Both private trade in foodgrains and government supported foodgrain distribution systems normally ensure adequate inflow of food into a region. In some areas, infrastructure bottlenecks and lack of purchasing power necessitate government-supported measures to ensure adequate supply.

Food availability by itself does not ensure adequate access to food. If people have access to a source of livelihood, they would in general have access to food and nutrition. Those who are unemployed, or employed on a casual basis or underemployed, would have limited economic and physical access to food. Persons with a low asset base and those engaged in non-viable enterprises tend to remain poor. Moreover, the poor spend a large percentage of their income on food and yet get very little to eat, let alone a balanced diet. This is because 80 to 90 per cent of the energy requirements of the lowest expenditure groups in various states come from cereals (NSSO, 1997). Food prices thus play an important role in determining the ability of the household to purchase an adequate diet.

It needs to be stated here, that food absorption relates to food assimilation which depends upon the state of health of the individual. Food consumption depends upon the habits, preferences, perceptions and knowledge of basic

Map 1
Food Insecurity in Rural India

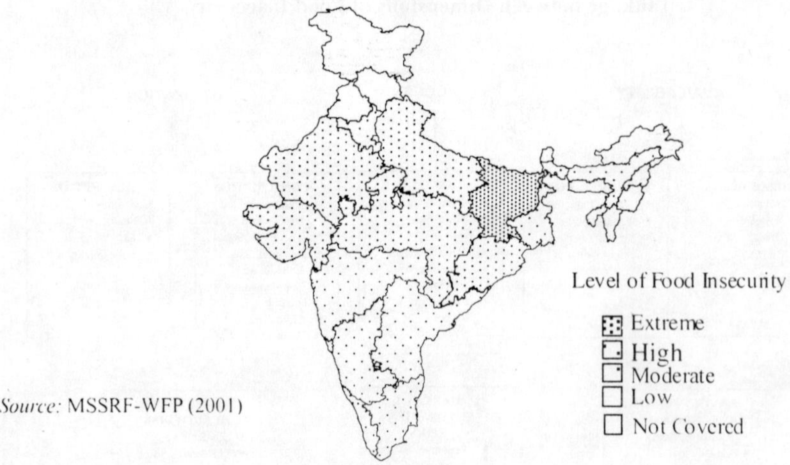

Source: MSSRF-WFP (2001)

nutrition which determine the intake of carbohydrates, proteins, fats and other basic nutrients. Low levels of nutrient intake may occur, if, people do not consume balanced diets, which may happen due to lack of knowledge of nutrition. Female literacy is known to enhance knowledge of nutrition and consequently, improve child health (Dreze and Sen, 1999). There are certain preconditions for the adequate absorption of each type of essential nutrient. For example, calorie adequacy is an essential pre-requisite for protein adequacy. A person who is not healthy cannot assimilate food even if she or he consumes a balanced diet. And one's state of health depends upon the state of sanitation and hygiene and the kind of surroundings and also upon the timely availability of medical facilities, which, in turn depend upon the level of health infrastructure.

Food availability, food access and food absorption are not separate phenomena, there are a number of overlapping elements among these dimensions. In rural areas, food production itself is linked to livelihood access, food access and food consumption. Livelihood access, in turn, influences the demand for food and better prices and incentives for further production. Better access to sources of livelihood also leads to better education, better living standards, better sanitation, better knowledge of nutrition, better absorption and better health.

Food insecurity may be present or potential. If a state overuses its natural resources and fails in making provision for containing environmental degradation, it could become potentially food insecure.

In this paper, we have considered the overall food insecurity map of India, in which the composite food insecurity indices[2] are reflected showing the relative positions of the states. The map is based on 19 indicators covering all the above dimensions and 15 major states (see appendices for the details of the indicators and the methodology used to arrive at the composite food insecurity index).

The composite food insecurity indices for different states have been translated into the final food insecurity map of India. The map shows that Bihar is the most food insecure state in every way. It is 'poor' in terms of almost all the indicators. The most food secure states are Punjab and Haryana, followed by Karnataka and Kerala, all of which have performed satisfactorily in terms of a number of indicators. There are moderately food secure states such as Tamil Nadu, Andhra Pradesh, Maharashtra, West Bengal and Assam. The set of states that comprise the highly food insecure category are Gujarat, Orissa, Rajasthan, Madhya Prádesh and Uttar Pradesh. The map categorises the states into different typologies based on the common problems of food availability, food access and food absorption among the group of states. None of the states including Punjab and Haryana, which have severe problems of long-term environmental sustainability is in the ideal position of being totally food secure.

III. CHILD WORK: TRENDS AND PATTERNS IN RURAL INDIA

The definition of child work is a contentious issue in contemporary research. There are wide differences in views as to who should be counted as a child worker. Officially in India, children in the age group, 5-14 years, who are engaged in production activities and services involving physical activities and/or wages, cash or kind are called child workers. Contemporary research, however, has established that children in this age group (5-14), who are out of school, are vulnerable to become child workers (called potential child worker) and could be counted as such. These children generally stay at home to help their parents with household chores including looking after younger siblings or engaging in non-wage physical activities. As a result, they prematurely lead adult lives, working for long hours for low wages under conditions detrimental to their health and mental development. Sometimes they are separated from their families and are deprived of meaningful education and training opportunities that could open up a better future for them (ILO, 1996). Thus, the children in this category are defined as 'nowhere' children and counted as child workers (Chaudhri, 1997; Burra, 1995). Most contemporary studies dealing with child work, include children in both these categories for the purpose of analysis.

1. Wide Variation in Estimates of Child Labour

Due to the multiplicity of definitions and the data collecting agencies, there is wide variability in the estimates of the number of working children in India. According to a report published by the Bureau of Statistics, ILO (1996), the number of working children in the developing countries of the world in the age group, 5-14 years is about 120 million, which increases to 250 million if secondary activities are also included. The same report reveals that India has the largest population of street and working children.

The figures from official agencies in India, however, vary between 11 million and 17 million. According to the National Sample Survey Organisations of India (1994), there are more than 230 million children in the age group, 5-14 years, out of which, more than 90 million children were out of school in 1994-95. According to the Census (1991), however, the number of children in the age group, 5-14, is 312 million and the number of those not attending school was 104 million in 1991, out of which 87 million alone were located in the rural areas, a majority of them being girls.

The Census report reveals that the number of working children was 11.3 million[3] in 1991 (of which 10.3 million were in rural India). The NSS[4] (1993-94) estimates are, higher than the Census figures. The number of child workers in this country was estimated to be 17.02 million, out of which about 13 million were in the rural areas. According to the National Council of Applied Economic Research, the number of working children in the rural areas of the country is estimated to be much lower — at about 9 million.

Nonetheless, if one adds the number of children who are not attending schools and those who are engaged in wage activities, both the NSS and Census figures yield similar figures with minor discrepancies. Importantly, estimates from all the agencies show the temporal trends in the regional pattern of child work to be declining in India since 1971. The NSS figures, on the other hand, show a decline in the proportion of children working in the rural areas over the 43rd and 50th Quinquennial rounds, from about 9.5 per cent to 7.5 per cent. The Census of India, however, shows that the proportion of children working as child work has marginally gone up from 6.11 per cent to 6.43 per cent during 1981-91, much of the increase being mainly due to the increase in the participation of girl children from 5.26 per cent to 6.29 per cent. It is, important to note that both of the above sources show an increase in the absolute numbers.

Notwithstanding the variability in the incidence of child work, all the major databases providing estimates of child work reveal that the percentage participation of girl children in the work activities has been increasing during the eighties and nineties. Further, the analysis of the state level census figures from 1971, 1981 and 1991 reveals that there has been a visible increase in work participation among the girl children in 13 major states, the increase being significant in the backward states like Orissa, Rajasthan and Uttar Pradesh.

2. Regional Pattern of Child Work

Given the similarity in the trends and patterns of various databases, we have analysed the Census data for the purpose of examining the regional pattern of child work (Figure 2). The level of child work in the rural areas is not uniformly distributed across the states. The incidence of child work is highly concentrated in some of the states like Andhra Pradesh, Karnataka, Madhya Pradesh, Rajasthan, Orissa, Bihar and West Bengal, most of which are less developed states. Further, there is wide variation in the inter-state incidence of child work in the rural areas. The proportion of working children in the main and marginal categories together is as high as 6.24 per cent in Andhra Pradesh and 0.4 per cent in Kerala. The inter-state variation in work participation among children (5-14 years) is high, the same being much higher for girl children as compared to boys.

Figure 2
Per cent Working and Nowhere Children

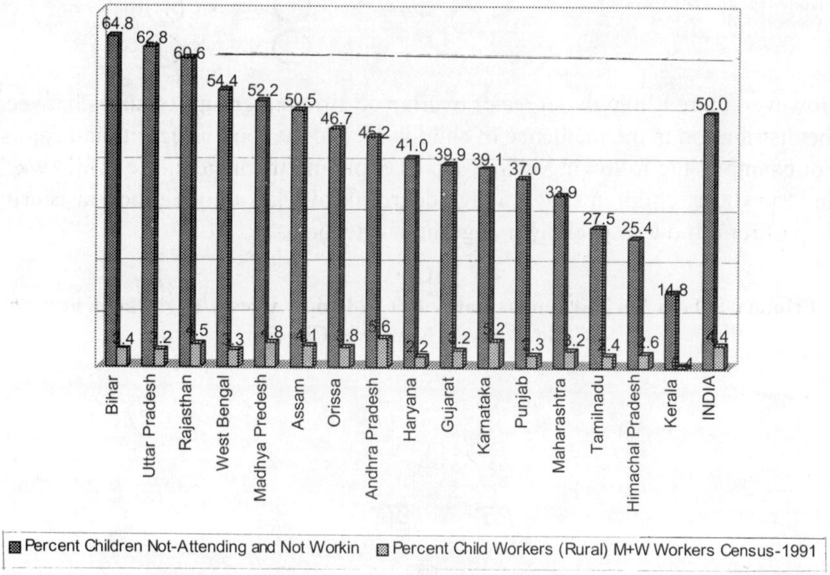

Percent Children Not-Attending and Not Workin | Percent Child Workers (Rural) M+W Workers Census-1991

The incidence of 'nowhere' children in the country has been declining during the last four decades, the decline in this category, being extremely uneven across states. While Kerala recorded the maximum decline in the incidence of the 'nowhere' children, Andhra Pradesh recorded the lowest.

Further, the incidence of 'nowhere' children is high in the relatively backward states like Bihar, Rajasthan, Orissa, Madhya Pradesh, Uttar Pradesh, West Bengal and Assam. Importantly, excepting Assam and West Bengal, the rate of female literacy in these states is much less than the national average. The southern states of Kerala, Karnataka, and Tamil Nadu, where the level of literacy is higher shows much lower incidence of 'nowhere' children.

A comparison of the socio-economic indicators across the states and the incidence of child work does not reveal any significant correlation between them.

Map 2
Child Work, 'Nowhere' Children and Food Insecurity in Rural India

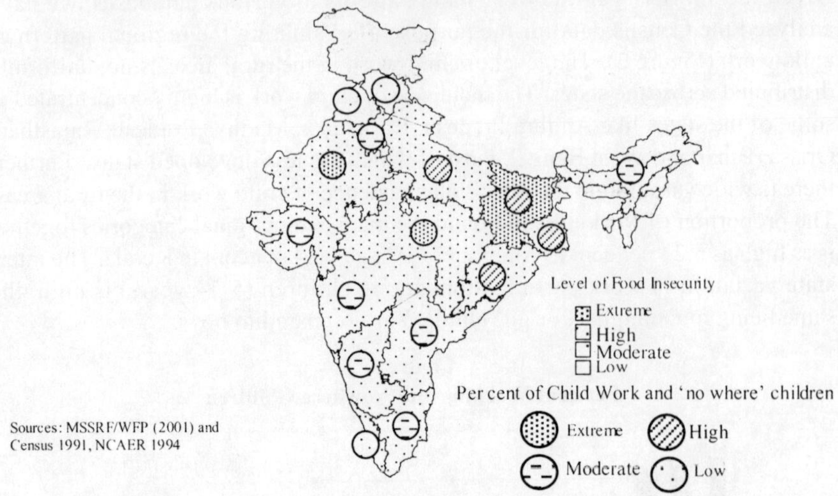

However, there is a high degree of overlap of different groups of states between the distribution in the incidence of child work and the food insecurity indicators. For example, the following map (Map 3) depicting the incidence of child work and 'nowhere' children shows a high degree of overlap with the food insecurity map of rural India (especially in high-high category).

Map 3
Primary School Net Enrolment Rate - 1997-98 and Extreme/High Incidences of Child Worker/'Nowhere' Children

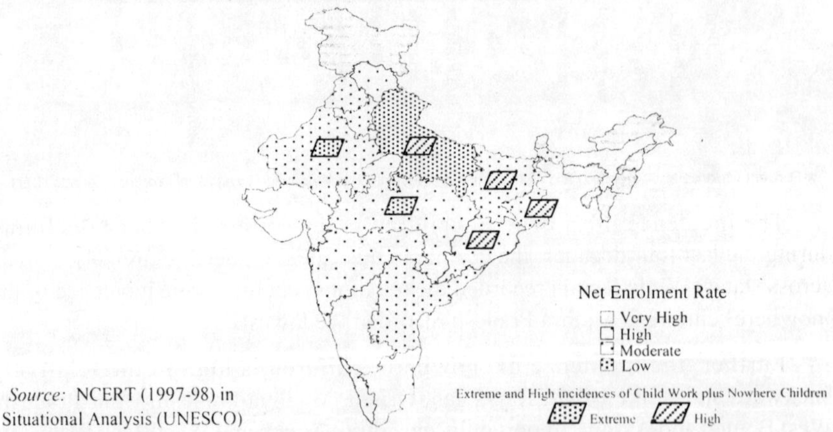

Source: NCERT (1997-98) in Situational Analysis (UNESCO)

A number of studies have classified the causes of child work into different categories, including the demand for and supply of child work and the demand for and availability of educational facilities which makes for the easy access of the children to schools (Deshpande, 2000). The demand for child work is a major factor explaining the incidence of child work.

The supply of child work is basically governed by two factors: (a) the need to supplement the family income, when the total family income is inadequate to meet household needs and (b) the suitability of the skills of children for crafts and related production activities (such as carpet and bangle industries). The major cause of child work, however, lies in household poverty and the inability of the households to meet their food and calories intake requirements, which is responsible for pushing the children to work for low wages.

Another standpoint from which scholars have attempted to explain the causes of child work is the dis-equilibrium in the demand and supply of educational facilities for children in the age group, 5-14 years. (Chaudhri, 2001). As primary schools are not available in sufficient numbers and potential students need to travel long distances to get to school, the children are discouraged from availing of this facility As a result, children stay at home and become prone to child work.

However, there is often shortage in the demand for schools in the rural areas. Particularly in the tribal dominated and economically backward locations. Because of the persistence of low income, poverty and food insecurity among families, poor households in the rural areas, either cannot afford to send their children to school or the opportunity cost involved in doing so is high. There is, therefore, a need to overcome both the supply and demand side constraints is accessing educational facilities to reduce the incidence of child work.

Although, the magnitudes are different, the statistics (e.g., Census/NSS/NCAER) show similar trends and patterns in the regional incidence of child work. School enrolment and drop out rates are indicators (Map 4), which reflect heavily on the incidence of child work. Indeed, the supply of child work does not get augmented automatically with the increase in the child population. The higher

Map 4
School Drop out Rate - 1997-98 and Incidence of Extreme/High Child Worker/ 'Nowhere' Children

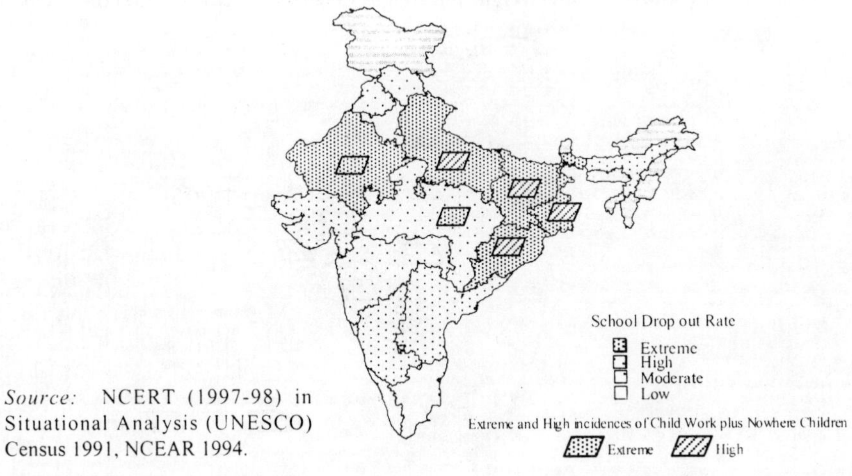

Source: NCERT (1997-98) in Situational Analysis (UNESCO) Census 1991, NCEAR 1994.

incidence of child work is basically a result of low enrolment and high drop-out rates. This manifests in the high absolute number of 'nowhere' children in rural India vis-à-vis its correlation with the regional pattern of school enrolment and school drop out rates.

One can see the overlapping nature of the maps depicting (a) child workers (plus 'nowhere' children), and primary school enrolment rate (Map 3) and (b) school drop-out rate[5] (Map 4). For example, most of the states in darkest shades in the enrolment map of India (like Tamil Nadu, Kerala, Maharashtra, Madhya Pradesh, etc.) appear in the lightest shades in the drop-out map of India. Similarly, the states with lighter shades (like Bihar, Orissa, Rajasthan, etc.) in the enrolment map of India appear in the darkest shade in the dropout map of India. The interdependent nature of the two indicators, implies that both the demand for and the supply of educational facilities are missing.

IV. CHILD WORK, 'NOWHERE' CHILDREN AND FOOD INSECURITY: AN ANALYSIS OF INTERRELATIONS

As mentioned earlier, no single indicator can explain the existence of child work; the causes are intertwined and need to be analysed in a holistic manner. We have thus analysed the food insecurity indicators, which have direct or indirect bearings on the spatial incidence of child work (plus 'nowhere' children) in India. The correlation analysis of the indicators reveals positive correlations of child work and 'nowhere' children with nutritional indicators like chronic energy deficiency among adults, wasting (Map 5) and stunting (Map 6) among under-5 children, proportion of people consuming less than 1890 kcal. (The values of all the correlation coefficients are higher than +0.42 and excepting for Chronic Energy Deficiency among adults, all other coefficients are significant at 10 per cent levels of significance.) The spatial distribution of child work and 'nowhere' children also shows positive correlations with indicators like drought, seasonality, poverty and the percentage distribution of the SC and ST population.

Map 5

Percentage of Children Underweight for Height (Wasted) in Rural India (0-5 years)

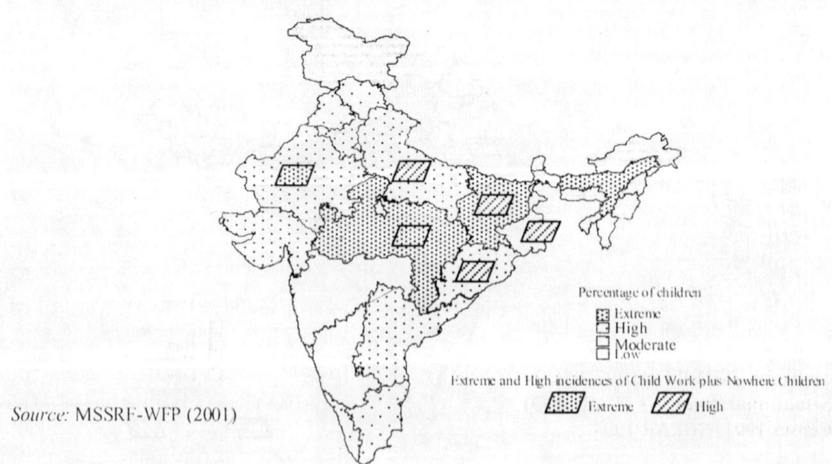

Source: MSSRF-WFP (2001)

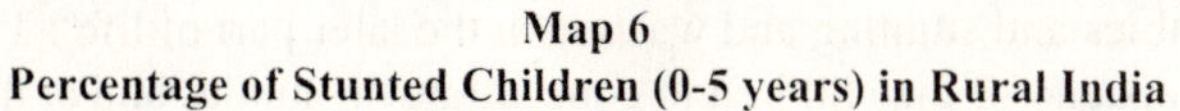

Map 6
Percentage of Stunted Children (0-5 years) in Rural India

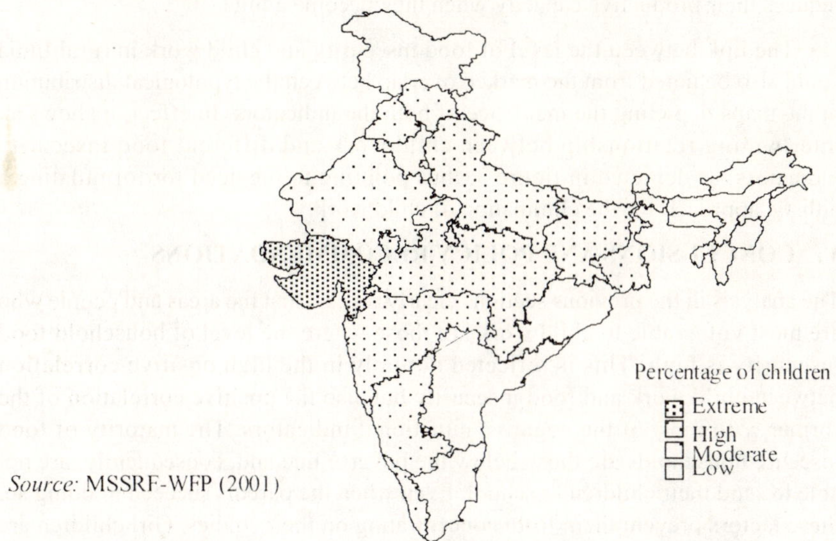

Source: MSSRF-WFP (2001)

The correlation analysis of child work and food insecurity indicators reveals strong linkages of the former with the level of food insecurity in the states. (The correlation coefficient of child work with the food insecurity index works out to be +0.54, significant at a 10 per cent level of significance). Although the distribution of child work does not show a significant correlation with the incidence of poverty at the state level, the causal link with poverty cannot be ignored (The correlation co-efficient is +0.34). The correlation coefficient between poverty and the overall food insecurity index reveals that the two factors are highly related to each other. It is the low income syndrome which restricts the purchasing power of the households, thus denying them access to sufficient food for a healthy and productive life. The lack of a balanced and sufficient calorie intake not only affects the mothers and other adult members of the households, but also accounts for the high mortality rate among infants and children, low birth

Figure 3
Food Insecurity and Child Work Interwined Connections

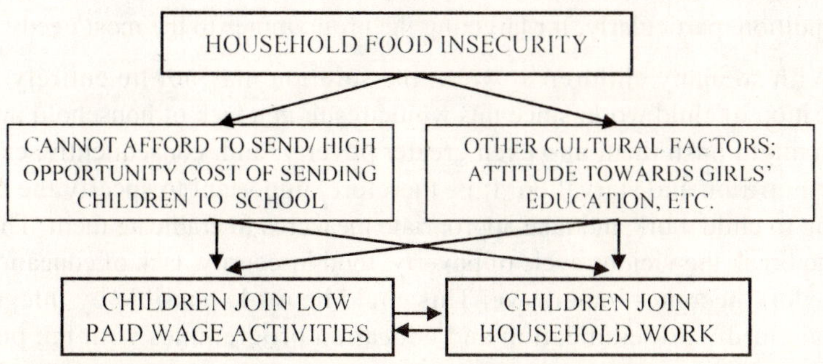

weight of babies and stunting and wasting in the later part of life[6]. This seriously affects the capacity of the children to concentrate on studies and at the same time reduces their productive capacity when they become adults.

The link between the level of food insecurity and child work in rural India could also be noted from the marked overlap between the typological distribution in the maps depicting the incidence of both the indicators. In effect, it shows an intertwining relationship between child work and different food insecurity indicators, as depicted in figure 3, thus pointing to the need for formulating a holistic approach for the elimination of child work.

V. CONCLUSIONS AND POLICY RECOMMENDATIONS

The analysis in the previous sections clearly reveals that the areas and people who are most vulnerable to child work are those where the level of household food insecurity is high. This is reflected not only in the high positive correlation between child work and food insecurity but also the positive correlation of the former with most of the negative nutritional indicators. The majority of food insecure households are those below the poverty line and, consequently, are not able to send their children to school. Even when the parents succeed in doing so, these factors prevent them from concentrating on their studies. Girl children are often engaged in more hazardous work (see sectoral distribution of employment for age group, 5-14 Census 1991) and receive lower wages than boy workers or are engaged in household chores.

As a result of the above factors, in most Indian states, there is both a demand for and supply of child workers and both these factors are associated with a number of intertwining factors. Thus, there is a need for a holistic development initiative which accounts for all these factors, and will help to break the vicious circle of poverty, food insecurity and child work. In the short term, however, food insecurity and child work can be combated through appropriate food safety nets (e.g., Food For Work that provides family rations, Public Distribution System, and nutritional support through programmes like Mid Day Meals and ICDS). It is noteworthy that the incidence of child work (plus 'nowhere' children) is high mostly in the states where the effective coverage of food entitlement schemes is not satisfactory.

Any programme for alleviating child work needs to clearly identify the target group and for this, a consensus on the definition of child work is an essential precondition, particularly, for targeting the programmes to the most needy.

With so many children at work, the solution may not lie entirely in the eradication of child work, since this would result in a lack of household income, which might push them into even greater poverty, and, consequently, extreme under-nutrition and starvation. It is, therefore, important to specify the causes leading to child work and take appropriate measures to eradicate them. Thus the need to break the vicious cycle of poverty, food insecurity, lack of education and child work becomes imperative. This could be made possible by integrating special child work eradication and education programmes with the poverty alleviation and employment generation programmes, which will help the poor households in an integrated manner.

Food plays a critical part with respect to interventions. It has been observed that external agencies such as the Government and local authorities, international organisations and non-governmental organisations all contribute to the task of overcoming the problem of food insecurity. Food insecure and child work prone households should be assisted by providing supplementary food to children through the Integrated Child Development Services (ICDS) and morning snacks and mid-day meals and supplemental nutrition packets in the primary schools to bridge the short-term nutritional gap. When safety nets are successfully cast, food insecurity is minimal. With the information that is currently available, such interventions should be carefully targeted geographically (preferably at the district and block levels) so that limited resources are utilised judiciously.

The effectiveness of the safety nets depends upon the need, the suitability of the programme, the awareness and participation of the community, and the competence of the implementing agency. The *panchayats* could play a useful role in mobilising the local community for working out solutions at the local level. The 11th schedule of the Article 243(Z) (73rd Constitutional Amendment Act) gives a list of 29 items which can respond to major causes of child work like poverty, lack of education, health care and so on. Panchayats can be involved in improving and monitoring the educational standards of the villages under their jurisdiction. In an effort to spread awareness, Panchayats should form citizen's groups such as village education committees and mother-teacher associations which could launch a door-to-door campaign aimed at highlighting the value of education and the disadvantages of child work.

There is also a need to strengthen the existing institutions, like Ashram Schools for SC/STs (social welfare departments of the state governments) which are located in the rural/tribal areas. In addition, assisting children with the provision of school books/uniforms will encourage children to attend school. Further, special emphasis must be placed on the needs of girl children because, they are more disadvantaged than boys. Furthermore, arousing public consciousness about the hazards of child work through posters/street plays depicting these hazards and organising meetings of community members, (particularly, women) will go a long way in making child work alleviation programmes successful. The formation of partnerships with local NGOs, which assist working children will help in the improved targeting of programmes at the local level.

Over the last 30 years, there have been a number of promising developmental initiatives, which have not always been presented in the most skillful manner, and as a result their positive impact has been somewhat limited These initiatives cover aspects such as Gender, Human Rights and Environment. It would be important for the initiatives directed at the eradicating of child work to be driven mainly by the needs and wisdom of individual countries and states. Also, it is important to draw on community leaders and exemplars who are engaged in the task of uplifting the poor to act as agents for promoting the development of their own communities.

Appendix

Sources of Indicators Used in the Food Insecurity Map of India (15 states)

Components

1. Deficit in production represented by the ratio of per capita consumption of cereals to per capita production of cereals

   a) Triennium average cereal production, for the triennium ending in 1993-94, (average of 1991-92,1992-93 and 1993-94); per capita per day in grams.

   Source: GOI (1995-96), Ministry of Agriculture, Area and Production of Principal Crops in India.

   b) Cereal consumption in kilograms per month in the year 1993-94.

   Source: NSSO, 50th Round, Report No. 402, (1993-94), *Level and Pattern of Consumer Expenditure, 1993-94,* Department of Statistics, GOI.

2. Instability of Cereal Production

   Calculated from the production data of 10 years from 1987-88 to 1997-98. Instability is calculated as the standard deviation of annual growth rates and expressed as a percentage. Annual growth rates are given by the first differences in the natural log of the production statistics. It represents a measure, which is free from the trend.

   Source: GOI, Ministry of Agriculture (1995-96) *Area, Production of Principal Crops in India* (Various Issues) and Ministry of Agriculture, (2000), *Agriculture in Brief,* 27th edition.

3. Sustainability Index

   Components

   a. Area not under forest as percentage of total geographical area.

   Source: GOI (1997), Ministry of Statistics and Programme Implementation, *Compendium of Environment Statistics.*

   b. Percentage of groundwater exploitation represented by net draft as a percentage of total available ground water resources

   Source: GOI (1997), Ministry of Statistics and Programme Implementation, *Compendium of Environment Statistics.*

   c. Percentage of area under non-leguminous crops to total gross cropped area.

   Source: Centre for Monitoring Indian Economy, Agriculture (1999), September. (Two-year average of 1994-95 and 1995-96)

   d. Percentage of problem area susceptible to soil erosion by wind and water as a percentage of total geographical area.

   Source: GOI, (2000), Ministry of Agriculture, Soil and Water Conservation Division, *Agriculture in Brief,* 27th edition.

4. Population affected by flood/cyclone/heavy rains/landslides in Lakhs

Source: India Disaster Report 2000 and 1999 data from GOI, Ministry of Statistics and Programme Implementation (1999), *Compendium of Environment Statistics.*

5. Percentage of drought prone area to total geographical area

   Source: GOI, Ministry of Statistics and Programme Implementation (1999), *Compendium of Environment Statistics.*

6. Calorie intake of the lowest deciles per capita per day (kcal)

   Source: NSSO, *Sarvekshana*, 50th Round, 1993-94, Vol. 21, No.2, 73rd Issue Oct-Dec'1997, Department of Statistics, Ministry of Planning and Programme Implementation, GOI.

7. Percentage of population consuming less than 1890 Kcal

   Source: NSSO, Sarvekshana, 50th Round, 1993-94, Vol. 21, No.2, 73rd Issue Oct-Dec'97, Department of Statistics, Ministry of Planning and Programme Implementation, GOI.

8. Percentage of population below poverty line (Rural, 1993-94)

   Source: Planning Commission estimates as quoted in Malhotra, 1997 represented in *India Rural Development Report (1999)*, National Institute of Rural Development, Hyderabad.

9. Percentage of population dependent on labour income

   Source: NSSO, 50th Round, Report No. 409, *Employment and Unemployment in India* (1993-94)

10. Rural Infrastructure Index:

    Components

    a. Percentage of households without electricity

       Source: Shariff, A. (1999), *India Human Development Report*, NCAER (2000).

    b. Percentage of households without piped water

       Source: Shariff, A. (2000), *India Human Development Report*, NCAER.

    c. Road length per thousand persons

       Source: GOI, Ministry of Surface Transport (1996-97), *Basic Roads and Statistics of India.*

    d. Percentage of villages without electricity

       Source: GOI, Ministry of Statistics and Programme Implementation, *Compendium of Environment Statistics* (1999), New Delhi.

11. Juvenile sex ratio - Ratio of females to 1000 males in the age group, 0-9 years of age.

    Source: GOI, Registrar General and Census Commissioner, *Census of India* (1991).

12. Percentage of female literacy - Number of literate females as a percentage to total females

Source: GOI, Registrar General and Census Commissioner, *Census of India* (1991).

13. Percentage of Scheduled Caste and Scheduled Tribe population in rural areas

    Source: GOI, Registrar General and Census Commissioner, *Census of India* (1991).

14. Life expectancy at age one

    Source: GOI, Registrar General and Census Commissioner, *Sample Registration Surveys* (1992-96).

15. Percentage of population with chronic energy deficiency

    Source: GOI, Ministry of Human Resource Development, Department of Women and Child development, *India Nutrition Profile* (1998).

    Data for Uttar Pradesh and West Bengal are taken from, NCAER, India Human Development Report 1999.

16. Percentage of severely stunted children under five (Rural)

    Severe stunting is defined as one whose weight for age is two standard deviations below the norm given by National Centre for Health Statistics, an international organization. International reference median is taken as the norm.

    Source: National Nutrition Monitoring Bureau (NNMB), (1996), and Ministry of Human Resource Development, Department of Women and Child development, India Nutrition Profile (1998) and Data for Uttar Pradesh and West Bengal are taken from, Shariff, A., NCAER, *India Human Development Report* (1999).

17. Percentage of children severely underweight for height (wasting) under five

    (Rural) Wasting in children is defined as children with lower weight for height, compared to National Centre for Health Statistics norm.

    Source: National Nutrition Monitoring Bureau (NNMB), (1996), and Ministry of Human Resource Development, Department of Women and Child development, India Nutrition Profile (1998) and Data for Uttar Pradesh and West Bengal are taken from, Shariff, A., *India Human Development Report* (1999), NCAER.

18. Infant mortality rate in rural areas (number of deaths per 1000 live births)

    Source: GOI, Registrar General and Census Commissioner, *Sample Registration Surveys* (1990 and 1997)

19. Health Infrastructure Index

    Computed from the data given in *Health Information of India,* Ministry of Health and Family Welfare (1995-96).

    Components

    a. Percentage of children immunised to total number of children in the age group of one and two.

       Source: National Family Health Surveys (NFHS-1) - (1992-93), International

Institute for Population Sciences (IIPS), Mumbai, India.

b. Percentage of population with access to safe drinking water in rural India

Source: GOI, Registrar General and Census Commissioner, Census of India (1991), in the publication of United Nations Population Fund, *India. Towards Population and Development Goals.* Oxford University Press.

Arunachal Pradesh data are taken for Assam, as there were no data for Assam.

c. Number of persons per bed in rural areas in all hospitals and dispensaries owned by government, private and local bodies and voluntary organizations.

Source: GOI, Ministry of Health and Family Welfare, *Health Information of India.* (1995-96).

d. Number of persons per Primary Health Centre, in rural areas

Source: GOI, Ministry of Health and Family Welfare, *Health Information of India.* (1995-96).

e. Number of persons per doctor in rural areas

Source: GOI, Ministry of Health and Family Welfare, *Health Information of India.* (1995-96).

Notes

1. The production of foodgrains has already crossed the 200 million-ton mark in the country.
2. The method of constructing the composite food insecurity indices involved the following steps;
   a) Ranks were assigned to the states for each of the indicators corresponding to their values in such a manner that rank 1 represented the worst possible situation and rank 15 represented the best possible situation for a particular indicator.
   b) The ranks of the states were then added up to arrive at the composite rank score of the states.
   c) The composite ranks of the states were then divided by 19 (the number of indicators) to arrive at the average food insecurity indices of the states.
   d) The values of the average ranks were then distributed among different classes (using the natural breaks to arrive at the typologies of food insecurity, viz. Extreme, High, Moderate and Low food insecure categories.
   e) These categories were then translated into the food insecurity map of India putting the different typologies to different shades of the red colour.
3. This figure includes only the main and marginal workers and not those in the non-worker category.
4. Includes child workers in both principal and subsidiary status categories.
5. Data from NCERT (1997-98) report on educational indicators have been used for the analysis of both these indicators.

6. All these indicators show positive correlations with the incidence of child work.

References

Burra, N. (1995), *Born to Work: Child Labour in India,* Oxford University Press, Delhi.

Centre for Monitoring Indian Economy (1999), *Report - Agriculture,* September.

Chaudhri, D. P. (1997), "A Policy Perspective on Child Labour in India with Pervasive Gender and Urban Bias in School Education", *The Indian Journal of Labour Economics,* Vol. 40, No. 4.

—— (2000), "Sources of Supply of Child Labour and the States: Explorations of Historical and Contemporary Evidence with Focus on States and Districts of India", in Compendium, *National Seminar on Child Labour: Realities and Policy Dimensions,* VV Giri National Labour Institute, NOIDA, Institute for Human Development, New Delhi.

Deshpande, Sudha (2000), "The Girl Child Labour in India", *National Seminar on Child Labour: Realities and Policy Dimensions,* VV Giri National Labour Institute, NOIDA and Institute for Human Development, New Delhi.

Dreze, Jean and Amartya Sen (1999), "Introduction", Dreze, Jean, Amartya Sen and Athar Hussain (eds.), *Political Economy of Hunger,* Clarendon Press, Oxford University Press.

Food Aid Organisation (2000), *The State of Food Insecurity in the World: A Report,* Second Edition.

GOI (1993), *73rd Constitutional Amendment Act,* Lok Sabha, New Delhi.

—— (1995-96), *Area and Production of Principal Crops in India,* Ministry of Agriculture.

—— (1996-97), *Basic Roads and Statistics of India,* Ministry of Surface Transport, Delhi.

—— (2000), *Agriculture in Brief,* (Vol.27), Soil & Water Conservation Division, Ministry of Agriculture.

—— *Sample Registration Surveys* (1992-96), Registrar General and Census Commissioner.

ILO (1996), *Child Labour and Targeting,* Bureau of Statistics, Geneva.

IIPS (1992-93), *National Family Health Surveys (1992-93),* 'NFHS-1', International Institute for Population Sciences (IIPS), Mumbai, India.

NCERT (1998), *6th All India Educational Survey,* National Council for Educational Research and Training, New Delhi.

National Institute of Rural Development(1999), *India Rural Development Report,* Hyderabad.

NSSO (1993-94), *Sarvekshana,* 50th Round, Vol. 21, No. 2, Oct-Dec, 1997, Department of Statistics, Ministry of Planning and Programme Implementation, Government of India.

NSSO (1993-94), 50th Round, Report No. 409, *Employment and Unemployment in India,* New Delhi.

—— (1997), *Sarvekshana.*

Shariff, A. (2000), *India Human Development Report,* NCAER, New Delhi.

UNICEF (1999), *The State of the World's Children,* Oxford University Press, New York.

United Nations World Food Programme (2001), *Food Insecurity Atlas of Rural India,* Delhi.

WFP (2000), *Country Strategy Outline (2002-2007),* World Food Programme, New Delhi.

Zutshi, Bhupinder (2000), *A Situational Analysis of Education for Street and Working Children in India,* UNESCO, New Delhi.

3

Bringing Rural Child Workers to School: Seasonal and Cultural Constraints

PIERRE SPITZ

I. INTRODUCTION

The 'Right to food' has received increased attention during the last five years. Heads of states and governments gathered at the World Food Summit in Rome in November 1996 adopted the "Rome Declaration on World Food Security", reaffirming "the right of everyone to have access to safe and nutritious food, consistent with the right to adequate food and the fundamental right of everyone to be free from hunger". As stated in the preamble of the International Code of Conduct on the Human Right to Adequate Food" subsequently drafted in 1997, the right to adequate food is a fundamental human right firmly established in international law. The Right flows from the Charter of the United Nations, the Universal Declaration of Human Rights and the International Covenant on Economic, Social and Cultural Rights of 1996 and has been reaffirmed in many pronouncements of the International Community over the last 50 years.

The Right to food has an instant appeal to deeply rooted human feelings, because food is vital to human sustenance. Furthermore, among the necessities of life, food shares with water a distinctive feature, so mundane that one tends to forget it: it is a basic human need without meeting which no living being can live beyond a certain number of days and certainly cannot perform manual work for very long. Food and water, therefore, need to be obtained within much stricter time constraints than other necessities of life (clothing, shelter, etc.). This daily anxiety has been voiced billions of times in popular sayings and prayers, such as, in Christian religions: "give us this day our daily bread". Beyond technical definitions, the notion of food insecurity reflects this anxiety and the uncertainty of realising the Right to Food for one's self, one's family, and one's community, in the near and more distant future.

The time dimensions of food insecurity are different in the urban and rural areas of a country such as India. As non-food producers, the urban poor depend entirely on the distribution through time of their earnings, on the one hand, and on availability of food and their prices, on the other. Although some employment opportunities available to them are linked to the season (construction activities, road repairs, processing of agricultural products, etc.) their earnings are generally erratic and not time-bound, and their livelihood depends on day-to-day make-shift arrangements. The extent of urban food insecurity is thus made of individual tragedies, each one surrounded by its own peculiar circumstances.

In rural areas, on the other hand, food insecurity has a very definite pattern, as resource flows and food availability are structured by time, that is, the seasons. This is so, not only for agricultural producers and labourers but also, to a large extent for rural artisans, craftsmen and workers in services and even workers in rural industries.

II. SEASONALITY DIMENSION OF RURAL FOOD INSECURITY

This seasonality dimension of rural food insecurity is particularly evident and clear-cut in the six states of Madhya Pradesh, Chhattisgarh, Jharkhand, Orissa, Rajasthan and Gujarat (WFP, 2001). The most food insecure districts of these states form part of a belt characterised by a uni-modal distribution of rainfall, dearth of irrigation facilities, a subsistence-oriented agriculture largely built on a single crop and in forested areas, cash income from forest products. The period for which the poor are food secure lasts, by and large, as long as self-provisioning of food is possible. When the household grain stocks are exhausted, a period of food insecurity steps in during which people have to undergo suffering and hardship due to hunger until the next harvest. The whole social fabric is adjusted to this qualitatively predictable seasonal pattern of food availability, employment, indebtedness and migration, with its likelihood of year-to-year fluctuations aggravating or partly alleviating food insecurity.

It is in within this seasonal framework, that time use of children needs to be determined. Rural children in the most food insecure districts can help to alleviate the food insecurity faced by their families, either in the short-term by paid or unpaid labour or in the longer term by attending school in the expectation of a more secure gainful employment because of having attained a better education status. The trade-offs between these time dimensions of the short-term vs. long-term as well as the nature (paid/unpaid) and location (within the family, the village or in more distant areas) of child work in contrast with what can be expected from the school system need to be clarified. Well-documented research is needed on the linkages between food insecurity, school attendance and child work, a nexus which WFP has attempted to explore. The following observations might contribute towards organising a more focused action/research effort in assessing the nature of these linkages and the most appropriate modalities to address the complex issues at stake.

Rural areas in India have, in spite of their great diversity, a common feature which, if not specific to India, is more prevalent here than anywhere else in the world. This is the tradition of family occupation, with its attendant opportunities and constraints attuned to a complex socio-economic and cultural system. It is within this framework that occupational patterns and employment opportunities for children need to be analysed. If the pursuit of agricultural activities is, by and large, neutral in relation to this system (although some specific activities might have some caste or gender dimensions), this is not the case with traditional occupations in crafts and services, except trade, which even if they are often dominated by caste appartenance does not have a closed access. The rural labour market, at least for a number of traditional occupations, is thus fragmented by rigid rules.

Among Muslim communities traditional occupations have built a near equivalent to the caste system, though more flexible, as in the case of traditional weavers. In Tribal societies, employment opportunities in traditional crafts are more widely open, even if transmission of skills along family or clans lines gives those who possess them a comparative advantage, like in any society. Through their participation, often at a very young age, in the family traditional craft and service activities, children learn skills, which they practice in their adult life. Families of potters, weavers, tailors, carpenters, blacksmiths offer employment opportunities, which are not available to the products of the prevailing school system. In addition, most of these activities in traditional crafts and services have a relatively continuous nature only interrupted, if at all, by seasonal constraints as for example, construction work or pot-making cannot be carried out during the monsoon. Very often during these periods of interruption, some agricultural work has to be done on the family land or on others' farms. Children are thus employed during most of the year. In such circumstances, it is difficult to convince parents not only to forgo their children's contribution to the household income but depending on their skill and experience, their future employment opportunities as well. Parents' reluctance, would, however, be reduced if an ad-hoc school time frame (e.g., late-afternoon classes) with a module approach could be adapted to the local patterns of home-based apprenticeship, providing, minimum literacy and an understanding of numeracy helping, thereby, children in their future home-based market-oriented productive activities. Once such a basic level of literacy is attained, education would be provided to further develop the children's abilities to master their understanding of the world and of their own lives, provided their teachers work in an environment conductive to enhancing and maturing their analytical capabilities, creativity, value system, their emotions as well as their capacity for rational thinking.

Out-of-school boys working for wages outside the family framework and even outside their village, as street vendors or in tea-stalls, shops, workshops, etc. have very uncertain job prospects. Some of them 'graduate' into slightly better positions thanks to on-the-job training, particularly in the field of mechanics or construction, but a number of them do not have the opportunities to develop their skills further. In such a situation, the education system faces an even stiffer challenge than in the preceding case, in which some scope for adjustment between family-based apprenticeship of traditional skills and schooling exists. What prospects can the rural primary schools of the most food insecure districts of India offer to the children of the poorest families so as to eliminate the need for child paid work?

III. NEED TO ADAPT SCHOOL CALENDAR TO FIELD REALITIES

For parents in these families who see no prospects of their children getting jobs except as unskilled or at best semi-skilled workers, primary schools are virtually becoming waiting rooms for paid work which they attend when their contribution is not required at home: as soon as opportunity for paid work arises, the child leaves the school to contribute to the family livelihood system.

While school meals might marginally increase school attendance by boys during this waiting period, they, along with take-home rations, may have a much better impact on girl attendance. In these vulnerable districts, girls work predominantly at home, or in their village and stay with their parents until their marriage. Household chores, care of siblings might be arranged differently if a synergy is built between the school and the *anganwadi* centre and its pre-school activities, with school-meals and take-home rations off-setting the opportunity cost of sending the girls to school. In tribal areas, with less unbalanced gender relationships, such an approach would be more feasible. Teaching in schools, however has to be kept in line with what is preached in *anganwadi* centers on health, hygiene and sanitation; such as separation of spaces for teaching, eating, cooking, food storing and well-kept latrines for boys and girls, as absence of these facilities have often been cited as a constraint to girls' attendance. The offer of support to residential schools for girls would also increase their access to secondary education. As there is generally no dowry system in tribal societies (but rather the reverse), the increased education level of girls is not perceived as a liability at marriage time.

In contrast to those households in which children are engaged almost full time in traditional crafts and services, families which have no such opportunity for the placement of their children in society and are mainly dependent on agriculture, require children's help at work only at certain times of the year, such as during harvesting. Moreover, many such families do not produce enough food for the whole year. For the most food-insecure households, with little opportunity of paid child work, provision of food at school may well contribute to an increase in attendance provided the school calendars are not rigidly fixed at the state level, but are flexible at the local level and adapted to circumstances. This includes not only holidays allowing children to help their parents in their agricultural tasks or to work in the fields of others for limited periods of time, but also relating school activities to the lean period. It needs to be mentioned here that, in some areas where school feeding programmes have been introduced schools are closed when food insecurity faced by poor families is at its peak. Appropriate solutions for avoiding such situations need, therefore, to be worked out in collaboration with committed teachers, local school committees and representatives of the education departments, so as to take into account the seasonality profiles of food availability, festivals, weather conditions and child labour requirements by gender, both locally and in relation to seasonal migrations. The need for such solutions becomes apparent from the experience of school teachers in Rajasthan, where, according to one study, for instance, "teachers mentioned that there are seasonalities in attendance of pupils" (Nambissan, 2001, p. 493), and not only in absence from school "during periods such as the peak agriculture season (October-November) and *mahua* collecting months (March-April)", but also during December-January, as children migrate with their parents for "cotton-crop related activities in neighbouring Gujarat".

It is comforting to note that in Rajasthan some steps in the right direction have already been taken. The same study notes: "Schools respond to poor enrolment as well as irregularity in attendance in a number of ways. In Jhadol, children are allowed re-admission to school two to three times a year before their names are struck off the register. They often return after a long absence and take re-admission. Efforts are also being made to introduce a revised school calendar that alters the time of vacations to suit local agricultural and social needs. Strategies evolved to increase awareness about the importance of education include *padyatras* in the villages, home visits by teachers and meetings with parents and the community. In Alwar, pre-school children are allowed to attend school without being formally enrolled. These are called *kachha* enrolments. This is done to encourage enrolment in Class I and also to facilitate 'school readiness' in pre-school children".

The lack of adaptation of the school to local realities is characteristics of an education system that is largely divorced from the rural context in which children live. There is no reference to agriculture in teaching and practical experience allowing for a better understanding of cause-effects relationships. People's perception of this alienation of the school from their world is reflected in a Hindi saying which states: "A child going to primary school is lost to the family, to secondary school lost to work, to high school lost to the village". At best, school crystallises hopes to escape from agriculture in the most food-insecure areas.

The introduction of some agriculture-related modules and school gardens, and the establishment of some links with agricultural extension workers, as well as health workers, might reduce the distance between the school and the community. The disjunction between the school calendar and the seasonal imperatives of the agricultural year are, clearly, a sign of the lack of integration of rural schools in the community. Schools are viewed as government enclaves and the community is unconcerned about the maintenance or the improvement of its building that require only a modest collective effort. To break this indifference, the Food for Work Programme could be introduced as an incentive for initiating the work of rehabilitating school buildings and the surroundings (playgrounds), making them more attractive. Labour participation could be a first step in bridging the gap between the school and the village, particularly, if schools are selected on the basis of their contribution in strengthening the relevance of the school to the prevailing socio-economic environment, and whose teachers have received awards in appreciation of their efforts in this direction. Further, increasing teachers' motivations and social status could contribute to improve relationships with parents. Once such a dynamic process is started, mutual reinforcements could take place and school committees would play a more active role.

The study on elementary education in rural India quoted above concludes as follows: "The community has a direct stake and is best placed to monitor performance. Ideally, it should appoint teachers and manage schools. However, this seems impossible in the face of fierce opposition from teachers' unions. At the very least, there should be a mechanism by which the *panchayat* is permitted to monitor the teachers' attendance, conduct of classes and teaching. In the public schools, poor performance should be brought to the notice of the educational authorities that are independent of the *panchayats* and necessary corrective measures taken. Communities should have greater flexibility to adapt strategies for construction and establishment of schools, determining teaching and vacation schedules and school timings in the light of local conditions (such as settlements, distances between them, the extent of development of roads and road transport and the seasonal pattern of activity requiring children's participation). The patterns appropriate to Kerala are unlikely to be appropriate for Rajasthan, or tribal areas of Orissa and Chota Nagpur, or the hills of UP" (op.cit., p. 45).

While agricultural tasks as such are governed by the seasons, livestock activities require continuity and, given the importance of grazing in the production systems of the selected districts, the work of livestock keeping falls predominantly on children. In some areas, girls are involved, at least until puberty, in others boys are the only livestock keepers. School attendance is, therefore, precluded as long as grazing is a predominant activity compared to stall-feeding and as long as adults place a low value on children's time. It would be revealing in this context to cite an interview of a nine year old Rajasthani girl by Ann. G. Gold in which the child demonstrates her acute consciousness of the trade-offs between attending school and tending the family's sheep (Gold, 2001). The interview is mentioned below:

Ann: So, do you go to school?

Kali: School, never! I never went to school, never.

(She talks about her work helping to graze the family's sheep)

Ann: Is grazing good or is studying good?

Kali: Grazing sheep is very good.

Ann: Why?

Kali: Sheep give us income, what does reading give? Sheep give us income . Suppose I do go to study, so, I'll hardly get a job!

Ann: So what is good about sheep?

Kali: Our own house's sheep?

They give us lambs. So we sell them; they give dung, and we sell it.

As seen in the agrarian history of European countries, children who look after sheep and cattle constitute the last group that do not go to school in rural areas. Some employment prospects open up with the intensification of livestock production systems through stall-feeding. This leads to the generation of fodder collection tasks, which are often shared between women and children, and are thus more amenable to adjustments to school attendance timings. In the most food insecure states/districts, it is to be expected that transformation of the livestock production systems will not be rapid, and as a consequence, livestock keeping might remain for a long time an obstacle to school attendance.

In dealing with child work, mainly in the framework of family occupation, whether agricultural or non-agricultural, we have not dealt with the worst forms of child labour. When the distance between the child and his family increases, working conditions tend to deteriorate and, at the end of the spectrum, in a far away city, the child is at the mercy of his/her employer. Such a situation results in the worst forms of child labour denounced by the ILO Convention 182, such as children in prostitution, slavery, forced and/or hazardous labour, or armed conflicts, the roots of which lie mainly in these food insecure rural families who have no other choice than to let their children migrate to the cities in order to survive. The deprivation of rural children is, however, less well perceived and known than the plight of the street children. Nevertheless, many of the latter are brothers and sisters of child workers in this field ,who have left the fields and come to the streets.

These children are, as underlined by Professor C.H. Hanumantha Rao[1], the labour force of tomorrow. What is more significant is that they are also the creative force of the future. In such a perspective, WFP endeavours towards the realisation of the Right to development of the most food insecure families through a synergy between the increased fulfilment of their Right to Food, their Rights to Health and Nutrition and their Right to Education, which are the three components of its intervention (food for work, support to *anganwadi* centres and food for education) constitute a noteworthy contribution.

In conclusion, it needs to be emphasised that by focusing on the realisation of the Rights of the Child to Food, Education and Health, it is Development itself, which is addressed, for the next generation. This is consistent with Amartya Sen's vision of development as an increase in the range of choices and opportunities, as a process of expanding freedom.

Note

1. Inaugural Address delivered at the *IHD-WFP Consultative Workshop on Food Insecurity and Child Work,* New Delhi, March 2001.

References

Gold, Ann G. (1996), New Light New Times? *Manushi* No. 123, March-April.

Nambbisan, Geetha (2001), "Social Diversity and Regional Disparities in Schooling: A Study of Rural Rajasthan", A. Vaidyanathan and P.R. Gopinathan Nair (eds.), in *Elementary Education in Rural India: A Grassroots View,* Sage Publications, New Delhi, 2001.

World Food Programme (2001), *India Country Programme, 2003-2007,* New Delhi.

4

Girl Child Labour and Food Insecurity in India

Sudha Deshpande

I. INTRODUCTION

Child labour is extensively used in small units in India as elsewhere in many countries of South Asia. These units are mostly own account enterprises but they may as well be small manufacturing and service establishments in the informal sector. They are found in almost all sectors of the economy ranging from agriculture, forestry and pastoral activities to handicrafts and other household industries like *beedi* rolling and informal services that include menial services like domestic services, petty trade, restaurants and garages, to name a few. The hours of work children put in as workers in these activities vary depending upon the nature of work they do or their occupation. In the context of child labour, the family is involved in two ways: firstly, as an employer; when the child works as a helper in the family enterprise, especially in agriculture or at home, in a home-based industry like handlooms and secondly, as a supplier of labour, whether the child works at home or outside. More importantly, in the case of children the decision to work is taken not by the child, who actually works, but mostly by the parents, though, at times by other members in the household.

There could be two reasons why parents send their child to work: firstly, to supplement the meager family income, when the total income which all workers in the household earn is inadequate to make the two ends meet. Alternatively, a similar situation may arise when the head of the family either loses his job or dies, in which case children may be sent for work for ensuring family survival. Secondly, it is believed that certain skills or crafts are acquired better if children are initiated in these crafts at a young age. This helps them get gainful employment later when these children are adults. Needless to say, child work has dire consequences on children as it prevents them from attending school and investing in human capital. This affects not only their current, but also their future income. All efforts, therefore, should be directed to reduce child work and even eliminate it altogether in future. In other words, it is poverty of the parents that pushes many children in the labour market.

The World Bank (1986) defines food security as assured access to enough food, which all people should have, at all times, so as to enable them to lead an active and healthy life. Thus, food security does not merely imply assured access to food but to food that is nutritionally adequate. The concept of "minimum level of living", which the Planning Commission adopted, way back in the early 1960s and later to define the poverty line income/consumption, comes very close to this concept of food security. The Task Force on Projections of Minimum Needs and Effective Consumption Demand (1979) estimated that, on an average, 2400 kcal per capita per day met the energy requirements of the population residing in rural India. For those residing in urban India, the corresponding required calorie intake was estimated at 2100 kcal, per capita per day (Malhotra, 1997, p. 69). Consumption of certain essential non-food items was included in the Planning Commission's definition of minimum level of living (World Bank, 1989). The working group on "Minimum Level of Living" under the chairmanship of Pitamber Pant, distinguished between public consumption such as housing and education, which was to be financed by the state directly, and private consumption, which was to be met by an individual's income. Calculated at 1960/61 prices, the minimum income required to purchase the calorie intake and a minimum of non-food items, was to be no less than Rs.20 per month on a per capita basis in rural and Rs.25 per month in urban India (Chakravarty, 1987). This has been accepted as the official poverty line in India. Households and persons living in households who did not have the per capita monthly income to access this nutritionally adequate diet, were considered poor. In India, data on household personal incomes are difficult to come by. Since at low levels of income, expenditure is most likely to equal income, data on monthly per capita consumer expenditure (which includes both food and non-food items), collected by the National Sample Survey Organisation (NSSO) have been used by the Planning Commission to estimate households and population below the poverty line.

We are aware that no one indicator can fully capture the numerous facets of poverty. Low average consumption, low wages, inadequate nutritional intake, vulnerability to various diseases, low literacy rates and gender-related disadvantages—all have been used for capturing different dimensions of poverty. Nonetheless, a single summary index of population "below poverty line" is a useful measure used by our planners for framing issues (World Bank, 1989). Hunger, food insufficiency, either chronic or seasonal, could be said to be important facets of poverty so defined. Hence, we can say that households and persons who are "below poverty line" consumption in India suffer from food insecurity. In this paper we have, therefore, treated poverty ratio, per cent of population below poverty line, as an index of food insecurity.

Threatened with either chronic or seasonal insecurity of food, poor households devise complex survival strategies to cope with such calamities. As food insecurity increases, the strategy adopted becomes increasingly more serious. Coping mechanisms which households adopt in a country like India may vary from one region to another. Temporary migration of male members of the family to nearby towns, collection of wild food from forests, taking up of casual wage employment in the non-farm sector in the face of droughts, borrowing from friends and relatives, sale of productive assets like bullocks or even land, selling gold and / or even brass utensils are some of the coping mechanisms that poor families are known to adopt. But the most basic, of all these mechanisms, is to have as many hands to work and earn some income in times of economic distress. This results in initiation of women and children into the labour market. It is under these circumstances, that poor households view the child as an economic asset that can be acquired most easily. The child is looked upon as an insurance against future hunger (World Bank, 1984). Having a large family is, in fact, a survival strategy that the poor adopt so that in difficult times children can be relied upon to work and contribute their mite to the family kitty.

It is against this backdrop that this paper tries to understand the relationship between the participation of girl child workers in the labour market and food insecurity that prevails in India. While by reviewing the trends in the volume of child labour and their participation in economic activity in India over the 1980s and the 1990s, we concentrate on a segment of child workers, namely, girls in the age group, 5-14, two Censuses, of 1981 and 1991, and four Employment-Unemployment surveys of the NSSO, conducted quinquennially since 1983, form our data base, for reviewing the trends in the volume of child labour in general and girl child labour, in particular.

For building the profile of girl workers in India we had to rely entirely on the Analytical Study Report on Working Children enumerated in 1991 (Registrar General, 1998) since data on child labour from the 2001 Census are not published as yet. The NSSO data on child labour are not as comprehensive as the Census data on economic characteristics of workers. Wherever possible we have tried to compare the Census data with those from NSSO's 50th round that are closest to the 1991 Census in time, as they relate to 1993-94. In addition, we have used the NSSO data to enrich our understanding of child workers especially those belonging to vulnerable social groups. As we shall see later, these data support many of the findings of case studies on child labour in India and help us identify problems that are specific to girl child labour.

We are aware that by defining work as "economically productive activity", both the Census and the NSSO exclude from its count of workers, women engaged exclusively in housework like cooking, cleaning and 'care activities' like looking after children and the aged. It is highly probable that in this group of women, enumerated as "non-workers who are out of labour force", there may be some who are engaged in economic activity but neither these women nor others in the household or society recognise the work they do as economic activity. This recognition dimension of work, generally undercounts women workers and this is likely to affect the count of girl workers too. As a consequence, girls working in family enterprises as family workers or helpers are most likely to be missed from the count of workers, than those working in small units as casual wage employees. Similarly, girls directly working under a middleman as contract workers under a putting out system are more likely to be counted as workers than those helping contract workers within the family.

Keeping these limitations in mind, we have analysed in Section II trends in the volume of child labour emerging from the Census and the NSSO's Employment-Unemployment surveys over the 1980s and the 1990s. Section III concentrates on the profile of a girl worker that emerges from the Census in 1991. Wherever possible we have supplemented this with the data from NSSO's 50th survey round of 1993-94, Section IV attempts to identify factors that determine the level of participation of girls in economic activity. In order to understand why economic participation of girls varied between states in 1991, Section V discusses consequences of child labour on children in general and highlights some specific problems relating to female child labour. Conclusions emerging from the first three sections and policy issues for reducing child labour, especially girl child labour, are enumerated in section VI.

II. TRENDS IN CHILD LABOUR IN INDIA

Estimates of Child and Girl Workers

In India, where a huge number of children start working from as early as five years of age, the magnitude of the problem of child work has assumed enormous proportions. We are aware of the existence of child labour, and that its incidence is spread unevenly across states. Unfortunately, our knowledge regarding child work is much more uneven and inadequate. Estimates of child workers differ widely from one source to another depending upon the definition used to identify a worker. Even the way in which we arrive at estimates of WPRs and the volume of child labour differs between sources. For instance, in the Census, child workers are enumerated and by relating them to relevant population, work participation rates are derived. In the case of NSSO data, however, the opposite is the case. We initially get the participation rates of the population sampled by the NSSO, and by applying them to the appropriate population estimates, arrive at the number of child workers in the economy.

Definitions used to identify workers in the Censuses have changed over time since we adopted the labour force approach to enumerate workers in 1961. The use of a uniform definition of a worker, however, enabled us to compare the count of workers between 1981 and 1991. Table 1 shows that the number of child workers, main and marginal, enumerated in the age group, 5-14, declined by just 2.5 m., from 13.7 m. in 1981 to 11.2 m. in 1991. Of the 11.2 m. child workers enumerated in 1991, 9.1 m. were boys working as main workers and nearly 38 per cent of them or 3.4 m., were girls. The share of girls in marginal child workers—76 per cent was higher-indicating that the availability of work in the labour market determined their work status, either as main or as marginal workers. Since most of the work in rural areas was seasonal and was more likely to be intermittent and casual than regular, the preponderance of girls among marginal workers was but natural.

Table 1
Volume of Child Labour and Work Participation Rates by Sex, 1981 and 1991

Status of workers	Number (in millions)		Percentage change	WPRs per cent	
	1981	1991	(1981-1991)	1981	1991
Boy workers					
Main	7.5	5.7	-2.7	8.0	5.2
Marginal	0.6	0.5	-1.8	0.7	0.5
Main + marginal	8.1	6.2	-2.7	8.7	5.7
Girl workers					
Main	3.8	3.4	-1.1	4.4	3.4
Marginal	1.8	1.7	-0.6	2.1	1.7
Main + marginal	5.6	5.1	-0.9	6.5	5.1
Total workers					
Main	11.3	9.1	-2.2	6.3	4.3
Marginal	2.5	2.2	-1.3	1.4	1.0
Main + marginal	13.7	11.3	-1.9	7.6	5.3

Note: Percentage rates of change (1981-1991) are compound rates of change per annum.
Source: Registrar General of India, 1984, 1998.

Work participation rates (WPRs) given in Table 1 show that both in 1981 and 1991, boys were economically more active than girls, irrespective of whether they were main or marginal workers. Table 1 further shows that the number of working boys and girls declined over the decade. As a result, work participation rates (WPRs), irrespective of sex, declined too. However, the number of boy workers who were counted as main workers declined much faster at 2.7 per cent per annum (compound) while the number of such girls declined at a much slower pace at 1.1 per cent per annum. This was true for marginal workers, too. So, though the absolute number of working girls declined during the decade they formed a larger share of the total child workers in 1991 than in 1981-1991: Girls formed 38 per cent of the main, 76 per cent of the marginal and 46 per cent of the main and marginal workers taken together as against 37 per cent, 73 per cent and 41 per cent, respectively, in 1981.

Table 2 gives the WPRs in the age group, 5-14, reported by the NSSO and the estimates of working children aged 5-14, derived by applying these WPRs to the appropriate population estimates, for the four survey rounds starting from 1983. WPRs reported in the table show that as in the Census, irrespective of the year to which the data relate, boys were economically more active than girls. But both were economically less active in 1999-2000 than in 1983. This indeed is an encouraging trend because (a) we expect children in these age group to attend school, not work (b) belying the expectations of economic distress, in the post-reforms decade of the 1990s, children were not drawn in to the labour market.

Table 2
Work Participation Rates and Estimates of Child Labour by Sex, 1983-1999/2000

Year	Boys	Girls	Total
WPRs (per cent)			
1983	11.9	10.6	11.2
1987-88	8.8	7.9	8.3
1993-94	6.4	6.0	6.2
1999-2000	4.0	3.6	3.8
Workers (in million)			
1983	12.06	9.49	21.45
1987-88	9.51	7.43	16.94
1993-94	7.24	5.94	13.18
1999-2000	5.18	3.98	9.16
Per cent change per annum			
1983-1987-88	-5.9	-6.1	-5.9
1987-88-1993-94	-4.5	-3.7	-4.2
1993-94-1999-00	-5.6	-6.7	-6.1

Source: Deshpande and Deshpande (2001), Table 3.

That the NSSO counts all workers, especially women workers, better than the Census is borne out by the higher estimates of child labour in Table 2. According to the NSSO, an estimated 21.45 million children worked in India in 1983, as against just 13.7 million, enumerated by the Census in 1981. Their number declined over the 1980s and the 1990s, at a much faster pace in the second than in the first half of the 1990s. According to the NSSO data, there were 13.2 million children working in 1993-94, about two years after India accepted economic reforms. Their number declined during the 1990s as a result of which an estimated 9.16 million children worked in India in 1999-2000, out of which 5.18 million were boys and 3.98 million girls. We hasten to add that as in the Census so also in the NSSO, children, especially girls, employed as helpers and in unpaid family work are likely to be missed from the count of workers. Yet, the NSSO probably counted girl workers a shade better than the Census-girls formed 44 per cent of the working children in 1983 and their share increased marginally to 45 per cent in 1993-94. But as a result of a faster decline in the number of girl child workers relatively to boys between 1993-94 and 1999-2000, their share in total child workers declined to 43 per cent in 1999-2000.

This brief overview of trends in child labour, based on the Census enumerated child workers and those estimated on the basis of WPRs reported in the NSSO's Employment-Unemployment surveys, is indeed encouraging. Irrespective of the source, the number of child workers declined over the last two decades. Contrary to expectations, the pace of decline in child work participation was faster in the 1990s than in the 1980s. NSSO data show that in the second half of the 1990s, participation of girls in the labour market declined faster than that of boys. It would indeed be interesting to know what these girls did in the labour market. Section II focuses on characteristics of girl child labour in India.

III. PROFILE OF A GIRL CHILD WORKER IN INDIA

We noted right at the outset, that our knowledge and understanding of child work is at best meagre. This section tries to present a rudimentary picture of a typical girl worker in India from the data available in the 1991 Census. In the attempt to do so we have, wherever possible, relied on comparable as well as supplementary data from the NSSO's 50th round (1993-94).

1. Rural-urban Distribution

The bulk of these children lived and worked in rural India. According to the 1991 Census, as against 75.0 per cent of main male workers of all ages, 87.6 per cent of male child workers, aged 5-14 were in rural India. In the case of female workers, the corresponding shares were even higher: 87.1 per cent for main female workers and 92.6 per cent for girl main workers. The provision of better remuneration for girl workers in the NSSO does not change this picture substantially. Nearly 85.5 per cent of the male and 89.6 per cent of the female children, according to the NSSO, worked in rural India in 1993-94, indicating probably that the NSSO count of urban workers was a little better than that of the Census. This concentration of child workers in rural India is not difficult to explain. Economic necessity caused by food insecurity and hunger is considered as one of the main causes of child work since most child labourers come from poor families. Given the higher incidence of poverty in rural than urban India (Malhotra, 1997), it was not surprising that child workers were concentrated in rural areas.

2. Social Characteristics

Data relating to the social background of child workers are not available in the Census. But the NSSO reports that in 1993-94, children belonging to scheduled castes (SCs) and scheduled tribes (STs), were far more active economically than those belonging to 'other castes', namely non-scheduled classes, both in rural and urban India. For instance, the WPR of rural boys belonging to SCs and STs were 11.9 per cent and 7.4 per cent, respectively compared to 5.9 per cent of boys belonging to the non-scheduled class. The corresponding rates for rural girls were even higher: 13.8 per cent, 8.8 per cent and 6.5 per cent. In urban India, the pattern for boys differed from that observed in rural India. Urban boys belonging to SCs and non-scheduled classes reported WPRs of 4.4 per cent and 3.5 per cent, respectively. But those belonging to STs surprisingly reported a lower rate of only 3.0 per cent. For urban girls, the corresponding rates were 6.2 per cent, 2.6 per cent and 2.9 per cent, respectively, in keeping with the pattern observed in rural India.

NSSO data draw our attention to a serious dimension of child labour. They report that children belonging to SCs and STs formed about 40 per cent of the working children in India. Given the higher incidence of poverty in these social groups and their inadequate access to either land or capital, their children were probably forced to work as hired labour in agriculture and at times, even as wage employees in hazardous occupations in manufacturing. More importantly, about 50 per cent of the child workers were employed in rural India while in urban India 60 per cent of the child workers belonged to families that were identified as poor in 1993-94. Nearly 59 per cent of children working in rural areas and 63 per cent of those working in urban areas reported that they worked to supplement their household income (Thorat, 1999). Hence, the link between poverty, food insecurity and child labour is not difficult to understand. Unfortunately, these data relate to all child workers; they do not tell us how many of these working children were girls. It is not possible to know how many of the girl child workers belonged to the socially and economically deprived classes. Though we would not be wrong in assuming that a large bulk of the girls who work at an age at which other children go to school, are likely to belong to these vulnerable groups that are poor and face chronic food insecurity.

3. School Attendance and Work Participation

Children are expected to start schooling when they are about six years old and complete it by the time they are about 14. Two age groups, 5-9 and 10-14, are identified universally as the school going age groups. Table 3 shows us that in 1991, school attendance was lower in rural India, more so for girls than boys; and that 38 per cent of the boys and only 30 per cent of the girls in the age group, 5-9, attended school. Urban India reported higher levels of school attendance in this age group-56 per cent for boys and 53 per cent for girls. Attendance ratios improved in the next age group, 10-14, especially for boys with 67 per cent of them in rural and 81 per cent in urban areas having attended school. Attendance ratios did not improve as much for girls; the corresponding figures (in percentage term) for them being 46 and 74 per cent, respectively.

Table 3

Distribution of Children by Age, Sex, Status and Rural-Urban Residence

(Per cent)

	Rural		Urban	
Status of children	Boys	Girls	Boys	Girls
Aged 5-9				
Students	38.4	30.3	56.0	52.9
Workers	0.8	0.6	0.4	0.1
Others	60.7	69.1	43.6	46.9
Total	100.0	100.0	100.0	100.0
Aged 10-14				
Students	66.8	46.2	81.2	74.0
Workers	11.6	8.6	4.9	1.9
Others	21.5	45.2	14.0	24.1
Total	100.0	100.0	100.0	100.0

Source: Registrar General, 1998, derived from Table 14.0, p. 469.

In the context of child labour, it is not attendance but non-attendance, which is a cause for concern. Children not attending school it is feared, are more likely to look for work and take it up if it were available. It is important, therefore, to know what children did if they were not in schools. Compulsions of poverty are often responsible for keeping children out of schools, but irrelevance of the education imparted by the school system may prevent parents from sending them to schools. It is difficult to guess how many of these children were 'drop-outs', defined as those who 'ever attended' school, but dropped out later. Children not attending school, are often referred to as 'deprived children', as they are deprived from having access to education. Their shares were higher in rural, than urban India.

It would be wrong to conclude that all children who did not attend school were working. Economic necessity compelled many children to pursue some economic activity whether they attended school or not. But the share of children who worked while attending school was negligible-being less than 0.3 per cent among boys and girls in the two school-going age groups, both in rural and urban India. The incidence of work, as expected, was higher among children who were not in schools, more so among those who were 10-14 years old, than those who were younger. Table 3 shows that less than one per cent, of the boys and girls aged 5-9, worked in rural and urban India. Work participation increased in the next age group, whereby nearly 12 per cent of the boys and 9 per cent of the girls, aged 10-14, worked in rural areas. The corresponding proportions were much lower-5 per cent for boys and 2 per cent for girls-in urban areas.

The table reveals the high incidence of children who were neither in schools nor working, and are often referred to in literature on child labour, as 'nowhere' children. Nearly 61 per cent of the rural boys aged 5-9 and 22 per cent of those aged 10-14, were neither in educational institutions, nor working. The corresponding proportions for rural girls were higher-69 per cent and 45 per cent, respectively, showing probably that they must have been engaged in housework and other related chores-the proportions of 'nowhere' children in both the age groups were lower in urban India.

These data presented slightly differently, however, bring out an alarming phenomenon of 'worklessness' that prevails in these juvenile ages. Of the children in age group, 5-9, who were not attending school, nearly 98 per cent were not in the labour market either. This was so in respect of both boys and girls in rural and urban India-in the age group, 10-14, nearly 65 per cent of the boys but 84 per cent of the girls could be classified as 'nowhere' children. Their shares were higher among boys (74 per cent) and girls (93 per cent) living in urban India. Girls were much more deprived than boys in this respect-nearly four of every five girls in rural, as against nine of every 10 girls in urban India were deprived of both, education, as they did not attend school and income, as they did not work.

Attendance ratios reported by the NSSO for 1993-94, given in Table 4 for both the school-going age groups, are much higher. Table 4 shows that 67 per cent of the boys and 56 per cent for girls aged 5-9 in rural and 84 per cent of the boys and 80 per cent of the girls in urban India in this age group attended school. Attendance ratios were higher in the next age group of school-going children, especially for boys—79 per cent of the rural and 87 per cent of the urban boys aged 10-14, were students. The ratios did not improve either for rural or urban girls (NSSO, 1997). It is difficult to explain the difference between the attendance ratios reported by the Census and the NSSO. Better enumeration in the latter, may probably explain only a part of it.

Table 4
Distribution of Children by Age, Sex, Status and Rural-Urban Residence

(Per cent)

	Rural		Urban	
Status of children	Boys	Girls	Boys	Girls
Aged 5-9				
Students	67.2	56.2	84.1	80.1
Workers	0.9	1.2	0.4	0.3
Others	31.9	42.6	16.5	19.6
Total	100.0	100.0	100.0	100.0
Aged 10-14				
Students	78.6	55.7	87.2	81.6
Workers	11.4	10.5	6.2	3.5
Others	12.0	33.8	6.6	14.6
Total	100.0	100.0	100.0	100.0

Source: NSSO, 1997.

Higher attendance ratios reported in the NSSO data for 1993-94 lowers the share of children not attending school compared to the Census. Nearly a third of the rural boys as against 43 per cent of the rural girls, aged 5-9, did not attend school in 1993-94. Their corresponding shares in urban India were still lower-17 per cent and 20 per cent, respectively. In the next age group, 10-14, with increased incidence of school attendance, among rural boys the share of those not attending school dropped to 23 per cent, but remained high at 44 per cent among rural girls. Higher overall attendance in urban India reduced the share of boys and girls aged 10-14 not attending school to 13 per cent and 18 per cent, respectively.

NSSO data for 1993-94 report a pattern of participation by age among both boys and girls that is similar to the Census. Irrespective of sex and rural-urban residence, children were economically more active in the age group, 10-14, than when they were younger (5-9 years old). As in the Census so also in the NSSO, barely one per cent of the boys and girls (aged 5-9 years) reported working in rural and urban India. But in the next age group, 10-14, about 11 per cent of the boys and 10 per cent such girls in the rural areas worked; as against 6.2 per cent boys and 3.5 per cent girls in the urban areas. Better enumeration of workers resulted in these higher participation rates than those reported in the Census, especially in urban India.

As we noted earlier, neither the share of children in schools nor in the labour market has been a matter of great concern to policy makers. Though their shares according to the NSSO in 1993-94 are low, because of higher attendance ratios and work participation rates, when we relate such children to those not attending school, they vividly bring out the incidence of 'worklessness' among children. Irrespective of sex and rural-urban location, nearly 98 per cent of the children aged 5-9 neither went to school nor did they work. Incidence of worklessness declined in the next age group with increased educational and economic participation. Still, 52 per cent of the boys and 76 per cent of the girls in rural India reported neither attending school nor working. The share of such children was marginally lower at 51 per cent among urban boys. But an overwhelming 81 per cent of the urban girls experienced worklessness.

Even if these data were corrected for the likely undercount of child workers in general and for girl workers in particular, incidence of 'worklessness' among these children was phenomenally high. It is difficult to guess how these children spent their time. Lack of adequate educational and particularly, vocational educational facilities combined with general apathy among parents towards school education probably kept many children out of schools, not many of whom could find work. Girls were doubly disadvantaged; they were victims of gender-based discrimination even before they entered the labour market. As a result, fewer girls than boys could have access to education. If at all, they entered the labour market, they suffered from employment discrimination since employers preferred boys. More often than not, social taboos and caste relations prevented girls from even trying to get work outside their own homes. Most of these girls probably ended up as 'invisible workers' helping their mothers and other members of the family in home-based work and at the same time with household chores like cleaning, fetching drinking water and fuel, looking after the siblings, etc., often putting in long working hours in them. They were enumerated not as unpaid family workers but as non-workers on the basis of the definition adopted to enumerate workers.

4. Sectoral Distribution

Our analysis so far was based on the 1991 Census data and those available from NSSO's 50th round (1993-94). In the analysis that follows, in the absence of comparable data in the NSSO, we shall be restricting ourselves to 1991 Census data for understanding the economic profile of working girl children in India.

The 1991 Census gives the distribution of child workers by the sector of the economy where they worked. Table 5 shows that, irrespective of sex, nine of every 10 child workers in rural India, worked in the primary sector. Even within the primary sector, they were more likely to work either as cultivators or as agricultural labourers than in allied agricultural activities like livestock, fishing, etc. This is surprising since the Time Use Survey (TUS) of the Central Statistical Organisation (GOI, 2000) reports that animal husbandry and taking care of animals was an important economic activity for children. It is possible that such children were not reported as workers to Census enumerators. In relation to boys, girls were more likely to work as wage workers in agriculture. Household and non-household industries were not important sectors of employment in rural India; together they accounted for about 5 per cent of boys and 7 per cent of the girls. Other sectors of the rural economy were not important employers of child labour in rural India.

The employment structure of the urban child workers was much more diversified than that of the rural workers. This was true for both, boys and girls. Non-household manufacturing was the most important sector of employment for boys where almost 30 per cent of them were employed. Other sectors of employment were trade presumably retail trade, which accounted for 20 per cent workers, services (about 15 per cent) and agricultural labour (13 per cent). Structure of employment of girls differed in some respects from that of boys. As for boys so also for girls, household and non-household manufacturing was the most important sector of employment. These two categories together employed nearly 36 per cent of the working girls in urban India. A little over a quarter of the girls, (26.4 per cent) were in services while about 22 per cent worked as agricultural labourers. Unlike for boys, trade was not a sector that employed girls.

Table 5

Distribution of Workers Aged 5-14 by Industrial Categories, Sex and Rural-Urban Residence, 1991

(Per cent)

	Rural		Urban	
Industrial category	Boys	Girls	Boys	Girls
Cultivation	42.6	33.1	6.2	5.6
Agri. labourers	43.4	54.5	13.4	22.7
Livestock etc.	4.9	2.8	2.3	1.2
Mining & quarrying	0.3	0.3	0.3	0.5
Household industry	1.7	3.9	5.4	14.5
Non-household industry	3.0	3.3	29.3	21.8
Construction	0.5	0.2	4.5	3.1
Trade & commerce	1.6	0.3	20.4	3.8
Transport	0.2	0.0	2.8	0.4
Services	1.9	1.4	15.4	26.4
Total	100.0	100.0	100.0	100.0

Source: Registrar General, 1998, Statement 13, p. 24.

The importance of non-household manufacturing as a sector of employment for children in urban India, both male and female, should be a cause for concern. A number of case studies in India highlight the irreparable damage done to children employed in manufacturing industries like fireworks, glass and bangle manufacturing, quarries, chemicals, *beedi* rolling and carpet making (Voll, 1999). Manufacturing units employing children were likely to be small units, where conditions of work were less likely to be congenial to the health of the employees.

But the Census data do not help us understand the harm such employment can cause to children in general and to girls in particular.

NSSO's 50th round furnishes us some information on employment of children working in specific hazardous occupations in manufacturing at the country level. Nearly 7 per cent of the child workers in rural areas and about 24 per cent in urban areas worked in these dangerous industries in 1993-94. Two industries, cloth painting/dyeing and weaving and *beedi* rolling which employed both boys and girls, were identified as the most hazardous in rural as well as urban areas (Thorat, 1999). Many boys and girls were likely to work in other hazardous occupations such as gem polishing, glass and bangle making, match and fireworks manufacturing, lock making, stone and slate quarries and even rag-picking that caused permanent damage to their health (Gupta and Voll, 1999). Very often, units in these industries preferred employing children because they constituted cheap labour. In the absence of proper supervision and implementation of child labour legislation, children continued to be exposed to unhealthy environment at the workplace. This not only affected their health but very often made them unemployable later when they could not continue working due to physical damage.

5. Employment Status

Table 6 shows that boy and girl workers in India, were mostly wage employees. This was true, much more for boys and girls working in urban India. Own account work or self-employment, as an employment status, was next in importance. About 27 per cent of the girls and 31 per cent of the boys in rural areas were single workers; their corresponding shares among urban workers were considerably lower—about 17 per cent and 22 per cent, respectively. With agriculture offering employment to a bulk of rural workers, family workers were more common in rural than urban areas. It is difficult to explain how some of these children were classified as employers by the Census. It is possible that they could be children working on their own farms and were therefore classified as employers.

Table 6

Percentage Share of Workers Aged 5-14 by Employment Status, Sex and Rural-Urban Residence, 1991

(Per cent)

	Rural		Urban	
Employment status	Boys	Girls	Boys	Girls
Employer	6.4	3.6	6.0	2.5
Employee	47.6	53.4	66.6	75.5
Single worker	30.7	25.8	22.0	16.7
Family worker	15.3	17.2	5.4	5.3
Total	100.0	100.0	100.0	100.0

Source: Registrar General, 1998, Statement 14, p. 26.

We earlier cited evidence from case studies in India to show that work in hazardous manufacturing industries can harm children physically, more so when they are employed in these small establishments as wage employees. One tends to assume and rightly so that children working within the family will suffer less since their parents will care for them more than an alien employer. This is probably generally true (Kumar, 1989). A predominance of wage employment in the employment structure for both boys and girls suggests that a large proportion of the working children were likely to be exposed to higher physical damage than those who worked within the family, as family workers. We do not know what kind of work children did as single workers, they could be street children working as hawkers or rag-pickers or hamals, who were extremely vulnerable and were likely to be exploited by police, municipal workers and even by drug peddlers. Girl street children, working as single workers were worse-off than boys; they were exploited in many ways and were often a victims of sex abuse and prostitution (Gupta and Voll, 1999).

6. Occupational Structure

The 1991 Census gives the share of boys and girls employed in selected occupations in rural and urban India. This classification excludes cultivators and agricultural workers and relates to non-farm work done by the workers. Table 7 gives the relevant shares of these children who were uneducated and very young. It was not surprising that they were mostly employed in traditional service occupations like sales and service work (Occupational division codes 4 and 5), farming (Occupational division 6) and production and related work (Occupational division codes 7, 8 and 9) and not in modern white-collar occupations like professions, administration and clerical work. Occupational structure of boys differed from that of girls, it also differed between rural and urban India. Together these six occupational divisions employed almost 96 per cent of the working boys and girls in rural and urban areas. In the rural sector relative to boys, girls were more likely to be employed as production and related workers. For both, farming occupations were next in importance, much more so for boys than girls. Though services were more or less of equal importance, sales work, where a worker is likely to come in contact with strangers, was important for rural boys but not girls. Occupational structure of urban child workers differed from that of the rural child worker. Nearly three-fourths of the boys and girls in urban areas were production process and related workers. Sales work was next in importance for boys, where nearly 19 per cent of them were employed. Twenty-eight per cent of the girls worked in service occupations, probably as domestics.

The census gives eight important occupation groups, at two-digit level, that employed child workers in rural and urban India. The occupational structure of urban boys was much more diversified than that of their rural counterparts. These eight occupation groups together employed nearly 54 per cent of the boys in rural but only 37 per cent of them in urban areas. The eight groups together employed a little over two-thirds of the girls both in rural and urban India, though the importance of each group differed in the two locations. Nearly a quarter of the

Table 7
Percentage Share of Workers* Aged 5-14 in Selected Occupational Divisions and Groups by Sex and Rural-Urban Residence, 1991

(Per cent)

Occupation division/ occupation group code and description	Rural		Urban	
	Boys	Girls	Boys	Girls
Dvn.4: Sales workers	9.1	3.0	18.4	4.8
Gr.40 Merchants, shopkeepers, wholesale and retail	5.6	1.9	9.0	2.5
Gr. 43 Salesmen, shop assistants and related	3.4	1.0	9.2	2.2
Dvn.5: Service workers	8.0	7.2	13.7	27.7
Gr.53 Maids and other housekeeping service workers n.e.c.	2.1	2.9	5.1	22.7
Dvn.6: Farmers, fishermen, hunters, etc.	33.5	23.0	2.6	1.6
Gr. 65 Other farm workers	24.9	13.1	1.4	0.7
Dvn.7-8-9: Production and related workers	44.5	63.0	60.0	61.3
Gr.75 Spinners, weavers, knitters, dyers etc.	7.9	10.0	7.8	14.0
Gr.78 Tobacco preparers and productmakers	2.8	27.5	1.4	16.1
Gr. 89 Glass formers, potters and related.	3.2	3.7	1.3	2.0
Gr. 99 Production and related workers n.e.c	3.5	7.1	1.8	6.1
Subtotal groups	53.5	67.2	37.2	66.2

Note: *Excluding cultivators and agricultural labourers.
Source: Registrar General, 1998, Statement 15, p. 28.

boys in rural India worked on farms, about 8 per cent were spinners, weavers, dyers, etc. and 9 per cent were sales workers, who worked most probably as hawkers and assisted in shops. Domestic work was not an important occupation group either for boys or girls in rural India. *Beedi* rolling and glass forming, which are identified as hazardous occupations, employed about 3 per cent each respectively, of the rural boys. In urban India none of these eight occupational groups employed more than 10 per cent of the boys. Sales work mainly retail trade and shop assistance, spinning, weaving etc. each employed about 8 to 9 per cent of the urban boys while domestic work accounted for employment of barely about 5 per cent of them.

For rural girls, tobacco preparing or beedi rolling was the most important occupation that employed almost 28 per cent of them, 13 per cent were employed as other farm workers and 10 per cent, as spinners, weavers, dyers, etc. Domestic work was the largest employer of girls in urban India; almost 23 per cent of whom were employed as domestics. While nearly 16 per cent rolled *beedis* and 14 per cent were spinners, weavers, dyers, etc.

Despite the aggregation, these data vividly showed that a large proportion of the child workers, especially girls, were in occupations identified as hazardous by the NSSO, as also in most literature on child work (Gupta and Voll, 1999). Occupational structure of children differed across states and the relative importance of different occupations as employers of child labour differed too. But in most states a large number of children were working in occupations, which were injurious to their health.

Given this profile of a girl worker in India we shall now discuss how participation of girls in economic activity differed across states and union territories. An attempt is also made to identify some determinants of girl child labour in India.

IV. DETERMINANTS OF GIRL CHILD PARTICIPATION IN INDIA

1. Age Specific Work Participation Rates (ASWPRs) Across States and Union Territories

Table 8 gives ASWPRs of child workers in India, across 24 states and seven union territories in 1991. At the all-India level, rural children were economically more active than urban children. In urban areas, boys were far more active than girls whereas in rural areas, they were so, only marginally. State-wise, Andhra Pradesh reported the highest while Kerala the lowest ASWPRs for both boys and girls living in their rural areas. Among the union territories, boys and girls living in rural areas of Dadra and Nagar Haveli were economically the most active while those in Lakshadweep were the least active. In urban India, Mizoram reported the highest ASWPRs for both boys and girls while the lowest rates were recorded in urban Kerala for boys and in urban Haryana for girls.

We noted earlier that in the rural sector, at all-India level, boys reported marginally higher participation in economic activity than girls. But this was not true for rural areas of all states and union territories. Table 8 shows that in 14 of the 24 states and three of the seven union territories, participation rates for rural girls were higher than those, reported for boys. This could happen if the rural labour market offered employment opportunities in agriculture that could absorb girls more easily than boys. But this could as well be the result of the higher female mortality in these age groups relative to boys, which by reducing the population in these ages, raised their age specific participation rates. This may also be a consequence of the general undercount of girl children in the general population, but better enumeration of female workers among them. It is difficult to say which of these factors was responsible for the reported higher participation of girls relative to boys.

2. Determinants of Economic Participation of Girls

We noted earlier that the total count of girl workers in India is an undercount due to various factors-definitional and social. In the foregoing analysis, we have tried to understand how the pattern of economic participation of girls differed from that of boys. For formulating any policy to reduce participation of children in economic activity in general and that of girls in particular, we need to identify crucial variables that determine the level of economic activity or WPRs. In the analysis which follows, with the use of regressions, we have tried to identify factors which could explain the variation in the ASWPRs for girls across 23 states and four union territories, both for rural and urban areas.

In the model we tested, ASWPR for girls in 1991 is treated as a dependent variable. The following three independent variables were included in the analysis: (i) percentage share of girls attending school in the age group, 11-13 in

Table 8

Work Participation Rates for Boys and Girls aged 5-14 for States and Union Territories by Rural-Urban Residence, 1991

(Per cent)

State	Rural		Urban	
	Boys	Girls	Boys	Girls
Andhra Pradesh	11.43	13.58	3.96	2.18
Arunachal Pradesh	4.95	7.38	2.42	2.11
Assam	7.19	4.20	2.96	2.82
Bihar	5.31	3.26	2.37	0.67
Goa	1.55	2.15	2.54	1.64
Gujarat	6.40	7.81	2.48	0.77
Haryana	3.59	2.24	1.80	0.39
Himachal Pradesh	3.75	5.90	1.59	1.07
Karnataka	10.70	11.34	4.59	2.38
Kerala	0.67	0.54	0.54	0.46
Madhya Pradesh	9.19	10.66	2.25	1.27
Maharashtra	6.51	9.86	2.10	0.96
Manipur	3.84	5.34	1.14	1.72
Meghalaya	9.59	7.57	1.43	1.52
Mizoram	10.31	11.57	7.41	7.44
Nagaland	5.50	6.67	1.67	0.95
Orissa	6.87	6.03	2.54	1.26
Punjab	5.91	1.07	2.69	0.35
Rajasthan	6.00	9.75	2.20	1.11
Sikkim	4.97	5.48	5.28	4.12
Tamil Nadu	5.26	6.63	3.15	2.02
Tripura	2.93	2.06	1.07	1.28
Uttar Pradesh	5.29	2.87	3.65	0.81
West Bengal	6.55	3.1	2.42	1.29
Andaman & Nicobar	2.55	1.49	1.86	0.35
Chandigarh	3.52	0.72	1.98	0.54
Dadra & Nagar Haveli	11.03	16.95	4.00	4.46
Daman & Diu	5.47	5.73	1.82	1.49
Delhi	1.41	0.39	2.18	0.35
Lakshadweep	0.38	0.08	0.46	0.12
Pondicherry	1.78	1.48	2.17	0.79
All-India	6.56	6.29	2.79	1.23

Source: Registrar General, 1998, Statement 10, pp. 21-23.

1991; (ii) percentage share of population below poverty line 1993-94; and (iii) per capita state domestic product in 1991-92.

We tried two regression equations, first, where our dependent variable was rural ASWPRs for girls and the second where it was urban ASWPRs for girls reported in the 1991 Census.

We noted earlier that children who attended school participated in economic activity only marginally. Not many children under 10 worked, irrespective of whether they attended school or not. Of the child workers reported in the Census, (male and female, rural and urban,) over 80 per cent were in age group, 10-14. It was, therefore, hypothesised that school attendance ratios of girls in the age group, 11-13, in 1991 would be negatively associated with ASWPR for girls: the higher the attendance ratio of girls aged 11-13 in the state in 1991, the lower would be the ASWPR for girls. This was expected to be true both in rural and urban areas of each state and union territory.

The Census fails to give us data on the economic background of child workers. But the NSSO data revealed that a large bulk of the children who work belong to poor households and are likely to belong to socially deprived classes who faced either chronic or seasonal food insecurity. The severity of food insecurity was likely to force children in poor families to enter the labour market. Notably, because of gender discrimination girls were also less likely to be sent to school and were readily available for work, however low paid it was. It was hypothesised that the level of economic participation of girls would be positively related to the incidence of poverty measured as a percentage share of population that lived in poverty in the state in 1993-94. We expected that ASWPR for girls would be high where the incidence of poverty was high. Data relating to the percentage of persons living in poverty, available separately for rural and urban areas, was used in the two equations.

The third independent variable, state domestic product (SDP) per capita, was used as a proxy for index of economic development in the state or the union territory. Our hypothesis was: the higher the level of development as indicated by the level of the SDP per capita, the lower would be the ASWPR for girls. This was logical since with economic development and rise in incomes, parents are less likely to send their children, (boys and girls) to work for supplementing family income. Secondly, with rising incomes we could expect greater awareness among parents about the need to educate children and view education as an investment in human capital. We expected to find a negative relationship between SDP per capita in a state and level of economic participation of girls, but had to make some compromises while using this variable. First, of the 24 states and seven union territories given in Table 8, data on SDP per capita was available only for 23 states and three union territories (GOI, 1999). This reduced the number of observations in our regression from 31 to 26. Secondly, SDP per capita was reported for the state or union territory as a whole and not for rural and urban areas separately. In its absence we have used SDP per capita for the state or union territory as a proxy variable for the level of economic development in both the equations.

The results of the first regression equation relating to rural ASWPRs are reported in Table 9. They show that the R-Square was 0.48 and the F-statistic was highly significant, at one per cent. Two hypothesised relationships, namely, (a) the negative relationship between the percentage of girls in the age group, 11-13, attending school in rural areas and female child participation; and (b) the positive one, between incidence of poverty in rural areas and female child participation were borne out in the results and the two relationships were significant at one percent. The expected negative relationship between SDP per capita and female child participation was not borne out. We obtained instead a positive relationship that was significant at 10 percent which needs an explanation.

Table 9

Results of Regression Equation: Determinants of Rural ASWPRs for Girls

Independent variables	Coefficient	t-statistic
Intercept	-4.7025	-0.7233
1. Percentage share of girls aged 11-13 attending school in rural areas of the state or union territory in 1991	-1.5296	-3.0624***
2. Percentage share of persons below poverty line in the rural areas of the state or union territory in 1993-94	0.7902	2.6038***
3. State domestic product per capita 1992-93	1.1046	1.4811*
R-Square 0.48		
F Statistic 0.0021***		

Note: Three, two and one asteriks indicate that the coefficient was statistically significant at 1, 5 and 10 per cent, respectively.

The participation rates for girls are higher in rural than urban areas. The structure of employment prevailing in rural areas fits well the supply of female labour determined by gender-based division of labour and preferences. Agriculture is a seasonal industry and many farm activities are sex-determined with women forming a high share of agricultural labourers. A typical housewife of a farmer can choose her hours of work on the farm or in the household industry. For various reasons cities are less conducive, if not hostile, places for women to work and do not offer as much freedom to combine housework and paid work as do villages. The encouraging and discouraging effects of rural and urban residence on women's participation may percolate to the girl child as well. However, since the SDP per capita is not available by rural-urban residence, the expected negative relationship we hypothesised between SDP and participation of girls was probably not borne out in rural India. So that SDP per capita may be higher because of higher levels of industrialisation and urbanisation. Either or both types of relationships may have been the result of neglect of rural areas. Hence, high SDP per capita may be positively associated with greater inequality and a higher female child participation in rural areas.

The results of the second regression, which tries to explain variation in the urban ASWPRs, are reported in Table 10. The three independent variables could explain only 18 per cent of the variation: R-Square was 0.18 and the F-Statistic was not significant. Factors other than these three determined the female child participation rates in urban areas. The Table shows that the two hypothesised negative relationships, first between urban school attendance ratios in respect of girls aged 11-13 and female child participation and second, between SDP per capita and female child participation rates were borne out. The expected positive relationship between incidence of urban poverty and female child participation was not borne out, though the observed relationship was significant at 10 per cent.

Table 10
Results of Regression Equation: Determinants of Urban ASWPRs for Girls

Independent variables	Coefficient	t-statistic
Intercept	10.7850	1.7823**
1. Percentage share of girls in ages 11-13 attending school in urban areas of the state or union territory in1991	-1.3080	-0.8670
2. Percentage share of persons below poverty line in the urban areas of the state or union territory in 1993-94	-0.2818	-1.4130*
3. State domestic product per capita 1992-93	-0.4784	-1.1329
R-Square 0.18		
F Statistic 0.2041		

Note: Two and one asterisks indicate that the coefficient was statistically significant at 5 and 10 per cent, respectively.

It has been observed (see Table 8) that the urban female child participation rates were low in almost all states and union territories. This low count of female child workers could be attributed to two factors. First, as we noted earlier, girls who helped at home in home-based industry or in the household who did contract work may not be reported as workers, since this work is not viewed by parents as work. In household industries, very often, a child worker who may work on a 'meagre' wage, which is paid partly in kind, may be reported as a family member not as a family worker (Gupta and Voll, 1999). Second, the definition used to identify workers in the Census excludes from the count of workers those engaged exclusively in house work. Labour market in urban areas gives very little freedom to women to choose their hours of work. In fact, poor women are forced to accept occupations that give them an opportunity to combine work with housework. To cite an instance, in a small case study of 300 working women living in three slums in Mumbai we found that many were either home-based workers or worked as domestics for households close to their slum. They reported being in these occupations because they could choose their hours of work and earn some income without neglecting their home. Very few were in occupations that kept them out of their homes the whole day. The most important finding was that these 300 households did not report a single girl child worker! This did not mean that all girls below age 15 were in schools. According to the data on the time disposition of these working women, in many households, girls helped their mothers in various household chores; such as getting water from the stand pipe outside their huts, getting rations from ration shops or vegetables and other things from the market, cleaning, looking after siblings and even cooking. Some of these activities were done by girls, even when they were attending schools, but were routinely done by many, who were not in schools either because they never went to one or because they had dropped out. The nature of their work was indeed important for the household as it involved releasing an adult to take up economic work. They were indirectly contributing to household income but were never reported as workers. In this study, we used the current weekly status approach of the NSSO to define workers, which, like the Census, did not treat housework as economic work (Deshpande and Deshpande, 1998). So the low count of female child workers in poor families in urban areas could be attributed to the invisibility of their work. This, in turn, lowered the participation of urban female child workers.

Having broadly identified the determinants of female child participation, we can now turn to the consequences of child work on workers in general and on female child workers, in particular.

V. CONSEQUENCES OF CHILD LABOUR

Earlier, while discussing the work performed by the girl child in India we enumerated characteristics of boy workers too and compared them with those of girls mainly to understand the differences, if any, between the two. Here we shall see what consequences child work has, on children themselves. In the process, some problems specific to girl children, which arise primarily because (a) they are girls and hence victims of gender-bias; and (b) the kind of work they do differs from that done by boys will be highlighted.

1. Impact on Children

The fact that a child works, rather than going to school or playing, has consequences for the child, the family to which the child belongs and the society in which children live. Many case studies in India support the finding that many types of child work, especially in hazardous occupations, can harm children physically. The physical damage could at times be irreparable and result in diseases of the respiratory system, causes eye-strain affecting their vision and at times may even lead to physical deformities. Children are vulnerable to accidents too. Therefore, it is felt that a child would be better cared for if he or she were to work at home as helpers or family workers, close to parents or relatives. However, the possibility of physical damage largely depends on the kind of work children do or the occupations in which they are engaged. Occupations like carpet weaving, *beedi* rolling, lock making, glass forming or making fireworks, are likely to impair the health of children, whether they work at home or outside in small factories, particularly of children are engaged in them for a long duration. Even work like fetching firewood or water or grazing cattle, if done for long hours can be harmful, though it is carried out often under the guidance of parents.

At times even parents, who care, may not be aware of the possible damage an activity can cause to their own children.

Time Use Survey (TUS) (GOI, 2000), supports many of these observations by indicating the actual number of hours which children in the age group, 6-14, spent in doing activities that were classified as economic activities. TUS reports that nearly 11 per cent of the boys and girls were in animal husbandry; they spent on an average almost 22 hours and 14 hours, respectively every week on this activity. About 5 per cent of the boys, but 15 per cent of the girls collected fuel, fruits, etc. for consumption in the family and spent 11 hours and nine hours on an average on this activity. It is heartening to learn that both boys and girls were not spending an unduly long time in these activities.

The most disturbing finding related to the weekly time spent by boys and girls employed in mining and quarrying and manufacturing. No doubt, barely half a per cent each of the boys and girls worked in mines and quarries. But boys so engaged spent 35 hours on an average or more than five hours per day if we consider a work-week of six days. Girls working in this industry spent longer hours-nearly 38 hours per week; and more than six hours per workday! Manufacturing too employed a very small share of child workers—1.44 per cent of boys and 2.23 per cent of girls, who also spent on an average 33 hours and 24 hours every week respectively doing this work (Hirway, 2001). Relatively to these two, work in animal husbandry which included grazing and taking care of animals and collecting fuel, fruits etc. for family consumption were less damaging physically for boys and girls working in them.

Apart from physical damage, child work can cause mental damage too among children. Long hours of repetitive work can impair mental abilities. Both the Census and the NSSO data highlight another serious problem in the context of children: a large bulk, neither went to schools nor were they engaged in work; many such girls possibly helped in housework. TUS (2000) reports that relatively to boys, girls spent longer hours every week, cooking and serving food, cleaning, upkeep of dwellings and surroundings, cleaning utensils, washing clothes, and taking care of siblings ,in short, in activities which are labeled as women's activities. The share of girls engaged in each of these activities varied between 15 per cent to 32 per cent, though the average time spent per week was relatively low; ranging between an average of 10 hours in cooking to about four hours in washing clothes in a week. We hasten to add that many of these activities in which the girls were engaged were likely to be done together with activities like attending school or even working. This was not so with boys, less than 6 per cent of whom reported participating in these activities and spent at the most five hours, mostly three hours in a week, in any one of these activities (Hirway, 2001). It is, therefore, not possible to guess what boys did if they were, neither students nor workers. This type of worklessness of long durations could be harmful for the child psychologically.

In general, we can say that parents by deciding to send children to work rather than to school, affect their future earnings. Some may argue that the low quality of education accessible to the poor may not do much good to the children either. But the correct policy initiative required here is to improve the quality of education and its content and make it more relevant. Secondly, it is often felt that some of the occupations provide vocational training if a child starts working at a young age. It is necessary to understand whether this, in fact, is so. We may need to know how much time is taken to acquire a given skill when a child is young, between 6-14 years, and later if the child is older—over 15 years of age. The possibility of combining such apprenticeship in the family trade and small manufacturing units with schooling should also be explored. Attempts made in this direction would not deprive such children of formal core education while they are in the process of acquiring skills.

2. Specific Problems of Female Children

We have seen how boys and girls are affected if they work instead of acquiring education when they are of school-going age. The consequences noted above affect boys and girls alike. But since girls are victims of discrimination based on gender, even within their own families there is a need to understand their specific problems, which arise because of their being girls. The most obvious outcome of this discrimination was visible both in the Census and the NSSO data reported in Section II. Pre-entry human capital discrimination against girls within the family resulted in lower school attendance ratios for girls than boys of school-going age. The probability of parents sending their sons to schools was higher than if they had daughters.

We also saw that the kind of work which girls do differs from that done by boys. Girls are more likely to work as family workers than boys. In the rural sector, many work with their mothers on farms either as helpers or casual wage employees or in household industry as family workers. Generally, girls are engaged in the most unskilled jobs, since parents are often reluctant to train their daughters for skilled jobs. It is felt that the effort in doing so is not worthwhile as girls leave their parents homes after marriage. Girls are the losers in the process; they neither acquire any skill, nor any education, since they are not sent to school.

Girls generally do housework, while most boys do not. We noted that the TUS is very eloquent on this dimension of girl child work. Most of the household chores have always been done by women in India and are regarded as belonging to the women's domain since all of them are carried out within the house. These activities are precious for the household, but their true worth is never recognised and much less respected, even by the parents. More importantly, girls are initiated in to housework when they are very young-at times even before they are 10. At that age they naturally take a long time to do any work which results in long hours of work. Unfortunately, when girls work outside their own homes and earn, they are often expected to help in household chores. This is not so with boys who are not expected to help in housework, mainly because they are boys, whether they attend school or work.

Religion has an important impact on work done, especially by women. This percolates down to girls in minority communities. In the case study of three slums, noted earlier, our respondents in one slum were predominantly Muslim. They did low-paid contract work at home since their husbands did not approve of their working outside their homes. These restrictions affected girls in their families too. Many girls were not sent to school, though there was a municipal primary school very close to this slum. More importantly, they were deprived of primary education even though it was free! Most of the time they stayed home, and helped not only in housework and in taking care of siblings but also in the contract work which was done by women in their households. (Deshpande and Deshpande, 1998).

Parents generally are not worried about where their son works and what kind of job he does because earning some money to supplement the family income is the sole aim of sending him to work. This is not so in the case of girls. Very often girls, especially among the higher castes, are not sent out of the house for work. Such inhibitions regarding work do not exist among lower caste women, which makes women and girls in these families, economically more active than those, belonging to higher castes. As a result, girls from these families are likely to be more independent and to enjoy greater autonomy in decision-making than those among the higher caste families. Further, women in the lower caste families may even send their girls to work outside their homes if work were available.

Girls are victims of discrimination based on gender, right from birth. Parents do not treat their daughters as well as their sons-daughters are underfed, relative to sons and often neglected when sick. Indeed, higher infant and childhood mortality among female than male children in India is attributed to this differential treatment As they grow up, parents tend to spend less on their education and training. The extent of this kind of discrimination differs in India across regions. This neglect of girls in some regions is known to lead to sex-selective foeticide and even infanticide (Kumar, 1989).

Women are biologically stronger than men. Though the number of boys exceed girls at birth, this excess of boys decreases with age, since boys experience higher age-specific mortality than girls in all subsequent age groups. It is expected that under normal circumstances in any population, there would be as many men as there are women. What is, however, forgotten in the Indian context is that this excess may also be partly a result of gender bias that leads to under-enumeration of women relative to men. This is equally an issue, as much as the physical neglect mentioned earlier. Indian women are also victims of social discrimination and have a low status within the family. They are not even recognised as human beings fit to be reported as individuals since generally men, as heads of households, report to the Census enumerators! Clearly, if woman's existence itself is not recognised, the economic work she does is less likely to be recognised and reported. This is likely to be true for girl children, as also the workers among them.

The National Family Health Survey-2 (NHFS-2) (IIPS, 2000) provides ample evidence of this neglect of the girl child. The infant mortality rate in the decade prior to the survey, i.e., 1988-98, was slightly higher for boys than girls-

75 and 71 infant deaths per 1000 live-births, respectively. But because of the neglect of girls in juvenile ages, 1-4, female mortality rate i.e., below five years was slightly higher than male mortality rate. As against, as many as 105 female children who died per 1000 female children born alive without celebrating their 5th birthday, the number of male children who died was 97. Excess female mortality occurred after the first year of life. This was not surprising since NFHS-2 gives evidence of a strong preference for male relative to female children among their women respondents. This preference probably translated itself into neglect of female children in the family. Be it full immunisation of children under three years of age or receiving vitamin A supplement or treating children with acute respiratory infection, parents revealed considerable gender-bias in their behaviour. For example, as against 43 per cent of the boys, only 41 per cent of the girls under three years of age, were fully vaccinated. Boys were more likely to receive each of the individual vaccinations than girls, be it BCG, Polio O, each of the three doses of DPT, or measles vaccine. The share of girls who were never vaccinated against any of these diseases, as a result, was higher than that of such boys. The survey report assures us that this gender-bias was evident much more in rural than in urban India. But since a majority of India's population still lives in rural areas, the bulk of all children and girls too, are likely to be found in rural areas and are likely to experience this discrimination.

Vitamin A supplement, provided to children under the National Programme for Prevention of Blindness was intended to reach all children under five years of age. The dose had to be administered orally every six months starting from the age of nine months. It was sad to see that in 1998-99, only three out of 10 children (12-35 months old) had received only one dose of vitamin A, while 17 per cent of all children reported taking it in the last six months. Worse still, here too, a larger share of boys than girls were likely to have received these doses. Though girls are biologically stronger, as was reflected in the lower morbidity levels among them relative to boys, when they were sick with acute respiratory infection, parents were less likely to approach health providers than they would had their son fallen ill. It is noteworthy, that while 67 per cent of the boys under three years of age had been taken for medical treatment to a health facility or health providers, only 60 per cent of such girls could expect to enjoy this privilege.

This continued neglect of the girl child was clearly reflected in the relatively greater extent of undernourishment among girls relative to boys. Using anthropometric measurements NFHS-2 showed, by applying weight for age measure, to find out whether the child was underweight or height for age measure if the child was stunted that the share of girls among underweight and stunted children was higher than that of boys. The third measure used was weight for height, which revealed wastage among children. This is a consequence of failure to receive adequate nutrition in the period immediately before the survey. The data did not show any difference in the incidence of wastage between girls and boys. This neglect of the girl child could, to a large extent, explain India's abnormally low sex ratio in the juvenile age group, 0-6 in the 2001 Census (Registrar General, 2001).

The kind of work, in which girls are engaged in the household is closely associated with the size of the household. In most families, these girls would generally do household chores enumerated earlier. The time they spend would not differ much between small and large families, but their utility as providers of child care obviously rises in poor households, as the size of the family increases. Even the treatment given to younger girls, can be different than that of older ones. Younger girls may be sent to schools while the older ones are kept at home to carry out the housework. It is also possible that girls of higher parity may be neglected much more by parents because of their preference for the male child leading to higher female mortality among higher parity children (Kumar, 1989).

It is possible that girls who do some economic work and earn income, however meager may be valued much more by their own parents and others in the household than others who are exclusively doing housework. In other words, if a girl has clear economic value, either because she directly contributes to total household income or indirectly to it by doing housework that permits older women in the family to go out and work, she is likely to be treated better, than a girl who does not do either. This hypothesis, has not been tested so far, and needs to be tested systematically.

We could conclude by saying that girls are discriminated against basically because they are girls, the most visible evidence of this being the lower school attendance ratios of girls compared to boys. They are often underfed and even neglected when sick, leading initially to higher levels of under nutrition, resulting ultimately in higher female than male mortality. They are mostly found doing housework, at times because they are not allowed to work outside their homes. Social factors play an important role here. In the context of female child labour, we need to consider two sets of questions: first, could we say that girls who do economic work are likely to be less discriminated against than those who do not? If so, what kind of work is likely to reduce discrimination against girls; does it have to be economic work or would housework do? And second, is the visibility of work a relevant factor? We need to incorporate these gender-related problems specific to girls while formulating policies to reduce child work, which we take up in the concluding section.

VI. CONCLUSION AND POLICY OPTIONS

In this paper we have argued that child labour, if carried out for long durations, by depriving children of even core-education, harms children, stunting not only their physical but mental development and affects their emotional adjustment. Child labour is cheap and hence used as a substitute for adult labour. Employment of children depresses adult wages thereby increasing the incidence of poverty in the population. Female child workers are confronted with additional problems. There is social reluctance to educate them or to impart skills to them. They are neglected relatively to boys, even within their own family and are victims of pre-entry human capital discrimination just because of their being girls. This neglect of girls reflects the low status of women in Indian society. These problems are of tremendous concern because the absolute number of even the visible female child workers is large. They are also likely to be missed from the count of workers, first because they are girls and second due to the invisibility of their work. It is absolutely essential to adopt policies to reduce child labour over time and eliminate it ultimately. But formulation of these policies is a complex issue since many of these children, especially girls, work in their own families.

Given such a dismal scenario, one can think of four types of policies: first, those that try to ban child work in all establishments, even on family farms; second, policies that ensure that all children of school-going age are in schools. Our analysis of determinants of female child participation confirmed that an increase in the school attendance would have a negative impact on the level of participation of girls in economic activity in rural and urban areas. Thirdly, we could think of measures that would release girls, from work in which they are currently engaged. Finally, we could think of how government policies need to be changed to help reduce child labour.

1. Policies Banning Child Labour

These policies constitute a set of legal measures that ban child labour, male and female. But experience shows that laws banning child labour are difficult to implement, especially in small establishments in the informal sector. In India, our experience is that factory inspectors are too few to cover thousands of small establishments in the country. They neither have the ability nor, sometimes, the will to enforce child labour laws. Family enterprises, being too small, often fall beyond the purview of labour legislation even though they are hazardous for children and adults alike. It is for instance unfortunate that the Child Labour (Prohibition and Regulation) Act of 1986, permits employment of children in hazardous industries if they are family enterprises (Kumar, 1989).

Enforcing labour legislation in large establishments is relatively easy. Small enterprises too are difficult to handle. As a result, they continue to use cheap child labour, often in occupations that could impair their health. Furthermore, inspecting or policing tiny family enterprises too is extremely difficult and very often employers of very small units are known not to report hired child labour by claiming that their enterprise is a family enterprise. Unpaid family work does not come under the purview of the existing laws but is a serious social problem, particularly since female child labour is involved.

One can think of many reasons why governments avoid interference in family life. The family in India is a basic social institution that can provide love, care and protection to a child, which no other government or voluntary agency can provide. Policing and punishments may be necessary if children are employed in dangerous work and even family enterprises should not be exempted from this, though this might be an expensive proposition.

Our knowledge of such types of activities is inadequate. We often assume that children work in traditional handicrafts but they work in modern chemical units, too. Also, we know very little about how effectively the small units are inspected, what difficulties confront the inspectors in the implementation of these laws and what ways and means small units use to bypass the legislation. These data gaps would have to be overcome while framing policies.

Finally, even in the Western developed countries child labour was eliminated not so much by enforcing of legislation aimed as preventing child labour, but by social changes which increased awareness of the society regarding the harm it can do to children and by transforming attitudes of parents. It must be remembered that child work would continue to exist until parents realize that it is harmful to children because the decision to send a child to work is ultimately their decision.

2. Policies for Ensuring Universal Education

Education is probably the most important field for framing policies which can help reduce child labour in general and that of girls, in particular. In India, an enormous number of boys and girls, who ordinarily should be in schools, do not attend them, because they are either just not sent to schools or even if they are sent to one, they drop out. Our regression results, restricted to participation of female children, conclusively revealed that improving school attendance of girls aged, 11-13, would go a long way in reducing their work participation. This is likely to be true for boys too. We need to find out how best this can be done. The policy of punishing parents for not sending their children to schools is not likely to work as this would be most difficult, if not impossible to implement. Improving schools, making the education system more relevant and even providing free mid-day meals have been thought of as incentives for improving school attendance and have been tried in different states in India. An appropriate policy mix, which combines compulsion with incentives would have to be tried.

While framing these educational policies, however, special attention needs to be given to education of girls. Female children are often denied access to education because of gender discrimination in the first place but also because of social factors. If efforts are made to improve access of girls to education, that may help improve their employability and income that they can earn. Education is likely to make them aware of the discrimination, they have to face within the family and may even make them resist it. Also, these girls are likely to be better mothers if they are educated.

Attempts would have be made to educate parents aimed at making them realise that education would result in better opportunities for their children in the future. Parents in rural areas often think that school education is irrelevant to their lives and that schools do not impart skills that would make their children employable. It is this view which makes parents feel that training children when young would assure them of their livelihood. Unless this perception changes, not much can be achieved. More importantly we must remember that children are sent to work because family incomes are inadequate. Our analysis identified incidence of poverty as an important determinant of female child labour. Efforts to increase school attendance are not likely to be successful, unless and until they are accompanied by growing employment opportunities for the poor. The increase in household income would help parents decide not to send their children, especially boys to work. But even in the case of girls, a decline in incidence of poverty may make parents withdraw girls from household chores and send them to schools instead.

3. Other Measures to Release Female Child Labour from Household Chores

One way to reduce female child labour is to devise substitutes for the services that are provided by girls. Many activities of girls in rural areas like fetching water or fuel are time consuming but are crucial for the very survival of the household. Girls in the household often do these activities routinely because that permits older women to go out and earn. If water and fuel are provided in rural areas through alternative measures, it is possible that many girls would be free from this work, and may be sent to schools instead, if schools are located nearer homes. For instance, provision of water within the hut may mean that there is no need for girls to fetch water. Similarly, provision of alternative arrangements for child care like *balwadies / anganwadies* and even mobile creches may release girls from the task of providing child care to siblings. Further, if this provision is accompanied by providing mid-day meals they are likely to succeed much more than otherwise. Initiatives in this direction have been made in certain states but need to be replicated on a large scale.

4. Changing Government Policies

Some government policies like encouraging small industry for promoting exports may indirectly encourage use of child labour. Financial and other incentives are given to units in the small sector especially when the units produce exclusively for exports. Very often labour legislation is not applicable to both large and small units located in export promotion zones especially created to encourage exports. Employers of establishments in export promotion zones often keep the size of their establishments small to reap the benefits of government policies designed to encourage small industry. But by locating their units in the export promotion zone they are in a position to flout labour legislation. In many such units child labour, especially female child labour is used extensively. Needless to add, girls working in these units are exploited; they are paid low wages and are made to work for long hours and that too even at night. These policies are likely to encourage child labour rather than discourage it. The Government may have to review its policies of giving financial and other incentives to units just because they are small and produce exclusively for exports.

We noted right at the outset that our knowledge about child labour in general and that about female child labour in particular is inadequate. Secondary data sources like the Census or the NSSO can at best provide merely a broad picture of the state of child labour in India. Even here, the Census data have an advantage over the NSSO as they are comprehensive and give valuable data on child labour at the district level in each state. These data on child workers are available by sex and rural-urban residence. They could be used profitably to study inter-state and intra-state differentials in the participation of children. But this should only be a starting point. The analysis of the secondary data may not answer some of the crucial questions that emerged earlier in our discussion: for instance how do parents view child work especially of their daughters; how do they value the housework done by their daughters; why don't they send their children to schools, etc. to mention a few. In-depth sample surveys using Census data as a base to derive the sample, if undertaken, to understand attitudes of parents would help answer some of these questions. They, no doubt, would go a long way in framing appropriate policies to reduce child labour in India over time.

References

Chakravarty, Sukhmoy (1987), *Development Planning: The Indian Experience*, Clarendon Press, Oxford.

Deshpande, Sudha and Ashish Deshpande (1998), *Impact of NEP on Women Workers in Slums of Mumbai*, Report of the Research Project Funded by Department of Women and Children, Ministry of Human Resource Development, Government of India, undertaken at the Department of Economics, University of Mumbai, February.

——— and Lalit Deshpande (2001), "Reforms and Labour Market in India", Paper presented at the *Seminar on Reforms and Employment in India*, Organised by the Institute of Applied Manpower Research, New Delhi, March 22-24.

Gupta, Manju and Klaus Voll (1999), "Child Labour in India: An Exemplary Case Study" in Voll Klaus (ed.), *Against Child Labour: Indian and International Dimensions and Strategies*, Mosaic Books, New Delhi.

GOI (1999), *Economic Survey 1998-99*, Government of India, Ministry of Finance, New Delhi.

——— (2000), *Report of the Time Use Survey*, Central Statistical Organisation, Ministry of Statistics and Programme Implementation, New Delhi.

Hirway, Indira (2001), "Understanding Children's Work in India: An Analysis of Their Time Use", Paper presented at a *Consultative Workshop on Food Insecurity and Child Work in Rural India*, jointly organised by World Food Programme and Institute for Human Development, New Delhi, March 15-17.

NFHS (2000), *National Family Health Survey (NHFS-2), India 1998-99*, International Institute for Population Sciences, Mumbai.

Kumar, Dharma (1989), *Child Work and Family Life in South Asia*, LAPTAP Working Paper No.1, ILO/LAPTAP, Bangkok.

Malhotra, Rajeev (1997), "Incidence of Poverty in India: Towards a Consensus on Estimating the Poor", *The Indian Journal of Labour Economics*, Vol. 40, No. 1, January-March, pp. 67-102.

National Sample Survey Organisation (1988), "A Note on the Third Quinquennial Survey on Employment and Unemployment: 38th Round (January-December 1983)", *Sarvekshana*, Vol. 11, No. 35, Department of Statistics, Government of India, New Delhi.

——— (1990), "Results of the Fourth Quinquennial Survey on Employment and Unemployment (All India), NSSO 43rd round (July 1987 - June 1988)", *Sarvekshana*, Special Number, Department of Statistics, Government of India, New Delhi.

——— (1997), *Employment and Unemployment in India (1993-94),* Fifth Quinquennial Survey, NSS 50th round (July 1993-June 1994), Department of Statistics, Government of India, New Delhi.

——— (2001), *Employment and Unemployment Situation in India, 1999-2000,* Quinquennial Survey, NSS 50th round (July 1999-June 2000), Department of Statistics, Government of India, New Delhi.

Registrar General and Census Commissioner (1984), *Census of India 1981, General Economic Tables,* Ministry of Home Affairs, Government of India , New Delhi.

——— (1997), *Working Children in India: An Analysis of the 1991 Census Data,* A Study Report in the Analytical Study Report Series on the 1991 Census Data, New Delhi.

——— (2001), *Provisional Population Totals, Paper I India,* Ministry of Home Affairs, Government of India, New Delhi.

Thorat, Sukhdev K. (1999), "Poverty, Caste and Child Labour in India: The Plight of Dalit and Adivasi Children", in Voll, Klaus (ed.) (1999).

Voll, Klaus (ed.) (1999), *Against Child Labour: Indian and International Dimensions and Strategies,* Mosaic Books, New Delhi.

World Bank (1984), *Population Growth and Economic Development,* World Development Report, The World Bank Oxford University Press, New Delhi.

——— (1986), *Poverty and Hunger: Issues and Options for Food Security in Developing Countries,* The World Bank Policy Study, Washington DC.

——— (1989), *India: Poverty, Employment and Social Services,* A World Bank Country Study, Washington DC.

5

Understanding Children's Work in India: An Analysis Based on Time Use Data

INDIRA HIRWAY

I. INTRODUCTION

There are two major sources of data on child labour in India, namely, the decennial Census of Population and the quinquennial NSSO (National Sample Survey Organisation) rounds on Employment and Unemployment. According to both the sources, there has been a decline in the incidence of child labour in India during the past few decades. The reports of the Census of Population, show a decline in the percentage of working children in the total child population, from 7.6 per cent in 1981 to 5.2 per cent in 1991, as well as in the share of child workers in the total workforce, from 6 per cent in 1981 to 3.59 per cent in 1991. (The 2001 Census data are not yet released). According to the NSSO also, there has been a consistent decline in the incidence of child labour in India during the past decades. Table 1 shows, the decline has been in respect of male and female children in both rural and urban areas.

The table also shows that the highest incidence of child labour is among rural females, in the age group, 10-14 years, followed by rural males—about 90 per cent of child labour live in rural areas.

Working children in India can be broadly divided into three categories, namely, full-time child workers employed in hazardous economic activities and processes as per the Child Labour (Prohibition and Regulation) Act, 1986; children employed for wages, but in activities that are not prohibited under the Child Labour Act, and children who are engaged as unpaid family workers in family enterprises, such as farms, household industries, petty trade and others. A

Table 1
Worker-population Ratios (Usual Status PS + SS) of Children

Age group/	Rural		Urban	
Years	Male	Female	Male	Female
5 - 9				
1983	2.5	2.3	0.7	0.7
1987-88	2.3	2.4	0.5	0.3
1993-94	1.1	1.4	0.5	0.5
1999-2000	0.6	0.7	0.3	0.2
10 - 14				
1983	23.8	22.4	10.6	6.4
1987-88	14.0	18.2	8.5	6.5
1993-94	13.8	14.1	6.6	4.5
1999-2000	9.1	9.6	4.9	3.6

Source: NSSO, (2001).

large number of children falling in the last category who are neither in schools nor are full-fledged workers are frequently described as 'nowhere' children (Chaudhri, 1996). Though the Census and the NSSO are able to provide some estimates of the first two categories of child workers, they do not give much information about 'nowhere' children. According to Chaudhri there were about 70 to 80 million 'nowhere' children in India in 1991, predominant among them being girls. However, not much information is available about who they are and how they spend their time.

It has been frequently argued by scholars that the Census-based and NSSO-based estimates of child labour are underestimates, partly because of the inadequacy of the concepts and methods (used in these surveys) to capture children's work, and partly because of the absence of a comprehensive definition of child labour used in these surveys. The Census and the NSSO are not able to net children's work because children are predominantly engaged in, what are called, 'difficult to measure' sectors like subsistence work, home-based work and other informal sector work. Children engaged in these sectors work during irregular periods, intermittently or seasonally and without any direct remuneration, with the results that their work is frequently not reported as work. In addition, there are biases of respondents (who do not consider their work as 'work') and investigators who do not frequently view children's activities as 'work'. Consequently, there is likely to be a gross underestimation of child workers.

As regards the definition of child labour too, the conventional definition, based on the time spent by children on economic work does not seem to be fully satisfactory because those children who are not engaged in market oriented economic work and who do not attend school are frequently engaged in collection of fuel wood, water, fodder, etc. and in non-economic work, such as taking care of younger siblings, helping in household chores, etc., to enable their parents to work. It is desirable to treat these children as child labour, as their needs and interests require the attention of policy makers. Somehow, information on how children spend their time on these activities is not available either from the NSSO rounds or from the Census of Population.

Thus, there is a significant data gap with respect to children's work, as well as non-work. In order to formulate any meaningful policy for child workers, it is necessary to have comprehensive information about how they spend their time. In other words, it is necessary to know (a) how many children are engaged in economic work (and what kind of economic work), and how much time they spend on such work, (b) how many of the working children go to school and (c) what do children do if they are neither engaged in work, nor go to school. Such comprehensive information will be useful in designing appropriate policies for the welfare of working and non-working children. It needs to be noted that such policies would be more important to girls who spend more time on economic as well as non-economic work, and whose school attendance rates are observed to be much lower than those of boys.

II. TIME USE STUDIES FOR UNDERSTANDING CHILDREN'S TIME USE

Since the conventional surveys like the Census or the NSS rounds are not likely to provide information on children's use of time, one has to explore some alternative survey techniques. In this context, time use studies are extremely relevant.

Historically speaking, time use surveys were first used in the early years of the twentieth century as a means of understanding the life style of people including their social life. These surveys were designed to understand that part of people's life for which no information was available from conventional data sources, such as, national income statistics, labour and employment statistics, population statistics, etc. In the second part of the twentieth century, and particularly during the last decades of the century, a need was felt to measure 'invisible' unpaid work of women and men to estimate the contribution of this work to human welfare. Several industrialised countries have been using these surveys to measure unpaid work of women, in terms of time as well as money (Goldschmidt-Cleremont and Pagnossin-Aligisakis, 1995). With the emergence of developing countries on the scene, however, time use surveys have acquired a new focus. These countries have seen several additional uses of this survey technique, such as, netting economic work of the poor or of those working in the informal sector, and improving thereby, the workforce/labour force statistics and national income statistics (Hirway, 1999).

1. The Indian Time Use Survey

The Department of Statistics, Government of India, decided to organise a pilot time use study at the national level. Since India was one of the first developing countries to undertake such a survey at the macro level, a technical committee was set up to undertake the following specific tasks:

(i) To advise the government on designing, planning and related matters leading to conducting a time use survey;

(ii) To suggest appropriate definitions and concepts, schedule of inquiry and a suitable reference period for the purpose of data collection through a survey;

(iii) To suggest an appropriate methodology for building up of the annual estimates of time disposition based on the survey data; and

(iv) To advise on any other matter referred to the technical committee by the Department of Statistics in respect of the time use survey.

After developing a suitable conceptual framework and methodology, the committee conducted the pilot time use survey in six states of India during the period, July 1998 to June 1999. The preliminary results of the survey are now available, though a detailed analysis of the data is still to be accomplished.

(i) Objectives

The Technical Committee laid down the following objectives of the pilot time use survey:

1. To develop a conceptual framework and a suitable methodology for designing and conducting time use studies in India on a regular basis, to evolve a methodology to estimate labour force/work force in the country and to estimate the value of unpaid work in the economy in a satellite account.

2. To collect and analyse the time use pattern of people in the selected states of India in order to have comprehensive information about the time spent by people on marketed and non-marketed economic activities covered under the UN-SNA 1993, non-marketed non-SNA (System of National Accounts) activities covered under the General Production Boundary and on personal care and related activities that cannot be delegated to others.

3. To use the data in generating more reliable estimates on work force and national income as per SNA 93, and in computing the value of unpaid work through a separate satellite account.

4. To infer policy/programme implications from the analysis of the data on (a) distribution of paid and unpaid work among men and women in rural and urban areas, (b) nature of unpaid work of women including the drudgery of their work and (c) sharing of household work by men and women for gender equity.

5. To analyse the time use pattern of the poor to understand the nature of their work so as to draw inference for employment and welfare programmes for them.

6. To analyse the data of the time use pattern of the weaker sections including the poor, the children and women in order to draw inferences for welfare policies for them.

(ii) Details of Sample Selection

Keeping in mind the wide socio-cultural diversities in India, six states were selected to represent each region of the country. Haryana, Madhya Pradesh, Gujarat, Orissa, Tamil Nadu and Meghalaya were chosen to represent northern, central, western, eastern, southern and north-eastern regions, respectively. The total sample size of 18, 628 households was first distributed among the states in proportion to the total number of estimated households as per the NSSO (1993-94) survey. The further distribution of the allocated sample in the states among the districts, villages and towns was done using a stratified sampling method. (Report of Time Use Survey, CSO, Government of India, New Delhi).

The Technical Committee developed suitable concepts and methods for conducting the survey. It developed a suitable system of classification for classifying time use activities. This system was designed in the SNA framework to classify activities in three major categories, namely SNA activities or economic activities which are covered under national income accounts; extended SNA activities which are not included in national accounts, but are covered under General Production Boundary; and non-SNA activities or personal activities which are for personal care and cannot be delegated to others (for example, sleeping, watching television, etc.). This classification is a three-digit classification, the first digit indicating the broad sector of activity, the second digit the sub-sector and the third digit the actual activity (see Appendix). Since this survey was of a different type than most others, a detailed Manual of Instructions was prepared and intensive training was imparted to investigators and supervisors at different levels.

The survey collected comprehensive information on how people, including children above six years, spend their time on different activities. The one-day recall method was used for data collection. The survey provides useful information for understanding children's work. This paper presents these data on children's contribution to economic work in terms of time spent on economic activities and to examine the time use pattern of children in respect of activities such as unpaid household work, education and learning, play and rest etc.

It needs to be stated at the outset that the data obtained through this survey has not yet been fully analysed as the first set of tables, published so far, present a preliminary analysis of the data. Consequently, the present analysis is limited to the broad pattern of the time use of children. For example, it presents data on how much time children spent on SNA work during the reference week, but does not provide separate data on how many of these children spent at least one hour on this work, with the result that we cannot compute workforce participation rates of children in economic activities. Also, the data provides information on how many children spent their time on each of the economic activities, but does not provide estimates of the net number of children participating in any economic activity, with the result that we cannot estimate the net number of children participating in economic work.

In spite of these limitations, however, these data are very useful in understanding children's work and non-work.

2. Time Spent on SNA Activities

Let us first examine how much time children spend on economic work as defined in the Systems of National Accounts. This work or activity has been divided into certain main categories, each of which is represented by a number. These are:

11 = Crop farming, kitchen gardening, etc.

12 = Animal husbandry

13 = Fishing, forestry, horticulture, gardening

14 = Collection of water, fodder, fuel, fruits, etc., hunting, storing

15 = Processing and storage

16 = Mining, quarrying & digging

21 = Construction activities

22 = Manufacturing activities

31 = Trade and business

32 = Services

It is clear that the activities from 11 to 16 refer to primary activities, 21 and 22 to secondary activities, and 31 and 32 to tertiary activities. These activity categories are divided into a three-digit classification as shown in the Appendix at the end of this paper. This classification provides details regarding the different economic activities carried out by the children.

Tables 2 and 3 present data on the number of children participating in different economic activities and the hours of work put in by them on these activities. The data presented are analysed as follows:

1. Table 2 shows that the most important economic activity for children in the age group, 6-14 years is animal husbandry. About 11.47 per cent of boys and 10.69 per cent of girls in this age group participated in this activity, particularly in animal grazing. The three-digit classification shows that boys are mainly engaged in animal grazing while girls are also engaged in tending animals. These boys and girls spent 21.54 hours and 13.94 hours, respectively on this activity, implying, on an average, a daily engagement of three and two hours respectively (Table 3).
2. The next important economic activity for children is the collection of fuelwood, water, fodder, fruits, etc. About 4.51 per cent of boys and 13.76 per cent of girls in the age group, 6-14, were engaged in this activity, which implies that this activity is more important for girls than for boys. However, boys spent 10.50 hours and girls 8.80 hours on an average during the reference week.

Table 2
Time Spent by Sample Persons on SNA Activities by Age and Sex

Economic activities	Activity code	6-9 years M	6-9 years F	6-9 years T	10-14 years M	10-14 years F	10-14 years T	6-14 years M	6-14 years F	6-14 years T
Crop farming, kitchen gardening, etc.	11	83	74	157	294	251	545	377	325	702
		(3.51)	(3.74)	(3.62)	(7.97)	(7.76)	(7.87)	(6.23)	(6.24)	(6.23)
Animal husbandry	12	161	126	287	533	431	964	694	557	1251
		(6.82)	(6.37)	(6.61)	(14.46)	(13.33)	(13.93)	(11.47)	(10.69)	(11.11)
Fishing, forestry, horti-culture, gardening	13	21	26	47	93	61	154	114	87	201
		(0.89)	(1.31)	(1.08)	(2.52)	(1.89)	(2.23)	(1.88)	(1.67)	(1.78)
Collection of fruit, water, plants etc., storing and hunting	14	65	111	176	208	606	814	273	717	990
		(2.75)	(5.61)	(4.06)	(5.64)	(18.74)	(11.76)	(4.51)	(13.76)	(8.79)
Processing and storage	15	6	15	21	23	52	75	29	67	96
		(0.25)	(0.76)	(0.48)	(0.62)	(1.61)	(1.08)	(0.48)	(1.29)	(0.85)
Mining, quarrying & digging, cutting, etc.	16	0	0	0	10	4	14	10	4	14
		(0.00)	(0.00)	(0.00)	(0.27)	(0.12)	(0.20)	(0.17)	(0.08)	(0.12)
Construction activities	21	16	8	24	40	20	60	56	28	84
		(0.68)	(0.40)	(0.55)	(1.08)	(0.62)	(0.87)	(0.93)	(0.54)	(0.75)
Manufacturing activities	22	12	14	26	75	102	177	87	116	203
		(0.51)	(0.71)	(0.60)	(2.03)	(3.15)	(2.56)	(1.44)	(2.23)	(1.80)
Trade, business and services	31	20	11	31	51	22	73	71	33	104
		(0.85)	(0.56)	(0.71)	(1.38)	(0.68)	(1.05)	(1.17)	(0.63)	(0.92)
Services	32	108	87	195	219	159	378	327	246	573
		(4.57)	(4.40)	(4.49)	(5.94)	(4.92)	(5.46)	(5.41)	(4.72)	(5.09)
Community services and help in other households	611	2	0	2	0	1	1	2	1	3
		(0.08)	(0.00)	(0.05)	(0.00)	(0.03)	(0.01)	(0.03)	(0.02)	(0.03)

Note: 1. The data presented in this and other tables are from the combined states which include Meghalaya, Tamil Nadu, Orissa, Gujarat, Madhya Pradesh and Haryana.
2. Figures in parenthesis show percentages of sample persons to total sample persons in respective categories.

Source: GOI (2000).

3. The other important economic activities of children are crop farming (about 6.23 per cent boys and 6.24 per cent girls participated in these activities) and petty services like informal sector services (in which 5.41 per cent boys and 4.72 per cent girls participated). The other activities of children are fishing and foresting manufacturing activities, etc.
4. Table 2 shows that the participation of children in the age group, 6-9 years is also significant. About 6.82 per cent of boys and 6.37 per cent of girls are engaged in animal husbandry, mainly grazing; 4.57 per cent of boys and 4.40 per cent girls are engaged in petty services; and 3.51 per cent of boys and 3.74 per cent of girls spend at least some time in crop farming.

Table 3
Weekly Average Time Spent on SNA Activities by Age and Sex (Participants)

Economic activities	Activity code	Age 6-9 years M	6-9 years F	6-9 years T	10-14 years M	10-14 years F	10-14 years T	6-14 years M	6-14 years F	6-14 years T
Crop farming, kitchen gardening, etc.	11	12.00	10.83	11.42	22.54	25.04	23.59	20.34	21.37	20.79
		(7.14)	(6.45)	(6.80)	(13.42)	(14.90)	(14.04)	(12.11)	(12.72)	(12.38)
Animal husbandry	12	19.71	14.44	17.37	22.12	13.79	18.22	21.54	13.94	18.02
		(11.73)	(8.60)	(10.34)	(13.17)	(8.21)	(10.85)	(12.82)	(8.30)	(10.73)
Fishing, forestry, horticulture, gardening	13	19.22	13.50	15.75	17.83	16.48	17.23	18.11	15.49	16.84
		(11.44)	(8.04)	(9.38)	(10.61)	(9.81)	(10.26)	(10.78)	(9.22)	(10.02)
Collection of fruit, water, plants etc., storing and hunting	14	12.28	7.26	8.93	10.02	9.10	9.34	10.50	8.80	9.27
		(7.31)	(4.32)	(5.32)	(5.96)	(5.42)	(5.56)	(6.25)	(5.24)	(5.52)
Processing and storage	15	13.15	13.73	13.52	5.79	8.95	8.09	7.59	9.82	9.18
		(7.83)	(8.17)	(8.05)	(3.45)	(5.33)	(4.82)	(4.52)	(5.85)	(5.46)
Mining, quarrying & digging, cutting, etc.	16	0.00	0.00	0.00	34.51	37.34	35.35	34.51	37.34	35.35
		(0.00)	(0.00)	(0.00)	(20.54)	(22.23)	(21.04)	(20.54)	(22.23)	(21.04)
Construction activities	21	4.83	9.48	6.70	32.75	16.62	27.96	26.16	14.27	22.30
		(2.88)	(5.64)	(3.99)	(19.49)	(9.89)	(16.64)	(15.57)	(8.49)	(13.27)
Manufacturing activities	22	10.31	11.13	10.82	35.54	25.87	29.90	32.70	23.97	27.57
		(6.14)	(6.63)	(6.44)	(21.15)	(15.40)	(17.80)	(19.46)	(14.27)	(16.41)
Trade, business and services	31	2.94	4.64	3.41	14.32	10.97	13.26	11.12	9.40	10.59
		(1.75)	(2.76)	(2.03)	(8.52)	(6.53)	(7.89)	(6.62)	(5.60)	(6.30)
Services	32	15.50	12.38	14.26	19.92	15.38	18.03	18.33	14.36	16.71
		(9.23)	(7.37)	(8.49)	(11.86)	(9.15)	(10.73)	(10.91)	(8.55)	(9.95)
Community services and help in other households	611	0.95	0.00	0.95	0.00	0.83	0.83	0.95	0.83	0.89
		(0.57)	(0.00)	(0.57)	(0.00)	(0.49)	(0.49)	(0.57)	(0.49).	(0.53)
All SNA activities		18.47	14.51	16.56	26.20	19.90	23.02	24.27	18.63	21.46
		(10.99)	(8.64)	(9.86)	(15.60)	(11.85)	(13.70)	(14.45)	(11.09)	(12.77)

Source: Same as in Table 2.

5. As per Table 3, children aged, 6-14, who participated in economic activities spent 21.46 hours a week (about three hours on a day), on an average, on SNA work, which comes to 12.77 per cent of their total weekly time. Boys spent 24.27 hours while girls spent 18.63 hours. The data show that boys engaged in mining, quarrying and digging spend maximum time on this work (34.5 hours), which implies that many of them are engaged in these activities on a full-time basis. This is followed by manufacturing work (32.70 hours), construction work (26.16 hours), animal grazing (21.54 hours) and crop farming (20.14 hours). In the case of girls engaged in SNA activities, maximum time, (37.34 hours), is spent by those who are

engaged in mining, quarrying & digging. This is followed by girls engaged in manufacturing activities (27.57 hours), construction work (22.30 hours), crop farming (20.79 hours) and animal husbandry (18.02 hours).

6. Working children in the age group, 6-9 years, spent, on an average, 18.47 hours (boys) and 14.51 hours (girls) on SNA activities. Boys engaged in animal husbandry (grazing) spent maximum time on work (19.71 hours), followed by those engaged in petty services (15.50 hours). In the case of girls, those engaged in animal husbandry spend maximum time on work (14.44 hours) followed by those engaged in processing and storage (13.73 hours) and petty services (12.38 hours).

It is not possible for us to find out the workforce participation rates, comparable to the NSS weekly status workforce participation rates, on the basis of the above data because the tables do not provide information on (1) the number of children working for at least one hour during the week and (2) the net number of children who participate in economic work. However, some broad observations can be made in this regard. To start with, if we consider certain activities as mutually exclusive (i.e. these cannot be undertaken by one person), we can say that animal husbandry, mining-quarrying, etc., and petty services are surely exclusive activities. This implies that at least 17 per cent of children aged 5-14 years do participate in economic activities. This is, of course, an underestimation.

The data presented in the tables also indicate that girls' participation is not less than boys. While girls have a higher participation in crop farming, collection of fuel, fodder, etc., processing and storage, and in manufacturing activities, boys' participation is higher in animal husbandry, fishing and forestry, mining, quarrying & digging, construction activities, trade and services. Also, though girls put in smaller number of hours in SNA activities at the average level, they spend more time than boys in crop farming, processing and storage, and in mining, quarrying & digging.

3. Time Spent on Other Activities

(i) Education and Learning

In order to estimate the incidence of child labour, it is important to know how many children go to school. Table 4, which presents these data, shows that 69.88 per cent of boys and 63.95 per cent girls in the age group, 6-14 attended school. The corresponding percentages were 72.23 and 69.72 respectively for boys and girls in the age group, 6-9, respectively. This implies that the school attendance declines considerably, particularly in the case of girls, as the age increases. The table also shows that about 30 per cent of boys and 36 per cent of girls did not attend school. In short, the goal of universal primary education appears to be quite distant even today.

How much time do children spend in school? The table shows that girls spend about 31.43 hours and boys about 31.21 hours in school. They also spend around 15 hours on homework or studies. Do the children who do not go to

Table 4
Time Spent by Sample Persons on Non-SNA Learning Activities by Age and Sex

Learning activities	Activity code	Age 6-9 years M	F	T	10-14 years M	F	T	6-14 years M	F	T
General education: school/university/other educational institutions attendance	711	1706	1379	3085	2521	1954	4475	4227	3333	7560
		(72.23)	(69.72)	(71.08)	(68.38)	(60.42)	(64.66)	(69.88)	(63.95)	(67.13)
Studies, homework and course review related to general education	721	1575	1263	2838	2394	1886	4280	3969	3149	7118
		(66.68)	(63.85)	(65.39)	(64.93)	(58.32)	(61.84)	(65.61)	(60.42)	(63.21)
Additional study, non formal education by children	731	35	34	69	70	55	125	105	89	194
		(1.48)	(1.72)	(1.59)	(1.90)	(1.70)	(1.81)	(1.74)	(1.71)	(1.72)
Non-formal education by children	741	12	5	17	6	11	17	18	16	34
		(0.51)	(0.25)	(0.39)	(0.16)	(0.34)	(0.25)	(0.30)	(0.31)	(0.30)
Work-related training	751	11	14	25	30	18	48	41	32	73
		(0.47)	(0.71)	(0.58)	(0.81)	(0.56)	(0.69)	(0.68)	(0.61)	(0.65)
Training under government programmes such as TRYSEM, DWCRA and others	761	7	3	10	6	13	19	13	16	29
		(0.30)	(0.15)	(0.23)	(0.16)	(0.40)	(0.27)	(0.21)	(0.31)	(0.26)
Other training/ education	771	34	28	62	76	67	143	110	95	205
		(1.44)	(1.42)	(1.43)	(2.06)	(2.07)	(2.07)	(1.82)	(1.82)	(1.82)
Learning not elsewhere classified	781	72	71	143	116	84	200	188	155	343
		(3.05)	(3.59)	(3.29)	(3.15)	(2.60)	(2.89)	(3.11)	(2.97)	(3.05)
Travel related to learning	791	1536	1217	2753	2315	1749	4064	3851	2966	6817
		(65.03)	(61.53)	(63.43)	(62.79)	(54.08)	(58.72)	(63.66)	(56.91)	(60.54)

Source: Same as in Table 2.

regular schools go to non-formal school? Table 4 shows that the number of such children is negligible, (around 0.30 per cent) both for boys and girls. Also, they spend less than one hour per day in these schools even when they do go to school. Non-formal education thus has not emerged as an effective alternative to regular schools. Some children, however, do spend their time on training and other kinds of education-which could be related to family enterprises. On an average, the children aged, 6-14, who participate in education-related activities spend 46.86 hours on these activities, with the boys spending 47 hours and girls 46.55 hours (Table 5).

Table 5
Weekly Average Time Spent by Participants on Non-SNA Learning Activities by Age and Sex

Learning activities	Activity code	Age: 6-9 years, Sex: M	F	T	10-14 years M	F	T	6-14 years M	F	T
General education: school/university/other educational institutions attendance	711	30.79	30.94	30.85	31.50	31.78	31.62	31.21	31.43	31.31
		(18.33)	(18.429)	(18.36)	(18.75)	(18.92)	(18.82)	(18.58)	(18.71)	(18.64)
Studies, homework and course review related to general education	721	13.73	13.97	13.83	16.81	16.62	16.73	15.57	15.54	15.56
		(8.17)	(8.32)	(8.23)	(10.01)	(9.89)	(9.96)	(9.27)	(9.25)	(9.26)
Additional study, non-formal education by children	731	8.93	9.59	9.33	7.88	9.18	8.53	8.25	9.37	8.86
		(5.32)	(5.71)	(5.55)	(4.69)	(5.46)	(5.08)	(4.91)	(5.58)	(5.27)
Non-formal education by children	741	7.51	8.06	7.69	3.10	6.31	4.98	5.61	6.87	6.20
		(4.47)	(4.80)	(4.58)	(1.85)	(3.76)	(2.96)	(3.34)	(4.09)	(3.69)
Work-related training	751	2.34	5.93	4.11	6.92	4.56	5.76	5.26	5.06	5.16
		(1.39)	(3.53)	(2.45)	(4.12)	(2.71)	(3.43)	(3.13)	(3.01)	(3.07)
Training under government programmes such as TRYSEM, DWCRA and others	761	1.39	2.66	1.76	1.68	2.67	2.19	1.57	2.67	2.06
		(0.83)	(1.58)	(1.05)	(1.00)	(1.59)	(1.30)	(0.93)	(1.59)	(1.23)
Other training/ education	771	12.91	8.69	11.21	9.61	7.40	8.58	10.74	7.77	9.41
		(7.68)	(5.17)	(6.67)	(5.72)	(4.40)	(5.11)	(6.39)	(4.63)	(5.60)
Learning not elsewhere classified	781	7.56	6.35	6.98	10.22	5.83	8.49	9.22	6.07	7.87
		(4.50)	(3.78)	(4.15)	(6.08)	(3.47)	(5.05)	(5.49)	(3.61)	(4.68)
Travel-related to learning	791	4.23	4.20	4.22	4.89	4.99	4.93	4.62	4.67	4.64
		(2.52)	(2.50)	(2.51)	(2.91)	(2.97)	(2.93)	(2.75)	(2.78)	(2.76)
Avg. for group		44.03	43.47	43.78	49.24	48.79	49.04	47.10	46.55	46.86
	7	(26.21)	(25.88)	(26.06)	(29.31)	(29.04)	(29.19)	(28.04)	(27.71)	(27.89)

Source: Same as in Table 2.

(ii) Extended SNA Activities

If, as we have seen, 67.13 per cent children are engaged in educational activities and about 17 per cent in economic activities, what do the rest of the children do? Or, how do they spend time when they are not engaged in economic activities or in studies? It is clear that those children are engaged either in extended SNA activities or in non-SNA activities.

As explained above, extended SNA activities are those activities which are not strictly economic activities, but which fall in the General Production

Boundary and which contribute to family welfare. These activities are: (a) household maintenance, management, etc, (b) care of children, sick, disabled or the old, and (c) community services and help in other households.

(a) Household Management and Maintenance: Tables 6 and 7 present data on the number and percentage of children participating in household maintenance activities, etc, and data on weekly average hours spent by the children on these activities, respectively. Both these tables clearly indicate that the number of children engaged in these activities is not small and that they spend considerable time on them. Table 6 shows that 32.02 per cent of girls in the age group, 6-14 participate in the cleaning and upkeep of dwellings, as against 4.10 per cent of boys, 25.50 per cent of girls clean utensils as against 2.10 per cent of boys, 22.93 per cent girls participate in cooking as against 3.60 per cent boys and 19.07 per cent of girls are engaged in washing, mending, ironing, etc. of clothes as against 6.93 per cent boys. This clearly indicates a gender bias in the distribution of household work between girls and boys. Table 7 also shows that on an average, the girls who participated in household work spent 13.01 hours a week on this work, while participant boys spent 5.32 hours on it.

It is worth noting that in the age group, 6-9 also, 17.04 per cent of girls are engaged in cleaning and upkeep of dwelling units as against 2.58 per cent of boys, 12.59 per cent girls and 1.40 per cent boys clean utensils and 7.38 per cent girls and 2.29 per cent boys spend some of their time in cooking and serving food. In the case of shopping for the family, however, the gender gap is much less, with 3.72 per cent of boys and 3.97 per cent of girls participating in these activities. Also, more boys than girls run errands (outside the house) for household maintenance and management.

Table 7 shows that girls engaged in cooking and serving food spend maximum time, 9.40 hours a week, on these activities: those engaged in cleaning, sweeping of dwelling units spend 4.37 hours; those engaged in cleaning utensils spend 3.92 hours and those engaged in washing clothes, etc. spend 3.57 hours a week on this activity. Even when boys participate in these activities, they spend much less time, on an average (3.17 hours a week) on these activities.

(b) Care of Children, Old, Sick and Disabled: Tables 8 and 9 present data on the number of children participating in care activities and the number of hours they spend on these activities. Table 8 shows that 7.06 per cent of girls in the age group, 6-14 years, and 7.18 per cent of girls in the age group, 6-9 years, spend their time on taking physical care of younger siblings. Also, 5.91 per cent of girls in the age group, 6-14 years, and 7.13 per cent girls in the age group, 6-9 years, take care of children by supervising them. The corresponding percentages for boys are much less—between 2 per cent and 3 per cent.

Children engaged in these activities spend considerable time on them (Table 9). For example, girls in the age group, 6-14 and 6-9 years spend 7.96

Table 6
Number and Percentage of Sample Children Engaged in Extended SNA Activities (Including Household Maintenance, Management and Shopping) for Own Households by Age and Sex

		Age								
		6-9 years			10-14 years			6-14 years		
		Sex								
Extended SNA activities	Activity code	M	F	T	M	F	T	M	F	T
Cooking food items, beverages and serving	411	54	146	200	164	1049	1213	218	1195	1413
		(2.29)	(7.38)	(4.61)	(4.45)	(32.44)	(17.53)	(3.60)	(22.93)	(12.55)
Cleaning and upkeep of dwelling and surroundings	421	61	337	398	187	1332	1519	248	1669	1917
		(2.58)	(17.04)	(9.17)	(5.07)	(41.19)	(21.95)	(4.10)	(32.02)	(17.02)
Cleaning utensils	422	33	249	282	96	1080	1176	129	1329	1458
		(1.40)	(12.59)	(6.50)	(2.60)	(33.40)	(16.99)	(2.13)	(25.50)	(12.95)
Care of textiles: sorting, mending, washing, ironing and ordering clothes and linen	431	71	126	197	348	868	1216	419	994	1413
		(3.01)	(6.37)	(4.54)	(9.44)	(26.84)	(17.57)	(6.93)	(19.07)	(12.55)
Shopping for goods, household appliances, equipment, food and various household supplies	441	51	39	90	174	168	342	225	207	432
		(2.16)	(1.97)	(2.07)	(4.72)	(5.19)	(4.94)	(3.72)	(3.97)	(3.84)
Household management: planning, supervising, paying bills, etc	451	0	6	6	10	27	37	10	33	43
		(0.00)	(0.30)	(0.14)	(0.27)	(0.83)	(0.53)	(0.17)	(0.63)	(0.38)
Do-it yourself home improvements and maintenance, installation, servicing and repair of personal and household goods	461	25	65	90	115	308	423	140	373	513
		(1.06)	(3.29)	(2.07)	(3.12)	(9.52)	(6.11)	(2.31)	(7.16)	(4.56)
Pet care	471	1	0	1	13	19	32	14	19	33
		(0.04)	(0.00)	(0.02)	(0.35)	(0.59)	(0.46)	(0.23)	(0.36)	(0.29)
Travel related to household maintenance, management and shopping	481	64	40	104	142	124	266	206	164	370
		(2.71)	(2.02)	(2.40)	(3.85)	(3.83)	(3.84)	(3.41)	(3.15)	(3.29)
Household maintenance, management and shopping not elsewhere classified	491	60	148	208	190	598	788	250	746	996
		(2.54)	(7.48)	(4.79)	(5.15)	(18.49)	(11.39)	(4.13)	(14.31)	(8.84)

Source: Same as in Table 2.

Table 7
Weekly Average Time Spent on Extended SNA Activities (Including Household Maintenance, Management and Shopping for Own Households) by Age and Sex

		Age								
		6-9 years			10-14 years			6-14 years		
		Sex								
Extended SNA activities	Activity code	M	F	T	M	F	T	M	F	T
Cooking food items, beverages and serving	411	5.72	5.53	5.57	5.08	9.99	9.30	5.21	9.40	8.76
		(3.40)	(3.29)	(3.32)	(3.02)	(5.95)	(5.54)	(3.10)	(5.60)	(5.21)
Cleaning and upkeep of dwelling and surroundings	421	2.79	3.12	3.07	3.58	4.68	4.54	3.39	4.37	4.23
		(1.66)	(1.86)	(1.83)	(2.13)	(2.79)	(2.70)	(2.02)	(2.60)	(2.52)
Cleaning utensils	422	4.00	2.91	3.01	3.00	4.16	4.06	3.21	3.92	3.86
		(2.38)	(1.73)	(1.79)	(1.79)	(2.48)	(2.42)	(1.91)	(2.33)	(2.30)
Care of textiles: sorting, mending, washing, ironing and ordering clothes and linen	431	1.50	2.43	2.07	2.01	3.74	3.21	1.92	3.57	3.05
		(0.89)	(1.45)	(1.23)	(1.20)	(2.23)	(1.91)	(1.14)	(2.13)	(1.82)
Shopping for goods, household appliances, equipment, food and various household supplies	441	2.35	1.95	2.16	2.51	2.70	2.61	2.47	2.55	2.51
		(1.40)	(1.16)	(1.29)	(1.49)	(1.61)	(1.55)	(1.47)	(1.52)	(1.49)
Household management: planning, supervising, paying bills, etc.	451	0.00	2.89	2.89	7.96	5.10	5.87	7.96	4.81	5.56
		(0.00)	(1.72)	(1.72)	(4.74)	(3.04)	(3.49)	(4.74)	(2.86)	(3.31)
Do-it yourself home improvements and maintenance, installation, servicing and repair of personal and household goods	461	7.41	4.35	5.24	6.76	6.41	6.51	6.89	6.01	6.26
		(4.41)	(2.59)	(3.12)	(4.02)	(3.82)	(3.88)	(4.10)	(3.58)	(3.73)
Pet care	471	1.00	0.00	1.00	5.57	4.17	4.76	5.46	4.17	4.72
		(0.60)	(0.00)	(0.60)	(3.32)	(2.48)	(2.83)	(3.25)	(2.48)	(2.81)
Travel related to household maintenance, management and shopping	481	3.29	1.74	2.73	3.09	3.13	3.11	3.16	2.76	2.99
		(1.96)	(1.04)	(1.63)	(1.84)	(1.86)	(1.85)	(1.88)	(1.64)	(1.78)
Household maintenance, management and shopping not elsewhere classified	491	3.28	4.25	3.98	4.33	5.51	5.23	4.10	5.26	4.97
		(1.95)	(2.53)	(2.37)	(2.58)	(3.28)	(3.11)	(2.44)	(3.13)	(2.96)
Avg. for		4.51	6.77	5.99	5.60	14.85	11.93	5.32	13.01	10.53
group	4	(2.68)	(4.03)	(3.57)	(3.33)	(8.84)	(7.10)	(3.17)	(7.74)	(6.27)

Source: Same as in Table 2.

Table 8
Sample Persons Who Have Spent Time on Extended SNA Activities Depending Upon the Mode of Payment in Care of Children, the Sick, Elderly and Disabled for Own Household

Extended SNA activities		Age 6-9 years M	F	T	10-14 years M	F	T	6-14 years M	F	T
Physical care of children: washing, dressing, feeding	511	73 (3.09)	142 (7.18)	215 (4.95)	71 (1.93)	226 (6.99)	297 (4.29)	144 (2.38)	368 (7.06)	512 (4.55)
Teaching, training and instruction of own children	521	17 (0.72)	9 (0.46)	26 (0.6)	20 (0.54)	21 (0.65)	41 (0.59)	37 (0.61)	30 (0.58)	67 (0.59)
Accompanying children to places: school, sports, lessons, etc./PHC/ doctors	531	35 (1.48)	32 (1.62)	67 (1.54)	59 (1.60)	52 (1.61)	111 (1.60)	94 (1.55)	84 (1.61)	178 (1.58)
Physical care of the sick, disabled elderly household members: washing, dressing, feeding, helping	541	15 (0.64)	18 (0.91)	33 (0.76)	15 (0.41)	51 (1.58)	66 (0.95)	30 (0.50)	69 (1.32)	99 (0.88)
Accompanying adults to receive personal care services: such as hari-dresser's therapy sessions, temple, religious place etc.	551	2 (0.08)	4 (0.20)	6 (0.14)	5 (0.14)	9 (0.28)	14 (0.20)	7 (0.12)	13 (0.25)	20 (0.18)
Supervising children needing care with or without other activities	561	72 (3.05)	141 (7.13)	213 (4.91)	67 (1.82)	167 (5.16)	234 (3.38)	139 (2.30)	308 (5.91)	447 (3.97)
Supervising adults needing care with or without other activities	562	4 (0.17)	4 (0.20)	8 (0.18)	3 (0.08)	14 (0.43)	17 (0.25)	7 (0.12)	18 (0.35)	25 (0.22)
Travel-related to care of children	571	3 (0.13)	10 (0.51)	13 (0.30)	4 (0.11)	10 (0.31)	14 (0.20)	7 (0.12)	20 (0.38)	27 (0.24)
Travel-related to care of adults and others	572	0.00 (0.00)	0.00 (0.00)	0.00 (0.00)	3 (0.08)	1 (0.03)	4 (0.06)	3 (0.05)	1 (0.02)	4 (0.04)
Taking care of guests/ visitors	581	3 (0.13)	2 (0.10)	5 (0.12)	8 (0.22)	6 (0.19)	14 (0.20)	11 (0.18)	8 (0.15)	19 (0.17)
Any other activity not mentioned above	591	12 (0.51)	13 (0.66)	25 (0.58)	20 (0.54)	27 (0.83)	47 (0.68)	32 (0.53)	40 (0.77)	72 (0.64)

Source: Same as in Table 2.

Table 9

Weekly Average Time Spent on Extended SNA Activities in Care for Children, the Sick, the Elderly and Disabled for Own Households According to Age and Sex (Participants)

Extended SNA activities	Activity code	6-9 years M	6-9 years F	6-9 years T	10-14 years M	10-14 years F	10-14 years T	6-14 years M	6-14 years F	6-14 years T
Physical care of children: washing, dressing, feeding	511	4.90 (2.92)	7.52 (4.48)	6.55 (3.90)	5.10 (3.04)	8.22 (4.89)	(4.49)	4.99 (2.97)	7.96 (4.74)	7.13 (4.24)
Teaching, training and instruction of own children	521	3.30 (1.96)	4.05 (2.41)	3.59 (2.14)	5.49 (3.27)	8.76 (5.21)	7.64 (4.55)	4.16 (2.48)	7.20 (4.29)	5.77 (3.43)
Accompanying children to places: school, sports, lessons, etc./ PHC/Doctors	531	14.01 (8.34)	11.95 (7.11)	12.91 (7.68)	19.07 (11.35)	14.98 (8.92)	17.16 (10.21)	17.32 (10.31)	13.75 (8.18)	15.57 (9.27)
Physical care of the sick, disabled elderly household members: washing dressing feeding, helping	541	2.16 (1.29)	2.86 (1.70)	2.53 (1.51)	5.93 (3.53)	4.79 (2.85)	5.14 (3.06)	4.26 (2.54)	4.25 (2.53)	4.26 (2.54)
Accompanying adults to receive personal care services: such as hari-dresser's therapy sessions, temple, religious place etc.	551	1.44 (0.86)	3.20 (1.90)	2.35 (1.40)	1.47 (0.88)	2.40 (1.43)	2.08 (1.24)	1.46 (0.87)	2.58 (1.54)	2.15 (1.28)
Supervising children needing care with or without other activities	561	10.04 (5.98)	12.33 (7.34)	11.53 (6.86)	8.63 (5.14)	12.20 (7.26)	11.08 (6.60)	9.33 (5.55)	12.26 (7.30)	11.29 (6.72)
Supervising adults needing care with or without other activities	562	1.01 (0.60)	2.76 (1.64)	2.04 (1.21)	2.57 (1.53)	4.56 (2.71)	4.36 (2.60)	1.53 (0.91)	4.12 (2.45)	3.60 (2.14)
Travel related to care of children	571	3.55 (2.11)	6.55 (3.90)	6.14 (3.65)	1.38 (0.82)	8.66 (5.15)	7.70 (4.58)	2.45 (1.46)	7.65 (4.55)	6.95 (4.14)
Travel related to care of adults and others	572	0.00 (0.00)	0.00 (0.00)	0.00 (0.00)	4.82 (2.87)	16.92 (10.07)	8.38 (4.99)	4.82 (2.87)	16.92 (10.07)	8.38 (4.99)
Taking care of guests/ visitors	581	3.19 (1.90)	1.00 (0.60)	2.66 (1.58)	2.19 (1.30)	0.66 (0.39)	1.60 (0.95)	2.52 (1.50)	0.73 (0.43)	1.90 (1.13)
Any other activity not mentioned above	591	5.50 (3.27)	3.77 (2.24)	4.60 (2.74)	3.33 (1.98)	7.65 (4.55)	5.80 (3.45)	4.02 (2.39)	6.59 (3.92)	5.45 (3.24)
Avg. for group	5	8.16 (4.86)	10.78 (6.42)	9.70 (5.77)	10.22 (6.05)	11.41 (6.79)	11.02 (6.56)	9.25 (5.51)	11.17 (6.65)	10.47 (6.23)

Source: Same as in Table 2.

hours and 7.52 hours on the physical care of children, respectively. The corresponding figures for the time spent by the girls in these age groups on supervising younger siblings are 12.26 hours and 12.33 hours. On the other hand, the boys spend much less time on these activities.

On an average, the girls engaged in care activities (including care of the old, sick and disabled) spend 11.17 hours on this activity (as against 9.25 hours by boys). These hours are slightly less (10.75 hours) for the girls in the age group 6-9 years.

(iii) Non-SNA Activities

How much time do children spend on non-SNA activities or on personal care-sleep, rest, personal hygiene, etc? Table 11 shows that children in the age group, 6-14 spend 68.33 hours on sleep, 9.45 hours on eating and drinking and 7.27 hours on personal hygiene. Girls spend slightly less time (68.30 hours) than boys (68.36 hours) on these activities.

Some noteworthy findings presented in tables 10 and 11 are:

(i) more boys than girls (a) participate in sports and games, (b) read magazines, (c) watch television, and (d) go to temples or religious places. On the other hand, relatively more girls (a) participate in religious activities at home and (b) gossip and chat.

(ii) The number of boys and girls who visit libraries or read newspapers is almost nil.

(iii) Boys and girls together spend about 99 hours on personal activities and 26 hours on sociocultural activities. Boys spend 27.38 hours and girls 24.60 hours in sociocultural activities.

Clearly, the above discussion on the time use pattern of girls and boys throws very useful light on how children spend their time on economic activities (covered under UN-SNA), extended SNA activities and non-SNA activities. The discussion also extensively dealt with the gender dimension of time use. To start with, the time use survey which formed the basis of the discussion has been able to capture children's work to a considerable extent. Though the data do not refer to WPRs, they show that a significant number of boys and girls in the age groups, 5-9 and 10-14 participate in economic activities. Secondly, though the percentage of girls engaged in economic activities is not less than the percentage of boys engaged in these activities, participant boys, on an average, spend much more time on SNA work during the week than participant girls. Both boys and girls are engaged in low-skilled activities, most of which are unpaid. Thirdly, the time use patterns of girls and boys in extended SNA activities and non-SNA activities clearly indicates a gender bias. Notably, the socialisation of children in India forces young girls to take on a significant burden of household activities like cleaning, washing etc. as well as child care. This gender bias in the distribution of extended SNA work, which is the root cause of low investment on women and their poorer access to developmental opportunities, starts right from the childhood. And lastly, young girls are also subjected to lower access to education,

Table 10
Number and Percentage of Sample Children Engaged in Personal Care and Self-maintenance Activities by Age and Sex

Care and self-maintenance activities		Age: 6-9 years			10-14 years			6-14 years		
		Sex: M	F	T	M	F	T	M	F	T
Sleep and related activities	911	2362 (100.00)	1978 (100.00)	4340 (100.00)	3687 (100.00)	3234 (100.00)	6921 (100.00)	6049 (100.00)	5212 (100.00)	11261 (100.00)
Eating and drinking	921	2360 (99.92)	1976 (99.90)	4336 (99.91)	3686 (99.97)	3230 (99.88)	6916 (99.93)	6046 (99.95)	5206 (99.88)	11252 (99.92)
Smoking, drinking alcohol and other intoxicants	922	4 (0.17)	4 (0.20)	8 (0.18)	13 (0.35)	14 (0.43)	27 (0.39)	17 (0.28)	18 (0.35)	35 (0.31)
Personal hygiene and health	931	2332 (0.17)	1961 (0.20)	4293 (0.18)	3654 (0.35)	3202 (0.43)	6856 (0.39)	5986 (0.28)	5163 (0.35)	1149 (0.31)
Walking, exercise, jogging, yoga etc.	932	179 (0.17)	116 (0.20)	295 (0.18)	366 (0.35)	169 (0.43)	535 (0.39)	545 (0.28)	285 (0.35)	830 (0.31)
Receiving medical and personal care from household members	941	6 (0.25)	7 (0.35)	13 (0.30)	14 (0.38)	14 (0.43)	28 (0.40)	20 (0.33)	21 (0.40)	41 (0.36)
Talking, gossiping and quarreling	942	1 (0.04)	2 (0.10)	3 (0.07)	4 (0.11)	4 (0.12)	8 (0.12)	5 (0.08)	6 (0.12)	11 (0.10)
Doing nothing or taking rest and relaxing	951	1422 (60.20)	1153 (58.29)	2575 (59.33)	2372 (64.33)	2198 (67.97)	4570 (66.03)	3794 (62.72)	3351 (64.29)	7145 (63.45)
Individual religious practices and meditation	961	1904 (80.61)	1562 (78.97)	3466 (79.86)	2935 (79.60)	2653 (82.03)	5588 (80.74)	4839 (80.00)	4215 (80.87)	9054 (80.40)
	962	36 (1.52)	31 (1.57)	67 (1.54)	58 (1.57)	91 (2.81)	149 (2.15)	94 (1.55)	122 (2.34)	216 (1.92)
Individual religious practices and meditation	971	160 (6.77)	150 (7.58)	310 (7.14)	357 (9.68)	367 (11.35)	724 (10.46)	517 (8.55)	517 (9.92)	1034 (9.18)
Other activities	981	283 (11.98)	257 (12.99)	540 (12.44)	431 (11.69)	419 (12.96)	850 (12.28)	0 (0.00)	0 (0.00)	0 (0.00)
Resting/ convalescing due to illness	982	6 (0.25)	10 (0.51)	16 (0.37)	15 (0.41)	16 (0.49)	31 (0.45)	0 (0.00)	0 (0.00)	0 (0.00)
Travel-related to personal care and self-maintenance	991	277 (11.73)	229 (11.58)	506 (11.66)	499 (13.53)	339 (10.48)	838 (12.11)	0 (0.00)	0 (0.00)	0 (0.00)

Source: Same as in Table 2.

Table 11
Weekly Average Time Spent by Sample Children on Non-SNA Activities Including Personal Care and Self-maintenance by Age and Sex

		Age								
		6-9 years			10-14 years			6-14 years		
		Sex								
Non-SNA activities		M	F	T	M	F	T	M	F	T
Sleep and related activities	911	70.85	71.44	71.12	66.76	66.35	66.57	68.36	68.30	68.33
		(42.17)	(42.52)	(42.33)	(39.74)	(390.49)	(39.63)	(40.69)	(40.65)	(40.67)
Eating and drinking	921	9.63	9.53	9.58	9.39	9.35	9.37	9.48	9.42	9.45
		(5.73)	(5.67)	(5.70)	(5.59)	(5.57)	(5.58)	(5.64)	(5.61)	(5.63)
Smoking, drinking alcohol and other intoxicants	922	2.24	2.79	2.57	3.10	3.49	3.27	2.89	3.22	3.05
		(1.33)	(1.66)	(1.53)	(1.85)	(2.08)	(1.95)	(1.72)	(1.92)	(1.82)
Personal hygiene and health	931	6.99	7.05	7.02	7.52	7.34	7.44	7.31	7.23	7.27
		(4.16)	(4.20)	(4.18)	(4.48)	(4.37)	(4.43)	(4.35)	(4.30)	(4.33)
Walking, exercise, jogging, yoga etc.	932	5.76	4.78	5.37	5.35	4.60	5.11	5.49	4.67	5.20
		(3.43)	(2.85)	(3.20)	(3.18)	(2.74)	(3.04)	(3.27)	(2.78)	(3.10)
Receiving medical and personal care from household members	941	1.38	1.43	1.41	3.51	2.30	2.91	3.01	1.96	2.43
		(0.82)	(0.85)	(0.84)	(2.09)	(1.37)	(1.73)	(1.79)	(1.17)	(1.45)
Talking, gossiping and quarreling	942	1.00	1.66	1.62	2.39	9.20	6.93	2.27	6.09	5.16
		(0.60)	(0.99)	(0.96)	(1.42)	(5.48)	(4.13)	(1.35)	(3.63)	(3.07)
Doing nothing, rest and relaxation	951	6.47	6.66	6.56	7.34	8.26	7.78	7.02	7.70	7.34
		(3.85)	(3.96)	(3.90)	(4.37)	(4.92)	(4.63)	(4.18)	(4.58)	(4.37)
Individual religious practices and meditation	961	8.99	9.54	9.24	8.67	9.95	9.27	8.80	9.80	9.26
		(5.35)	(5.68)	(5.50)	(5.16)	(5.92)	(5.52)	(5.24)	(5.83)	(5.51)
Forced leisure	962	9.90	19.94	14.56	12.95	14.41	13.79	11.89	15.80	14.02
		(5.89)	(11.87)	(8.67)	(7.71)	(8.58)	(8.21)	(7.08)	(9.40)	(8.35)
Individual religious practices and meditation	971	2.41	2.11	2.27	2.17	2.41	2.28	2.25	2.31	2.28
		(1.43)	(1.26)	(1.35)	(1.29)	(1.43)	(1.36)	(1.34)	(1.38)	(1.36)
Other activities	981	4.10	5.31	4.68	3.89	4.29	4.09	3.97	4.67	4.31
		(2.44)	(3.16)	(2.79)	(2.32)	(2.55)	(2.43)	(2.36)	(2.78)	(2.57)
Resting/ convalescing due to physically unwell persons	982	6.63	5.52	5.88	28.79	18.15	23.55	21.21	11.55	15.68
		(3.95)	(3.29)	(3.50)	(17.14)	(10.80)	(14.02)	(12.63)	(6.88)	(9.33)
Travel related to personal care and self-maintenance	991	3.03	2.96	3.00	3.20	3.06	3.15	3.14	3.02	3.09
		(1.80)	(1.76)	(1.79)	(1.90)	(1.82)	(1.88)	(1.87)	(1.80)	(1.84)
Avg. for group		99.92	101.11	100.46	97.19	98.33	97.72	98.26	99.39	98.78
	9	(59.48)	(60.18)	(59.80)	(57.85)	(58.53)	(58.17)	(58.49)	(59.16)	(58.80)

Source: Same as in Table 2.

training and self-development activities. They also get marginally less time (than boys) for rest and play.

In brief, girls suffer from gender-based discrimination and exploitation right from their childhood.

III. TIME USE PATTERN OF CHILDREN AND ADULTS

Data on the weekly average time spent by children and adults on different activities is presented in Table 12. Some of the important observations emerging from the table are listed below:

1. Girls (6-14) participating in economic activities spend much less time (18.63 hours) on SNA activities as compared to boys (24.27 hours). However, both of them combined spend 21.46 hours a week on SNA activities, which is about 47 per cent of the time spent by an adult on SNA activities.

2. Girls (6-14) participating in extended SNA activities spend much more time on extended SNA activities than participant men (covering all ages). The girls spend, for example, 13.01 hours on household management, 10.64 hours on community services and 11.17 hours on care activities. The corresponding data on time spent by men are 6.76 hours, 7.99 hours and 6.12 hours.

3. Also, girls (6-14) bear a much higher burden of total work-SNA and extended SNA work combined - than boys, reflected in the time spent by them. On an average, girls spend about 53.45 hours and boys 44.54 hours on total work, which is 83 per cent of the time spent by girls.

Table 12

Time Spent by Sample Children and Adults on Different Activities

Age group	Sex	SNA activities	Household management etc.	Community services	Learning	Cultural activities	Personal care	Care activities
6-14	Male	24.27	5.32	5.70	47.40	27.38	98.82	9.25
	Female	18.63	13.01	10.64	46.55	24.60	99.39	11.17
	Total	21.46	10.53	8.47	46.86	26.13	98.98	10.47
15-59	Male	57.55	6.76	7.99	45.59	15.23	98.02	6.12
	Female	31.39	37.61	8.57	38.53	14.49	93.22	12.29
	Total	46.28	27.91	8.23	42.76	14.91	95.73	10.54
60 +	Male	47.43	8.38	9.92	5.79	17.33	126.88	9.44
	Female	27.03	26.24	12.24	7.30	16.92	126.77	15.34
	Total	39.70	19.89	10.80	6.25	17.16	126.83	13.22
Total	Male	54.65	6.73	7.91	44.50	18.57	100.83	6.65
	Female	30.06	34.38	9.33	44.30	17.44	97.31	12.38
	Total	44.02	25.59	8.52	45.66	18.07	99.23	10.69

Source: Same as in Table 2.

Inter-state Differences in Time Use Pattern of Children

So far we have used data of combined states to understand children's work and non-work. Though, strictly speaking, the six selected states together, do not represent the all-India scenario, they do represent the six broad regions of the country. Therefore, the data used in our study, has been examined to understand the broad patterns of time use of girls and boys in India. It is useful, however, to examine state-wise variations in the time use pattern of children. Table 13 presents data on participation of children in SNA activities in the six states. The table shows that:

(i) There are wide interstate variations in the percentage of children engaged in economic activities. The lowest participation of children in economic activities is in Tamil Nadu, followed by Haryana, Gujarat, Meghalaya, Madhya Pradesh and Orissa. For example, in Tamil Nadu about 4.13 per cent of children spend time on animal husbandry and about 7.87 per cent are engaged in collection of fuelwood, fodder, water, fruit, etc. while the corresponding percentage in some of the other states are: 35.61 in Meghalaya, 14.63 in Orissa and 11.44 per cent in Haryana. In terms of the average number of hours put in by these children on these activities, however, the differences (between the figure for Tamil Nadu and the other states) are much less. Except for Haryana, where child workers, on an average, put in 14 hours in SNA work, in the rest of the states children work for 20 to 22 hours a week.

(ii) Animal husbandry and collection of fuelwood, fodder, fruits, etc., are the most important activities of child workers in all the states, though the percentages of children engaged in these activities vary across the six states. In Tamil Nadu, however, petty services are also important in terms of participation by children.

(iii) As regards children's participation in education, Meghalaya is at the top with 78.04 per cent children in the age group, 6-14 attending school, followed by Tamil Nadu (77.29 per cent) and Haryana (73.08 per cent). Madhya Pradesh is at the bottom with only 57 per cent children in this age group attending school. Participation of children in non-formal education is less than 1 per cent in all the states except Meghalaya where 2.08 per cent children go to non-formal school, and spend 3.25 hours at these schools as compared to less than half an hour in the other states.

(iv) Gender gap in the time use pattern of boys and girls is prevalent in all the states, particularly in respect of extended SNA activities. However, the gender gap is the highest in Haryana and Gujarat and the least in Tamil Nadu. It is not possible to arrive at specific ratios with the given data (which are overlapping in many ways), but it is hoped that it will be possible to compute these ratios when further analysis of the time use data is undertaken.

Table 13
Children's Time Use in Economic Activities in the Six Selected States

Economic activities	Activity code	Combined state 6 - 9 years M	F	T	6 - 14 years M	F	T	Meghalaya 6 - 9 years M	F	T	6 - 14 years M	F	T	Tamil Nadu 6 - 9 years M	F	T	6 - 14 years M	F	T
Crop farming, kitchen gardening, etc.	11	12 (3.51)	10.8 (3.74)	11.42 (3.62)	20.34 (6.23)	21.37 (6.24)	20.8 (6.23)	0 (0.00)	0 (0.00)	0 (0.00)	36.01 (5.03)	28.6 (3.93)	31.94 (4.45)	9.31 (3.02)	5.92 (0.54)	8.16 (1.83)	22.19 (4.17)	18.35 (2.67)	20.78 (3.44)
Animal husbandry	12	19.71 (6.82)	14.4 (6.37)	17.37 (6.61)	21.54 (11.47)	13.94 (10.69)	18 (11.11)	36.57 (7.32)	18.84 (9.59)	28.89 (8.39)	42.22 (13.84)	8.71 (8.43)	30.37 (10.98)	3.23 (0.75)	3.34 (2.17)	3.31 (1.43)	18.27 (4.17)	9.98 (4.09)	14.29 (4.13)
Fishing, forestry, horticulture, gardening	13	19.22 (0.89)	13.5 (1.31)	15.75 (1.08)	18.11 (1.88)	15.49 (1.67)	16.8 (1.78)	0.5 (1.22)	4.5 (1.37)	2.35 (1.29)	11.14 (5.03)	8.66 (2.81)	10.15 (3.86)	0 (0.00)	2.38 (0.54)	2.38 (0.26)	17.95 (0.92)	8.63 (0.98)	12.43 (0.95)
Collection of fruit, water, plants, etc., storing and hunting	14	12.28 (2.75)	7.26 (5.61)	8.93 (4.06)	10.5 (4.51)	8.8 (13.76)	9.27 (8.79)	6.13 (17.07)	4.83 (19.18)	5.49 (18.06)	8.43 (25.16)	7.14 (44.94)	7.53 (35.61)	5.95 (1.51)	2.25 (6.23)	2.88 (3.78)	4.76 (3.25)	3.76 (12.80)	3.94 (7.87)
Processing and storage	15	13.15 (7.83)	13.7 (8.17)	13.52 (8.05)	7.59 (4.52)	9.82 (5.85)	9.18 (5.46)	0 (0.00)	0 (0.00)	0 (0.00)	17.94 (10.68)	7.26 (4.32)	10.03 (5.97)	2.04 (1.21)	1.29 (0.77)	1.57 (0.93)	2.46 (1.46)	1.26 (0.75)	1.85 (1.10)
Mining, quarrying & digging, cutting, etc.	16	0 (0.00)	0 (0.00)	0 (0.00)	34.51 (0.17)	37.34 (0.08)	35.4 (0.12)	0 (0.00)	0 (0.00)	0 (0.00)	0 (0.00)	0 (0.00)	0 (0.00)	0 (0.00)	0 (0.00)	0 (0.00)	2.5 (0.08)	0 (0.00)	2.5 (0.04)
Construction activities	21	4.83 (0.68)	9.48 (0.40)	6.7 (0.55)	26.16 (0.93)	14.27 (0.54)	22.3 (0.75)	0 (0.00)	0 (0.00)	0 (0.00)	3.5 (0.63)	0 (0.00)	3.5 (0.30)	0.5 (0.25)	0 (0.00)	0.5 (0.13)	63 (0.67)	12.55 (0.44)	45.13 (0.56)
Manufacturing activities	22	10.31 (0.51)	11.1 (0.71)	10.82 (0.60)	32.7 (1.44)	23.97 (2.23)	27.6 (1.80)	0 (0.00)	0 (0.00)	0 (0.00)	0 (0.00)	4.94 (2.25)	4.94 (1.19)	16.63 (1.51)	24.06 (2.17)	21.43 (1.83)	37.19 (2.92)	38.33 (3.56)	37.8 (3.23)
Trade, business and services	31	2.94 (0.85)	4.64 (0.56)	3.41 (0.71)	11.12 (1.17)	9.4 (0.63)	10.6 (0.92)	0 (0.00)	0 (0.00)	0 (0.00)	0 (0.00)	5.75 (1.12)	5.75 (0.59)	3.36 (1.51)	4.68 (1.08)	3.87 (1.30)	17.01 (1.33)	12.77 (1.33)	15.01 (1.33)
Services	32	15.5 (4.57)	12.4 (4.40)	14.26 (4.49)	18.33 (5.41)	14.36 (4.72)	16.7 (5.09)	11.93 (9.76)	18.8 (2.74)	12.49 (6.45)	14.31 (7.55)	18.22 (3.37)	15.56 (5.34)	28.07 (7.54)	24.09 (8.13)	26.57 (7.82)	28.07 (8.75)	21.64 (8.27)	25.29 (8.52)
Community services and help in other households	611	0.95 (0.08)	0 (0.00)	0.95 (0.05)	0.95 (0.03)	0.83 (0.02)	0.89 (0.03)	0 (0.00)	0 (0.00)	0 (0.00)	0 (0.00)	0 (0.00)	0 (0.00)	0 (0.00)	0 (0.00)	0 (0.00)	0 (0.00)	0.83 (0.09)	0.83 (0.04)
	All-SNA activities	18.47	14.5	16.56	24.27	18.63	21.5	18.16	11.11	15.23	29.56	13.8	20.43	20.65	14.49	17.73	28.51	17.41	22.78

Table 13 contd.

Economic activities	Activity code	Orissa						Gujarat						Madhya Pradesh					
		Age																	
		6 - 9 years			6 - 14 years			6 - 9 years			6 - 14 years			6 - 9 years			6 - 14 years		
		Sex																	
		M	F	T	M	F	T	M	F	T	M	F	T	M	F	T	M	F	T
Crop farming, kitchen gardening, etc.	11	15.83 (1.49)	13.29 (3.51)	13.92 (2.45)	25.43 (4.42)	26.58 (6.16)	26.09 (5.27)	4.28 (2.04)	5.52 (1.55)	4.67 (1.82)	18.54 (4.86)	22.33 (3.53)	19.7 (4.27)	14.37 (6.53)	11.72 (7.87)	13.1 (7.14)	19.48 (9.34)	19.53 (11.58)	19.5 (10.36)
Animal husbandry	12	29.58 (2.97)	26.4 (1.62)	28.24 (2.33)	29.57 (7.12)	23.86 (5.35)	27.01 (6.26)	15.12 (5.70)	10.86 (9.28)	12.8 (7.28)	18.63 (8.89)	11.67 (14.43)	14.73 (11.36)	22.81 (13.74)	21.55 (9.02)	22.4 (11.60)	25.53 (18.85)	17.12 (13.92)	22.38 (16.62)
Fishing, forestry, horti-culture, gardening	13	15.04 (1.98)	14.61 (2.43)	14.76 (2.20)	12.91 (3.46)	23.86 (2.93)	27.01 (3.20)	7.93 (0.41)	10.5 (0.26)	8.49 (0.34)	3.84 (0.34)	7.49 (0.31)	5.38 (0.32)	25.8 (1.36)	13.6 (2.13)	18.9 (1.71)	25.04 (2.79)	21.96 (2.34)	23.65 (2.59)
Collection of fruit, water, plants, etc., storing and hunting	14	19.12 (3.71)	8.06 (6.22)	12.2 (4.91)	15.23 (6.44)	9.34 (23.23)	10.73 (14.63)	13.41 (1.63)	8.83 (5.15)	10.2 (3.19)	9.34 (3.35)	11.12 (9.45)	10.55 (6.08)	10.18 (2.59)	15.04 (3.77)	12.7 (3.12)	13.36 (3.01)	12.23 (5.66)	12.69 (4.21)
Processing and storage	15	0 (0.00)	0 (0.00)	0 (0.00)	5.6 (3.33)	6.14 (3.65)	5.85 (3.48)	22.14 (13.18)	22.88 (13.62)	22.5 (13.40)	12.85 (7.65)	11.47 (6.83)	11.71 (6.97)	9.39 (5.59)	15.56 (9.26)	14.2 (8.46)	7.03 (4.18)	10.36 (6.17)	9.42 (5.61)
Mining, quarrying & digging, cutting, etc.	16	0 (0.00)	0 (0.00)	0 (0.00)	36.96 (0.19)	63 (0.10)	43.66 (0.15)	0 (0.00)	0 (0.00)	0 (0.00)	0 (0.00)	0 (0.00)	0 (0.00)	0 (0.00)	0 (0.00)	0 (0.00)	34.39 (0.32)	25.18 (0.20)	31.36 (0.26)
Construction activities	21	6 (0.25)	0 (0.00)	6 (0.13)	22.1 (0.48)	0 (0.00)	22.1 (0.25)	0 (0.00)	0 (0.00)	0 (0.00)	61.65 (0.25)	60.53 (0.21)	61.16 (0.23)	5.2 (1.77)	9.48 (1.31)	7.12 (1.56)	11.05 (1.99)	7.93 (1.30)	9.99 (1.68)
Manufacturing activities	22	10.21 (0.74)	2.97 (0.81)	5.92 (0.78)	28.56 (1.63)	17.85 (1.52)	22.65 (1.58)	0 (0.00)	1.75 (0.26)	1.75 (0.11)	43 (1.17)	20.28 (3.01)	27.31 (1.99)	3.48 (0.41)	3.37 (0.33)	3.44 (0.37)	16.12 (0.97)	12.28 (1.24)	14.13 (1.09)
Trade, business and services	31	0 (0.00)	49 (0.27)	49 (0.13)	17.36 (0.19)	49 (0.10)	19.05 (0.15)	6.64 (0.41)	0 (0.00)	6.64 (0.23)	13.66 (0.84)	7.75 (0.62)	10.65 (0.74)	1.89 (1.36)	2.75 (0.98)	2.13 (1.19)	8.44 (1.88)	3.28 (0.59)	7.59 (1.29)
Services	32	2.86 (0.74)	1 (0.27)	2.38 (0.52)	60.58 (1.15)	9.63 (0.61)	49.46 (0.89)	25.1 (0.61)	0 (0.00)	25.1 (0.34)	28.58 (1.59)	40.39 (1.35)	33.83 (1.48)	5.19 (8.44)	4.95 (8.85)	5.08 (8.62)	5.44 (9.34)	4.58 (8.33)	5.09 (8.88)
Community services and help in other households	611	0 (0.00)	0 (0.00)	0 (0.00)	0 (0.00)	0 (0.00)	0 (0.00)	0 (0.00)	0 (0.00)	0 (0.00)	0 (0.00)	0 (0.00)	0 (0.00)	0.95 (0.27)	0 (0.00)	0.95 (0.15)	0.95 (0.11)	0 (0.00)	0.95 (0.06)
	All-SNA activities	22.5	16.33	18.87	28.63	19.11	23.05	16.45	13.61	15	22.2	20.42	21.28	19.07	15.57	17.5	24.34	19.04	22.04

Table 13 contd.

Economic Activities	Activity code	Haryana Age Sex 6-9 years M	F	T	6-14 years M	F	T
Crop farming, kitchen gardening, etc.	11	11.43	3.73	8.61	18.02	16.42	17.55
		(2.78)	(2.98)	(2.86)	(6.89)	(3.58)	(5.52)
Animal husbandry	12	5.73	8.46	7.4	8.35	9.12	8.74
		(4.37)	(8.33)	(5.95)	(15.29)	(21.48)	(17.85)
Fishing, forestry, horticulture, gardening	13	0	0	0	1.04	1.89	1.54
		(0.00)	(0.00)	(0.00)	(0.50)	(0.72)	(0.59)
Collection of fruit, water, plants, etc., storing and hunting	14	1.66	1.81	1.77	6.03	9.48	8.43
		(1.19)	(4.76)	(2.62)	(5.21)	(20.29)	(11.44)
Processing and storage	15	0	0	0	3.55	8.39	6.54
		(0.00)	(0.00)	(0.00)	(2.11)	(4.99)	(3.89)
Mining, quarrying & digging, cutting, etc.	16	0	0	0	19.25	0	19.25
		(0.00)	(0.00)	(0.00)	(0.17)	(0.00)	(0.10)
Construction activities	21	2	0	2	1.52	42.58	16.6
		(0.40)	(0.00)	(0.24)	(0.34)	(0.24)	(0.30)
Manufacturing activities	22	0	0	0	40.13	8.53	11.4
		(0.00)	(0.00)	(0.00)	(0.50)	(2.15)	(1.18)
Trade, business and services	31	5.46	0	5.46	4.61	0	4.61
		(0.79)	(0.00)	(0.48)	(1.34)	(0.00)	(0.79)
Services	32	1.77	0	1.77	14.52	0	14.52
		(0.79)	(0.00)	(0.48)	(0.84)	(0.00)	(0.49)
Community services and help in other households	611	0	0	0	0	0	0
		(0.00)	(0.00)	(0.00)	(0.00)	(0.00)	(0.00)
All-SNA activities		6.7	7.41	7.05	12.74	15.62	14.14

IV. CONCLUDING OBSERVATIONS AND ISSUES

The time use survey data have provided useful information about children's economic and non-economic activities. It has clearly shown that the participation of children's work in economic activities is much more than what is revealed by conventional statistics. Broadly, around 20 per cent of boys and girls in the age group, 6-14, participate in economic activities, and they spend, on an average, about 22 hours (3 hours per day) on these activities. It is also significant that children in the age group, 6-9 years, also participate in economic activities, and spend, on an average, 17 hours on economic work.

The major activities in which children are engaged are low-skilled unpaid or subsistence activities or activities on family enterprises, like animal husbandry including grazing and collection of fuel, fodder, water, fruits, etc., as well as crop farming and petty services. Considering the fact that the first two activities are closely linked with environmental degradation, one can say that poor families are forced to depend on child workers for their basic needs of fuelwood, water, etc., and for animal grazing as they cannot spare time for these activities. This implies that environmental protection and ecological regeneration can go a long way in reducing children's economic work.

Children, particularly girls, participate in extended SNA activities in a big way. The gap between the numbers of girls and boys participating in these activities and the time devoted by them is significant. While one-third of the girls in this age group participate in these activities and spend about three hours per day, about 6-8 per cent of boys participate in these activities and spend around one hour per day. It is important to note here that child care-physical care and supervision-is done by children in both the age group, 6-9 as well as the age group, 10-14. While the former put in 17 hours on child care during the week, the latter put in around 18 hours on this work.

When one combines SNA and extended SNA work, one realises that children's contribution to this total work in the society is more than marginal, in terms of both number of participants as well as hours put in. The contribution of girls is greater than that of boys.

This burden of work on children has implications for children's enrolment in schools. More than 32 per cent 'nowhere' children, who do not go to school, are largely engaged in economic or in extended economic activities. In the case of girls, their low attendance in school is not only due to their participation in economic activities but also due to the responsibilities borne by them in extended SNA activities.

In sum, children's participation in economic work is influenced by: (a) environmental degradation leading to children's involvement in grazing, collection of fuelwood, fodder, fruits, etc., and (b) poor incomes of families who earn low wages due to low productivity and earnings in agriculture, poor development of the non-farm sector in rural areas and low employment and low wages/earnings in unorganised sector activities in urban areas. The fact that environmental degradation and low productivity agriculture are closely connected with less than satisfactory management of natural resources, has important policy implications in that agriculture and environment need to be accorded high priority. We believe that once land, water and vegetation receive the attention they deserve, the need for children's work in the economy will decline considerably. It is imperative that policies are initiated for the generation of employment with an assured package of social protection. These policy implications do not include the supply side factors, such as, issues regarding educational infrastructure, quality of education, etc. as these are outside the purview of this paper.

While concluding this paper we would like to draw attention to the fact that the time use survey data are not yet fully analysed. An in depth analysis of the data can throw much more useful light on the nature and extent of children's SNA, extended SNA and non-SNA activities.

Appendix

Time use Survey: Classification used in the Indian Time use Survey

I. Primary Production Activities

11. Crop Farming, Kitchen Gardening, etc.

111 Ploughing, preparing land, cleaning of land

112 Sowing, planting, transplanting

113 Application of manure, fertiliser, pesticides and watering, preparing organic manure, harvesting, threshing, picking, winnowing

114 Weeding

115 Supervision of work

116 Kitchen gardening - backyard cultivation

117 Stocking, transporting to home, guarding or protection of crops

118 Sale and purchase-related activities

119 Travel to work

12. Animal Husbandry

121 Grazing animals outside

122 Tending animals - cleaning, washing shed, feeding, watering, preparation of feed

123 Caring for animals: breeding, shearing, medical treatment, grooming, shoeing, etc.

124 Milking and processing of milk, collecting, storing of poultry Products

125 Making dung-cakes

126 Poultry rearing-feeding, cleaning

127 Other related activities

128 Sale and purchase-related activities

129 Travel to work

13. Fishing, Forestry, Horticulture, Gardening

131 Nursery - seedings

132 Planting, tending, processing of trees

133 Collecting, storing and stocking of fruits, etc.

134 Wood cutting, chopping and stocking firewood

135 Fish farming, cleaning sea-bed, feeding fish catching fish, gathering other aquatic life

136 Care of house plants, indoor and outdoor garden work

137 Flower gardening - landscaping, maintenance, cutting, collecting, storing

138 Sale and purchase-related activities

139 Travel to work

14. Fetching of Fruits, Water, Plants, etc., Storing and Hunting

141 Fetching of water

142 Fetching of fruits, vegetables, berries, mushrooms, etc., edible goods

143 Fetching of minor forest produce, leaves, bamboo, etc.

144 Fetching of fuel/fuel wood/twigs

145 Fetching of raw material for crafts

146 Fetching of building materials

147 Fetching of fodder

148 Sale and purchase of related activities

149 Collection of other items

15. Processing and Storage

152 Milling, husking, pounding

153 Parboiling

154 Sorting, grading

155 Grinding, crushing

156 Any other related activities

157 Sale and purchase related activities

158 Travel to work

16. Mining, Quarrying, Digging, Cutting, etc.

161 Mining/extraction of salt

162 Mining/digging/quarrying of stone, slabs, breaking of stones for construction of building road, bridges, etc.

163 Digging out clay, gravel and sand

164 Digging out minerals — major and minor

165 Transporting in vehicles

166 Storing and stocking

167 Any other related activities

168 Sale and purchase related activities

169 Travel to work

II. Secondary Activities

21. Construction Activities

211 Building and construction of dwelling (laying bricks, plastering, thatching, bamboo work, roofing) and maintenance and repairing of dwelling.

212 Construction and repair of animal shed, shelter for poultry, etc.

213 Construction of wells, storage facilities, fencing, etc. for farms, irrigation work

214 Construction of public works / common infrastructure — roads, buildings, bridges, etc.

217 Any other activity related

218 Sale and purchase related activities

219 Travel to work

22. Manufacturing Activities

221 Food processing and cooking for sale — making pickles, spices and other products; canning fruits, jams and jellies; banking; beverage preparation; selling readymade food, etc.

222 Butchering, curing, processing, drying, storing, etc. of meat, fish, etc.

223 Manufacturing of textiles — spinning, weaving, processing of textiles; knitting, sewing, garment making of cotton, wool and other materials

224 Making handicrafts, pottery, printing and other crafts made primarily with hands (wood based, leather based crafts, embroidery work, etc.)

225 Fitting, installing, tool setting, tool and machinery — moulding, welding, tool making

226 Assembling machines, equipment and other products

227 Production-related work in large and small factories in different industries — as production workers, maintenance workers paid trainees and apprentices, sales administration and management activities

228 Sale and purchase activity

229 Travel for the work

III. Trade, Business and Services

31. Trade and Business

311 Buying and selling goods — such as capital goods, intermediate goods, consumer durable, and consumer goods in the organised and formal sectors.

312 Petty trading, street and door to door vending, hawking, shoe cleaning, etc.

313 Transporting goods in trucks, tempos and motor vehicles

314 Transporting in hand carts, animal carts, cycle rickshaws, etc. or manually

315 Transport of passengers by motorized and non-motorized vehicles

32. Services

321 Services in government and semi-government organisations (salaried)

322 Services in private organisations (salaried)

323 Petty services: domestic servants, sweepers, washers, priest, cobbler, gardener, massaging, prostitution, (wages) watching and guarding

324 Professional services: medical and educational services (private tuition, non-formal teaching, etc.) financial services and management and technical consultancy services

325 Professional services: computer services, xerox/photocopying services, beauty parlors, hair cutting saloons, etc.

326 Technical services: plumbing, electrical and electronic repair and maintenance and other related services

327 Others

328 Travel to work

IV. Household Maintenance, Management and Shopping for Own Household

411 Cooking food items, beverages and serving

421 Cleaning and upkeep of dwelling and surroundings

422 Cleaning of utensils

431 Care of textiles: sorting, mending, washing, ironing and ordering clothes and linen

441 Shopping for goods and non-personal services; capital goods, household appliances, equipment, food and various household supplies

451 Household management: planning, supervising, paying bills, etc.

461 Do-it-yourself home improvements and maintenance, installation, servicing and repair of personal and household goods

471 Pet care

481 Travel-related to household maintenance, management and shopping

491 Household maintenance, management and shopping not elsewhere classified

V. Care for children, the Sick, Elderly and Disabled for Own Household

511 Physical care of children: washing, dressing, feeding

521 Teaching, training and instruction of own children

531 Accompanying children to places: school, sports, lessons, etc. /PHC/doctor

541 Physical care of sick, disabled, elderly household members; washing, dressing, feeding, helping

551 Accompanying adults to receive personal care services such as hairdresser's therapy sessions, temple, religious places, etc.

561 Supervising children, needing care with or without other activity

562 Supervising adults, needing care with or without other activity

571 Travel related to care of children

572 Travel related to care of adults and others

581 Taking care of guests/visitors

591 Any other activity not mentioned above

VI. Community Services and Help to Other Households

611 Community organized constructions and repairs; buildings, roads, dams, wells, ponds, etc. community assets

621 Community organized work: cooking for collective celebration, etc.

631 Volunteering with/for an organisation (which does not involve working directly for individuals)

641 Volunteering work through organisations extended directly individuals and groups

651 Participation in meetings of local and informal groups / caste, tribes, professional associations, union, fraternal and political organisations

661 Involvement in civic and related responsibilities; voting, rallies, attending meetings, panchayat

671 Informal help to other households

681 Community services not classified elsewhere

691 Travel related to community services

VII. Learning

711 General education: school/university/other educational institutions attendance

721 Studies, homework and course review related to general education

731 Additional study, non-formal education under adult education program

741 Non-formal education for children

751 Work - related training

761 Training under government program such as TRYSEM, DWCRA and others

771 Other training/education

781 Learning not elsewhere classified

791 Travel related to learning

VIII. Social and Cultural Activities, Mass Media, etc.

811 Participating in social events: wedding, funerals, births and other celebrations

812 Participating in religious activities: church services, religious ceremonies, practices, *kirtans,* singing, etc.

813 Participating in community functions in music, dance, etc.

814 Socialising at home and outside the home

821 Arts, making music hobbies and related courses;

822 Indoor and outdoor sports participation and related courses

831 Games and other past-time activities

832 Spectator to sports, exhibitions/museums, cinemas/theater/concerts and other performances and events

841 Other related activities

851 Reading other than newspaper and magazines

852 Watching televisions and video

853 Listening to music/radio

861 Accessing information by computing

862 Visiting library

863 Reading newspaper and magazine

871 Mass media use and entertainment not classified elsewhere

891 Travel-related to social, cultural and recreational activities, social cultural and recreational activities not elsewhere classified, mass media use and entertainment

892 Travel-related in search of job

IX. Personal Care and Self-Maintenance

911 Sleep and related activities

921 Eating and drinking

922 Smoking, drinking, alcohol and other intoxicants

931 Personal hygiene and health

932 Walking, exercise, running, jogging, yoga, etc.

941 Receiving medical and personal care from professional

942 Receiving medical and personal care from household members

951 Talking, gossiping and quarreling

961 Doing nothing, rest and relaxation

962 Forced leisure or forced rest & relaxation-willing and available for work

971 Individual religious practices and meditation

981 Other activities

982 Resting / convalescing due to physical illness and physical unwell persons

991 Travel-related to personal care and self-maintenance

References

Chaudhri, D.P. (1996), *A Dynamic Profile of Child Labour in India 1951-1991,* ILO, New Delhi.

Goldschmidt-Clermont, L. and E. Pagnossin-Aligisakis (1995), *Measures of Unrecorded Economic Activities in Fourteen Countries,* Human Development Report Office, Occasional Papers 20, United Nations Development Programme, New York.

GOI (2000), *Report of the Time Use Survey,* Government of India, Central Statistical Organisation, Ministry of Statistics and Programme Implementation, New Delhi.

Hirway, Indira, Jacqui Cottyn and Pushkar Pandya (eds.) (1991), *Towards Eradication of Child Labour,* Oxford & IBH Publishing Co. Pvt. Ltd., New Delhi

—— (1999), "Conceptual and Methodological Issues of Time Use Studies in India", Paper presented at the *International Seminar on Time Use Studies,* Ahmedabad, December 7-9, 1999.

—— (1999), "Estimating Workforce Using Time Use Study: Results and Its Implications for Employment Policy in India", Proceedings of the *International Seminar on Time Use Studies,* CSO, Government of India, New Delhi.

NSSO (2001), *Employment and Unemployment in India, 1999-2000,* Key Results, New Delhi.

PART II

Understanding the Links: A Causal Analysis

6

Nutritional Poverty, School Education and Supply of Child Labour: Explorations with States, Districts and Household Data for Rural India

D.P. CHAUDHRI AND E.J. WILSON

International agencies and national policy makers have so far been mainly focusing on the demand side of child labour. Instruments and policies to deal with the problem clearly reflect this focus. Policies and programmes dealing with nutritional poverty do sometimes consider their impact on child nutrition and school attendance, but do not deal with their implications for child labour. This is partly because of the lack of conceptual clarity, and partly because of the difficulty in accessing reliable data at the household level and at higher levels of aggregation necessarily required in operationalising the conceptual framework. To understand the sources of supply of child labour and its causal link with poverty, one has to carefully analyse household decision making processes in the context of their access to assets and policy supported entitlements or lack of them.

The paper attempts to explore the issue of the interaction between poverty and child labour in Rural India. We use NSS 50th round (1993-94) rural household data, some 1991 Census-based district data and time-series and cross-sectional data for major states of India (1970-94) for the years for which poverty data is available. A battery of statistical and econometric analysis tools are used in the exploration process.

The paper is divided into seven sections. Section I deals with the specific characteristics of the rural poor. Section II explores the determinants that influence the number of children in a household using a sample of 69, 205 rural households. The third section is devoted to children's participation in school education, household duties and labour force. Section IV deals with the econometric analysis derived from formal modelling. Section V presents evidence from the best and worst districts and section VI summarises the international and Indian experience of school feeding programmes and their efficacy. The final section provides conclusions and policy implications.

I. IDENTIFYING ATTRIBUTES OF THE RURAL POOR

A Working Group (1962) defined the absolute poverty line on a consumption expenditure basis as under:

(i) The national minimum for each household of five persons (four adult consumption units) should be not less than Rs.100 per month in terms of 1960-61 prices or Rs. 20 per capita. For urban areas, this figure should be raised to Rs.125 per month per household or Rs. 25 per capita to cover the higher prices of the physical volume of commodities on which the national minimum is calculated.

(ii) This national minimum excludes expenditure on health and education, both of which should be provided by the state according to the Constitution and in the light of its other commitments.

This was the first officially defined poverty line and implied that head-count poverty measurement is the most appropriate measurement for use in the Indian Republic. It was revised and updated by the Expert Group. Ravallion (1998a, b) provides an excellent summary of the various measures of poverty, with head-count poverty being a convenient and popular measure. He also provides cogent analytical arguments regarding poverty comparisons over time. Suryanarayana (2000), Mehta and Venkatraman (2000) comment on the overestimation of poverty reduction, which needs to be examined with appropriate analytical tools. It may be noted that the Indian absolute poverty line deals with nutritional poverty but derives it from consumer expenditure. This poverty line is below that of the World Bank's one dollar per capita per day measure. Expenditure on health and education, being a constitutional duty of the state, is explicitly excluded from the absolute poverty measure and, therefore, the household's consumption expenditure.

That poverty and high total fertility rates translate into population growth have been examined extensively and their mutually reinforcing nature has been commented upon and is now well understood. UNICEF (1999) summarises this interrelationship as a poverty-population growth and environmental degradation (PPE) triangle. Caldwell (1990) provides cogent demographic reasons and Manna (1998) recent evidence from Indian states. Family size and the number of children in each household and its relationship to poverty is now consuming the attention of poverty experts. It needs emphasis in the Indian context because of its enormous implications for equity, poverty and child labour eradication and educational policy. Based on NSS 50th round (1993-94), rural household data

(69,205 households), we derived information on family size and number of children per household (Table 1). Notably, in every state of India the poor and very poor have a relatively larger family size and a larger number of children providing a basis for four sensitive policy issues. First, compulsory or semi-compulsory family planning can be seen by the poor as an attempt to eliminate the poor, rather than any real attempt to deal with the problem of poverty. In a democratic polity, this would be a rather sensitive issue. Second, all efforts at improving rural primary school education will benefit the poor households at twice the rate of the non-poor. As such, moving rural primary education to the centre of the anti-poverty programme would help the poor and also the economic growth process. It needs to be noted that the PROBE Report (1999) explodes the myth of demand deficiency in rural primary education. Any policy failure resulting in supply constraint in states with a high incidence of poverty needs to be addressed urgently. Third, over 90 per cent of child labour is in rural areas, affecting some states more than others. Chaudhri and Wilson (2001a) highlight the fact that 97.5 per cent of child labourers are in the age group, 10-14 years. Any attempt to address this problem requires extending the period of compulsory education from primary school level to middle school level. Do we have the political will and moral stamina to achieve this objective? It is significant to note here that The Supreme Court of India (with its decision of December 1996)[1] or world opinion on human rights will ensure its realisation. Furthermore, the schooling of rural youth and vocational training need a policy shift. In a report to the ILO, New Delhi, Visaria (1999) provides an outline for such a shift, which needs research and policy orchestration. Fourth, half the poor in rural India are under 15 years of age, and the proportion of children among the ultra-poor is higher than 60 per cent (Chaudhri, 2001). Investment in their health, education and capability enhancement is good for poverty reduction, economic growth and human rights.

Apart from nutritional deprivation that forms the core of poverty measurement in India, literacy and education, or rather lack of it, is an important identifier of poverty. Table 2 provides information on the incidence of illiteracy among all adult males and females in rural households, based on NSS 50th round (1993-94) household data. The incidence of illiteracy among females of very poor households in Andhra Pradesh, Bihar, Haryana, Jammu & Kashmir, Madhya Pradesh, Rajasthan, and Uttar Pradesh is 91-95 per cent compared to 53-66 per cent for the non-poor higher income groups in those states. Within groups, gender differences are sharper among the poor than among the non-poor. Kerala has an illiteracy rate of 27 per cent among females and 15 per cent among males in the poorest group. Differences are also more pronounced among the non-poor than among the poor across states. Educational level of the heads of rural households in different states of India follow similar patterns (Table 3). Except in Kerala, the poorest households are predominately headed by illiterates. This changes progressively as we move to better-off groups.

The non-poor have a higher proportion of heads with more than primary school and technical education. The inference that the incidence of education and

Table 1

Family Size, Number of Children Per Household among Rural Poor and Non-poor in Major States of India, 1993-94

State	Family size				Number of children (0-14) per household			
	Very poor	Moderately poor	Non-poor low	Non-poor high	Very poor	Moderately poor	Non-poor low	Non-poor high
	1	2	3	4	5	6	7	8
Andhra Pradesh	5.1	4.4	4.2	3.9	2.2	1.5	1.2	1.0
Arunachal Pradesh	5.7	5.4	4.6	4.1	2.1	2.1	1.5	1.4
Assam	5.7	5.4	5.1	4.7	2.6	2.0	1.6	1.2
Bihar	5.7	5.1	4.9	4.5	2.6	1.9	1.7	1.3
Gujarat	6.4	5.7	5.5	4.5	2.8	2.2	1.9	1.2
Haryana	6.3	6.0	6.3	5.6	3.3	2.7	2.6	1.9
Himachal Pradesh	6.2	6.3	5.3	4.3	2.7	2.5	1.8	1.2
Jammu & Kashmir	6.8	6.3	6.0	4.9	3.4	2.9	2.3	1.6
Karnataka	6.2	5.6	5.5	4.5	2.6	2.0	1.7	1.2
Kerala	5.6	5.3	4.7	4.2	2.2	1.9	1.3	1.0
Madhya Pradesh	5.7	5.5	5.2	4.9	2.5	2.1	1.8	1.5
Maharashtra	5.5	5.1	4.9	4.3	2.4	1.7	1.5	1.2
Manipur	6.0	5.9	5.5	4.8	3.0	2.4	1.8	1.4
Meghalaya	5.2	5.2	5.0	3.7	2.5	2.1	1.7	0.9
Mizoram	6.6	5.4	5.8	4.6	1.8	2.5	2.3	1.4
Orissa	5.3	5.1	4.8	4.3	2.2	1.6	1.4	1.0
Punjab	6.3	5.7	5.7	5.3	3.3	2.4	2.0	1.5
Rajasthan	6.3	5.9	5.6	4.7	3.1	2.5	2.2	1.6
Sikkim	5.6	5.2	4.4	3.2	2.4	1.8	1.4	0.8
Tamil Nadu	4.7	4.3	4.0	3.7	1.8	1.4	1.1	0.8
Uttar Pradesh	6.2	6.0	5.8	5.2	2.9	2.5	2.2	1.7
West Bengal	5.6	5.4	5.1	4.9	2.8	2.1	1.7	1.3
All-state average	5.9	5.5	5.2	4.5	2.6	2.1	1.8	1.3

Notes: 1. "-" = Not compiled. 2. *a* TFR for both Rural and Urban Indian Population.

Source: Computed from National Sample Survey, 50th round (1993-94), Household Data CD, NSS Organisation, Calcutta. Chaudhri, D.P. (2000), Poverty and Equity Issues in Indian Agriculture, an invited paper presented at the Plenary Session, *Indian Agriculture: The Perspectives for 21st Century*, at the Third Conference of Asian Agricultural Economists, Jaipur, India.

Table 2

Illiteracy Rates of Rural Poor and Non-poor, Aged Above 15 years, in Major States of India, 1993-94

Per cent

State	Very poor 15y+		Moderately poor 15y+		Non-poor (low) 15y+		Non-poor (high) 15y+	
	Female	Male	Female	Male	Female	Male	Female	Male
Andhra Pradesh	91.1	70.4	85.4	60.5	75.0	48.5	57.3	29.2
Arunachal Pradesh	88.6	78.2	88.4	71.2	86.5	64.2	82.6	63.6
Assam	71.4	45.6	58.8	32.2	37.3	18.4	23.1	11.1
Bihar	92.9	66.1	83.8	48.7	74.1	35.6	56.8	20.8
Gujarat	88.3	51.6	79.5	43.8	68.1	35.3	53.6	24.6
Haryana	91.3	62.2	82.2	49.9	76.2	41.7	67.1	26.8
Himachal Pradesh	81.5	56.3	63.7	39.2	59.8	30.8	46.7	20.1
Jammu & Kashmir	94.0	72.1	83.3	56.7	71.7	36.6	57.7	29.7
Karnataka	88.4	64.9	78.6	50.6	65.9	36.2	45.9	22.9
Kerala	27.4	15.3	17.2	11.0	14.2	6.9	7.9	2.6
Madhya Pradesh	92.7	66.4	85.3	51.6	77.2	40.2	66.4	28.0
Maharashtra	77.8	48.4	67.7	34.5	58.3	24.8	44.2	15.2
Manipur	71.5	45.2	45.4	24.5	51.3	23.4	47.9	18.4
Meghalaya	64.0	52.6	53.4	40.2	49.9	31.8	39.6	25.5
Mizoram	66.7	60.0	38.5	23.2	10.7	3.6	14.3	6.0
Orissa	85.0	61.2	40.6	15.6	44.0	22.2	25.4	9.0
Punjab	86.0	70.3	72.2	41.5	59.7	26.6	41.2	14.9
Rajasthan	95.5	69.9	80.1	60.7	71.5	50.1	51.5	33.5
Sikkim	78.5	35.7	92.6	58.5	89.1	49.6	82.6	40.1
Tamil Nadu	77.8	50.5	65.7	33.3	54.6	28.4	24.7	7.5
Uttar Pradesh	91.5	59.9	58.6	30.5	43.3	23.6	25.5	9.2
West Bengal	75.6	57.0	85.2	48.3	77.4	40.5	64.9	31.2

Source: Same as in Table 1.

Table 3
Educational Level of the Rural Poor and Non-poor Household Heads in Major States of India 1993-94

	Very poor (Per cent)				Moderately poor (Per cent)				Non-poor low (Per cent)				Non-poor high (Per cent)			
State	Illiterate	Below primary	Above primary	Technical	Illiterate	Below primary	Above primary	Technical	Illiterate	Below primary	Above primary	Technical	Illiterate	Below primary	Above primary	Technical
Andhra Pradesh	77.3	12.0	10.5	0.3	70.2	13.9	15.7	0.2	59.1	14.1	25.8	1.0	35.3	15.1	41.7	7.9
Arunachal Pradesh	90.8	4.9	3.7	0.6	80.2	9.0	10.5	0.3	73.5	7.3	17.5	1.7	72.2	4.6	20.0	3.2
Assam	54.5	20.2	25.1	0.2	39.0	25.0	35.1	0.8	23.3	26.0	48.6	2.1	14.0	15.6	61.0	9.4
Bihar	73.1	10.6	15.5	0.8	57.0	12.2	28.8	2.0	41.6	13.9	38.8	5.7	24.9	14.0	49.6	11.5
Gujarat	62.7	16.4	20.6	0.3	55.5	19.9	24.5	0.2	44.2	18.3	36.5	1.0	30.0	18.8	45.7	5.5
Haryana	69.3	8.9	21.8	-	61.8	12.6	25.6	-	54.4	8.3	36.0	1.3	41.9	10.5	42.7	5.0
Himachal Pradesh	70.2	8.8	20.5	0.6	56.8	16.0	27.0	0.2	49.2	19.7	30.3	0.8	35.1	13.8	46.3	4.9
Jammu & Kashmir	80.4	3.9	15.7	-	72.6	6.7	20.7	-	57.4	7.2	34.0	1.3	44.6	8.1	42.7	4.6
Karnataka	73.4	12.3	14.0	0.3	60.5	16.2	22.3	1.0	48.4	17.4	32.3	1.9	31.5	16.1	46.4	6.0
Kerala	31.3	31.3	37.5	-	23.9	27.5	48.6	-	15.1	21.5	62.5	0.8	6.5	17.2	69.1	7.1
Madhya Pradesh	73.1	13.9	12.6	0.4	59.5	18.7	21.0	0.9	49.4	21.0	27.7	1.8	34.6	20.0	40.9	4.5
Maharashtra	57.2	14.7	27.8	0.2	45.8	14.6	38.6	1.0	35.1	16.0	46.6	2.4	24.5	13.9	54.0	7.6
Manipur	55.6	13.9	30.6	-	38.3	12.6	47.2	1.8	37.9	11.3	46.0	4.8	31.3	10.9	45.3	12.5
Meghalaya	58.3	16.7	25.0	-	55.5	19.7	24.8	-	46.3	14.0	38.7	1.0	37.5	16.7	43.0	2.8
Mizoram	75.0	-	25.0	-	28.2	12.8	59.0	-	8.6	19.5	71.9	-	8.2	17.7	70.4	3.7
Orissa	67.2	20.8	11.9	0.1	48.3	27.8	23.2	0.8	34.2	32.5	30.6	2.8	19.2	24.0	48.6	8.1
Punjab	75.4	4.3	20.3	-	72.2	9.6	17.8	0.4	63.7	6.9	28.3	1.1	45.0	7.4	43.9	3.7
Rajasthan	77.3	9.1	13.1	0.5	69.1	12.8	16.9	1.3	62.1	16.0	20.0	2.0	51.4	13.0	30.8	4.9
Sikkim	50.0	28.6	21.4	-	48.1	25.6	26.4	-	36.1	19.4	41.7	2.8	8.5	16.4	64.8	10.3
Tamil Nadu	62.5	15.1	22.4	-	49.8	21.1	28.6	0.6	38.6	21.5	38.2	1.7	22.4	16.8	53.3	7.5
Uttar Pradesh	70.1	10.3	19.1	0.5	59.4	12.2	26.2	2.2	51.3	13.9	32.3	2.5	38.6	12.1	41.5	7.7
West Bengal	62.2	18.9	18.7	0.1	46.8	21.9	30.2	1.0	33.2	20.1	43.4	3.4	16.2	15.4	56.5	11.9

Sources: Same as in Table 1.

that of poverty are inversely related is unmistakable. The intensity varies across states with Kerala at one extreme and Bihar at the other.

Nutritional poverty, educational poverty and larger number of children per household are the three main identifying characteristics of the poor in rural India. In the absence of easily accessible comparable data on health poverty we did not explore the issue. However, Radhakrishna et al. (1998) provide the fourth important identifier of poverty. The reinforcing nature of the three identifiers is explored in sections II and IV below.

II. CHILDREN IN A RURAL HOUSEHOLD: A SEARCH FOR DETERMINANTS

Table 1 shows that the poor and ultra-poor have a larger number of children per household compared to the non-poor. To establish the relative role of poverty in determining the number of children, when other plausible influencing factors are held constant, we estimate a linear regression equation using the entire 50th round (1993-94) NSS sample of 69,205 rural households. Other factors that are expected to have an influence on the number of children in a household are the literacy status (or rather the lack of it) and the occupational status (measured dichotomously as agricultural or non-agricultural) of adult females in the household. These two variables reflect the knowledge deprivation and employment levels in traditional occupations of the households. Government policy aimed at helping the poor is incorporated in the Integrated Rural Development (IRD) Assistance Programmes covering the household and household's purchases of foodgrains (rice or wheat) from the public distribution system (PDS). Household assets holdings are represented by the ownership of land as well as animals (including milch, draught and small animals), landholdings represent the ability of households to provide for children directly and cattle ownership, being labour-intensive in nature, represents both children's usefulness as labour and also the household's ability to maintain them. Income is proxied by household consumption expenditure which is grouped into four classes—very poor, moderately poor, low non-poor and high non-poor.

Whilst transforming the data into Naperian logs gives the convenient interpretation of elasticity estimates, this was not possible because of the dichotomous specifications of the variables. The number of children vary from zero to a maximum of 22 in the entire sample. As explained earlier, the Consumer Expenditure Class variable takes values one to four for the increasing expenditure classes. The IRD support and PDS purchase variables are zero for no support/ purchases and take value one when the household receives support and makes purchases. The measure of adult female illiteracy takes the number reported for the household. Land and animals ownership are measured as zero for no ownership and one for ownership, regardless of the relative sizes of the holdings. The occupational status of the household is defined as either 'non-agricultural' with value zero or 'agricultural' with value one. The educational level of the household head ranges in value from zero for no training, to one for primary school, two for post-primary education and four for technical training.

The results of the OLS estimation of the regression are reported in Table 4a. Importantly, the inverse relationship between the four increasing consumer expenditure classes and the number of children in the household clearly show that the poor have larger numbers of children in their family. The estimated OLS co-efficient with respect to poverty is -0.417 with very significant t-statistic. The coefficients for IRD and PDS support are smaller but positive, significant at the one per cent level, and similar in magnitude at just below 0.1. Households with more children, therefore, are more likely to access the IRD and PDS support schemes. The number of illiterate adult females has a positive effect of 0.211 on the number of children, suggesting that illiteracy of adult females indeed adds to the number of children in the family. Land ownership has a positive and significant coefficient of 0.185, whilst cattle holdings has double this value of 0.365. Increasing household assets are also indicative of more children. It needs to be remembered that these positive effects combine the negative income effects on the number of children. A household with lower income will have more children on an average, whilst greater security and assets allows a family to have more children. Finally, agricultural occupation has a positive value of 0.4, which implies that households characterised as having agricultural occupations, have more children. This reinforces the income effect on these households. All coefficients are very significant at the one per cent level.

Table 4a
Determinants of the Number of Children in Indian Rural Households, 1993-94

Dependent variable: Number of children in a household
Sample size: 69205 households

Explanatory variables	OLS	
	Co-efficient	t-value
Consumer expenditure class	-0.417	-71.256 ***
IRD support	0.093	3.795 ***
PDS purchases	0.086	6.027 ***
Illiterate adult females	0.211	27.807 ***
Landownership	0.185	16.702 ***
Agricultural occupation	0.400	26.136 ***
Animals owned	0.365	25.537 ***
R^2= 0.134	S.E. = 1.5516	F = 1039.48

Note: *** significant at one per cent.
Source: Computed from 50th round (1993-94) NSS database for rural households.

Given the dichotomous nature of these variables, an alternative measure of the number of children was derived. The new variable takes value zero when the number of children are below the average for all households and one for above average number of children. The regression was re-estimated using the logistic procedure, which is relevant for binary choice dependent variable models. These results, overall, are strikingly similar despite the differently specified dependent variable as reported in Table 4b.

Table 4b
Determinants of the Number of Children in Indian Rural Households, 1993-94

Dependent variable: Number of children in a household
Sample size: 69205 households

Explanatory variables	Logistic regression	
	Co-efficient	Wald statistic
Consumer expenditure class	-0.536	3871.052 ***
IRD support	0.016	5.944
PDS purchases	-0.063	-9.667 ***
Illiterate adult females	0.226	421.755 ***
Landownership	0.242	1065.397 ***
Agricultural occupation	0.800	4.473
Educational level of HH head	0.232	534.836 ***
Constant	-0.5	35.464 ***

Note: *** significant at one per cent.
Source: Computed from 50th round (1993-94) NSS database for rural households.

The expenditure class variable has a marginally larger estimate of -0.536 (compared to -0.417 for OLS estimation), implying that lower income households have an increased probability of having above average number of children. This effect is very significant with the Wald statistic significant at the one per cent level. The positive coefficient effect of the number of illiterate adult females is 0.226, which is very similar to the OLS estimate of 0.211. This also applies to the estimated coefficients for the ownership of land. The inclusion of the educational level of the household head gives a significant and positive effect, which reinforces the positive asset holding coefficients. However, there are differences between the two coefficients in that the PDS coefficient changes sign and the agricultural occupation coefficient becomes insignificant with the logistic regression method. Whilst some further examination is required, the different approaches give very similar results for the major variables. This implies a remarkable degree of robustness in the estimates for the effects of consumer expenditure classes, illiterate adult females and asset ownership.

The strong conclusion that emerges from our analysis is that poverty increases the number of children in the family. Assuming poverty to be constant, land and cattle ownership increases the number of children, whilst illiteracy of adult females and the predominance of agricultural occupation (reflecting traditional activity) also positively affects the number of children in the family.

The effect of the number of children on 'nowhere' children (who are neither in the labour force nor in schools) has been reported and analysed (Chaudhri, 2000a). The results of linear regression estimates using OLS on district data obtained from the 1991 Census is reproduced in Tables 4c and 4d. The estimated coefficients from the sample of 374 districts show the positive impact of child population and 'nowhere' children on child labour. The elasticity of male child population with respect to male child labour is a high 1.08. The 'nowhere' children elasticities for child labour are very similar with value 0.72 for male child labour and 0.71 for female child labour. The inescapable conclusion from this finding is that poverty (via larger numbers of children) increases the number of deprived children and children engaged as labourers. It needs to be noted that our specification in two alternative estimation procedures is slightly different. Standard regression requires real valued variables while the logistic regression handles binary variables. Also, the household schedules that we analysed did not report child labour directly. Accordingly, we decided to deal with the theme of this paper, in a step-wise manner. The emphasis on the supply side remains unaffected.

Table 4c

Determinants of the Supply of Male Child Labour in Districts of India, 1991

Dependent variable: Ln (Number of male child workers, 5-14 years)
Sample size: 374 districts

Explanatory variables	OLS	
	Co-efficient	t-value
Male child population	1.080	2.10 **
Male students	-0.750	-2.33 ***
Male 'nowhere' children	0.720	3.47 ***
Average household size	-0.230	-3.44 ***
Urbanisation	0.070	1.15 *
Infrastructure index	0.150	1.17 *
Constant	-4.000	-5.28 ***
R^2= 0.710	S.E. = 0.5492	F = 143.70

Notes: 1. *** significant at one per cent. 2. ** significant at 5 per cent. 3. * significant at 10 per cent.

Source: Computed from Census of India 1991, Data Diskettes.

Table 4d

Determinants of the Supply of Female Child Labour in Districts of India 1991

Dependent variable: Ln (Number of female child workers, 5-14 years)
Sample size: 374 districts

Explanatory variables	OLS	
	Co-efficient	t-value
Female child population	0.792	0.59
Female students	0.845	2.96 ***
Female 'nowhere' children	0.711	2.63 ***
Average household size	-0.479	-3.99 ***
Urbanisation	0.083	0.79
Infrastructure index	-0.692	-4.26 ***
Constant	0.792	0.59
R^2= 0.316	S.E. = 0.9980	F = 28.54

Notes: 1. *** significant at one per cent. 2. ** significant at 5 per cent. 3. * significant at 10 per cent.

Source: Computed from Census of India 1991, Data Diskettes.

III. POVERTY, CHILD LABOUR AND SCHOOL EDUCATION

The National Sample Survey has provided detailed information about the economic activity of children (5-14 years) and their school attendance by expenditure class. Table 5 shows a three-way classification on an all-India basis for male and female children separately. The first three expenditure classes represent the ultra-poor of rural India.

Five interesting patterns with implications for public policy are discernable. First, the proportion of children who help in household activity reveals an important gender bias. The proportion of boys from ultra-poor households on a per thousand basis who participate in household activities is lower than that from their non-poor counterparts-the figures being 237-247 and 302-314 per thousand, respectively. The reason for this can be found in Table 5 where we report child participation in full-time labour force. As the table shows 359 children per thousand in the poorest households are fully occupied in activities that directly compete with school education, as against 366 and 342 children from the highest expenditure classes. The figure for ultra-poor being 359 is comparable. The incidence of child labour is higher among the poorer households than the non-poor households. However, even among the high expenditure non-poor, child labour is not totally absent, being 40-50 per thousand compared to 81-112 among the poor.

Second, the observed pattern for the girl child is very similar. The phenomenon is evident from a comparison of columns 6 and 7 and lines 1 and 2 with 10 and 11. On the basis of expenditure class, only 374-438 girls per thousand of the ultra-poor household work full-time: 291-320 per thousand in household activity and 83-118 per thousand in full-time child labour. Comparable figures for the top groups are 338-398 in household work and 56-89 per thousand in child labour.

Third, the proportion of rural girls found in full-time labour is higher than boys for virtually all expenditure classes-from the poorest to the richest. This clearly reflects the gender bias inherent in Indian society. More importantly, it provides glaring evidence of the state's wanton neglect of its constitutional duties on two counts: failing to provide education for all as per the directive principles or the Constitution and allowing gender bias to persist violating the spirit of the preamble.

Fourth, girls of ultra-poor households participate in household activities as well as child labour at higher rates compared to boys from similar poverty backgrounds. The alarming disparity in the participation rates and worsening situation analysed there (Chaudhri, 1997a) calls for an effective social policy response.

Finally, an overwhelmingly high proportion of households in all expenditure classes report that child labour is economically an asset for the households. The difference between the ultra-poor and non-poor is noticeable with 923 households reporting economic contribution of child labour to the household, compared to 765 who do not.

Table 5
Per Thousand Distribution of Rural Children (aged 5-14) Working for each MPCE Class in India

Monthly per capita consumption expenditure MPCE	Number of children helping in HH chores per 1000 children	Number of children working per 1000 children (aged 5-14)	Male number of children whose work helps HHS. economically per 1000 children working	working Number of children		Number of children helping in HH chores per 1000 children	Number of children working per 1000 children (aged 5-14)	Female number of children whose work helps HHS. economically per 1000 children working	Number of children working	
				Estd. Number	Sample				Estd (00)	Sample
	1	2	3	4	5	6	7	8	9	10
Less than 120	247	112	923	4,449	215	320	118	826	4,859	199
120 - 140	237	84	906	4,067	186	291	83	859	3,451	162
140 - 165	240	81	913	6,357	293	310	78	831	5,544	259
165 - 190	251	73	879	6,781	305	325	85	866	6,765	317
190 - 210	238	70	911	4,969	239	330	78	848	4,895	261
210 - 235	263	70	920	5,491	288	333	79	840	5,314	270
235 - 265	257	65	886	5,107	282	335	78	885	5,355	304
265 - 300	260	54	895	3,987	218	337	69	881	4,148	243
300 - 355	287	56	880	4,103	270	356	63	904	3,909	237
355 - 455	298	58	730	3,665	239	375	61	720	3,186	223
455 - 560	302	40	765	1,155	104	338	89	739	2,336	118
560 and above	314	52	827	1,474	146	398	56	769	1,292	130
N.R	305	64	968	418	19	363	46	728	226	11
All-classes	263	69	885	52,023	2,804	335	78	842	51,280	2,734

Source: National Sample Survey Organisation, Economic Activities and School Attendance by Children Of India (1997).

Table 6 shows school attendance and working boys by expenditure class of households and Table 7 provides similar information for girls. It is clear from the tables that full-time attendance in school and not working are, as expected, directly related to the household's monthly per capita expenditure. In other words, fewer children from poorer households are full-time students, their number being 466 per thousand compared to 855 per thousand among the richer households (Table 6, column 2).

As can be seen from Table 6 very few children are in the category of never having attended school, irrespective of the household's consumption expenditure class (columns 7, 8 and 9). Though the proportion of children who have never been to school (3-4 per cent) is small it cannot be ignored. Clearly, the expansion of school facilities that is being advocated would directly help this tiny part of the deprived child population.

A majority of working children and those in the 'nowhere' category belong to the group who attended school but dropped out. As expected, their proportion among working boys is almost three times higher among the children from the poorest households as compared to those from richer ones. The gap is even more glaring among children who are not working and have dropped out (our category of 'nowhere' children). The proportion of boys from the poorest households who dropped out is 396 per thousand compared to 94 per thousand among boys from richer households. Thus it is clear that the crux of the problem lies in the ability of schools to retain children in school once they are enrolled. This directly vindicates the results of the PROBE Report (1999). The problem of dropouts in rural schools seems to be one that can be attributed mainly to the poor quality education-a supply-side problem (Chaudhri, 1996).

The pattern observed for girls as reported in Table 7 is very similar to that discussed above for boys with two major differences. First, the proportions of girls dropping out from schools in all expenditure classes is much higher than that which was observed among boys. Second, girls from the poorest households drop out at rates at least 50 per cent higher than that of boys. The most effective way of dealing with the problem of gender bias is to focus on participation and retention of girls in the school system up to the age of 14 as is specified in the Constitution of India.

IV. ECONOMETRIC ANALYSIS OF POVERTY AND CHILD LABOUR: STATE LEVEL DATA ANALYSIS

The econometric analysis of rural poverty and child labour requires the estimation of two specifications. The determination of rural poverty is modelled in Chaudhri and Wilson (2001a, b) as a growth process where short-term factors such as the public distribution of foodgrains and long-term factors such as total factor productivity growth are important. Rural poverty is measured in terms of rural head count poverty (RHCP), defined as the proportion of rural poor to the total rural population. Unfortunately, the state data for rural poverty are only available for 11 years: 1970, 72-73, 77, 83, 86-87, 89-90 and 92-93, which leaves 13 missing years during this period—nine in the first half of the sample and four in

Table 6

Per Thousand Distribution of Rural Male Children (Aged 5-14) by Status of School Attendance and Work for Each Household MPCE in India

Monthly per capita expenditure	School attendance: Attending			Dropped out			Never attended			Number of children		
	Working	Not working	All	Working	not working	All	Working	Not working	All	All	Estd (00)	Sample
	1	2	3	4	5	6	7	8	9	10	11	12
Less than 120	16	466	483	94	396	490	2	25	27	1,000	39,798	1,892
120 - 140	6	531	537	75	355	429	3	31	34	1,000	48,280	2,305
140 - 165	14	588	601	67	287	354	1	44	45	1,000	78,140	3,845
165 - 190	8	624	633	64	269	333	1	34	35	1,000	92,722	4,672
190 - 210	14	652	666	56	242	298	-	36	36	1,000	70,784	3,815
210 - 235	16	697	713	53	205	258	1	28	29	1,000	78,661	4,418
235 - 265	15	739	754	50	164	214	1	32	33	1,000	78,160	4,736
265 - 300	12	763	775	41	154	196	1	29	30	1,000	73,182	4,531
300 - 355	13	789	802	42	129	172	1	26	26	1,000	72,866	5,030
355 - 455	18	807	825	40	106	147	-	28	29	1,000	62,994	4,890
455 - 560	19	837	855	21	94	115	-	30	30	1,000	29,045	2,280
560 and above	24	818	842	30	93	123	1	35	36	1,000	34,625	2,950
All-classes	14	689	703	54	210	264	1	32	33	1,000	759,257	45,364
Estd.children ('00)	10,558	523,365	533,923	40,806	159,678	200,484	659	24,190	24,850	759,257	X	X
Sample children	853	32,733	33,586	1,917	8,398	10,315	34	1,429	1,463	45,364	X	X

Source: National Sample Survey Organisation, Economic Activities and School Attendance by Children Of India (1997).

Table 7

Per Thousand Distribution of Rural Female Children (Aged 5-14) by Status of School Attendance and Work for each Household MPCE in India

Monthly per capita expenditure	School attendance										Number of children	
	Attending			Dropped out			Never attended					
	Working	Not working	All	Working	Not working	All	Working	Not working	All	All	Estd (00)	Sample
	1	2	3	4	5	6	7	8	9	10	11	12
Less than 120	8	311	319	105	638	643	5	34	38	1,000	41,257	1,883
120 - 140	2	372	374	79	509	588	2	36	38	1,000	41,775	2,012
140 - 165	6	436	442	71	448	518	1	39	40	1,000	70,764	3,472
165 - 190	7	449	456	76	421	496	2	46	48	1,000	79,853	4,067
190 - 210	8	511	519	70	370	440	1	40	41	1,000	62,420	3,354
210 - 235	7	542	549	73	343	415	-	36	36	1,000	66,882	3,810
235 - 265	11	573	583	66	311	377	1	39	40	1,000	69,025	4,220
265 - 300	7	649	657	62	243	305	-	38	38	1,000	60,210	3,839
300 - 355	10	672	681	52	230	283	1	35	36	1,000	62,196	4,381
355 - 455	13	703	715	48	210	257	-	27	27	1,000	52,526	4,182
455 - 560	19	724	743	71	167	237	-	20	20	1,000	26,113	2,102
560 and above	13	748	761	41	162	203	-	36	36	1,000	27,999	2,449
All-classes	8	545	554	68	341	408	1	37	38	1,000	661,021	39,771
Estd.children ('00)	5,603	360,348	365,951	44,925	225,083	270,009	752	24,310	25,062	661,021	X	X
Sample children	551	23,943	24,494	2,149	11,710	13,859	34	1,384	1,418	39,771	X	X

Source: National Sample Survey Organisation, (NSSO, 1997) Economic Activities and School Attendance by Children Of India.

the second half. The presence of missing values rules out the possibility of including lagged values in dynamic form specifications.

The expected major explanatory variables of poverty are: the rural wage rate (RWAGE), total factor productivity (TFP), the public distribution of foodgrains (PDS), development expenditure (DEVEX), rural population (RPOP), literacy rates (LIT) and child labour (CL). It is hypothesised that child labour will be a function of supply and demand variables. The variables to be considered are rural head count poverty (RHCP), rural wage rate (RWAGE), rural population (RPOP), 'nowhere' children (NC) and students enrolled in middle schooling (SE). These variables are listed with relevant details below.

Major Explanatory Variables of Poverty

Variables	Name	Unit of measurement
Rural head-count poverty	RHCP	Proportion of rural poor to total rural population, percentage
Child labour	CL	Number of rural children (aged 4-15) working
'Nowhere' children	NC	Number of rural children (aged 4-15) dropped out or never attended school
Student enrolment	SE	Number of children enrolled in middle schooling (VI-VIII)
Rural wage rate	RWAGE	Constant 1960-61 prices, Rs.
Total factor productivity	TFP	Index, 1970=100
Development expenditure	DEVEX	Constant 1980-81 prices, Rs million.
Total fertility rate	TFR	Proportionate increase in population, percentage
Rural literacy	LIT	Proportion of rural population literate, percentage
Rural population	RPOP	Numbers, 000's
Public distribution of total foodgrains	PDS	Total central and state governments' distribution, constant 1980-81 prices, Rs.

The data for these variables are available for 15 major Indian states: Andhra Pradesh, Bihar, Gujarat, Haryana, Himachal Pradesh, Karnataka, Kerala, Madhya Pradesh, Maharashtra, Orissa, Punjab, Rajasthan, Tamil Nadu, Uttar Pradesh and West Bengal. The availability of 11 years of data for 15 states allows a pooled cross-section time series econometric estimation procedure where the variables stack the 11 observations for each of the 15 states to give 165 observations for each variable. All variables are in Naperian logs so that the estimated coefficients using OLS will be elasticities. In order to determine possible state effects, state-specific dummy variables were also included in the regressions.

The preliminary Shazam econometric results showed evidence of extreme multicollinearity in the variables with high adjusted coefficients of determination,, and t-statistics, which were very sensitive to the specification of the included variables in the regressions. The calculated for linear regressions of the variables against other explanatory variables are above 0.8 with many having the value over 0.95. The condition numbers were typically much greater than the benchmark level of thirty, according to Judge et al. (1985). It was, therefore, necessary to use the principal components (PC's) estimation procedure for both equations.

As shown in the study by Chaudhri and Wilson (2001a, b), there are significant structural breaks between the pre- and post-liberalisation periods. We tested for change using the CUSUM squared tests and the identified structural breaks can be grouped into three broad periods, early 1980's, late 1980's and early 1990's. The second period coincides with the drought of 1987 and the emerging foreign exchange problems which forced the economic reforms in the early 1990's. Chaudhri and Wilson (2001a, b) identify changes to the structure of poverty in the rural sector as those that occurred in 1988 for the period of interest. Inspection of the time series of the rural head count poverty ratio, (Fig. 1) below, shows the possible structural change around 1988 and 1993.

Whilst our interest lies in the changes since liberalisation in 1991 our data sample ends in 1993 and so there are not enough data points to compare the effects of events since 1991. We therefore select 1989 as the change point and estimate the RHCP and CL equations allowing for structural change over the final four data points. The regression results for the estimation of the equations using principal components are recorded in Tables 8 and 9. The coefficient estimates are elasticities because of the double-log representation, various specifications were estimated for each equation and it was found that the parameter estimates were sensitive to the selection of the number of principal components. The criterion adopted for the selection of the principal components for each regression was based on the condition index which was greater than 100 (which is the relevant benchmark for extreme multicollinearity). The structural change dummy variables are listed on the right of Tables 8 and 9.

Figure 1

Rural Head Count Poverty Ratio, All-India, 1966-67 to 1995-96

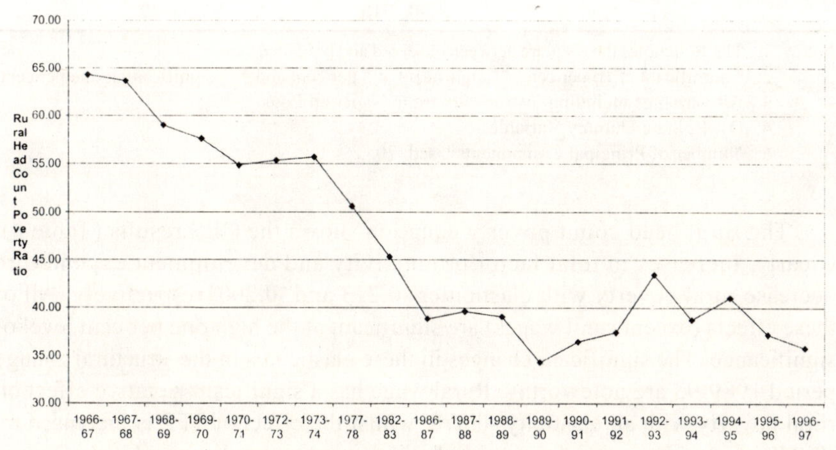

Table 8
Estimated Co-efficients of the Determinants of Rural Head Count Poverty in Major States of India, 1970-1993

Dependent variable: Rural head count poverty		Principal components (Condition indices >100)			
		Full sample 1970-1993		Structural change effects 1989-1993	
	N=165	Co-efficient	t-values	Co-efficient	t-values
X1	Rural wage rate	-0.018	-0.459	-0.078	-3.489***
X2	Total factor productivity	-0.213	-7.148***	-0.043	-2.245**
X3	Public distribution of foodgrains	0.058	3.006***	0.001	0.039
X4	Development expenditure	-0.200	-6.845***	0.155	4.364***
X5	Rural population	0.196	6.973***	-0.086	-3.353***
X6	Literacy	-0.031	-1.213	0.036	1.770*
X7	Child labour	0.126	5.618***	-0.006	-0.197
D1	Andhra Pradesh	-0.219	-4.779***	-0.108	-4.988***
D2	Bihar	0.045	1.044	-0.022	-1.019
D3	Gujarat	-0.003	-0.097	0.020	1.206
D4	Haryana	-0.120	-2.918***	-0.020	-1.090
D5	Himachal Pradesh	0.021	0.553	0.039	1.799*
D6	Karnataka	0.052	1.113	0.027	1.229
D7	Kerala	0.057	2.259**	0.000	0.022
D8	Madhya Pradesh	0.056	1.184	0.041	1.812*
D9	Maharashtra	0.134	2.946***	0.060	2.918***
D10	Orissa	0.081	1.693*	0.040	1.641
D11	Punjab	-0.158	-3.581***	-0.037	-2.005**
D12	Rajasthan	0.054	1.220	-0.004	-0.193
D13	Tamil Nadu	0.085	1.813*	0.063	2.781***
D14	Uttar Pradesh	0.046	1.395	0.06	3.321***
D15	West Bengal	-0.129	-3.224***	-0.154	-5.205***
C	Constant	1.400	3.049***		
		R^2=0.7718		S.E.=0.20	

Notes: 1. The R^2 denotes the r-square between observed and predicted values.
2. * significant at 10 per cent, ** significant at 5 per cent and *** significant at one per cent.
3. All variables including instruments are in Naperian Logs.
4. D1-15 State Dummy Variables.
5. Number of Principal Components Used: 20.

The rural head count poverty equation shows the OLS results (Table 8). Clearly, increases in total factor productivity and development expenditure decrease rural poverty with elasticities -0.213 and -0.200, respectively. All of these effects (except rural wages) are significant at the high one per cent level of significance. The significant changes in these elasticities in the structural change period 1989-93 are noteworthy. Rural wage has a significant negative effect on rural poverty with an elasticity -0.078, whilst the effect of TFP is increased by -0.043. A comparison of this with development expenditure whose effect is

Table 9
Estimated Co-efficients of the Determinants of Child Labour in Major States of India, 1970-1993

Dependent variable: Child labour		Principal components (Condition indices >100)			
		Full sample 1970-1993		Structural change effects 1989-1993	
N=165		Co-efficient	t-values	Co-efficient	t-values
X1	Rural head count poverty	0.177	6.754***	0.143	8.755***
X2	Rural wage rate	-0.171	-6.001***	-0.301	-13.770***
X3	Rural population	0.113	4.772***	0.087	3.056**
X4	'Nowhere' children	0.828	41.270***	0.004	0.136
X4	Student enrolment in middle schooling (VI-VIII)	-0.144	-5.602***	-0.127	-4.289***
D1	Andhra Pradesh	0.676	18.350***	0.309	18.180***
D2	Bihar	-0.526	-15.030***	-0.218	-12.820***
D3	Gujarat	0.036	0.946	0.035	2.037**
D4	Haryana	-0.297	-8.576**	-0.187	-11.470***
D5	Himachal Pradesh	0.043	1.596	0.003	0.211
D6	Karnataka	0.340	9.330***	0.197	11.400***
D7	Kerala	-0.764	-30.020***	-0.301	-18.690***
D8	Madhya Pradesh	0.143	3.812***	0.09	4.925***
D9	Maharashtra	0.384	10.510***	0.211	12.390***
D10	Orissa	-0.215	-6.148***	-0.065	-3.644***
D11	Punjab	0.067	1.971**	-0.011	-0.692
D12	Rajasthan	-0.140	-3.892***	-0.092	-4.800***
D13	Tamil Nadu	0.340	9.378***	0.201	11.380***
D14	Uttar Pradesh	0.045	3.948***	-0.054	-2.953***
D15	West Bengal	-0.130	-4.291***	-0.137	-7.693***
C	Constant	-0.109	-0.351		
		R^2=0.9824		S.E.=0.16	

Notes: 1. The R^2 denotes the r-square between observed and predicted values.
2. * significant at 10 per cent, ** significant at 5 per cent and *** significant at one per cent.
3. All variables including instruments are in Naperian Logs.
4. D1-15 State Dummy Variables.
5. Number of Principal Components Used: 18

reduced by a large 0.155, gives an overall elasticity of -0.045 during this period. The supply side pressure of rural population clearly increase rural poverty with an elasticity 0.196. The concomitant increase in public distribution (0.058) and child labour (0.126) coincide with increases in rural poverty. The positive coefficient on public distribution can have the interpretation that a 10 per cent increase in public distribution will cause around a 6 per cent increase in rural poverty. However, care should be taken in interpreting this result. The positive co-efficient captures bi-directional causation in terms of the increase (or decrease) in the public distribution of foodgrains by the authorities when rural poverty increases (decreases). Chaudhri and Wilson (2001b) decompose this into short and long-term effect, which allow for the bi-directional causality and which derives an unambiguous negative effect on rural poverty.

The state differences are as expected with Haryana, Punjab and West Bengal having significantly less than average rural poverty. Significantly, the structural change effects are important for many of these variables.

Table 9 shows the elasticities for the determinants of child labour. All explanatory variables are significant for the full sample, 1970 to 1993, at the 1 per cent level. Rural head count poverty, rural population and 'nowhere' children have positive effects on child labour with the latter elasticity, a high value of 0.828, which is also very significant with t-statistic of 41.27. The rural wage rate and student enrolments have inverse effects on child labour with respective elasticities of -0.171 and -0.144. There are significant increases in these elasticities in the post-1989 period with the exception of 'nowhere' children. The state differences are also important with Andhra Pradesh well above average and Bihar and Kerala below average.

All these results are encouraging because the estimates are significant at the one per cent level despite the very high levels of multicollinearity. The relatively close fits of the equations are indicated by the reported coefficients of determination of 0.77 for the rural head count poverty regression and 0.98 for the child labour regression. Given the mutual interdependence between these two equations in terms of the RHCP and CL variables appearing in both, we calculate the semi-reduced form and report the estimates in Table 10. Only the coefficients from tables 8 and 9, which are significant at the 5 per cent level, are included in the calculations. The results include the structural change effects and the estimates are called impact elasticity multipliers.

Table 10 shows some interesting results. Total factor productivity has the largest effect on rural head count poverty with an elasticity multiplier (-0.267),

Table 10
Reduced Form Impact Elasticity Multipliers Major States of India, 1970-1993

(Including structural change effects for 1989-93)

	Rural head count poverty	Child labour
Total factor productivity	-0.2673	-0.0856
Public distribution of foodgrains	0.0607	0.0194
Development expenditure	-0.0469	-0.0150
Rural population	0.1416	0.3237
Rural wage rate	-0.0617	-0.4914
Nowhere children	0.1083	0.8627
Middle school enrolment	-0.0354	-0.2820

Note: Only structural coefficients which are significant at 5 per cent or one per cent levels are included in the calculation of the reduced form.

one-third of which is the impact multiplier effect on child labour. However, the supply effects of rural population and 'nowhere' children have large positive effects on child labour with elasticity multipliers of 0.324 and 0.863, respectively. The rural wage effect is also pronounced in reducing child labour with the impact elasticity multiplier of -0.491. Thus, development expenditure and middle school enrolments both reduce rural poverty and child labour.

V. EVIDENCE FROM BEST AND WORST DISTRICTS OF INDIA

In Tables 11 and 12, we report details on the labour force participation rates, proportion in school and the proportion of 'nowhere' children in 20 best and 20 worst performing districts in India as per 1991 Census. The worst performing districts are in a number of states with Andhra Pradesh, Madhya Pradesh and Karnataka having more than one district in this category. It may be noted that Kerala, Tamil Nadu, Punjab, Haryana and Himachal Pradesh are excluded from this group. The highest participation rate was reported in district Jhabua in Madhya Pradesh at 15.2 per cent in this category while the 20th worst performing district was Jaintia Hills in Meghalaya with a labour force participation rate of 9.7 per cent. These rates are more than 2-3 times that of All-India average of 4.3 per cent.

Table 11

Ranks of Child Labour Participation Rates of Districts of India (Aged 5-14), 1991 in Twenty Worst-performing* Districts

Ranks*	Districts (States)	Main workers participation rates	Marginal workers participation rates	Per cent in schools	Per cent of children nowhere
1	Jhabua (Madhya Pradesh)	15.2	10.3	28.7	45.8
2	Bellary (Karnataka)	14.3	1.5	52.0	32.2
3	Mahbubnagar (Andhra Pradesh)	14.0	0.6	39.2	46.2
4	Kurnool (Andhra Pradesh)	13.5	0.5	44.8	41.1
5	Bastar (Madhya Pradesh)	13.4	4.3	38.0	44.3
6	Raichur (Karnataka)	12.8	1.1	40.6	45.6
7	Mon (Nagaland)	12.7	0.0	44.7	42.6
8	Betul (Madhya Pradesh)	11.2	2.6	62.4	23.8
9	Guntur (Andhra Pradesh)	11.2	0.8	56.6	31.4
10	Karimnagar (Andhra Pradesh)	11.2	0.6	57.1	31.1
11	Vizianagaram (Andhra Pradesh)	11.1	1.4	49.7	37.7
12	Nizamabad (Andhra Pradesh)	10.7	0.6	46.9	41.8
13	Khammam (Andhra Pradesh)	10.5	0.9	52.8	35.8
14	Medak (Andhra Pradesh)	10.4	0.5	43.2	45.9
15	Tawang (Arunachal Pradesh)	10.2	0.4	42.6	46.8
16	Anantapur (Andhra Pradesh)	10.2	1.0	50.3	38.5
17	Gulbarga (Karnataka)	10.1	1.2	46.5	42.3
18	West Nimar (Madhya Pradesh)	9.8	2.8	40.5	46.8
19	Prakasam (Andhra Pradesh)	9.7	0.8	52.8	36.7
20	Jaintia Hills (Meghalaya)	9.7	0.8	37.7	51.8
	All-India Average	4.3	1.0	50.7	44.0

Note: *Ranked according to 1991 total child labour participation rates.

Sources: Computed from: Census of India, 1991, *Census Handbook*, Registrar General & Census Commissioner, India, 1996.

Chaudhri, D.P. (1997), "Policy Perspectives on Child Labour in India" (work-in-progress).

Among the 20 best performing districts, we find that Kerala, and Himachal Pradesh have more than one district in this category with a participation rate of much less than one per cent. The others that have achieved this distinction are Dhanbad district of Bihar and Hoshiarpur district of Punjab with a participation rate of one per cent of children in labour force, as against the all-India average of 4.3 per cent.

Table 12
Ranks of Child Labour Participation Rates of Districts of India (Aged 5-14) 1991 (Twenty Best-performing* Districts

Ranks*	Districts (States)	Main workers participation rates	Marginal workers participation rates	Per cent in schools	Per cent of children nowhere
1	Kozhikode (Kerala)	0.2	0.1	86.5	13.2
2	Kannur (Kerala)	0.2	0.1	86.6	13.1
3	Alappuzha (Kerala)	0.2	0.1	89.5	10.2
4	Pathanamthitta (Kerala)	0.3	0.1	89.7	9.9
5	Malappuram (Kerala)	0.3	0.1	83.2	16.4
6	Kottayam (Kerala)	0.3	0.0	90.0	9.6
7	Kollam (Kerala)	0.4	0.1	88.3	11.2
8	Idukki (Kerala)	0.5	0.2	84.8	14.6
9	Ernakulam (Kerala)	0.5	0.1	91.0	8.4
10	Trivandrum (Kerala)	0.6	0.1	86.8	12.5
11	Hamirpur (Himachal Pradesh)	0.6	1.5	84.5	13.4
12	Thrissur (Kerala)	0.7	0.1	89.9	9.4
13	Kangra (Himachal Pradesh)	0.7	1.0	79.7	18.6
14	Wayanad (Kerala)	0.7	0.4	82.8	16.1
15	Mahendragarh (Haryana)	0.7	0.9	67.2	31.2
16	Rewari (Haryana)	0.8	0.3	74.2	24.7
17	Palakkad (Kerala)	0.9	0.2	85.9	13.0
18	Hoshiarpur (Punjab)	1.0	0.2	73.4	25.4
19	Una (Himachal Pradesh)	1.0	0.8	78.7	19.5
20	Dhanbad (Bihar)	1.0	0.2	54.5	44.3
	All-India Average	4.3	1.0	50.7	44.0

Note: As in Table 11.
Source: As in Table 11.

Participation in the school system in the two groups of districts is vastly different. Among the best performing districts with the exception of Dhanbad and Wayanad, all others had a participation rate in full time schooling of 75-91 per cent. In the worst performing districts the participation rates in the school system ranged from 28.7 per cent in Jhabua (the worst performer) to 62.4 per cent in Betul (Madhya Pradesh). The differences in the proportion of 'nowhere' children in these two groups of districts were even sharper. In the best performing districts, the proportion of 'nowhere children' was generally below 20 per cent with the exception of Dhanbad (Bihar), Hoshiarpur (Punjab) and Mahendragarh (Haryana). The inference that the solvent of both the categories of deprived children, namely, 'nowhere' children and full-time child labour being full time school education is inescapable. We had subjected this to formal, simple econometric modelling with data from 374 districts pertaining to all major states of India from 1991 Census. The results are reported in Section III.

VI. SCHOOL FEEDING PROGRAMMES AND THEIR EFFICACY

School feeding programmes have been used to achieve some or all of the three objectives. First, school feeding programmes are used to improve school enrolments and the participation of children from poorer households in education. An extensive body of literature reporting experiments in developing countries around the world unambiguously support the expectation that the use of school feeding has a significant and positive impact on school enrolments. Levinger (1986) providing an evaluation of a number of studies on the impact of school feeding programmes confirms country specific evidence. She also presents a representative literature survey of this issue. It was earlier pointed out, that the proportion of children who have never attended school is rather small—about 3-4 per cent of all children. However, the evidence from the states and districts, which was examined by us due to lack of data—may suggest wide variations. Generally, school feeding programmes would help a small proportion of children on an all-India basis, but may be a useful instrument in states and districts with large proportions of children who never attended schools.

Second, the school feeding programmes as reported in the literature have been successfully used as an instrument for targeting dropout rates. In India, as reported in Tables 6 and 7, a very high proportion of children do attend schools, but dropout, the proportion of girls in this category being larger than that of boys. The evidence summarised in Levinger (1994), among many others, on the efficacy of school feeding programmes in improving retention rates is generally positive, but is qualified in some ways. Its usefulness in eliminating short-term hunger is firmly confirmed. However, in situations of chronic hunger, the results depend on the effect of associated health problems, orchestration of the programme with community, state and family initiatives and an enduring nature of the feeding programme.

Third, the impact of the school feeding programmes that evoke interest among educationalists, development economists and policy makers is its positive impact on active learning capacity (ALC) of the child. Levinger (1996) building on her earlier work (1977) states:

"Earlier in this book, the notion of active learning capacity (ALC) was introduced as critical in understanding how child quality acts as a determinant of learning outcomes. ALC was defined as a child's propensity and ability to interact with and take optimal advantage of the full complement of resources offered by any formal or informal learning environment. If the quality of instruction (including the availability of teaching-learning resources and teacher quality) and quality of the school plant are held constant, then the following relationship is posited: As a child's ALC increases, the child's school achievement will also rise (assuming that the school does not penalize or discriminate against children with high ALC).

"Three sets of variables influence ALC. Primary variables are those that significantly affect ALC both directly and, through their effects on the secondary variable set, indirectly. The variables within the primary set interact with one another, at most, to a moderate degree. Primary variables are also influenced by the set of secondary variables, although this relationship is not as intense as its reciprocal. Among variables in the secondary set, the level of interdependence is high"

"Both the primary and secondary sets of variables focus on child quality, that is, those characteristics the learner brings to the classroom that play a significant role in determining school outcomes. Mitigating variables, the third set, have potential to alter, for better or worse, the impact of primary and secondary variables. The processes and interactions that occur in school to determine ALC and, through ALC, school achievement, are the focus of the mitigating variable set. In other words, mitigating variables capture those moments when child quality and school quality encounter each other. The nature of this encounter , its content and proccsses , will largely determine whether a child completes basic education or be among those who are almost assuredly confined to the margins of society."

The conceptual model, proposed by Levinger (1996) is presented in Figure 2. The potential for understanding the interaction of nutritional interventions with secondary and tertiary variables is rather high. In this context it would be interesting to cite the concluding observations of a study dealing with child feeding experiment in Gujarat:

"The State Government of Gujarat provides a mid-day meal to about three million Primary School pupils every day of term, about 200 days a year. The Programme is organised by a Mid-Day Meals Commission which reports directly to the Chief Minister. A School Health Package, consisting of biannual treatments with an anthelmintic, vitamin A and iron, was integrated into the MDMP in 1994 and is implemented by the Government of Gujarat."

The results of this controlled experiment generated certain conclusions, which are listed below:

(a) The prevalence of intestinal parasitic infections was 40 per cent in the Resurvey compared with 71 per cent in the Baseline Survey;

(b) The average haemoglobin concentration was 119 g/L in boys and 117 g/L in girls in the Resurvey compared with 107 g/L and 104 g/L, respectively during the Baseline Survey;

(c) The prevalence of signs of vitamin A deficiency was 22 per cent in the Resurvey compared with 48 per cent in the Baseline Survey;

(d) The prevalence of stunting showed no difference between the surveys, but more children had a normal Body Mass Index at the Resurvey compared with the Baseline Survey (12 per cent vs. 7 per cent in younger children and 34 per cent vs. 24 per cent in older children); more than 70 per cent of

Figure 2
Factors Affecting the Active Learning Capacity of Primary School Children

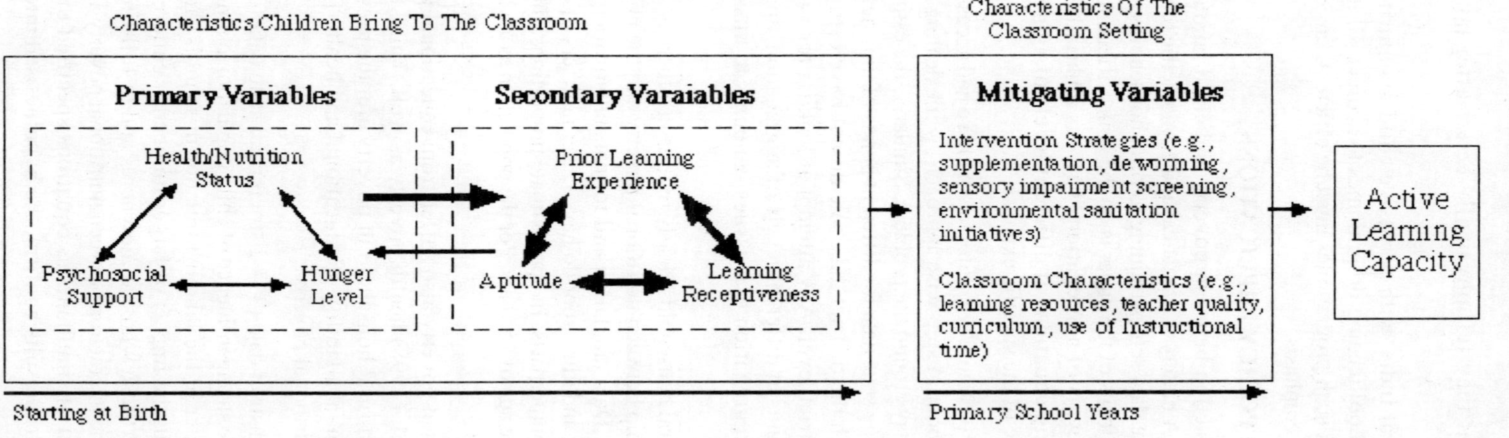

Source: Levinger, B. (1996), Nutrition Health and Education for All, UNDP, New York, http://www.edc.org/INT/NHEA/index.html, <accessed on 1 March 2001>.

children reported that they felt physically better after taking the treatments than before.

Thus, we find that in rural India, with pervasive child malnutrition and hunger the potential of the school feeding programmes to achieve all the three objectives, is rather high. That such programmes must be efficient, targeted and orchestrated hardly needs any emphasis.

VII. CONCLUSIONS AND POLICY IMPLICATIONS

The paper explores the interaction between poverty and child labour in the specific context of rural India. A battery of statistical and econometric techniques are used in the analysis of large data sets pertaining to rural households, districts and major states of India. The focus of the paper is on the issues affecting supply of child labour at different levels of aggregation. There is a variation in the specification of the estimating equations at different levels of aggregation, because of the underlying logic of the specific exercise.

It merits mention that the household schedules to which we had access did not report the incidence of child labour. A step-wise approach , while dealing with the household data was the only way around the problem. Similarly, the estimates of the simultaneous equations using state data for different points of time deal with a different issue compared with the district data. We do not have estimates of nutritional poverty at the district level. Any attempt at looking for symmetry among the estimated coefficients at different levels of aggregation, apart from being inappropriate due to aggregation bias issues, amounts to missing the message of the paper.

The analysis of 69, 205 rural households clearly reveals that there is a strong, discernable, inverse relationship between nutritional poverty and the number of children in a rural household. Data tabulation and formal statistical regression analysis suggests that the poor and ultra-poor do have larger numbers of children compared to their non-poor counterparts. In approximate proportions, more than half the rural poor are below the age of 15 years. For the population as a whole, the proportion is about 36 per cent.

Households with nutritional poverty also suffer from educational poverty, and as per Radhakrishna et al. (1998) health poverty as well. Thus, the four distinctive characteristics of a rural household in poverty are: the presence of larger number of children, non-availability of educational and health facilities along with the existence of nutritional poverty.

Econometric analysis of district data (374 districts) and state data for 1970-1993 unambiguously shows the strong influence of child population on 'nowhere' children (those who are neither in the labour force nor in schools) and child labour. This clearly brings out the impact of larger number of children in the family on deprived children (those who are 'nowhere' and in full-time child labour). In order, to examine the interaction between nutritional poverty and child labour we had estimated a set of simultaneous equations specified through a formal model. The econometric results confirm, the hypothesised interaction between nutritional poverty and child labour with positive and significant elasticities. The reinforcing nature of child labour and rural poverty is confirmed by our findings.

Among the other conclusions emerging from our study are:

1. Only 3-4 per cent of rural children have never attended school. A large proportion, (643 girls and 490 boys per thousand among poorest households) dropped out of school, over 90 per cent of them are not working ('nowhere' category) while others are in full-time child labour.
2. One-third of all children helped in household chores irrespective of expenditure class with the proportion of girls in this category being larger. Full-time child labour participation rates are higher among children of poorer households and that of girls from these households is even higher. The deprivation of the girl child increases in intensity with poverty.
3. The efficacy of school feeding programmes in increasing school enrolment is now well established. However, since only 3-4 per cent of rural children have never been to schools in India, the benefit of increased enrolment, though very important, will be small in the Indian context.
4. School feeding programmes, when properly designed, implemented with long-term commitment and orchestrated with other school improvements, community and family involvement do help substantially increase retention rates and also the active learning capacity of children. Evidence in this regard from the state of Gujarat is also very encouraging and international experience is positive.

For policy makers, three messages emerge: First, improved retention in schools and girl-focused school education is good for faster demographic transition, future productive life of these potential workers and accelerated economic growth; second, the most effective means of social development is to eliminate gender bias in non-participation in the school system through various educational improvement programmes and third, widespread use of school feeding programmes, designed with sensitivity and orchestrated with improvements of school facilities, if implemented with community and family support (probably through the Panchayati Raj institutions) would yield very high social returns. Thus we need to target nutritional poverty among children, substantially reduce drop out rates from schools and also participation in full time child labour through an orchestrated strategy. Above all, number of focussed action-research projects all over India are needed urgently, particularly in areas of endemic poverty and child labour.

(Thanks are due to Mei Ball, Linda Munoz and Silvana Noveska for competent research assistance and efficient word processing. We have benefited from discussions with Uday Balakrishnan, Robert Castle, late Ajit Dasgupta, Meena Gupta, Andrew Frazer, Mahaveer Jain, M.P. Joseph, L.D. Mishra, A.L. Nagar, Chris Nyland, Uma Pillai among many others. Usual academic caveat applies.)

Appendix

CLASSIFICATION OF CHILD WORK AND CHILD LABOR

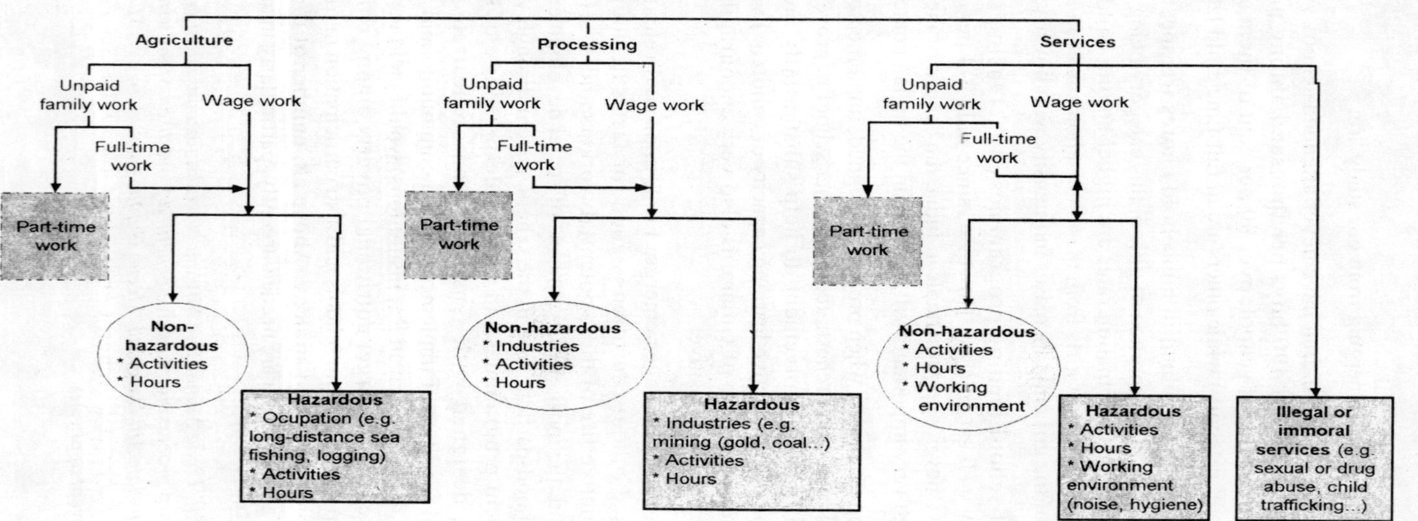

CLASSIFICATION	POTENTIAL MEASURES
[Box] Problem areas with strong conflict of interest between the State-Community, Family and the Employers of cheap child labor	* Strengthening the legal basis (national and international) and its enforcement * Improving monitoring and awareness raising
[Oval] Areas where the State-Community, Family and the Employers do not have major conflict of interest	* Institutional reforms * Making school education cheaper, more flexible and accessible combining with awareness raising and provision of technical supports
[Shaded box] Areas where there is minimal conflict between the State-Community, Family and the Users of child work, particularly between school education and part-time work	* Institutional strengthening * Decrimination of child labor of non-hazardous, part-time non-conflicting with schooling

References

Caldwell, J.C. (1990), *The Soft Underbelly of Development: Demographic Transition in Conditions of Limited Economic Change.* World Bank Annual Conference of Development Economics, Washington DC.

Chaudhri, D.P. (1996), *Dynamic Profile of Child Labour in India, 1951-1991,* CLASP, ILO, New Delhi.

—— (1997), "A Policy Perspective on Child Labour in India with Pervasive Gender and Urban Bias in School Education", *The Indian Journal of Labour Economics,* Vol. 40, No. 4, October-December, p.789.

—— (2000a), "Basic Human Rights, Core Labour Standards and Relative Educational Deprivation of Youth in Modern Indian States", *The Indian Journal of Labour Economics,* Vol. 43, No. 1, January-March, pp. 35-58.

—— (2001), "Targeted Action Plan for Breaking the Unholy Alliance Between Hunger and Poverty in India: Generating Synergy Between the State, Civil Society and the Market," Invited paper prepared for *the 88th Indian Science Congress.*

—— and E. Wilson (2000b), "Challenge of Child Labour in Rural India: A Multi Dimensional Problem in Need of an Orchestrated Policy Response," Prepared for Australian Centre for International Agricultural Research Project, *Equity Driven Trade and Marketing Strategies for Improved Performance of Indian Agriculture: A Scoping Exercise.* Project Number ANRE 1/98/91, Department of Economics Working Paper No 6, University of Wollongong, Australia.

—— and E. Wilson, (2001a), "Agricultural Growth, Employment and Poverty: Theoretical and Empirical Explorations with Indian Data (1967-1998)", in Acharya S.S. and D.P. Chaudhri (eds.), *Indian Agricultural Policy at the Crossroads: Priorities and Agenda,* Rawat Publications, Jaipur (in press).

—— and E. Wilson (2001b), "Rural Poverty, Government Response and Agricultural Growth in India (1970-1993)", Paper presented at the *Australian Agricultural and Resource Economics Society,* 45th Annual Conference, Adelaide.

—— (1994), *Nutrition, Health and Education for All,* United Nations Development Programme, New York.

Levinger, B. (1977), *A Conceptual Model to Improve Educational Delivery Systems to Rural Children in Developing Nations: Colombia as a Case Study.* Ph.D. dissertation, The University of Alabama.

——(1996), *Critical Transitions: Human Capacity Development Across the Lifespan,* US Agency for International Development, Washington DC.

Manna, M. (1998), "Factors Affecting Fertility Decline and Fertility Variation in 1990s : An Inter-State Analysis", *Economic and Political Weekly,* December 19, p. 3283.

MDMP (1996), *Improved Mid Day Meal Programme (MDMP),* Gujarat, India, http://www.ceid.ox.ac.uk/child/MDMP.htm.

Mehta, J. and S. Venkatraman (2000), "Poverty Statistics: Bermicide's Feast", *Economic and Political Weekly,* July 1.

Mishra, L. (2000), *Child Labour in India,* Oxford University Press, New Delhi.

NSSO (1997), *Household Consumer Expenditure and Employment Situation in India,* Department of Statistics, Government of India, New Delhi.

—— (1997), *Sarvekshana Analytical Report,* Vol. 20, Nos. 2 and 3, 70th Issue, January-March, Department of Statistics, Government of India, New Delhi.

—— (1997), *Sarvekshana Analytical Report,* Vol. 21, No. 2, 73rd Issue, October-December, Department of Statistics, Government of India, New Delhi.

PROBE Team (1999), *Public Report on Basic Education in India,* Oxford University Press, New Delhi.

Radhakrishna, R., S. Indrakant and C. Ravi (1998), *India's Integrated Child Development Services Program Assessment and Options for Reform,* Centre for Economic and Social Studies, Hyderabad, September, p. 54

Ravallion, M. (1998a), *Poverty Lines in Theory and Practice,* Living Standards Measurement Study Working Paper, No. 133, World Bank, Washington DC.

—— (1998b), *Poverty Comparisons: A Guide to Concepts and Methods,* Living Standards Measurement Study Working Paper No. 88, World Bank, Washington DC.

Suryanarayana M.H. (2000), "How Real is the Secular Decline in Rural Poverty?", *Economic and Political Weekly,* June 17, p. 2129-2140.

UNDP (1999), *State of the Worlds Children,* UNICEF and Oxford University Press, New York

Visaria, P. (1999), *Youth Unemployment in India,* A Report prepared for the ILO, New Delhi.

7

Household Food Security and Activity Status of Children in Rural India: Some Dimensions and Correlates

ANIL GUMBER AND D.B. GUPTA

I. INTRODUCTION

Since the dawn of Independence, India has made considerable progress in the production of foodgrains and provision of food security to the growing population. The per capita food availability has increased from 395 gm per day to 511 gm during 1951-91 with an annual growth rate of 0.28 per cent. The rise in the level of food availability, no doubt, has enhanced the nutritional level of the Indian people and to some extent led to the progressive decline in mortality rate, particularly since 1980. However, the effect of growth has not been uniform across states and population groups. Even today two-fifths of the country's population continues to live in poverty and/or is hardly able to afford minimum level of daily food requirements and other basic needs. The available literature suggests a strong inverse relationship between food security and various parameters of well-being. Further, food insecurity affects children and women much more than men. Several studies have pointed out that the levels of malnutrition and morbidity among children, especially among pre-school children, are higher among the food insecure households compared to the food secure ones.[1] The child's growth and development continues to remain subdued in food-insecure environment.

This paper primarily focuses on various dimensions of household food security and their likely effect on the activity status of children. As the older children (aged five years and above) are involved in diverse activities, defined in terms of economic and social needs, the paper exclusively emphasises on their activities under different food security environments.

It is based on large-scale household survey data collected by NCAER in 1994, covering more than 33000 rural households from all major states of the country except Jammu & Kashmir.[2] A multiple-topic questionnaire was canvassed amongst the sampled households to elicit information on various human development indicators (including income, expenditure, assets, food security, employment, education, health, etc.).

At the outset, an attempt is made to present the current food consumption and nutrition scenario from both published and unpublished data sources. Later, a detailed exercise is undertaken on the basis of NCAER-HDI survey data to explore various dimensions of food security and their association with the activity status of children. Select indicators are based on income and their sources, food consumption both in terms of physical quantity and nutrition intake and expenditure on foodgrains and other food items are considered to measure the level of household food security. We have also tried to explore one critical indicator for defining the level of household food security—that is the quantity of and consumption expenditure on fats and edible oil incurred by the household members. It is mostly, the low-income rural households who purchase edible oil more frequently and some times on a daily basis, from the market to meet their day-to-day requirements. The other important measurement aspect of this indicator is that this tends to be affected least by reporting bias, recall problems and seasonality. Also, this indicator would reflect on their purchasing power as well as vulnerability.

II. DIMENSIONS OF FOOD SECURITY

1. Pattern of Food Consumption

In the survey, detailed information regarding food consumption on various items both home produced and purchased from the market, including a ration shop, were collected for a reference period of one month prior to the date of survey. The data were collected between January to June 1994. The seasonal variations may not be important in estimating the consumption needs and actual consumption of food grains.

For rural India as a whole, the per capita consumption of foodgrains averaged around 14 kg. per month, which corresponds to 467 grams per day (Table 1A). This estimate is marginally less than the norms for intakes set by nutritionists for the rural population. Those, whose food intake is below this average, are perhaps, consuming less than the nutritional requirements. There are some variations across states—it is only around 10 kg in Kerala and Gujarat compared to an average consumption of more than 17 kg. per person per month in Himachal Pradesh and Rajasthan. A part of this variation is explained by the difference in food habits. In Kerala, for example, the consumption of cereal substitutes such as Tapioca and non-cereal items such as nuts, fruits and vegetables are considered to provide substantial nutrition. Similarly, in Gujarat food habits favour greater use of edible oils, fruits and vegetables which explains the relatively low cereal consumption among people in the state. The climatic extremes and lack of cereal substitute in Rajasthan and Himachal Pradesh may account for the higher level of foodgrain consumption in these states.

Consumption of foodgrains per capita vary only marginally according to population groups. The consumption levels are lower for landless labourers and those living in the lower segment below the poverty line, and in larger households. The lower levels of consumption among all these groups appear to be due to lack of purchasing capacity or lack of resources. The consumption of cereals is also low among the STs and Christians, which is more likely to be due to geographic and cultural reasons. Most of the Christians belong to Kerala, which has recorded lower levels of consumption of foodgrains (Table 2A). The lower intake of cereals by STs is attributed to the fact that they live in remote, probably hilly and forest areas, thus reducing their access to foodgrains. The food items consumed by STs may also contain smaller amounts of foodgrains and larger amounts of nuts, roots, leaves, fruits and so on, which are available from the common property resources.

2. Level of Food Intake

Overall, the average food intake per consumption unit per day for rural population, estimated by the National Institute of Nutrition (NIN), Hyderabad, was found to be adequate in respect of cereals but marginally deficient in pulses compared to the recommended dietary allowances (RDA). However, the consumption of other foodstuffs such as milk and milk products, fats and oils, and sugar was inadequate (Table 1).

Table 1

Average Food Consumption in Rural India during Mid-1990s (in g/cu/day)

Food stuff	RDA	DNP (rural 18 states & UTs)	NNMB (rural eight states)	NCAER (rural 16 major states)
Cereal	460	488	464	582
Pulses	40	32	33	30
Vegetables	150	201	102	139
Fruits		15	22	3
Flesh food		22	14	15
Milk and milk products	150	126	95	153
Fats and oils	20	14	13	19
Sugar	30	20	23	43

Note: DNP- District Nutrition Profile; NNMB - National Nutrition Monitoring Bureau of National Institute of Nutrition, Hyderabad.

Source: India Nutrition Profile (1998), Department of Women & Child Development, MOHRD, GOI; NCAER-HDI Survey, 1994.

The NCAER survey, which elicited information on the consumption of various food items during the reference month through recall, provides a fairly optimistic scenario of cereal consumption. Unlike NIN estimates, where dietary measures were used to caliber and record the daily food consumption of the individuals, the NCAER survey relied mainly on the production and consumption of food items at the household level. The consumption of vegetables, milk and milk products, fats and oils estimated from the NCAER data are very close to RDA.

According to the NCAER data, there are wide inter-state differentials in food consumption (Table 3A). Consumption of cereals was found to be higher in Rajasthan, Himachal and Orissa and lower in Kerala, Gujarat and the Northeast region, than the country's average consumption. The consumption of pulses was significantly (more than 50 per cent) higher in Himachal Pradesh and Punjab and lower in Kerala and Orissa. The Northern states (Punjab and Himachal Pradesh) have also reported higher consumption of *gur* and sugar, milk and milk products, and *ghee* and edible oils. On the contrary, people in Kerala, Tamil Nadu, West Bengal, Northeast region and Orissa have reported higher consumption of flesh food. This is due to fact that people in these states consume fish almost on a daily basis and "rice and fish" is a very common meal. Overall, the level of food consumption in Punjab, Himachal Pradesh, Rajasthan and Haryana was higher than the national average, whereas it was lower in Madhya Pradesh, Kerala, Tamil Nadu and Bihar.

3. Expenditure on Foodgrains and Other Food and Non-food Items

In the NCAER-HDI survey, disaggregated information on household expenditures on various types of day-to-day needs for a living was collected. Information on expenditures on foodgrains and other food items, as also on health care of all household members and children's education were separately collected in the survey. However, expenditures on other non-food items, including that on purchase of household assets, information on which would have provided complete information on household expenditure was not collected. In this discussion, however, the proportion of expenditure on these items (excluding expenditure on health and education) available from NSS 44th round for the year 1988-89 is used for adjusting the estimates. Complete information regarding the distribution of per capita expenditure per month on foodgrains, other food items, health care, children's education and other non-food items is discussed below.

Tables 4A and 5A present the estimated total expenditure per capita per month in current prices. The mean monthly per capita household expenditure (MPCE) for rural India has worked out to be Rs. 287, and ranges from a high of Rs. 554 in Punjab to a low of Rs. 208 in Madhya Pradesh and Rs. 210 in Orissa. The actual expenditure in rupees on foodgrains, other food items, health, education and other non-food items are Rs. 87.5, Rs. 96.8, Rs. 21.3, Rs. 9.0 and Rs. 73.5, respectively. In percentage terms, these corresponding figures are 30.6, 33.4, 7.4, 3.1 and 26.6 of the total expenditure, respectively for rural India.

The expenditure on foodgrains alone is about 31 per cent, but this proportion is low in Haryana, Punjab and Rajasthan. On the other hand, expenditure on this item in Bihar and Orissa is as high as 43.3 per cent and 42.7 per cent, respectively. But for Rajasthan these proportions are in the expected direction. It is normally expected that the proportion of expenditure on basic food items will be relatively high in areas and population groups with low levels of income.

III. ACTIVITY STATUS OF CHILDREN

Table 2 presents the distribution of population aged five and above by broad usual activity status. The proportion of children reporting for work in the age group, 5-9 was found to be negligible whereas it was around 8 per cent among children aged 10-14. This fact conforms to published information in both the Census and National Sample Survey pertaining to the early 1990s.

Table 2
Distribution of Population Aged Five and Above in Rural India by Broad Usual Activity Status, 1994

(Per 1000 persons)

Broad activity status	5-9	10-14	15-19	20-24	25-29	30-34	35+	All 5+	15-24	All 15+	All-ages
Male											
Worker	8	82	409	746	925	973	913	594	562	818	524
Unemployed	N	16	79	99	43	14	4	27	88	34	23
Student	599	749	460	132	17	2	N	261	311	94	231
Others	392	153	53	23	15	11	83	119	39	54	222
Female											
Worker	10	91	294	376	419	447	408	295	335	393	259
Unemployed	N	7	24	16	7	1	1	6	20	7	5
Student	507	597	247	34	2	2	1	185	141	41	164
Others	482	305	436	574	571	551	590	513	505	559	571
Person											
Worker	9	86	358	565	669	714	676	453	456	616	398
Unemployed	N	12	54	59	25	8	3	17	56	21	15
Student	556	678	365	84	10	2	1	225	232	68	199
Others	435	224	223	292	297	276	321	305	256	294	388

Note: N - Negligible.
Source: Computed from NCAER-HDI Survey Data, 1994.

A comprehensive review of the impact of reforms on employment attempted by Shariff and Gumber (1999) suggests: "One of the positive features of the growth in employment over time is a definite decline in the participation of children aged 5 to 14 years in the workforce". The total number of child workers which was 21.5 million in 1983 declined to 17 million in 1988 and to 13 million in 1994. Compared with adult participation rates, where male-female ratio is 3:1 the participation rate among male and female children is the same, suggesting a disproportionate increase in the participation of female children in the female labour market. Further around 90 per cent of the child labour during all periods come from the rural areas, although this proportion has declined over the period. The proportion of child labour has declined at the rate of 5.1 per cent during 1983-88 and 4.1 per cent in the post-reform period (1988-94).

One fall out of a decline in child labour is the substitution effect, which favours the employment of adult females in the economy. For example, the adult female work participation rate (WPR) increased from 32.3 to 34.9 during 1988 to 1994, while the over-all rates remained stagnant at about 28 per cent (Table 3). The increase in the rural female WPRs has been substantial, i.e., from 39.9 to 46.7

per cent. Thus, even a stable female WPR over the period actually indicates an increase in the WPR of adult females.

Table 3

Child Labour in India by Sex and Residence according to NSS Rounds

Round/Reference/	Person			Male			Female		
Date	Rural	Urban	All	Rural	Urban	All	Rural	Urban	All
Child workers (in millions)									
38 July 1, 1983	19.36	2.09	21.45	10.69	1.37	12.06	8.67	0.72	9.49
43 Jan. 1, 1988	14.75	1.86	16.94	8.56	1.11	9.51	6.98	0.75	7.43
50 Jan. 1, 1994	11.51	1.67	13.18	6.19	1.04	7.24	5.32	0.62	5.94
Growth rate of child workers									
1983 to 1988	-5.86	-2.56	-5.11	-4.81	-4.58	-5.14	-4.72	0.85	-5.29
1988 to 1994	-4.05	-1.78	-4.1	-5.26	-1.05	-4.44	-4.42	-2.97	-3.66
Work participation rate of children									
38 July 1, 1983	13	4.9	11.2	13.5	6.1	11.9	12.5	3.6	10.6
	(56.4)	(43.5)	(47.6)	(70.9)	(65.9)	(69.6)	(41.6)	(18.1)	(36.1)
43 Jan. 1, 1988	9.9	3.9	8.3	10.2	4.5	8.8	9.7	3.4	7.9
	(55.5)	(43.3)	(52.4)	(70.4)	(65.1)	(69.0)	(39.9)	(18.9)	(32.3)
50 Jan. 1, 1994	7.2	3.5	6.2	7.2	3.7	6.4	7.1	2.5	6
	(56.3)	(43.5)	(53.0)	(71.5)	(66.2)	(70.0)	(46.7)	(19.1)	(34.9)

Note: Figures in parenthesis refer to work participation rate for population aged 15 years and above.

IV. RELATIONSHIP BETWEEN HOUSEHOLD FOOD SECURITY AND ACTIVITY STATUS OF CHILDREN

As discussed earlier, three types of household insecurity indicators-in terms of food, nutrition and income-are identified and analysed by relating them to the activity status of children.

In the analysis we have used a number of food security parameters. Apart from per capita monthly expenditures (in money terms) on foodgrains, fats and edible oils, and all food items we have considered the first two parameters in quantity terms, too. For activity status, we have classified children aged 6-14 years into workers, unemployed, students and others. Further, these have been classified according to their gender.

In the NCAER survey, 5.2 per cent of rural children aged 6-14, were classified as workers; the incidence of child workers was marginally higher among girls (5.5 per cent) than among boys (4.9 per cent). However, the gender differentials were more pronounced among children attending schools. The proportion of students among rural boys was as high as 73 per cent as compared to only 60 per cent in the case of girls (Figure 1) and the gender differential was reversed in the case of children who were neither studying nor participating in the labour force, thus categorised as 'others'.

One of the important factors influencing activity status of children and associated gender differentials is the economic status of the household usually measured in terms of income. Figure 2 shows the activity status of children across

Figure 1
Children Aged 6-14 Years by Activity Status

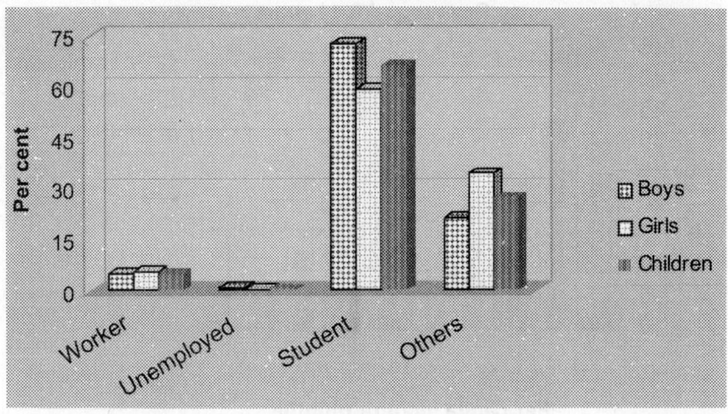

Figure 2
Activity Status of Children (Aged 6-14 Years by Per Capita Income Quintile)

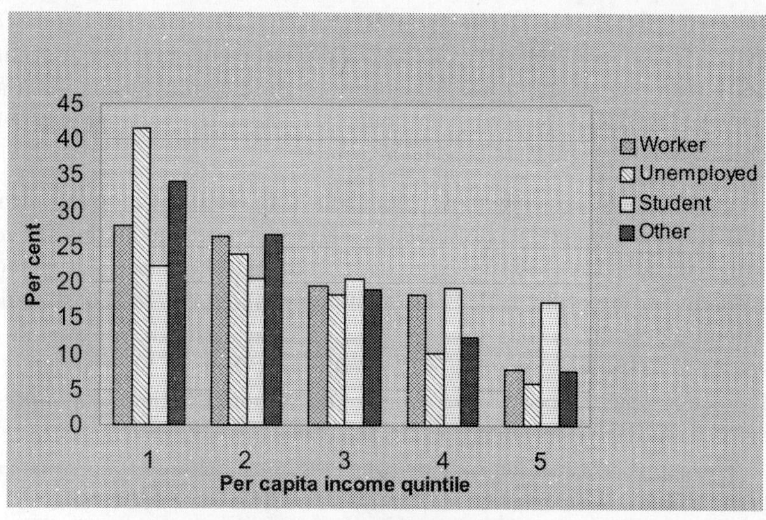

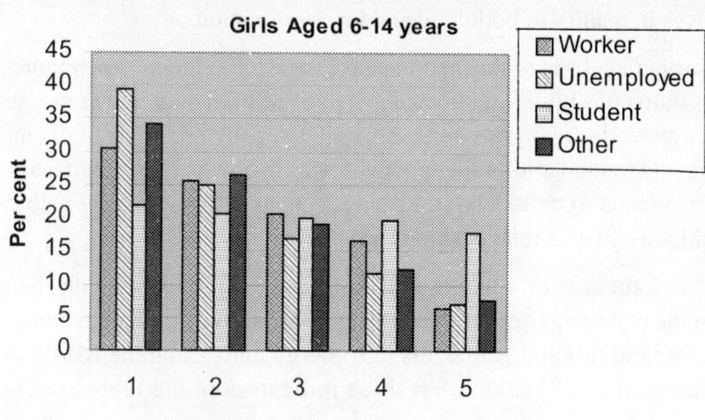

(Figure 2 contd.)

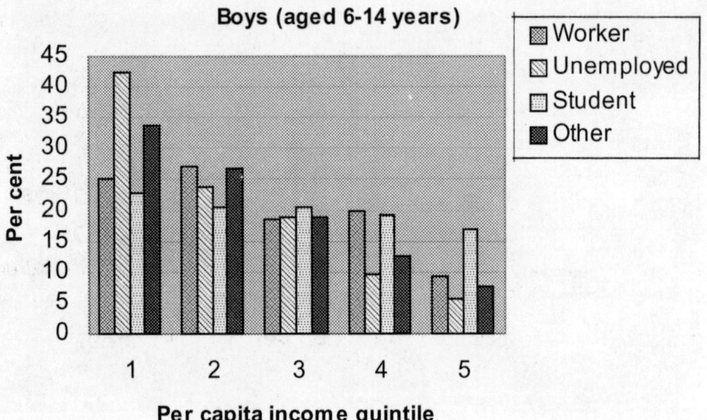

quintiles of households based on per capita income. Interestingly, the student-population ratios across income quintiles remained the same (i.e., number of students are fairly distributed), whereas the proportion of child labour declined steadily with income quintiles. A majority of child workers as well as those unemployed were concentrated in the bottom two quintiles. A similar pattern had emerged when we segregated the data by gender.

In terms of the association of child labour with food, nutrition and income security indicators, the data presented in Table 4, shows that all the five food security indicators have been disaggregated according to the households quintiles. The salient feature of the table is the monotonic increase in the consumption/expenditure over the various quintiles. Also, in value terms, the top quintile has about three times the expenditure on food grains than the bottom one. This difference is very sharp when we compare the bottom and the top quintiles in terms of the monthly expenditure on fats and edible oils. The ratio comes to about 1:10. The gap is however not so wide, when the consumption of foodgrains and 'fats and edible oil' is compared in quantity terms. This is easily explained by the differences in quality of both food and fat consumption.

A further analysis of the relationship between foodgrain expenditure and the activity status of children indicated a U-type relationship. However, when we consider expenditure on fats and edible oil a negative relationship is indicated, which is understandable as the most vulnerable households will usually report higher incidence of child labour. Further, gender differentials show that for the girl-child, this inverse relationship is less sharp.

Table 5 focuses on relating nutrition security indicators with the activity status of the children. The nutrition indicators are derived from converting various food items, and fats and edible oils into energy units using the ICMR yardstick (Gopalan et al., 1971). The first three indicators in the table are classified

Table 4
Usual Activity Status of Children Aged 6-14 Years by Household Food Security Indicators, Rural India, 1994

Expenditure indicators		Mean value	Children				Boys				Girls			
			Worker	Unemployed	Student	Others	Worker	Unemployed	Student	Others	Worker	Unemployed	Student	Others
Per capita monthly expenditure on foodgrains — quintile (Rs.)	1	47.4	5.6	0.7	63.8	29.9	5.1	0.9	69.7	24.3	6.2	0.5	57.5	35.8
	2	67.6	3.9	0.5	65.2	30.4	4.0	0.7	71.3	24.0	3.8	0.3	58.2	37.8
	3	83.2	4.7	0.6	66.9	27.8	4.5	0.6	73.0	21.9	4.9	0.6	59.9	34.6
	4	101.7	5.3	0.7	68.9	25.1	4.9	1.1	75.2	18.8	5.8	0.3	61.6	32.3
	5	144.5	6.8	1.0	69.8	22.4	6.5	1.4	76.4	15.7	7.1	0.5	62.2	30.2
		88.8	5.2	0.7	66.6	27.6	4.9	0.9	72.8	21.4	5.5	0.4	59.6	34.5
Per capita monthly expenditure on fats and edible oil — quintile (Rs.)	1	4.33	5.9	0.7	56.1	37.4	6.2	0.8	63.8	29.2	5.5	0.6	47.5	46.4
	2	8.99	5.9	0.8	62.6	30.7	5.4	1.3	68.7	24.7	6.6	0.2	55.9	37.3
	3	13.08	5.3	0.7	69.2	24.9	5.0	0.9	74.6	19.6	5.6	0.4	63.2	30.8
	4	18.23	4.7	0.6	74.2	20.6	3.8	0.7	79.4	16.1	5.7	0.4	67.8	26.0
	5	40.92	3.3	0.5	78.7	17.5	3.2	0.8	84.0	12.0	3.3	0.3	72.4	24.0
		16.93	5.2	0.7	66.6	27.6	4.9	0.9	72.8	21.4	5.5	0.4	59.6	34.5
Per capita monthly expenditure on all food items — quintile (Rs.)	1	93.1	6.4	0.8	55.5	37.3	6.1	1.0	62.1	30.8	6.8	0.5	48.3	44.4
	2	131.7	4.9	0.6	63.4	31.1	4.5	0.7	69.9	24.9	5.4	0.4	56.5	37.6
	3	162.6	5.2	0.6	68.5	25.7	4.9	0.9	74.7	19.5	5.6	0.4	61.3	32.7
	4	202.9	4.7	0.7	74.0	20.7	4.6	1.1	80.0	14.3	4.9	0.2	66.8	28.1
	5	309.2	3.7	0.6	80.4	15.4	3.7	0.7	84.3	11.2	3.6	0.4	75.3	20.6
		179.8	5.2	0.7	66.6	27.6	4.9	0.9	72.8	21.4	5.5	0.4	59.6	34.5
Per capita monthly consumption of food-grains — quintile (kg.)	1	8.35	4.3	0.8	69.8	25.1	4.4	1.2	73.8	20.7	4.3	0.4	65.4	30.0
	2	11.46	5.0	0.5	65.3	29.2	4.5	0.6	71.1	23.7	5.5	0.5	59.1	34.9
	3	13.89	4.6	0.6	65.7	29.1	3.9	0.8	72.6	22.7	5.4	0.3	57.8	36.5
	4	16.69	5.5	0.8	66.0	27.8	5.2	1.0	72.5	21.2	5.7	0.5	58.4	35.3
	5	23.23	7.0	0.7	66.0	26.3	7.0	1.0	74.1	18.0	7.0	0.4	56.1	36.5
		14.71	5.2	0.7	66.6	27.6	4.9	0.9	72.8	21.4	5.5	0.4	59.6	34.5
Per capita monthly consumption of fats and edible oil — quintile (gm)	1	176	5.7	0.6	58.8	34.9	5.7	0.8	66.1	27.4	5.6	0.4	50.8	43.2
	2	320	6.0	0.9	63.2	29.8	5.6	1.4	69.7	23.3	6.5	0.4	56.1	37.0
	3	453	5.1	0.6	70.2	24.1	4.6	0.7	75.7	19.1	5.6	0.5	64.0	29.9
	4	583	3.5	0.5	76.4	19.6	3.2	0.7	81.6	14.4	3.8	0.1	69.8	26.2
	5	961	3.7	0.7	79.8	15.8	3.4	0.9	83.8	11.9	4.0	0.4	75.0	20.6
		461	5.2	0.7	66.6	27.6	4.9	0.9	72.8	21.4	5.5	0.4	59.6	34.5

Table 5

Usual Activity Status of Children of Aged 6-14 Years in Rural India by Nutrition Security Indicators, 1994

Nutrition indicators		Mean value	Children				Boys				Girls			
			Worker	Unemployed	Student	Others	Worker	Unemployed	Student	Others	Worker	Unemployed	Student	Others
Per person per day energy intake—quintile (kcal)	1	1264	5.0	0.8	64.6	29.7	4.7	1.1	69.6	24.5	5.2	0.5	59.1	35.1
	2	1685	5.0	0.7	64.8	29.6	4.6	0.8	70.2	24.4	5.4	0.5	58.7	35.4
	3	2010	4.9	0.5	66.0	28.6	4.4	0.7	72.7	22.1	5.4	0.2	58.5	35.9
	4	2398	5.5	0.7	68.3	25.4	5.3	1.0	75.5	18.2	5.9	0.5	59.9	33.7
	5	3340	5.8	0.6	71.5	22.1	6.0	0.8	78.1	15.2	5.5	0.4	63.2	30.9
		2125	5.2	0.7	66.6	27.6	4.9	0.9	72.8	21.4	5.5	0.4	59.6	34.5
Per consumption unit per day energy intake — qunitile (kcal)	1	1592	5.4	0.8	65.2	28.7	5.2	1.1	70.1	23.6	5.6	0.4	59.5	34.4
	2	2112	4.8	0.7	65.0	29.4	4.3	0.9	70.8	24.0	5.5	0.5	58.5	35.6
	3	2505	5.2	0.6	66.1	28.0	4.7	1.0	72.6	21.8	5.8	0.3	58.9	35.0
	4	2994	5.4	0.6	68.6	25.5	5.7	0.7	76.1	17.4	5.0	0.4	60.1	34.5
	5	4226	4.9	0.5	70.9	23.7	4.6	0.5	78.0	16.8	5.3	0.5	62.3	32.0
		2655	5.2	0.7	66.6	27.6	4.9	0.9	72.8	21.4	5.5	0.4	59.6	34.5
Per consumption unit per day food intake— qunitile (gm.)	1	557	5.8	0.9	63.0	30.3	5.5	1.2	68.5	24.7	6.0	0.5	56.8	36.6
	2	756	5.2	0.7	64.6	29.5	4.4	1.0	69.7	24.9	6.0	0.4	58.8	34.8
	3	912	5.7	0.5	66.5	27.3	5.5	0.8	74.0	19.7	5.9	0.3	58.1	35.8
	4	1115	4.8	0.6	69.7	25.0	4.7	0.7	76.3	18.3	4.9	0.4	62.2	32.5
	5	1670	3.4	0.4	74.6	21.6	3.5	0.5	81.2	14.7	3.3	0.2	66.6	29.8
		986	5.2	0.7	66.6	27.6	4.9	0.9	72.8	21.4	5.5	0.4	59.6	34.5
Per person per day energy intake — by kcal groups*	1	1448	5.0	0.8	64.5	29.7	4.8	1.0	69.6	24.6	5.3	0.5	58.9	35.3
	2	1947	4.6	0.4	66.1	28.9	4.0	0.6	72.6	22.8	5.2	0.2	58.9	35.7
	3	2241	5.6	0.9	67.6	25.9	5.0	1.1	75.1	18.9	6.4	0.7	59.0	33.9
	4	3068	5.6	0.6	70.4	23.4	5.9	0.8	77.1	16.2	5.3	0.3	62.0	32.4
		2125	5.2	0.7	66.6	27.6	4.9	0.9	72.8	21.4	5.5	0.4	59.6	34.5
Per consumption unit per day energy intake— by kcal groups*	1	1517	5.2	0.8	64.9	29.0	5.2	1.1	70.0	23.6	5.2	0.5	59.1	35.2
	2	1954	5.2	0.8	65.2	28.9	4.7	0.9	70.0	24.4	5.8	0.6	59.6	34.1
	3	2251	4.6	0.5	65.7	29.2	4.0	0.8	72.0	23.2	5.3	0.2	58.6	35.9
	4	3296	5.4	0.6	68.3	25.7	5.2	0.8	75.5	18.6	5.6	0.4	60.2	33.8
		2655	5.2	0.7	66.6	27.6	4.9	0.9	72.8	21.4	5.5	0.4	59.6	34.5

Note: * kcal groups are: 1 -1 799, 1800 - 2099, 2100 - 2399, and 2400 and above.

according to household quintiles, the last two indicators are classified into four groups according to caloric intake up to 1799, 1800-2099, 2100-2399 and 2400 kcal and above. A perusal of the figures reveals that almost 75-80 per cent of people have a calorie intake below the prescribed norm of 2400 kcal. However, when we adjust for age and sex, then only 50 to 55 per cent of households are below the prescribed norms. In terms of calorie intakes, the other three nutrition levels exhibit similar trends. It should, however, be noted that nearly 25 per cent of the households were not able to afford even 1800 kcal. In contrast to food security indicators where we observed an inverse relationship with child labour, no such relationship is indicated when we consider nutrition security indicators.

Finally, an attempt is made to relate income security indicators with the use of child labour. Table 6 shows the incidence of child labour across per capita income quintiles, household income groups, poverty groups and land holding size groups. Except for the top quintile where the percentage of child workers is distinctly low, the other lower quintiles do not indicate any income effect. The incidence of child labour tends to decline with the size of land holding, except for the 'large' landholding group, which reported the highest incidence of child labour. This may be because the child was involved in the family farm activity.

V. CONCLUDING REMARKS

To sum up the discussion on correlates of child labour, we have presented the strong and mild association of child work with food, nutrition and income security indicators in Table 7. It is clear from the table that all the four indicators relating to fats and edible oils measured in terms of quantity, nominal value, diet intake (gms per consumption unit per day) and energy (kcal) were strongly and negatively related with the incidence of child labour. Also, it was found that the incidence of child labour was higher among wage earning households, particularly those receiving agricultural wages as income.

The exercise undertaken here is exploratory in nature. It has, however, thrown up some major issues for more detailed work, which essentially relate to examining whether the differences in child labour behaviour vary with food, nutrition and income security. Also, consumption (both in quantity and nominal values) of fats and edible oils is indicated to capture better the extent of vulnerability among households. To get clearer insights into these relationships, perhaps a multivariate analysis would be more instructive.

Table 6
Usual Activity Status of Children Aged 6-14 Years by Income Security Indicators, Rural India, 1994

Nutrition indicators		Mean value / Per cent distribution	Children: Worker	Children: Unemployed	Children: Student	Children: Others	Boys: Worker	Boys: Unemployed	Boys: Student	Boys: Others	Girls: Worker	Girls: Unemployed	Girls: Student	Girls: Others
Per capita annual income—quintile	1	1207	5.6	1.1	57.2	36.2	4.9	1.5	65.1	28.5	6.3	0.6	48.7	44.4
	2	2236	6.0	0.7	60.7	32.5	5.9	1.0	67.3	25.8	6.1	0.4	53.5	40.0
	3	3335	5.1	0.6	68.0	26.4	4.5	0.8	74.5	20.1	5.7	0.3	60.4	33.5
	4	5052	5.4	0.4	74.5	19.7	5.5	0.5	78.9	15.1	5.4	0.3	69.2	25.1
	5	12396	2.9	0.3	81.8	15.1	3.1	0.3	85.0	11.5	2.6	0.2	77.9	19.4
	All	4846	5.2	0.7	66.6	27.6	4.9	0.9	72.8	21.4	5.5	0.4	59.6	34.5
Annual household income groups	1-20	57.6	6.2	0.8	60.2	32.8	5.8	1.1	67.4	25.7	6.7	0.5	52.1	40.7
	21-40	26.8	4.9	0.6	70.3	24.1	4.7	0.8	75.9	18.6	5.2	0.4	64.0	30.5
	41-61	8.9	3.1	0.4	77.0	19.4	3.2	0.5	81.9	14.4	3.1	0.3	71.1	25.5
	62-85	3.3	2.3	0.2	80.6	17.0	2.5	0.3	84.7	12.5	2.1		75.7	22.2
	86+	3.4	1.3	0.2	85.8	12.7	1.4	0.3	88.5	9.8	1.3	0.1	83.2	15.5
	All	100.0	5.2	0.7	66.6	27.6	4.9	0.9	72.8	21.4	5.5	0.4	59.6	34.5
Poverty groups														
BPL- Lowest	1	15.9	5.5	1.0	57.1	36.4	4.9	1.5	64.9	28.7	6.2	0.5	48.8	44.5
BPL-Upper	2	18.8	5.4	0.9	59.3	34.4	5.2	1.1	65.8	27.9	5.6	0.6	51.9	41.9
APL-Lowest	3	43.8	5.7	0.5	70.3	23.5	5.4	0.7	76.2	17.7	6.0	0.3	63.4	30.3
APL-Upper	4	21.6	2.9	0.4	80.2	16.5	3.2	0.5	83.5	12.8	2.6	0.3	76.3	20.8
	All	100.0	5.2	0.7	66.6	27.6	4.9	0.9	72.8	21.4	5.5	0.4	59.6	34.5
Landholding grp.														
Landless — wage	1	31.4	4.9	0.7	66.6	27.8	5.0	0.8	73.6	20.7	4.9	0.5	58.9	35.7
Landless — other	2	17.2	4.1	0.9	71.2	23.8	3.9	1.2	75.0	19.9	4.5	0.5	66.9	28.1
Marginal	3	18.1	4.1	0.3	69.6	25.9	4.2	0.5	75.3	20.0	3.9	0.2	62.8	33.1
Small	4	8.8	3.3	0.4	71.2	25.2	2.9	0.5	78.3	18.2	3.7	0.2	63.3	32.9
Medium	5	5.0	3.2	0.3	74.0	22.5	3.1	0.4	80.0	16.5	3.3	0.2	67.5	29.0
Large	6	19.4	9.6	1.2	53.4	35.8	8.3	1.6	60.7	29.4	11.2	0.6	45.0	43.2
	All	100.0	5.2	0.7	66.6	27.6	4.9	0.9	72.8	21.4	5.5	0.4	59.6	34.5

Table 7
Significant Association of Child Work with Food, Nutrition and Income Security Indicators

Indicators	Type of association	Child work all (aged 6-14)	Child work boys	Child work girls
I. Food Security Indicators				
PC Value of foodgrains	None	-	-	-
PC Value of fats and edible oils	Negative	S	M	S
PC Value of total food	Negative	S	S	S
PC Quantity of foodgrains	Positive	M	M	M
PC Quantity of fats and edible oils	Negative	S	M	M
II. Nutrition Security Indicators				
PC kcal from foodgrains	Positive	M	M	M
PC kcal from fats and edible oils	Negative	S	M	M
PC kcal from total food	None	-	-	-
Adult equivalent kcal from total food	Negative	M	M	NS
GCUD cereals	Positive	NS	M	M
GCUD pulses	Negative	M	M	NS
GCUD Gur and Sugar	Negative	S	M	S
GCUD Milk and its products	Negative	S	S	S
GCUD Fats and edible oils	Negative	S	M	S
GCUD Flesh food	None	-	-	-
GCUD Vegetables	Negative	S	M	S
GCUD Fruits	None	-	-	-
GCUD Meals taken outside home	None	-	-	-
GCUD All food items	Negative	S	S	S
III. Income Security Indicators				
Household size	Negative	NS	M	M
Household annual income	Negative	S	S	S
Per capita annual income	Negative	S	M	S
Agricultural income	Negative	S	S	S
Agricultural wage income	Positive	S	S	S
Non-agricultural wage income	Positive	S	M	-
Draft animals	None	-	-	-
Milch animals	None	-	-	-
Productive assets (scores)	Negative	S	S	S
Durable assets (scores)	Negative	S	S	S
Gross cropped area	Negative	S	S	S
Gross irrigated area	Negative	S	S	S
Number of sampled household with child aged 6-14		20528	15043	13580

Note: PC - per capita, GCUD - gram per consumption unit per day, S: strong, M: mild, NS: not significant.

Appendix

Table 1A
Consumption of Foodgrains and Utilisation of PDS in States

Regions/States	Household income (Rs. per year)	Per capita income (Rs. per year)	Per capita consumption of foodgrain (kg/month)	Per cent of households using PDS	Quantity of cereals (kg.) bought from PDS (per household/ month)	Percentage requirement of cereals met from PDS
North						
Haryana	39956	6368	12.8	9.0	18.1	32.4
Himachal Pradesh	23973	4168	17.4	75.6	43.8	41.4
Punjab	37418	6380	14.3	5.6	23.4	5.5
Upper Central						
Bihar	22459	3691	14.8	5.0	49.5	29.2
Uttar Pradesh	26733	4185	15.2	5.2	33.4	24.5
Lower Central						
Madhya Pradesh	25319	4166	13.5	34.2	15.7	20.4
Orissa	17208	3028	16.4	5.2	18.6	16.7
Rajasthan	27184	4229	17.6	23.6	33.1	14.7
East						
North-Eastern Rg	28160	5070	12.5	21.7	20.5	31.9
West Bengal	18113	3157	16.3	11.3	38.4	45.6
West						
Gujarat	29356	5288	10.1	47.6	17.3	18.1
Maharashtra	29929	5525	13.2	50.7	13.8	13.2
South						
Andhra Pradesh	24776	5046	14.3	66.4	18.6	30.6
Karnataka	27372	4769	15.1	70.1	15.0	22.8
Kerala	29101	5778	9.8	78.0	23.7	51.9
Tamil Nadu	23271	5122	12.6	82.4	12.0	21.6
Rural India	25653	4485	14.3	33.2	19.0	23.5
C.V.	21.25	20.7	15.66	78.24	44.87	45.84

Source: NCAER/HDI Survey, 1994.

Table 2A
Consumption of Foodgrains and Utilisation of PDS by Population Groups, Rural India

Population groups	Average household income	Per capita income	Per capita consumpt. foodgrain	Percentage of household using PDS	Average cereals from PDS	Percentage requirement from PDS
Household Income Groups						
Up to 20000	11027	2192	14.2	34.3	19	26.3
20001-40000	28141	4506	14.3	32.4	19	22
40001-62000	49072	7132	14.4	31.9	19.8	20.5
62001-86000	72178	9309	14.6	28.1	18.7	16.4
Above 86000	147855	17865	14.7	28	17.6	13
Poverty Line Groups						
Lower segment below	6950	1095	13.7	30.1	23	26.3
Upper segment below	12379	2026	14.1	29.5	19.7	22.7
Lower segment above	22138	3931	14.2	37.1	18.7	23.9
Upper segment above	58100	11396	15.4	30.6	16.6	21
Landholding Groups						
A. Landless wage earner	11313	2308	13.5	44.3	17.5	25.8
Marginal	19586	3502	14.4	31.4	21.1	28
Small	29377	4803	14.7	27	17.1	18.7
Medium	44695	6516	15	25.7	17.3	14.7
Large	85969	10930	15.1	29.7	20.1	13.6
Landless others	21574	4111	13.6	35.2	19.8	28.1
B. Land owners	31154	5108	14.7	29.2	19.5	21.5
Landless	16141	3187	13.6	40	18.4	26.8
Occupation Groups						
Cultivators	32374	5408	14.8	28	18.3	19.5
Salaried+Self-employed	35760	5857	14	33.8	23	28.3
Wage earners	12580	2450	13.8	43	18.3	26
All others	21010	3709	13.9	30.3	19.1	25.9
Social Groups						
Caste						
STs	19556	3504	13.7	37.5	21.6	25.7
SCs	17465	3237	14.4	32.1	17.3	22.5
Other Hindus	29786	5113	14.5	34.2	18.4	22.5
Religion						
Hindus	25712	4514	14.4	34.1	18.6	22.9
Muslims	22807	3678	14	21.8	23.6	28.8
Christians	28860	5920	12.5	66.1	22	38.3
Other minorities	30330	5427	13.8	15.7	18.1	11.4
Household Size Group						
Up to 4	18399	5687	15.5	37.9	16.7	31.1
5-7	25060	4326	14.2	33	19.3	23
8 and above	40449	4019	13.8	24.9	24.9	16.8
Adult Literacy Group						
None literate	15271	3138	14.5	29	18.1	23.6
Female literate	19060	3987	13.7	50.7	16.3	27.2
Male literate	24367	4137	14.7	29.9	18.2	20.4
Both literate	36187	5683	13.9	38.2	20.6	25.6
Village Development Groups						
Low	24149	4045	14.9	18	22.2	20.8
Medium	25173	4369	14.5	33.4	20.2	24.6
High	27628	5079	13.5	46.8	16.8	23.8
All-groups	25653	4485	14.3	33.2	19	23.5

Source: NCAER/HDI Survey, 1994.

Table 3A

Diet Intake Across States and Recommended Dietary Allowance for Rural India, 1994

(in gm/ consumption unit per day)

State	Cereals	Pulses	*Gur* and sugar	Milk and milk products	Fats and edible oils	Flesh foods	Vegetables	Fruits	Meals taken outside home	Total
Andhra Pradesh	582.9	24.0	29.8	140.7	20.1	17.0	129.3	3.6	1.5	948.8
Bihar	599.4	27.1	20.5	72.9	15.9	10.0	124.5	2.4	0.4	873.0
Gujarat	417.9	33.3	65.6	212.6	37.3	3.3	138.8	0.1	2.0	910.9
Haryana	519.0	22.7	83.6	493.5	18.9	2.3	100.1	0.6	0.2	1241.0
Himachal Pradesh	685.3	58.2	75.7	424.0	31.3	8.8	142.7	5.2	10.1	1441.3
Karnataka	603.9	35.5	59.1	109.7	17.7	15.8	80.6	16.2	1.1	939.7
Kerala	410.0	17.0	37.9	140.8	17.1	47.7	159.8	1.0	10.6	841.8
Maharashtra	552.3	32.4	55.2	106.9	19.3	9.6	108.8	3.3	0.1	888.0
Madhya Pradesh	556.7	35.5	34.7	97.0	17.2	4.6	90.2	0.6	1.0	837.5
Orissa	681.3	20.4	20.2	30.2	12.2	18.9	137.7	0.7	2.1	923.7
Punjab	554.8	51.8	150.4	592.9	30.8	6.7	218.1	2.5	2.4	1610.3
Rajasthan	744.1	22.5	57.7	416.9	20.7	6.3	115.5	3.9	0.4	1387.9
Tamil Nadu	526.9	26.1	34.5	97.5	18.8	20.1	141.8	0.8	2.0	868.5
Uttar Pradesh	616.7	40.5	49.8	201.4	17.7	8.4	155.2	3.8	0.4	1093.9
West Bengal	657.2	22.4	31.2	40.6	19.6	31.3	218.5	0.8	1.0	1022.6
Northeast region	499.2	24.8	29.2	96.2	19.3	36.1	176.5	1.2	1.4	883.9
Rural India	582.2	30.0	43.3	153.3	19.3	14.9	138.6	2.9	1.4	985.9
RDA	460	40	30	150	20		150			850

Table 4A
Estimated Per Capita Expenditure Per Month for Rural India

(In Rs.)

Region/ State	Food expenditure Foodgrains	Other food	Total food	Non-food Health	Education	Other non-food	Total non-food	Total expenditure	CPI 1993-94 (BASE 1960-61) = 100
North									
Haryana	58.9	152	210.5	20.3	17	101.5	138.8	349.3	939
Himachal Pradesh	111.5	153.9	265.4	38.5	30.9	105.6	175	440.4	1173
Punjab	87.7	232.6	320.3	32.4	17.5	184.3	234.2	554.5	1258
Upper Central									
Bihar	94.4	57.2	151.6	22.2	7.4	36.9	66.5	218.1	1183
Uttar Pradesh	90.3	102.2	192.5	20.2	8.4	84.8	113.4	305.9	1250
Lower Central									
Madhya Pradesh	71.9	56.7	128.6	20.1	4.9	54.4	79.4	208	1133
Orissa	89.6	55.6	145.2	12.4	6.3	46.7	65.4	210.6	1118
Rajasthan	80.7	162.8	243.5	27.5	10.2	129.1	166.8	410.3	1170
East									
Northeastern Region	102.3	84.4	186.7	16.5	11.8	45.3	73.6	260.3	
West Bengal	111.3	90.1	201.4	24.2	8.2	52.1	84.5	285.9	1074
West									
Gujarat	69.2	122.3	191.5	15.4	8.4	75.8	99.6	291.1	1012
Maharashtra	64.5	82.4	146.9	18	7.8	67.7	93.5	240.4	1033
South									
Andhra Pradesh	91.3	93.9	185.2	29	7.2	91.4	127.6	312.8	939
Karnataka	87	88.3	175.3	21.3*	9.9	76.5	60.8	236.1	1093
Kerala	75.1	132.6	207.7	21.7	17.8	87	126.5	334.2	1274
Tamil Nadu	99.9	101.4	201.3	31.2	8.1	69.6	108.9	310.2	1039
Rural India	87.5	95.8	183.3	21.3	9	73.5	103.8	287.1	1114

Note: * The figures are the same as the national average.
Source: NCAER/HDI survey, 1994.

Table 5A
Estimated Per Capita Expenditure as a Percentage of Total Expenditure for Rural India

Region/ State	Food expenditure			Non-food and CPI 1993-94				
	Food-grains	Other food	Total food	Health	Education	Other non-food	Total Non-food	Total expenditure
North								
Haryana	16.9	43.3	60.2	5.9	4.9	29.0	39.8	100.0
Himachal Pradesh	25.3	35.0	60.3	8.7	7.0	24.3	39.7	100.0
Punjab	15.8	41.9	57.8	5.8	3.2	33.2	42.2	100.0
Upper Central								
Bihar	43.3	26.2	69.5	10.2	3.4	16.9	30.5	100.0
Uttar Pradesh	29.5	33.4	62.9	6.6	2.7	2.8	37.1	100.0
Lower Central								
Madhya Pradesh	34.6	27.3	61.9	9.7	2.4	26.0	38.1	100.0
Orissa	42.5	26.4	68.9	5.9	3.0	22.2	31 1	100.0
Rajasthan	19.7	39.7	59.4	6.7	2.5	31.4	40.6	100.0
East								
Northeastern region	39.9	32.4	71.7	6.3	4.5	17.4	28.3	100.0
West Bengal	38.9	31.5	70.4	8.5	2.9	18.2	29.6	100.0
West								
Gujarat	23.7	42.2	65.9	5.3	2.9	26.0	34.1	100.0
Maharashtra	26.8	34.3	61.1	7.5	3.2	28.2	38.9	100.0
South								
Andhra Pradesh	29.2	30.0	59.2	9.3	2.3	29.2	40.8	100.0
Karnataka	32.5	33.0	65.6	8.0	3.7	22.7	34.4	100.0
Kerala	22.5	39.7	62.2	6.5	5.3	26.0	37.8	100.0
Tamil Nadu	32.2	32.7	64.9	10.1	2.6	22.4	35.1	100.0
Rural India	30.5	33.4	63.9	7.4	3.1	25.6	36.1	100.0

Source: NCAER/HDI Survey, 1994.

Notes

1. For a comprehensive review of such linkages in several developing countries see, Haddad et al. (1998), "Estimating the Interactions between Household Food Security and Preschool Diarrhea", *Food Policy*, Vol. 23, Nos. 3 and 4, pp. 241-261.
2. For details of sampling design see Shariff, A. (1999), *India: Human Development Report — A Profile of Indian States in the 1990s*, Oxford University Press, New Delhi.

References

Gopalan, C., B.V. Rama Sastri and S.C. Balasubramanian (1971), *Nutritive Value of Indian Foods*, National Institute of Nutrition, Indian Council of Medical Research, Hyderabad.

Shariff, A. and A. Gumber (1999), "Employment and Wages in India: Pre- and Post-reform Scenario", *The Indian Journal of Labour Economics*, Vol. 42, No. 2, p. 197.

8

Child Work, Schooling, and Household Resources in Rural North India

FRANÇOIS LECLERCQ

I. INTRODUCTION

This paper aims to investigate the determinants of schooling and child work in rural north India and test the relevance of alternative explanations of why some children work. Work impedes with human capital acquisition, as it competes for children's time in schools and affects health and nutrition. Furthermore, while child work participation rates are not very high in rural India compared to other South-Asian and Sub-Saharan African countries, the size of India's population translates into large absolute numbers of working children. Reducing child work is thus an important policy issue in India (Basu, 1999, for cross-country comparative figures, and Jensen, 1999 on Pakistan).

Microeconomic literature stresses that child work can arise due to a variety of factors and circumstances. Several recent papers have tried to test the empirical validity of Basu and Van's (1998) 'luxury axiom', a formalisation of the common idea that 'a household would not send its children out to work if its income from non-child labour sources were sufficiently high'. Long-run poverty would thus be the main cause of child work. Another strand of research focuses on capital market imperfections. For example, the lack of insurance markets may force households to respond to adverse income shocks by sending their children to work, temporarily or permanently. The first two explanations relate to 'food insecurity'.

However, at least two alternative explanations of child work are equally plausible. First, labour market imperfections may make it difficult for land-cultivating parents to hire extra labour, for example, during peaks of agricultural activity, making it imperative for children to work even though their household's resources may be well above subsistence levels. Finally, educating children in dysfunctioning schools may result in yielding returns that are insufficient for parents to meet the often substantial direct costs of schooling. Parents may then want their children do some work even though their income contribution is not necessary (PROBE, 1999).

This paper discusses these ideas in the rural Indian context, focusing on the 'BIMARU states' of north India, i.e., Bihar, Madhya Pradesh, Rajasthan, Uttar Pradesh as they were defined before 2000, and now also including Chattisgarh, Jharkhand, and Uttarakhand. This region constitutes a more or less homogenous block with socio-economic and institutional characteristics clearly distinct from those prevalent in other parts of India. To sum up, it has the lowest levels of human development, though perhaps not the highest incidence of child work-it seems that among all Indian states, child work is most frequent in Andhra Pradesh. The core of the analysis is the estimation of a bivariate probit model of work participation and school enrolment, including individual, household, school and village-level explanatory variables that reflect the different hypotheses mentioned above. The data used are drawn from the 1994 NCAER-HDI survey.

At the outset, it is necessary to define child work and to clarify its links with schooling. Children are conventionally defined as individuals aged up to 14, for example by the International Labour Organisation (ILO), which conveniently corresponds to the age range for compulsory education in many countries, including India, as stipulated in the Constitution. According to the data at hand, work participation rates are negligible until the age of nine, and this paper, therefore, focuses on a relatively narrow age range, children aged 10-14. Thus, child work, as observed here, refers to the early transition to work of pre-adolescents: never-enrolled children start working earlier than enrolled ones, and some enrolled children leave school and start working before the age of 15. The main issue is the anticipated end of childhood in rural North India rather than a high incidence of work in early childhood.

Child work is very heterogeneous in nature, for children are engaged in diverse activities, paid or unpaid, within or outside their families, and they may work part-time or full-time. All activities outside the family can be considered as work and are the most likely to be caused by long-run poverty. Participation in household chores or labour on the family farm is much more ambiguous-most children are likely to carry out such activities at least seasonally or for a short duration every day. These activities may represent children's participation in family life, the acquisition of household and farm skills which enter children's human capital, or undesirable child work. They become really problematic when they conflict with schooling, affect the child's health, or deprive her from leisure, but defining a general threshold beyond which this happens is difficult.

Turning to the links between child work and schooling, conventional wisdom has it that the low school enrolment rates observed in rural India are caused by child work: Poverty forces households to send their children to work and thus preclude schooling. The ground reality is, however, much more complex. It is now a well-established stylised fact that a majority of the children who do not attend school do not work either, at least full time: They are 'nowhere' (Chaudhri, 1997), and thus schooling and work are not perfect substitutes. Indeed, non-enrolment is more plausibly explained by other factors than child work. Recent studies have emphasised the roles of the direct (rather than opportunity) costs of schooling (Tilak, 1996) and dysfunctionings of the school system in rural North India in explaining non-enrolment (De, et al., 2000; Drèze and Kingdon, 2001; Drèze and Sen, 1995 1997; Lanjouw and Stern, 1998; Leclercq, 2001a; PROBE, 1999). Having said this, the question remains as to why a significant share of out-of-school children are at work rather than 'nowhere'. The primary aim of this paper is to address this issue: Section II reviews recent developments in the literature on child work in developing countries, section III presents the data and section IV highlights stylised facts on the incidence of child work in rural north India. Section V discusses the specification of a bivariate probit model of the determinants of work participation and school enrolment of children aged 10-14. Section VI comments on estimations results. Section VII provides the conclusion emphasising the implications of the results for methodology and policy making.

II. RECENT DEVELOPMENTS IN THE LITERATURE ON CHILD WORK IN DEVELOPING COUNTRIES

Recent years have witnessed a renewal of interest in child work among development economists, with several important theoretical papers to their, credit, though the success achieved in the rigorous empirical implementation of their recommendations has been limited-primarily because of data constraints. Basu (1999) provides a comprehensive survey of historical and contemporary theory and empirical evidence. Recent papers focus on alternative explanations for child work, each of which is more closely associated with a given type of child work.

A first strand of research has investigated the hypothesis that working children belong to poor households which could not survive without their income contribution. Indeed, Basu and Van (1998) show that if this is the case, and if adult labour can be substituted by child labour, a ban on child labour has ambiguous consequences for children, depending on the level of the aggregate demand for labour. Some economies may feature multiple equilibria, with a 'bad' equilibrium characterised by low wages and child work, and a 'good' one by adult wages which are high enough to make children's contribution superfluous. In the former case, a ban raises adult wages and child labour permanently disappears. However, if the aggregate demand for labour is low enough, only the 'bad' equilibrium exists, and deeper changes in economic conditions are required to suppress child labour.

A rigorous test of the poverty hypothesis is proposed by Bhalotra (2000), who develops a theoretical model of child wage labour supply as a function of child and adult wages and household life-cycle income. As per the poverty hypothesis, children work only to earn the difference between other household members' income and the subsistence level. An increase in life-cycle income thus reduces the number of hours worked, and the income effect of an increase in child wages dominates the substitution effect. The wage elasticity of hours worked by children is thus negative, if households are 'poor enough' ('weak poverty hypothesis') and equal to minus -1 for households who are just at the subsistence level ('strong poverty hypothesis'). If poverty is not the cause of child work, the substitution effect dominates and a more usual labour supply curve obtains, with a positive elasticity. Estimations run for children aged 10-14 living in rural Pakistani yield a significant, negative elasticity for boys, ranging from - 0.3 to - 0.6, but an insignificant one for girls. Bhalotra's paper thus simultaneously proves the relevance of the poverty hypothesis in certain situations and points to the need for alternative explanations.

Like much of the literature, these papers focus on wage labour, which is an extreme form of child work, with the worst consequences for children (see for example, Weiner, 1991), and a major problem in itself, though it is not the most common type of child work in rural areas of North India as in probably many other countries. Massive poverty-induced child wage labour is perhaps mainly a problem of urban India.[1]

Capital market imperfections are the focus of another series of papers. Baland and Robinson (2000) show that credit constraints can prevent poor households from borrowing the amount of money needed to cover the direct and opportunity costs of schooling, though the amount borrowed for children's education could be repaid from the earnings of the children when they become adults and work. Ranjan (2001) and Rammohan (2001) also consider the role of credit constraints on child work.

Jacoby and Skoufias (1997) analyse the impact of adverse income shocks on school participation in ICRISAT villages (Maharashtra and Andhra Pradesh). Households faced with such shocks can only imperfectly contain their expenditure, and some of them can no longer bear the direct or opportunity costs of schooling. More generally, shocks due to bad monsoons or illness or demise of household members are likely to cause children to work either temporarily or permanently. Cameron and Worswick (2001) find that crop losses in Indonesia is more like to affect expenditure on girls' education than on boys', and that a similar gender bias is likely in India both in schooling and work.

Long-run poverty and capital market deficiencies that explain child work relate to the economic vulnerability of rural households in North India and this constitutes 'food insecurity'. At least two alternative explanations have been investigated in the literature which focus on the two types of child work most frequently encountered in rural North India, namely farm labour and household work. Two papers by Bhalotra and Heady (2000) and Cockburn (2000) argue that agricultural households who do not need their children's income to survive, may still use child farm labour if labour market imperfections prevent them from hiring extra adult labour, notably during seasonal peaks of activity. Cockburn stresses that the ownership of productive assets increases the marginal returns to child labour, though some assets are rather labour-decreasing. He provides evidence of this in rural Ethiopia-probably the country with the highest incidence of child work in the world today, but his estimates mix up the contribution of assets to household income and their impact in terms of substitution between child and adult labour.

Bhalotra and Heady focus on farm size and estimate probit models of the number of hours of work by children belonging to land-operating households in Ghana and Pakistan. They include a proxy for household income among regressors, namely food consumption instrumented to correct for possible endogeneity, and find that land size has a positive impact on hours worked by girls but not on boys in both countries.

Household work is the most common type of female child work, and its incidence is linked to household composition. Garg and Morduch (1998) have shown that credit and labour market imperfections can result in implicit competition for scarce resources between siblings. If the returns to male human capital perceived by parents are higher than those to female human capital, a child will benefit from having less siblings but more sisters among them. In a previous paper (Leclercq, 2001b), It was shown that this economic version of 'sibling rivalry' influences school enrolment decisions in rural North India, but only in nuclear households: Joint-family households have more substitution possibilities between adult's household work and are less dependent on their children's activities. Comparable phenomena should be observed for child household work.

Finally, child work may be the consequence, rather than the cause of non-enrolment (PROBE 1999): If the returns to schooling are very low, parents may not incur the direct costs of schooling, even in the absence of high opportunity costs, and instead make their children do some work because they are not at school — this is more likely in the case of part-time rather than full-time work. Furthermore, children working within their family acquire experience that which is useful in developing their human capital, and there is a trade-off between these skills and those acquired through schooling.[2] Bommier and Lambert (2000) show that this can explain why rural Tanzanian children typically start schooling at a late age i.e., the age of eight or nine rather than six years: They are sent to school only when the marginal returns to schooling become larger than those to work experience. It is noteworthy here, that increasing the returns to schooling through improvements in school quality should have a dramatic impact on this type of child work.

Thus, there are many explanations for child work, long-run poverty being only one of them. Any econometric analysis of child work must, therefore, rely on a precise characterisation of the case under study, section III.

III. THE DATA

The data used in this paper are based on a household survey carried out in 1994 by the National Council for Applied Economic Research (NCAER, Delhi) in cooperation with the United Nations Development Programme (UNDP), for preparing the first Human Development Report for India (Shariff, 1999). The resulting NCAER-HDI dataset covers 194,473 individuals constituting 33,230 households, selected from 1,762 villages in the rural areas of India's 16 major states. It is a large, representative, multipurpose survey with detailed information on topics such as household income and assets, expenditure and food security, education, fertility and health. The survey also covers village-level information pertaining mostly to physical and social infrastructures and to agricultural prices.

As explained in the introduction, the analysis is restricted to North India defined as the former 'BIMARU' states. This region accounts for 39.1 per cent of the rural population of the states covered by NCAER-HDI data, about 270 millions persons in 1994. Accordingly, sample size remains large: 76,050 individuals, 12,337 households, and 653 villages.

The main source of information on child work is each individual's primary and secondary occupation. These variables distinguish between schooling, different types of work, and a residual category labelled 'child below 15 years'. One hundred out of 30,562 children aged below 14 are reported to have a secondary occupation, and only 36 combine work and schooling. Whether this is a reflection of reality or whether the questionnaire design is problematic is unclear, as it is very likely that 'nowhere' children include seasonal or part-time workers. The participation rates mentioned in section IV may be considered as lower bounds to the actual rates, though the consistency of their patterns suggests that the data are reliable as far as full-time work is concerned.

For most children, no information on the number of hours or days worked is available and the income generated is not available or retrievable from the rest of the dataset. The only exception concerns wage labour - detailed information on the labour supply of households earning income from wage labour is available, covering the number of days worked over the year of reference for income data (1993), daily wage rates, and earnings, distinguishing between several types of agricultural (sowing, harvesting, other operations), and non-agricultural (domestic services, other services, skilled labour, construction labour, other unskilled labour) wage labour. Unfortunately, the data do not pertain to individuals but are strangely aggregated at a sub-household level, distinguishing between female and male children and adults. There are less than 300 observations of rural North Indian children, so that little robust econometric analysis of these data is possible.

While the next section displays some descriptive statistics using this information, the econometric analyses of child work proposed in sections V and VI concentrate on children's occupation status, i.e., 'enrolled', 'working', 'nowhere', or, in a few cases, 'enrolled and working'.

IV. INCIDENCE AND PATTERNS OF CHILD WORK IN RURAL NORTH INDIA

1. The Incidence of Child Work

How common is child work in the rural areas of North India ? The data at hand suggest that full-time child work is a significant but limited phenomenon. Work is the primary occupation of 9.4 per cent of girls and 4.2 per cent of boys aged 5 to 14. Figure 1 shows the evolution of participation rates with age: full-time work is negligible among young children (1.7 per cent of girls and 0.9 per cent of boys aged five to nine), but affects relatively a large proportion of pre-adolescents (18.3 per cent of girls and 7.8 per cent of boys aged 10 to 14).

To clarify the relation between work and schooling, Figure 2 also includes the proportions of enrolled and 'nowhere' children. Until age nine, almost all out-of-school children do not work, so that it would not be true to conclude that work causes non-enrolment, and the proportion of 'nowhere' children decreases as schooling increases. From the age 10 onwards, the proportion of 'nowhere' children more or less stabilises, while enrolment in schools decreases and the number of children at work increases. This however, does not mean that many pre-adolescents leave school to start working: quite to the contrary, once enrolled, most children remain at school until age 12 at least,[3] and, as Figure 3 shows, work participation rates hardly rise above 10 per cent among ever-enrolled children. Meanwhile, the rates for never-enrolled children reach more than 50 per cent by age 14. The bulk of working children aged 10 to 14 — 83.3 per cent of girls and 72.4 per cent of boys — were never enrolled. Thus, initial enrolment seems to condition work, rather than the reverse.

The bottom part of Figure 2 displays the differences between the figures for female and male children. They show that girls are strikingly disfavoured compared to boys at all ages: they work more and are less likely to be enrolled. Furthermore, the gaps sharply increase with age—with the boys remaining in school much longer than girls, and girls starting to work much earlier. Girls

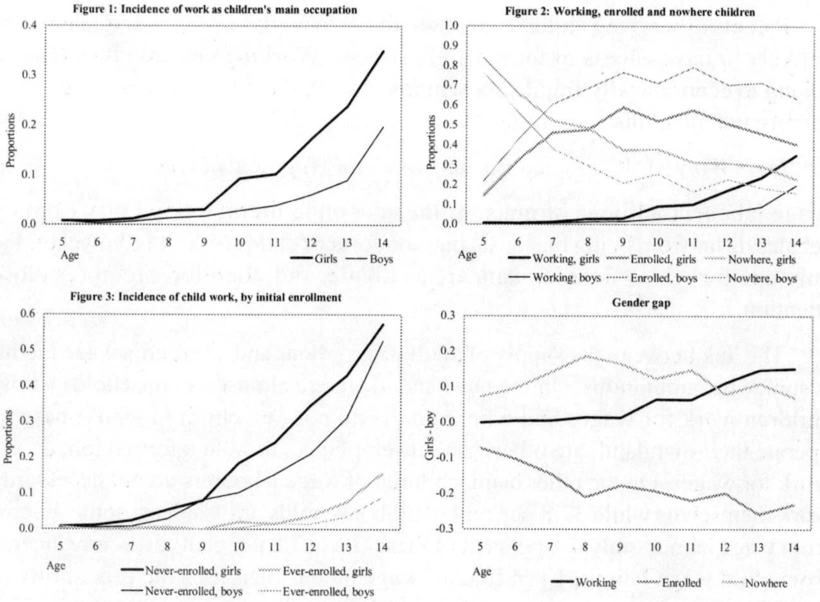

represent 65.4 per cent of workers, and only 36.0 per cent of school-going children aged 10 to 14.

Finally, schooling and child work are unequally distributed within households, so that the proportion of households affected by child work is higher than individual participation rates: 21.4 per cent of households with at least two children aged 10 to 14 have at least one worker, including only 3.7 per cent in which all children work. Overall, 16.4 per cent of households with children aged 10 to 14 have at least one child worker.

2. Types of Child Work

Figure 4 displays the distribution of working children aged 10 to 14 across six activity categories. There is a striking difference in the type of work performed between boys and girls. Almost all working girls (84.6 per cent) do household work, and farm and wage labour constitute the bulk of the remaining 15 per cent, while boys' activities are much more diversified, with household work being relatively frequent (24.1 per cent), but not more than farm labour, wage labour or informal non-agricultural activities.

These figures are remarkably similar to those for adults, aged 15 to 59, belonging to the same gender. In keeping with the view of rural North India's patriarchal social norms, women have very few employment opportunities outside their home, and do mostly household work. Agriculture employs more than half of the men — 46.2 per cent on their own farm, and roughly 10 per cent as agricultural wage workers — but non-agricultural wage work, (informal and formal non-agricultural employment) is also widespread. Household work is negligible among adult males, unlike in the case of male children among whom it is widely prevalent.

Parents of working children are more likely to work for wages and fathers are unlikely to have access to formal employment. Working children thus tend to belong to economically fragile households, though the differences between their parents and all adults aged 15 to 59 are not substantial.

(i) Days Worked, Wages and Earning of Child Wage Labourers

Wage labour, the focus of much of the economic literature and many policy debates, is far from being the most common form of child work. It is, however, the only one for which detailed data are available, and, therefore, requires close attention.

The link between the supply of adult wage labour and children's wage labour is somewhat ambiguous. On the one hand, there are almost no households whose children work for wages and whose adults do not i.e., children whose parents operate their own land, are otherwise self-employed, or hold a formal job, do not work for wages. On the other hand, children of wage labourers do not necessarily work themselves while 37.8 per cent of all households draw at least some income from wage labour, only 4.1 per cent of these (i.e., 37.8 per cent) draw any income from child wage labour. Even if adult wage labour increases the probability of

Figure 4
Distribution of Working Children and Adults by Activity

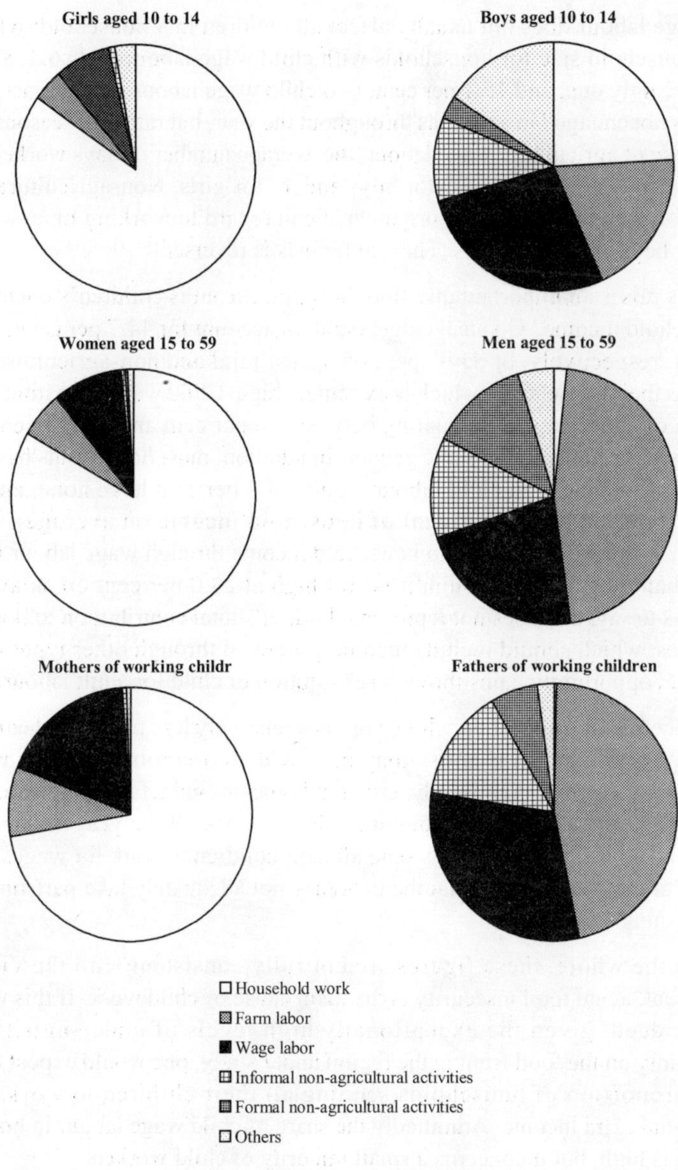

child work, children are likely to compensate for their parents' time spent at work and do household chores rather than work with them, a practical consequence is that this sub-section is based on 213 observations, pooling genders and all types of agricultural and non-agricultural wage labour together.

Wage labour does not usually affect all children in a household: while the mean household size for households with child wage labourers is 6.4, 81.3 per cent have only one, and 15.1 per cent, two child wage labourers. Similarly, wage labour is not engaged in activities throughout the year, but rather in seasonal ones. In the case of agricultural wage labour, the average number of days worked in the year of reference (1993) is 75 for boys and 43 for girls. Non-agricultural wage labour, on the other hand, is more intensive in regard to working time, with 126 days for boys and 73 for girls. The gender bias is reversed.[4]

This raises an important question: how significant is children's contribution to household income? On an average, children account for 44.7 per cent and 52.9 per cent, respectively, of days spent on agricultural and non-agricultural wage labour in their households, which is extremely high. Child wages constitute only a fraction of adult wages, fluctuating between 50 per cent and 80 per cent of the wages paid to adults of the same gender. In addition, most households have other sources of income than child labour—only 24.4 per cent have none, and wage labour represents 61.7 per cent of household income on average—so that children's direct contribution to household income through wage labour is much lower than 50 per cent, though it is still high at 21.0 per cent on an average.[5] Needless to say, this does not represent children's total contribution to household resources, which should include income generated through other types of child work and opportunity gains through substitution of child for adult labour.

To conclude this section, child work is a relatively less frequent phenomenon in rural North India. It is not synonymous with non-enrolment. Most working children work within their family, either at home or on the family farm, and most of them are girls. Even wage labourers do not work all the year round in most cases, and almost no households send all their children to work for wages. This is subject to the qualification that the data may not adequately take part-time work into account.

On the whole, these figures are not fully consistent with the view that permanent, acute food insecurity is the main cause of child work. If this were the case, indeed, given the exceptionally high levels of under-nutrition and uncertainty on the food front in the region under study, one would expect to find a large proportion of households sending all their children to work to earn substantial extra income. Admittedly the share of child wage labour in household income is high, but it concerns a small minority of child workers.

This is certainly not to deny that food insecurity is a major problem in India — it indeed is. The point is that there is, after all, no reason why child work should provide the affected households with a major additional source of income. Adult labour markets are known to be very imperfect in rural India, with heavy constraints on women's employment and widespread underemployment of men, and so it would be rather surprising to find smoothly functioning child labour markets enabling households to fill the gap between their current resources and subsistence levels or other minimal consumption levels, especially in periods of crises due, for example, to bad monsoons. It could well be possible that food-insecure households cannot even rely on their children's work to improve their living standards, and that, as a consequence, some children find themselves in a situation that is even worse than being at work, a possibility emphasised by Basu (1999).

It is, therefore, necessary to disentangle the alternative explanations for child work presented earlier through an econometric analysis of children's work and school enrolment, which is the focus of the next sections.

V. AN EMPIRICAL MODEL OF CHILD WORK PARTICIPATION AND SCHOOL ENROLMENT FOR RURAL NORTH INDIA

1. Econometric Framework: The Bivariate Probit Model

The richness of NCAER-HDI data makes possible the introduction of numerous independent variables accounting for the alternative hypotheses on the causes of child work, reviewed earlier. The major data constraint concerns the dependent variable itself: The only variable available for all children is their occupation status, a qualitative variable, and so a bivariate probit of work participation and school enrolment decisions is estimated, clubbing all child workers together, but keeping in mind that most regressors are closely linked to a specific kind of work.

The estimated model is:

$$\Pr(\text{work}_i) = f(\alpha_0 + C_i\,\alpha_1 + H_h\,\alpha_2 + S_v\,\alpha_3 + V_v\,\alpha_4 + \varepsilon_i^{\text{work}})$$

$$\Pr(\text{school}_i) = g(\beta_0 + C_i\,\beta_1 + H_h\,\beta_2 + S_v\,\beta_3 + V_v\,\beta_4 + \varepsilon_i^{\text{school}})$$

$$\text{Cov}(\varepsilon^{\text{work}}, \varepsilon^{\text{school}}) = \rho$$

where work is a dummy equal to 1 if the child works and to 0 otherwise and school another dummy equal to 1 if the child is enrolled and to 0 otherwise. For 'nowhere' children, both variables equal 0, and, as mentioned earlier in section III there is a negligible number of children for whom both variables equal 1. C is a vector of child individual variables, H, a vector of household variables, S, a vector of school variables (actually aggregated at the village level), and V, a vector of village variables. The significance of (provides a test that the two decisions are independent.

The rest of this section discusses the choice of independent variables, focusing on their impact on child work and concludes with shorter discussion in terms of schooling.

2. Long-run Wealth and Exposure to Shocks as Elements of Food (In) Security

As shown by Bhalotra (2000), a rigorous test of the long-run poverty hypothesis involves testing the sign of the elasticity of hours worked by children to their wages (or their marginal productivity in unpaid activities). Unfortunately, with the exception of wage labourers, such variables are neither available nor retrievable from the rest of the dataset.[6] Less formal inference can be gained from the impact of household non-child labour income. A strong negative impact is consistent with the poverty hypothesis, but does not prove it, for income affects child work through other channels, notably its positive impact on schooling. On the contrary, an insignificant coefficient on income would be evidence that poverty is not the issue.

An obvious practical problem is that household current income is endogenous to child work, so that one has to find another measure of household long-run resources. In other contexts, total or food consumption is often found to be a good alternative, but if the food insecurity hypothesis is valid, children's income will be devoted exclusively to food consumption, which will then be as endogenous as total income. Filmer and Pritchett (1998) have argued that information on household unproductive assets, consumer durables and housing conditions can be used to generate an index of long-run household wealth through the principal components analysis (PCA). The index is just a linear combination of the asset and housing variables, the weights being determined by the PCA.

Table 1 shows how such an index can be computed using NCAER-HDI data, taking great care to select only variables that are completely independent of child work, for example, by including the nature of the house, but excluding its state, or the availability of water, which is a direct determinant of household work.[7] Figure 5 displays kernel regressions of child work participation of boys and girls on the wealth index, per capita income and per capita food consumption. Work is a decreasing function of the three variables, but the relationship is expectedly clearest for the wealth index, and least distinct for food consumption. Focusing on the wealth index, child work declines more sharply in the left part of the graph.[8] Participation rates are 25.4 per cent for girls and 22.4 per cent for boys of the first quartile, and decline to 7.2 per cent and 3.2 per cent respectively in the last one. While not definitive, univariate non-parametric evidence is thus not inconsistent with the food insecurity hypothesis.

A second set of variables proxies for households' exposure to adverse income shocks. As the dataset is a cross-section without retrospective information on income, it is not possible to measure income shocks directly, but several indicators of economic vulnerability are available. The number of deaths in the household in the year preceding the survey and the number of adult household members (aged 15 and above) currently suffering from a long-duration disease are used. The specification also includes dummies for female-headed households, mothers working outside the home (in wage or farm labour), and children whose father or mother is missing from the household. Given women's status in rural North India, most female-headed households are widow-headed and do not have adult male members, which is a heavy constraint on their economic opportunities. While girls may benefit by depending on a female rather than a male head, the net impact is likely to be negative. Given the limited employment opportunities open to women, mothers working for wages or doing farm labour belong to economically and socially fragile households, and children may do household work to compensate for the time their mother spends outside the home.[9]

Two more dummies indicate households buying subsidised cereals from fair-price-shops (FPS), and the existence of a bank in the village. They should reduce child work, the former if the food insecurity hypothesis is valid, and the latter as an inverse proxy for credit constraints.

Table 1
Generating an Index of Household Wealth through Principal Components Analysis

Variable	Scoring factor	Mean	Standard deviation
Household owns:			
Property besides the place of dwelling	0.105	0.121	0.326
Radio	0.205	0.313	0.464
TV	0.284	0.078	0.268
VCR	0.104	0.004	0.066
Air-cooler	0.149	0.008	0.088
Fan	0.297	0.116	0.320
Housing:			
Kuccha house	-0.325	0.606	0.489
Pucca house (reference: semi-pucca)	0.345	0.148	0.355
Floor in wood, stone, or bricks	0.084	0.084	0.277
Floor in cement	0.316	0.078	0.268
Floor in other materials (reference: mud)	0.032	0.002	0.049
Walls in wood	-0.014	0.039	0.193
Walls in bricks and mud	0.121	0.280	0.449
Walls in bricks and cement, concrete	0.289	0.086	0.281
Walls in other materials (reference: thatch, mud)	0.010	0.054	0.225
Number of rooms in the house	0.263	2.300	0.864
Separate kitchen	0.306	0.227	0.419
Ventilation in kitchen	0.303	0.200	0.400
Chimney / smoke outlet at the cooking place	0.148	0.048	0.215
Toilet	0.195	0.079	0.270
$R^2 = 0.1988$			

Notes: Apart from the number of rooms in the house, all variables are dummies. The principal component analysis relies on household data including all households surveyed in north India. The index of household wealth is computed as the first principal component from the scoring factors, using only the first eigenvector. The index is computed, for each observation, as the sum of the standardised values of each variable (value-mean / standard deviation) weighted by the scoring factor, so that its mean value (for the full sample of households) is 0. It captures 19.88 per cent of the variance in the included variables.

3. Alternative Explanations: Household Composition, Farm Size, and Costs of Schooling

Household composition affects child work in a variety of ways. Given their size, households with more economically dependent members are likely to rely more on their children's economic contribution. The number of adults should have the opposite effect. Household size and the numbers of individuals belonging to different age / gender categories are therefore included in them, along with birth order, as it has often been observed that younger siblings are less likely to work.

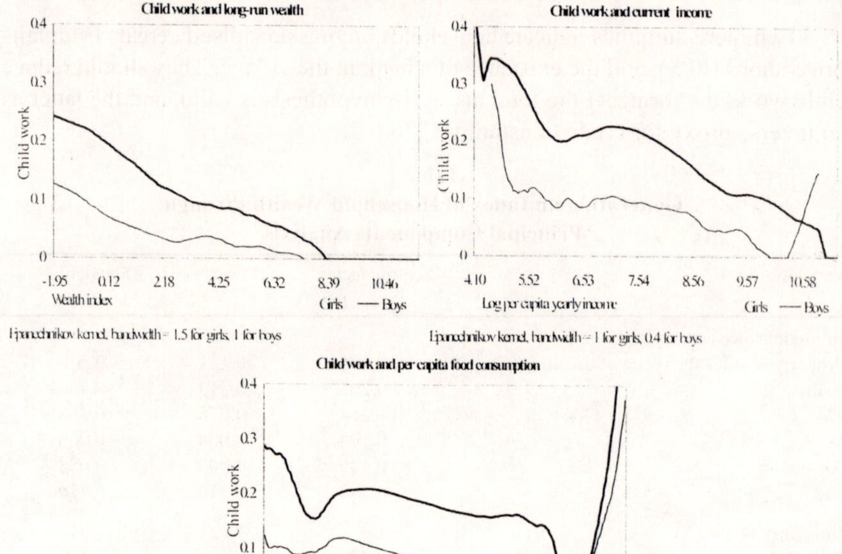

Figure 5: Kernel regressions of child work on measures of household resources

The 'distance' to the nearest source of drinking water, measured in minutes taken to walk to the source, is also used, as fetching water is often cited as one of the main tasks performed by working children.

Models of child farm labour predict that, in the presence of adult labour market imperfections, and controlling for long-run wealth and household size, the marginal productivity of child labour increases with farm size. The per capita amount of land and number of farm animals owned by the household are included, along with a dummy for the ownership of a tractor. The latter, which is unlikely to be operated by children, greatly increases adult labour productivity and should dramatically reduce the need for child labour on the family farm.

NCAER-HDI data include a limited amount of information on schools. Dummies for the existence of an *anganwadi* (pre-primary school) and a primary school within the village and an index of the distance to middle, secondary, higher secondary, and upper education institutions are included along with dummies for the availability of midday-meals, free textbooks and other incentive schemes. The existence of educational institutions in the village should reduce child work, either directly—by enabling children aged 10 to 14 to enrol in these schools, which would be difficult if they have to go to another village—or indirectly, with the help of *anganwadis*, which can free girls from the burden of taking care of their younger siblings. Incentive schemes reduce the costs of schooling. In particular, if children work to earn their own food consumption, mid-day-meals can contribute towards making their work superfluous.

4. Parental Characteristics and Village Controls

It is necessary to control for parental characteristics affecting child work besides its other determinants. Parents' education determines their economic opportunities and their ability to invest in children's human capital. Fathers' education also proxies for their earnings. Few mothers earn any independent income, but, given their husband's income, their education proxies for their bargaining power within the household.

Agriculture wage labour, as well as informal and formal non-agricultural activities are associated with more or less irregular income and are more or less human-capital intensive. Children whose father has a formal, salaried employment are the least exposed to income shocks, while (daily) wage labour yields very uncertain earnings. Furthermore, boys are likely to have the same occupation as their fathers, so that the human-capital intensity of the latter's occupation influences the returns to their education.

Finally, additional controls include children's age, dummies for the household's socio-religious background (Scheduled Tribes, Scheduled Castes, Muslims), village size, and an index of infrastructures (other than schools, banks and fair-price shops).

5. Interpretation of the Specification in Terms of Schooling

Schooling and work compete for children's time. A variable that has a positive (negative) impact on child work should thus have an indirect negative (positive) impact on schooling. Most variables also have a direct impact on schooling that may or may not operate in the same direction as the indirect one. For example, long-run wealth reduces the opportunity costs of child work, while also making it easier to bear the direct costs of schooling. Per capita land owned reduces schooling through its impact on work, but also contributes positively to household income. If the wealth index correctly proxies for household resources, it should pick up the income effect, and the coefficient on land owned should be positive for work and negative for schooling.

VI. ESTIMATION RESULTS

The dataset provides information on the activities of 4356 girls and 5374 boys, aged 10 to 14; the exclusion of a few outliers slightly reduces sample size, to 4296 girls and 5283 boys. The model was estimated using stata 7.0. Separate regressions were run for girls and boys, taking survey weights into account and controlling for clustering at the village level. Table 2 displays the definitions of all variables, their means and standard deviations. Table 3 displays coefficients and Table 4 the marginal effects on the marginal probabilities of working and being enrolled, respectively. Wald tests of joint significance for relevant groups of variables are reported in Table 5.

Table 2
Definitions, Means and Standard Deviations of Variables
(Girls and Boys Pooled)

Variable	Definition	Mean	St. Dev.
Work	Dummy: 1 if child's primary or secondary occupation is work	0.128	0.334
School	Dummy: 1 if child's primary or secondary occupation is school	0.612	0.487
Age	Age of the child, in years	11.825	1.454
Wealth index	PCA index of household long-run wealth (see table 1)	0.274	2.136
Deaths	Number of deaths in the household in the previous year	0.077	0.309
Sick adults	# hh. members aged 15 + suffering from long-duration diseases	0.356	0.608
Female head	Dummy: 1 if household head is a female	0.019	0.135
Mother working outside	Dummy: 1 if mother's main occupation is wage / farm labour	0.157	0.364
No father	Dummy: 1 if father absent from the household	0.053	0.223
No mother	Dummy: 1 if mother absent from the household	0.042	0.200
Use of FPS	Dummy: 1 if household buys cereals from a fair-price-shop	0.134	0.340
Bank in the village	Dummy: 1 if there is a bank in the village	0.209	0.406
Birth order	Age-rank among individuals aged upto 21 in the household	2.386	1.299
Size	Household size	7.863	3.614
Males aged 0 to 4	# of males aged 0 to 4 in the household	0.381	0.642
Females aged 0 to 4	# of females aged 0 to 4 in the household	0.380	0.671
Males aged 5 to 10	# of males aged 5 to 10 in the household	0.910	0.928
Females aged 5 to 10	# of females aged 5 to 10 in the household	0.772	0.873
Males aged 11 to 14	# of males aged 11 to 14 in the household	0.708	0.704
Females aged 11 to 14	# of females aged 11 to 14 in the household	0.600	0.703
Males aged 15 to 59	# of males aged 15 to 59 in the household	1.985	1.225
Males aged 60 +	# of males aged 60 and above in the household	0.226	0.433
Females aged 60 +	# of females aged 60 and above in the household	0.176	0.388
Distance to water	'Distance' to the main source of drinking water, in minutes	6.348	10.318
Land per capita	Per capita amount of land owned by the household, in acres	0.481	0.768
Animals per capita	Per capita # of cows, buffaloes, goats owned by household	0.430	0.645
Tractor	Dummy: 1 if the household owns a tractor	0.044	0.204

(Table 2 contd.)

Anganwadi	Dummy: 1if there is an anganwadi in the village	0.268	0.443
Primary school	Dummy: 1 f there is a primary school in the village	0.843	0.364
Middle school and above	Index of distance to schools above the primary level (weights taken from NCAER-HDI data, scaled 0 to 1)		0.251
0.221			
Midday-meals	Dummy: 1 if there is a midday-meal programme in the village	0.039	0.193
Free textbooks	Dummy: 1 if there is a corresponding programme in the village	0.229	0.420
Other incentives	Dummy: 1 if other schooling incentives are available	0.563	0.496
Parents' education (reference category is 'none'):			
Father: Below primary	Dummy: 1 if father's education is below primary	0.070	0.255
Primary	Dummy: 1 if father's education is primary	0.112	0.315
Middle	Dummy: 1 if father's education is middle or above	0.350	0.477
Mother: Below primary	Dummy: 1 if mother's education is below primary	0.033	0.179
Primary	Dummy: 1 if mother's education is primary	0.053	0.224
Middle	Dummy: 1 if mother's education is middle or above	0.061	0.239
Father's main occupation (reference category is 'agriculture')			
Wage labour	Dummy: 1 if wage labour	0.190	0.392
Informal activities	Dummy: 1 if informal non-agricultural activities	0.136	0.342
Formal employment	Dummy: 1 if formal non-agricultural employment	0.152	0.359
Others	Dummy: 1 if none of the above	0.018	0.132
Scheduled Tribes	Dummy: 1 if the household belongs to a Scheduled Tribe	0.094	0.292
Scheduled Castes	Dummy: 1 if the household belongs to a Scheduled Caste	0.208	0.406
Muslims	Dummy: 1 if the household is Muslim	0.095	0.294
Village population	Village population, '000s	2.407	2.480
Village infrastructures	Index of village infrastructures (weights taken from NCAER-HDI data, scaled 0 to 1)	0.385	0.136

Table 3
Bivariate Probits of Work and School Enrolment of Children Aged 10 to 14
(Coefficients)

	Girls aged 10 to 14		Boys aged 10 to 14	
	Work	School	Work	School
Age	0.273	-0.188	0.300	-0.081
	(9.31)***	(8.28)***	(9.78)***	(3.98)***
Household long-run wealth				
Wealth index	-0.079	0.130	-0.070	0.136
	(3.60)***	(7.77)***	(3.31)***	(7.21)***
Exposure to shocks				
Deaths	-0.117	-0.020	0.141	-0.147
	(1.21)	(0.24)	(1.57)	(1.91)*
Sick adults	0.121	0.021	0.009	0.063
	(2.23)**	(0.48)	(0.15)	(1.30)
Female head	-0.135	0.078	0.356	-0.355
	(0.70)	(0.39)	(1.86)*	(1.91)*
Mother working outside	0.316	-0.170	0.176	-0.030
	(4.17)***	(2.06)**	(1.85)*	(0.41)
No father	0.244	0.345	0.102	0.213
	(1.47)	(2.45)**	(0.61)	(1.61)
No mother	0.617	-0.411	0.155	-0.182
	(4.36)***	(2.80)***	(0.94)	(1.48)
Use of FPS	-0.049	0.176	-0.058	0.026
	(0.58)	(2.29)**	(0.58)	(0.35)
Bank in the village	-0.080	0.221	-0.138	0.272
	(0.79)	(2.17)**	(1.26)	(2.96)***
Household composition				
Birth order	-0.007	-0.106	0.027	-0.027
	(0.18)	(3.06)***	(0.54)	(0.81)
Size	-0.063	0.124	-0.082	0.086
	(1.45)	(3.04)***	(1.69)*	(2.19)**
Males aged 0 to 4	0.153	-0.319	0.227	-0.134
	(1.83)*	(4.72)***	(2.95)***	(2.11)**
Females aged 0 to 4	0.141	-0.229	0.161	-0.156
	(1.78)*	(3.39)***	(1.90)*	(2.32)**
Males aged 5 to 10	0.102	-0.216	0.078	-0.150
	(1.56)	(3.52)***	(1.19)	(2.75)***
Females aged 5 to 10	0.086	-0.184	0.073	-0.062
	(1.40)	(3.35)***	(1.12)	(1.22)
Males aged 11 to 14	0.059	-0.147	0.075	-0.138
	(0.79)	(2.22)**	(0.93)	(2.18)**
Females aged 11 to 14	0.039	-0.016	0.044	0.005
	(0.60)	(0.26)	(0.52)	(0.07)
Males aged 15 to 59	0.002	-0.051	0.059	-0.133
	(0.03)	(0.90)	(0.80)	(2.41)**
Males aged 60 and above	0.020	-0.087	0.176	-0.169
	(0.18)	(0.92)	(1.66)*	(1.95)*
Females aged 60 and above	0.042	-0.122	0.070	-0.008
	(0.43)	(1.50)	(0.69)	(0.10)
Distance to water	-0.005	-0.008	-0.008	0.001
	(1.46)	(2.84)***	(1.66)*	(0.27)
Productivity of farm labour				
Land per capita	-0.056	-0.082	-0.050	0.051
	(1.32)	(2.14)**	(0.99)	(1.33)

(Table 3 contd.)

Animals per capita	0.047	-0.086	0.084	-0.046
	(1.00)	(2.17)**	(2.10)**	(1.11)
Tractor	-0.006	0.322	-0.415	0.191
	(0.03)	(1.98)**	(2.04)**	(1.12)
School availability and schooling incentives				
Anganwadi	0.009	0.094	-0.014	0.120
	(0.11)	(1.33)	(0.17)	(1.70)*
Primary school	-0.086	0.052	-0.020	-0.045
	(0.65)	(0.47)	(0.19)	(0.43)
Middle school and above	-0.055	0.410	0.254	0.090
	(0.28)	(2.29)**	(1.23)	(0.54)
Mid-day meals	0.034	0.061	0.118	-0.084
	(0.26)	(0.46)	(0.84)	(0.79)
Free textbooks	0.009	0.061	-0.030	-0.057
	(0.09)	(0.70)	(0.33)	(0.71)
Other incentives	0.038	0.031	-0.075	0.034
	(0.46)	(0.41)	(0.84)	(0.45)
Parental education and father's main occupation				
Father' education:				
Below primary	-0.054	0.218	-0.131	0.597
	(0.55)	(2.17)**	(0.91)	(5.97)***
Primary	-0.175	0.334	-0.313	0.552
	(1.86)*	(3.76)***	(2.86)***	(6.81)***
Middle	-0.248	0.693	-0.584	0.742
	(2.65)***	(9.07)***	(5.31)***	(8.60)***
Mother's education				
Below primary	-0.286	0.670	-0.680	0.962
	(1.69)*	(4.15)***	(2.35)**	(4.74)***
Primary	-0.692	0.653	-0.339	0.621
	(3.80)***	(4.98)***	(1.77)*	(3.74)***
Middle	-0.530	0.771	0.164	0.289
	(2.65)***	(4.77)***	(0.76)	(1.72)*
Father's main occupation:				
Wage labour	0.123	-0.144	0.261	-0.139
	(1.40)	(1.57)	(2.51)**	(1.64)
Informal activities	0.094	-0.064	0.244	-0.073
	(0.85)	(0.71)	(2.20)**	(0.79)
Formal employment	-0.162	0.291	-0.154	0.238
	(1.34)	(3.12)***	(1.17)	(2.41)**
Others	0.219	-0.206	0.648	-0.164
	(1.01)	(1.17)	(2.48)**	(0.68)
Scheduled Tribes	0.020	-0.031	0.225	-0.352
	(0.19)	(0.28)	(2.14)**	(4.05)***
Scheduled Castes	0.096	-0.209	0.226	-0.139
	(1.27)	(2.82)***	(2.70)***	(1.96)**
Muslims	0.126	-0.275	0.133	-0.396
	(1.09)	(2.68)***	(1.12)	(4.48)***
Village controls				
Village population	0.009	-0.012	-0.008	-0.034
	(0.40)	(0.82)	(0.35)	(2.27)**
Village infrastructures	-0.274	-0.038	-0.007	-0.179
	(0.80)	(0.13)	(0.02)	(0.55)
Constant	-3.891	1.801	-5.038	1.528
	(9.93)***	(5.70)***	(11.59)***	(5.18)***
p	-0.901***	-0.881***		
Wald test of p = 0	$\chi2(1)=260.38$; p-value=0.000		$\chi2(1)=312.50$; p-value=0.000	
Log likelihood	-13029140 (5 iterations)		-12586152 (5 iterations)	
Wald test of all coefficients	$\chi2(92)=1095.8$; p-value=0.000		$\chi2(92)=1092.9$, p-value=0.000	
Observations	4296		5283	

Notes: Weighted estimation taking clustering at the village level into account. Robust *z*-statistics in parentheses. ***, **, and * indicate significance at the one per cent, 5 per cent, and 10 per cent level respectively.

Table 4
Wald Tests of Joint Significance

		Girls aged 10 to 14		Boys aged 10 to 14	
		Work	School	Work	School
Exposure to income shocks	(2(8)	52.91	27.38	19.71	20.87
	P-value	0.000***	0.001***	0.012**	0.008***
Household composition	(2(11)	20.37	43.89	12.07	16.71
	P-value	0.041**	0.000***	0.358	0.117
Productivity of farm labour	(2(3)	2.61	13.84	10.71	4.49
	P-value	0.455	0.003***	0.013**	0.214
School availability and schooling incentives	(2(6)	0.74	11.62	2.78	5.28
	P-value	0.994	0.071*	0.836	0.508
Parental education and father's main occupation	(2(10)	219.06	219.06	228.67	228.67
	P-value	0.000***	0.000***	0.000***	0.000***

Note: ***, **, and * indicate significance at the one per cent, 5 per cent, and 10 per cent level respectively.

Table 5
Bivariate Probits of Work and Enrolment of Children Aged 10 to 14 (Marginal Effects)

	Girls aged 10 to 14		Boys aged 10 to 14	
	Work	School	Work	School
Age	0.0635	-0.0748	0.0300	-0.0257
Wealth index	-0.0184	0.0518	-0.0070	0.0433
Deaths				-0.0466
Sick adults	0.0282			
Female head			0.0468	-0.1243
Mother working outside	0.0804	-0.0674	0.0192	
No father	0.1359			
No mother	0.1833	-0.1594		
Use of FPS	0.0703			
Bank in the village	0.0878	0.0815		
Birth order	-0.0424			
Size	0.0496	-0.0082	0.0275	
Males aged 0 to 4	0.0354	-0.1271	0.0226	-0.0427
Females aged 0 to 4	0.0328	-0.0915	0.0161	-0.0494
Males aged 5 to 10	-0.0860	-0.0475		
Females aged 5 to 10	-0.0733			
Males aged 11 to 14	-0.0586	-0.0437		
Females aged 11 to 14				
Males aged 15 to 59	-0.0423			
Males aged 60 and above	0.0176	-0.0537		
Females aged 60 and above				
Distance to water	-0.0030	-0.0008		
Land per capita	-0.0329			
Animals per capita	-0.0343	0.0084		
Tractor	0.1271	-0.0302		
Anganwadi	0.0376			
Primary school				
Middle school and above	0.1637			
Mid-day meals				
Free textbooks				

(Table 5 contd.)

Other incentives				
Father's education: Below primary	0.0865	0.1547		
Primary	-0.0378	0.1321	-0.0256	0.1480
Middle	-0.0545	0.2692	-0.0481	0.2070
Mother's education: Below primary	-0.0574	0.2521	-0.0399	0.2049
Primary	-0.1124	0.2469	-0.0262	0.1569
Middle	-0.0941	0.2855	0.0833	
Father's main occupation: Wage labour	0.0297			
Informal activities	0.0284			
Formal employment	0.1153	0.0709		
Others	0.1055			
Scheduled Tribes	0.0257	-0.1208		
Scheduled Castes	-0.0838	0.0239	-0.0448	
Muslims	-0.1086	-0.1373		
Village population	-0.0109			
Village infrastructures				

Notes: Only marginal effects significant at 10 per cent are reported (see Table 3 for levels of significance). These marginal effects relate to the marginal probabilities of child work and school enrolment. They are computed at the mean value of each variable, except for dummies, for which they represent the effect of a discrete change in the variable, from 0 to 1.

Given the eclecticism of the specification, both regressions yield reasonable numbers of significant coefficients (some of them only at 10 per cent). All the groups of variables proxying for different causes of child work comprise individually significant variables in most regressions, though they are not always jointly significant. As the work variable relatively rarely equals 1, results are more visible for schooling than for work: More of the coefficients are significant, and the marginal effects are larger.

ρ is strongly significant and close to 1 in both cases, confirming that child work and school participation decisions depend on each other. Coefficients that are simultaneously significant in the work and school equations have opposite signs: Work and schooling are substitutes.

It must noted that age is associated with a decline in schooling and an increase in work which is much larger for girls than for boys, reflecting patterns observed in figures 1 and 2. Over the narrow age range under consideration, the effect of age is linear. Additional regressions (not shown) yielded insignificant coefficients for quadratic terms.

1. Child Work, Schooling and Food Insecurity

Does food insecurity cause child work? The wealth index attracts highly significant coefficients with expected signs for both genders and both equations, but its impact is linear: Attempts to include quadratic terms were unsuccessful. Similarly, introducing wealth quartile dummies and interaction terms, or estimating the model separately by quartile, yielded no significant coefficients for the first quartile.

Interpreting the marginal coefficients requires understanding variations in the wealth index. An extremely poor household with none of the consumer durables, living in a completely kuccha house with mud floor and walls and only one room and no provision for cooking, ventilation, or chimney, and a toilet would have an index of –1.88. Shifting to a semi-pucca house with wooden floor and walls brings the index to –0.98. A further shift to a pucca house with a cement floor, brick-and-cement walls, with three rooms and a separate, ventilated kitchen — a good house by rural North Indian standards, but still without any of the consumer durables or a toilet — yields a value of 4.06. Now the two shifts would reduce a girl's probability to work by 1.6 and 9.3 percentage points respectively, which is somewhat lower than what one would expect, if only the poorest households had working children — the first shift should have more sizeable consequences, since 40.4 per cent of households have an index below –0.98. The corresponding increases in school attendance would be 4.6 and 26.1 percentage points, respectively.

Considering the incidence of poverty in the region under study, it is likely that most households with working children are poor by conventional standards, but child work is not limited to those living in the deepest poverty.

The variables introduced to proxy for the exposure to shocks are always jointly significant at 5 per cent at least, and each of them is individually significant in at least one equation. There is some evidence that the death or disease of household members affect children, but the crucial variables are those associated with adult women. Female-headed households are economically fragile, with very large impacts on boys (work increases by 4.7 percentage points, schooling by 12.4). As explained in the previous section, it is possible that, for girls, the opposite impacts of living in a poor household and depending on a head of the same gender neutralise each other: No net impact is observed. Meanwhile, given the magnitude of the marginal effects, girls whose mother works outside the household or is absent are bound to work: Young daughters — but not sons — rather than fathers compensate for mother's work when the latter is not available.

Caution is required in interpreting the lack of impact of buying cereals from a fair-price shop. Indeed, as the Public Distribution System is supposed to target the poor, if it were efficiently implemented, a purposive-programme-placement bias would result in spuriously insignificant coefficients. However, the PDS is known to be functional only in areas with reasonably good administrative structures. At the state level, the poorer regions of North India benefit from it much less than relatively well-off states like Kerala. Locally, villages with better infrastructure and 'governance' are more likely to have functional fair-price shops, but this is accounted for by the village infrastructure index, so that the actual impact of the availability of subsidised cereals should be observed. Furthermore, if the food insecurity hypothesis is valid, households will send their children to work only if they do not reach subsistence consumption levels including what they may purchase from an FPS without children's income contribution: The variable will be exogenous. On the whole, therefore, I believe that the insignificance of the FPS variable constitutes, admittedly informal, evidence of the inefficiency of the Public Distribution System, rather than evidence against the food insecurity hypothesis.

The dummy for the presence of a bank in the village is significant for schooling, but not for child work. Credit constraints may limit educational investments without child work generating enough additional income to relax them. However, a formal test of the impact of credit on child work is much more involved and would often require more detailed data: poor households are unlikely to have access to formal credit by banks, so that the dummy may rather signal a small number of villages with better overall infrastructures, or situated in more prosperous areas.

2. Household Composition

Household composition variables have a decisive influence on child work and schooling, with numerous individually significant coefficients — the lack of joint significance for boys is surprising. Overall, children fare better in larger households with more adults and less dependent persons, especially young children. More subtle gender-specific effects can also be observed. Birth order does not have the expected sign, but it is significant only for girls' schooling.

Controlling for household size, the key element of age composition is the number of children aged up to 10 years, especially very young ones, which makes it more probable that the child will work than get enrolled in a school. This reflects the competition between siblings for scarce household resources, both in terms of income — households with more children need additional income to feed them — and time, since someone has to take care of the children. Girls are more frequently asked to do so, and the impacts are, unsurprisingly, larger on girls than on boys.

The gender composition of the household is crucial. Among, children, there is evidence of 'sibling rivalry' as defined by Garg and Morduch (1998). Indeed, the negative impact of male children is usually larger than that of female children, and the numbers of girls, aged 5 to 10 and 11 to 14, do not affect child outcomes significantly in all cases, but one. As a consequence, substituting female for male other children in the household, improves a child's situation.

Meanwhile, the number of males of all ages negatively affects boys' schooling, contrarily to the number of females (except those aged 0 to 4) — while one would expect positive income effects associated with adults males to dominate. In a context, where under-employment is frequent and the marginal productivity of labour may be low, it is possible that adult men divert scarce resources away from pre-adolescents. Compared to all other categories, the presence of girls and women aged 11 and above improves the situation of children (remember that women aged, 15 to 59, are the reference category) — unlike men, women do not compete with each other. The household composition coefficients thus give important information on the functioning of households with scarce resources, patriarchal social norms and gender-wise unequal returns to human capital perceived by decision-makers (parents or male household heads).

3. Productivity of Farm Labour

The variables included as determinants of the productivity of farm child labour are significant for girls' schooling and boys' work. Per capita animal ownership expectedly increases boys' work, and tractor ownership reduces it. The evidence for female schooling has interesting implications. Indeed, controlling for household wealth removes income effects associated with land, animals and tractors, so that the coefficients indirectly reflect the expected impact of the variables through child work.

Now very few girls are reported to do farm labour, and no impact of farm size on female child work is observed. How is this possible, given that farm size has no obvious direct impact on schooling once wealth is accounted for?[10] This may be a sign that a larger farm size is associated with part-time child labour, which is not reported as a main occupation but affects the probability of enrolment.

4. School Availability and Schooling Incentives

School variables are hardly ever significant. I consider this to be a feature of the data rather than the population under study, for several reasons. Most villages now nominally have a primary school, and therefore, it is not surprising that the primary school dummy has no impact: Information on the capacity and quality of existing schools is required to get reliable evidence. Likewise, the nominal existence of an anganwadi does not imply that it is functional, or that it has the capacity to take in all very young children in the village, or that all children have social access to it. Qualitative field studies consistently stress the importance of school availability and quality, but collecting adequate school-level data for econometric analysis is remarkably difficult, and extremely few satisfying databases exist.[11]

In this context, the respective significant impacts of anganwadis and middle and secondary schools on male and female schooling are evidence that school institutions matter.

5. Parental Variables

Along with household composition, parental variables yield the largest numbers of significant coefficients, and are jointly significant at the one per cent level in all equations.

Parents' education is a key determinant of schooling. Because of hypergamy, children who have an educated mother (even 'below the primary level') also have an educated father, usually up to the 'middle and above' level, so that the mother's education has an additional impact on a child's education. Female enrolment is more dependent on parents' education, and here the impact of the mother is crucial. Many more uneducated parents send their sons than their daughters to school, so that parental education has a relatively less impact on boys, and having an educated father is more discriminatory.

The impacts of parental variables on child work are large compared to those of many other variables in the specification. Interestingly, in regard to the impact of educational level of fathers, the main difference is between the impact of those who have and have not completed primary schooling, rather than between educated and uneducated ones. The small number of mothers educated at the middle level and above may account for the insignificant coefficients for boys' work.

Parental education can reduce child work, whatever its direct causes: Educated parents are more likely to escape poverty, have access to credit, use human-capital intensive agricultural technologies altering the relative gains from child labour and schooling, and thus help their children through the schooling process. The point is that the difficulties faced by uneducated parents in enrolling their children and in preventing them from working have serious dynamic consequences, limiting socio-economic upward mobility.

The nature of the father's occupation has implications for the regularity of household income, and hence the positive coefficients of formal employment in the schooling equations, which supplement the coefficient on mother's occupation in the group of variables proxying for economic insecurity. The coefficients on boys' work may also reflect the idea of a trade-off between specific human capital acquired through work and general human capital acquired through schooling (Bommier and Lambert, 2000). Indeed, the main occupation of the father and that of his son are highly correlated, and son may acquire skills while working on the family enterprise. The equivalent for men having a formal job is to enroll their sons. This however, does not apply to girls, most of whom will work in the home of their husband's family; which accounts for the absence of a direct impact of the father's occupation on their probability of working.

Finally, while the village controls are insignificant but for one coefficient, many of the community dummies remain significant, especially for schooling, with large marginal impacts. This constitutes another constraint on the individual's upward mobility. The absence of any impact on girls' work suggests that female child work is directly linked to the status of women in North Indian society and a gender repartition of tasks that cuts across communities.

VII. CONCLUSIONS AND IMPLICATIONS FOR RESEARCH AND POLICY

The aim of this paper was, to (a) assess the incidence of child work in rural North India, and study its determinants, and (b) compare the impacts of long-run wealth and household exposure to income shocks with those of alternative factors to examine the validity of the food insecurity hypothesis. A number of results emerge from the analysis, that go beyond Duraisamy's (2000) earlier results.[12]

Full-time child work is not very common in rural North India, but affects a significant fraction of children aged 10 to 14. With few exceptions, girls, who constitute two-thirds of all working children, do household work, while boys activities are more diversified, as they also include wage and child labour as well as informal non-agricultural activities.

Turning to the determinants of child work, there is evidence that food insecurity increases child work, but it is difficult to ascertain that it is its only or even its main direct cause. Indeed, exogenous long-run wealth significantly reduces child work, but this relationship is linear and the slope is not very steep, so that admittedly lower levels of child work are observed in relatively well-off households, which one would not consider as subsistence-poor. The variables proxying for households' exposure to income shocks and the impact of the father's main occupation provide additional evidence that economic vulnerability is associated with higher levels of child work.

As far as girls are concerned, the ultimate cause of child work is the gender-distribution of tasks in rural North Indian society, that is orthogonal to income levels. Besides parental education, the few variables that are found to significantly affect child work relate to the substitution between child and adult females' work. Indeed, household work is the sole responsibility of women, with the consequence, that female child work, rather than male adult work is substituted for female adult work if the latter is not available. Female child work entirely depends on household structures. The need to take care of younger siblings and do household chores, clearly, is a major constraint on girls' leisure and schooling. The burden of pre-adolescent and adolescent girls is heavier in food-insecure, or more generally, poor households, but this comes as the next important constraint and compounds the impact of the gender-repartition of tasks. For example, food insecurity could cause mothers to work for wages, and thus raise the time for which girls aged 10 to 14 are asked to spend on household work. Food insecurity would not lead children to engage in direct income-generating activities, but it would be an indirect cause of other forms of child work.

As boys engage in more diverse activities, the picture for them is less monochromatic. Joint significance indicates that, besides long-run wealth and parental characteristics, only exposure to income shocks and the productivity of farm labour matter, but more household composition variables are individually significant for them than for girls. Many boys, at least those performing tasks other than wage labour, are thus likely to work for other reasons than food insecurity.

The implications of these activities for schooling are consistent with those of previous studies in India and other developing countries. School and work are, unsurprisingly, substitutes, and respond both positively and negatively to all variables that affect them both. Household structures are once again decisive, and there is evidence of 'sibling rivalry', i.e., children benefit from having sisters rather than brothers.

The implications of the results in terms of methodology concern data collection above all. The limited information on child work available in NCAER-HDI data constrains the analysis. Future surveys should aim to collect information on the time spent by children and adults on different activities, thus allowing a finer analysis of the substitution between schooling and work and between different types of work. The fact that, in this paper, the impact of the productivity of farm labour on child work is observed through schooling suggests that occupation status variables miss part-time workers, understating the actual incidence of child work, as shown by Hirway (2001), who presents the first results of the recent and pioneering Indian Time Use Survey. Coupling time-use data with classical information on households, schools, and villages should be a major source of improvement in existing theoretico-empirical models.

It is, however, likely that choice-based sampling will become necessary: where the incidence of child work is not very high, sampling methods not targeting child workers are unlikely to yield sufficient numbers of observations for each type of work.

A second implication relating to methodology is that substitution between different household members' time is a crucial element of decisions on child work. Systems of simultaneous equations allowing the time parents and siblings devote to different activities to directly influence each child's work and schooling would improve our knowledge of intra-household processes, and our capacity to predict possible harmful effects of policy measures aimed at reducing child work.

Finally, as far as policy making is concerned, three observations deserve consideration:

1. Reducing female child work and increasing female schooling requires effectively setting up (a) institutions like *anganwadis* in an effective manner and, as importantly, (b) pre-primary schools, which would take care of very young children. A better implementation of the Integrated Child Development Programme (ICDS) could have a major impact on children's general well-being. It would also make it easier for women to engage in income-generating activities, and to challenge prevailing social norms suppressing their agency.
2. Given the fact that child work and schooling can be substituted for each other, it is clear that improvements in school availability and quality, as well as limited school costs or subsidies to poor households who enroll their children, would reduce child work in non-subsistence poor households. This is important since the recent increase in enrolment rates observed, for example, from the results of the last Census, is in large part due to the hasty development of private schools (De, et al., 2000). Given the impact of household wealth on child work and schooling, the latter are unlikely to contribute much towards reducing child work.
3. Growth in the income of the poor can go a long way towards reducing directly income-generating child work, but one should keep in mind the fact that even relatively well-off households have working children. Thus, providing more *anganwadis* and schools, as also the development of rural capital markets become essential requirements. Needless to say, mechanisms to ensure food security more effectively than the existing Public Distribution System are needed independently of their impact on child work. Finally, and importantly, public policy has a major role to play, not only in enhancing household incomes, but also in developing adequate rural infrastructure.

(I thank Lionel Massün (WFP) and Nira Ramachandran (IHD) for inviting me to participate to the Consultative Workshop on Child Work and Food Insecurity in Rural India, World Food Programme and Institute for Human

Development, New Delhi, March 15-17, 2001, Assit Datta and other workshop participants for their comments on a previous version of this paper, as well as Jean Drèze and Sylvie Lambert for helpful advice on ongoing research linked to this paper. Any errors and shortcomings in this paper are entirely mine.

Support from the National Council of Applied Economic Research (NCAER), especially from Abusaleh Shariff, in obtaining NCAER-HDI data is gratefully acknowledged.)

Notes

1. Madhura Swaminathan (1998), analyses of the situation in the city of Bhavnagar, Gujarat, where industries like ship-breaking employ large numbers of children in hazardous activities with tragic consequences for their welfare and life expectancy.

2. This does not apply to most types of wage labour, whatever exploitative employers may assert (Weiner, 2001).

3. See Leclercq (2001a) for a discussion of this controversial topic.

4. Provided those children do not also perform other types of work, the numbers of days worked could leave many of them enough time to attend school outside work periods. That they do not is consistent with high direct costs of schooling combined with conflicting school and work timings.

5. Children's earnings recorded in the database include the cash value of the in-kind component of children's wage.

6. Bhalotra (2000) does focuses on wage labourers. Her approach involves estimating a Heckman selection model with a first-stage regression of participation in wage labour for all children, and a second-stage regression of hours worked by wage labourers that includes a selectivity correction term computed from the first-stage regression. Conditioning on participation in the second-stage regression drastically reduces observation numbers, making the use of asymptotic estimators problematic. Moreover, the model is identified only if the first-stage regression includes variables that determine participation in wage labour but not the number of hours worked. As the two decisions are likely to be taken simultaneously, it seems impossible to find suitable candidates. Unfortunately, Bhalotra does not mention her identification restrictions. In the absence of any plausible ones using NCAER-HDI data, I do not attempt to replicate her approach.

7. The index is based on variables that are commonly used as instruments for income in the literature, and its use may be seen as a simpler alternative to instrumental variable techniques.

8. The distribution of the wealth index is lognormal, so the right end of the graph concerns a small number of very rich (by rural north Indian standards) households.

9. Meanwhile, there is little doubt that expanding women's employment opportunities should play a major role in increasing their bargaining power within and outside the household and raising household income, with positive consequences on child work and schooling (see the discussion of women's agency by Drèze and Sen, 1995). The point is that given current circumstances, most women do not have access to gainful activities, for example, extremely few women hold a formal non-agricultural job, as is evident on Figure 4, and work only when necessary. Prevailing social norms concerning women's economic opportunities have dire consequences on their own and their children's well-being.

10. Except for tractor ownership, which may pick up non-linearities in household wealth, as productive assets are excluded from the PCA index and only a few very rich households (4.4 per cent) actually own tractors.
11. Using unique school data collected in 1996 by the PROBE team in a sub-sample of NCAER-HDI villages, Drèze and Kingdon (2001) find that several elements of school quality improve enrolment, retention and grade attainment, with a large impact of midday meals, especially for girls. Coupling the same school data with a larger number of household observations drawn from the NCAER-HDI base, I obtain similar results in Leclercq (2001a). Unfortunately, the low incidence of child work in NCAER-HDI data makes the use of this smaller dataset for the analysis of child work difficult. Drèze and Kingdon argue that schooling incentives are generally poorly implemented in North India, so restricting attention to these states makes a precise evaluation of their impact difficult. Sipahimalani (1999), using NCAER-HDI data for all India, finds significant impacts of incentives programmes on elementary school participation.
12. Using NCAER-HDI data for all-India, Malathy Duraisamy displays tabulations of child work across several household variables and presents estimations results for the determinants of child work and schooling. Her basic specification includes age, gender, parental education, uninstrumented current income, caste and religion dummies, availability of electricity, and middle school and state dummies and thus does not allow to disentangle the impact of food insecurity from that of other factors, which is the focus of the present paper.

References

Baland, Jean-Marie, and James A. Robinson (2000), "Is Child Labour Inefficient?", *Journal of Political Economy,* Vol. 108, No. 4, pp. 663-679.

Basu, Kaushik (1999), "Child Labour: Cause, Consequence and Cure, with Remarks on International Labour Standards", *Journal of Economic Literature,* No. 37, September, pp. 1083-1119.

—— and Pham Hoang Van (1998), "The Economics of Child Labour", *American Economic Review,* Vol. 88, No. 3, pp. 412-427.

Bhalotra, Sonia (2000), "Is Child Work Necessary?", *DPEP* No. 26, STICERD, London School of Economics, August.

—— and Chris Heady (2000), "Child Farm Labour: Theory and Evidence", *DEDP* No. 24, STICERD, London School of Economics, July.

Bommier, Antoine, and Sylvie Lambert (2000), "Education Demand and Age at School Enrolment in Tanzania", *Journal of Human Resources,* Vol. No 351, Winter, pp. 177-203.

Cameron, Lisa A. and Christopher Worswick (2001), "Education Expenditure Responses to Crop Loss .in Indonesia: A Gender Bias", *Economic Development and Cultural Change,* pp. 351-63.

Chaudhri, D. P. (1997), "A Policy Perspective on Child Labour in India with Pervasive Gender and Urban Bias in School Education", *Indian Journal of Labour Economics,* Vol. 40, No. 4, pp. 789-808.

Cockburn, John (2000), "Child Labour versus Education: Poverty Constraints or Income Opportunities?" (mimeo), Cambridge University, Paper presented at *Journées d'Economie du Développement.* Distribution des Revenus, Pauvreté, Bien-Être, IRD, Paris, October 26-27.

De, Anuradha, Claire Noronha, and Meera Samson (2000), "Private Schools and Universal Elementary Education: A Case Study of Three Districts", (mimeo), Collabourative Reasearch and Dissemination and Institute for Human Development, Delhi

Drèze, Jean, and Geeta Kingdon (1999), "School Participation in Rural India", *Development Economics Discussion Paper,* Series No. 18, STICERD, London School of Economics, London.

—— and Amartya Sen (1995), *India: Economic Development and Social Opportunity,* Oxford University Press, Delhi, Oxford and New York.

—— (eds.) (1997), *Indian Development: Selected Regional Perspectives,* Oxford University Press, Delhi, Oxford and New York.

Duraisamy, Malathy (2000), "Child Schooling and Child Work in India", Paper prepared for the Programme of Research on Human Development, NCAER-UNDP, Delhi, December.

Filmer, Deon, and Lant Pritchett (1998), "Estimating Wealth Effects without Expenditure Data — or Tears: An Application to Educational Enrolments in States of India", *Working Paper,* World Bank, September.

Garg, Ashish and Jonathan Morduch (1998), "Sibling Rivalry and the Gender Gap: Evidence from Child Health Outcomes in Ghana", *Journal of Population Economics,* Vol. 11, No. 4, December, pp. 471-493.

Hirway, Indira (2001), "Understanding Children's Work in India: An Analysis of Their Time Use", Paper presented at the IHD-WFP *Consultative Workshop on Food Insecurity and Child Work,* March 15-17.

Jacoby, Hanan G. and Emmanuel Skoufias (1997), "Risk, Financial Markets, and Human Capital in a Developing Country", *Review of Economic Studies,* Vol. 64, No.3, July.

Jensen, Robert T. (1999), "Child Labour in Pakistan: Patterns, Causes and Consequences for Children", (mimeo) John F. Kennedy School of Government, Harvard University, September.

Lanjouw, Peter, and Nicholas Stern (eds.) (1999), *Economic Development in Palanpur over Five Decades,* Oxford University Press, Delhi.

Leclercq, François (2001a), "Patterns and Determinants of Elementary School Enrolment in Rural North India", University of Paris I, April, Paper presented at *XVIII èmes Journées de Microéconomie Appliquée,* Nancy, France, June 7-8.

—— (2001b), "Household Structures and School Participation: Is There 'Sibling Rivalry' in Rural North India?" (mimeo), University of Paris I, June.

PROBE Team (1999), *Public Report on Basic Education in India,* Oxford University Press, Delhi.

Rammohan, Anu (2001), "Development of Financial Capital Markets and the Role of Children as Economic Assets", *Journal of International Development.* No 13, pp. 45-58.

Ranjan, Priya (2001), "Credit Constraints and the Phenomenon of Child Labour", *Journal of Development Economics,* No. 64, pp. 81-102.

Shariff, Abusaleh (1999), *India: Human Development Report: A Profile of Indian States in the 1990s,* NCAER and Oxford University Press, Delhi.

Sipahimalani, Vandana (1999), "Education in the Rural Indian Household: The Impact of Household and School Characteristics on Gender Differences" Department of Economics, Yale University, August, (mimeo).

Swaminathan, Madhura (1998), "Economic Growth and the Persistence of Child Labour: Evidence from an Indian City", *World Development,* Vol. 26, No 8, August, pp. 1513-1528.

Tilak, Jandhyala B.G. (1996), "How Free is 'Free' Primary Education in India?", *Economic and Political Weekly,* Vol. 31, No. 5, February 3, pp. 275-282, and No.6, February 10, pp. 355-366.

Weiner, Myron (1991), *The Child and the State in India: Child Labour and Education Policy in Comparative Perspective,* Oxford University Press, Delhi.

9

Food Security and Child Work in South India: Determinants and Policies

S. MAHENDRA DEV AND C. RAVI

I. INTRODUCTION

The dismal plight of India's children between six and 14 years of age is vividly brought out by Myron Weiner: "Less than half of India's children between ages six and 14—82.2 million—are not in school. They stay at home to care for cattle, tend younger children, collect firewood, and work in the fields. They find employment in cottage industries, tea stalls, restaurants, or as household workers in middle-class homes. They become prostitutes or live as street children, begging or picking rags and bottles from trash for resale. Many are bonded labourers and working as agricultural labourers for local landowners"..." India's policy makers have not regarded mass education as essential to India's modernisation" (Weiner, 1991).

The Convention on the Rights of the Child recognises that every child should have a right to education. In India many children are being deprived of this right. In this context, it may also be noted that neglect of primary education is one of the biggest failures of Indian development policies. The 52nd round of NSS shows that there were about 230.8 million children in the age group, 6-14 in 1995-96, of which around 61 per cent were attending school. In other words, 39 per cent of the children in this age-group were out of school. In absolute terms, 90 million children were out of school in India during the year 1995-96 and were thus deprived of education security which is their right.

South India accounted for 33 per cent of child labour in the country in 1993-94. Interestingly it comprises the states with contrasting experiences, such as Andhra Pradesh with the highest incidence and Kerala with the lowest incidence of child labour. Also, Kerala and Tamil Nadu were more successful with the enrolment and food security as compared to Karnataka and Andhra Pradesh. These contrasts in south India present an interesting study.

The objective of this paper is to examine child work across Indian states and across regions/districts in south India as well as the relationship between food security in a broader sense and child work. Finally, it discusses some policy issues. Section II provides dimensions of child work at state, region and district level, while section III examines the determinants of child work. Section IV discusses policy issues relating to child work and the last section presents the conclusions.

II. DIMENSIONS OF CHILD WORK AT DIFFERENT LEVELS

1. The Concept

Conventionally, a working child is defined as a child in the age group, 5-14 who is engaged in some kind of work, either paid or unpaid. Here one can distinguish between 'child labour' and 'child work' in that 'child labour' is a conventional concept, whereas 'child work' is a broader one.

One can broaden the definition of child labour to child work by defining a child labourer as one who is deprived of the right to education and childhood. The child population can be grouped into three categories: school-going children, child labourers and 'nowhere' children (non-labour and non-school goers).[1] According to NSS data, the last category of 'nowhere' children forms about 35 per cent of the child population and they are potential child labourers. Therefore, the child labour problem should address not only the category of child labour, but also that of 'nowhere' children. In this study, we take up both the dimensions i.e., conventional and broader definitions.

2. Dimensions at State Level

The Population Census, conducted once in 10 years and the quinquennial sample surveys of the National Sample Survey Organisation (NSSO) on Employment and Unemployment are two main sources of data on overall employment and unemployment in the country. These two sources also provide workforce data by age distribution, which can provide information on the incidence of child labour. The employment data from the NSS is more reliable than the Census as the former has well-trained investigators. However, data at the district level can be obtained from the Census. As part of its Human Development Survey, National Council of Applied Economic Research (NCAER) provides data on various aspects of child labour for the year 1994, which refers only to rural areas. It is better to look at different sources because child labour data is quite sensitive to the nature of data collection.

Within states there are significant regional disparities in the incidence of child labour (Table 1). The Table below shows that south Indian states like Andhra Pradesh and Karnataka have a higher incidence of child labour as compared to those of poorer states like Bihar, Orissa and Uttar Pradesh. It may be emphasised here that the high proportions of child labourers in the southern states (except Kerala) could be due to the existence of job opportunities in economically better developed regions. Crops like cotton and groundnut in Andhra Pradesh, sericulture in Karnataka, match industries in Tamil Nadu, etc. can, to some extent, explain the higher levels of child labour in these states. However, this link may not be straightforward since, states like Maharashtra and Gujarat have higher areas under these crops, but their incidence of child labour is lower. The data on child labour is sensitive to the way the data is collected. Thus, there are some differences in its incidence and rank in some states. If we take NSS, data even Tamil Nadu has a higher incidence of child labour.

Table 1
Incidence of Child Labour (Age Group, 5-14) in Rural Areas Across Indian States

State	Incidence			Ranks		
	Census 1991	NSS 1993-94	NCAER 1994	Census 1991	NSS 1993-94	NCAER 1994
Andhra Pradesh	12.5	17.8	9.0	15	17	16
Karnataka	11.0	13.9	7.4	14	16	14
Kerala	0.6	0.8	0.4	1	1	1
Tamil Nadu	5.9	10.4	5.6	8	13	11
Assam	-	2.6	2.6	-	3	6
Bihar	4.4	3.7	3.9	5	5	9
Gujarat	7.1	4.1	6.2	10	6	12
Haryana	3.0	2.6	1.9	2	2	5
Himachal Pradesh	4.8	13.6	0.8	6	15	2
Jammu & Kashmir	-	5.6	-	-	9	-
Madhya Pradesh	9.9	8.4	3.5	13	12	8
Maharashtra	8.1	6.5	8.0	12	10	15
Orissa	6.5	7.4	5.1	9	11	10
Punjab	3.6	2.7	3.4	3	4	7
Rajasthan	7.8	12.2	1.2	11	14	3
Uttar Pradesh	4.2	5.0	1.5	4	7	4
West Bengal	4.9	5.1	6.7	7	8	13
All-India	6.4	7.2	4.3	-	-	-
CV Across states(%)	49.0	65.0	63.0			

Note: CV-Coefficient of Variation.
Sources: 1. Census 1991. 2. NSS 50th round on Employment and Unemployment. 3. Duraisamy (2000) for NCAER data.

According to the wider definition of child labour (i.e., child work), the number of child workers is derived by adding the percentage of 'nowhere' children (neither going to school nor working) to the number as per the conventional definition total child work is quite substantial (38 per cent in rural areas). The percentage of 'nowhere' children is quite high among girls and poorer states.

As mentioned above, the wider definition indicates that those who are not going to school can be considered as child workers. The addition of the last two categories (child labour and 'nowhere' children) gives us the number of total child workers in a broad sense because 'nowhere' children are considered as potential child labourers. The regional disparities are quite high in the percentages of non-school going children ('nowhere' + working children) (Table 2).

Table 2
Activity Status of Children, Age Group, 5-14

State	Currently enrolled	Reported working	'Nowhere' children (Not working and not enrolled)	Total child work	All-children
Andhra Pradesh	68.7	9.0	22.3	31.3	100.0
Karnataka	67.0	7.4	25.6	33.0	100.0
Kerala	91.1	0.4	8.5	8.9	100.0
Tamil Nadu	73.0	5.6	21.3	26.9	100.0
Assam	68.6	2.6	28.8	31.4	100.0
Bihar	51.8	3.9	44.3	48.2	100.0
Gujarat	67.8	6.2	25.9	32.1	100.0
Haryana	69.0	1.9	29.1	31.0	100.0
Himachal Pradesh	86.8	0.8	12.4	13.2	100.0
Maharashtra	73.7	8.0	18.3	26.3	100.0
Madhya Pradesh	52.1	3.5	44.4	47.9	100.0
Orissa	60.4	5.1	34.6	39.7	100.0
Punjab	78.8	3.4	17.8	21.2	100.0
Rajasthan	54.8	1.2	44.0	45.2	100.0
Uttar Pradesh	56.7	1.5	41.8	43.3	100.0
West Bengal	57.1	6.7	36.2	42.9	100.0
All-states	61.9	4.3	33.8	38.1	100.0

Source: Duraisamy (2000).

The poorer states like Bihar, Madhya Pradesh, Rajasthan and Uttar Pradesh have a high proportion of 'nowhere' children. The incidence of 'nowhere' children for girls is quite high in the poorer states possibly because of gender bias. The South Indian states have lower incidence of non-school going children. Table 3 shows incidence of child labour and non-school going children across regions, and significant regional disparities within and across states.

III. DETERMINANTS OF CHILD WORK

We examine the determinants of child labour at three levels using a simple linear regression model. The first exercise relates to the 17 major states of India. Next we concentrate on regional (NSSO) and district level analysis. We have used both child labour and non-school going children as dependent variables.

Several supply and demand factors determine the incidence of child labour. The poor send their children to work to augment their income. Therefore, the poverty variable is one of the important determinants for the supply side factor of child labour. It is not, however, clear which is the cause and which the effect between poverty and child labour. It is possible that child labour can perpetuate poverty. We have taken the head count ratio as well as percentage of calorie intake derived from non-cereal food as the poverty indicators. The latter reflects the food poverty. The assumption is that the better-fed derive more nutrition from non-cereal food than from cereal. Economic development (State Domestic Product), is another variable, which is supposed to reduce child labour with better opportunities for adult labour, which in turn may reduce the pressure on child labour. It is also possible that economic development might increase child labour for the same reason, i.e., better opportunities. Here, wage rate is crucial. If the wage rate for adults is high, there is a possibility for reduction in child labour. The related variable that reflects the demand for opportunities is work participation rate. Another factor that is generally related to low fertility and in turn reduction of child labour is female literacy. Availability of schooling facility in the village is crucial to the reduction of child labour. Therefore, we have also included the percentage of villages having a primary school in each state as one of the explanatory variables.

Table 3
Incidence of Child Labour and Percentage of Non-school Going Children, 1991

State/Region	Incidence of child labour	Percentage of non-school-going children
Andhra Pradesh		
1 Coastal	11.8	5.3
2 Inland Northern	13.2	62.1
3 South Western	15.2	63.4
4 Inland Southern	9.4	45.5
Karnataka		
1 Coastal and Ghat	5.3	29.5
2 Inland Eastern	8.3	39.9
3 Inland Southern	10.3	45.6
4 Inland Northern	13.1	55.1
Kerala		
1 Northern	0.6	16.4
2 Southern	0.6	11.9
Tamil Nadu		
1 Coastal Northern	5.3	34.7
2 Coastal	4.4	28.5
3 Southern	6.1	29.8
4 Inland	8.0	35.89

Source: Census 1991 and CMIE District Profile reports.

Child labour is concentrated in agriculture and food security is one of the important variables that determine variations in child labour. We have used agriculture-related variables such as value of agricultural production per-capita (rural), irrigation and per capita rural expenditure, as important explanatory variables. Our hypothesis is that human development indicators such as female literacy, and food security variables together explain variations in child labour and deprivation. In what follows we have discussed the results of our regression analysis.

At the state level, we tried different combinations of determinants of child labour in the regression analysis. In all our results, poverty as measured by the headcount ratio performed poorly with perverse signs. On the other hand, calorie intake from non-cereal food reveals significant depressing effect on child labour. Work participation rate, calorie intake and percentage of indebted rural labour households together explained about 83 per cent of the interstate variation in child labour. All the estimated coefficients are significant at one per cent level. If we take female work participation, female literacy and calorie intake, the regression equation (2) could explain almost 76 per cent of the variation in child labour. However, in this equation female literacy is not significant. To see the effect of growth and availability of primary schools on child labour, we regressed these variables on child labour along with work participation and percentage of indebted labour households. The results indicate that almost 90 per cent of the variability in child labour is explained by these four variables. Thus, at state level, factors like work participation, percentage of indebted rural labour households, calorie intake from non-cereal food, female work participation, and SDP are important determinants of child labour. Also the results are robust with respect to work participation rate and percentage of indebted households in the sense that their coefficients remain more or less invariant to the choice of other independent variables.

1. Regression Results at State Level

Dependent Variable cpr = Child Worker Participation Rate

(1) cpr = -16.3690 + 0.5414 wp - 0.1518 cal + 0.1099 debt $R^2 = 0.8289$

(0.0734) (0.0664) (0.0679)

(2) cpr = 3.4719 + 0.2910 fwp - 0.0414 fl - 0.1544 cal $R^2 = 0.7579$

(0.0523) (0.0458)n (0.0845)

(3) cpr = -15.0025 + 0.5778wp - 0.0005 sdp - 0.0768psch + 0.1110 debt $R^2 = 0.8950$

(0.0608) (0.0002) (0.0356) (0.0567)

In the case of non-school going children, the regression analysis suggests that female literacy alone can explain almost 84 per cent of interstate variations in the percentage of 'nowhere' children. Though the poverty (head count ratio) shows positive relationship with the dependent variable, it is insignificant in most cases. An interesting result of our analysis is that female work participation is negatively related to the percentage of 'nowhere' children. Together with calorie intake and female literacy, female work participation could explain 92 per cent of the variation in 'nowhere' children.

Results at State Level

Dependent Variable cnw = 'Nowhere' + Working Children

(1) cnw = 58.0626 - 0.7162 fl $R2 = 0.8456$

(0.0829)

(2) cnw = 72.6150 -0.6978 fl - 0.2617 cal - 0.2094 fwp $R2 = 0.9203$

(0.0696) (0.1282) (0.0796)

cpr: child participation rates
cnw: non-school going children (nowhere+child labour)
wp- work participation rates
fwp- female work participation rates
cal- percentage of calories from non-cereals.
debt- percentage of indebted rural labour households
psdp- per capita state domestic product
psch- percentage of villages with primary school.

Region Level in South India

Here we examine variations across NSS regions within South India. The results given below show that percentage of irrigated area, value of agricultural out put per hectare, female literacy and percentage of agricultural labour are important determinants of child labour participation., In the case of non-school going children, the variations are explained by irrigation, female literacy and per capita expenditure.

Results for Nsso Regions Data — 4 Southern States — 14 Observations

Dependent Variable cpr = Child Worker Participation Rate

(1) cpr = 19.4822 - 0.2298 fl $R2 = 0.8681$

(0.0259)

(2) cpr = -11.6102 + 0.3091 agw $R2 = 0.5224$

(0.0853)

(3) cpr = 19.7243 -0.0022 value $R2 = 0.5862$

(4) cpr = 22.1552 -0.07913 irr -0.2378 fl $R2 = 0.9396$

(0.0219) (0.00185)

Region Level Results

Dependent Variable cnw = 'Nowhere' + Working Children

(5) cnw = 111.6002 - 0.5862 fl - 0.4445 pce $R2 = 0.9000$

(0.1816) (0.2442)

(6) cnw =121.6246 - 0.2118 irr - 0.5869 fl - 0.4844 pce

(0.0224) (0.2451) (0.2245) $R2=0.9412$

Note: Figures in parenthesis refer to standard errors.

2. District Level Results for South India

The district level results are similar to those of region level results. The important explanatory variables are female literacy, and per capita expenditure. Foodgrains per capita shows a positive and significant relationship with child labour probably due to the labour-intensive nature of food crops.

Results of Regression for The District Level Data-74 Observations

Dependent Variable: Child Labour Participation Rate

(1) cpr = 45.5611 - 0.3885 pce R2 = 0.7390

(0.00271)

(2) cpr = 3.8761 + 0.0340 fgrain R2 = 0.2476

(0.0069)

(3) cpr = 18.345 - 0.2167 fl R2 = 0.7932

(0.0126)

(4) cpr = 29.6221 - 0.1402fl - 0.1523 pce R2 = 0.8906

(0.0678) (0.1298)

District Level Results

Dependent Variable: cnw = 'Nowhere' + Working Children

(5) cnw = 176.2554 - 1.4127 pce R2 = 0.7973

(0.0833)

(6) cnw = 77.5463 - 0.7689 fl R2 = 0.8664

(0.0354)

(7) cnw = 115.875 - 0.5310 fl - 0.5177 pce R2=0.8906

(0.0678) (0.1298)

Note: Figures in parenthesis refer to standard errors.

pce. — per capita expenditure
irr. — percentage of irrigated area
fgrains. — foodgrain production per capita
fl. — female literacy

IV. POLICY ISSUES

In this section we discuss the need for new policy initiatives and some issues relating to eradication of child labour and sending the children to school.

Our results in respect of regions and districts showed that food security variables represented by the agriculture variable and human development indicators are important for reducing the number of child labourers and non-school going children.

1. Food Security and Child Work

What type of policies are needed to improve food security for the households and children in particular so that the number of non-school going children would be reduced? The lessons from Kerala and Tamil Nadu would be useful here. In Kerala, as shown in Table 4, around 50 per cent of the eligible children are covered under the government's scheme for providing free noon-meals to school children (Kannan, 2000) and the Public Distribution System has also proved to be a success. Tamil Nadu has introduced a large number of nutrition programmes. Its Chief Minister's Noon-meal Programme is well known (Rajivan, 1999). There has also been an improvement in the enrolment in primary schools and decrease in school drop-out rates. India can also emulate the example of Bangladesh's food for education programme. There is a need to have more schools with schemes for providing free noon-meals for children like those in Kerala and Tamil Nadu, which attracted a large number of students.

Table 4

Free Noon-meal for School Children

Years	Total eligible students (in lakhs)	Students enrolled in the scheme (in lakhs)	Col.3 as percentage of col.2
1978-79	25.70	18.27	71
1988-89	44.43	32.00	72
1989-90	44.44	20.56	46
1990-91	44.27	20.57	46
1991-92	44.02	24.10	55
1992-93	43.54	23.42	54
1993-94	42.80	24.00	56
1994-95	41.92	21.21	51
1995-96	40.90	20.86	51
1996-97	40.11	23.75	59

Source: Kannan (2001).

Notably, as a result of appropriate public action, the levels of malnutrition in Kerala and Tamil Nadu are much lower than in the other two southern states (Table 5). In Karnataka and Andhra Pradesh total malnutrition (moderate + severe) was around 50 per cent even in the late 1990s. In the latter, malnutrition is high, despite the prevalence of the PDS.

Another observation is that the per capita calorie intake is low in Kerala and Tamil Nadu as compared to other southern states (Table 6). However, the chronically energy deficient (CED) population is comparatively lower in Tamil Nadu and Kerala, which indicates that health and sanitation, etc., are given more importance as compared to energy intake.

Table 5
Per cent Distribution of Children (Age group, 1-5) Having Malnutrition

State	Period	Moderate	Severe	Total (moderate + severe)
Andhra Pradesh	1975-79	46.1	15.4	61.5
	1988-90	44.3	7.5	51.8
	1996-97	41.5	7.2	48.7
Karnataka	1975-79	50.0	14.3	64.3
	1988-90	48.8	8.3	57.1
	1996-97	45.5	6.4	51.9
Kerala	1975-79	46.5	10.3	56.8
	1988-90	32.9	2.0	34.9
	1996-97	25.3	2.0	27.3
Tamil Nadu	1975-79	47.0	12.6	59.6
	1988-90	45.8	4.2	50.0
	1996-97	33.9	3.0	36.9

Source: NNMB Surveys, National Institute of Nutrition.

Table 6
Per Capita Calorie Intake and Percentage of Chronically Energy Deficient Adults

State	Per capita calorie intake (kcal/day) 1993-94	Chronically energy deficient (CED) (%) 1994
Andhra Pradesh	2052	49.4
Karnataka	2073	53.8
Kerala	1965	37.3
Tamil Nadu	1884	33.2

Source: NSS Report, No. 405 and NNMB Report.

2. Economic Growth, Poverty and Child Labour

The policies that improve economic growth and reduce poverty would certainly help in reducing child labour. For example, an increase in adult wages, an outcome of growth, is important to reduce the supply of child labour. But, a micro study by Swaminathan (1998) argues that economic growth alone is not sufficient to eradicate child labour. Her study examines features of child labour in an area of high economic growth in western India, where growth was associated with an increase in the number of child workers over the last 15 years. The analysis shows that children work on repetitive manual tasks that do not require long years of training or experience. The work is low paying, monotonous and hazardous. It forecloses the option of school education for most children. Thus, aggregate economic growth is not a sufficient condition for reduction in child labour.

3. Need for Compulsory Education

The establishment of compulsory education for children is an essential prerequisite for the reduction and abolition of child labour. In a narrow sense, compulsory education is understood as a law making it compulsory for parents to send their children to school and providing for the punishment of parents who do not comply with it. In a broad sense, compulsory education may be interpreted as "(a) a compulsion on the state to provide adequate schooling facilities to all children, and (b) subject to that, an obligation of the parental community to send all children to school. Thus understood, compulsory education is a broad notion" (Dreze, 1997). The most important thing is that compulsory education would put much needed pressure on the state to expand schooling facilities. The argument against compulsory education is that it leads to official harassment of parents and deprives poor families of the earnings from child labour. It may be noted here that non-coercive means can be used for promoting compulsory education. The girl child in particular would benefit from the establishment of compulsory education.[2]

The 83rd constitutional amendment for India speaks of 'the right to compulsory education'. The provision for compulsory education and right to education makes sense on the fulfillment of two conditions: (a) availability of adequate school facilities at a convenient distance, and (b) provision of free education. To introduce compulsory education before these conditions are met would be to put the cart before the horse (Dreze, 1999).[3] Some of these and other factors that need to be taken into consideration for ascertaining the feasibility of the provision for compulsory education are:

1. Reasons for not going to school and drop-outs: NSS 52nd round provides reasons for those who 'never enrolled' and for those who 'drop out from school'. The reasons are grouped into three factors: lack of interest, direct school-related factors, and direct economic factors. The major factor (nearly 50 per cent) for not enrolling is lack of interest followed by economic factors (25 to 26 per cent). Regarding drop-out from school, lack of interest is the major factor but direct school-related factors are also important. These are: (a) education not considered useful, and (b) schooling/higher education facilities not being made available conveniently.

Lieten's study (2000) on Uttar Pradesh also reveals that school-related factors are important. Some of the findings of his study are the following:

i) Access to education is a general wish among parents and children.
ii) The access remains limited due to the ill-equipped and ill-functioning government schools.
iii) The appropriation of child labour power to augment family income is generally rejected.
iv) Dissatisfaction with the school functioning may induce the child and the parents too forego 'education' of their children, enforcing them to start earning.

2. Availability of teachers and other facilities: We have seen above that school-related factors constitute a significant proportion of the reasons for drop-

out rates among children. Some data show that 22 per cent of the rural primary schools have only one teacher at the all-India level. This percentage is higher in government schools. In an absolute sense, one lakh and 12 thousand schools in rural areas have only one teacher. As regards infrastructure, about 36 per cent of primary schools and 34 per cent of upper primary schools do not have pucca buildings. Other ancillary facilities like drinking water and toilet facilities are also low for primary and upper primary schools .

3. Children can either drop-out of school because they have to work; or work because they dropped out of school: The general perception, is that children do not attend school because they have to work. Contrary to this perception, some time utilisation studies for the children suggest that most of the children who are not attending school are not doing much work either (Table 7). Also, the direction of causation does not necessarily run from child labour to non-attendance. This can be the other way round in the sense that 'drop-out' children take up productive work of their own choice or through parental pressure as a 'default occupation' (Dreze, 1997). A case study of Calcutta shows that two thirds of working children are 'working as they have nothing else to do as the schools are not very attractive and teaching conditions are poor. Thus, the schooling system is partly responsible for the persistence of child labour.

Table 7
Work Patterns of Out-of-school Children (Probe States)

Category	Boys	Girls
Proportion who worked more than eight hours on the day preceding the survey	20 per cent	22 per cent
Proportion who performed wage labour on the day preceding the survey	5 per cent	1 per cent
Average time of work on the day preceding the survey	4.2 hours	5.1 hours
Extra time of work, compared with children who are attending the school	2.1 hours	2.2 hours

Source: PROBE Survey (random sub-sample of 333 out-of-school children in the age group, 6-12.

The study by Ravallion and Wood (2000) on Bangladesh shows that education subsidies have improved school enrolment, but their impact on child labour is much lower. The study points out that the poverty trap argument cannot be used to explain the persistence of child labour in every case, because child work is not the major reason for not going to school.

In some areas, children are concentrated in large numbers. For example, in the cotton cultivation areas of Andhra Pradesh, there is a large concentration of girl child labourers. As shown in Table 8, girls work for more days and get less income. Parents work less when children are working.

Table 8
Details of Number of Working Days and Income Earned by Different Family Members

(Rs. per month)

Family	Girl		Female		Male		Total
	Days	Income	Days	Income	Days	Income	income
1.	30	420 (32%)	24	408 (31%)	18	500 (38%)	1328
2.	56*	784 (50%)	18	306 (20%)	9	480 (31%)	1570
3.	30	360 (24%)	23	390 (26%)	15	750 (50%)	1500
4.	30	420 (27%)	22	374 (19%)	50**	1200(60%	1994
5.	60*	690 (42%)	24	408 (26%)	20	490 (31%)	1588
Total	204	2674	111	1886	112	3420	7980

Notes: 1. *Two girl children are working. 2. ** Two adult males are working.
Source: Venkateswarulu (1998).

However, a study on Andhra Pradesh has shown that both parents and others make several adjustments when the children are withdrawn from work and put into the school (Table 9).

Table 9
Adjustments by Parents and Adults When Children go to School

(in per cent)

Nature of work	Adjustment in the family when the child goes to school						
	Mother	Father	Both parents	Sisters	Brothers	Other adults	Others
Domestic work	63.4	3.4	14.9	13.8	1.9	2.6	
Caring for siblings	13.0	—	17.8	13.7	2.7	0.8	52.0*
Taking care of plough bullocks	3.6	33.3	19.0	—	22.6	2.4	19.1**
Cattle herding	6.6	8.7	4.6	11.2	12.6	18.3	38.0***
Goat herding	7.8	9.6	4.8	7.9	7.1	3.0	59.8#
Bonded labour		4.1	—	—	8.1	2.0	85.9# #

Notes: 1. *Children old enough to be on their own. 2. **plough bullock sold in the market. 3. ***cattle sold in the market. 4. #Goats sold in the market. 5. # # Debt stood cancelled by use of the Act on bonded labour abolition system act (1970).

4. Role of Government

(i) Need to Focus on the Girl Child

We have seen above that the percentage of 'nowhere' children are higher for girls as compared to boys. Many of the older girls may be doing household work and taking care of younger siblings so that the parents can go out and work as labourers. One solution to this problem could be to set up institutions where there can be collective arrangements for child care such as anganwadis. PROBE (1999) survey says that the performance of anganwadis in the PROBE states is very poor. There is, therefore, a need too strengthen these institutions. In Himachal Pradesh, by contrast, about half of the villages have functioning anganwadis, and 85 per cent of these anganwadis are considered as 'satisfactory' by the local head teacher (PROBE, 1999).

Education for girls is a prerequisite for enabling them to contribute to economic growth as well as effecting improvements in living standards. The government can make special investments on residential, bridge and camp schools in the form of non-formal education which can help in bringing back working girls to mainstream education and in reducing future drop outs.[4]

(ii) Credit Availability

It has been shown in the literature that the major reasons for the emergence and existence of child labour may be credit market imperfections and the high costs of education (Grote et al., 1998). Credit availability for parents can help them improve the education of their children. Here, the government can contribute towards filling this need though of course it has to move towards free and compulsory education.

(iii) Learning from Innovative Alternative Programmes

Shiksha Karmis is an innovative programme, which has become popular with many state governments. In this programme, state governments hire part time teachers to supplement the regular teaching staff. The Shiksha Karmi programme in Rajasthan proved to be effective in carefully identifying and training local village youth to take the place of 'absentee' teachers who had abandoned remote rural schools. In Himachal Pradesh, voluntary teachers are hired at about half the salary of a regular teacher. The education Guarantee Scheme of Madhya Pradesh is another example of a low cost alternative for education. These alternative programmes can be successfully tried in different parts of the country.

5. Role of NGOs

Many NGOs have been doing good work in the field of education and child work. PROBE (1999) discusses the work of three NGOs viz., Eklavya in Madhya Pradesh, Lok Jumbish in Rajasthan and MV Foundation in Andhra Pradesh. While Eklavya and Lok Jumbish concentrate directly on education, the MV Foundation focuses on child labour.

The M.V. Foundation (2000) in Hyderabad focuses on the elimination of child labour and putting children back in schools. According to the charter of the Foundation, every child out of school is considered a child labourer. The Foundation works in about 400 villages in rural Rangareddy district in Andhra Pradesh and is said to have pulled out several thousands of children from work and put them into schools in the last few years. Some overall improvements were also found in the areas where the foundation had worked. Wages for adults seem to have improved with the withdrawal of children from the labour market; while there has been a shift in the cropping pattern so that agriculture could be managed without child labour and adults became more organised in their work. There have also been improvement in the schooling facilities. More such efforts are, however, needed in a state like Andhra Pradesh where large numbers of the country's child labourers are concentrated.

V. CONCLUSION

This paper examines the dimensions, determinants and policies regarding child labour and non-school going children in India with emphasis on the south Indian states. The share of child labour as understood in the conventional sense is highest in south India as compared to other regions (33 per cent of the child labour are in these states). However, if we look at non-school going children, the percentages are higher in states like Bihar, Uttar Pradesh and Orissa.

The determinants of child labour and non-school going children are examined at three levels: state level for the major states of India, region level (below the state) and district level for south India. The results at the state level show that factors like work participation rates, percentage of indebted rural labour households, percentage of calories from non-cereal food, percentage of agricultural labour households, female literacy, etc., explain the variations in child labour across states. Surprisingly, the poverty variable is showing perverse signs. In the case of non-school-going children, the results show that female literacy and per capita expenditure are relatively much more important. The results at the regional level for south India show that the value of major crops per hectare, irrigation, female literacy and per capita expenditure are factors that explain most of the variations in child labour. In the case of non-school-going children, the variations are explained by factors such as irrigation, female literacy and per capita expenditure. The availability of foodgrains per capita shows a positive relationship with child labour, probably due to the labour intensive nature of food crops. The district level results are also similar to those at the regional level.

The results show that food security variables and human development variables are important for reducing the incidence of child labour and the number of non-school-going children. In this respect, the experiences of Kerala and Tamil Nadu are noteworthy. These two states have more or less taken care of the food security of their population and are also in a much better position in terms of health and education, as compared to states like Karnataka and Andhra Pradesh. We have also stressed the importance of supply side factors like quality of education, role of teachers, etc., for improving the enrolment rates. One has to go beyond the poverty argument and move towards universalisation of primary education. It has been observed that even poor families make adjustments when the children are withdrawn from work and put to school.

Appendix

Table 1A
State-wise Basic Data

State	Incidence of child labour	Percentage of working and 'nowhere' children	Poverty	Total work participation rates	Female work participation rates	Female literacy	Percapita SDP	Total adult work participation rates	Adult female participation rates	Per centage of calorie from non-cereal food items
Andhra Pradesh	17.77	40.70	15.92	57.50	52.10	24.80	7006	81.00	72.40	25.57
Assam	2.60	24.20	45.01	35.30	15.90	52.10	5520	54.50	23.90	23.54
Bihar	3.65	50.30	58.21	35.10	17.20	19.70	3417	56.60	26.90	22.49
Gujarat	4.14	31.20	22.18	48.80	39.60	36.10	9054	73.20	57.90	40.39
Haryana	2.60	26.50	28.02	37.20	27.10	34.00	10526	62.20	44.00	41.02
Himachal Pradesh	13.62	14.00	30.34	55.40	52.00	51.50	6896	79.90	72.90	34.35
Jammu & Kashmir	5.56	Na	30.30	45.60	39.10	38.70	5400	72.20	59.70	32.40
Karnataka	13.92	32.20	29.88	51.70	43.00	34.60	7242	74.90	61.30	27.57
Kerala	0.76	6.80	25.76	38.10	23.80	81.70	6524	53.40	32.30	40.64
Madhya Pradesh	8.39	46.50	40.64	49.40	41.00	22.10	5516	76.50	63.00	24.95
Maharashtra	6.52	21.90	37.93	51.40	47.70	39.70	12010	77.70	70.50	31.20
Orissa	7.41	39.30	49.72	44.20	31.70	30.50	4662	65.30	45.70	16.69
Punjab	2.65	23.50	11.95	39.20	22.00	43.90	12934	58.70	32.40	49.32
Rajasthan	12.20	48.40	26.46	50.00	45.70	15.00	5315	77.60	67.20	32.89
Tamil Nadu	10.36	21.60	32.48	53.90	47.80	42.80	8051	74.80	64.70	28.68
Uttar Pradesh	5.00	43.20	42.28	37.80	21.90	22.90	4794	61.90	34.70	31.92
West Bengal	5.07	34.80	40.80	37.60	18.50	40.70	6247	58.90	28.50	22.41
All-states	7.20	36.70	37.27	44.40	32.80	32.10				28.97

Source: Results of NSSO 50th round sample survey on 'Employment and Unemployment' and 'Consumer Expenditure'.

Table 1A Contd.

State	Percentage villages with primary school within	Percentage of villages with middle school within	Percentage of agrl. labour households	Percentage of rural labour households	Per capita rural labour expenditure/ annum	Percentage of indebted rural labour households	Average amount of debt/ rural labour
Andhra Pradesh	68.40	21.60	41.48	49.81	3000.25	49	3642.00
Assam	80.40	30.40	22.98	34.81	2641.35	42	581.00
Bihar	63.40	20.90	39.22	42.62	2193.79	27	1476.00
Gujarat	81.30	31.50	37.85	47.84	3175.05	35	2576.00
Haryana	77.30	43.80	15.87	30.14	3331.65	50	5158.00
Himachal Pradesh	40.50	17.00	2.85	15.22	3389.75	21	3322.00
Jammu & Kashmir	86.90	19.10	3.33	14.85	3548.71	30	2022.00
Karnataka	74.80	38.50	37.74	41.51	2702.74	37	2962.00
Kerala	87.00	73.40	28.22	47.78	3805.68	29	6957.00
Madhya Pradesh	78.10	22.80	34.85	39.84	2466.59	24	3858.00
Maharashtra	74.10	31.50	41.17	49.63	2736.73	33	3690.00
Orissa	72.80	25.00	25.46	29.12	2240.68	26	2361.00
Punjab	78.00	26.10	27.69	34.82	3994.37	31	4176.00
Rajasthan	75.50	27.90	9.97	26.38	3321.40	40	5698.00
Tamil Nadu	90.30	35.70	42.08	54.65	2981.73	33	3497.00
Uttar Pradesh	46.20	16.90	15.31	19.25	2583.83	39	3272.00
West Bengal	72.50	16.80	32.57	42.83	2707.51	40	1405.00
All-states	67.00	24.20	30.34	38.29	2778.57	35	3169.00

Source: Villages primary scholl and middle school—NSSO 47th round on 'Availability of some Educational and Culture Related Facilities in Indian Villages' Data on labour households and their debt and expenditures are taken from 'Rural Labour Enquiry Reports'.

Table 2A
Region-wise Basic Data

State	NSSO regions	Child labour participation rates			Percentage of working and 'nowhere' children			Percentage of irrigated area	Value of major crops/ha	Female literacy	Work participation rates	Percentage of agrl. workers	Per capita foodgrain prodn.	Per capita expenditure	Poverty
		Rural	Urban	Total	Rural	Urban	Total								
Andhra Pradesh															
	1) Coastal	11.76	3.65	9.74	55.25	35.29	50.30	48.024	5570.34	36.60	42.48	71.35	199.40	85.46	31.91
	2) Inland northern	13.24	2.31	9.95	62.06	31.10	52.75	24.055	2978.70	29.93	43.13	67.43	127.76	87.18	26.98
	3) South western	15.16	4.64	12.60	63.43	42.66	58.38	13.004	3630.04	26.85	44.22	75.53	83.32	84.70	38.65
	4) Inland southern	9.43	3.17	8.11	45.52	31.99	42.68	27.609	4590.03	34.77	41.92	73.57	78.72	85.74	22.80
Karnataka															
	1) Coastal and ghat	5.26	2.97	4.69	29.47	22.29	27.69	32.416	5704.76	64.58	39.37	48.91	103.00	95.24	11.89
	2) Island eastern	8.32	2.91	7.20	39.89	25.36	36.89	20.712	6824.59	50.28	38.98	76.60	190.52	94.40	19.67
	3) Island southern	10.28	3.43	7.58	45.58	26.09	37.90	20.475	3803.11	47.63	37.08	57.30	102.21	92.55	38.86
	4) Island northern	13.09	3.78	10.76	55.13	34.95	50.07	13.831	2856.39	35.64	39.21	71.00	164.77	88.08	44.59
Kerala															
	1) Northern	0.64	0.47	0.60	16.41	13.03	15.64	13.893	5963.68	82.64	26.63	49.39	41.09	115.40	38.43
	2) Southern	0.57	0.53	0.56	11.86	10.92	11.61	13.205	8015.64	88.51	29.95	45.54	33.87	117.15	30.00
Tamil Nadu															
	1) Coastal	5.33	1.66	3.86	34.65	22.56	29.80	56.804	6269.74	52.25	37.21	55.63	117.75	95.53	54.28
	2) Coastal	4.39	1.73	3.79	28.47	22.09	27.04	56.177	6136.21	50.87	40.24	71.54	215.10	102.27	28.57
	3) Southern	6.09	3.02	5.12	29.84	22.55	27.53	37.678	4488.15	55.61	41.65	62.03	94.78	95.67	45.65
	4) Inland	8.00	4.44	6.88	35.89	25.81	32.70	28.082	6554.72	45.14	45.55	60.99	89.21	105.68	34.75

Source: Census 1991 and CMIE district profile reports.

Table 3A
District-wise Basic Data

Sl. No.	District	Child work participation rates			Percentage of working nowhere children			Percentage of irrigated area	Value of major crops/ha	Female literacy	Total literacy	WPR participation rate	Percentage of agrl. workers	Foodgrain prodn/person	1993-94 (NSSO)	
		Rural	Urban	Total	Rural	Urban	Total								PCE	Poverty
1	Srikakulam	11.63	4.65	10.78	56.61	35.28	54.02	50.11	3796.00	23.52	36.22	48.64	78.16	127.00	85.46	31.91
2	Vizianagaram	14.40	3.80	12.55	60.88	35.93	56.53	34.88	4149.00	22.47	34.19	49.86	74.73	107.00	85.46	31.91
3	Visakhapatnam	13.63	1.66	8.94	61.61	31.47	49.79	29.40	4420.00	34.60	45.51	43.11	62.24	60.00	85.46	31.91
4	East Godavari	7.79	3.29	6.77	56.04	38.35	52.03	68.10	7338.00	42.26	48.79	38.48	67.89	219.00	85.46	31.91
5	West Godavari	11.11	4.83	9.83	49.82	35.28	46.86	86.29	8088.00	46.98	53.38	43.34	71.99	342.00	85.46	31.91
6	Krishna	12.16	3.86	9.21	51.80	34.33	45.60	59.28	5500.00	45.54	53.16	43.29	66.27	265.00	85.46	31.91
7	Guntur	14.87	4.71	11.95	54.43	39.48	50.12	43.79	6595.00	35.85	46.35	47.86	73.29	214.00	85.46	31.91
8	Prakasam	11.79	3.81	10.54	56.11	34.95	52.80	27.83	3451.00	27.06	40.30	48.64	79.43	141.00	85.46	31.91
9	Nellore	10.65	3.89	9.13	52.97	31.27	48.09	75.85	6250.00	36.99	47.76	45.62	71.82	230.00	85.46	31.91
14	Mahbubnagar	16.01	4.12	14.64	70.87	33.62	66.58	13.00	1764.00	18.03	29.58	50.20	83.40	95.00	87.18	26.98
15	Rangareddy	12.23	2.31	7.78	60.25	32.83	47.94	15.64	2042.00	36.91	49.07	40.75	55.77	71.00	87.18	26.98
17	Medak	12.43	2.19	10.93	66.45	32.84	61.51	24.41	2713.00	19.25	32.41	47.77	78.11	144.00	87.18	26.98
18	Nizamabad	13.51	3.21	11.33	63.78	38.59	58.45	50.75	5005.00	21.35	34.18	49.64	66.42	208.00	87.18	26.98
19	Adilabad	12.39	1.84	9.87	64.65	37.23	58.10	9.08	1213.00	30.60	32.96	44.38	70.06	91.00	87.18	26.98
20	Karimnagar	14.27	3.11	11.74	55.80	28.28	49.57	43.23	5040.00	23.37	37.17	50.33	68.02	196.00	87.18	26.98
21	Warangal	12.32	2.30	10.40	58.18	28.59	52.51	40.10	4058.00	26.08	39.30	47.77	75.56	137.00	87.18	26.98
22	Khammam	13.77	2.17	11.41	59.38	29.33	53.27	29.20	3828.00	30.53	40.50	45.87	76.83	149.00	87.18	26.98
23	Nalgonda	11.17	2.42	10.10	57.65	27.02	53.90	30.04	3283.00	24.92	38.00	48.31	76.56	212.00	87.18	26.98
12	Anantpur	13.28	4.12	11.20	59.42	41.63	55.37	14.28	4595.00	27.61	42.18	46.20	75.86	64.00	84.7	38.65
13	Kurnool	17.19	5.12	14.05	67.76	43.60	61.49	13.89	2740.00	26.04	39.97	46.51	75.18	104.00	84.7	38.65
10	Chittoor	9.58	2.91	8.30	43.41	29.61	40.76	36.42	4778.00	36.44	49.75	45.93	74.75	66.00	85.74	22.8
11	Cuddapah	9.20	3.46	7.85	48.54	34.63	45.27	26.77	4360.00	32.36	48.12	43.94	71.76	97.00	85.74	22.8
9	Dakshini Kannada	5.05	3.33	4.62	25.86	20.78	24.58	33.46	5684.00	67.96	75.86	43.17	42.53	103.00	95.24	11.89
20	Uttara Kannada	5.69	2.19	4.86	36.98	25.67	34.28	16.48	5746.00	56.77	66.73	38.78	65.45	103.00	95.24	11.89

Table 3A contd.

7	Chikmagalur	7.92	2.86	7.04	38.43	22.13	35.61	10.59	6083.00	51.31	61.05	45.96	78.11	169.00	94.4	19.67
12	Hassan	9.42	2.98	8.30	40.93	26.04	38.33	14.28	7257.00	44.90	56.85	44.24	78.90	161.00	94.4	19.67
13	Kodagu	6.33	3.17	5.81	36.91	28.10	35.46	4.01	8914.00	61.22	68.35	47.16	73.85	168.00	94.4	19.67
18	Shimoga	8.05	2.84	6.70	40.53	25.67	36.70	48.03	6034.00	51.42	61.53	40.88	74.70	232.00	94.4	19.67
2	Bangalore (rural)	8.97	6.89	8.58	41.09	33.43	39.68	17.43	2771.00	38.15	50.17	43.01	74.05	215.00	92.55	38.86
14	Kolar	12.50	3.53	10.44	46.45	27.48	42.09	24.27	3104.00	37.75	50.45	43.42	76.12	111.00	92.55	38.86
15	Mandya	9.72	3.69	8.74	41.72	27.73	39.43	43.06	5725.00	36.70	48.15	44.51	80.83	189.00	92.55	38.86
16	Mysore	9.40	3.00	7.60	55.09	28.51	47.62	19.06	3401.00	37.95	47.32	40.20	69.15	123.00	92.55	38.86
19	Tumkur	11.96	4.16	10.70	43.07	27.55	40.57	14.89	4517.00	41.93	54.48	47.68	77.99	136.00	92.55	38.86
3	Belgaum	10.10	2.50	8.39	47.87	27.95	43.38	26.30	4699.00	38.69	53.00	42.35	71.87	153.00	88.08	44.59
4	Bellary	19.37	6.59	15.81	62.21	40.61	56.19	30.22	3561.00	31.97	45.57	45.13	75.55	184.00	88.08	44.59
5	Bidar	8.07	1.96	6.90	53.76	32.80	49.75	7.32	2374.00	30.53	45.11	39.86	76.22	130.00	88.08	44.59
6	Bijapur	11.43	3.11	9.52	50.40	33.39	46.50	14.19	2045.00	40.06	55.13	41.64	76.37	178.00	88.08	44.59
8	Chitradurga	12.14	3.93	9.97	46.45	30.94	42.35	22.36	3986.00	43.36	55.48	43.05	71.67	207.00	88.08	44.59
10	Dharwad	13.81	4.27	10.61	48.24	35.20	43.87	9.39	2970.00	45.20	58.68	42.14	70.45	116.00	88.08	44.59
11	Gulbarga	13.99	2.43	11.26	65.94	35.51	58.76	3.32	1671.00	24.49	38.54	43.07	77.09	142.00	88.08	44.59
17	Raichur	16.13	4.73	13.81	69.93	45.77	65.01	20.14	2809.00	22.15	35.96	44.43	51.01	229.00	88.08	44.59
1	Kasaragod	1.32	0.93	1.26	19.46	15.07	18.77	17.96	4057.00	76.29	82.51	33.33	48.21	30.00	115.4	38.43
2	Kannur	0.25	0.38	0.31	14.59	12.63	13.64	5.59	7922.00	87.65	91.48	28.87	39.74	16.00	115.4	38.43
3	Wayanad	1.10	1.68	1.12	18.16	17.33	18.13	9.40	5831.00	77.69	82.73	38.77	74.84	67.00	115.4	38.43
4	Kozikode	0.29	0.27	0.29	14.58	12.21	13.71	2.99	6349.00	86.79	91.10	26.57	32.26	7.00	115.4	38.43
5	Malappuram	0.37	0.34	0.37	17.25	15.43	17.09	12.86	7019.00	84.09	87.94	24.29	53.16	28.00	115.4	38.43
6	Palakkad	1.12	1.04	1.11	15.40	12.89	15.03	25.24	4232.00	75.72	81.27	35.48	59.82	117.00	115.4	38.43
7	Thrissur	0.79	0.68	0.76	11.18	9.68	10.80	41.75	7200.00	86.94	90.20	31.96	38.45	49.00	117.15	30
8	Ernakulam	0.84	0.41	0.63	9.81	9.29	9.56	30.26	6409.00	89.27	92.35	33.44	32.21	44.00	117.15	30
9	Idukki	0.67	0.64	0.66	15.92	12.78	15.78	2.24	11122.00	82.96	86.94	39.71	76.83	12.00	117.15	30
10	Kottayam	0.34	0.48	0.36	10.50	9.47	10.32	6.12	8962.00	94.00	95.72	31.23	49.65	35.00	117.15	30
11	Alappuzha	0.32	0.32	0.32	11.06	10.16	10.79	15.86	6945.00	91.12	93.87	34.09	40.13	59.00	117.15	30
12	Pathanamchitta	0.32	0.42	0.34	10.95	8.23	10.58	4.73	7676.00	92.38	94.39	29.73	59.30	24.00	117.15	30
13	Kollam	0.40	1.07	0.53	11.72	14.29	12.21	2.10	8202.00	87.00	90.47	32.10	46.28	22.00	117.15	30

Table 3A contd.

14	Thiruvanantha-puram	0.74	0.48	0.66	13.86	13.60	13.77	5.31	6922.00	85.76	89.22	32.60	46.98	14.00	117.15	30
2	Chengalpattu MGR	5.14	1.59	3.62	30.36	22.29	26.91	80.68	6691.00	55.22	66.38	38.06	51.30	140.00	95.53	54.28
3	N. Arcot Ambedkar	5.17	2.52	4.33	30.03	27.37	29.19	56.67	4012.00	48.58	60.87	40.42	56.99	169.00	95.53	54.28
5	Tiru' Sambuvaryar	6.32	2.50	5.88	35.25	26.21	34.19	0.00	0.00	39.25	53.07	45.64	80.28	0.00	95.53	54.28
6	South Arcot	5.07	1.60	4.57	39.22	23.27	36.90	60.21	7966.00	39.70	52.86	43.68	80.16	200.00	95.53	54.28
12	Tiruchirapalli	5.80	1.78	4.76	31.57	22.21	29.16	29.20	5773.00	48.94	61.22	46.39	69.68	131.00	102.27	28.57
13	Thanjavur	2.93	1.80	2.68	25.63	22.44	24.92	72.57	6980.00	54.77	66.02	40.58	72.34	301.00	102.27	28.57
14	Pudukkottal	5.07	1.13	4.56	28.95	19.53	27.73	51.00	4922.00	43.62	57.63	44.25	75.37	184.00	102.27	28.57
11	Dindigul Anna	7.44	2.51	6.37	34.44	21.81	31.70	29.31	5288.00	43.94	56.68	49.11	73.03	117.00	95.67	45.65
15	Patumpon 'M-Thevar	4.64	1.35	3.77	28.18	21.71	26.46	56.78	4456.00	49.74	63.04	46.11	73.41	103.00	95.67	45.65
16	Madurai	6.69	2.67	4.95	32.99	22.10	28.29	51.95	7077.00	54.74	66.41	43.99	61.82	118.00	95.67	45.65
17	Kamarajar	10.17	6.59	8.89	35.80	25.86	32.25	33.09	3392.00	50.17	62.91	50.08	52.71	55.00	95.67	45.65
18	Ramanatha-puram	5.31	1.99	4.59	30.26	25.12	29.15	30.45	2718.00	48.70	61.59	45.43	74.21	111.00	95.67	45.65
19	Chidambaranar	5.48	2.50	4.26	28.55	21.69	25.74	0.00	0.00	64.57	73.02	41.59	55.30	80.00	95.67	45.65
20	T' Katta-bomman	7.02	3.26	5.87	30.17	23.06	28.00	45.10	2830.00	54.23	65.58	47.18	55.84	97.00	95.67	45.65
21	Kannlyakumari	1.33	1.36	1.33	17.01	17.60	17.10	48.57	8696.00	78.39	82.06	30.51	58.82	52.00	95.67	45.65
4	Dharmapuri	8.55	3.44	8.09	41.06	27.18	39.80	19.65	5054.00	34.23	46.02	47.59	80.76	141.00	105.68	34.57
7	Salem	7.21	6.49	7.00	34.01	29.60	32.70	27.52	7175.00	41.45	53.31	49.25	61.04	98.00	105.68	34.57
8	Periyar	9.97	4.56	8.55	37.45	27.15	34.76	41.84	5017.00	41.58	53.80	52.31	63.46	105.00	105.68	34.57
9	Nilgiri	1.09	1.40	1.25	22.20	22.67	22.44	0.84	21288.00	61.47	71.70	40.69	66.37	6.00	105.68	34.57
10	Coimbatore	8.15	3.86	5.84	31.91	23.33	27.30	40.83	6479.00	55.73	66.35	45.14	44.50	50.00	105.68	34.57

Correlation Matrix for State Level Data

	|cpr	nwh	povrt	wp	fwp	fl	psdp	tawp	afwp	cal	psch	msch	aglhh	rlhh	pexp	debt	debtam
cpr|	1.0000																
nwh|	0.1569	1.0000															
pvrt|	-0.2410	0.4362	1.0000														
wp|	0.8541	-0.1282	-0.3923	1.0000													
fwp|	0.8016	-0.2150	-0.3975	0.9790	1.0000												
fl|	-0.3745	-0.7072	-0.2322	-0.1816	-0.1842	1.0000											
psdp|	-0.1349	-0.3635	-0.6103	0.1492	0.1763	0.2471	1.0000										
tawp|	0.8181	-0.0621	-0.3208	0.9544	0.9683	-0.3758	0.1225	1.0000									
afwp|	0.7730	-0.1952	-0.3738	0.9555	0.9917	-0.2512	0.1798	0.9818	1.0000								
cal|	-0.3224	-0.5240	-0.7328	-0.0800	-0.0073	0.3618	0.6751	-0.0829	-0.0006	1.0000							
psch|	-0.2881	-0.2601	-0.2338	-0.0547	-0.0338	0.2628	0.2357	-0.1164	-0.0415	0.1246	1.0000						
msch|	-0.3208	-0.3778	-0.2653	-0.1578	-0.1047	0.6525	0.2402	-0.2983	-0.1459	0.3937	0.5133	1.0000					
aglh|	0.0650	0.4171	0.0648	0.1479	0.0382	-0.0608	0.2152	0.0271	-0.0022	-0.2452	0.3244	0.1752	1.0000				
rlhh|	0.0141	0.2124	-0.0921	0.1576	0.0764	0.1531	0.2888	0.0067	0.0235	-0.0919	0.4825	0.4046	0.9336	1.0000			
pexp|	-0.1280	-0.7214	-0.8269	0.0598	0.1233	0.5114	0.5115	0.0008	0.1043	0.8595	0.2503	0.3901	-0.3895	-0.1592	1.0000		
debt|	0.0779	0.1728	-0.2827	-0.1122	-0.1026	-0.1980	0.1816	-0.0675	-0.0903	0.0502	0.1335	0.0904	0.0921	0.1716	0.0299	1.0000	
dbtam|	0.0451	-0.2459	-0.5430	0.1627	0.2532	0.2235	0.3229	0.1259	0.2470	0.5886	0.1434	0.6359	-0.1184	0.0780	0.5794	0.0496	1.0

Correlation Matrix for Region Level Data

	cprr	nwr	irr	value	fl	wp	agw	fgrains	pce	poverty
cprr|	1.0000									
nwr|	0.9863	1.0000								
irr|	-0.1541	-0.0812	1.0000							
value|	-0.7656	-0.7623	0.2305	1.0000						
fl|	-0.9317	-0.9390	-0.1197	0.6933	1.0000					
wp|	0.7295	0.6992	0.2884	-0.4196	-0.8461	1.0000				
agw|	0.7227	0.7236	0.0895	-0.4242	-0.8212	0.6704	1.0000			
fgrains|	0.3634	0.3957	0.5167	-0.1038	-0.4744	0.4285	0.6408	1.0000		
pce|	-0.8802	-0.8973	-0.1334	0.7195	0.8902	-0.7167	-0.7050	-0.4523	1.0000	
poverty|	0.0509	0.0511	0.1290	-0.2210	-0.0613	-0.1103	-0.0848	-0.1321	0.0306	1.0000

Correlation Matrix for District Level Data

	cprr	nwr	irr	value	fl	tl	wp	agw	fgrains	pce	poverty
cprr|	1.0000										
nwr|	0.9439	1.0000									
irr|	0.1409	0.1400	1.0000								
value|	-0.5175	-0.4951	0.0639	1.0000							
fl|	-0.8906	-0.9308	-0.2335	0.4930	1.0000						
tl|	-0.8971	-0.9501	-0.2309	0.4872	0.9928	1.0000					
wp|	0.7339	0.6791	0.2478	-0.3377	-0.8226	-0.8015	1.0000				
agw|	0.5577	0.6050	0.0745	-0.2260	-0.7065	-0.6968	0.6468	1.0000			
fgrains|	0.4976	0.5097	0.6060	-0.1575	-0.5332	-0.5373	0.4443	0.4734	1.0000		
pce|	-0.8598	-0.8929	-0.3105	0.4494	0.8800	0.8785	-0.6872	-0.6208	-0.5787	1.0000	
poverty|	-0.0131	-0.0594	0.0721	-0.2112	-0.0319	0.0110	-0.0587	-0.0105	-0.0632	-0.0119	1.0000

Notes

1. See Chaudhri (1997) for this classification.
2. See Sinha (1994) on the need for compulsory education.
3. On basic education, see PROBE, 1999.
4. World Bank's 'District Poverty Initiative Project' (DPIP) in six districts of Andhra Pradesh has given emphasis to girls education in the form of investments in bridge schools.

References

Chaudhri, D.P. (1997), "A Policy Perspective on Child Labour in India with Pervasive Gender and Urban Bias in School Education", *The Indian Journal of Labour Economics,* Vol. 40, No.4.

Dreze, J. (1997), "Primary Priorities , Lesson in Compulsory Education", *Times of India,* October 15.

Duraisamy, M. (2000), "Child Schooling and Child Work in India," Paper prepared for NCAER, New Delhi under its "Programme of Research in Human Development" (mimeo).

Grote, U., A. Basu and D. Weinhold (1998), "Child Labour and the International Policy Debate," *ZEF Discussion Papers on Development Policy.*

Kannan, K.P. (2000), "Food Security in a Regional Perspective: A View from Food Deficit Kerala", *Working Paper No.304,* Centre for Development Studies, Thiruvananthapuram.

—— (2001), "Food Security for Reducing Child Deprivation: Kerala's Remarkable Record," Paper presented at IHD-WFP *Workshop on Food Insecurity and Child Work,* New Delhi, March 2001.

Lieten, G.K. (2000), "Children, Work and Education", *Economic and Political Weekly,* Vol. 35, Nos. 24 and 25.

MV Foundation (2000), *Annual Report, 1999-2000,* M. Venkatarangaiya Foundation, Hyderabad.

PROBE (1999), *Public Report on Basic Education in India,* Oxford University Press, New Delhi.

Rajivan, Anuradha (1999), "Incentives in Nutrition: The Story of Noon Meals in Tamil Nadu", Paper presented at the *Seminar on Social Security in India,* April 15-17, Institute for Human Development, New Delhi.

Ravallion, M. and Q. Wodon (2000), "Does Child Labour Displace Schooling? Evidence on Behavioural Responses to an Enrollment Subsidy?" *Economic Journal,* Vol.110, March 2000, pp.158-176.

Sinha, Shantha (1994), "Child Labour and Compulsory Education", *The Child and the Law,* UNICEF, New Delhi.

Venkateswarulu, D. (1998), "Girl Child Bonded Labour in Cotton Seed Fields: A Study of Two Villages in Rangareddy District of Andhra Pradesh", A study commissioned by MV Foundation.

Weiner, Myron (1991), *The Child and the State in India,* Oxford University Press, Delhi.

PART III

Regional Variations: Profiles of Vulnerable States

10

Child Work in Bihar: A Leeway for Household Food Insecurity

PIUSH ANTONY

I. INTRODUCTION

The causes of the existence and perpetuation of child work have been articulated from many perspectives, which, in turn, have facilitated the formulation of various interventions. Food based intervention, though widely advocated and practiced as a poverty alleviation strategy, is, however, yet to find a legitimate space in the discourse on interventions towards eliminating child labour. This is attributed to two primary reasons. First, a direct linkage between food security of the households and child work has not been successfully established. Second, as a corollary, food-based interventions with different target groups have not been analysed for their potential to impact on the magnitude of child work. In the recent decades, a few select programmes such as the Public Distribution System with its protective element for household food security, and more recently, the noon-meal scheme for school-going children with a high priority on the nutritional aspect can be seen as exceptions to this. Although these programmes have made some desultory engagements with food-based interventions towards child work, their exact impact is unknown.

This paper makes an attempt to highlight a rather simple relationship that is too opaque to be considered while formulating many other specific interventions. For this, food as the most essential of basic needs, the insecurity of which can lead to the deprivation of other basic entitlements, is taken up to understand the nuanced relationship it holds with a set of other economic, social and cultural factors in perpetuating child labour.

II. METHODOLOGY

The data used for this study have been drawn from a larger survey conducted in the year 1999-2000 in the six districts of Bihar. A cluster analysis was done to select the districts, which were clustered from the north and south plains of Bihar on the basis of differentiation across the districts in terms of seven indicators. These were population growth, population density, urbanisation, tenancy, cropping intensity, use of high-yielding varieties (HYV) of paddy and tubewell cultivation. Further, from each cluster of districts obtained by using the above indicators, one district was selected with a probability proportional to the rural population. The districts selected for the final survey were Nalanda, Rohtas, Gopalgunj, Gaya, Madhubani and Purnea. From each of these districts, three villages spread over two representative blocks were chosen for the household survey. Out of these villages, a Census survey was conducted in one village, while a sample survey was undertaken in the remaining two villages. On the basis of the Census survey in the 12 villages across all the selected districts, a proportionate random sampling resulted in the selection of 20-25 per cent of the households for the second round of detailed survey. The present paper is based on this detailed survey of 12 villages.

III. FRAMEWORK OF THE STUDY

Bihar, with about 85 per cent of rural population, ostensibly has a more pronounced agrarian base for its economy. According to the latest NSS 55th round on employment, 80.6 per cent of the total rural workforce is engaged in agriculture and allied activities. Juxtaposed with the rural poverty ratio of 58 per cent in the state, it can be inferred that an overwhelming majority of rural households live at a subsistence level. In other words, these households tend to function more on the basis of a food economy with comparatively less market engagements. However, this marginalisation exposes them to a series of vulnerabilities vis-a-vis the household food economy which works at a subsistence level. The term 'food economy' refers to the production, consumption and distribution of food within the household and any shortfall in any of these adversely affects the food security of the household. As in other rural economies in India, traditional mechanisms used by households to cope with food insecurity are steadily being eroded due to the sustained incursions caused by the market. Added to this has been the large-scale influx of state-sponsored strategies designed to counter food insecurity which are affected by a cortex of inter-linked factors related to targeting, efficiency, appropriateness and adequacy. The households are thus left with the single option of relying completely on the labour market, which is in turn highly segmented.

The labour market segmentation in Bihar needs to be understood in terms of its crucial linkage with the institution of caste. The demand for and supply of labour are determined by the dynamics of the social composition of the population with semi-feudalism at one end of the continuum and the strict social caste hierarchy with its undertone of political clout at the other end (Jeffery and Jeffery, 1997). This strong caste-class nexus in the labour market, naturally, has a significant bearing on the food security of the household. One of the few options that the households exercise is to have 'more hands' in the labour market to overcome the contingencies of such a segmented and pre-determined labour market.

This paper attempts to understand the existence of child workers in Bihar in the context of the specificities and contingencies of the rural labour market in India with its spill over effect on the food insecurity of the household leading to the incidence of child work. Based on the field data the, paper, therefore, tries to understand:

(i) the prevalence and intensity of child work and the nature of the work engaged in by children;

(ii) the food security of the households defined in terms of social and economic accessibility and availability of main food items and of culturally accepted alternate dietary supplements as a determining factor behind the magnitude of child work found in the surveyed villages.

The basic premise on which this analysis rests are:

a) the 'rational choices' of a poor household tend to be dominated by the choices they have to make vis-a-vis the food economy;

b) food is a social commodity and, therefore, food insecurity of the household needs to be juxtaposed with the social choices the household has in terms of accessing other entitlements in the market;

c) given the labour market specificities, the presence of child workers in a household is one of the mechanisms for coping with the problem of food insecurity of the household.

With these premise as the backdrop, the household survey data was analysed to bring out the incidence of child workers and their nature of work which in turn have been cross-tabulated against the social and economic status of their households (caste and ownership of land). Food consumption expenditure groupings of the households are used as indicative of food security which is further analysed for its linkages with the incidence of child labour.

Such an analysis aims at understanding the exigency, if any, for food-based interventions and to provide policy directions for such interventions wherein social factors are taken into consideration.

IV. INCIDENCE AND CHARACTERISTICS OF CHILD WORK IN THE SURVEYED VILLAGES

The data in this section shows a disheartening bias reflected in the caste-class composition of child workers. It is well established that the Indian rural economy is still in the grip of a strong caste-class nexus. While there has been considerable group mobility in India, the so-called lower caste groups still account for a major portion of the poorest. Poverty, the most popular argument in explaining the perpetuation of child labour in India, also emanates from this nexus. In our data too, one sees a strong association between incidence of child labour and the socio-economic status of the households (Table 1).

Table 1
Percentage of Child Workers by Caste, Class and Land-size

Category	Worker	Non-worker
Caste		
Forward caste	5.06	94.94
Other backward caste (I)	29.68	70.32
Kurmi	10.26	89.74
Yadav	18.39	81.61
Koeri	10.20	89.80
Other backward caste (II)	16.22	83.78
SC/ST	17.97	82.03
Muslims	19.21	80.79
Class		
Agrl. labour	26.06	73.94
Poor and marginal peasants	8.57	91.43
Middle peasants	9.72	90.28
Big peasants	7.72	92.28
Landlords	4.39	95.61
Non-agriculture	11.58	88.42
Land-size (acres)		
Nil	23.27	76.73
Up to 1	14.19	85.81
1 to 2.5	10.10	89.90
2.5 to 5	10.48	89.52
5 to 10	1.08	98.92
10 to 20	100.00	
More than 20		100.00
All	15.49	84.51

Although the highest concentration of child workers is seen in households belonging to the category of 'other backward castes' (OBC (I)), a substantial proportion of child workers are seen amongst Muslim, SC/ST and Yadav households (see Table 1). The caste-class correlation is apparent in that the majority of child workers belong to either agricultural labour households or to families with marginal landholdings. Next to agriculture labour households, it is non-agriculture households that show the highest incidence of child labour. The size of landholdings further substantiates this clustering of child workers in the lowest caste/class category of the sample. Land being an indicator of class status, it can be seen from our data that households with land size of up to 5 acres have more child workers, compared to those with more than 5 acres of land. It is significant that landless households show the highest incidence of child work in the land size category.

1. Emerging Consensus

A consensus is emerging among scholars that in rural India, child work gets institutionalised in the 10-14-age cohort (Mishra, 2000) as is substantiated by our data. It shows that across caste and class groups, a higher proportion of older children participate in commonly accepted and valued 'productive' work. In fact,

9.3 per cent of the total workers, who constitute to 15.5 per cent of the total children in the sample households, fall in the age group, 10-14 (Table 2).

Table 2
Percentage of Workers in Different Age Groups

	Age group (broad)			
Category	5-9	10-14	15-59	60 & above
Caste				
Forward caste	0.44	4.22	88.00	7.33
Other backward caste (I)	5.03	14.20	73.08	7.69
Kurmi	1.82	5.45	87.27	5.45
Yadav	3.64	10.91	80.00	5.45
Koeri		8.77	84.21	7.02
Other backward caste (II)	2.45	12.27	80.37	4.91
SC/ST	4.20	8.62	81.12	6.06
Muslims	4.47	11.73	76.54	7.26
Class				
Agrl. labour	5.12	12.81	76.95	5.12
Poor and marginal peasant		6.00	90.00	4.00
Middle peasant		5.93	84.75	9.32
Big peasant	2.11	4.82	84.34	8.73
Landlord	0.45	4.05	87.39	8.11
Non-agriculture	1.00	10.00	81.50	7.50
Land size (acres)				
Nil	5.06	11.50	78.00	5.44
Up to 1	1.31	9.97	82.94	5.77
1 to 2.5	1.81	7.53	82.53	8.13
2.5 to 5	2.24	7.46	80.60	9.70
5 to 10		0.90	90.99	8.11
10 to 20			82.76	17.24
More than 20			100.00	
Total	3.03	9.26	81.02	6.68

While interpretations of the strong caste-class correlation in Bihar are varied, the field evidence shows that there is a clear occupational stratification in Bihar, which determines the age and type of occupation in which younger members of particular caste categories will participate. It is important to note that amongst the various caste groups, a higher proportion of Muslim child workers are employed as non-agricultural labour, while a majority of SC and OBC children are involved in agriculture and allied activities (Table 3).

At the same time, it is important to note that the highly agrarian base of Bihar's economy precludes much economic activity and, therefore, productive work in fields other than agriculture (Das, 1992). This is reflected in children's occupational profile—about 13.7 per cent of the child workers are productively employed as agricultural labour and in cultivation. Further, if animal grazing is also taken into account, approximately 25 per cent of all working children belong to agriculture and the allied sector. Another interesting feature is that nearly one half of all working children are engaged in household work and a large proportion

Table 3
Occupational Structure of the Working Children

Category	Occupational structure of working children							
	Cultivation	Agriculture labour	Non-agriculture labour	Servants	Animal grazing	Collecting wood/ cowdung	House-work	Others
Caste								
Forward caste	4.76	4.76	0.00	0.00	0.00	9.52	76.19	4.76
Other backward caste (I)	1.54	6.15	4.62	1.54	21.54	21.54	43.08	0.00
Kurmi	0.00	50.00	0.00	0.00	0.00	25.00	25.00	0.00
Yadav	6.25	0.00	0.00	0.00	18.75	12.50	62.50	0.00
Koeri	60.00	0.00	0.00	0.00	0.00	0.00	40.00	0.00
Other backward caste (II)	12.50	8.33	0.00	4.17	4.17	29.17	29.17	12.50
SC/ST	1.82	14.55	1.82	3.64	20.00	12.73	45.45	0.00
Muslims	6.90	3.45	13.79	0.00	3.45	17.24	55.17	0.00
Class								
Agrl.labour	5.84	11.69	3.25	1.95	15.58	18.18	42.86	0.65
Poor and marginal peasant	0.00	0.00	0.00	0.00	0.00	0.00	100.00	0.00
Middle peasant	0.00	0.00	0.00	0.00	14.29	14.29	71.43	0.00
Big peasant	13.04	0.00	4.35	0.00	0.00	13.04	69.57	0.00
Landlord	0.00	0.00	0.00	0.00	10.00	20.00	70.00	0.00
Non-agriculture	0.00	0.00	9.09	4.55	18.18	18.18	36.36	13.64
Land size (acres)								
Nil	3.05	12.21	4.58	1.53	15.27	19.85	40.46	3.05
Up to 1	9.30	2.33	4.65	2.33	6.98	16.28	58.14	0.00
1 to 2.5	9.68	3.23	0.00	3.23	19.35	6.45	58.06	0.00
2.5 to 5	7.69	0.00	0.00	0.00	7.69	23.08	61.54	0.00
5 to 10	0.00	0.00	0.00	0.00	0.00	0.00	100.00	0.00
Total	5.48	8.22	3.65	1.83	13.70	17.35	47.95	1.83

of children (17.35 per cent) are engaged in fuel wood and cow dung collection. Household work, being of an informal nature implies work without any monetary payment. This work is mostly done by girl children and includes taking care of younger siblings. Several studies have also come out with concurring evidence that girl children are normally engaged in assisting in home-based production, including animal husbandry, etc.

Poor educational status has always been one of the critical indicators of the prevalence and magnitude of child labour. Many scholars have effectively demonstrated the direct relationship between the lack of education and child labour (Wiener, 1992). The field data adds substance to this argument, in that, 89.5 per cent of child workers have never had any schooling and 9.5 per cent have marginally participated in primary education (Table 4). A clear caste-class relationship can be seen in the proportion of child workers who have attended primary schools. The child workers belonging to the landlord households and to Kurmi and Koeri caste groups (upwardly mobile middle caste groups) seem to have had at least an opportunity to enroll in schools. In comparison, child workers belonging to OBC I, Muslim, SC and ST households have had no exposure to formal education. In fact, the field data seems to point to their complete lack of access to education. This is further substantiated by the field data on the level of education amongst working and non-working children, wherein one can clearly identify a causal caste-class relationship in the context of child workers.

Table 4 shows educational attainment of workers and non-workers across caste, class and land size. It can be seen that child workers from the most backward, SC and Muslim communities are mostly illiterate. The illiteracy level among SC/ST is over 96 per cent and that among Muslims is over 93 per cent. When it comes to class groups, child workers from agricultural labour, poor and marginal peasants have substantially high illiteracy when compared to other groups. A similar level of illiteracy is seen among the landless households and those possessing land of up to one acre in size.

The field data reveals that more than a quarter (27 per cent) of the total children in the age group, 5-14 have never enrolled in any school in the plains of Bihar (Table 5). Interestingly, it can be seen that never enrolled children appear across all caste groups. While over 43 per cent children from SC/ST families are never enrolled, the corresponding percentage from the OBC (I) is around 52 per cent. Even among the Upper castes, 8 per cent of the children have reportedly never enrolled in school. The proportion of non-enrolled children is also high among agriculture labour households (44 per cent), non-agriculture households (18 per cent) and to a smaller extent among the landlord households (4 per cent). This phenomenon needs to be understood in the light of a multitude of factors such as lack of infrastructure, economic compulsions, practice of involving children in household chores as well as in home-based production.

Table 4
Level of Education among Working and Non-working Children Aged 5-14

Category	Worker			Non-worker			
	Illiterate	Primary	Middle	Illiterate	Primary	Middle	High school
Caste							
Forward caste	66.67	28.57	4.76	11.42	77.16	11.42	0.00
Other backward caste (I)	95.38	4.62	0.00	42.21	51.95	5.84	0.00
Kurmi	75.00	25.00	0.00	8.57	60.00	31.43	0.00
Yadav	93.75	6.25	0.00	16.90	76.06	5.63	1.41
Koeri	60.00	40.00	0.00	13.64	81.82	4.55	0.00
Other backward caste (II)	79.17	16.67	4.17	27.42	63.71	8.06	0.81
SC/ST	96.36	3.64	0.00	47.41	47.81	4.78	0.00
Muslims	93.10	6.90	0.00	42.62	53.28	4.10	0.00
Class							
Agrl.labour	95.45	3.90	0.65	46.00	48.97	5.03	0.00
Poor & marginal peasant	100.00	0.00	0.00	21.88	68.75	9.38	0.00
Middle peasant	71.43	14.29	14.29	21.54	63.08	12.31	3.08
Big peasant	86.96	13.04	0.00	14.55	72.73	12.73	0.00
Landlord	40.00	60.00	0.00	9.17	80.28	10.55	0.00
Non-agrl. labour	77.27	22.73	0.00	32.14	63.69	4.17	0.00
Land size (acres)							
Nil	94.66	5.34	0.00	47.92	47.92	4.17	0.00
Up to 1	86.05	11.63	2.33	26.92	65.38	7.31	0.38
1 to 2.5	80.65	16.13	3.23	15.58	75.72	8.33	0.36
2.5 to 5	69.23	30.77	0.00	8.11	80.18	11.71	0.00
5 to 10	100.00	0.00	0.00	6.52	72.83	20.65	0.00
10 to 20	0.00	0.00	0.00	0.00	72.73	27.27	0.00
More than 20	0.00	0.00	0.00	50.00	50.00	0.00	0.00

Table 5
Enrolment Status of Children Aged 5-14

Category	Enrolment status of children		
	Never enrolled	Enrolled but not regular	Enrolled and regular
Caste			
Forward caste	8.52	4.44	87.04
Other backward caste (I)	52.26	6.45	41.29
Kurmi	17.65	35.29	47.06
Yadav	15.38	9.23	75.38
Koeri	4.08	16.33	79.59
Other backward caste (II)	18.27	16.35	65.38
SC/ST	43.17	16.94	39.89
Muslims	35.44	15.19	49.37
Class			
Agriculture labour	44.15	12.17	43.68
Poor and marginal peasants	10.53	10.53	78.95
Middle peasants	10.53	10.53	78.95
Big peasants	13.54	6.77	79.69
Land lords	4.48	8.21	87.31
Non-agriculture	18.33	17.50	64.17
Land Size			
Nil	42.20	12.14	45.66
Up to 1	26.36	15.45	58.18
1 to 2.5	15.38	12.09	72.53
2.5 to 5	8.05	0.00	91.95
5 to 10	8.70	2.90	88.41
10 to 20	0.00	11.76	88.24
More than 20	0.00	0.00	100.00
District			
Gaya	26.72	7.76	65.52
Gopalgunj	18.71	8.63	72.66
Madhubani	21.64	11.94	66.42
Nalanda	51.72	8.62	39.66
Purnea	35.47	10.81	53.72
Rohtas	13.41	15.64	70.95
Total	26.57	11.06	62.36

2. Regional Disparity in the Education System

At first glance it seems that there is a clear regional disparity in the educational system in the state. Almost half the child population, 51 per cent in Nalanda have never been enrolled in schools; and a third (31 per cent) of the children in Purnea too have never attended school. This finding however, needs to be explained and interpreted beyond the stylised facts and empirical evidence that seem obvious. In the case of Purnea, secondary data too points to the poor educational infrastructure and, given the high concentration of certain communities (Muslim and OBC I) that lack access to formal education in the district it, is not surprising that the enrolment rate is comparatively very low. In the case of Nalanda, the reasons are more complex and one that is a result of the caste composition of the sample households. On the one hand, Nalanda district has a substantially higher SC population and on the other, the villages chosen for the survey were clearly divided along caste lines. As an aside, the caste-class relationship was most stark in Nalanda and this is reflected in the enrolment figures of the sample households. It is to be noted that education status, especially enrolment is linked to ownership of assets, especially size of landholdings. As the land size of the household increases, an increase in the education participation can be seen. For example, among the landless, the proportion never enrolled stands at around 42 per cent, while the same is as low as 8.7 per cent among the households with 5-10 acres of land. In respect of households with land sizes above 10 acres, all children are enrolled.

In general, across districts, caste and class groups, as expected, a majority of the child workers have never been enrolled in schools and the few privileged who have been a part of the formal educational system have been unable to cross the glass ceiling of primary education. However, this becomes important when seen in the context of the economic status of the child labour families. Children help their families in several ways. As seen from Table 6, children have been reported undertaking different types of work, irrespective of their education status. Predominantly, children are engaged in tending animals and taking care of younger siblings (Table 6). Children irrespective of their enrolment status largely handle these two activities. While among the never enrolled, over 34 per cent of children are involved in sibling care, among the other two categories (irregular and regularly attending school) over 27 per cent reported sibling care. This is also the case with animal husbandry wherein never enrolled, irregular and regular school going children are almost equally involved in this activity.

Table 6

Distribution of Enrolled and Non-enrolled Children Aged 5-14 by Working Status and Types of Work

Type of work performed by children	Enrolment status of children					
	Never enrolled		Enrolled not regular		Enrolled and regular	
	Count	Col %	Count	Col %	Count	Col %
Not working	99	40.41	41	40.20	293	50.96
Wage labour	9	3.67	1	0.98	0	0.00
Help in family cultivation	4	1.63	5	4.90	6	1.04
Looking after animals	42	17.14	20	19.61	102	17.74
Help in other domestic work	4	1.63	0	0.00	2	0.35
Looking after younger siblings	84	34.29	28	27.45	158	27.48
Others	3	1.22	7	6.86	14	2.43
Total	245	100.00	102	100.00	575	100.00

3. High Proportion of 'Nowhere' Children

However, what is more intriguing is that a high percentage of children are reported not working-It is as high as 40 per cent among the never enrolled. This phenomenon of children not being part of either the school or the work force (formal or informal) is referred to as 'nowhere' children (Chaudhri, 1996).

Though it can be convincingly argued that 'nowhere' children are potential child workers, their existence needs deeper probing. The main reason for counting out these children from the work force lies largely in what is culturally understood as 'work'. These children are not sent to the school mainly because the concept of work in the state-is such that it does not carry the intrinsic value of education.

Although there are many demand-side factors that contribute to the existence of 'nowhere' children, in the case of Bihar, the social construct of work is particularly significant. For parents who have to start the day early in the morning, a school-going child is a liability at least in the earlier classes. Their daily nutritional requirements are affected not only by the availability or accessibility of the food items in the households, but also by the timings at which food is served.

V. UNDERSTANDING FOOD SECURITY FROM SOCIOLOGICAL STANDPOINT

In this section, an attempt is made to understand food security from a sociological angle as the findings in the above section clearly bring out the social composition of child work heavily skewed towards the lower caste groups. Many of the qualitative findings are garnered from the focus group discussions and social mapping exercises undertaken in the study villages.

The concept of social commodities has been very significant in explaining the dynamics of Indian villages. Many anthropological studies in the early part of the 20th century highlighted the social distances between the different social groups but overlooked the social constructs of differential values ascribed to essential needs across the categories of social groups. However, the latter half of the century witnessed a deluge of literature pertaining to this. Most of these studies, which attempt to understand rural poverty, caste-class nexus in the villages, marginalisation of certain communities, migration, etc. recognised social accessibility as an explanatory variable in relating to many of the developmental problems of rural India. Of significance was the finding on lack of social accessibility of education, and health. No less significant was the almost total exclusion of public places by certain social groups. Though various social movements, political developments and policy interventions in the country have contributed to the disappearance of many of the overt forms of social exclusion from the public places, there is enough evidence to prove that village India is still grappling with it. Food, a concept with a cultural connotation has been the least discussed in the discourse on social exclusion, mainly because of the sensitivity of the issue coupled with the pre-conceived notions about the food basket and practices of different social groups. This lacuna in our knowledge system on social exclusion had various policy backlashes. While many micro-level studies reveal that there is a two-class system in the villages alongside, there were research studies conducted to investigate the lack of access to the public distribution system by the targeted groups. Similarly, many studies focused on the failure of noon-meal schemes to attract children to school. Though these studies overlooked social exclusion that is in practice, they did contribute suggestions such as for community-sponsored schools and area-specific health centres, which becomes a basis for taking policy initiatives. While these ostensibly solved the problems of physical proximity, they contributed very little towards solving the problems of social exclusion.

Food: A Social Commodity

Food security of the households being largely a problem of the lower income groups, which are mostly from the lower castes necessitates an understanding of food as a social commodity. A social commodity possesses besides its economic value, a socially ascribed value, which is maintained through the various social mechanisms of maintaining *status quo*. In the case of Bihar, this is most evident in the diversity of food basket and in the availability of the foodgrains to the various social groups. While the richer households have a wider choice of main cereals pulses and grains throughout the year, the poorer households with a strong caste bias towards the lower caste groups, possesses a limited choice in terms of their consumption basket. This is clearly brought out by the focus group discussions with the communities. Most of the lower caste groups use alternate main cereal throughout the year due to cultural preferences and affordability, and any shortage in the income adversely affects the already limited food basket.

Another important point in this context would be the continued practice of making payment of wages in kind in rural Bihar. This practice constitutes both demand and supply factors for child labour and brings out a saga of causal factors of a vicious nature. The prevalence of wages in kind undoubtedly brings down the adult wage rate, and lower wage rates in a highly segmented labour market of a semi feudal social structure implies high indebtedness among the labourers. The patron-client relationship that presupposes the practice of wages in kind further substantiates this inference. Family indebtedness as a major cause for child work is well established and in our study, though indebtedness did not get reflected as a major factor, the focus group discussions reveal that most of the child workers are not paid labour. This came out very clearly for those child workers who are engaged in animal husbandry as most of those who are involved in cattle grazing for the landlord's house are not paid but are given one full meal. Based on this qualitative information which came out quite clearly in the focus group discussions, and which is of importance in understanding the food insecurity of the household and the coping mechanisms that the family chooses, we have tried to classify the households with child workers into food consumption categories. Food expenditure is given in rupee terms for the main food items consumed for the month of the survey and we have taken the clusters based on the averages for these categories.

Food is treated as a key private resource in this paper. There have been studies in India, which have documented the fact that a household's social security is closely and inextricably interlinked to its food sufficiency. Taking cognisance of this, in India, poverty is quantified in nutritional terms. Although, this has generated a plethora of debates on the deterministic measure of a concept like poverty, it remains to be said that food sufficiency is a vital and important indicator of a household's well-being. From the above discussion it is evident that the class-caste background of working children determines their access to formal education. However, a closer look at the economic status of these households reveals that both per capita consumption and per capita expenditure are abysmally low.

Table 7 presents the data related to household level food sufficiency. It can be seen that as one moves down the caste ladder, food insecurity becomes visible. Among different classes, agriculture and non-agriculture labour have reported food sufficiency of the order of 55 and 54 per cent, respectively. In terms of land size, one can see a clear situation of food insecurity among the landless and marginal farmers, those who own land of sizes exceeding 5 acres are found to be completely self-sufficient in food.

Table 7
Distribution of Working Children by Households with Food Sufficiency

Category	Food sufficient for whole year?
Caste	
Forward caste	90.48
Other backward caste (I)	60.00
Kurmi	50.00
Yadav	75.00
Koeri	40.00
Other backward caste (II)	70.83
SC/ST	41.82
Muslims	51.72
Class	
Agriculture labour	55.19
Poor and marginal peasants	100.00
Middle peasants	85.71
Big peasants	56.52
Land lords	100.00
Non-agriculture	54.55
Land size (acres)	
Nil	46.56
Up to 1	76.74
1 to 2.5	77.42
2.5 to 5	76.92
5 to 10	100.00
Total	58.90

Table 8 shows the relationship between child work and food sufficiency in households. It can be seen that child workers across all castes, class and categories of farmers, mostly come from households who have reported food insufficiency conceived in term of expenditure on consumption of man food items. This relationship is particularly pronounced in the case of Kurmi, OBC II and Muslim castes.

Table 8
Distribution of Working and Non-working Children by Households with Food Sufficiency

Category	Is there food sufficiency for whole year?			
	Yes		No	
	Worker	Non-worker	Worker	Non-worker
Caste				
Forward caste	5.01	94.99	5.56	94.44
Other backward caste (I)	25.83	74.17	38.24	61.76
Kurmi	5.41	94.59	100.0	—
Yadav	15.38	84.62	44.44	55.56
Koeri	5.41	94.59	25.00	75.00
Other backward caste (II)	12.78	87.22	46.67	53.33
SC/ST	14.02	85.98	22.54	77.46
Muslims	13.51	86.49	35.00	65.00
Class				
Agriculture labour	23.22	76.78	30.67	69.33
Poor and marginal peasants	8.82	91.18	100.00	—
Middle peasants	8.96	91.04	20.00	80.00
Big peasants	4.80	95.20	37.04	62.96
Landlords	4.67	95.33	100.00	
Non-agriculture	8.70	91.30	19.23	80.77
Land size (acres)				
Nil	18.77	81.23	29.41	70.59
Up to 1	13.36	86.64	17.86	82.14
1 to 2.5	8.54	91.46	26.92	73.08
2.5 to 5	8.33	91.67	75.00	25.00
5 to 10	1.08	98.92	—	—
10 to 20	—	100.00	—	—
More than 20	—	100.00	—	—
Total	11.83	88.17	27.78	72.22

A substantial proportion, 32 per cent of the total number of child workers belong to the households whose consumption expenditure on food is the lowest and about 29 per cent of those workers come from household, which fall in the next consumption expenditure category. Thus, the lowest two categories account for over 60 per cent of the child workers. This correlation is further corroborated by the fact that a majority of the households with child workers come from the lower-caste groups. (Table 9)

What are the implications of this correlation at the household level and for the child worker? At the household level, we can argue that food insecurity of the household exposes the child to work, especially where food is given as wages. Here it is important to recall the existence of a substantial section of 'nowhere' children or potential child labourers who will be absorbed into the labour force without wages, but for a square meal per day, while a large section of child workers engaged in animal husbandry is already working for wages in kind. At the same time, for the parents of the child workers this forms a short-term coping mechanism in two ways. One, the provision of food for a non-earning member is

Table 9
Percentage Distribution of Child Workers by Food Consumption Class

Category	Per capita consumption expenditure on food					
	1	2	3	4	5	Total
Caste						
Forward caste	0.00	0.00	100.00	0.00	0.00	100.00
Other backward caste (I)	42.42	27.27	9.09	9.09	12.12	100.00
Kurmi	0.00	0.00	33.33		66.67	100.00
Yadav	50.00	50.00	0.00	0.00	0.00	100.00
Koeri	0.00	100.00	0.00	0.00	0.00	100.00
Other backward caste (II)	28.57	21.43	35.71	7.14	7.14	100.00
SC/ST	26.09	34.78	34.78	4.35	0.00	100.00
Muslims	36.36	18.18	18.18	0.00	27.27	100.00
Class						
Agrl.labour	38.16	27.63	21.05	5.26	7.89	100.00
Poor & marginal farmers	0.00	0.00	0.00	0.00	0.00	100.00
Middle peasants	0.00	0.00	100.00	0.00	0.00	100.00
Big peasants	0.00	75.00	0.00	0.00	25.00	100.00
Landlords	0.00	0.00	0.00	50.00	50.00	100.00
Non agriculture	0.00	28.57	42.86	0.00	28.57	100.00
Land Size (acres)						
Nil	33.90	33.90	18.64	1.69	11.86	100.00
Up to 1	31.25	18.75	31.25	12.50	6.25	100.00
1 to 2.5	36.36	9.09	18.18	18.18	18.18	100.00
2.5 to 5	0.00	40.00	60.00	0.00	0.00	100.00
5 to 10	.	.	.	.	.	.
10 to 20	.	.	.	.	.	.
Above 20	.	.	.	.	.	.
District						
Gaya	44.44	5.56	44.44	5.56	0.00	100.00
Gopalgunj	87.50	12.50	0.00	0.00	0.00	100.00
Madhubani	10.00	30.00	40.00	10.00	10.00	100.00
Nalanda	33.33	50.00	16.67	0.00	0.00	100.00
Purnea	23.81	33.33	14.29	7.14	21.43	100.00
Rohtas	14.29	57.14	28.57	0.00	0.00	100.00
All	31.87	28.57	23.08	5.49	10.99	100.00

Notes: Per capita consumption expenditure on food: 1. lowest 20 per cent of the households in terms of consumption 2. next 20 per cent of the households 3. next 20 per cent of the households 4. next 20 per cent of the households 5. highest 20 per cent of the households (80 per cent to 100 per cent).

taken care of and two, the food requirements of the children are ensured even during the periods of food insufficiency. It merits mention here, that in a situation when the consumption basket or the income levels are at the lowest, especially, during seasonal distress due to lack of employment, the family makes the rational choice of ensuring food for their children by making them work in less hazardous jobs in agriculture and allied activities. However, this short-term arrangement introduces the child to the labour market, which absorbs the cheap labour very efficiently. This, however, adds to the food insecurity of the household in the long run as the child may not add to the food economy for a long time and even when it does the contribution would be meagre as his/her wages may not be adequate to meet the consumption requirements.

With this understanding, what is the scope for food-based interventions in eliminating child labour?

As our focus group discussions reveal, food as an incentive in the school is not yet a popular measure in our study villages. This was to the extent that none was sure of the availability of such a scheme in the schools. But those who were sure of it complained about the low quality and insufficiency of grain. Even regarding access to the public distribution system, it was reported that many did not possess the below poverty line card. Those who possessed, accessed rations when other buyers recommended the quality. However, it was observed that the caste of the proprietor of the shop, (the shop being located in the main village where social accessibility is limited was) also brought up as an issue affecting the accessibility of the public distribution system.

As we found that the maximum number of child workers are in the 10 to 14 age group and this is the age group where macro level data report maximum dropout, food based interventions as an incentive for school attendance exhibit the potential of an effective strategy. Experiences of other states are also in support of this. However, given the extremely polarised social exclusions in rural Bihar, to ensure efficiency at the policy level, any food-based intervention should be self-selective with minimum value addition components in it to avoid leakages. A cooked meal, which is culturally acceptable, is one possibility. It has to be mentioned here that many micro-level studies reveal that the efficiency of distribution of nutritive food packets for the school-going children is low. For, it was not a self-targeted intervention and the value added component at the hand of providers or in the family being high, the target optimisation is minimal.

Social exclusion being the strongest in the case of food, delivery channels have to sensitised in terms of actual delivery of the intervention to accommodate the specificities of the target group. Though Bihar is the only state where decentralised governance is yet to take off, any interventions to eliminate child labour have to incorporate the village communities into the task as they possess both the conventional strappings of security, as well as the means to effect efficient delivery.

(The author wishes to acknowledge the help she received from Anup K. Karan in data analysis and contributions from V. Gayathri in preparing this paper.)

References

Chaudhri, D.P. (1996), *Dynamic Profile of Child Labour in India,* 1951-1991, CLASP, ILO, New Delhi.

Das, Arvind N. (1992), *The Republic of Bihar,* Penguin, New Delhi.

Jeffery R. and P. Jeffery (1997), *Population, Gender and Politics,* Cambridge University Press, Cambridge.

Mishra, Lakshmidhar (2000), *Child Labour in India,* Oxford University Press, New Delhi.

Weiner, Myron (1991), *The Child and the State in India,* Oxford University Press, New Delhi.

11

Hunger, Illiteracy and Child Deprivation in a Tribal Region: A Study of Jharkhand

NIRA RAMACHANDRAN AND ANUP K. KARAN

I. THE STUDY AREA

The newly constituted state of Jharkhand includes 18 districts falling within four administrative divisions of the erstwhile state of Bihar (Table 1). Carved out of the southern plateau region, the formidable terrain and dense forests have rendered the area relatively inaccessible and inhabited largely by tribal population. Prior to the formation of the new state, Jharkhand accounted for approximately 45 per cent of the total geographical area of Bihar, with only one-fourth of its population.

Table 1
Administrative Divisions of Jharkhand

Administrative division	District
North Chotanagpur	Dhanbad, Bokaro, Giridih, Hazaribagh, Koderma, Chatra
South Chotanagpur	Lohardaga, Gumla, Ranchi, East Singhbhum, West Singhum
Palamau	Palamau, Garhwa
Santhal Pargana	Dumka, Deogarh, Godda, Sahebganj, Pakur

Seven out of the 18 districts have a population density of less than 200 persons per sq. km (Table 2), the lowest being Gumla with only 127 persons per sq. km. Only two of the 18 districts have a density of over 500 persons per sq. km. (Dhanbad—950, Bokaro—507). Although there are about 30 different tribes in the area characterised by diverse social and economic conditions, but they can be broadly classified into three groups—the Scheduled tribes (STs), the Christian Scheduled tribes (ST Chs.) and the primitive tribal groups (PTGs) based on their income, educational levels and their interactions with the non-tribal population in the region. The incidence of poverty and deprivation is highest among the primitive tribal groups, who have a poor resource base and live in remote and relatively inaccessible areas (Dayal and Karan, 2000). The Christian tribals have a higher level of education and employment status in comparison to their non-Christian counterparts. Other settlers in the region include the *sadans* or non-tribals who have been living in the area for a long time and have more or less adapted to tribal culture and customs, and the new migrants who have settled in the urban centres to work in industry and related occupations.

Table 2
Some Demographic Indicators of Selected Study Districts

Characteristics	Gumla	Palamau	Dumka
Population growth per annum	1.34	2.78	2.32
Population density (per sq. km.)	127	192	241
Urban population (per cent)	4.53	5.34	6.12
Rural population (per cent)	94.47	91.66	93.88
S.T. population (per cent)	70.79	9.94	41.55
S.C. population (per cent)	5.31	14.59	6.93
Male population (per cent)	50.32	51.79	51.12
Female population (per cent)	49.68	48.21	48.88
Literacy rate (per cent)	39.67	31.10	34.02

Source: Census of India, 1991.

More than one quarter of the overall population, i.e., 27.67 per cent is tribal, with districts like Gumla reporting 71 per cent of its population as tribal. Tribal population is lowest in the north towards the boundary with the neighbouring state of Bihar and in the urban-industrial mining zones. Although tribals live mostly in rural areas, only about 14 per cent of the villages are purely tribal in nature. Over 50 per cent of the villages are inhabited by both tribal and non-tribal population.

Based on Census data, Jharkhand records a higher work participation rate (WPR) than Bihar — 31.34 per cent compared to 29.14 per cent (Census, 1991). However, the survey data reveals substantially higher participation rates – 54.5 per cent in the age group, 15-59. In fact, if main and subsidiary occupations are clubbed together, the overall WPR becomes as high as 92 per cent (95.48 per cent for males and 88.50 per cent for females) reflecting the level of poverty in the region. The major proportion of the workers, about 85 per cent, are engaged in agricultural activities. Of these, 63 per cent are cultivators and 23 per cent agricultural labourers.

Overall literacy levels are about 41 per cent ranging from 33 per cent in Palamau to 49 per cent in Dumka. Literacy levels are highest among the forward castes, closely followed by the Christian scheduled tribes. Even the children in the age group, 5-14 record only about 74 per cent literacy levels.

About 30 per cent of the area is under forests, while net sown area (NSA) accounts for only 25 per cent. Irrigation is available to only a small proportion of the net sown area. Except in Palamau, where 21 per cent of the NSA is irrigated, all other districts record less than 12 per cent of the NSA under irrigation. The problem of soil erosion is acute due to which a large portion of the cultivable land is destroyed every year, thus further straining the resource base. Apart from cultivation, the forest is a major resource for the local people providing edible roots, fruit, vegetables, flowers, honey, birds and animals. The *mahua* tree alone provides food, liquor and oil both for cooking and lighting. It has been estimated that access to three *mahua* trees is adequate for the survival of a tribal household for over a year.

Since only a single crop is sown in the region, agriculture does not provide employment throughout the year. Thus, over 12 per cent of the workers migrate during the lean season i.e., mid-November to mid-June to work as casual labour, both in the agricultural and non-agricultural sector. In the latter, brick kilns, construction sites, small hotels and roadside eateries provide the best employment opportunities. Migration is not restricted to neighbouring districts or states, but is often to far-off metropolitan cities as well. (Dayal and Karan, 2000). A large number of tribals live below the poverty line. The 44th round of the NSS estimated that 63 per cent of the tribals live below the poverty line. According to an occupation-wise estimate of poverty among the tribals of this region, almost 75 per cent of small and marginal farmer households, 100 per cent of agricultural labour households and about 50 per cent of households engaged in other occupations may be classified below the poverty line.

II. METHODOLOGY

This paper is based on the analysis of primary data collected from all 1103 households of 12 sample villages selected from three representative districts of Jharkhand, i.e., Gumla, Palamau and Dumka. The survey was conducted during December, 2000. The details of the sampling methodology are given below. An additional survey of a sub-set of 301 households yielded more specific information on child labour and food security issues which has helped enrich the data base.

The selection of districts for the study was carried out on the basis of a cluster analysis using six variables: 1. Forest Cover; 2. Tribal Population, 3. Urban Population, 4. Population Growth Rate, 5. Irrigated Area; and 6. Yield of Paddy. These variables represent a combination of the natural resource base, the level of agricultural and industrial development and the human resource base. One district, each, was selected from the emerging clusters i.e., Palamau, Dumka and Gumla. Within each of the selected districts, two representative blocks were chosen on the basis of block values closest to the district values. The selection of sample villages within these blocks was based on two criteria, (i) village size between 100-300, and (ii) proportion of tribal population at least 10 per cent. The main survey covered all households in the 12 sample villages, while the sub-set questionnaire was canvassed in 20-25 per cent of the households in each village (depending on village size), covering a total of 301 households.

Moreover, participatory rural analysis techniques including Focus Group Discussions, Food Calendars, etc. were also used to gather more detailed qualitative information to supplement the quantitative data base.

III. FOOD INSECURITY IN THE REGION

The threat of food insecurity is very real in the region, particularly in the case of the landless, engaged as casual labour in agricultural or non-agricultural occupations. Seasonal food shortages affect almost every household cutting across caste and class barriers, with the sole exception of large land holders. As food insecurity is an intrinsic part of rural life, traditional coping mechanisms have evolved which include the collection of edible forest products as well as gleanings from fields and other commons. The level of food distress varies from a few months of food shortages when harvest supplies run out, to near-starvation levels for small landholders and the landless during the monsoons, when both food and employment are in short supply. A large proportion of the households face food shortages for at least part of the year. As landholdings are small and irrigation facilities inadequate, the area is single-cropped and productivity is low. Food production even in a good agricultural year meets food requirements barely for six months. For the rest of the year, food intake is reduced to minimal levels and in extreme situations, the diet consists of berries, leaves and other forest gleanings.

A seasonal food calendar (Table 3) prepared on the basis of participatory techniques carried out in 12 sample villages of Jharkhand, reveals that food distress is an integral part of village life. While there are essential variations based on location, an assured food supply exists for only about three to four months of the year, i.e., in winter following the harvest in late October-early November. Food supplies tend to run short by the end of winter, and the starvation period begins by mid-summer (June) and in many cases, continues till the end of October.

During periods of starvation, people consume small amounts of coarse grains and home-grown vegetables and turn to the forest for supplies of berries, herbs, edible leaves and wild vegetables. As Mukerjee (2000) states "the commons provide a safety net for the poor villagers to tide over the hunger period". Even among the sample districts, there are variations in the level of food distress. While in Gumla, people turn to coarse cereals like maize during periods of food shortages, Dumka and Palamau do not have even maize stocks available. The villagers in these districts thus resort to consuming inferior cereals such as *goda, gondli and mahua*. The response to food shortages is in the form of cutting down amount of intake and number of meals, as well as turning to forest gleanings.

Table 4 brings out the level of food sufficiency among the sample households. Only 70 per cent of the households felt that they had access to sufficient food throughout the year. Inter district variations are evident with Dumka being worst-off with almost 41 per cent of the sample households

Table 3
Seasonal Food Calendar

Village	Availability	Shortage	Starvation
Andhradih	Nov-Feb (4)	Sep-Oct, Mar-Apr(4)	May-Aug (4)
Baradih	Dec-Mar (4)	Sep-Nov, Apr-May(5)	Jun-Aug (3)
Sarapmunda	Oct- May (8)	Aug-Sep (2)	Jun- Jul (2)
Gujharia	Nov-Feb (4)	Mar-Jun (4)	Jul- Oct (4)
Udaipura	Dec-May (6)	Sep-Nov (3)	Jun-Aug (3)
Ghutwa	Apr-Jul & Dec-Jan (6)	Feb-Mar, Nov (3)	Aug-Oct (3)
Baherakalan	Nov-Mar (5)	Oct, Apr-May (3)	Jun-Sept (4)
Karma	Dec-Mar (4)	Apr-May, Sep-Nov (5)	Jun-Aug (3)
Rampur	Dec-May (6)	Jun, Oct-Nov (3)	Jul-Sep (3)
Maheshpur	Dec-Apr (5)	May-Jun, Nov (3)	Jul-Oct (4)
Karmatand	Nov-Feb & May-Jul(7)	Mar-Apr (2)	Aug-Oct (3)
Indravani	Dec-Mar (4)	Apr-Jun, Oct-Nov (5)	Jul-Sep (3)

Note: Figures in brackets indicate number of months.

claiming to being food insecure for at least some part of the year. Across the caste groups, not even the upper caste households are totally food secure. Almost 8 per cent among upper castes felt that food supplies were not sufficient throughout the year. Among the other groups, the scheduled caste households were the worst-off with 48 per cent being food insecure, followed by the Christian Scheduled Tribes, the Muslims and the Scheduled Tribes (37, 31 and 31 per cent, respectively). Across occupational groups, the proportion of food insecure households ranged from 7 per cent (other occupations) to as much as 59 per cent of the households engaged in agricultural labour. Based on landownership, the landless, as expected were the worst-off with 48 per cent being food insecure. The proportion reduced progressively with the increasing size of land owned till households owning 10 acres and above recorded no food insecurity.

While 30 per cent of all households reported some degree of food insecurity, the extent to which the households are food insecure can be seen in Table 5. The Table reveals that two-thirds of the households experience at least two months of food distress every year, while about 8 per cent of the overall households report as much as four months of food scarcity. This seems to corroborate the findings from the food calendar, where seasonal food shortages with starvation periods from mid-summer to autumn have emerged in the exercises conducted in all the 12 villages. Similar experiences have been recorded in other areas of the country. In the hill districts of Uttaranchal, the monsoon months are the critical period with not only food stocks running out, but also the drying up of the main source of income from agriculture or construction work which also ceases during this period (Ramachandran, 2000).

Table 4
Food Sufficiency by Caste, Occupation of HH, Land Size and District

Category	Per cent households with sufficient food for the whole year
Caste group	
Upper caste	92.3
OBC I*	80.0
OBC II	76.9
SC	52.2
ST	69.1
ST (Ch)	63.2
PTG	76.5
Muslims	69.0
Occupation of HH	
Self-employed in agriculture	71.2
Agricultural labourer	41.2
Non-agriculture labourer	66.2
Salaried worker	88.9
Petty job	72.7
Petty business	70.0
Other occupation**	93.3
Non-worker	69.2
Land size (in acres)	
Landless	51.7
Up to 1	62.4
1 to 2.5	78.0
2.5 to 5	80.0
5 to 10	84.6
10 and more	100.0
District	
Gumla	76.7
Palamau	78.0
Dumka	59.5
All	70.3

Notes: 1.* OBC I connotes the lower social strata among the other backward classes.
2.** Other occupation include the gathering of firewood, cowdung for fuel, animal grazing, *jajmani* system, etc. The *jajmani* system is a traditional form of employment in villages, where a professional household provides its services to the villagers in return for foodgrain, a piece of land or other payment. The range of services provided is varied including the services of priests, carpenters, masons, barbers, etc.

IV. SCHOOL ENROLMENT AND OTHER OCCUPATIONS

While the questionnaire does not deal with class-wise enrolment at the school level, it does include the number of children in the school-going age group who are students. Among the different social groups, the upper castes recorded 84.4 per cent of their children as students, while the scheduled tribes had the lowest recorded enrolment—only 45 per cent (Table 6). The Christian scheduled tribes recorded the second highest value of 72 per cent, undoubtedly due to the

Table 5
Level of Food Insecurity by Caste, Occupation of HH, Land Size and District

Category	Per cent households by number of food deficient months in a year			
	1	2	3	4
Caste group				
Upper caste	0	100.0	0	0
OBC I	0	75.0	25.0	0
OBC II	0	50.0	16.7	33.3
SC	0	63.6	27.3	9.1
ST	10.9	67.4	17.4	4.3
T(Ch)	0	57.1	28.6	14.3
PTG	0	50.0	25.0	25.0
Muslims	22.2	77.8	0	0
Occupation of HH				
Self-employed in agriculture	6.3	75.0	12.5	6.3
Agricultural labourer	20.0	60.0	20.0	0
Non-agricultural labourer	12.5	58.3	16.7	12.5
Salaried worker	0	50.0	50.0	0
Petty job	0	66.7	0	33.3
Petty business	0	75.0	25.0	0
Other occupation	0	0	0	100.0
Non-workers	0	50.0	50.0	0
Land size (in acres)				
Landless	0	71.4	21.4	7.1
Up to 1	7.9	55.3	21.1	15.8
1 to 2.5	11.1	72.2	16.7	0
2.5 to 5	9.1	72.7	18.2	0
5 to 10	0	100.0	0	0
District				
Gumla	0	70.0	20.0	10.0
Palamau	6.9	69.0	13.8	10.3
Dumka	10.2	63.3	20.4	6.1
All	8.0	65.9	18.2	8.0

availability of good mission schools and missionary influence on the families. The Muslim community also scores low with only 62 per cent of their children enrolled.

What perhaps needs looking into is the substantial proportion of children recorded as unable to work—26.5 per cent. Since this category includes both handicapped children and those who are perceived as too young to work, the proportion ranging from 9 to 39 per cent across caste and class categories, it also raises questions of their health status, perhaps capaciously acute malnutrition, stunting or wasting which could result from nutritional deficiencies. Stunted children are often perceived as being too young to work or to enrol in school, while those subject to wasting may actually be too weak to work or study. This group of undernourished children swells the ranks of the already large pool of 'nowhere' children existing in the region. Even average values at district level for this category range between 18 to 32 per cent, Dumka scoring lowest.

Table 6
Occupational Structure (Main Occupation) of Children Aged 5 to 14 years old

Category	Cultivator	Agriculture labour	Non-agriculture labour	Petty jobs	Petty business	Other occupations	Student	Household work	Unable to work
Caste group									
Upper caste	0	0	0	0	2.2	84.4	4.4	8.9	
OBC I	0	2.6	0	1.3	1.3	9.1	58.4	9.1	18.2
OBC II	0.7	0.7	0	0.7	0	1.4	70.9	5.4	20.3
SC	0.9	0	0	0	0	11.7	55.9	10.8	20.7
ST	1.6	0.6	0.5	0.2	0.1	12.7	45.2	7	32.0
ST (Ch)	0	0	0	0	0	3.4	71.9	2.2	22.5
PTG	0	2.9	4.4	0	0	11.8	51.5	2.9	26.5
Muslims	0	0	0.4	0.4	0	7.7	62.1	7.7	21.7
Occupation of HH									
Self- employed in agriculture	1.3	0.2	0.1	0.2	0	11.2	48.8	7.6	30.6
Agriculture labour	0	4.8	1.6	3.2	0	12.9	29.0	9.7	38.7
Non-agriculture labour	0.4	0	0.4	0	0	10.7	53.9	6.6	28.0
Salaried worker	1.4	0	1.4	0	0	2.7	81.1	2.7	10.8
Petty Job	0	0	0	0	0	6.7	82.2	0	11.1
Petty business	0.6	0.6	0	0.6	1.3	3.9	71.6	5.2	16.1
Other occupation	0	3.3	4.9	0	0	14.8	54.1	6.6	16.4
Non-workers	1.3	2.5	1.3	0	0	6.3	61.3	7.5	20.0
Land size (in acres)									
Landless	0	1.5	0	0.8	0	4.5	64.4	6.1	22.7
Up to 1	0.7	0.7	0.7						
0.6	0	10	50.6	7.4	29.1				
1 to 2.5	1.2	0.4	0.4	0.2	0.2	9.8	55.1	6.3	26.4
2.5 to 5	1.0	0.3	0	0	0.3	11.5	55.7	6.6	24.6
5 to 10	0	0	0	0	0	14.8	52.5	11.5	21.3
10 and more	7.7	0	0	0	0	0	76.9	0	15.4
District									
Gumla	0.4	1.3	0	0.9	0	9.4	50.2	5.8	31.8
Palamau	1.5	0.5	0.9	0.1	0	13.5	43.3	8.4	31.7
Dumka	0.3	0.5	0.2	0.3	0.3	5.1	70.5	5.1	17.6
All	0.9	0.6	0.5	0.3	0.1	9.8	54.4	6.8	26.5

Taking all children in the age group, 5-14, only 54 per cent are in school. About 7 per cent are engaged in household work and 12 per cent in other occupations, cultivation, agricultural and non-agricultural labour, petty jobs or petty business taken together.

Children of large farmers (owning more than 10 acres of land) seem to be more actively involved in agriculture as a full-time occupation (8 per cent), smaller landholders can perhaps manage their land independently or with marginal help from their children. However, upon analysis of the proportion of children engaged as cultivators as a subsidiary occupation (Table 7), the values ranged from 12-19 per cent among all categories of landowners. The occupational status of the head of the household, whether a farmer, agricultural / non-agricultural labourer or salaried employee, does not seem to impact on the proportion of children working as cultivators. Across all the three categories, it ranges between 11 and 22 per cent.

On an average, 54 per cent of the children in the age group, 5-14 are enrolled in school, while 26 per cent form the 'nowhere' children who are neither in school nor at work (see Table 6). As Chaudhri (2000) states, sources of supply of child labour do not arise directly from increase of child population. These arise from a large pool of 'nowhere' children augmented by dropouts from school who also join this category. Looked at in terms of social groups, the scheduled tribes record 32 per cent as 'nowhere' children, while all groups other than the upper castes, have proportions ranging from 18-26 per cent. The primitive tribal group also records as much as 26 per cent of school-age children in this group.

In terms of occupation, the agricultural labour households report as much as 39 per cent of their children in this category followed by non-agricultural labour at 28 per cent. Across the districts, one finds that Dumka with the lowest incidence of child workers—12 per cent and the highest school enrolment ratio of 70 per cent, also records a considerably lower proportion of 'nowhere' children i.e., 18 per cent as compared to the other two districts (32 per cent).

Of all the children in the school-going age group, 40 per cent are illiterate (Table 8). The upper castes record the lowest levels of illiteracy, while among the Scheduled Tribes, almost half the children are illiterate. The primitive tribal groups followed by the Muslims and OBC I group record the next largest proportion of illiterate children ranging between 32-44 per cent. In terms of occupation, households headed by agricultural labourers record 61 per cent followed by farming households and casual labourers. From the landless to the small farmers, all households record 32-44 per cent as illiterate. Only amongst the large farmers owning above 10 acres, the level of illiteracy is about 15 per cent.

About 43 per cent of all the children have completed three years of pre-primary schooling (see Table 8). However, only 13.5 per cent have completed the primary stage, while a mere 3 per cent have studied further, but have not completed middle schooling.

Table 7
Occupational Structure (Secondary Occupation) of Children Aged 5 to 14

Category	Culti-vator	Agriculture labour	Non-agriculture labour	Petty business	Other occupa-tions	Student	House-hold work
Caste group							
Upper caste	10.0	0	0	0	50	0	40.0
OBC I	13.3	0	0	6.7	56.7	0	23.3
OBC II	3.3	3.3	0	6.7	66.7	0	20.0
SC	15.4	5.1	2.6	0	66.7	0	10.3
ST	15.8	2.6	0	2.9	64.7	.7	13.2
ST (Ch)	23.1	0	0	0	69.2	0	7.7
PTG	16.7	5.6	0	0	50.0	0	27.8
Occupation of HH							
Muslims	22.4	2.0	0	0	63.3	0	12.2
Self-employed in agriculture	14.1	1.1	0	2.3	68.8	.8	12.9
Agriculture labour	22.2	22.2	0	0	38.9	0	16.7
Non-agriculture labour	20.3	1.4	1.4	0	65.2	0	11.6
Salaried worker	19.0	0	0	0	57.1	0	23.8
Petty Job	11.1	0	0	0	72.2	0	16.7
Petty business	21.4	2.4	0	11.9	47.6	0	16.7
Other Occupation	0	5.9	0	5.9	41.2	0	47.1
Land size(in acres)							
Non-workers	15.4	15.4	0	0	61.5	0	7.7
Landless	7.4	0	0	11.1	70.4	0	11.1
Up to 1	14.2	3.2	.6	2.6	66.5	0	12.9
1 to 2.5	18.6	3.4	0	3.4	60.0	.7	13.8
2.5 to 5	17.3	1.0	0	0	58.2	1.0	22.4
5 to 10	14.3	0	0	0	71.4	0	14.3
10 and more	12.5	0	0	0	75.0	0	12.5
Districts							
Gumla	18.1	1.4	0	1.4	52.8	0	26.4
Palamau	17.4	2.7	.4	.4	65.9	.8	13.0
Dumka	11.7	3.1	0	7.8	64.8	0	12.5
All	15.6	2.6	.2	2.6	63.6	.4	15.0

V. PROFILE OF CHILD WORKERS

As mentioned above, WPRs are generally higher than average in Jharkhand — a reflection of the high level of poverty in the state. In the working-age group of 15-59 years, the WPR is as much as 54 per cent and remains as high as 45 per cent even in the above-59 year category (Table 9). A sizeable proportion of children in the age group, 5-14 years are full-time workers i.e., 19 per cent. If main and subsidiary occupations are clubbed, the proportion of children engaged in, either full-time or part-time work, rises to 33 per cent. In fact 13.7 per cent of the primary workforce is comprised of children. Children also account for about the same percentage of the workforce, when considering main and subsidiary occupations together (Table 10).

Table 8
Level of Education among Children Aged 5-14 by Caste, Occupation of HH, Land Size and District

Category	Percentage of children by level of education			
	Illiterate	Pre-primary*	Primary	Above primary below middle
Caste group				
Upper caste	15.6	53.3	28.9	2.2
OBC I	32.5	49.4	16.9	1.3
OBC II	22.1	46.3	20.1	11.4
SC	36.3	52.2	8.0	3.5
ST	49.1	37.8	11.0	2.1
ST(Ch)	24.4	50.0	18.9	6.7
PTG	43.5	49.3	7.2	0
Muslims	32.8	48.7	16.8	1.7
Occupation of HH				
Self-employed in agriculture	44.4	40.9	12.4	2.2
Agricultural labourer	61.3	32.3	6.5	0
Non-agricultural labourer	42.9	42.5	13.2	1.5
Salaried workers	14.5	53.9	23.7	7.9
Petty job	17.8	53.3	22.2	6.7
Petty business	22.1	57.1	15.6	5.2
Other occupation	40.7	44.1	11.9	3.4
Non-workers	37.0	38.3	14.8	9.9
Land size (in acres)				
Landless	31.9	45.9	17.8	4.4
Up to 1	43.3	43.4	10.9	2.4
1 to 2.5	40.6	43.6	13.0	2.6
2.5 to 5	36.2	42.4	16.1	5.3
5 to 10	44.3	36.1	19.7	0
10 and more	15.4	53.8	26.9	3.8
District				
Gumla	48.0	39.9	11.7	0.4
Palamau	49.2	39.9	9.5	1.4
Dumka	24.8	49.2	19.6	6.4
				6.4
All	39.9	43.4	13.5	3.1

Note: * Pre-primary schooling refers to the classes conducted at government run *anganwadis* for children aged three to six years. *Anganwadis* existed in all the sample villages of the study area. However, in two villages,they had become dysfunctional.

A further breakup (see Table 9) reveals that while 35 per cent of the children in the age group, 10-14 are full-time workers, even the age group, 5-9 records 6 per cent as full-time workers. Taking main and subsidiary occupations together, the proportions rise as high as 58 per cent for the age group, 10-14 and 11 per cent for the age group, 5-9.

This could be looked at in another way, i.e., 11.5 per cent of all main workers are children in the age group, 10-14 and as much as 2.2 per cent of the main workforce are below nine years of age. For main and subsidiary occupations taken

Table 9
Work Participation Rates Among Children and Adults

Age group	Workers (main occupation)			Workers (main and subsidiary occupation)		
	Non-workers	Others	Workers	Non-workers	Others	Workers
5-14	93.2	1.2	5.7	87.4	1.2	11.4
10-14	65.3		34.7	42.2		57.8
15-59	45.2	0.3	54.5	8.5	0.3	91.2
>59	54.8		45.2	45.2		54.8
Total	56.7	0.4	42.9	28.8	0.4	70.8

Table 10
Share of Workers by Age Groups

Age group	Workers (main occupation)			Workers (main and subsidiary occupation)		
	Non-workers	Others	Workers	Non-workers	Others	Workers
5-14	27.4	50.0	2.2	50.6	50.0	2.7
10.14	16.3		11.5	20.8		11.6
15-59	50.0	50.0	79.6	18.5	50.0	80.8
>59	6.2		6.8	10.1		5.0
Total	100.00	100.00	100.00	100.00	100.00	100.00

together, the corresponding figures are 12 per cent and 3 per cent respectively (see Table 10).

1. Caste and Class Variations

The incidence of child workers is often related to social causes. Table 11 brings out this relationship. The table reveals that children in the age group, 5-14 belonging to the upper castes or to the Christian Scheduled Tribes are least involved in the work force — only 6.7 and 5.6 per cent, respectively. The other backward classes (II) also have less than 10 per cent of their children engaged in full-time work. Of the Muslim children, a little over 16 per cent are employed full-time, while of the children belonging to the Scheduled Castes, Scheduled Tribes, the Primitive Tribal Groups and the Other Backward Castes (OBC I), over 22 per cent are full-time workers. The proportion of children engaged as full-time workers varies according to the family occupation. Of the different occupational groups, agricultural labourers have the largest proportion of child workers—32 per cent. Next in importance are the farm households where 20.6 per cent of the children work. Even among those households, where the head is engaged in non-agricultural work, about 18 per cent of the children are employed. Surprisingly, small business-men, petty job workers and salaried workers also report between 7-12 per cent of their children as full-time workers.

Table 11
Percentage of Working Children (as per Main Occupation) by Caste, Land Size, and District

Category	Percentage of workers (main occupation)		
	Non-workers	Others	Workers
Caste group			
Upper caste	93.3		6.7
OBC I	76.3		23.4
OBC II	90.6	0.7	8.7
SC	75.2	1.8	23.0
ST	76.7	0.6	22.7
ST (Ch)	93.3	1.1	5.6
PTG	76.8		21.7
Muslims	83.8		16.2
Occupation of HH			
Self-employed in Agriculture	78.8	0.6	20.6
Agricultural labourer	67.7		32.3
Non-agriculture labourer	81.3	0.7	17.9
Salaried workers	89.5	2.6	7.9
Petty job	93.3		6.7
Petty business	87.7		12.3
Other occupation	70.5		29.5
Non-worker	80.2	1.2	18.5
Land size (in acres)			
Landless	85.2	2.2	12.6
Up to 1	79.5	0.4	20.1
1 to 2.5	80.8	0.8	18.3
2.5 to 5	80.3		19.7
5 to 10	73.8		26.2
10 and more	92.8		7.7
District			
Gumla	82.1		17.9
Palamau	74.7	0.4	24.9
Dumka	87.1	1.2	11.7
All	80.4	0.6	19.0

In terms of landownership, households owning some land, i.e., below 10 acres, report between 18-26 per cent of their children as full-time workers, while among families owning more than 10 acres, this figure drops sharply to about 8 per cent. The explanation could lie in the large landowner's capacity to engage hired labour. Surprisingly, the landless households record a much smaller proportion of full-time child workers—about 13 per cent only. This would indicate the large-scale involvement of children in the agricultural work on their family farms, rather than as hired labourers. District-wise, the percentage of primary child workers ranges from about 12 per cent in Dumka to as much as 25 per cent in Palamau whereas Gumla records about 18 per cent.

Taking main and subsidiary occupations together, the proportion of child workers goes up steeply in all categories with even the upper castes recording around 18 per cent (Table 12). Among the SC and ST groups, it reaches as high as 38-42 per cent. Agricultural labour households report over 40 per cent of their children as part-time workers. In all the landowning households, over 32 per cent of part-time child workers, are recorded, while even the relatively large farmers admit to the involvement of their children (27 per cent)in farm work as a subsidiary occupation .

Table 12

Percentage of Working Children (as per Main and Subsidiary Occupation) by Caste, Land Size, and District

	Percentage of workers (main and subsidiary occupation)		
Category	Non-workers	Others	Workers
Caste group			
Upper caste	82.2		17.2
OBC I	57.1		42.9
OBC II	79.2	0.7	20.1
SC	56.6	1.8	41.6
ST	61.8	0.6	37.6
ST (Ch)	82.2	1.1	16.7
PTG	66.7	1.4	31.9
Muslims	74.9		25.1
Occupation of HH			
Self-employed in agriculture	64.3	0.6	35.1
Agricultural labourer	59.7		40.3
Non-agricultural labourer	67.8	0.7	31.5
Salaried workers	75.0	2.6	22.4
Petty job	66.7		33.3
Petty business	72.9		27.1
Other occupation	65.6		34.4
Non-worker	74.1	1.2	24.7
Land size (in acres)			
Landless	72.6	2.2	25.2
Up to 1	66.7	0.4	32.9
1 to 2.5	66.3	0.8	32.9
2.5 to 5	65.6		34.4
5 to 10	60.7		39.3
10 and more	73.1		26.9
District			
Gumla	66.4		33.6
Palamau	60.7	0.4	38.9
Dumka	74.5	1.2	24.3
All	66.7	0.6	32.7

2. Impact of Family Education

It would be revealing to analyse whether the educational level of the members of the household affects the induction of children into the workforce. In Table 13, the highest level of education attained by any one family member has been taken as representing the level of education of the household. The table shows that of all child workers, the largest segment, i.e., 33 per cent come from illiterate households, another 29 per cent come from households where no member has completed even primary schooling. The proportion of child workers progressively reduces with the educational attainment of the family which is conclusively evident from the fact that only 0.65 per cent of the child workers come from families where at least one member is a graduate.

Table 13
Percentage of Working Children by Highest Educational Attainment in the Household

Level of education	Percentage of contribution to child workforce
Illiterate	32.69
Below primary	29.13
Primary	16.50
Middle	12.62
Secondary	6.80
Higher secondary	1.29
Graduate	0.65
Others	0.32

This relationship can be further refined by taking the educational attainment of the best-educated female member of the family (Table 14). Here one finds that 71 per cent of the child workers come from the families where the mother or other women in the household are illiterate. With even a few years of schooling, i.e., below primary level, there is a dramatic drop of 53 per centage points in the proportion of child workers, i.e., to 17.8 per cent. Again, households with the best-educated female member having reached the primary level of schooling, account for only 7 per cent of the total child workers. Households which have any female member attaining secondary or higher secondary levels of education, contribute less than one per cent of the child workforce. This serves to highlight the importance of educating the women as a first step in the crusade against child work.

Table 14
Percentage of Working Children by Highest Educational Attainment of Female Member

Level of education	Percentage contribution to child workforce
Illiterate	71.20
Below primary	17.80
Primary	7.12
Middle	1.62
Secondary	0.97
Higher secondary	0.32
Graduate	-
Others	0.32

VI. OCCUPATIONAL STRUCTURE OF CHILD WORKERS

Half of the child workers are engaged in 'other occupations' which consist of the collection of firewood, cowdung for fuel, animal grazing or working under the *Jajmani* system (Table 15). A little over one-third are employed in their own households, while the rest are engaged in different agricultural and non-agricultural occupations – about 5 per cent as cultivators, 3 per cent each, as agricultural and non-agricultural labour and 1.6 per cent in petty jobs.

Caste-wise, the pattern changes with the upper castes—the OBC II and the scheduled castes reporting higher proportions of child workers engaged in their own household work and correspondingly lower proportions in other work. Across occupations, the highest proportions of child labourers remain concentrated in the 'other occupations' category. However, where landownership is concerned, large farmers owning up to 10 and more acres of land tend to employ their children as cultivators in their own fields, while the children of the smaller landholder families continue to be absorbed in housework and 'other occupations'.

Table 15
Occupational Structure (Main Occupation) of Child Workers

Category	Culti-vator	Agriculture labour	Non-agriculture labour	Petty jobs	Petty business	Other occupations	Homework
Caste group							
Upper caste	0.0	0.0	0.0	0.0	0.0	33.3	66.7
OBC I	0.0	11.1	0.0	5.6	5.6	38.9	38.9
OBC II	7.7	7.7	0.0	7.7	0.0	15.4	61.5
SC	3.8	0.0	0.0	0.0	0.0	50.0	46.2
ST	7.0	2.7	2.2	1.1	0.5	55.9	30.6
ST (Ch)	0.0	0.0	0.0	0.0	0.0	60.0	40.0
PTG	0.0	13.3	20.0	0.0	0.0	53.3	13.3
Muslims	0.0	0.0	2.6	2.6	0.0	47.4	47.4
Occupation of HH							
Self-employed in agriculture	6.3	1.1	0.6	1.1	0.0	54.0	36.8
Agriculture labourer	0.0	15.0	5.0	10.0	0.0	40.0	30.0
Non-agriculture labourer	2.0	0.0	2.0	0.0	0.0	59.2	36.7
Salaried workers	16.7	0.0	16.7	0.0	0.0	33.3	33.3
Petty job	0.0	0.0	0.0	0.0	0.0	100.0	0.0
Petty business	5.3	5.3	0.0	5.3	10.5	31.6	42.1
Other occupation	0.0	11.1	16.7	0.0	0.0	50.0	22.2
Non-workers	6.7	13.3	6.7	0.0	0.0	33.3	40.0
Land size in (acres)							
Landless	0.0	11.8	0.0	5.9	0.0	35.3	47.1
Up to 1	3.7	3.7	3.7	2.8	0.0	49.5	36.7
1 to 2.5	6.6	2.2	2.2	1.1	1.1	52.7	34.1
2.5 to 5	5.0	1.7	0.0	0.0	1.7	58.3	33.3
5 to 10	0.0	0.0	0.0	0.0	0.0	56.3	43.8
10 and more	100.0	0.0	0.0	0.0	0.0	0.0	0.0
District							
Gumla	2.5	7.5	0.0	5.0	0.0	52.5	32.5
Palamau	6.2	2.1	3.6	0.5	0.05	54.1	33.5
Dumka	2.9	4.3	1.4	2.9	2.9	42.9	42.9
All	4.9	3.3	2.6	1.6	0.7	51.3	35.5

VII. LITERACY AND EDUCATIONAL ATTAINMENT OF CHILD WORKERS

Among all the working children, 78 per cent are illiterate, whereas 17 per cent have studied till the pre-primary level. A mere 3 per cent have studied up to the primary level while only one per cent have completed primary schooling (Table 16).

Table 16
Working and Non-working Children by Level of Education

(Per cent)

Category of worker		Percentage of children by level of education			
		Illiterate	Pre-primary	Primary	Above primary-below middle
Worker (main occupation)	Non-workers	30.4	49.9	16.1	3.7
	Others	100.0	0	0	0
	Workers	78.3	17.4	3.3	1.0
Worker (main and subsidiary occupation)	Non-workers	36.6	47.4	13.2	2.8
	Others	100.0	0	0	0
	Workers	45.6	36.0	14.6	3.8

Taking working children by their occupation, it was found that of child cultivators, one-third are illiterate, 60 per cent have studied up to pre-primary level, 7 per cent at primary level and no one above that (Table 17). Among children working as agricultural labourers 50 per cent are illiterate, 30 per cent, below primary level and 20 per cent have reached upto the primary level. The child workers engaged as non-agricultural labourer are uniformly illiterate. Even children engaged in petty jobs are largely found to be illiterate, with none having reached even primary level. It is only among child workers engaged in petty business, that 50 per cent have reached the primary level of schooling. Among child workers in other occupations, about one per cent have even crossed the primary stage of schooling.

Table 17
Percentage of Children by Occupational Status (Main) and Level of Education

Occupational status (primary occupation)	Percentage of children by level of education			
	Illiterate	Below primary	Primary	Above primary-below middle
Cultivator	33.3	60.0	6.7	0
Agricultural labourer	50.0	30.0	20.0	0
Non-agricultural labourer	100.0	0	0	0
Petty jobs	80.0	20.0	0	0
Petty business	50.0	0	50.0	0
Other occupations	87.8	10.9	0	1.3
Student	0	71.3	23.4	5.3
Household work	72.2	21.3	5.6	0.9
Unable to work	92.4	6.2	1.2	0.2

Gender Disparities

Gender differences emerge sharply both at the state and district levels. While in the age group, five to nine years, 3 per cent of the boys work, the corresponding figure for girls is 8.5 per cent (Tables 18 and 19). In the age group, 10-14 years, 21.5 per cent of boys work as against 49 per cent of girls in the same group. At district level, workers account for 7-14 per cent of the male child population, but the figures for girls range from 17 to 36 per cent. Cutting across caste and class differences, the girl child in rural areas is discriminated against in terms of work. The difference is least among the upper castes but becomes conspicuous when the SC and ST groups are considered. The proportion of girl child workers is three to six-fold that of male child workers. Even among the Muslim community, 23 per cent of girl children work as against 9 per cent of boys.

Table 18
Distribution of Male Child Workers by Caste, Class and Occupation of Household

		Workers (main occupation)	
Category	Non-workers	Others	Workers
Caste group			
Upper caste	94.7		5.3
OBC I	80.5		19.5
OBC II	96.8		3.2
SC	91.7	1.7	6.7
ST	85.1	0.4	14.4
ST (Ch)	100.0		
PTG	83.8	2.7	13.5
Muslims	91.3		8.7
Occupation of HH			
Self-employed in agriculture	88.2	0.5	11.4
Agricultural labourer	77.8		22.2
Non-agricultural labourer	90.3	0.7	9.0
Salaried workers	93.5	2.2	4.3
Petty job	92.6		7.4
Petty business	88.3		11.7
Other occupation	83.8		16.2
Non-workers	82.5		17.5
Land size (in acres)			
Landless	94.3	1.4	4.3
Up to 1	88.1	0.3	11.5
1 to 2.5	86.9	0.4	12.7
2.5 to 5	87.6		12.4
5 to 10	92.3		7.7
10 and more	86.7		13.3
District			
Gumla	86.8		13.2
Palamau	85.1	0.5	14.4
Dumka	92.2	0.6	7.1
Age group			
5-9	96.0	0.9	3.1
10-14	78.5		21.5

VIII. EXPLORING THE LINKS

The foregoing analysis clearly brings out the existence of a seasonal cycle of food insecurity in the region. Most households face two to four months of food shortages with at least two months of near-starvation levels. Food insecure people devise their own coping mechanisms, the most basic of which is to have as many hands to work and earn as possible, furnishing a kind of insurance against future hunger (Ramachandran, 2001). As observed, the area is characterised by high levels of child work participation. Taking main occupations alone, 19 per cent of

Table 19
Distribution of Female Child Workers by Caste, Class and Occupational Structure

Category	Workers (main occupation)		
	Non-workers	Others	Workers
Caste group			
Upper caste	92.3		7.7
OBC I	72.2		27.8
OBC II	86.0	1.2	12.8
SC	56.6	1.9	41.5
ST	66.5	0.8	32.7
ST (Ch)	87.0	2.2	10.9
PTG	68.8		31.3
Muslims	76.7		23.3
Occupation of HH			
Self-employed in agriculture	69.6	0.7	29.7
Agricultural labourer	53.8		46.2
Non-agricultural labourer	71.1	0.8	28.1
Salaried workers	83.3	3.3	13.3
Petty job	94.4		5.6
Petty business	87.2		12.8
Other occupation	50.0		50.0
Non-workers	78.0	2.4	19.5
Land size (in acres)			
Landless	75.4	3.1	21.5
Up to 1	69.1	0.4	30.5
1 to 2.5	74.7	1.2	24.1
2.5 to 5	73.0		27.0
5 to 10	60.0		40.0
10 and more	100.0		
District			
Gumla	77.8		22.2
Palamau	63.7	0.3	36.1
Dumka	81.1	1.8	17.1
Age group			
5-9	90.0	1.5	8.5
10-14	51.4		48.6

Note: Child workers include children working in their own households.

the age group, 5-14 are engaged in the workforce. If main and subsidiary occupations are taken together, then one-third of all children in the school-going age group are workers, at least on a part-time basis.

While the coincidence of the two variables is unquestionable, establishing a link between the two needs further analysis. This section attempts to explain the incidence of child work in the region through various causal factors, food insecurity in particular.

The existence of caste-wise variations in both food insecurity levels and the incidence of child labour has already been established. Table 20 compares the per capita foodgrain consumption with the average number of child workers per household for the top 20 per cent and the bottom 20 per cent of households ranked on the basis of per capita foodgrain consumption. The Table reveals that of the top

20 per cent households which consume between 20-22 kg of foodgrain per capita per month, there are, on an average, no child workers, cutting across all social groups. The lone exception being the Scheduled Tribe households with an average of 0.16 child workers per household or in other words, one child worker in every sixth household.

Table 20
Per Capita Foodgrain Consumption and Incidence of Child Labour by Caste

	Top 20 per cent households		Bottom 20 per cent households	
	Per capita foodgrain consumption (kg. per month)	Average no. of child workers per household	Per capita foodgrain consumption (kg. per month)	Average no. of child workers per household
Upper caste	22.00	0	11.75	0.50
OBC I	21.05	0	10.63	0
OBC II	20.00	0	10.88	0.57
S.C.	20.91	0	11.71	0.50
S.T.	20.65	0.16	11.85	0.29
PTG	21.67	0	11.28	0.20
S.T. (Christians)	20.00	0	11.98	0.50
Muslims	21.02	0	12.50	0.08
All	20.86	0	11.64	0.28

Note: Foodgrain consumption has been calculated on the basis of data collected for the month of the survey (December). While the results may not be precise because of the lack of comparable data for other months, it must be remembered that December is a month of plenty and consumption levels are at the highest.

On the other hand, among the bottom 20 per cent of households ranked on the same basis, i.e., those consuming between 10.63 and 12.50 kg of foodgrain per capita, per month, the average number of child workers ranges between zero and 0.57. This implies that cutting across caste differences, among the upper castes, the OBC II, the SC and the SC Christians, every alternate household has one child worker, while among the STs, one in every three households has a child worker. Across all groups, every third household has child workers among the food deficient households, while none has a child worker among those households that are food sufficient.

It must be noted that on an all-India basis, the average requirement of foodgrain per capita, per month amounts to about 12 kg. However, among the poor, larger amounts of foodgrain are required to offset the lack of other more expensive food items in the diet. Thus, high levels of grain consumption indicate higher levels of food security in this particular region, as there is almost no consumption of meat, fish, eggs or fruit on a regular basis. (Table 21).

That households with a certain degree of food security do not put their children to work, while its reverse holds true for the most food insecure households in the region is now evident. However, whether these relationships are statistically significant remains to be seen. Table 22 tabulates the correlations between four variables basic to understanding the issue:

(i) number of food deficient months a year;

(ii) ratio of school-going children to total children in the household;

(iii) ratio of child workers to total children in the household; and

(iv) per capita foodgrain consumption per month.

Table 21
Average Number of Days of Consumption Per Month of Different Food Items

Food items	Upper caste	OBC I	OBC II	SC	ST	ST(Ch)	PTG	Muslims	All
Rice	30	30	26	24	27	30	27	26	27
Wheat	10	4	7	4	6	7	3	7	6
Other grains	4	9	12	14	14	8	19	15	13
Pulses	22	14	17	15	14	15	17	17	15
Vegetables	27	24	25	23	24	24	25	25	24
Milk	21	4	6	3	4	0	6	5	5
Eggs	0	1	1	0	0	1	1	1	1
Fish	1	1	1	1	1	1	3	1	1
Meat	2	0	1	1	1	1	1	1	1
Fruit	0	0	0	0	0	1	0	0	0

Note: Consumption of different food items has been calculated on the basis of data collected for the month of the survey (December).

Table 22
Correlation Matrix

Category	Number of food deficient months in the year	Ratio of school-going children to total children in HH	Ratio of child-workers to total children in HH	Per capita food-grain consumption per month
Number of food deficient months in the year	1			
Ratio of school-going children to total children in HH	-0.160*	1		
Ratio of child-workers to total children in HH	-0.067	-0.258**	1	
Per capita food-grain consumption per month	-0.098	-0.089	-0.143*	1

Note: 1.* implies significant with 95 per cent level of confidence.
2.** implies significant with 99 per cent of confidence .

The matrix reveals three significant correlations:

1. The number of food deficient months in the year faced by the household is negatively correlated with the ratio of school-going children. The relationship is significant at 95 per cent level of confidence.

2. There is a strong negative correlation between the proportion of school-going children and the proportion of child workers per household as expected, significant at 99 per cent level of confidence.

3. There is a strong negative relationship between per capita foodgrain consumption per month and the ratio of child workers significant at 95 per cent level of confidence. This serves to substantiate the findings of the previous Table.

IX. SUMMARY OF FINDINGS

1. Food Insecurity

(i) The state is characterised by a high degree of food insecurity.

(ii) Food scarcity is seasonal with shortages beginning by the end of the winter and culminating in starvation levels through summer and the monsoon.

(iii) Two-thirds of all households experience at least two months of acute food distress.

(iv) Food insecurity is highest among the scheduled castes with 48 per cent of all SC.

(v) Households reporting food shortages. The next most vulnerable caste groups are the Christian Scheduled Tribes, the Scheduled Tribes and the Muslims with about one-third of them being food insecure.

(vi) Across occupational groups, agricultural labourers are the most prone to being food insecure (59 per cent).

(vii) As regards land ownership, the landless labourers, expectedly, are the most food insecure (48 per cent).

2. School Enrolment, Literacy and Educational Status

(i) School enrolment also follows a caste-based pattern with the upper castes sending about 84 per cent of their children to school, while the scheduled castes have an enrolment ratio of only 45 per cent.

(ii) 26.5 per cent of the children in the age group, 5-14 are neither in school nor at work.

(iii) These 'nowhere' children are perceived by their families as either 'too young to work' or 'not fit for work' which raises questions of ill-health, perhaps, stunting or wasting due to undernutrition or malnutrition.

(iv) 40 per cent of children in the school-going age group are illiterate. Here again caste emerges as a dominant factor. Among the Scheduled Tribes, almost half the children in this age group are illiterate.

(v) Across occupations, agricultural labourers record 61 per cent of their children as illiterate, while in terms of landownership, the landless as well as the small farmers report between 32-44 per cent of the school-going age group as illiterate.

(vi) 43 per cent of all children are educated up to only pre-primary level, 13.5 per cent up to primary level and only 3 per cent above primary level.

3. Child Work

(i) 35 per cent of the children in the age group, 10-14 are full-time workers, while as much as 6 per cent of the age group, 5-9 are also main workers.

(ii) Taking main and subsidiary occupations together, 33 per cent of the age group, 5-14 are engaged in work.

(iii) About 12 per cent of the main workforce is comprised of children aged 10-14, while about 2 per cent consist of children aged 5 to 9 years.

(iv) Caste-wise, the SC, ST, PTG, and OBC I groups account for over 22 per cent of all main child workers, with Muslims following close behind with 16 per cent.

(v) Across occupational groups, agricultural labour households contribute 32 per cent of the main child workers, with farmers accounting for 21 per cent. With the high level of poverty in the region, it is not surprising that the children of small businessmen, salaried workers and those engaged in petty jobs also account for 7-12 per cent of the main child workers.

(vi) In terms of landownership, the landless households record smaller proportions of full-time child workers than smaller farmers who report between 18-26 per cent.

(vii) About one-third of all child workers come from illiterate households and another 30 per cent from households where no member has completed even primary schooling. On the other hand, where even one family member is a graduate, the contribution to the child workforce drops sharply to just 0.65 per cent.

(viii) 71 per cent of child workers come from households where women are illiterate. Even a few years of schooling (at primary levels) has a dramatic impact, i.e., a drop of 53 percentage points to 17.8 per cent.

(ix) About half the child workers are engaged in 'other occupations' i.e., the gathering of firewood, dung, fodder and animal grazing, while one-third work in their own households. Of the remaining child workers, 5 per cent are cultivators, 3 per cent labourers—either agricultural or non-agricultural, and the remaining, about 2 per cent, in petty jobs.

(x) Of the working children, 78 per cent are illiterate, 17 per cent have studied up to pre-primary levels, 3 per cent have studied at primary level and only one per cent have completed primary schooling.

(xi) Gender differences emerge sharply– of the age group, 5 to 9, only 3 per cent of the boys work, while the corresponding figure for girls is 8.5 per cent. Of the age group, 10-14, 21.5 per cent of the boys work, while for girls, the proportion is as high as 49 per cent.

(xii) At district level, boy workers account for 7-14 per cent of the male child population, while the girls account for 17-36 per cent.

(xiii) Caste-wise differences persist—Among the upper castes, the difference between work participation rates of boys and girls is the least, while gender disparities become more glaring among the SCs and STs, where the girl child participation rate is 3-6 times that of boys. Even among the Muslim households, the girl child's work participation rate is 23 per cent as against 9 per cent for boys.

4. The Links between Food Insecurity and Child Work

(i) Of the top 20 per cent households ranked on the basis of per capita foodgrain consumption, (between 20-22 kg per month), there are, on an average, no child workers.

(ii) On the other hand, of the bottom 20 per cent households consuming between 11-13 kg per capita per month, every alternate household cutting across caste groups, has a child worker. Among the ST households, the ratio is one in every three.

(iii) The number of food deficient months in the year facing by the household is negatively correlated with the ratio of school-going children. The relationship is significant at 95 per cent level of confidence.

(iv) There is a strong negative relationship between per capita foodgrain consumption per month and the ratio of child workers significant at 95 per cent level of confidence.

5. Policy Implications

The initial evidence from the region seems to point to the possibility of using food-based interventions to effect a reduction in child work. The obvious seasonality of food shortages indicates the need to focus interventions in these months of deprivation.

As caste is a major determinant of all three factors, i.e., child work, school enrolment and illiteracy, interventions may be targeted to the most vulnerable caste groups in order to achieve effective results.

Gender disparities continue to be sharp across most groups, warranting a clear focus on the girl child.

The positive impact of literacy and even more so, of a few years of primary schooling of parents or other family members, on keeping children out of the workforce is evident. Women's education seems to have even more dramatic impact. This indicates the importance of focusing on adult literacy and education, particularly female literacy and education as a basic strategy in the fight against child work. School meal programmes do not necessarily have to be restricted to children in schools, but may well be extended in different form, perhaps as dry rations to adults attending classes under adult literacy and education programmes. Such a strategy could prove effective in this and other starvation-prone regions.

References

Alagh, Y.K. (1999), "Grain of Truth", *The Indian Express*, November, quoted in Mukerjee, (2000).

Census of India (1999), *Primary Census Abstract*, Census of India Series B, Registrar General of India, Government of India, New Delhi.

Chaudhri, D.P. (2000), "Source of Supply of Child Labour and the State: Explorations of Historical and Contemporary Evidence with Focus on States and Districts of India", Paper presented at the *National Seminar on Child Labour: Realities and Policy Dimensions,* Organised by the V.V. Giri National Labour Institute, Noida and Institute for Human Development, New Delhi, December 5-7.

Dayal, H. and A.K. Karan (2000), "Social and Economic Security for the Scheduled Tribes" in Mahendra Dev S. et al. (eds.), *Social and Economic Security in India*, Institute for Human Development, New Delhi.

—— (2000), "Poverty and Livelihood in a Tribal Region", Institute for Human Development, New Delhi (mimeo).

Mukerjee, A. (2000), *Perspectives of Rural Women on Food Security from a Tribal Village (in West Bengal) 1993 to 1998* (A longitudinal study through PRA), Paper presented at the IHD-CESS *Seminar on Food Security in India: The Emerging Challenging in the Context of Economic Liberalisation,* Hyderabad, March 2000.

Ramachandran, N. (2000), "Review and Fieldtesting of Guidelines for Formulating and Implementing National Plans of Action for Nutrition", Prepared for the *Nutrition Planning Assessment and Evaluation Service,* Food and Nutrition Division, FAO, Rome.

—— (2001), "Food Insecurity and Child Work", A Concept Paper prepared for the *IHD-WFP Consultative Workshop on Food Insecurity and Child Work,* New Delhi, March.

12

Food Insecurity and Children in Madhya Pradesh: A Need for Structural Change

ASEEM PRAKASH

I. DISCOURSE ON CHILDHOOD AND FOOD INSECURITY

The present understanding about children of the country was derived from the 'development model', which did not evolve according to the specific socio-economic requirements of the country but was 'universally given' based on the experience of the industrial west. This model required replicating the trajectory of the development model of western capitalism the thumb rule being that if the set rules of development were followed, the required shift from an agriculture-based economy to an industry-based one would take place, resulting in similar socio-economic advancement. This model does give an idea of 'backwardness' but only in the context of the western concept of 'advancement'; it fails to give any insight into 'backwardness' *per se*. Accordingly, development was understood and operationalised as allocation of resources for a faster growth at the national level, which would, it was presumed finally trickle down to the lowest rung of society, thereby resulting in similar growth at the local level. In this model, those without any property are to be supported by the state to enable them to acquire assets manifested in the form of knowledge and perform the economic activities required by the service sector.

In this concept, childhood is seen as a distinct and separate phase of life where children are deliberately moved away from the real world of work, sexuality and politics and confined to the classroom (Aries, 1986). Childhood is construed as a period when the child is to be protected, and his/her growth processes are to be enhanced through schooling. In other words, the child's world and that of the adult were sharply delineated (Raman, 2000), so that the children's activities are limited to playing and learning, while the economic cushion to the children is to be provided by the adult member(s) of the household till they grow up and acquire the required qualifications to earn their living.

However, the dominant view within the same school of thought argues that the problem of achieving the goal of universalisation of primary education, at least in India, is closely related to the 'stage of development'. This implies that the backward nature of the economy does not permit poor families to invest money in the education of their children. In this situation, it is argued that children can also contribute to the aggregate resource base of the family through their direct and indirect action within the market or by helping their parents in the household work.[1] As against this view, it is strongly contended by experts that children can be pulled away from both domestic and market labour and pushed to school, if food is guaranteed to them by the state through measures like mid-day meal schemes. Thus, it is vehemently believed that poverty and the consequent food insecurity pushes the children out of school to join the ranks of labour and that if some provision of food security is made, the integral components of primary schooling, enrolment rate and retention rate can be drastically improved. This would not only allow the dissemination of education, but also provide the much-needed supplement to the family's food basket.

The paper attempts to examine the structures, which sustain the incidence of child labour. It is divided into five sections. Section II discusses the typology of child labour. The third section analyses the reasons for the labour of children with particular emphasis on existing educational provisions. Section IV discusses the Madhya Pradesh Government's initiatives towards tackling the problem of food insecurity through watershed development schemes with the help of a case study of *kakradhar* village in *Jhabua* district. It brings out the inherent difficulties in implementing the scheme, which further enhances the vulnerability of the marginalised social categories.

The last section argues that the strategy of ensuring compulsory primary education through the provision of mid-day meal schemes as the core element of policy initiatives to end child labour, obfuscates the complex web of the discursive structures in which the families facing shortage in food items, push their children to get embedded, reproduced and sustained in the labour market. It also favours a holistic development effort based on an understanding of the local political economy.

II. TYPOLOGY OF LABOUR OF CHILDREN

The paper makes a distinction between two types of labour, child labour and labour of the working child. Child labour operates at the level of a social construct where children are not supposed to be the sole bread-winners for the family and their income is always subsidiary and/or additional income to the family. This allows the employer to give less wages to the child worker than to an adult worker, despite the fact that the quantity and quality of work done by child labour might be only marginally different from that by the adult worker. In such a scenario, the child worker is in direct interaction with the labour market. An external agent(s) invariably extracts the profit earned through payment of lower wages to the child. The incidence of such child labour can be exemplified through the labour of children in the mine quarrying belt (Katni, Satna, Damoh etc.), stone quarrying belt (Vidisha, Raisen, Chhatarpur etc.), coal mining (Betul, Chindwara, etc.) of Madhya Pradesh, and construction activities throughout the state. Other examples of child labour can be children working in hotels and restaurants or working as porters, etc.

A working child connotes labour of the child in a family-based income generation activity or processes where s(he) is not in direct interaction with the market. This type of child labour is mainly found in the traditional caste/ community-based activities, which are usually done under the piece-wage system. In most cases, the skills required for the job are inherited from the family. In many such cases, the child attends school and during, free time helps her/ his parents. These activities may (as witnessed in the *beedi*-making belt of Madhya Pradesh—Sagar, Jabalpur, Damoh, etc.) or may not (as in family-based brick kilns in Madhya Pradesh) be carried out through subcontracting. Other examples of this type of labour are child hawkers, children working in garages/tea stalls owned by the family, etc. However, the family as a unit invariably carries out the task in each case. The surplus generated from the child's labour in such family-based activities is shared within the family. This type of children's labour is most widely prevalent in the state.

III. REASONS FOR LABOUR OF CHILDREN IN MADHYA PRADESH

A Study Report in the *Analytical Study Report Series on the 1991 Census Data* (1996) points out that there are 16,740,647 children in the age group, 0-14, out of which 1,352,563 are either main or marginal workers. This means that 7.73 per cent of the total child population are working either as main or marginal labourers in the state, the estimate varying substantially between 1.7 per cent (Bhind), 10.5 per cent (Chindwara) and 25.5 per cent (Jhabua) across various districts and regions.

The reasons for the perpetuation of children's labour are varied. We will try to capture the causes of child labour by analysing the available data, and draw broad generalisations based on the analysis in order to understand the issue at hand.

1. Causes of Child Labour

(i) Poverty

It is often argued that the underlying cause behind the phenomenon of labour of children is the perpetuation of poverty. Poverty is generally the result of the inadequate availability of resources that may be required to satisfy the livelihood needs of the family. In such a situation, the labour of the children, contributes to the aggregate income of the household. However, an analysis of the available data for the state of Madhya Pradesh (Figure I) does not fully support the view that poverty is the only reason for pushing children into the labour force. For instance,

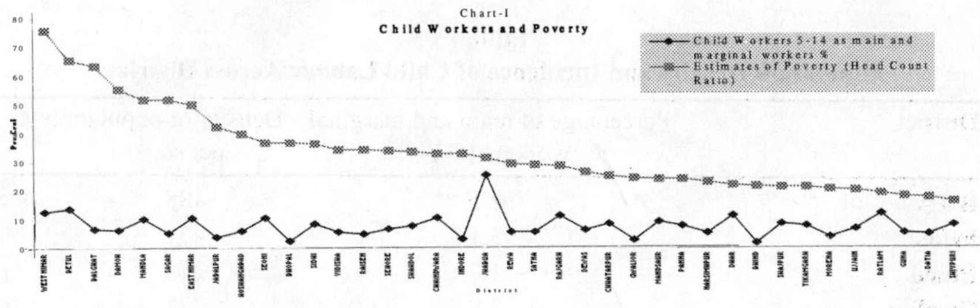

in Jhabua, which has the highest percentage of child labour in the state, the incidence of poverty is estimated to be relatively low. Similarly, the district of west Nimar tops the table of poverty estimates but has a relatively lower incidence of child labour. There are numerous such examples in the state of Madhya Pradesh, but these should suffice to establish the validity of the argument that the push factor of poverty may not be the only contributor to high incidence of child labour in the state. At best, it may be one of the causative factors, so that the high incidence of child labour may be traced to a combination of factors.

(ii) Density of Population

A high density of population leading to a mismatch between the available supply of livelihood resources and the demand for them may also necessitate the generation of extra income from an additional member of the family. This might also result in pushing the children into the labour market. However, when we analyse the data with the help of the following table (Table 1), there appears to be a negative relationship between the high incidence of children's labour and population density. This suggests a weak link between demographic pressures translating into a pressure on land and degradation of common property resources, and other avenues of income generation and the high incidence of children's labour.

However, before we analyse the causes of children's labour emerging from the demand side, it would be essential to understand the linkages of the labour of children with education.

(iii) Lack of Education

It is often argued that the absence of resources required for enrolling children in school, may push them into the labour market as child labour or working child. In order to refute/ support/ partially negate this argument, it would be essential to analyse the available educational statistics.

Table 2 shows that:

(a) Out of 37 districts in the state, 18 have a larger number of dropouts at the primary level than at the secondary level.

(b) Sixteen districts in the state have more children in the labour force than the state's average. Out of these 16 districts, six districts have a higher drop-out rate than the state's average at the primary level, implying that

Table 1
Population Density and Incidence of Child Labour Across Districts

District	Percentage of main and marginal workers (5-14)	Density of population per sq. km.
Bhopal	2.5	488
Indore	3.1	471
Bhind	1.7	273
Gwalior	2.9	271
Jabalpur	3.8	261
Rewa	5.5	246
Ujjain	6.6	227
Ratlam	12.1	200
Satna	5.8	195
Datia	4.8	194
Tikamgarh	7.7	186
Dhar	11.4	168
Jhabua	25.5	167
Shajpur	8.4	167
Rajgarh	11.2	161
Sagar	5.3	161
Mandsaur	9.3	159
Narsimhpur	5.4	153
West Nimar	12.6	151
Balghat	6.7	148
Morena	3.8	148
Dewas	6.2	147
East Nimar	10.6	133
Chhindwara	10.5	133
Chhatarpur	8.5	133
Vidisha	5.5	132
Sidhi	8.5	130
Sehore	6.6	129
Hoshangabad	5.9	126
Shahdol	7.9	124
Damoh	6.4	123
Betul	13.8	118
Guna	5.4	118
Seoni	10.7	114
Shivpuri	8.0	110
Raisen	4.9	104
Mandla	10.3	97
Panna	7.9	96
Madhya Pradesh	7.87	167

Note: Percentage of main and marginal workers (5-14) means percentage of children working as the labourers out of total child population in the district.

Source: MPHDR, 1998.

the retention rate at the primary level may or may not reduce the incidence of child work. This, in turn, connotes that enrolment and retention rate as well as high/low incidence of children's labour is possibly dependent on the perception of the value of education in the eyes of parents as well as the value of education in the local labour market.

(c) The relatively more disturbing fact that emerges from the table is that 18 districts show a higher drop-out rate, which is more than the state's average at the middle level. Moreover, 10 out of the 16 districts, which have a higher incidence of children's labour than the state's average also have a higher drop-out rate at the middle level (the most vulnerable age for entering into the labour market) than the state's average. The labour at this stage is of both types, i.e., child labour as well as well as working children, a fact which primarily depends on the demands of the nature of the local economy. For instance, in the *beedi* belt of Madhya Pradesh, the effort of children's labour is primarily concentrated in the household trade, whereas, in the mining and quarrying belt it is in direct interaction with the market.

2. National Programme for Nutritional Support to Primary Education

Before we analyse the implications of the above tabulated evidences and discussions, it would be worthwhile to discuss briefly the impact of the National Programme for Nutritional Support to Primary Education (NPNSPE) in Madhya Pradesh.[2]

The programme was started in 1995-1996 with the objective of working towards universalisation of primary education by providing the incentive of free noon-meal to the students attending school .The programme is also expected to enhance nutritional security of the children belonging to the poor households. Under it, 37 districts (289 blocks) were covered in phase I and 36 districts (156 blocks) under phase II.

In order to assess the impact of the scheme, the Operations Research Group (ORG) carried out a primary survey in selected blocks of four districts, namely, Guna, Raisen, Rajnandgaon and Rewa. The study documents the enrolment, attendance as well as the retention rate of the pre-and post-programme periods. As shown in Table 3, an increase in enrolment was recorded in the first year of the programme though the subsequent years were marked by a decline.

The trends in attendance were also not very encouraging as indicated in Table 4. The percentage of students having an attendance of more than 80 per cent dropped substantially from 53 per cent in the pre-reform period to 45 per cent in the post-programme period, though there was an increase of 9 per cent in the percentage of students whose attendance was between 70 and 79 per cent. There was no marked difference between the percentage of students in the pre-and post-programme periods with an attendance of between 51 and 60 per cent and below 50 per cent between the pre-and post-programme period.

Table 2
Drop-out Rate at Primary and Secondary School Level and Incidence of Child Workers Across Districts

Districts	Percentage of child workers (5-14) as main and marginal workers	School drop-out rate at primary stage	School drop-out rate at middle stage
Jhabua	25.5	40	23.8
Betul	13.8	16	18.19
West Nimar	12.6	21	27.17
Ratlam	12.1	44	26.37
Dhar	11.4	19	36.67
Rajgarh	11.2	23	35.32
Seoni	10.7	58	33.39
Chhindwara	10.5	18	26.53
Mandla	10.3	41	51.27
Mandsaur	9.3	47	39
Sidhi	8.5	39	10
Chhatarpur	8.5	11	14.13
Shajpur	8.4	10	35
Shivpuri	8	18	30.4
Shahdol	7.9	24	14.55
Panna	7.9	16	8.23
Tikamgarh	7.7	2	6.41
Balghat	6.7	13	31.94
Ujjain	6.6	16	21.28
Sehore	6.6	10	22.66
Damoh	6.4	20	18.59
Dewas	6.2	30	19.37
Hoshangabad	5.9	19.5	26.28
Satna	5.8	15	5
Rewa	5.5	48	6
Vidisha	5.5	33	22.51
Guna	5.4	40	20.53
Narsimhpur	5.4	32	30.78
Sagar	5.3	13	11.39
Raisen	4.9	19.2	10.29
Datia	4.8	18	14.34
Morena	3.8	43	21.2
Jabalpur	3.8	5	31.07
Indore	3.1	18	21.19
Gwalior	2.9	20	30.64
Bhopal	2.5	14	17
Bhind	1.7	15	15
Madhya Pradesh	7.65	24.02	22.53

Note: Data for East Nimar is not available.

Source: Data compiled from *Women in Madhya Pradesh—A Stastical Profile*, 1997 and MPHDR, 1998.

Table 3
Growth in Enrolment During Pre-and-Post-Programme Period

Period	Per cent
1992-93 to 1993-94	3
1993-94 to 1994-95	-1
1994-95 to 1995-96	16
1995-96 to 1996-97	2
1996- 97 to 1997-98	-2

Source: UNICEF-ORG (1999).

Table 4
Trends in Attendance

Attendance	Percentage of students	
(%)	Pre-programme	Post-programme
1- 50	16	15
51-69	15	15
70-79	16	25
80 and above	53	45

Source: Same as in Table 3.

In order to assess the impact of NPNSPE on the retention of the children at primary level, a cohort analysis for the pre-programme period (1992-93) was undertaken. In all, 814 class I students were traced (i.e. the pre-programme period) and 1078 students enrolled in class I during the post-programme period. As is evident from Table 5, the dropout rates have increased from 20 per cent in the pre-programme period to 25 per cent.

Table 5
Drop-out Rates during Pre- and Post-return Period

Period	Percentage of drop-out children
Pre-programme	20
Post-programme	25

Source: Same as in Table 3.

The above evidence indicates that the meal incentive schemes can, perhaps, provide the needed impetus for increasing the initial enrolment rate, but offer no guarantee for the continued retention of students at school. There can be two possible reasons for this phenomenon of increased initial enrolment, but failure to maintain the retention of students: (a) absence of satisfactory delivery mechanisms and (b) social values existing in society that give a low premium to education *per se*.

The limited data pertaining to a sample of 61 schools collected by the UNICEF-ORG study does not seem to point to the first reason for sustaining the retention of students at school.

Table 6 reveals that in all the 61 sample villages, the noon-meal was provided in all the schools and more than 60 per cent of the schools provided scholarships to their students. Cost-free uniforms were supplied to only 31 per cent of the schools, free stationery was provided to just 2 per cent of the schools, while free bags were not provided to any of them. However, the last three factors cannot be a deterrent in maintaining the retention rate, since wearing a uniform was never made compulsory in these schools, nor is the cost of stationery at a level which cannot be met by the parents. Therefore, it can be safely concluded that the delivery mechanism could not be the cause of the increased dropout rate.

Table 6
Percentage of Schools Providing Incentive

Incentive	Per cent
Free textbook	86
Mid-day meal	100
Free stationery	2
Free uniform	31
Scholarship	63
Free bag	-

Source: Same as in Table 3.

The above discussion and interpretation of data suggest that the high incidence of child labour is not driven solely by poverty and demographic pressures. These conditions may be necessary, but as the available data points out, are not sufficient conditions for increasing the demand for child labour. Moreover, the incentive-based schooling may also not be sufficient to deter children from joining the labour force. This should induce us to look into the structural factors contributing to a high drop-out rate and pushing the children into the labour force either as working children or child labourers.

3. Factors Promoting Labour of Children

It is argued that there are a combination of factors, which cause the emergence and perpetuation of the phenomenon of child labour. These are:

(i) Workers' Participation Rate and Child Labour

The production relations in a district(s) may require a large labour force. In such a scenario, the market for child labour may also be large.

As the above figure shows, the most proximate cause of child labour may be the demand side creation, that is, increased labour opportunity available in the district(s). The demand side pressure may create a selective market for cheap labour, possibly served by the children of the poorer households but not

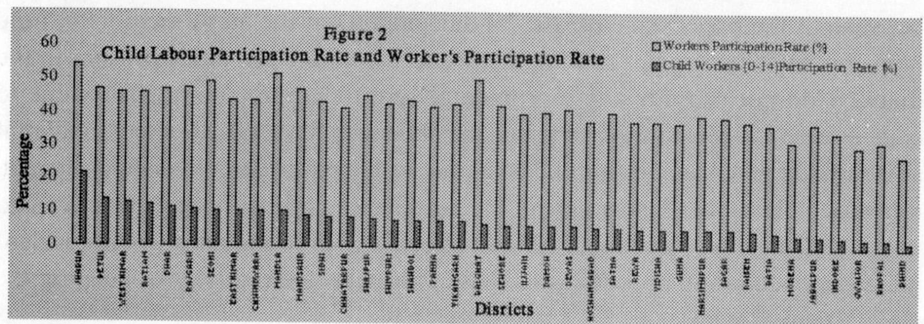

necessarily the poverty stricken households. Poverty, in combination with the demand side pull, creates a situation in which child labour is perpetuated and sustained. There are combinations of reasons for such a demand side pull:

(a) Dynamics of the Labour Market: It is argued that the requirement for children's labour may be a demand side creation. It might be that economic activity performed by the child gets socially defined as less productive and hence warrants lower wages which would be unacceptable to the adult. This process gives surplus profit to the persons controlling/owning the production process. Therefore, this might be one of the many reasons for the perpetuation of child labour.

(b) Experience of Adults and Expansion of the Labour Market: The search for a job by an adult member of the household may force her/him to enter the labour market with very low wages. This might be due to lack of economic activity in the districts resulting in a situation marked by high supply and low demand of labour power. When such jobs can be accessed without education, even children of the households who can afford to wait for returns from education, enter the labour market at an early stage. The entry of additional workforce in the labour market further pushes the wages down, which might again require another member of the family to work. *Poverty might not be the proximate cause of child labour but it provides sufficient space for the pull factor to generate a corresponding push.* In a word, child labour is primarily a result of low wages which do not allow the labour power to reproduce itself and those dependent on him.

(ii) Education and Child Labour

It is true that the Educational Guarantee Scheme coupled with the mid-day meal scheme and *Anganwadis and balwadis* have increased the initial enrolment of students but the limited evidences provided by the UNICEF-ORG study show that it has not been able to contain the dropout rate. This may be due to the absence of any forward linkages between education and economic opportunities in the districts. The dominant viewpoint presumes that lack of education and skill leads to unemployment and underemployment and hence, acts as a push factor for the children to join the labour force. However, the complex dynamics of the labour market in the labour intensive economy of Madhya Pradesh reveal a slightly different picture. The whole exercise of schooling as indicated above is considered futile even by the households who can afford the cost of education because of the experience (of the labour market) of the adult members of the households. This implies that the nature of economic activities present in the districts do not provide any incremental benefit to the labour efforts due to education. It is thus quite possible that the child may have joined school, but left it at the middle level and, even if he is not formally employed in the labour market, might be helping her/his parents in the household work, as both productive and unproductive labour (working child). In effect, high drop-out rates are the result of underpaid economic opportunities that in turn act as a catalyst for keeping the children out of school.

IV. BID TO TACKLE FOOD INSECURITY IN MADHYA PRADESH

The paper looks at the development schemes promoted by the present government of Madhya Pradesh and its efforts to tackle the problem of food insecurity faced by the landless and marginal farmers through primary data generated with the help of field visits to Jhabua district in Madhya Pradesh. It therefore focuses on the Rajiv Gandhi Watershed Development Mission and its impact on the livelihood demands of poor and landless households in rural areas. However, before we proceed further, there are two caveats in order.

1. The following data pertaining to the watershed development scheme was collected in order to judge the efficacy of such a development initiative from the standpoint of the poor and landless.[3] Therefore, there are no explicit tables and graphs depicting the causes of child labour and its linkages with food insecurity. However, the structural constraints of the food security/ insecurity of the family as a whole are taken into account and certain facts which were not gathered systematically but were explicit during the field visit are brought to light.
2. It is essential to point out the reasons behind not using the commonly used indicators, i.e., Integrated Child Development Schemes (ICDS) and the Public Distribution System (PDS), for understanding the problem of food insecurity at the household level in general and children in particular. Firstly, the benefits that may be generated from the two above-mentioned schemes may be limited in nature because it is not able to capture the complex socio-economic dynamics that result in the perpetuation of poverty and consequently promote or hinder food insecurity. Secondly, procurement from the PDS is dependent not only on the economic status but also on the access to these institutions. It is also possible that the districts having a relatively higher level of food security may show low procurement through the PDS. Thirdly, for most of the poor households in Madhya Pradesh, the effort is to meet the daily food requirement, which is directly dependent on the nature of the labour opportunities available in the districts. It may be pointed out that the watershed schemes are the major sources of labour opportunities both, directly and indirectly. Lastly, it enables us to take the household as the unit of analysis as well as the complex socio-economic dynamics that results in unequal power

relationship between different social categories rather than isolating the child from these dynamics and analysing the results independently.

Rajiv Gandhi Mission for Watershed Development in Madhya Pradesh

The agenda of The Rajiv Gandhi Mission scheme for watershed development (RGMWD) has been implemented in all the districts of the state and is funded by both the state and central government. All funds under the drought-prone area programme and Integrated Watershed Development Programme are spent on watershed treatment, while 50 per cent of the funds from the employment assurance scheme are earmarked for it along with sectoral funds at the district level and the Jawahar Rojgar Yojna fund at the panchayat level.

(i) Kakradhar Village (Jhabua District)

Kakradhar is a predominantly tribal village surrounded by small hills, with a population of around 800 and 115 households. Incidentally, this village is also regarded as a model village of the state government for the 'successful' implementation of the watershed scheme. It covers an area of 1,156 ha, and is rainfed, though a few big farmers have the resources required for tapping ground water. The average landholding per household in the village is between 2-3 ha. But due to its successive divisions over the generations, the quantity of land left with the majority of the families is very little and does not allow them to earn their livelihood and support their respective families through personal agricultural cultivation. Therefore, most of the households earn their livelihood by dividing their time between working as agricultural labour on the agricultural fields of *patidars,* a landed upper caste, and putting in their effort in some other activities in the district, while also working on their fields during *kharif.* Till recently most of the families used to migrate to other cities to work; watershed treatment has created avenues for work as agricultural labourers in the same district itself.

In all, 53 (about 46 per cent of the total households) tribal households having 457 members were interviewed and the summary of the findings is discussed below. The interviews do not cover each and every member of the household but mostly the head of the family or some other person who had an idea about the family resource base and intra family distribution of income and expenditure.

Table 7 shows that all the families, except seven earn their livelihood primarily through agricultural labour. Members of 42 families work on their field and engaged as agricultural labour since the produce/income from their own agricultural fields does not suffice to meet the demands of their respective families. There are more women and children in these families who work on their own fields than men, who normally work as wage agricultural labours or take any other available opportunity. Children mostly help their mothers in daily household tasks as well as lend a helping hand in the agricultural activities, if they are not employed in construction activities or in some other sundry jobs.

Table 7
Economic Activities of the Sample Families

Activity	Number	Average land holding	Permanent labour in the family	Casual labour in the family
Farmers families (working on own land only)	7	5-10 ha	29	-
Farmers families (working on own land as well as agriculture labour)	42	2-3 ha	142	73
Landless	4	-	13	9

The work of agriculture labour or other form of labour (mainly in construction activities) gives an income of Rs. 30-35 per day to the male and Rs. 20-25 to the female members, while the children who work can only manage Rs. 10-15 per day. As indicated in Table 8, there is a major disparity between the average annual income of the large farmers, marginal farmers' families (who also work as agricultural labour) and the landless families. The average annual income of the landless household stands at Rs. 19,000, whereas that for marginal farmers families and large farmers stands at Rs. 25,500 and Rs. 46,000 respectively. However, it should be noted that the watershed treatment and consequent growth in agricultural productivity has created an avenue for labour activities in the district, resulting in a considerable drop in migration. However, this has also brought down the wages due to increased supply of labour, since most of the families prefer to work at home.

Table 8
Average Annual Income of the Sample Families

Sample families	Income from crop	Income from labour
Farmer families (working on own land only)	46000	-
Farmer family (working on own land as well as agriculture labour or other form of labour)	12500	13000
Landless	-	19000

The study tabulated families' expenditure on food by taking two variables i.e., size of the families and its relationship with the percentage of income spent on food. However, we ignored this criterion for calculating the expenditure on food by big farmers, because in spite of having relatively larger families (average size is more than 8), their expenditure on food is much less.

As indicated in Table 9, a family with a size of more than six members spends more than 75 per cent of their income on food, whereas those with between four-six members spend more than 50 per cent but less than 75 per cent on food items.

Table 9
Percentage Expenditure on Food out of Total Earning by Sample Households

Sample families	Number of households	Expenditure out of total
Families with more than 6 members	29	More than 75 %
Families (less than 6 members)	17	Between 50 % and 75 %
Landed class Families (Average size being 8.5)	7	Less than 30 %

The consequences of low wages are :

(a) The expenditure on food is unusually high for the labouring families irrespective of their size. In such a situation, when the wages are not adequate for the labour to reproduce its own labour power and sustain its family, children may be drawn into the labour market in order to contribute their bit to the family food basket. This may possibly lead to the vicious web of poverty and its linkages with the labour of children. This initial push factor is further encouraged by the vast opportunities work available for labour in the construction activities in the district, which have shown a significant decadal growth rate of nearly 100 per cent (MPHDR, 1998), for enabling the absorption of the underpaid child labour. However, the children also assist their parents in the fields or work as labourers in the fields of big farmers throughout the year. The level of attendance and enrolment in schools is not satisfactory in the district when compared with the state average.

(b) This unusually high expenditure on food is even higher for families comprising more than six members The limited data pertaining to 29 household indicates that having large families with many working hands does not necessarily mean higher economic/food security. In a labour surplus economy with minimal economic activity, (apart from dry land agriculture) as in Jhabua, the simple demand and supply logic pushes down the wage rate, triggering off the cycle of low wage and expansion of the labour market as discussed earlier.

The problem becomes even more serious during the season when there are relatively fewer work opportunities for agricultural labour for a few months after the harvest of Kharif crops. The families are forced to migrate either outside the village or outside the district because of the following reasons:

(a) Lack of resources to tap ground water during the *rabī* season. It is true that soil and water conservation measures have increased the moisture retention capacity of the soil but the best and most profitable use of this is availed of by the farmers who have the capacity to invest in water augmenting devices.

(b) The economic insecurity and consequent lack of capacity to invest optimally in the food basket, forces them to look for employment avenues outside the village.

The families that migrate more or less regularly have a very low level of literacy—only around 23 per cent among the adults and 33 per cent among the children (Table 10). In such families, children between 12 and 15 years of age are mostly illiterate or drop-outs and they either work as labourers or help their parents in their work thus reducing the latter's workload.

Table 10
Relationship between Migration and Literacy

Status of migrants	Member	Literacy: Literate	Literacy: Illiterate
Full families migrating during *rabi* season	17		
Adult members	49	12	37
Children	21	Primary level- 6 Middle level - 1	14

Some of the village children do attend the schools promoted under NPNSPE. The availability of supplementary nutrition has been a major incentive to join the *balwadis*. However, the initial enrolment rate is not matched by the retention rate. According to the school teacher's attendance register, out of 29 students in the year 1997-98, only 18 continued to attend the school in the year, 1998-99. However, the enrolment of the children increased from 29 to 37 during the same time period.

The educational rate of children among those households who migrate along with their whole family is very low because of the absence of a fixed location of stay throughout the year. Depending on their age, the children may be either drawn into the labour market or simply assist their parents. However, the migration of the full family has been considerably reduced with the landed class taking up the cultivation of two crops and the resultant enrolment of labour. However, this has not been matched with a high enrolment and retention rate, in schools due to the perceived redundancy of education systems.

The evidences gathered from the village point overwhelmingly to the major disparity in the economic earnings of the various social and economic groups of the village. However, in the absence of cohort data for the pre-and post-watershed development, we have to rely on the observations made during the field visits and general discussion with the villagers. The low productivity of the agricultural fields in the absence of any new technological inputs and institutionalised credit support results in the migration of a substantial number of people from the village to the big cities of Madhya Pradesh and the neighbouring state of Rajasthan, mostly at the expense of the education of their children. Moreover, not being residents, of the city/town to which they migrate, they are not entitled to any of the benefits of the development schemes in the city. Due to their absence from their native place, they also miss the benefits accruing from the various development initiatives in their own village.

Nevertheless, the successful implementation of the watershed schemes in the district has resulted in slowing the migration process and the consequent availability of the opportunity to work as agricultural labourers on the fields of rich farmers who cultivate two crops a year. The biggest beneficiary of the soil and water conservation measures has been the relatively rich farmer who can tap the re-charged ground water and invest in fertilisers and improved variety of seeds.[4] However, the increase in labour supply due to the decline in migration has led to fall in the daily wage. As a result, most of the sample households have to invest more than 75 per cent of their income on food items. The sample household data points out that while the larger household may provide additional working hands, it also demands a greater proportion of investment in food items leaving no or very little surplus. This invariably triggers off the vicious cycle of debt trap in the event of any spending on health-related contingency or for fulfilling social responsibilities (marriage, etc.). Further, a few sample households who exercise control over productive resources (land, water, etc.), spend the least on food items and are also food secure.

The lowering of income not only affects the food security of the family adversely but also drastically retards the normative development of their children. This is due to the perceived redundancy of education in the local labour market as a result of which the children either join the ranks of labour (child labour) or just help their parents in both 'productive' and 'unproductive' work of the household (working child), particularly at the middle school level.

The combination of factors discussed above explains why Jhabua district has the highest incidence of child labour in the state.

V. CONCLUSION

The dominant structures in the society are maintained even by the development schemes, which professedly seeks to challenge the status quo and usher in the winds of change through participatory development initiatives. The case study of watershed schemes in Madhya Pradesh shows that schemes like the Rajiv Gandhi Mission, which was launched with the explicit purpose of making a dent in food insecurity and utilises almost all the funds allocated for poverty alleviation programmes, do result in the creation of work opportunities for labour but only in the short-run. Initially, the scheme helped the landless by providing wage labour for creating various water harvesting structures and later through increased labour opportunities. The experience of successful watershed development initiatives tells us that the profit that accrued to the landed class from cash crops made them shift to mechanisation, resulting in increased marginalisation of the labour force. Therefore, it can be safely argued that such schemes launched with the objective of addressing the problem of food security do not tackle the problem of 'relative poverty' of the marginalised social groups by omitting provisions for giving them control over productive resources, and perpetuates not only poverty but also food insecurity of the whole family, which directly affects the children. At best, it serves only as a short-term relief measure for tackling the problem of absolute poverty. The labour of children in various forms is the direct fallout of the incapacity of the adult workers to reproduce their labour power and sustain those who are dependent on them.

In the context of children, the dominant view supports the argument that low enrolment rate, high drop-out rate and child labour are sustained because of the high level of food insecurity that emerges due to poverty. This scheme of things can be changed if the importance of compulsory primary education is emphasised. Parents can be coaxed to send their children to school through schemes like the mid-day meal scheme. This rationalist argument ignores the structural causes of poverty, food insecurity and illiteracy, on which the subordination of marginalised social groups is sustained.

The increased primary school enrolment rate resulting from the provision of incentives of nutritional support has not been successful in ensuring the retention of the same students in subsequent years. The experience of Madhya Pradesh also shows that there are very high drop-out rates at the middle level. This is generally due to the absence of any forward linkages with livelihood prospects available in the local economy. Understandably, in such a situation the investment of time and other precious resources on education is not considered meaningful even by those households who can afford to send their children to school.

This, in effect, encourages the children as well as their parents to make efforts to look for labour opportunities in the local labour market. If the local economy has the potential to absorb the additional labour force, children readily join the ever-growing strength of child labourers as unskilled labourers. This again triggers off the vicious circle of poverty discussed earlier. It is stressed that this process is self-sustaining in the absence of any initiative towards evolving structural remedies. In the case of a weak local economy, which does not have the potential for encouraging new entrants, the perceived redundancy of education probably not only keeps the children out of the school system, but also forces them to join the ranks of the working children where they might not be in directly interaction with the market, but supply their labour efforts for making a livelihood for their family.

It is argued that the targeted approach has been of limited value. Unless the wider political economy is taken into account and all facets of economic activity are paid due attention, the prospects of change appear bleak.

(The author is thankful to the editorial committee for comments on the initial draft of the paper.)

Notes

1. This conceptual difference is made clear in the coming section.
2. This section is based on the impact evaluation study carried out by Operation Research Group and UNICEF of NPNSPE for the Ministry of Human Resource Development, Government of India (ORG, 1999).
3. For the impact of watershed development initiatives on marginalised social categories see Datar and Prakash (2000).

4. It is essential to take into account the fact that, most of the watershed treatment follows the ridge to valley approach. This means that all the structures for water harvesting are built on the ridge area. It is a well known fact that the land owned by lower classes which are less fertile are on the ridge and land owned by big farmers are in the valley. Therefore, these measures primarily benefit the big farmers.

References

Aries, P. (1986), *Centuries of Childhood*, Penguin, UK.

Datar, Chhaya and Aseem Prakash (2000), *Women Demand Land and Water*, Tata Institute of Social Sciences, Mumbai.

Raman, Vasanthi (2000), "Politics of Childhood: A Perspective from South", *Economic and Political Weekly,* November 11.

MPHDR (1998), *Madhya Pradesh Human Development Report,* 1998, Sanket, Bhopal.

UNICEF-ORG (1999), "Evaluation Study to Assess the Efficiency and Effectiveness of the National Programme for Nutritional Support to Primary Education in Madhya Pradesh," New Delhi (mimeo).

RGI (1996), *Working Children in India: Analytical Study Report Series on the 1991 Census Data,* Registrar General of India, New Delhi.

13

Food Insecurity, Education and Child Work in Rural Rajasthan

DIPAYAN BHATTACHARYYA, RITU MATHUR AND BAL PARITOSH DASH

I. INTRODUCTION

Despite the accumulation of large stocks of foodgrains, there is a high incidence of malnutrition[1] in India. The high level of undernourishment imperils women's health and increases the incidence of underweight births. This reflects on the health of infants and young children. The susceptibility of these children to diseases and death is reflected in the high incidence of infant mortality rate (IMR), stunting and wasting among them, particularly in the rural areas. Thus, a large number of school-age children either are not able to concentrate on studies or do not go to school at all. All this manifests in the increasing pressure on children to join work activities at an early age. It merits mention here that millions of children leave school and get engaged in different kinds of jobs which are often hazardous in nature.

Child work is a complex phenomenon. In India, children in the age group, 5-14 years, who are engaged in production activities and services involving physical activity and are paid wages in cash or kind are officially called 'child workers'. Contemporary literature and research, however, has established that children in the age group, 5-14 years, who are out of school, are forced by circumstances to become child workers. These children either engage in helping with household chores like looking after younger siblings, collecting water, washing clothes etc. or in non-wage physical activities. Children falling in this category are defined as 'nowhere' children (Choudhri, 2000).

Most of the studies on child work include children in both the categories for the purpose of analysis. However, the programming implications of both the definitions are different. While the first one can be dealt with by enforcing the legislations on child labour, the second calls for a more holistic approach to the problem of child work.

The causes of child work are generally identified as lack of education among children consequent to the low rate of enrolment and high drop-out rate, malnutrition among children and household poverty leading to the inability of parents to send their children to school. Poverty resulting in a lack of purchasing power among the households, pushes their children to work at an early age to supplement the family income. In most cases, however, children are forced to help with the household chores (Burra, 1995). In the rural areas, these children, especially the girl children, are engaged in cooking, cleaning the house, washing clothes, fetching water, etc., whereby their mental and physical growth gets constrained. These children suffer from worse forms of deprivation and denial of basic necessities like education, health, food, shelter, physical protection, security and recreation. (ILO, 1996).

The attempt to link food insecurity with child work whereby it is identified as a major cause of the latter is of recent origin. Very little literature, investigating the link between the incidence of child work and food insecurity is available. The most important issue is to understand the implications of food insecurity at the community and household levels and examine its repercussions on child work and education of children. Furthermore, it is also important to understand food insecurity in its broader context rather than consider it merely as an issue of availability or production of foodgrains.

The main objective of this paper is to analyse the level of food insecurity in Rajasthan, its spatial pattern across the districts in the state and to examine its implications for the incidence of child labour. Section II presents the trends and patterns in the level of child labour and its linkages with food insecurity in Rajasthan. The second part of the section gives a macro overview of the level of food insecurity in the state. Here, an attempt has also been made to identify the most food insecure districts in the state. This section is primarily based on secondary data and suggests the broad trends in the patterns of food insecurity vis-à-vis child labour. Section III presents the findings of a community level study which was undertaken in five districts of Rajasthan representing different agroclimatic and socio-economic zones of the state. Here an attempt has been made to understand the community level dynamics of food insecurity and their possible bearing on the incidence of child labour. The last section summarises the findings of the paper and delineates the possible policy interventions for food security aimed at reducing the level of child work.

II. CHILD WORK AND FOOD INSECURITY IN RURAL RAJASTHAN

1. Trends and Patterns in Child Work in Rural Rajasthan

As mentioned in the introductory section, the definition of child labour has been widely debated over the last four decades. For official purposes, children in the age group, 5-14, engaged in wage activities are considered as child workers. Researchers and policy makers however, argue for inclusion of those who may not be engaged in wage activity but are out of school. These children are highly susceptible to the pressures to become child labour and in literature, are defined as 'nowhere' children. Most of the official databases provide information on both the aspects of child labour. In this paper, we have considered both the categories of children for the purpose of analysis.

The multiplicity of definitions and methods of data collection have resulted in a number of estimates for working children in the age group, 5-14, in Rajasthan. While the Census of India (1991) shows that 7.8 per cent children were engaged in work activities[2] in the rural areas of Rajasthan, NSS[3] (1994) shows the figure to be 12.2 per cent. The National Council of Applied Economic Research (NCAER), however, reports an incidence of 1.2 per cent child labour for the rural areas, which is much lower than the national average of 5.8 per cent (Shariff, 2000). The wide divergence of the NCAER figures from the others is attributed to the relatively smaller size of the sample survey. Importantly, except NCAER all other data sources (Census, 1991; NSS, 1994; Zutsi, 2000) show the incidence of child labour in Rajasthan to be much higher than the national average. While according to the Census, the incidence of child labour in Rajasthan is one per cent higher than the national average, the NSS figure for Rajasthan is higher by about 6 per cent than the national average (Figure 1). This points to the gravity of the problem of child labour in rural Rajasthan.

While the provisional results of the 2001 Census on child labour are yet to be released a UNESCO project report on child labour (Zutsi, 2000), provides

Figure 1
Percentage of Child Work by Different Sources

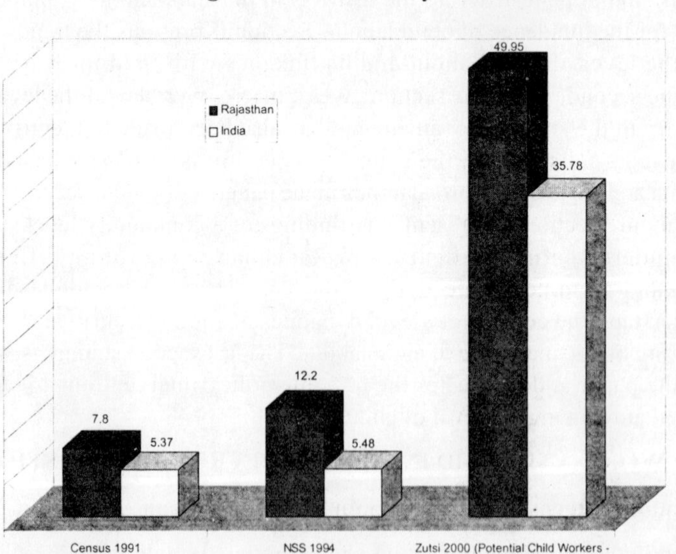

estimates of child labour for different states of India. The report shows an alarmingly high estimate of about 50 per cent working and nowhere children in rural Rajasthan for the year 2000, which is much higher than the figure estimated for the country as a whole. This establishes the case for special interventions for containing the growing incidence of child labour in the state. What is intriguing is that the incidence of child labour has gone up from 5.64 per cent to 7.8 per cent during 1981-91 (Census, 1991) in rural Rajasthan. This is solely due to the increase in the work participation of girl children. While the work participation rate of boys in the age group, 5-14 years has come down from 5.98 per cent to 5.19 per cent, that for girls has gone up from 5.26 per cent to 7.88 per cent in the state during 1981-91. What is more disturbing is that there has been a steep increase in the already high percentage participation of girl children in work activities in the rural areas during the eighties. The figure has increased gone up from 6.38 per cent in 1981 to 9.75 per cent in 1991 (Figure 2). This clearly brings home the plight of the girl child in the state and should receive the foremost attention of researchers, policy planners and programme implementation agencies.

Figure 2
Work Participation Rate (Census 1981 and 1991)

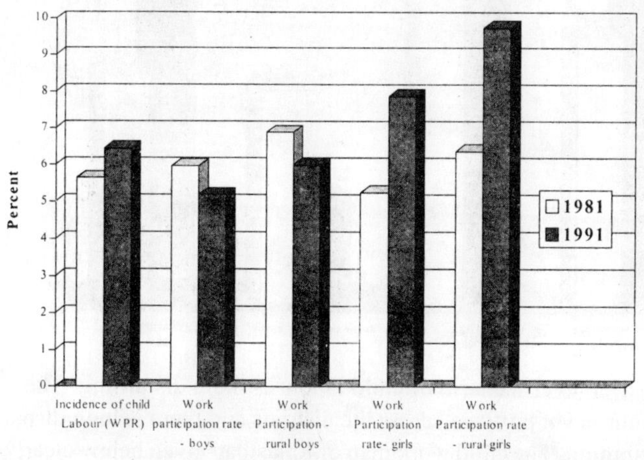

An analysis of the occupational structure in child work participation unravels many miseries of the girl children. A majority of the children in rural Rajasthan is engaged in the farming sector, where the work participation of the girl children is higher than that of the boys. Also, the work participation rate (WPR), in the hazardous industries like manufacturing and related activities the WPR is much higher for the boys than girls. Specifically, the percentage of girl children working in the hazardous glass industry is much higher than that of boys.

The incidence of 'nowhere' children in the state is much higher than the national average—while about 50 per cent of the children in the country are out of school but are not engaged in paid activities, the corresponding figure for the state is about 60 per cent. Here too, the percentage of girl children in the age group, 5-14 years, who do not attend school is 66 per cent, which is much higher than the figure for boys in the same age group. This, however, gives a partial explanation of the relatively high incidence of girl child labour in the state.

All these findings reflect the low educational indicators for the state. A comparison of there and those of the country as a whole reveals that the drop-out rate for the state is 55.6 per cent, which is one of the highest in the country. This could be explained in terms of the low level of female literacy in the state, which is a dismal 20 per cent as compared to the national average of 40 per cent. The average increase in the enrolment rate of the state is offset by the high drop-out rates (Figure 3). In order to reap the benefits of the relatively better performance in enrolment, the state must improve the retention rates.

Figure 3
Educational Indicators

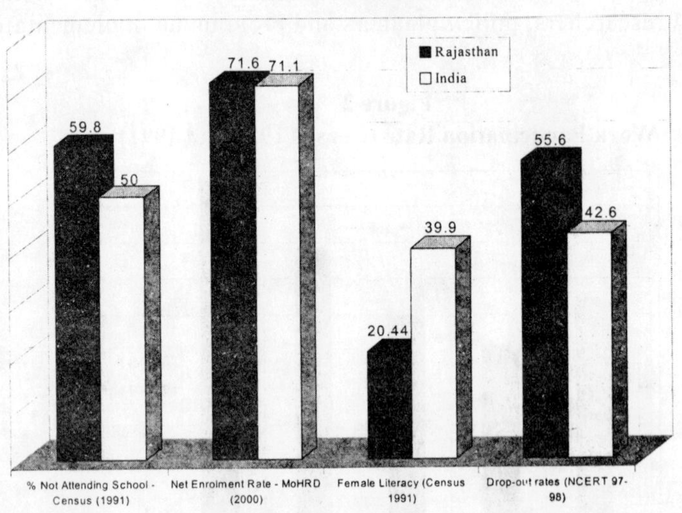

The district level scenario of child labour is more disturbing. The incidence of child labour is not uniform across the districts and there is high disparity in its spatial distribution. The child work map of Rajasthan given below clearly shows a clustering in the incidence of child labour in a corridor between the southern and northern parts of the state, the southern part stretching a bit towards the west covering three districts like Barmer, Jalore and Sirohi. Importantly, the north-arid region, which is highly fertile and is marked by higher agricultural production, shows a higher incidence of child labour than the other agroclimatic regions of the state. Five of the seven districts in this region fall in the extreme and high categories of child work (Figure 4). Higher inter-district migration and linked agricultural bonded labour[4] in the region (WFP, 2000) could be the main reason for such a spatial pattern of child labour.

The other two regions showing a higher incidence of child labour are the Southern Aravali Range and the Southern Banas-Chambal Range, where there is a high concentration of textile and carpet industries. Most of the districts in these

Figure 4
Work Participation Rate - Census (1991)

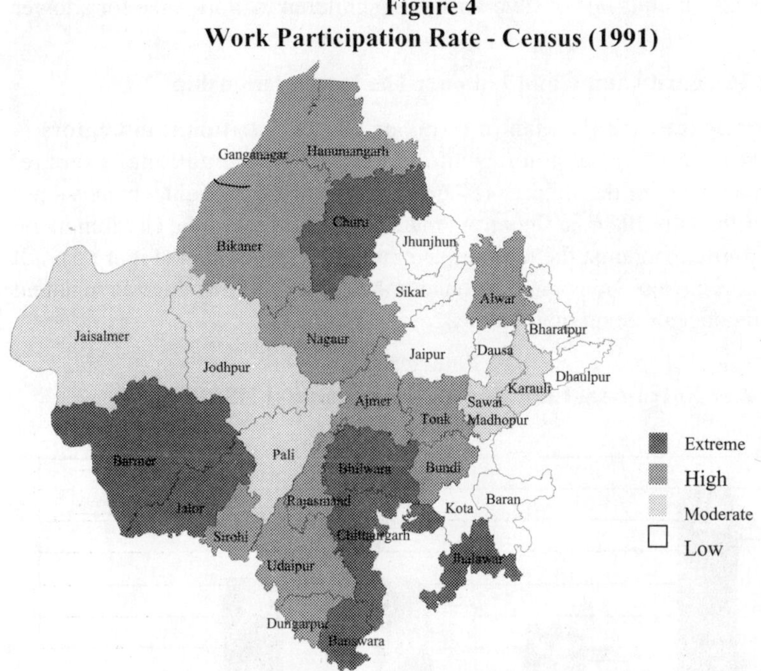

ranges have a high incidence of child labour and fall in the 'extreme' or 'high' categories in the child work map of the state.

This implies that in districts where there is a lack of adequate employment opportunities or availability of low-paid agricultural activities, family income is not able to fully meet the household's requirements. Further, because of differential pattern of growth and the concentration of economic activities in certain regions, there has been large scale inter-district migration to these regions. When the families migrate during the lean season or for a part of the year, the children miss school and tend to join their parents at work. Further, even if the children do not migrate with their parents, because of the high opportunity cost involved, they are not sent to schools and are assigned the duty of taking care of household activities.

The causes of child work can be looked at from two perspectives—low household income trap and suitability of children for some production activities. In the first case, because of the low family income among the most vulnerable households in the rural areas, children in these families are compelled to engage in economic activities to supplement the family income. Secondly, there are certain production activities like crafts and related production activities (such as carpet and bangle industries) where children are more suitable for enhancing productivity. The instances of the latter are much higher in Rajasthan compared to other states because of the location of a large number of carpet industries in the state (WFP, 2000a). The major factor behind child labour, however, is household poverty and inability of the households to meet their food and calorie intake requirements, which is responsible for forcing children to work even for a lower wage.

2. Food Insecurity and Child Labour: The Interrelationship

The performance of Rajasthan in terms of all the nutritional indicators is amongst the worst in the country and is lower than the national average. Approximately half of the children (50.6 per cent) are underweight which is 4 per cent higher than the all-India figure. As much as 52 per cent of the children in the state are stunted[5] against the national average of 45.5 per cent (Figure 5). All these findings have obvious implications for the capacity of the children to attend school and concentrate on their studies.

Figure 5
Key Nutritional Indicators in Rajasthan (NFHS, 1998-99)

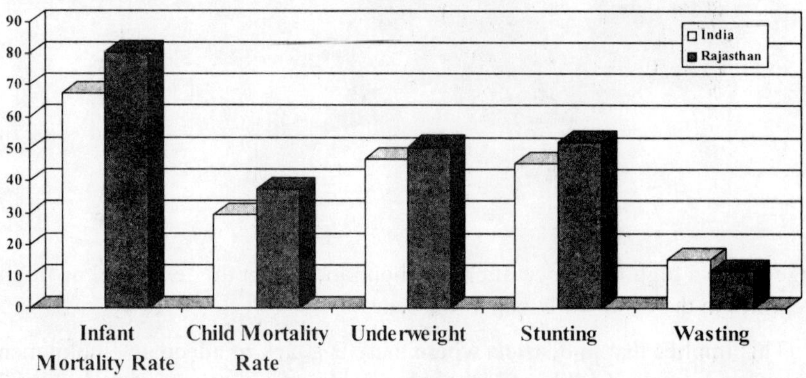

The recently released Food Insecurity Atlas of Rural India (WFP and M.S. Swaminathan Research Foundation, Chennai, 2001) identifies four principal interacting dimensions of food insecurity: Availability of food, Access to food, Utilisation of food, and Vulnerability to Natural Disasters like drought, flood, earthquake, etc. All these dimensions of food insecurity reveal that Rajasthan is one of the most food-insecure states, ranking second only to Bihar.

World food programme (WFP) has also prepared a Food Insecurity Map of Rural Rajasthan (Figure 6) considering all the indicators of food insecurity for which data are available (see Appendix I for preparation of Composite Index). The map depicts the most food insecure districts in four typologies viz., 'extreme', 'high', 'moderate' and 'low' food insecure districts, there being as many as 10 extremely food insecure districts and five highly food insecure districts. It is important to note here, that there is a marked overlap between the different typologies in the map for child work and food insecurity in Rajasthan. However, unlike the mid-way corridor in the child work map, food insecurity in the state is mostly concentrated around the south and south-west districts like Banswara, Dungarpur, Udaipur, Sirohi, Jalore, Barmer, Jaisalmer, and Pali and the south-eastern districts like Bara, Jhalawar, Kota, Madhopur, Karauli, Tonk and Ajmer.

Figure 6
Degree of Food Insecurity in Rural Rajasthan

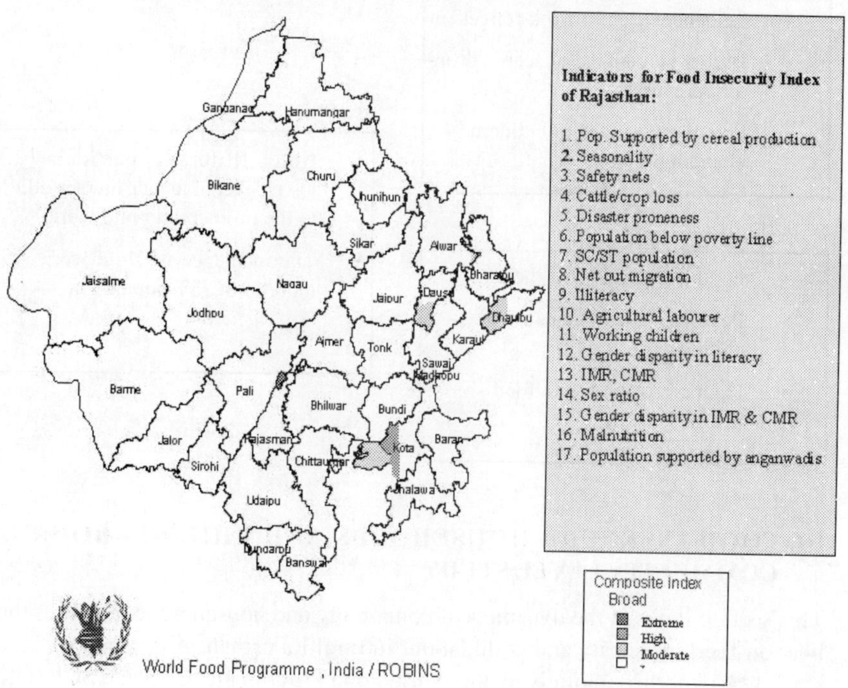

The exceptions in the south east are Bhilwara, Chittaurgarh and Bundi, where food security and child labour are co-existent. This is probably because of the concentration of textile and carpet industries in these districts.

Thus, except the northern arid plain region, all other regions overlap with the child work map of Rajasthan. This is perhaps because it receives a number of migrant labourers due to the relatively better agricultural assets and higher level of farming activities in the region (WFP, 2000b). These farmers migrate with their families including the children, as a result of which the participation of children in this area is high.

Notwithstanding the relatively diversified locations of child labour vis-à-vis food insecurity in the state, the above analysis reveals that there is significant overlap between the two indicators. This could be confirmed from the high and significant correlation between child labour and many of the food insecurity indicators, among which the important ones are percentage of people below the poverty line, illiteracy, seasonality, sex ratio and cattle and crop loss. Importantly, the correlation between child labour and the food insecurity index is also positive and significant. Thus, there is a clear link between the level of food insecurity and child labour (Figure 7).

Figure 7
Degree of Food Insecurity in Rural Rajasthan

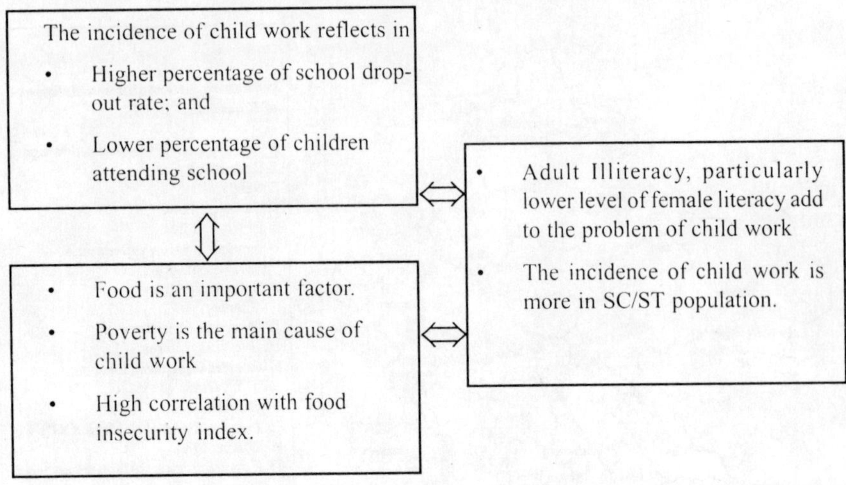

III. FOOD INSECURE HOUSEHOLDS AND CHILD LABOUR: A COMMUNITY LEVEL STUDY

This section looks at the dynamics of community and household level issues that bear on food insecurity and child labour in rural Rajasthan. A community level study was undertaken jointly by the World Food Programme, CRS and SCF (UK) in five districts of Rajasthan, viz., Ajmer, Baran, Barmer, Banswara and Churu, representing different agro-ecological and socio-economic divisions[6] of the state, during October-November 2000. The study was based on focused group discussions followed by house-listing and collecting qualitative information on the food security dynamics of the communities. Its findings presented interesting revelations regarding community perceptions of food security and their implications for child labour. In the study, all children who are not attending school have been considered as 'child workers'.

The study revealed that of the five study districts, three districts viz., Barmer, Banswara and Churu had a high incidence of child workers. More than 50 per cent of the children in these districts did not go to school, of which more than 20 per cent were engaged in economic wage activities which are hazardous to their health. Although in Ajmer the percentage of children engaged in work activities in the rural areas was lower than in the other three districts, it was still alarming at around 10 per cent.

The study revealed that illiteracy in general and socio-economic factors in particular, were the major determinants of child work. Because of cultural reasons, female literacy is much lower in all the study districts. This reflects the passive attitude of the community towards the education of girl children. Discrimination against girl children starts right from birth. At the household level, boys are favoured over girls with regard to food distribution and education. Mothers start teaching girls how to manage household activities like washing clothes, cleaning the house, collecting water, taking care of the younger siblings, collecting fodder and fuel-wood, etc., at an early age, as a matter of cultural practice. As a result, in most of cases, children, particularly girls, stay back at home[7] and later engage in wage activities. Apart from helping in the household chores, girls also engage in embroidery work and agricultural activities in most of the villages studied. This also partially explains the higher incidence of child marriage in these regions. Such practices are largely prevalent among the SC/ST communities.

Further, as a result of the lack of demand for schooling, particularly at the middle and higher level, and lack of social consciousness, the availability of schooling facilities are meagre. One could see the high incidence of child labour in districts where most or all of the study villages did not have middle level schools. In the villages of Banswara, Churu and Barmer covered by the study, no middle school was found. As a result, enrolment at this level of schooling was very low and the children were thus compelled to either stay at home or go to an alternative place to work. The incidence of both working and 'nowhere children' in these districts was high.

Nonetheless, the most important factors governing the low enrolment rates, and the high incidence of child labour and 'nowhere' children were poverty and household food insecurity which were mainly the outcome of high seasonality in agricultural activities in the studied districts in particular and Rajasthan in general. It was found that child work was mainly prevalent among households below the poverty line. The study revealed a positive correlation between the number of food insecure households (see Appendix for the food definition of insecure households) and incidence of child work. The small income from the younger members of the households significantly supplemented the household income and as a result children in the below poverty line households were usually not enrolled in schools or, if enrolled, did not attend classes because of the high opportunity cost involved in going to school.

Seasonality in agricultural activities and migration thereof have an important bearing on the incidence of child work. Needless to say, seasonality has a very strong influence on food security in Rajasthan. Rajasthan has been witnessing droughts for three consecutive years and this has had implications for the economic well-being of the community. Many households are forced to migrate with the entire family including children. Most of the labour households in Barmer and Banswara reported families migrating during the lean season to the north arid and Banas-Chambal regions, where the agricultural and economic activities are higher. This disrupts the education of children in the middle of the year. Children who migrate with their parents, work at very low wages and some are even forced into begging by their parents. The recurring nature of poverty and food insecurity had forced the children into activities like animal rearing and fodder collection as also in farming activities like harvesting, weeding, grass cutting in most of the studied villages, even during years of normal monsoon.

All this underscores the immediate need to work out Suitable policy programme to curb the incidence of child labour in the state. Since the factors influencing child work embrace multiple but interlinked dimensions, the programmes for aimed at its alleviation need to take an integrated and holistic approach to the issue.

IV. CONCLUSION AND POLICY RECOMMENDATIONS

Both secondary and community level analyses in the preceding sections clearly reveal that child work is a multi-dimensional issue and involves a number of socio-economic and cultural factors. It is not only the lack of schooling facilities but also a shortage of demand for such facilities, which underlies the problem of child labour. The shortage of demand for schooling, which implies low enrolment and high drop-out rates in the primary and middle level schools, makes children vulnerable to the pressures to join the labour force. This could be attributed to cultural factors like passive attitude towards female literacy/ education of girls, seasonal factors like uncertain monsoon and loss of productivity and socio-economic factors like household poverty and food insecurity. Child labour is thus a vicious cycle of a number of intertwined dimensions.

It should be evident from this study that any attempt to reduce or eliminate child labour requires a holistic approach to break the vicious cycle. Viewed in this broad context, the issue could be tackled through two strategies: first, strengthening of the education system to improve the rate of retention and reduce the school drop-out rate and second, providing sustainable livelihoods to households who are below the poverty line and are thus vulnerable to child labour.

The former could be achieved by providing sustainable training and organising awareness camps on the values of sending children to school, as also on the hazards of child work for the mental and physical development of children. Here, efforts should be initiated by the government and non-governmental organisations working for the cause of 'nowhere' and working children to ensure wider coverage of primary schools by providing incentives like provision of books, education kits etc. Special emphasis needs to be placed on providing education to the children who migrate with their parents.

Further, food could play an important role in the interventions aimed at enhancing the rate of school attendance among children. It would, therefore, be important to provide nutritional support to children at schools through the effective implementation of schemes like mid-day meals, morning snacks, etc. Also the children of school-going age who have never been enrolled in school could be brought into the system through, formal education and the provision of school meals to help them attain the minimum physical standard required for effective learning. It would, therefore, be important to link up the existing integrated child development scheme (ICDS) programme with primary level education and extend it to all parts of the state. The ICDS could also then act as a creche for small children, so that older siblings would be free to attend school. For this to happen, the timing of ICDS centres should be the same as that of schools.

However, the educational and nutritional support programmes would succeed only when the opportunity cost of sending the children to the school is substantially low or zero in the poor households. It would, therefore, be important to break the cycle of poverty and food insecurity to make a dent on the level of child labour. This requires providing sustainable livelihood opportunities to members of the households below the poverty line. Ensuring sustainable returns from agriculture by minimising effects of drought through effective watershed management would be critical for the agricultural economy of Rajasthan. This could also be achieved by developing rural community asset building and watershed management to reduce the impact of seasonality and enhance the productive capacity of the regions, which could check forced migration. Further, during drought years, timely relief work will help in checking migration, which could also make a significant dent in tackling the problem of education and reducing child work.

Since livestock and animal husbandry is one of the important means of livelihood in rural Rajasthan, particularly among the food insecure households, development of pasture land and improved watershed management would help strengthen their livelihood security. Also, better infrastructure and cooperation for the production and marketing of animal products will go a long way towards enhancing the incomes of the food insecure households. Further, building up of effective partnerships with the local level NGOs, CBOs and the communities at large will help in harnessing the experiences and needs at the local level for better programming and targeting of the programmes.

Appendices

Appendix I
Mapping of Food Insecurity Indicators

The composite food insecurity map of rural Rajasthan considered 17 food insecurity indicators, covering all the dimensions of food insecurity. Most of these indicators were mapped in the Food Insecurity Atlas of Rural India (FIARI). However, all of them suggested in the FIARI could not be considered in the Food Insecurity Atlas of Rajasthan because of the non-availability of district level data for many of the indicators listed below:

1. Number of persons supported per ton of cereal production per annum
2. Seasonality in cereals production
3. Availability of safety nets for food security
4. Total loss of cattle/crop loss; such losses are higher during the drought years
5. Proneness to disasters like drought, flood, earthquake etc.
6. Percentage of people below the poverty line
7. Percentage of SC and ST population
8. Net out migration from the state to other states
9. Rate of illiteracy (100-rate of literacy)

10. Percentage of agricultural labourer
11. Percentage of children engaged in work activities
12. Gender disparity in the rate of literacy
13. Infant mortality rate, child mortality rate
14. Sex ratio
15. Gender disparity in IMR and CMR
16. Malnutrition among the children below the age of five years
17. Number of people supported per *anganwadi* centre

Methodology

The method of constructing the composite food insecurity indices involved the following steps:

a) Since, individual indicators chosen for working out vulnerability indices are measured in different units, the division by mean method has been used to convert the indicators into indices. This makes them scale-free and comparable.

b) The composite food insecurity index has been arrived at by taking the average of the food insecurity indices for the districts.

c) The values of the average ranks were then distributed into different classes (using the natural breaks to arrive at the typologies of food insecurity, viz. 'Extreme', 'High', 'Moderate' and 'Low' food insecure categories) .

d) These categories were then translated into the food insecurity map of rural Rajasthan with the districts in different typologies.

Appendix II
Identification of food insecure households for the village level community study

The identification of the food insecure/ vulnerable households/ groups was based on two modules:

1. A household listing to collect information on socio-economic characteristics of the households in the sampled communities, and
2. A vulnerability ranking to distribute the entire community across four groups according to their food security base.

The ranking or grouping of households was carried out according to the following group definitions:

Group I: Households which can obtain sufficient food for themselves in normal times without assistance (gift/loan) and who may actually be able to provide (gift/loan) assistance to others.

Group II: Households which can obtain sufficient food for themselves in normal times without assistance (gift/loan) but who cannot provide (gift/loan) assistance to others.

Group III: Households which can obtain sufficient food for themselves in normal times with or without assistance (gift/loan) from others (including food aid)

Group IV: Households which cannot obtain sufficient food for themselves in normal times without assistance (gift/loan) from others (including food aid)

In the paper, households in Groups III and IV have been considered as 'food insecure'.

Appendix III
Classification of Districts into Different Agro-climatic and Socio-ecological Regions

Northern Arid Plain	:	Ganganagar, Bikaner, Nagaur, Sikar, Jhunjhunam, Hanumangarh and Churu
Northern Aravali Range	:	Alwar, Dausa, Jaipur and Ajmer
Southern Arid Plain	:	Jaisalmer, Barmer, Jalore, Pali and Jodhpur
Southern Aravali Range	:	Sirohi, Udaipur, Dungarpur, Banswara, Chittaurgarh and Rajsamund
Banas-Chambal Range	:	Bhilwara, Bundi, Kota, Jhalawar, Bara, Sawai-Madhepur, Tonk, Karaul, Dhaulpur and Bharatpur

Notes

1. There are 208 million undernourished people in India (FAO, 1999)
2. Includes only the main and marginal workers; does not include the children in the non-workers category.
3. Includes children in both principal and subsidiary status.
4. In most of the cases the families migrate with the children to the areas with higher agricultural activities within the state.
5. Both moderately and severely stunted children have been considered in the analysis.
6. The state was divided into five agro-ecological and socio-economic zones viz. Northern Arid Plain, Northern Aravali Range, Southern Arid Plain, Southern Aravali Range and the Banas-Chambal Range. This geographical classification, by and large overlaps with the National Sample Survey sub-regions in the state.
7. The school drop-out rate among the children is high in the studied villages. For example, the average drop-out rates in the villages surveyed in Banswara is 77 per cent, which is much higher than the national as well as the state average.

References

Burra, N. (1995), *Born to Work: Child Labour in India*, Oxford University Press, Delhi.

Chaudhri, D. P. (2000), "Sources of Supply of Child Labour and the States: Explorations of Historical and Contemporary Evidence with Focus on States and Districts of India", *National Seminar on Child Labour: Realities and Policy Dimensions*, VV Giri National Labour Institute, Noida and Institute for Human Development, New Delhi, December 5-7.

FAO (2000), *The State of Food Insecurity in the World*, Food and Agriculture, Second Edition, Rome.

GOI (1998), *India Nutrition Profile.* Government of India, National Nutrition Monitoring Bureau (NNMB) and Department of Women and Child Development, New Delhi.

ILO (1996), *Child Labour and Targeting*, International Labour Organisation Bureau of Statistics, Geneva.

Shariff, A. (2000), *India Human Development Report*, NCAER, New Delhi.

WFP (2000a), *Food Insecurity and Vulnerability Profile of Rajasthan*, New Delhi.

—— (2000b), *Country Strategy Outline (2002-2007)*, New Delhi.

—— (2001), *Food Insecurity Atlas of Rural Rajasthan*, Delhi.

Zutshi, Bhupinder (2000), *A Situational Analysis of Education for Street and Working Children in India*, UNESCO, New Delhi.

14

Household Food Insecurity and Child Labour: Some Evidences from Rural Orissa

NIKHIL RAJ AND ANOOP KUMAR SATPATHY

I. INTRODUCTION

The problem of child labour has generated intense debates at several platforms. A number of initiatives have been taken by various social partners to counter the problem. These range from providing schooling facilities to children, efforts aimed at raising income levels of the parents/guardians of the child labour, effective enforcement of child labour legislations to several micro-interventions by way of raising the awareness level among the communities, where child labour is present. These interventions and initiatives by all the social partners are based on research findings, which suggest that among several determinants of child labour, poverty and lack of compulsory education are crucial ones. Poverty is, indeed, symptomatic of insecurities of sorts faced by the households. One such insecurity is related to food. The varying levels of household food insecurity have recently been recognised as proximate determinants of child labour. Therefore, this paper attempts, empirically, to ascertain the correlation between household food insecurity and child labour.[1] The study area chosen for this purpose is rural Orissa, where people quite often experience hunger, malnutrition and starvation deaths. This paper is divided into four sections. Section II focuses on review of literature. Section III provides a background of socio-economic and demographic composition as well as child labour profile of the three sample districts, namely, Bargarh, Sambalpur and Bolangir. Section IV deals with the methodology of data collection and analysis. Section V presents the survey findings. Section VI discusses the conclusions of the study.

II. REVIEW OF LITERATURE

The concept of food security i.e., "access by all people at all times to enough food for an active and healthy life" (World Bank, 1986) is a global concern. In a broader sense, it is defined as, not just secure and stable access to a sufficient quantity of food, but also as access to food that is adequately nutritious, culturally acceptable, procured without any loss of dignity and self-determination and consistent with the realisation of other basic needs. In the 1970s, 'food security' was mostly concerned with national and global food supplies. But in the 1980s it became an important 'organising principle' in development and the focus shifted to the question of household and individual levels with emphasis on access, vulnerability and entitlements. The focus on access has largely resulted from the pioneering work of Sen (1981) on food entitlements. Entitlement involves the quantum of food the household actually has; an access to their own production, income and gathering of wild foods, community supports (claims), assets and migration. Using his entitlement framework, he demonstrated that a decline in food availability was neither a necessary nor a sufficient condition for creating hunger. He showed that famine could occur in the absence of any change in production, if the value of people's production and work activities declined vis-a-vis to the cost of staple food. Therefore, Dreze and Sen (1989) suggested that public policy should concentrate on alleviating the costs of entitlement failure in the form of 'entitlement protection'. The concept of secure access to enough food at all the times, also involves the 'time' factor. The World Bank (1986) draws a distinction between chronic and transitory food insecurity. A household faces chronic food insecurity when the members continually run the risk of inability to meet their food requirements, while transitory food insecurity results when a household faces a temporary decline in its entitlement and the risk of failure to meet its food requirements for a short duration.

Ensuring food security to the population has been one of the major objectives of India's development planning since its independence. It has been broadly interpreted to mean the adequate availability of foodgrain in the country as a whole and the necessary availability of purchasing power to have access to the minimum food requirement at the household level. At the time of independence, India faced the threat of famine, acute starvation and undernutrition largely due to the absence of a proper food security system and also due to the abysmal lack of purchasing power amongst the poorer sections of the population. Therefore, the first priority of the planners was to achieve national food security via increasing the production and productivity through investment in agriculture and the green revolution.[2] The fact that famines and acute starvation have not been witnessed since the last five decades testifies to the success of these efforts. Though the country achieved self-sufficiency in foodgrain production at the national level, and is currently holding huge buffer stocks (45 million tones in 1999-2000), yet food security at the household level has not been achieved due to lack of access to basic foods. The problem of access is more acute among the vulnerable sections of the society, i.e., Scheduled Castes (SCs), Scheduled Tribes[3] (STs), landless labourers, marginal farmers, etc., especially in the case of deficit and inaccessible regions.

The Public Distribution System[4] (PDS) set up to ensure availability of foodgrains at affordable prices to the vulnerable section of the population is one of the key elements of the government's food security system. In spite of the mounting food subsidy bill (Rs. 192000 crore in 1999-2000) (GOI, 2001), evaluation studies of the PDS have shown that it has utterly failed to translate sufficiency of foodgrain to household level food security at the national level.

In the inaccessible and interior parts of rural India, poor illiterate landless labourers and marginal farmers live in conditions of acute poverty. As they are illiterate, they always get a low return from agricultural production because of lack of knowledge and information about improved agricultural practices. Their only asset, labour, is undervalued because physical access to markets is difficult for them as they live in remote areas. Secondly, as the agricultural productivity in the region is very low, the market wage rate is much below the minimum wage rate, especially for females. Due to their involvement in small transactions, access to financial markets also remains limited. Moreover the absence of non-farm activities, and the desire to fulfil the minimum needs of the households, forces the family members including children into different types of low-paid work. This survival strategy continues year after year, thereby keeping the households in a more or less permanent condition of inadequate consumption, poor education and ill health.

Households that are prone to food insecurity develop complex strategies to cope with these problems. Although coping strategies vary with local conditions, there is a common pattern in the sequences of responses (Corbett, 1988). As the severity of food insecurity increases, the trend of household response became progressively more serious and threatening. Examples of coping mechanisms vary from change in cropping pattern, seasonal migration of farm labourers to towns, collection of wild food, diversification of income through joining non-farm employment, use of inter-household transfer and loans, rationing of current food consumption, sale of productive and liquid assets, sale of the girl child, sending children to work and finally distress-induced permanent migration.

On the issue of coping mechanisms, substantial differences exist among the scholars. Some argue (Kochar, 1999; Jacoby and Skoufias, 1997) that poor people themselves develop several mechanisms such as sale of assets to deal with such risks arising out of food insecurity. However, most of these measures provide short-term protection at high economic costs in the long term thus preventing any escape from poverty (World Bank, 2000). These are the situations that lead to child labour and malnourishment with irreparable damage to child health and the breakdown of families. If these mechanisms fail, households may increase their labour supply, start working for longer hours, pushing more household members (women and/or children) to join work or migrating to unaffected areas. If the local labour market is rigid in absorbing the new entrants to the labour force, then shock migration is the only answer. And if the male member migrates, women and children may need to work in the local labour market at usually very low wage rates. And finally, if all these fail, households tend to reduce consumption and prefer to remain hungry, wherein risk sharing falls disproportionately and mainly on women and children. In rural landless households, child mortality rates are found to rise during drought like conditions. Studies in India show that nutrition of girl children suffered more than boys during periods of low consumption in slack agriculture season (Behrman, 1988). Frequent fluctuations in the price of foodgrains have also been found to adversely affect education of girl children as compared to their male counterparts (Behrman and Deolalikar, 1990).

In some parts of rural India, child labour is found to play a significant role in household response to seasonal variations in household income (Barrett and Carter, 1999). During the lean season, they are taken out of school and sent to work on farms, tend cattle or carry out the household tasks, in exchange for food (Jacoby and Skoufias, 1997). This is because the opportunity cost of sending children to school is perceived as high by the food-insecure household during this period and in the process whatever income the child earns becomes significant. Food security is also related to the family size, sex composition within the family and the level of socio-economic development. Rural India has witnessed changes like rising unemployment, lower old-age dependency ratio, and higher child dependency ratio quite contrary to the national scenario, which affects food security in more than one way. For the poor families, food insecurity is certainly a major factor underlying the worst form of child labour.

Moreover, it has also been found that lack of assets – personal, public and social—is both a cause as well as an outcome of poverty. Most poor people lack assets due to stark inequalities in the distribution of income and wealth, poor health, inadequate skills and inhabitation in the poor areas within the country. These assets interact with the market and social opportunity to generate income, a better quality of life and a sense of psychological well-being. Assets are also central to coping with stress arising out of food insecurity faced at the household level (World Bank, 2000). Low assets and low incomes are mutually reinforcing: low education translates into low incomes, which translate into meagre wealth and reduced educational opportunity for the next generation.

III. SOCIO-ECONOMIC PROFILE OF ORISSA AND SAMPLE DISTRICTS

According to the 2001 Census, Orissa had a population of 36.7 million, with 85 per cent living in rural areas. Nearly 22 per cent of the population in the state is designated as Scheduled Tribes and another 16 per cent as Scheduled Castes (Census, 1991). Level of literacy in the state is quite low, as only 76 per cent of males and 51 per cent of females above seven years are literate.

Orissa is an agro-based backward economy, which is prone to natural calamities like floods, droughts and cyclones. Agriculture is the mainstay of the states' economy with a contribution of about 33 per cent to Net State Domestic Product (NSDP) during 1997-98. Over 64 per cent of its population is dependent on agriculture for its livelihood. Of the total active labour force in the state, around 28.7 per cent are agricultural labourers, with a work participation rate of 37.53 per cent (see Appendix Table 1). The per capita income of the state, which was estimated at Rs. 1668 in 1997-98[5] (at 1980-1 prices), has grown at a much lower rate as compared to other states.

Of the total gross cropped area (GCA) of 87.46 lakh hectares, only 18.76 lakh hectares are irrigated. Because of the high pressure of population, per capita cultivable land declined from 0.39 hectares in 1950-51 to 0.18 hectares in 1997-98 and the per capita foodgrain production from 230.44 kg. to 187.65 kg per annum during the same period. The intensity of fertiliser consumption is lowest in Orissa (30.52 kg per hectare in 1996-97) compared to other states in the country (see Appendix Table 1). It is a food-deficient state and contributes only 4.23 per cent to the country's food grain basket. The major causes of low productivity of the state's agriculture are inadequate capital formation, inadequate irrigation facilities and uneconomic size of holdings to name a few. About 70 per cent of the total cropped area is rainfed and dependent on monsoon rainfall. The state has about 31.54 lakh small and marginal farmers who do not have the means to make appropriate investment in agriculture owing to poverty.

The major food crop of the state is paddy, which covers more than 70 per cent of the GCA under principal crops. The average yield rate of rice in the state was 9.93 quintals per hectare in 1997-98, which was nearly half the national average of 18.8 quintal per hectare in the same year (see Appendix Table 1), and also much lower than that in the agriculturally developed states like Punjab (31.3 qtl. /hect.) and Haryana (22.2 qtl. /hect.). Fibre and cash crops cover only about 3 per cent of GCA.

In Orissa, almost half of the population lives below the poverty line (Table 1). According to recently released estimates of the Planning Commission (1999-2001), it ranked highest in terms of percentage of population living below the material poverty line (47.15 per cent).

Table 1

Percentage of Population Living below Poverty Line, (Orissa and India)

Year	Orissa			India		
	Rural	Urban	Combined	Rural	Urban	Combined
1983-84	67.53	49.15	65.29	45.65	40.79	44.48
1987-88	57.64	41.53	55.58	39.09	38.20	38.36
1993-94	49.72	41.64	48.56	37.27	32.36	35.97
1999-2000	48.01	42.83	47.15	27.09	23.62	26.10

Source: Planning Commission, Government of India.

It also ranked highest in the country in terms of crucial non-income measures of poverty like Infant Mortality Rate (IMR), Child Mortality Rate (CMR), etc. The number of infants who may die before their first birth day among the children ever born (IMR) is considered as a significant indicator to determine the socio-economic, demographic and environmental development of a region. Infant and child mortality in India is still very high and Orissa has the highest incidence of child deaths in India (Figure 1 and Appendix Table 2). The IMR and

Figure 1

Key Nutritional Indicators of Orissa and India, NFHS-2, 1998-99

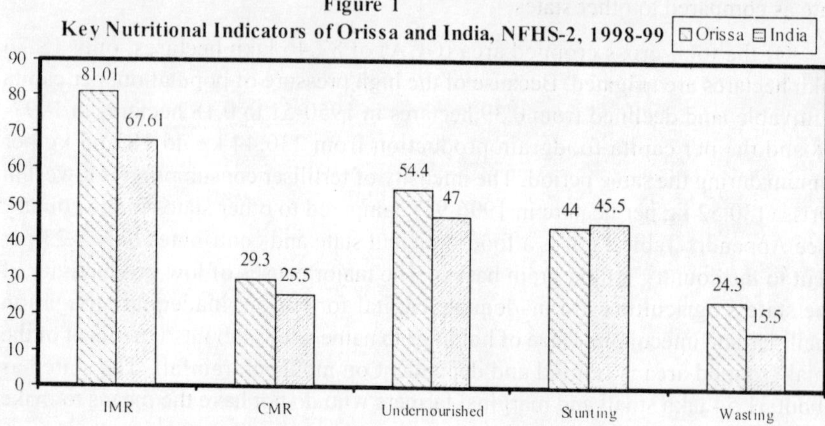

CMR among girls are higher compared to that of boys, which also indicates a certain degree of gender bias in access to basic health and sanitation facilities. The major factors that determine the deaths of infants and children are, poor and insufficient nutritional status of children as well as of pregnant women, unavailability of or inability to provide proper pre and post-natal care, surroundings in which the child is given birth, and the incidental contagious diseases. Nutritional status of children is directly related to that of their mothers. The National Family Health Survey-2, reveals that the percentage of children under the age of three years, who are undernourished (weight-for-age) in Orissa is quite high and ranks second in the country with more than 54 per cent of undernourished children (Figure 1). These rates are even higher in the sample districts[6]. Indigenous and social groups consisting of Scheduled Castes and Scheduled Tribes and casual labour that constitute the major chunk of the population in the state show high incidence of poverty, due to social barriers, lack of access to 'economic resources' and low literacy, especially among females. The problem gets compounded when we add to this, 9.9 lakh unemployed at the start of the Ninth plan (1992-1997) in the state.

Child Labour in Orissa and Sample Districts

The estimate of child labour in India varies from 11.28 million as per the Census 1991 to over 100 million as estimated by some NGOs. As per the NSS data on employment and unemployment, the estimate of child labour was 13.6 million in 1993-94 (50th round) and has declined to 10.4 million (approximately) in 1999-2000 (55th round). Although India has the largest child labour population in the world, the proportion of working children to total labour force is lower in India than in many developing countries. The incidence of child labour is a violation of the child's human rights and it curtails the potential development of the child. The architects of the Indian Constitution were fully aware of this menace and incorporated articles 15(3), 23, 24, 39(e), (i) and 45 which mandate non-employment of children and their induction into schools. These were augmented with the Prohibitive Laws namely Bonded Labour System Abolition Act 1976 and

Child Labour (Prohibition and Regulation) Act, 1986. The abundance of prohibitive laws, international conventions and even the constitutional mandate has not been able to completely eradicate the problem. In India, one out of every four persons is a child. The three districts selected for this study in Orissa are Bargarh, Sambalpur and Bolangir. These have a higher proportion of both female and male child workers than the state and national average. Orissa accounts for about 3.78 per cent of India's total child labour. Bolangir district ranks fourth within the state in terms of its colossal magnitude of child workers. Sambalpur and Bolangir districts have also a higher incidence of rural child work, especially among girls (Tables 2 and 3).

Table 2
Characteristics of Children in India, Orissa and in the Study Districts (per cent)

	India	Orissa	Sambalpur	Bolangir
Child population (5-14 yrs)				
Total	25.04	24.34	23.38	23.82
Males	25.13	24.22	23.06	23.77
Females	24.95	24.46	23.71	23.88
Male child workers	2.76	2.84	3.07	4.03
Non-workers	48.94	49.11	49.54	51.24
Percentage of non-students among non-workers	39.96	36.15	28.36	34.00
Female child workers	5.68	6.39	6.39	6.89
Non-workers	30.46	29.20	30.91	29.48
Percentage of non-students among non-workers	53.42	52.01	47.54	59.35

Note: Figures for Bargarh are not available for 1991 as it is a new district carved out of Sambalpur in 1993.
Source: Calculated from the Census of India, 1991, B-Series of Tables.

Table 3
Percentage of Workers among Children, 1991

State/	Total			Rural			Urban		
District	Total	Boys	Girls	Total	Boys	Girls	Total	Boys	Girls
India	5.37	5.66	5.06	6.43	6.56	6.29	2.04	2.79	1.23
Orissa	5.87	6.30	5.43	6.46	6.87	6.03	1.92	2.54	1.26
Sambalpur	7.75	7.58	7.92	8.97	8.72	9.22	2.04	2.49	1.54
Bolangir	8.52	9.87	7.15	9.17	10.63	7.70	2.51	3.00	2.00

Note: Figures for Bargarh are not available for 1991 as it is a new district carved out of Sambalpur in 1993.
Source: Calculated from the Census of India, 1991, B-Series of Tables.

Children are usually sent to work to supplement the family income, when the income earned by other family members is not enough to meet the needs of the family. Even though there are legislative provisions, which prohibit child labour in the organised sector in India, it fails to address the problem in home-based activities, family enterprises and agriculture and the unorganised sector. Even the strict enforcement of laws has not been enough to minimise the magnitude of child labour in India. Several micro level surveys and studies have corroborated the fact that economic compulsions in the backward areas compel parents to send their children to work (Gupta and Voll, 1999). It is found that majority of the children work either as agricultural labourers (42.5 per cent) or as cultivators (35.2 per cent) in India (VVGNLI, 2001). As the task of sending the children to school is an added burden on the respective families, this may be the reason for higher rate of dropouts in the state. In 1991, the dropout rate in the state was as high as 65 per cent.

IV. METHODOLOGY

This paper seeks to analyse the problem of child labour vis-à-vis the problem of food insecurity among rural households[7] in six representative villages spread across three districts of western Orissa. The study is based on primary household level data which were collected from 282 households[8] in these villages. The distribution of sample households is given below (Table 4)

Table 4
Number of Districts and Villages Surveyed in the Sample

District	Village	Number of house-holds surveyed
Bargarh	Tukura	60
	Nileswara	46
	Total	106
Sambalpur	Gumuloi	40
	Jaladihi	40
	Total	80
Bolangir	Jagua	42
	Patherla	54
	Total	96
	Grand total	282

The study was undertaken in the backward region of western Orissa as it provides a classic case to assess the current status of household food insecurity and its impact on child labour in rural areas. Due to its geographical location in arid and semi-arid regions, drought conditions and intermittent rainfall are a recurrent phenomenon in most parts of these districts except the canal-irrigated belt of Sambalpur and Bargarh district. This type of agro-climatic situation renders poor households vulnerable to different kinds of shocks or disaster events. The Government of India has classified most of the districts[9] (nine out of 10) in this region as endemic child labour out of 133 such districts in India. Other factors like level of agricultural development defined in terms of agricultural productivity, net area irrigated and rate of fertiliser consumption, etc. were also taken into consideration in the selection of sample districts. For the selection of the study villages, listing of all villages in the districts was done according to the ratio of workers engaged in agriculture and manufacturing within households from the Primary Census Abstract (PCA) data of 1991 (Sector I and VA as per the National Industrial Classification). On the basis of these criteria, two villages were selected from each district. To increase the homogeneity of the units of analysis and for the intensive study of the effect of food insecurity on child work, the survey attempted to cover more households from fewer numbers of villages per district.

Both quantitative and qualitative data were collected with the help of four research scholars belonging to the study area. The unit of analysis is the household. All the sample households have been selected on the basis of systematic sampling with random start. The information from all the households in six villages was collected during the period December 2000 to January 2001. In order to stem any data gaps, local investigators also visited these villages later. The survey collected detailed information on each household on a variety of indicators like demographic and socio-economic features, availability of work opportunity, asset and indebtedness profile of the household, average size of the land holdings, expenditure pattern of the households on food and non-food items[10], household perceptions about food sufficiency/insufficiency, coping mechanisms adopted by the households to deal with inadequacy of food resources, and a detailed profile of child labour.

In addition to this, an attempt has been made to collect information from households about the varying degrees of severity of food insecurity[11] by using the multiple indicator interview schedule discussed below.

To examine the relationship between food insecurity and child labour, in terms of responses to relative perception regarding food insecurity, an index has been worked out. This index categorises households into four groups:-

1. Food Secure (FS): Household shows no or minimal evidence of food insecurity.
2. Food Insecure without Hunger (FISWH): Food insecurity is evident in household member's concern about adequacy of household food supply and in adjustments to household food management including reduced *quality* of food. Little or no reduction in member's food intake is reported.
3. Food Insecurity with Hunger - Moderate (FISM): Food intake of adults in the household is reduced to an extent that implies that adults have repeatedly experienced the physical sensation of hunger. Reduction/ skipping of children's diet are not observed.
4. Food Insecurity with Hunger - Severe (FISS): At this level all households with children have reduced or skipped children's food intake

The above index represents the condition of household members as a group and not necessarily the condition of a particular member in household. A household classified as food insecure with hunger as per the indices, indicates that at least one member, or members of the household are experiencing hunger due to insufficiency of resources and not necessarily all members and not necessarily on all, or even on most days.

Based on the perception of the sample households for the preceding month[12] (last 30 days) of the survey concerning kinds of household conditions, events, behavioral patterns, etc. were combined to construct the index. These parameters specifically include perceptions of households on:

(i) Adequacy of the quantity of food.

(ii) Anxiety that the food budget or food supply may be insufficient to meet basic needs.

(iii) The experience of running out of food, and without money to obtain more.

(iv) Perceptions of the respondent that the food eaten by household members was inadequate in either quality or quantity or both.

(v) Instances of reduction/skipping of food intake by adults in the household and its frequency.

(vi) Instances of reduction/skipping of food intake by children in the household and its frequency.

V. SURVEY FINDINGS

In this section, an attempt has been made to analyse and establish the interrelationship between food insecurity and child labour based on the broad findings of our survey.

1. Basic Socio-economic Characteristics of the Surveyed Households

A general profile of the six sample villages included in the study shows a dominance of Scheduled Castes and Scheduled Tribe communities. Nearly 65 per cent of all households belong to these communities. This holds for the districts of Sambalpur and Bolangir as well. In the case of Bargarh, it is the Other Backward Classes[13] (OBCs), which constitutes nearly 62 per cent of the population (Appendix Table 3). A population dominated by OBCs, SCs and STs also necessitates an enquiry into the levels of literacy, occupational pattern and land ownership among these households. It is evident from the data that nearly 70 per cent of all sample households belong to the landless or marginal (0-1 acres) landholding category. The proportion is, however, slightly less in Sambalpur. A significant proportion of such households in the sample belongs to the socially backward castes and communities. This is further reflected in the low literacy rate among the heads of the households, which is around 50 per cent. The case of Bolangir is even more distressing, with nearly 58 per cent of households being headed by illiterates (Appendix Table 3).

As regards the occupational distribution of the heads of the households, our findings indicate that about 35 per cent are working as labour—both in agricultural and non-agricultural activities and another 36 per cent are working as cultivators (Appendix Table 3). Sambalpur, which is relatively an agriculturally developed district, shows a slightly different picture. More than half of the heads of the households in Sambalpur are working as cultivators and less than a quarter working as labour. In this context, it is important to note that the average landholding size among the sample households was 1.24 acres (Appendix Table 3). Sambalpur ranks highest (1.78 acres) and Bolangir lowest (0.60 acres) in landholding size. It is natural, therefore, that in districts other than Sambalpur, the heads of the households are primarily working as labour—either in agriculture or non-agriculture related activities.

The weak economic position of the households is also indicated by the average level of indebtedness (Appendix Table 3), the debts having been mainly incurred for non-productive consumption purposes. While this average for all the households in the sample villages in the three districts is more than Rs. 2000, it is 1.5 times higher in Bolangir—a district placed at a lower level of agricultural and infrastructural development where the main source of earning of the heads of the households is wage income from various forms of labour. The age distribution is typical of populations that have recently experienced a moderate to high fertility increase, with relatively higher proportions in the younger and lower proportion in the older age groups. About 36 per cent of the sample population is below the age of 14 and 7 per cent is in the above 59 years category. Landlessness coupled with wage work, and the presence of large number of SC and ST illiterate poor women appears to lead to higher fertility rates and hence higher youth dependency ratio, though in Orissa and India fertility continues to decline. The average family size among the landless households is above six (Appendix Table 3). A higher family size for this group of households is explained by their need to maximise their wage earnings. However, as found in a study by Sarap et al (2000) on the working of the PDS in Kalahandi district in Orissa, in the case of the households having landownership of more than two acres, the family size is even higher (6.68). This is attributed to the typical insulating strategies adopted by peasant households to supply more family labour to their farms with a view to cutting down the wage cost and also to avoid peak season insecurities on account of engagement of hired labour. Moreover, such households appear to have a relatively higher sense of security because of better reserved incomes, hence the observation that even such households are found to have larger family size.

2. Profile of Child Labour

Among the 282 households in the sample, there were 214 child labourers, in the school going age (i.e., 5-14 years), thereby implying 1.32 child labourers per household (Appendix Table 4). Given an average family size of six persons, including the parents and four children, it may be safely assumed that even if all the children in these families are in the age group, 5-14 years, at least one child of families in rural western Orissa could be classified as child labour. It was also found that households headed by illiterates contributed to nearly half of the child labour in the surveyed regions (Appendix Table 4).

If child labour in agriculture and livestock related activities are combined, then Bargarh accounts for 40 per cent of the child labour in the sample households, followed by 36 per cent in Sambalpur and less than seven per cent in

Bolangir. In the case of Bolangir, field observations indicate that there is an acute problem from the demand side and even adults do not have adequate employment opportunities. Under such circumstances, it is natural that employment of children is rather low. In this context, it has been noted that among all the child labour, less than 30 per cent is accounted for by Bolangir district alone. At the other extreme, Bargarh (a relatively developed agricultural district), accounts for nearly 45 per cent of all child labour among the sample households. It is thus obvious that the problem of child labour is also governed by demand side factors and moves in tandem with development processes in the rural areas (Appendix Table 5).

A significant proportion (nearly 30 per cent) of child labour is also found to be working primarily either as attached labour in agriculture or even as casual labour within this sector.

(i) Gender Distribution of Child Labour

The data does not indicate any significant difference between male and female child labour. While male children constitute 52 per cent of all child labour in the sample households, the rest is comprised of female children. The proportion of child labour involved in domestic activities, including sibling care is nearly 30 per cent of all child labour (Appendix Table 4). Therefore, even though no specific difference in the percentage of male and female children is observed at an aggregate level, there are indicators which suggest that most of the domestic work and sibling care work is done by the female children.

As, several types of work by girl children are not clearly visible in undeveloped or backward areas, it is very likely that from the 'rights' perspective, these activities by girl children are also a denial of their basic rights to education—as they become the first casualty when households try to meet their food insecurity problems in particular, and other economic insecurities, in general.

Who is the Casualty? — A Case of *Jaldihi* in Sambalpur

Lochan Beriha, aged 60 years recalls, "When I was young and the family needed support, my daughter was asked to stop going to school. My wife and my daughter-in-law could join work only thereafter". History, for Lochan Beriha seems to have come full circle. Last year, severe food problems faced by the villagers, and his family in particular forced both his grand daughters to drop out of school and help in collecting firewood and work as part-time domestic helps in the neighbourhood.

Source: As obtained from a focus group discussion in the village.

(ii) Land Ownership and Child Labour

In terms of landownership (Appendix Table 4), it was found that nearly three-fourths of the child labour belong to households which are either landless or have marginal landholdings (0-1 acre). In this context, one should recall that the majority of the households in the sample were from this category and that they also belong to socially backward castes and communities. Social as well as economic backwardness is thus once again empirically verified to be an important determinant of child labour.

3. Consumption Pattern of the State

An analysis of the pattern of consumption expenditure and Engel's ratio is made on the basis of the 32nd round (1977-78), 50th round (1993-94) and 55th round (1999-2000) National Sample Survey (NSS) data to assess the standard of living and well-being of the people of Orissa compared to other states and the national average.

The average Monthly Per Capita consumer expenditure (MPCE) in rural areas in Orissa is estimated to be Rs. 373.17 as per the 55th round, having registered an increase of 611.20 per cent over the 32nd round. The corresponding figure for the urban areas is Rs. 618.48 with an increase of 610.98 per cent[14] during the same period. It is important to mention here that, the per capita (rural/ urban) consumer expenditure in Orissa has remained below that of the all India level all through from the 32nd to the 55th round.

Analysis of the 50th and 55th round of NSS data[15] shows that the standard of living of people as measured by the Engel's Ratio[16] both in rural and urban areas of Haryana, Karnataka, Kerala, Andhra Pradesh, Maharashtra and Punjab was higher as compared to Orissa as these states show a smaller Engel's ratio. The position of Orissa in rural areas has improved recently as the ratio decreased from 68.1 per cent in the 50th round to 64.1 per cent in the 55th round. However, for urban areas it shows marginal improvement as the ratio came down from 57.8 per cent to 56.98 per cent during the same period. Further, the Engel's ratio both in rural and urban areas of Orissa is higher than the all-India level during both the rounds indicating a higher incidence of poverty and a lower standard of living of the people as compared to the average at all-India level (Figure 2).

Figure 2
Engel's Ratio for Orissa and India, NSS Rounds

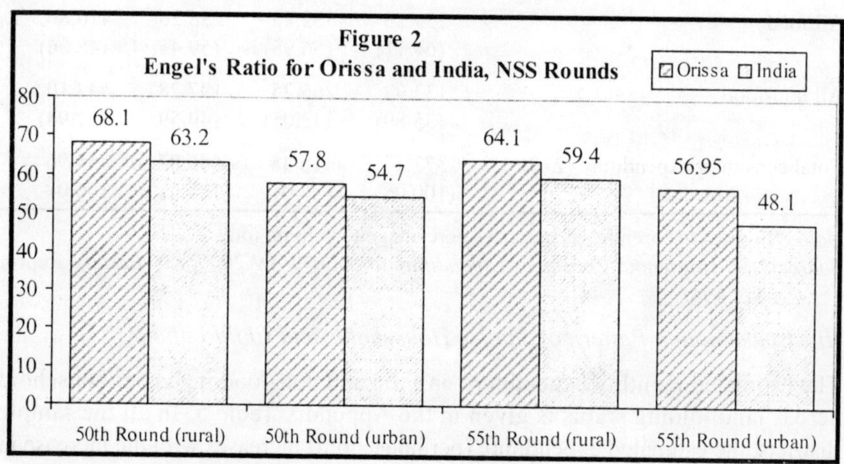

Analysis of average monthly per capita consumer expenditure (in Rs.) on food and non-food items as per the 55th round of NSS data reveals wide disparity between rural and urban areas, both in the case of Orissa and at an all-India level. The gap is more pronounced in the case of the non-food component. (Table 5) Both in case of Orissa and India, monthly per capita expenditure (MPCE) on food and non-food items in urban areas is higher than in rural areas. But if one takes percentage expenditure as an unit of analysis then in case of food items the expenditure is higher in rural areas and non-food expenditure is higher in urban areas both at state and national level (see Table 5). From the above analysis, it is observed that the people living in the urban areas both at state and national level are comparatively more affluent than those who live in the rural areas.

A disaggregated analysis of expenditure on food items only (NSS 55th round) further reveals that in Orissa, per capita consumer expenditure on foodgrain, particularly for cereals is relatively higher as compared to other developed states, whereas in the case of non-foodgrain it is relatively lower.[17] This observation is more pronounced, in case of the rural areas (Table 5). The higher per capita consumption for cereals is notable, despite the fact that the allocation and off-take of cereals from PDS in the state is not high (Thamarajakshi, 1997). According to scholars, due to the successful advent of the green revolution, rice production in the state has been accelerated enabling higher consumption of cereal and hence food items.

Table 5

Average Monthly Expenditure Per Person on Different Groups of Items of Consumption for Orissa and India, 55th Round, 30 Days Reference Period

(in Rs.)

	Orissa		India	
Items	Rural	Urban	Rural	Urban
Cereals	134.38 (36.01)	140.39 (22.70)	107.25 (22.2)	105.58 (12.35)
All food	239.25 (64.11)	352.23 (56.95)	288.20 (59.41)	410.86 (48.06)
All non-food	133.92 (35.89)	266.25 (43.05)	197.28 (40.59)	444.10 (51.94)
Total consumer expenditure (2+3)	373.17 (100.0)	618.48 (100.0)	486.07 (100.0)	854.96 (100.0)

Note: *Figures in parentheses indicates percentage to column total.

Source: NSS *Household Consumer Expenditure in India, 1999-2000, Key Results.* Report No. 454.

(i) Consumption Pattern of Sample Households and Child Labour

The estimated monthly expenditure on food and non-food items per household across landholding status is given in the Appendix Table 5. In all the sample districts, the estimated expenditure (per household) increases with the increase in landholding status. The expenditure (per household) in Bolangir is lower across all landholding category (except the landless) as compared to the other two districts. It is a relatively backward district agriculturally and infrastructurally. It is also evident from the data that per household expenditure in Sambalpur is higher than in Bargarh across all but large landholding size.

The percentage expenditure on food items constitutes about four-fifths of the total expenditure in all three districts and decreases marginally with the increase in land ownership (Appendix Table 5). In other words, it means that expenditure on non-food items increases with the increase in landholding status. This is because households make a huge expenditure on cereals particularly, on rice when they are poor. However when their need for the basic food items is fulfilled with the increase in landholding status and hence income, expenditure on food declines progressively. Among these districts, in the case of Bolangir, percentage expenditure on food is highest and it is the lowest in Bargarh. This implicitly indicates that the standard of living of the household is better in Sambalpur and Bargarh as compared to Bolangir.

Studies on changes in the standard of living and measurement, and prevalence of poverty[18] categorise people into different MPCE classes on the basis of level of expenditure. The percentage distribution of households according to monthly per capita expenditure (MPCE) classes shows that in all the six villages of the three districts, about 66 per cent of the households (Appendix Table 5) come under the lower two classes, i.e., Rs. 0-255 and Rs. 255-34019. This also holds good for the entire state (both for rural and urban areas), if one analyses the NSS consumer expenditure data pertaining to the 55th round (1999-2000).

The inter-district analysis (as per the present study) shows that in Bolangir, nearly 70 per cent households come under these two MPCE classes, whereas in the case of the other two districts it is around 62 per cent. A higher concentration of population in the lower expenditure class is indicative of a higher ratio of population living below the poverty line. If one assumes consumption expenditure as a proxy for income, it is natural to expect that the highest number of child labourers will be concentrated in households under these two MPCE categories (Appendix Table 5) who are poor and food insecure in all districts and where the dependency ratios are also high (Appendix Table 5). Although our field result confirmed the above generalisations, on another front it is contradictory. For example, in Bolangir where all the proximate determinants of food insecurity i.e., presence of relatively higher illiterate (58 per cent) and labouring (agricultural and non-agricultural) households with less than one acre of landholdings, (where the dependency ratios and households in the lowest MPCE class are also high), proportionately less child labour are concentrated (27 per cent) compared to Bargarh (45 per cent) and Sambalpur (28 per cent). The rationale behind the existence of this sort of contradiction lies in an analysis of the problem from the demand side. In Bolangir, though agriculture is the dominant economic activity of the masses, its production and productivity is the lowest in the state due to its geographical location in the arid and semi-arid areas with non-availability of irrigation and other supportive infrastructure. The agricultural crops are also ravaged continuously by frequent droughts. All this makes agriculture a non-profitable venture, thereby reducing the demand for labour to a great extent. Secondly, the virtual non-existence of non-farm and industrial employment further accentuates the problem. As such, in the face of less labour demand in Bolangir, even adult members of the food insecure households find it difficult to get employment. The above battery of arguments reasonably explains the prevailing contradiction, that causes lower incidence of child labour vis-a-vis the presence of higher number of food insecure households in Bolangir. Analysis of information obtained through the participatory rural appraisal, (PRA) shows that parents are quite willing to send their child to work, in case of employment opportunity.

The above discussion gives us enough reasons to conclude that, though household food insecurity is a necessary condition for the existence of a higher incidence of child labour, it does not appear to be sufficient. For a higher incidence of child labour, other factors like relative levels of development of a district and the existence of demand for labour, among other factors have to coexist simultaneously vis-a-vis household food insecurity.

4. Food Insecurity, Child Labour and Coping Mechanisms

It has already been mentioned in the section on methodology that, based upon certain quantitative and qualitative responses, an index of food insecurity was developed. The households were then classified into four groups, depending upon varying degrees of food insecurity. To repeat, these categories are FS, FISWH, FISM and FISS.

An examination of the distribution of child labour across households confronting varying levels of food insecurity shows that while FS households account for only 8.4 per cent of child labour, the FISWH households record nearly 20 per cent and those facing moderate (FISM) to severe food insecurity (FISS) account for more than 70 per cent of all child labour in the sample districts of Orissa (Appendix Table 7). A disaggregated picture also reveals that at the household level, the transition from FISWH to FISM adds to child labour, with the trend continuing intensively as one moves to households facing severe food insecurity. It is evident, therefore, that households may try to adapt certain other coping mechanisms till their food insecurity reaches a certain intensity. Policy interventions are indeed required to arrest such transition among households, if withdrawal of children from school and their subsequent pushing into work have to be avoided.

In fact, in terms of several *coping mechanisms* adopted by the households, child labour emerges as a first preference for nearly 10 per cent of the households. Almost 20 per cent of the FISS households adapt to the problem of food insecurity by withdrawing their children from schools and putting them to work. The proportion of such households is much lower (7.67 per cent) in the case of Food Secure (FS) households. It may also be noted that among the various alternatives available to households to cope with the problem of food insecurity, child labour emerges as an option only when some changes have already taken place in terms of dietary patterns, or some loan (grain or cash) has been incurred and in severe cases, some sale of assets has already taken place and the accruals from all these changes have not been found to be sufficient.

The distribution of child labour across the occupational pattern of the heads of the households reflects that about 42 per cent of child labour in rural Orissa are drawn from households where the head of the households is a wage laboures—in agriculture and non- agriculture activities, more prominently in the former (Appendix Table 7). The remaining child labourers belong to households headed by cultivators or those working in the service sector. Among these households, less than 5 per cent of child labours belong to households that are Food Secure (FS). The remaining child labour is drawn from households which face varying levels of food insecurity—without hunger to moderate with hunger (FISM) and severe with hunger (FISS). Also, among food insecure households, nearly 91 per cent are either landless or possess marginal landholdings (Appendix Table 7).

An idea of the incidence of child labour could also be obtained by looking at the ratio of child labour to adult labour in each district across households grouped by varying degrees of food insecurity (Appendix Table 7). The findings in this regards suggest that the ratio of child labour to adult labour goes on rising from 18.1 in FISWH households to 22.0 among FISM households and finally to 39.64 among households confronting severe food insecurity. In Bargarh and Sambalpur districts, the corresponding figures are slightly higher, the main reason being the availability of some employment for adults, which is lacking in Bolangir district. The demand side factors explain these the inter-district variations in the child labour to adult labour ratio.

Three food items namely rice, wheat and pulses were considered to get an idea of overall spread of household food insecurity and the relative sufficiency of the households on these consumption items was examined. The overall picture suggests that nearly 80 per cent of all households are sufficient in terms of rice (Appendix Table 6). As regards wheat and pulses, the corresponding figures are much lower at 40 per cent and a mere 5 per cent, respectively. In this context, it is important to note that rice cultivation occupies 70 per cent of GCA under principal crops and also the major staple diet in Orissa and it is also distributed through the PDS channel. On the other hand, production of wheat in the state is very low and it is also not distributed through the PDS/TPDS in the study areas.

A disaggregated analysis of the above type of sufficiency across landownership of the households in the three sample districts indicates that in terms of rice, at least in Bargarh and Sambalpur most of the households across all land size categories are sufficient (Appendix Table 6). However, as the land size increases in the district of Bolangir, the proportion of households having rice sufficiency is seen to rise from 60 per cent of all households in the landless category to more than 80 per cent in the category where average land owned is above two acres. The relative agricultural backwardness of a particular region has thus a significant impact on relative food sufficiency. A more or less similar observation holds in the case of wheat (Appendix Table 6). On the other hand, though pulse sufficiency is found to emerge in a marginal way in the Sambalpur and Bargarh district among households, which have more than one acre of land it doesn't provide any conclusive trend across the land holding category in the three study districts. Thus, even in terms of sufficiency of basic cereals, there is some insufficiency in terms of wheat and to a larger degree in terms of pulses.

The Reach of PDS/TPDS

Out of the three study districts, the Targeted Public Distribution System (TPDS)[20] is present only in two districts. i.e., Sambalpur and Bolangir, while the general Public Distribution System (PDS) facility is available in Bargarh district only. The present study results shows that, in all the three districts around 82 per cent of the sample households have a ration card (Appendix Table 6). Out of this only 76 per cent get their rations from the PDS/TPDS. In Bolangir district where most of the sample households come under the lowest two Monthly Per capita Consumption Expenditure (MPCE) classes and where the dependency ratios are also high, only 67 per cent of the households have their own ration card. Of these only 65 per cent of the people are actually getting their rations from the PDS (Appendix Table 4). But in case of Sambalpur it is as high as 90 per cent the major reasons for not having a ration card are: (a) division of earlier extended family as a wiring mechanism against the recent drought condition and (b) malpractice and delay in the distribution of Below Poverty Line (BPL) card as a result of which most of the needy and poor families are virtually out of this system. Our PRA results confirm this conclusion. Around 63 per cent of the total households held that the quality of cereals distributed at the Fair Price Shop (FPS) is either good or satisfactory (Appendix Table 6). Most of the households also indicated that the FPS's opens only for one to three days in a month. The main problem that people faced at the FPS which results in low off takes are: (i) lack of hard cash at the time of distribution; (ii) lack of information about the number of days of opening of the FPS; (iii) one time monthly distribution; (iv) irregularities in the distribution; (v) no supply of coarse cereal (Appendix Table 6). With a view to improving the system, most of the villagers in the sample villages felt that the rice distributed to the BPL families should be given at FPS shops instead of at the *Panchayat* Office. To make the system leakage free, the monitoring of the distribution could be preferably taken up by the teachers of the local schools. Also, these households expressed the need for off take on credit basis for a short period, especially during the lean agricultural season, which would help them to tide over small periods of food insecurity.

Source: Based upon group discussions and household survey findings.

Deprivation in terms of pulse intake could have an adverse impact on the growth of children, as the main source of protein intake in the rural areas is also missing. Food insecurity and malnutrition appear to be closely related. This could in fact be an independent area of study.

VI. CONCLUSION

In brief, the preliminary evidences from this small sample survey conducted in rural areas of the three Western districts of Orissa indicate that social and economic backwardness as reflected in terms of land ownership, caste of the households and the literacy levels of the heads of the households, apart from the family size determine the degree of food insecurity of households. The greater the intensity of this insecurity, the more the children would be forced to join work, even though it is a first option for only one-fifth of the households. The transition of households from the FISM to FISS needs to be checked urgently to avoid further increase in the proportion of child labour. Analysis of household consumption expenditure shows that the standard of living of the households is higher in Bargarh and Sambalpur compared to Bolangir district. Further it is found that the highest proportion of child labour was concentrated in households who fall in the lowest MPCE classes. Lastly, it was established beyond reasonable doubt that, though household food insecurity is a necessary condition for child labour, it is by no means, a sufficient one. For a higher incidence of child labour, other factors like relative levels of development of a district and existence of demand for labour, among others have to coexist simultaneously vis-a-vis household food insecurity.

Appendix

Table 1

A Comparative Profile of Study Districts vis-a-vis Orissa and India

Indicators	Bargarh	Sambalpur	Bolangir	Orissa	India
Infrastructure development index	-	115.39	100.13	101.45	100
Total population (in '000)	1207	809	123	31660	846303
Percentage share of population	-	0.32	0.20	3.74	100
Annual population growth rate (81-91)	-	1.69	1.59	1.83	2.14
SC population (in %)	18.44	17.07	15.39	16.2	16.48
ST population (in %)	19.56	35.08	22.06	22.21	8.08
Total literacy rate (in %)	47.65	51.65	38.63	49.09	52.2
Total illiteracy rate (in %)	52.35	48.44	61.37	50.91	47.8
Female literacy rate (in %)	-	33.35	21.88	34.68	39.29
Rural literacy rate (in %)	-	45.61	36.71	45.46	44.69
Sex ratio @	979	956	981	970	927
Density $	207	121	188	203	274
Urbanisation (in %)	6.67	25.40	10.51	13.38	25.73
Child labour to total children (5-14 years)#	7.75	7.75	8.52	5.87	5.37
IMR (1991)	103	103	101	81.0**	67.61**
CMR (1991)	131	131	139	29.3**	25.5**
Percentage workers in agriculture	65.6	58	67.8	63.7	69
Work participation Rate, (in %)	44.3	44.08	40.74	37.53	37.46
Net sown area in hectares	288540	134379	287345	5017499	144.2+
Rate of fertilizer consumption, (1996-7)=	60.8	57.6	10.22	30.52	77.5
Yield rate of rice* (1996-7)	15.3	12.79	3.57	13.7	18.6

Notes:
1. @ No. Of females per'000 males; $ Population per sq. Km.
2. = In Kg. Per Hectare; * In Qtls. per hectare
3. ** The figures are for the year 1998-99 and taken from NFHS-2; + The figures are in million hectares # The figure for Sambalpur and Bargarh is same, as the later was earlier a part of Sambalpur. The figures are given in percentages.
4. % Indicates total workers as a percentage of total population; - data not available as the district was created in 1993.

Source:
1. Government of India. (GOI): *Census Report, 1991.*
2. Ministry of Finance, (GOI): *Economic Survey, 2000-2001.*

Table 2
Basic Demographic and Nutritional Indicators of Orissa and India

Indicators	Orissa	India
Birth rate (1999)	24.1	26.1
Death rate (1999)	10.6	8.7
Rural IMR (1998)	101	77
Life expectancy at birth (in years)	57.2	61
Enrolment ratios in school education from Class I to VIII	27.3	23.6
Total fertility rate (NFHS, 1998-99)	2.46	2.85
Maternal mortality rate, 1997 (in Number)	361	408
No of undernourished women #	48	35.4
Population expected to survive beyond 40 Years of Age	81.0	84.3
Two year old babies immunized from all principal child disease	36.1	35.4
Children (Under 5 years) suffering from the problem of underweight and malnutrition*	54.7	46.6
Household with safe drinking water	51.4	70.6
Percent age of population living below poverty line (1999-2000)	47.15	26.10
Per-capita NSDP at constant prices, 1995-96 (in Rs.)	1634	2608
Per-capita in dollar PPP's	804.58	1,240

Source:
1. Government of India (GOI), Census Report, 1991
2. Ministry of Health and Family Welfare, GOI, Health Information of India, Planning Commission, CSO and Directorate of Economics and Statistics, Government of Orissa.
3. Sample Registration System (SRS); National Family Health Survey, (NFHS) 1998-99.
4. Percentage of women with BMI Value < 18.5 Kg/m^2 * NFHS-2, 1998-99
5. # Percentage of women with BMI Value < 18.5 Kg/m^2 * NFHS-2, 1998-99.

Table 3
Key Survey Results

Indicators	Bargarh	Sambalpur	Bolangir	All
Total number of households surveyed	106	80	96	282
Caste of head of household				
SC	24.53	12.50	31.25	23.40
ST	3.77	75.00	58.33	42.55
OBC	62.26	12.50	8.33	29.79
Others	9.43	0.00	2.08	4.26
*Land holding status of household**				
Landless	50.94	15.00	66.67	46.10
Marginal	18.87	37.50	18.75	24.11
Small	15.09	22.50	8.33	14.89
Big	15.09	25.00	6.25	14.89
Literacy levels among the head of household				
Illiterate	39.62	55.00	58.33	50.35
Primary	41.51	30.00	31.25	34.75
Middle	13.21	10.00	8.33	10.64
Matric and above	5.66	5.00	2.08	4.26
Occupational (primary) distribution of head of household				
Cultivator	26.42	67.50	20.83	36.17
Agricultural labour	28.30	2.50	14.58	16.31
Non-agricultural labour	9.43	12.50	35.42	19.15
Service	11.32	2.50	8.33	7.80
Others	24.53	15.00	20.83	20.57
Average landholding size (in acre)	1.36	1.78	0.60	1.24
Average indebtedness (in Rs.)	1385.79	2265.85	3233.98	2262.62
Age distribution of population				
0-4 years	5.84	7.59	12.88	8.62
5-14 years	29.56	22.77	27.04	26.68
15-59 years	58.39	62.95	51.07	57.46
59 years and above	6.20	6.70	9.01	7.25
Total number of persons	548	448	466	1462
Dependency ratios	448	466	1462	
Total dependency ratios	71.25	58.87	95.80	74.05
Youth dependency ratios	60.63	48.23	78.15	61.43
Old-age dependency ratios	10.63	10.64	17.65	12.62
Average family size (in number) by landholding status of household				
Landless	5.5	7.2	5.4	6.0
Marginal	5.2	5.6	5.3	5.4
Small	5.5	6.0	5.0	5.5
Big	6.4	6.5	7.1	6.7
All households	4.5	5.0	4.6	4.7
Gender distribution of head of household				
Male	84.91	95.00	87.50	88.65
Female	15.09	5.00	12.50	11.35

Note: (As a percentage to column total for each variable in the district);
*Marginal - (up to 1) Acres, Small - (1 to 2) Acres, and Big - (more than 2) Acres.

Source: Field Survey.

Table 4
Key Survey Results

Child Labour Profile in the Study Area

Indicators	Bargarh	Sambalpur	Bolangir	All
Number of child labour (5-14 years)	96(44.85)	60(28.03)	58(27.10)	214(100.0)**
Prevalence of child labour by education level of the head of the household				
Illiterate	50.00	40.00	58.62	49.53
Primary	35.42	56.67	37.93	42.06
Middle	14.58	3.33	3.45	8.41
Primary occupation of the child labour (5-14 Years)				
Attached labour	16.67	6.67	20.69	14.95
Casual labour	8.33	26.67	17.24	15.89
Agricultural labour	31.25	30.00	3.45	23.36
Livestock	10.42	6.67	3.45	7.48
Non-agricultural labour	8.33	6.67	0.00	5.61
Domestic labour	22.92	23.33	41.38	28.04
Sibling care	2.08	0.00	13.79	4.67
Gender distribution (child labour)				
Male	54.17	46.67	55.17	52.34
Female	45.83	53.33	44.83	47.66
*Ratio of child labour across land holding status**				
Landless	60.42	30.00	65.52	53.27
Marginal	16.67	30.00	13.79	19.63
Small	14.58	20.00	6.90	14.02
Big	8.33	20.00	13.79	13.08

Note: Figures in brackets are percentage to column total for each variable in the district);
*Marginal - (up to 1) Acres, Small - (1 to 2) Acres, and Big - (more than 2) Acres;
** Figure in the parentheses indicates percentage to row total.

Source: Field Survey Data.

Table 5
Expenditure Pattern of Households Across Landholding Status

Land-holding	Districts	Total monthly expenditure (in Rs.)	% expenditure on food items	% expenditure on non-food items
Landless				
	Bargarh	973.94	76.09	23.91
	Sambalpur	1291.65	82.81	17.19
	Bolangir	1031.76	79.62	20.38
	Total	1032.64	78.49	21.52
Marginal				
	Bargarh	1248.69	75.80	24.20
	Sambalpur	1379.34	81.02	18.98
	Bolangir	1139.37	81.69	18.31
	Total	1280.31	79.70	20.30
Small				
	Bargarh	1451.42	68.72	31.29
	Sambalpur	1795.77	80.14	19.86
	Bolangir	1109.53	79.79	20.22
	Total	1533.88	75.72	24.28
Big				
	Bargarh	2145.48	74.84	25.16
	Sambalpur	1854.63	71.94	28.07
	Bolangir	1300.27	83.22	16.78
	Total	1886.23	74.65	25.35
Total				
	Bargarh	1280.47	74.71	25.30
	Sambalpur	1573.84	78.88	21.12
	Bolangir	1075.20	80.25	19.75
	Total	1295.90	77.80	22.20

Indicators	Bargarh	Sambalpur	Bolangir	All
Total number of households surveyed	106	80	96	282
Number of child labour (5-14 years)	96 (44.85)	60 (28.03)	58 (27.10)	214 (100.0)
Distribution of household according to monthly per capita consumption expenditure (MPCE) classes				
Rs.0 to 255	28.85	36.59	50.00	38.30
Rs.255 – 340	34.62	24.39	20.83	26.95
Rs.340-420	15.38	19.51	14.58	16.31
Rs.420 & above	21.15	19.51	14.58	18.44
Dependency ratio according to households MPCE classes (in Rs.)				
Rs.0 to 255	100.00	71.15	100.00	90.57
Rs.255 – 340	82.35	68.75	105.00	82.52
Rs.340-420	78.26	51.85	130.77	77.78
Rs.420 & above	62.16	41.38	81.25	58.54
Distribution of child labour according to households MPCE classes (in Rs)				
Rs.0 to 255	35.42	41.94	46.43	40.19
Rs.255 – 340	39.58	35.48	25.00	34.58
Rs.340-420	14.58	9.68	21.43	14.95
Rs.420 & above	10.42	12.90	7.14	10.28

Note: *Marginal - up to 1 acres, Small - 1 to 2 acres, and Big - more than 2, acres.
Source: Field Survey.

Table 6
Key Survey Results

Indicators		Bargarh	Sambalpur	Bolangir	All
Total number of households surveyed		106	80	96	282
Distribution of household in terms of sufficiency/insufficiency in rice across land size					
Landless	Sufficient	82.14	66.67	60.71	70.77
	Insufficient	17.86	33.33	39.29	29.23
Marginal	Sufficient	90.00	93.33	55.56	82.35
	Insufficient	10.00	6.67	44.44	17.65
Small	Sufficient	100.00	100.00	40.00	85.71
	Insufficient	0.00	0.00	60.00	14.29
Big	Sufficient	100.00	100.00	83.33	95.24
	Insufficient	0.00	0.00	16.67	4.76
All	Sufficient	88.68	90.00	60.42	79.43
	Insufficient	11.32	10.00	39.58	20.57
Distribution of household in terms of sufficiency/insufficiency in wheat across land size					
Landless	Sufficient	57.14	22.22	10.71	32.31
	Insufficient	42.86	77.78	89.29	67.69
Marginal	Sufficient	40.00	53.33	11.11	38.24
	Insufficient	60.00	46.67	88.89	61.76
Small	Sufficient	57.14	55.56	20.00	47.62
	Insufficient	42.86	44.44	80.00	52.38
Big	Sufficient	75.00	71.43	0.00	52.38
	Insufficient	25.00	28.57	100.00	47.62
All	Sufficient	56.60	50.00	10.42	39.01
	Insufficient	43.40	50.00	89.58	60.99
Distribution of household in terms of sufficiency/insufficiency in pulses across land size					
Landless	Sufficient	0.00	0.00	14.29	6.15
	Insufficient	100.00	100.00	85.71	93.85
Marginal	Sufficient	0.00	0.00	11.11	2.94
	Insufficient	100.00	100.00	88.89	97.06
Small	Sufficient	14.29	11.11	0.00	9.52
	Insufficient	85.71	88.89	100.00	90.48
Big	Sufficient	0.00	0.00	0.00	0.00
	Insufficient	100.0	100.0	100.0	100.0
All	Sufficient	1.89	2.50	10.42	4.96
	Insufficient	98.11	97.50	89.58	95.04
Distribution of household in terms of sufficiency and insufficiency across all land size					
Rice	Sufficient	88.68	90.00	60.42	79.43
	Insufficient	11.32	10.00	39.58	20.57
Wheat	Sufficient	56.60	50.00	10.42	39.01
	Insufficient	43.40	50.00	89.58	60.99
Pulses	Sufficient	1.89	2.50	10.42	4.96
	Insufficient	98.11	97.50	89.58	95.04
Percentage households having a ration card					
Yes		86.79	92.50	66.67	81.56
No		13.21	7.50	33.33	18.44
Percentage households actually availing ration from PDS					
Yes		77.36	90.00	64.58	76.60
No		22.64	10.00	35.42	23.40
Perceptions on the quality of cereals distributed through the PDS/FPS					
Good		15.09	12.50	8.33	12.06
Satisfactory		49.06	52.50	50.00	50.35
Not Satisfactory		13.21	25.00	22.92	19.86
Inferior		22.64	10.00	18.75	17.73

Table 6 contd.

Problems faced by the household in availing PDS/FPS facility				
Too Far	3.77	2.50	4.17	3.55
Frequent Migration	0.00	0.00	2.08	0.71
One time monthly distribution	26.42	5.00	27.08	20.57
Lack of information about distribution time	24.53	25.00	18.75	22.70
Lack of Hard Cash	28.30	47.50	20.83	31.21
Irregularities in distribution	15.09	12.50	18.75	15.60
No supply of coarse material	1.89	7.50	8.33	5.67

Note: *Marginal - (up to 1) Acres, Small - (1 to 2) Acres, and Big - (more than 2) Acres.
Source: Field Survey.

Table 7
Key Survey Results

Indicators	Bargarh	Sambalpur	Bolangir	All
Number of child labour (5-14 years)	96	60	58	214
Type of occupation of head of household and child labour				
Cultivator	22.92	40.00	13.79	25.23
Agricultural labour	33.33	16.67	20.69	25.23
Non-agricultural labour	4.17	16.67	37.93	16.82
Service	16.67	3.33	17.24	13.08
Others	22.92	23.33	10.34	19.63
Distribution of food insecure households by landholding status				
Land / Food security	FS	FISWH	FISM	FISS
Landless	23.08	30.56	45.45	70.27
Marginal	15.38	33.33	21.82	21.62
Small	23.08	16.67	20.00	2.70
Large	38.46	19.44	12.73	5.41
Ratio of child labour to adult labour across food security status of households				
Food secure (FS)	24.00	0.00	33.33	20.93
Food insecure without hunger (FISWH)	18.37	14.29	27.78	18.10
Food insecure with hunger–moderate (FISM)	27.27	20.75	18.87	22.00
Food insecure with hunger–severe (FISS)	50.00	40.00	28.21	39.64
All households	30.00	21.28	24.37	25.48
Distribution of child labour across food insecurity status of households				
Food secure (FS)	12.50	0.00	10.34	8.41
Food insecure without hunger (FISWH)	18.75	23.33	17.24	19.62
Food insecure with hunger–moderate (FISM)	25.00	36.67	34.48	30.84
Food insecure with hunger–severe (FISS)	43.75	40.00	37.93	41.12

Note: *Marginal - up to 1 acres, Small - 1 to 2 acres, and Big - more than 2 acres
Source: Field Survey.

Notes

1. Child labour refers to any work by children (under 14 Years of age), paid or unpaid, that restricts their physical and mental development, their opportunity for a desirable level of education and recreation. Many believe that children who are not going to school or to the work are highly vulnerable to child work. In the literature, these children are defined as "Nowhere Children" and should also be counted as child labour (Chaudhri, 2000). This study defines child labour as children who work either full time or part-time for the purpose of analysis.
2. Green Revolution or the new "Agricultural Strategy" was put into practice in '*selected regions*' of the country in the Kharif season of 1966 and was termed as High-Yielding Varieties Programme (HYVP). It was introduced in the form of a package of a programme since it depends crucially on regular and adequate irrigation, fertiliser, and high-yielding varieties of seeds, pesticides and

insecticides. Its main aim was to increase the agricultural production and productivity in the face of continuing stagnation in production on the one hand, and rapidly increasing demand on the other.

3. Scheduled Castes and Scheduled Tribes are castes and tribes the Government of India officially recognises as socially and economically backward and in need of special protection from injustice and exploitation.

4. Public Distribution System (PDS) is a social security measure, whereby the government tries to achieve household food security by providing essential consumer goods at cheap and subsidised prices to the consumer so as to insulate them from the impact of rising prices of commodities and to maintain the minimum nutritional status of our population. To run this system, the government resorts to levy purchases of a part of the marketable surplus with traders/millers and producers at the procurement prices (fixed somewhere between minimum support prices and open market prices). The grain (mainly wheat and rice) thus procured, is used for the distribution to the consumer through a network of ration and fair price shops (FPS) or for building up buffer stocks. The system is in operation since the mid-sixties.

5. See *Economic Survey of Government of India* for various years.

6. See Appendix Table 1 and 3 to get a comparative picture of various demographic, nutritional and development indicators at the district, state and national level.

7. A household is a group of persons normally living together and taking food from a common kitchen. A boarding house, a hotel, or a hostel is treated as a cluster of households, where each individual boarder (with his dependents or guests) forms a separate household for itself. Households maintained and provided food directly by government, such as those in prisons, asylums and relief camps etc., are however, excluded from the scope of the survey.

8. Overall sample size is smaller in this paper as only six rural villages across three districts are taken up for the survey. Again sample size for each village was set according to the size of the village. The initial target sample size was three hundred.

9. The names of the districts are Kalahandi, Sambalpur, Bargarh, Bolangir, Nawarangpur, Nawapara, Deogarh, Jharsuguda and Sundergarh. It is important to mention here that out of 133 child labour endemic districts across 13 states of India, Orissa's contribution is 16 districts (2nd highest after Maharashtra state)

10. The reference period used for household consumption expenditure on food and non-food items is a moving one in the sense that this period is always linked with the date of enquiry. For all items of consumption expenditure the reference period is the last 30 days preceding the date of survey.

11. The authors are thankful to Mr. Gary Bickel and Mr. Mark Nord of USDA for providing this methodology and also for their constant encouragement and guidance. The original methodology was changed slightly to suit the local conditions.

12. The data collected on household perception pertained to a moving reference period of 30 days preceding the date of survey.

13. Other Backward Classes (OBCs) are castes and communities that have been designated by the Government of India as socially and educationally backward and in need of protection from social injustice.

14. This increase was not adjusted for inflation.

15. The Engel's ratios for Orissa and India are calculated from NSS Report No. 402 (50th round) and 454 (55th round)

16. Engel's Ratio is an index of the standard of living of the people indicating the percentage of total consumer expenditure on food items. A small ratio indicates a higher standard of living and vice-versa.

    Consumption expenditure on food includes items directly purchased from the market and imputed values of self-produced items.

17. See NSS Report No. 454, Household Consumer Expenditure in India 1999-2000, *Key Results* (55th round).

18. In India population below the poverty line is measured on the basis of monthly per capita consumer expenditure data published by National Sample Survey Organisation (NSSO).

19. MPCE class is made on the basis of corresponding NSS standard.

20. To make the general PDS more effective the Government of India introduced TPDS with effect from June 1, 1997. Under this system two set of prices namely, a highly subsidised price for the allocations meant for the poor (below poverty line population) and near open market prices for the non-poor (above poverty line population) was introduced. The maximum income level for the population to be covered under BPL was kept at Rs. 15000 per annum. In Orissa, the TPDS is in operation only in 143 Integrated Tribal Development Project (ITDP) and Drought Prone Areas Programme (DPAP) blocks.

References

Barrett, Christopher. and Michel Carter (1999), *Can't Get Ahead for Falling Behind: New Directions for Development Policy to Escape Poverty and Relief Traps*, USAID, Washington D.C.

Behrman, J. (1988), "Intra-Household Allocation of Nutrients in Rural India: Are Boys Favoured? Do Parents Exhibit Inequality Aversion?", *Oxford Economic Papers*, Vol. 40, No.1, pp. 32-54.

—— and Deolalikar (1990), "The Intra-Household Demand for Nutrients in Rural South India: Individual Estimates, Fixed Effects and Permanent Income," *Journal of Human Resources*, Vol. 24, No. 4, pp. 665-696.

CMIE (2000), *Profiles of District*, Centre for Monitoring Indian Economy, Mumbai, India.

Chaudhri, D.P (2000), "Sources of Supply of Child Labour and the State: Explorations of Historical and Contemporary Evidence with Focus on States and Districts of India", Paper presented at the *National Seminar on Child Labour: Realities and Policy Dimensions*, December 5-7, Noida.

Corbett, J. E. M (1988), "Famine and Household Coping Strategies," *World Development*, Vol.16, No.9, pp.1099-1112.

Dreze, J. and A. K. Sen (1989), *Hunger and Public Action*, WIDER Oxford University Press, Oxford.

GOI (2001), *Economic Survey, 2000-2001*, Government of India, Ministry of Finance, New Delhi.

Gupta, Manju and K. Voll (1999), "Child Labour in India: An Exemplary Case Study" in Voll Klaus (ed.), *Against Child Labour: Indian and International Dimensions and Strategies*, Mosaic Books, New Delhi, pp. 85-144.

Jacoby, H.G. and Emmanuel Skoufias (1997), "Risk, Financial Markets and Human Capital in a Developing Country," *Review of Economic Studies*, Vol.64, No.3, pp. 311-335.

Kochar, Anjini (1999), "Smoothing Consumption by Smoothing Income: Hours of Work Responses to Idiosyncratic Agricultural Shocks in Rural India," *Review of Economics and Statistics*, Vol. 81, No.1, pp. 50-61.

Raj, Nikhil (2000), *Tools for Convergence – Orissa*, V.V. Giri National Labour Institute, NOIDA, India.

Satpathy, A.K (1998), *Consumption Pattern and Expenditure Elasticities: An Inter-State Analysis*, M. Phil. Dissertation (Unpublished), Jawaharlal Nehru University, New Delhi, India.

Sarap, K. (2000), "Food Security System and its Operation in Orissa: Evidences from Some Villages in Semi-arid Area," Paper Presented in the *National Seminar on Food Security in India: The Emerging Challenges in the Context of Economic Liberalization*", Centre for Economic Studies, Hyderabad and Institute for Human Development, New Delhi.

Sen, A. K (1981), *Poverty and Famines: An Essay on Entitlement and Deprivation*, Clarendon Press, Oxford.

Thamarajakshi, R (1997), "Economic Reforms and State Intervention in Food Grain Market", *Economic and Political Weekly*, Vol. 30, No.30, July 26- August 1, pp. 1894-1900.

VVG NLI (2001), *Child Labour in India: An Overview*, NRCCL, p. 22, V.V. Giri National Labour Institute, NOIDA, India.

World Bank (1986), *Poverty and Hunger: Issues and Options for Food Security in Developing Countries*, World Bank Policy Study, Washington D.C.

—— (2000), *World Development Report 2000/2001: Attacking Poverty*, Washington D.C.

15

Educational Deprivation and Employment Status of Children in Rural Areas of Andhra Pradesh, Madhya Pradesh and Orissa: Evidences from NFHS-2

Parveen Nangia and Nizamuddin Khan

I. INTRODUCTION

The Constitution of India declares that the state shall endeavour to provide for the free and compulsory education all children until they complete the age of 14 years within 10 years from the commencement of the Constitution (Article 45). This means that by 1960 education should have been made compulsory throughout the country. Though the government failed to achieve the objective of providing free and compulsory education to the expanding child population, it has sought to fulfil its commitments time and again by formulating different policies and passing various Acts to regulate the education and employment of children. But the policies/programmes aimed at providing elementary education could not be successfully implemented. Even various Acts formulated to control child labour could not be strictly enforced.

The National Family Health Survey (NFHS-2), conducted under the aegis of Ministry of Health and Family Welfare, Government of India, recently shows that 21 per cent of children (aged 6-14 years) in the country were not attending school as late as in 1998-99. It further showed that compared to 12 per cent children in urban areas, 24 per cent in rural areas do not attend school and that 17 per cent boys against 26 per cent girls do not do so indicating that a large number of girls, particularly in the rural areas were deprived of elementary education.

Among children aged 6-17 years, 16 per cent never attended school. Twelve per cent boys and 21 per cent girls in this age group could never attend school. The major reasons why these children never attended school are given as high cost of education (25 per cent), absence of interest in studies (20 per cent), pressure of household work (12 per cent), and education given low priority (11 per cent). Nearly 7 per cent of the children could never attend school because they were required to work on farm/family business or work for payment. Overall, 21 per cent children (17 per cent boys and 24 per cent girls) could never attend school because they were required to work or help in household chores or take care of siblings.

It was also observed that school attendance drops rapidly with age—as against 82 per cent children (aged 6-10 years) attending school the percentage of school-going children in the age group, 5-17 was less than 50 per cent. The drop-out is more pronounced among female children, particularly in rural areas. Of the children who dropped out, two out of every five did so because they were not interested in studies or had failed repeatedly, 13 per cent because their parents felt that the cost of education was too high, another 13 per cent because they were required to do household work and 10 per cent because they were required to work on farm or family business or outside for payment in cash or kind. In all, 26 per cent of children who ever attended school dropped out because they were required to work or help in the household chores or take care of siblings. Interestingly, among girls, 8 per cent had to stop schooling because they got married and for another 5 per cent further education was not considered necessary (IIPS and ORC Macro, NFHS-2: India, 2000).

The National Family Health Survey, conducted in all the states in India, collected data on various aspects of population, such as household living conditions, educational attainment, fertility and family planning, nutritional status of children, immunisation, and child health. Apart from this information collected in the first round of NFHS in 1992-93, additional information on the quality of health and family planning services, reproductive health, nutritional status and consumption of various food items by women, and domestic violence was collected in the second round of NFHS conducted in 1998-99. In the latter round, data were also collected on the haemoglobin level of women and their children up to three years of age by testing their blood. The NFHS covered a sample of nearly 90,000 representative households from all the 26 states of India, which are inhabited by 99 per cent of the population of the country.

Sample Design

The NFHS sample is designed to provide estimates for a state as a whole and for its rural and urban areas, separately. The required sampling rates for rural and urban areas were determined by allocating the sample proportionally to the population of the two areas. Within each domain (rural and urban areas), the sample was selected in two stages: the selection of primary sampling units (PSU), which are villages in the rural areas and census enumeration blocks in the urban areas, with probability proportional to the population size (PPS) at the first stage, followed by the selection of households within each sample area, so as to achieve a self-weighting sample of households within each domain. In other words, every household in the domain is given the same chance of being included in the survey (IIPS and ORC Macro, NFHS-2: India, 2000).

This paper attempts to assess the educational deprivation of children (aged 6-14 years) and their participation in the labour force in the rural areas of some selected states of India (Andhra Pradesh, Madhya Pradesh and Orissa). The overall sample size used in the survey is 3,872 households from Andhra Pradesh, 6,749 from Madhya Pradesh, and 4,689 from Orissa. The rural sample sizes from these states are 2,854, 4,950 and 3,757 households, respectively.

This study, analyses the reasons for never attending school as well as for dropping of school. The study also looks into the determinants and characteristics of child labour. Although NFHS did not have a direct question on child labour, it had one for every member of the household who was more than six years old: 'what kind of work does the person do most of the time' and 'does he/she earn cash for that'. In addition, the study also looks into the consumption of intoxicants by children, since the initial taste of such things may make them addicted at a later stage, which would be detrimental to their health.

II. BASIC CHARACTERISTICS OF POPULATION IN THREE STATES

This section throws some light on the socio-economic and demographic characteristics of the population in the three states discussed in this paper.

1. Andhra Pradesh

According to the provisional population figures of the 2001 Census, Andhra Pradesh has a population of 75.7 million with a density of 275 persons per square kilometre. The level of literacy in the state is quite low (lower than the Indian average) as only 71 per cent of the males and 51 per cent of the females above 7 years of age are literate in the state (Registrar General and Census Commissioner, India, 2001). According to the 1991 Census, nearly 16 per cent of the population in the state was designated as scheduled caste and another 6 per cent as scheduled tribe. Nearly, three-fourth of the population live in rural areas. More than 70 per cent of the working population in the state was engaged in the agricultural sector. The NFHS-2 results show that 45 per cent of the rural households are landless (IIPS and ORC Macro, NFHS-2: Andhra Pradesh, 2000).

In 1998, about 3.2 million job seekers were registered with the employment exchanges in the state. According to the Planning Commission estimates for 1993-94, nearly 16 per cent of the rural population and 38 per cent of the urban population in the state lives below the poverty line (CSO, 1999). However, NFHS-2 data show that among the rural households in the state, 48 per cent have a low standard of living, 43 per cent a medium standard of living, and 9 per cent a high standard of living.

An overwhelming majority of the households (88 per cent) were headed by Hindus, 6 per cent by Muslims, and 6 per cent by Christians. Muslims are concentrated in the urban areas; they constitute 15 per cent of the urban households, but only 3 per cent of the rural households. One-third of the population in the state was below 15 years of age (IIPS and ORC Macro, NFHS-2: Andhra Pradesh, 2000).

2. Madhya Pradesh

According to the provisional population figures of the 2001 Census, Madhya Pradesh has a population of 60.4 million with a density of 196 persons per square kilometre. (This does not include the population of Chhatisgarh, which was a part of Madhya Pradesh at the time of NFHS-2.) The level of literacy in the state is very close to the national average with 77 per cent of the males and 50 per cent of the females above the age of seven years found to be literate in the state (Registrar General and Census Commissioner, India, 2001). According to the 1991 Census, 14 per cent of the population in the state is designated as Scheduled Caste and another 23 per cent as Scheduled Tribe. Nearly 77 per cent of the population lives in the rural areas. Agriculture is the mainstay of the state's economy. However, about 44 per cent of the area of the state is cultivable. According to NFHS-2, 31 per cent of the rural households are landless (IIPS and ORC Macro, NFHS-2: Madhya Pradesh, 2001).

In 1998, about 2.5 million job-seekers were registered with the employment exchanges in the state. According to the Planning Commission estimates for 1993-94, nearly 41 per cent of the rural population and 48 per cent of the urban population in the state lives below the poverty line (CSO, 1999). However, according to the NFHS-2, 42 per cent of the rural households in Madhya Pradesh have a low standard of living, 49 per cent have a medium and more than 8 per cent a high standard of living.

Nine out of every 10 households in the state are headed by Hindus, 5 per cent by Muslims, and one per cent by Christians and Jains, each. Muslims are concentrated in the urban areas; they constitute 14 per cent of the urban households, but only 2 per cent of the rural households. Nearly two-fifths of the population in the state is below 15 years of age (IIPS and ORC Macro, NFHS-2: Madhya Pradesh, 2001).

3. Orissa

According to the provisional population figures of the 2001 Census, Orissa had a population of 36.7 million with a density of 236 persons per square kilometre. The level of literacy in the state is almost the same as in the nation as a whole. Seventy-six per cent of the males and 51 per cent of the females above seven years of age are literate in the state (Registrar General and Census Commissioner, India, 2001). According to the 1991 Census, 16 per cent of the population in the state is designated as Scheduled Caste and another 22 per cent as Scheduled Tribe. Agriculture is the dominant sector in the state's economy. Nearly 87 per cent of the population in the state lives in the rural areas and nearly 65 per cent of the working population in the state is engaged in this sector. According to NFHS-2, 39 per cent of the rural households are landless (IIPS and ORC Macro, NFHS-2: Orissa, 2001).

In 1998, about one million job-seekers were registered with the employment exchanges in the state. According to the Planning Commission estimates for 1993-94, nearly 50 per cent of the rural population and 42 per cent of the urban population in the state lives below the poverty line (CSO, 1999). However, according to the NFHS-2, among the rural households in Orissa, 63 per cent have a low standard of living, 31 per cent have a medium, and 6 per cent a high standard of living.

Most of the households in the state (97 per cent) are headed by Hindus, less than 2 per cent by Muslims and less than 2 per cent by Christians. One-third of the population in the state is below 15 years of age (IIPS and ORC Macro, NFHS-2: Orissa 2001).

III. EDUCATION : A COMPARATIVE ANALYSIS

Education is the key to human development. It enhances one's productive capacity by effecting improvements, in knowledge and skills and provides opportunities to an individual to develop and nurture his or her sense of social and moral responsibilities. It also plays an important role in the promotion of culture and transmission of knowledge from one generation to another. This section looks into certain features of the education system in the three states in the light of their socio-economic characteristics.

1. Educational Attainment of Children

In the rural areas of Andhra Pradesh, Madhya Pradesh and Orissa, less than one-fifth of the children in the age group, 6-14 years, have never attended school. The situation in Orissa is slightly better than in Andhra Pradesh and Madhya Pradesh, as 85 per cent children in Orissa, 83 per cent in Andhra Pradesh and 81 per cent in Madhya Pradesh have ever attended school. Moreover, in Orissa 79 per cent children still attend school, whereas in Andhra Pradesh and Madhya Pradesh the proportion of such children is 72-73 per cent, respectively.

In terms of educational attainment, female children are at a disadvantage in all the three states, which is also true for the country as a whole. In all the three states the per centage of boys who ever attended school is 85 per cent or more, whereas that of girls varies from 76 to 80 per cent. Even among those who attend school a higher proportion of girls than boys drop out. The highest level of school dropout and gender differential in dropout is seen in Andhra Pradesh, where 9 per cent boys and 16 per cent girls dropped out before completing 15 years of age. In comparison, only 7 per cent of children dropped out in Orissa with hardly any variation by sex (Table 1).

School attendance rate is much lower in the age group 11-14, than 6-10 years, in all the three states (Table 2). Although in the younger cohort (6-10 years), school attendance is lower in Madhya Pradesh (77 per cent) compared to Andhra Pradesh and Orissa (83 per cent, each), in the older cohort (11-14 years) school attendance is lowest in Andhra Pradesh (58 per cent) compared to Madhya Pradesh (65 per cent) and Orissa (73 per cent). In all the three states, a much lower proportion of female children attend school compared to male children. The

Table 1
Educational Status of Children Aged 6-14 years by Sex in Rural Areas of the Three States, 1998-99

Educational status	Male	Female	Total
		Andhra Pradesh	
Ever been to school	87.3	77.8	82.6
Currently attending school	79.5	65.6	72.6
Drop outs	8.8	15.7	12.1
		Madhya Pradesh	
Ever been to school	84.6	76.3	80.5
Currently attending school	78.1	66.5	72.4
Drop outs	7.7	12.7	10.0
		Orissa	
Ever been to school	88.4	80.4	84.5
Currently attending school	83.0	74.7	79.0
Drop outs	6.2	7.0	6.6

Note: This table and all the subsequent tables are computed from NFHS-2, 1998-99.

decline in school attendance rate from age group '6-10' to 11-14, is much higher for female children, particularly in Andhra Pradesh.

Table 2
Percentage of Children Aged 6-14 Years Attending School by Sex in Rural Areas of the Three States, 1998-99

Age	Per cent attending school		
	Male	Female	Total
		Andhra Pradesh	
6-10	86.3	79.3	82.9
11-14	68.8	47.0	57.6
		Madhya Pradesh	
6-10	80.1	73.9	77.1
11-14	75.4	54.9	65.0
		Orissa	
6-10	85.4	81.0	83.2
11-14	79.9	64.8	72.7

The gender discrimination is also evident in terms of educational attainment. Table 3 shows the sex-wise distribution of children by level of education. In all the three states, a higher proportion of girls than boys are illiterate and a lower proportion of girls than boys have passed at least primary school. Madhya Pradesh shows the lowest achievement in the level of education of children, where, compared to 28 per cent boys, 37 per cent girls are illiterate. Only 20 per cent boys and 16 per cent girls have completed at least primary school education. On the other hand, illiteracy is lowest in Orissa, where 15 per cent boys and 23 per cent girls are illiterate in the rural areas and 30 per cent boys and 24 per cent girls have completed at least primary school.

Table 3
Level of Education of Children, Aged 6-14 Years, by Sex in Rural Areas of the Three States, 1998-99

Level of education	Male	Female	Total
		Andhra Pradesh	
Illiterate	21.3	30.6	25.9
Lit.< Primary	49.8	44.7	47.3
Primary complete	23.3	19.9	21.6
Middle school complete and above	5.6	4.8	5.2
		Madhya Pradesh	
Illiterate	27.6	36.5	32.0
Lit.< Primary	52.5	47.2	49.9
Primary complete	18.1	14.7	16.4
Middle school complete and above	1.7	1.6	1.7
		Orissa	
Illiterate	14.6	22.6	18.5
Lit.< Primary	55.6	53.6	54.6
Primary complete	24.2	18.9	21.6
Middle school complete and above	5.6	4.8	5.2

2. Reasons for Non-Enrolment of Children

The data obtained from The National Statistical Survey Organisation (NSSO) reveal that poverty and economic compulsion are the most important factors accounting for the non-enrolment of children. This is followed by lack of interest in studies, which is primarily due to faulty curriculum, poor teaching-learning practices and inadequate class room infrastructure and basic facilities (Visaria et al., 1993; Nautiyal, 1995).

The NFHS, carried out in the states, was aimed at finding out the main reason why children (a) never attended school and (b) dropped out of school and were currently not attending its. The findings of the survey, are presented in tables 4 and 5 respectively.

In Andhra Pradesh, the major reason why children were never sent to school is that they were required to work either on farm or family business or outside for payment in cash or kind (27 per cent). Another 20 per cent children were required for household work or taking care of siblings. While, an equal proportion of children was not interested in studies. A larger proportion of boys than girls could never go to school because they were required to work. On the other hand, a larger proportion of girls than boys could never attend school because they were required to do the household work or take care of their siblings.

In Madhya Pradesh, one in every four children could never attend school because they were required to work or take care of the household chores or younger siblings. The high cost of education is reported to be another major reason why some children were never sent to school (19 per cent). Either the parents did not know that education in government schools is free or they wanted to put their children in private schools, which charge a heavy fee. The other major reason for never attending school is that children are not interested in studies (15 per cent).

In Orissa, 30 per cent of children were deprived of education because of its high cost. Another 27 per cent were not interested in education, and 19 per cent were required for work or taking care of the household chores or siblings. Prevalence of widespread poverty in the state is one of the reasons for educational deprivation of children.

In every state a higher proportion of boys than girls are not interested in studies. This reflects on the poor education system, which is unable to attract a sizable proportion of children. The problem lies not only with the education system but also with the parents who do not understand the importance of education in the overall development of a child. Moreover, there are some cultural factors which affect the education of children. What is worse, some parents do not consider education to be necessary for a child—a perception that is reported to be the main reason why 10 per cent children in Madhya Pradesh, 11 per cent in Andhra Pradesh and 13 per cent in Orissa have never attended school. In all the three states with reference to girls, rather than boys, education is not considered to be necessary for a child's overall development. This emphasises the need to create an awareness among certain sections of the population about the necessity of education, particularly for girls.

As mentioned earlier, a much higher proportion of girls drop out compared to boys. Table 5 shows that the main reasons why children drop out from school are child labour, requirement of children for household chores and care of siblings. The proportion of children who dropped out because of these reasons is 39 per cent in Andhra Pradesh, 31 per cent in Madhya Pradesh and 29 per cent in Orissa. In all the three states, a higher proportion of boys drop out because they are required to work (on farm/family business or for payment in cash or kind) and a higher proportion of girls do so because they are required for household work or for taking care of siblings. For example, in Orissa 13 per cent boys and 4 per cent girls drop out because they are required for work on family farms or business units or because they work for payment in cash or kind, whereas, 12 per cent boys and 30 per cent girls drop out because they are required for household chores or taking care of siblings. Given the reasons, one way of reducing the school drop out substantially could be to provide some kind of scholarship (equivalent to the income of the child through labour) to children who are required to work, to augment their meagre family income. Similarly, if other family members could also share the household work, many of the girls who drop out could be retained in the education system. Therefore there is a need to change the social ethos and move away from compartmentalisation of the roles of different family members.

The higher cost of education is responsible for the drop out of 10-18 per cent of children in these states. More than one-third of the children (with a higher proportion of boys than girls) dropped out in every state because they were not interested in studies or experienced repeated failures. The male-female difference is particularly large in Orissa, where more than half of the boys and nearly one-

Table 4
Per cent Distribution of Children Aged 6-14 Years By Reason for Never Attending School in Rural Areas of the Three States 1998-99

Main reason for never attending school	Andhra Pradesh			Madhya Pradesh			Orissa		
	Male	Female	Total	Male	Female	Total	Male	Female	Total
School too far way	1.6	2.8	2.3	2.5	4.6	3.8	4.4	2.7	3.3
Transport not available	1.0	0.9	1.0	0.6	1.0	0.8	-	-	-
Education not considered necessary	6.9	13.2	10.9	7.4	11.2	9.7	10.8	14.4	13.0
Required for household work	13.8	20.2	17.9	6.9	15.9	12.3	5.6	14.6	11.2
Required for work on farm/ family business	12.9	9.3	10.6	9.7	3.8	6.1	1.2	2.2	1.8
Required for outside work for payment in cash or kind	16.2	16.8	16.6	5.0	2.0	3.2	4.8	2.2	3.2
Cost too much	13.9	12.7	13.1	18.9	19.2	19.1	27.9	31.5	30.1
No proper school facilities for girls	-	1.2	0.8	-	0.8	0.5	-	0.2	0.2
Required for care of siblings	1.1	2.8	2.2	2.1	8.2	5.7	0.4	3.4	2.3
Not interested in studies	25.7	17.4	20.4	18.1	13.4	15.3	32.3	23.9	27.1
Other	6.5	2.1	3.7	28.4	19.3	22.9	12.0	4.6	7.4
Don't know	0.5	0.6	0.6	0.6	0.6	0.6	0.8	0.2	0.5

Table 5
Per Cent Distribution of Children Aged 6-14 Years by Reasons for Drop Out From School in Rural Areas of the Three States 1998-99

Main reason for never	Andhra Pradesh			Madhya Pradesh			Orissa		
attending school	Male	Female	Total	Male	Female	Total	Male	Female	Total
School too far away	2.6	4.6	3.8	1.8	7.1	5.0	-	2.6	1.3
Transport not available	-	1.2	0.7	0.9	2.2	1.7	-	0.9	0.9
Further education not considered necessary	3.6	3.4	3.5	2.7	2.2	2.4	2.5	5.2	3.8
Required for household work	4.4	16.5	11.8	7.7	19.4	14.7	11.9	23.3	17.5
Required for work on farm/ family business	15.0	4.6	8.6	14.5	4.9	8.8	5.9	0.9	3.4
Required for outside work for payment in cash or kind	22.2	12.6	16.3	4.5	3.1	3.7	6.8	3.4	5.1
Cost too much	10.6	9.0	9.6	13.2	9.8	11.2	16.1	19.8	17.9
No proper school facilities for girls	-	1.1	0.7	-	3.7	2.2	-	0.9	0.4
Required for care of siblings	-	3.4	2.1	4.1	4.3	4.2	-	6.9	3.4
Not interested in studies	35.5	32.3	33.5	37.3	26.8	31.0	51.7	28.4	40.2
Repeated failures	0.9	2.8	2.1	5.5	4.0	4.6	1.7	3.4	2.6
Got married	-	0.6	0.3	-	4.3	2.6	-	0.9	0.4
Other	2.6	3.9	3.4	7.7	8.0	7.9	1.7	2.6	2.1
Don't know	2.7	4.0	3.5	-	0.3	0.2	1.7	0.9	1.3

third of the girls dropped out for these reasons. It clearly shows that our education system is not able to retain all those children in school who are keen to study. There is, therefore, a need for a reexamination of the entire education system, particularly at the school level. At the outset it should be made attractive to the students. If the teachers are affectionate, friendly, hard working and innovative, they can develop various ways to evoke the interest of students in studies. Similarly, the course curriculum should be designed in a way such that it can be helpful in the growth and development of children, retain their interest in education and prepare them for a career, even if they have to drop out for some compelling reasons.

3. Determinants of School Attendance

In this subsection an attempt is made to find out the determinants ot current school attendance of children in all the three states separately (Table 6) by using logistic analysis. The results show that rural girls are significantly less likely to attend school than boys in all the three states. The Odds ratios for attending school for girls compared to boys are 0.4 for Andhra Pradesh, 0.8 for Madhya Pradesh and 0.6 for Orissa.

Religion plays a significant role in the current school attendance of children only in Madhya Pradesh and Orissa, where Muslim children are less likely to attend school compared to Hindu children and children from other religions are more likely to attend school compared to Hindus. In Andhra Pradesh, religion does not play an important role in determining the school attendance of children.

Children belonging to scheduled tribes are less likely than those from scheduled castes to attend school in all the three states. The odds ratios for attending school by scheduled caste children compared to scheduled tribe children are 2.5 times higher for Andhra Pradesh and Orissa and 1.25 times higher for Madhya Pradesh. Children belonging to other groups (i.e., those other than scheduled castes scheduled tribes) are more likely to attend school than children belonging to scheduled castes.

In Andhra Pradesh and Madhya Pradesh, children from households, which possess agricultural land, are less likely to attend school than those from households which do not have any agricultural land. The plausible explanation for this might be that children coming from households which own some land are required to work on the farm and, are therefore, unable to attend school. On the other hand, in Orissa, children coming from households, which possess agricultural land (up to two acres or more than five acres), are more likely to attend school compared to children belonging to households which do not possess any agricultural land.

The household size plays a negative role in the school attendance of children in Andhra Pradesh, but a positive role in Madhya Pradesh. In other words, in Andhra Pradesh, children from the bigger households (more than four members) are less likely to attend school than children from smaller households (up to four members), whereas the situation in Madhya Pradesh is just the reverse. In Orissa, the direction of relationship is not very clear.

In all the three states children coming from households with a medium and high standard of living are much more likely to attend school compared to those from households with a low standard of living.

Table 6

Determinants of School Attendance (Current)

Variable	Andhra Pradesh Odds ratio	Madhya Pradesh Odds ratio	Orissa Odds ratio
Sex			
Male R	1.00	1.00	1.00
Female	0.43***	0.77***	0.59***
Religion			
Hindu R	1.00	1.00	1.00
Muslim	0.78	0.89*	0.26***
Other	0.88	1.27**	2.74**
Caste/Tribe			
Scheduled Caste R	1.00	1.00	1.00
Scheduled Tribe	0.39***	0.79***	0.43***
Others	1.12	1.08*	1.33**
Landholding			
None R	1.00	1.00	1.00
< 2 Acre	0.95	0.84**	1.69**
2-5 Acre	0.72*	0.84***	0.84
5 + Acre	0.65***	0.88***	1.27*
Household size			
Small R	1.00	1.00	1.00
Medium	0.64***	2.12***	0.83
Large	0.53***	1.65***	0.73*
Very large	0.75	1.91***	1.56
Standard of living			
Low R	1.00	1.00	1.00
Medium	2.15***	1.22***	3.66***
High	11.03***	1.29***	6.19***

Note: 1. Logistic regression showing the effect of different variables on current attendance in school.
2. R Reference category
3. * 0.05 level of significant. ** 0.01 level of significant. ***0.001 level of significant.

4. Relationship between Drop Out, Marriage and Child-Birth

Although for a small proportion of girls the reason given for drop out was marriage, it raises some interesting questions pertaining to what happens to the those who drop-out from school—at what age do they get married and when do they have their first child. The NFHS data can not answer these questions. However, an attempt is made here to see how those women (currently age group, 15-49) who got married during childhood (before the age of 15) are different from those who got married after age 15 in terms of their level of education and age at first birth. The results of the analysis are presented in Table 7.

Early marriage has a bearing upon the educational attainment of the girls. In all the three states the proportion of women who are illiterate is much higher among those who got married before the age of 15 than those who married after that age. The proportion of illiterate women varies from 72-78 per cent in the group which got married in childhood. Compared to 47-53 per cent of those who got married after the age of 15. Furthermore, women who got married after net age of 15 have a higher level of educational achievement than those who were married in childhood. For example, while less than one per cent of women in all the three states who got married in childhood had completed at least high school education, 11-18 per cent of those who got married after age 15 had completed the same level of education.

In India, where proving their fecundity becomes important for married women, spacing for the first child is usually not attempted. More than three out of every five women who got married before they were 15 had their first child by the age of 16 and nearly four-fifths by the time they were 18. In contrast, more than half of the women who got married after they were 15 had their first child after they become 19. In terms of relationship between age at marriage, women's level of education and age at first birth, the three states are not different from each other.

Table 7
Per cent Distribution of Ever Married Women Who Married during Childhood by Educational Level and Age at First Birth in Rural Areas of the Three States, 1998-99

	Married before age 15			Married at age 15 or after		
Demographic and background characteristics	Andhra Pradesh	Madhya Pradesh	Orissa	Andhra Pradesh	Madhya Pradesh	Orissa
Respondent's education						
Illiterate	75.0	77.6	72.0	46.8	52.6	49.5
Incomplete primary	9.2	10.5	13.8	9.4	10.5	13.0
Complete primary	7.9	6.8	5.4	9.1	9.4	8.6
Middle school complete	7.1	4.3	7.9	16.5	12.7	18.3
High school complete	0.8	0.4	0.7	10.0	3.4	5.4
Higher secondary or more complete	-	0.4	0.2	8.2	11.5	5.2
Respondent's age at first birth						
<= 14 years	29.6	23.9	32.8	-	-	-
15–16 years	33.4	38.3	38.4	17.1	14.2	12.3
17–18 years	16.0	18.5	12.2	27.5	26.4	26.0
19 years and above	13.6	11.7	10.0	41.1	45.4	50.2
No birth	7.4	7.6	6.6	14.3	14.0	11.5

IV. EMPLOYMENT OF CHILDREN

In rural areas, employment of children is usually participatory, whereby the child joins adults to internalise the adult roles and understand the working environment. In the agricultural sector, many children work as family labour—the boys join adults to learn how to handle the wooden plough, reap the harvest, and sell and purchase articles in the market. Similarly, girls are expected to be proficient in weeding paddy fields, harvesting, cooking meals, fetching water, taking care of siblings, sweeping and washing the house, etc. (Dube, 1981).

1. Work Status of Children

The work participation rates for children are 15 per cent for Andhra Pradesh, 8 per cent for Madhya Pradesh and 3 per cent for Orissa. The NFHS-2 data show that in Andhra Pradesh, 13 per cent of the boys and 17 per cent of the girls aged 6-14 are reported to be working (Table 8). In Madhya Pradesh, work participation rates for female children are slightly lower than for male children (6 and 8 per cent, respectively). In Orissa, there is hardly any difference in the work participation rate of male and female children (3 per cent each).

Table 8
Work Status of Children Aged 6-14 Years by Sex in Rural Areas of the Three States, 1998-99

Work status	Male	Female	Total
		Andhra Pradesh	
Non-worker	86.6	82.8	84.7
Worker	13.4	17.2	15.3
Total	100.0	100.0	100.0
		Madhya Pradesh	
Non-worker	91.3	93.8	92.5
Worker	8.7	6.2	7.5
Total	100.0	100.0	100.0
		Orissa	
Non-worker	96.7	97.1	96.9
Worker	3.3	2.9	3.1
Total	100.0	100.0	100.0

Table 9 shows that there is a wide variation in the occupational distribution of children between the states. For example, in Andhra Pradesh 47 per cent of child workers are engaged as agricultural labourers compared to only 11 per cent in Orissa. Again, the proportion of plantation and farm workers varies from 37 per cent in Madhya Pradesh to 13 per cent in Andhra Pradesh and as against 35 per cent of child workers employed as labourers in Orissa, only 8 per cent of working children work as labourers in Madhya Pradesh.

In Andhra Pradesh, one-third of the boys work as agricultural labourers and another one-fifth as plantation and farm workers. In percentage terms, 12 per cent of the boys work as cultivators and 15 per cent as labourers. Among the girl child workers, a majority (58 per cent) work as agricultural labourers, 11 per cent as cultivators and 7 per cent as plantation and farm workers. As many as 18 per cent working girls are employed as labourers.

In Madhya Pradesh, 47 per cent boys work as plantation and farm workers and 23 per cent as cultivators, while 13 per cent work as agricultural labourers and 6 per cent as other labourers. As against this pattern of occupational distribution among boys in the state, among girl child workers more than one-third are engaged as agricultural labourers, one-fourth as cultivators and one-fifth as plantation and farm workers.

In Orissa, the highest proportion of both boys (32 per cent) and girls (39 per cent) work as labourers, while a much higher proportion of boys (24 per cent) than girls (9 per cent) are involved in plantation and farm activities, respectively On the other hand, compared to 8 per cent boys, 15 per cent girls work as agricultural labourers.

Table 9
Occupational Distribution of Children Aged 6-14 Years in Rural Areas of the Three States, 1998-99

Occupation	Male	Female	Total
		Andhra Pradesh	
Cultivator	11.9	10.6	11.2
Agricultural labourer	33.7	57.6	47.0
Plantation and farm worker	20.8	7.1	13.2
Labourer	14.9	17.7	16.3
Other	18.8	7.1	12.3
Total	100.0	100.0	100.0
		Madhya Pradesh	
Cultivator	23.0	24.3	23.5
Agricultural labourer	13.0	35.2	22.2
Plantation and farm worker	47.0	21.4	36.5
Labourer	5.7	11.4	8.0
Other	11.3	7.6	9.8
Total	100.0	100.0	100.0
		Orissa	
Cultivator	10.8	3.4	7.5
Agricultural labourer	8.1	15.3	11.3
Plantation and farm worker	24.3	8.5	17.3
Labourer	32.4	39.0	35.3
Other	24.3	33.9	28.6
Total	100.0	100.0	100.0

Table 10 shows the work participation rate of children from different socio-economic groups. By religion work participation rate in Andhra Pradesh is highest for Christian children (18 per cent), followed by Hindu children (15 per cent) in Madhya Pradesh and Orissa it is highest for Hindu children (8 per cent). By sex, work participation rates are quite similar for different religious groups. However, the widest gender gap in work participation rate is observed among Muslims in Andhra Pradesh, among whom 14 per cent of the female children participate in the labour force compared to only 4 per cent of the male children.

By caste/tribe, work participation rate is highest among the scheduled tribe children, followed by scheduled castes in all the states. Twenty-five per cent of the scheduled tribe children in Andhra Pradesh, 13 per cent in Madhya Pradesh and 5 per cent in Orissa participate in the workforce. Among scheduled caste children work participation rate varies from 18 per cent in Andhra Pradesh to 3 per cent in Orissa. The work participation rate of children from other backward classes is also higher than that of children who do not belong to SC/ST or other backward classes. Gender wise, in Andhra Pradesh work participation rate of female children is higher than of male children (in caste/tribe category), whereas in Madhya Pradesh and Orissa, the trend is just the opposite.

By household size, work participation rate of children does not show any definite pattern in the three states. Child labour is comparatively low in the very large households (more than 12 members), which may be because in the larger families there might be so many working hands that children are not required to work.

Child labour is found to be high among the landless households or the households which have more than 5 acres of land compared to those with small landholdings (up to 5 acres). The differences are much higher in Andhra Pradesh compared to Madhya Pradesh or Orissa. A higher work participation rate in the landless households could be attributed to poverty, which forces children to work for a livelihood. In the households with bigger landholdings (more than 5 acres), children might be providing additional labour input to the adults to maximise the agricultural produce from the fields. Since hiring of labour from outside might be more costly for such households, they may prefer to engage their own children in farm work.

Table 10 reveals that in all the three states, as the standard of living of the household increases, the work participation rate of children declines rapidly: In Andhra Pradesh, it declined from 20 per cent in households with a low standard of living to 3 per cent in those with a high standard of living; in Madhya Pradesh it declined from 10 per cent in households with a low standard of living to 3 per cent in those with a high standard of living and in Orissa, from 5 per cent in low SLI households to one per cent in medium SLI households. No child is reported to be participating in the labour force in Orissa from households with high SLI. In respect of gender differences, however, in each category of SLI, work participation among girls is strikingly higher than that of boys in Andhra Pradesh. In Madhya Pradesh, in the low SLI category the rate for females is much lower than for males, but in the other categories there is not much variation in the work participation rate of male and female children. In Orissa, there is hardly any variation by sex in the work participation rates of children in different economic categories.

2. Characteristics of Child Labour

Table 11 shows that an overwhelming majority of working children fall in the age group, 10-14. By and large, only a small proportion of working children in the states start working before 10 years of age (13 per cent in Andhra Pradesh, 14 per cent in Madhya Pradesh and 11 per cent in Orissa). In Andhra Pradesh and Madhya Pradesh a higher proportion of boys than girls start working at a younger age (6-9 years), whereas in Orissa, girls start working much before boys. The age-wise distribution data (not shown in the table) show that the work participation rate of girls is higher than of boys after age 11 in all the states.

Working children are educationally at a disadvantage because they cannot attend school, they have to work. As mentioned earlier, a substantial proportion of

Table 10
Work Participation Rate of Children in Rural Areas of The States by Socio-economic Groups, 1998-99

Socio-economic groups	Andhra Pradesh			Madhya Pradesh			Orissa		
	Male	Female	Total	Male	Female	Total	Male	Female	Total
Religion									
Hindu	13.5	17.3	15.3	8.9	6.4	7.7	3.3	2.9	3.1
Muslim	3.8	14.1	9.8	3.8	3.9	3.8	3.2	-	1.9
Christian	16.3	18.8	17.5	4.1	3.5	3.8	-	2.0	1.2
Caste/Tribe									
Scheduled Caste	15.6	19.9	17.6	8.1	4.6	6.4	3.5	3.4	3.4
Scheduled Tribe	21.8	31.5	25.7	16.1	10.8	13.3	5.5	5.0	5.2
Other Backward Class	13.2	16.8	15.1	6.0	5.0	5.5	3.5	2.6	3.0
Others	6.2	11.4	9.0	2.9	1.5	2.2	1.0	0.8	0.9
Household size									
Small (1-4)	11.2	12.0	11.4	8.5	8.0	8.3	4.2	3.6	3.9
Medium (5-8)	14.4	18.9	16.7	8.6	5.4	7.0	3.8	3.0	3.4
Large (9-12)	13.9	15.6	15.1	9.8	8.4	9.1	1.4	2.8	2.2
Very large (13+)	4.8	18.9	11.5	7.5	5.4	6.3	-	0.6	0.3
Landholding									
None	14.5	16.6	15.5	8.6	5.0	6.8	4.8	3.8	4.3
< 2 Acre	8.8	14.7	11.7	6.1	5.8	5.9	3.5	0.7	2.2
2-5 Acre	8.6	16.9	13.0	6.8	7.0	6.9	1.5	2.0	1.8
5 + Acre	16.9	20.8	18.8	9.9	6.6	8.3	2.2	2.9	2.5
Standard of living									
Low	18.5	22.4	20.4	12.5	7.6	10.1	5.2	4.2	4.7
Medium	9.2	14.4	11.8	7.2	6.0	6.6	0.9	1.0	1.0
High	1.8	4.0	3.4	2.4	2.8	2.6	-	-	-

children drop out because they are required to work. A minority of working children have ever been to school (41 per cent in Andhra Pradesh, 32 per cent in Madhya Pradesh and 38 per cent in Orissa). In comparison, in all the three states more than 85 per cent of the non-working children have ever been to school (data not shown). In all the states a higher proportion of boys than girls (both working and non-working) have ever been to school. Generally, the educational level of working children is much better in Orissa than in Andhra Pradesh or Madhya Pradesh. As against only 17 per cent of illiterate working children in Andhra Pradesh and Madhya Pradesh the corresponding percentages are 64 and 77, respectively. On the other hand, compared to 27 per cent working children in Orissa, 18 per cent in Andhra Pradesh and 11 per cent in Madhya Pradesh have completed at least primary education. A gender-wise comparison shows that as against 56 per cent of working boys in Andhra Pradesh, 73 per cent in Madhya Pradesh and 61 per cent in Orissa who are illiterate, the corresponding percentages for illiterate working girls are: 71, 83 and 21. In Orissa, among working female children 55 per cent are literate but have not completed primary education and 24 per cent have completed at least primary education.

Chronic poverty is the major factor responsible for the prevalence and perpetuation of child labour (Kulshreshtra, 1978; Ministry of Labour, 1979; Sawhney, 1979; UNICEF, 1980; Rodgers and Standing, 1981; Princy, 1998). In NFHS, the standard of living is used as a proxy indicator of poverty. The standard of living index (SLI) is prepared on the basis of the ownership of a house, agricultural land, livestock, durable goods, type of house, and availability of basic amenities in the house (for details see Appendix). On the basis of this criteria 64 per cent of working children in Andhra Pradesh, 50 per cent in Madhya Pradesh and 90 per cent in Orissa belong to poor households (See Table 11). While another 34 per cent working children in Andhra Pradesh, 46 per cent in Madhya Pradesh and 10 per cent in Orissa belong to households with a medium standard of living. A negligible proportion of working children belong to households with high SLI in Andhra Pradesh and Madhya Pradesh, but none of the working children in Orissa belong to this category. Generally, working children from better off families are the ones who are not interested in studies and their parents prefer to send them to work to learn something which would assure them a secure future, rather than letting them remain at home where they would idle away their time and possibly join the company of vagabonds (Nangia, 1987).

3. Determinants of Child Labour

A logistic regression analysis is computed to see the effect of different socio-economic variables on the chances of participation of children in the labour force. The analysis is done for all the three states separately. The independent variables selected for the analysis are sex of the child, religion, caste/tribe, size of the landholding, household size and the standard of living index. All the households, which had children in the age group, 6-14 were considered for this analysis. The results given in Table 12, confirm some of the findings shown earlier through cross tabulations. The logistic analysis shows that in Andhra Pradesh, female children are much more likely to work, whereas in Madhya Pradesh they are less

Table 11

Per cent Distribution of Child Workers by Background Characteristics in Rural Areas of the Three States, 1998-99

	Andhra Pradesh			Madhya Pradesh			Orissa		
Background characteristic	Male	Female	Total	Male	Female	Total	Male	Female	Total
Age									
6-9 years	15.1	10.4	12.5	15.1	12.9	14.1	8.2	13.3	10.5
10 -14 years	84.9	89.6	87.5	84.9	87.1	85.9	91.8	86.7	89.5
Ever been to school	47.4	35.0	40.5	36.8	26.2	32.4	48.6	25.4	38.2
Education									
Illiterate	55.6	71.4	64.4	72.8	83.3	77.1	61.1	20.9	16.9
Literate < Primary	23.2	13.7	17.9	13.8	8.6	11.6	20.8	54.7	55.8
Primary completed	20.2	13.7	16.6	11.4	8.1	10.1	18.1	19.4	22.0
Middle school Completed and above	1.0	1.2	1.1	2.0	-	1.2	-	4.9	5.4
Standard of living									
Low	68.5	60.6	64.1	54.5	43.8	50.1	90.4	88.3	89.5
Medium	30.0	37.4	34.1	42.8	51.4	46.4	9.6	11.7	10.5
High	1.5	2.0	1.8	2.7	4.8	3.5	-	-	-

likely to do so than male children. In Orissa, sex is not a determining factor for participation of children in the labour force. Compared to scheduled caste children, scheduled tribe children are more likely to enter the labour force in Andhra Pradesh and Madhya Pradesh. The odds ratios of participation of scheduled tribe children in the labour force are 1.6 times higher in Andhra Pradesh and 2.3 times higher in Madhya Pradesh. In Orissa belonging to a caste or tribe does not make any difference in the participation of children in the labour force.

Compared to those households which do not possess any agricultural land, children from households with 5 or more acres of land are far more likely to enter the labour force in Andhra Pradesh. In Madhya Pradesh, children belonging to households with more than 2 acres of land are more likely to enter the labour force than those belonging to households which do not possess any agricultural land. This could be because of the greater requirement of labour at the bigger farms, which could be easily fulfilled by the available labour of children within the household. In Orissa, the size of landholding does not make any difference to work participation rate of children.

Table 12
Logistic Regression Showing Effect of Different Variables on Child Labour

Variables	Andhra Pradesh Odds ratio	Madhya Pradesh Odds ratio	Orissa Odds ratio
Sex			
Male [R]	1.00	1.00	1.00
Female	1.45***	0.66***	0.83
Religion			
Hindu [R]	1.00	1.00	1.00
Muslim	0.66	1.06	0.84
Other	1.12	0.33*	0.33
Caste/tribe			
Scheduled Caste [R]	1.00	1.00	1.00
Scheduled Tribe	1.64**	2.30***	1.53
Others	0.91	0.77	0.91
Landholding			
None [R]	1.00	1.00	1.00
< 2 Acre	0.97	1.11	1.03
2-5 Acre	1.32	1.47*	1.69
5 + Acre	1.76***	1.31*	0.94
Household size			
Small [R] (1-4)	1.00	1.00	1.00
Medium (5-8)	1.43*	0.88	0.98
Large (9-12)	1.49*	1.35	1.02
Very large (13+)	1.16	1.22	0.24
Standard of living			
Low [R]	1.00	1.00	1.00
Medium	0.51***	0.63***	0.22***
High	0.13***	0.29***	0.00

Note: [R] Reference category, * 0.05 level of significant, ** 0.01 level of significant, *** 0.001 level of significant.

In Andhra Pradesh, the children from medium and large households (5-12 members) have a significantly higher chance of joining the labour force than those of the smaller households (up to four members). However, the size of the household does not make any significant difference on the participation of children in the labour force in Madhya Pradesh and Orissa.

The effect of poverty on child labour is clearly visible in the last panel of Table 12. Compared to children from households with low standard of living, children from the households with medium and higher standard of living are significantly less likely to join the labour force in all the states.

4. Work Participation and Consumption of Intoxicants

This section compares the pattern of consumption of intoxicants (chewing of tobacco, drinking of alcohol and smoking) by working and non-working children. Consumption of intoxicants is not appreciated, particularly in childhood. It is presumed that some working children consume intoxicants not only to derive pleasure, but also to develop confidence to survive in the adult world, where they become easy prey to exploitation. Moreover, the loosening of family control over working children and their financial independence also prompts them to derive pleasure from certain habits, such as consuming various intoxicants, gambling, watching movies, etc. Sometimes adults also induce these habits among working children so that they could share the earnings of these children (in the form of intoxicants or movies, etc.) under the guise of friendship. The data reveal that the consumption of intoxicants is particularly high among working children in Orissa and Madhya Pradesh—in Orissa, 17 per cent of working children chew tobacco, 8 per cent drink alcohol and 3 per cent smoke and in Madhya Pradesh, 7 per cent of the working children chew tobacco, 3 per cent drink alcohol and one per cent smoke. In comparison, the proportion of non-working children who consume such intoxicants is negligible in both the states. A higher proportion of working boys than working girls consume these intoxicants. Nevertheless, 17 per cent of the working girls in Orissa chew tobacco, 7 per cent drink alcohol and 2 per cent smoke (Table 13). In Andhra Pradesh, a negligible proportion of working and non-working children consume intoxicants. However, these estimates might be very conservative as the information was elicited from the head or any other adult member of the household, who might not be aware of the habits developed by these children.

V. SUMMARY AND RECOMMENDATIONS

The results of NFHS-2 show that more than 80 per cent of the rural children in Madhya Pradesh and Orissa have ever attended school. Out of those children who ever attended school, a small proportion (7-12 per cent) had already dropped out by the time of the survey. Girls are at a greater disadvantage than boys, in regard to schooling. In relation to boys a smaller proportion of them ever attend school and a higher proportion drop out. The educational status of children in Orissa is slightly better than in Andhra Pradesh and Madhya Pradesh. The requirement of children for work or taking care of the household chores and siblings, lack of interest in studies and high cost of education are the major reasons for children not

Table 13
Per cent of Children Who Consumed Intoxicants in Rural Areas of the States, 1998-99

Intoxicants	Non-worker Male	Non-worker Female	Non-worker Total	Worker Male	Worker Female	Worker Total
			Andhra Pradesh			
Chew tobacco	0.1	0.1	0.1	-	0.4	0.2
Drink alcohol	1.7	1.2	1.4	1.5	1.6	1.6
Smoke	0.1	0.1	0.1	1.5	0.8	1.1
			Madhya Pradesh			
Chew tobacco	1.5	1.8	1.6	9.1	4.8	7.3
Drink alcohol	0.6	0.5	0.6	3.7	2.4	3.1
Smoke	0.1	-	0.1	1.7	-	1.0
			Orissa			
Chew tobacco	1.6	2.4	2.0	18.1	16.7	17.4
Drink alcohol	1.3	1.3	1.3	8.2	6.8	7.6
Smoke	0.1	0.1	0.1	4.2	1.7	3.0

attending school. For about one-tenth of children (higher in the case of girls) education is not considered necessary, which clearly shows that there is a need to create more awareness about the importance of education for each individual and to make education more interesting and useful so that children do not drop out. Teachers whose attitude is friendly and who can make learning interesting can play an important role in retaining children in school. Vocational training should be provided from the early classes so that those children who can not continue in school for long should be equipped with some skill to enable them to establish a place in the labour market and earn better. Scheduled tribe children in all the three states are less likely to attend school. Poverty is an important factor which prevents children from attending school. Children of the poor are either required to work or take care of the household responsibilities or are unable to bear the cost of education.

As regards working children, 15 per cent of children in Andhra Pradesh, 8 per cent in Madhya Pradesh and 3 per cent in Orissa participate in the labour force. In Andhra Pradesh, female work participation rate is more than that of males, in Madhya Pradesh a higher proportion of males participate in the labour force than females, but in Orissa there is no difference in the work participation rate of male and female children. The agricultural sector and plantations employ a majority of workers in rural Andhra Pradesh and Madhya Pradesh, but in Orissa a majority of child workers are employed as labourers and other workers. The work participation rates are highest among children from scheduled tribes followed by scheduled castes. Most of the child workers start working after 10 years of age. Among males less than half and among females less than two-fifths of the working children have ever been to school in any of the three states.

Poverty is closely related to child labour. As the standard of living goes up, the likelihood of children participating in the labour force declines. In Andhra Pradesh and Madhya Pradesh scheduled tribe children, and children from households which own more land, are more likely to work. In Andhra Pradesh female children are more likely to work than male children, while in Madhya Pradesh the reverse situation prevails. Scholarships offered to children from the poor families for attending school could to a large extent mitigate the problem of child labour and enhance the school attendance rate.

Some of the children, particularly working children in Madhya Pradesh and Orissa, start consuming intoxicants. Seventeen per cent children in Orissa and 7 per cent in Madhya Pradesh chew tobacco, 8 per cent in Orissa, 3 per cent in Madhya Pradesh and 2 per cent in Andhra Pradesh drink alcohol and a smaller proportion smoke. Consumption of intoxicants is higher among boys than among girls. There is thus a need to create an awareness among the public in general and child labour, in particular, about the detrimental effects of consumption of intoxicants.

Appendix

Construction of Standard of Living Index

Standard of living index (SLI) is calculated by adding the following scores:

House type: 4 for *pucca*, 2 for semi-*pucca*, 0 for *kachha*;

Toilet facility: 4 for own flush toilet, 2 for public or shared flush toilet or own pit toilet, 1 for shared or pubiic pit toilet, 0 for no facility;

Source of lighting: 2 for electricity, 1 for kerosene, gas, or oil, 0 for other source of lighting;

Main fuel for cooking: 2 for electricity, liquid petroleum gas, or biogas, 1 for coal, charcoal, or kerosene, 0 for other fuel;

Source of drinking water: 2 for pipe, hand pump, or well in residence/yard/plot, 1 for public t, hand pump, or well, 0 for other water source;

Separate room for cooking: 1 for yes, 0 for no;

Ownership of house: 2 for yes, 0 for no;

Ownership of agricultural land: 4 for 5 acres or more, 3 for 2.0-4.9 acres, 2 for less than 2 acres or acreage not known, 0 for no agricultural land;

Ownership of irrigated land: 2 if household owns at least some irrigated land, 0 for no irrigated land;

Ownership of livestock: 2 if owns livestock, 0 if does not own livestock;

Ownership of durable goods: 4 each for a car or tractor, 3 each for a moped/scooter/ motorcycle, telephone, refrigerator, or colour television, 2 each for a bicycle, electric fan, radio/transistor, sewing machine, black and white television, water pump, bullock cart, or thresher, 1 each for a mattress, pressure cooker, chair, cot/bed, table, or clock/watch.

Index scores range from 0-14 for a low SLI to 15-24 for a medium SLI and 25-67 for a high SLI.

Note

1. These states are selected because by the time this paper was completed NFHS-2 datasets were available only for these states.

References

CSO (1999), *Selected Socio-economic Statistics, India,* Government of India, Ministry of Statistics and Programme Implementation, Central Statistical Organisation, New Delhi.

Dube, Leela (1981), "The Economic Roles of Children in India: Methodological Issues", in Rodgers and Standing (eds.) *Child Work, Poverty and Underdevelopment,* Geneva, ILO.

IIPS-ORC Macro (2000), International Institute for Population Sciences and ORC Macro, *National Family Health Survey (NFHS-2), India, 1998-99,* Mumbai.

——, *National Family Health Survey (NFHS-2), India, 1998-99, Andhra Pradesh,* Mumbai.

——, *National Family Health Survey (NFHS-2), India, 1998-99, Madhya Pradesh,* Mumbai.

——, *National Family Health Survey (NFHS-2), India, 1998-99 , Orissa,* Mumbai IIPS.

Kulshreshtra, J.C. (1978), *Child Labour in India,* Ashish Publishing House, New Delhi.

Ministry of Labour (1979), *Report of the Committee on Child Labour,* Government of India, New Delhi.

Nangia, Parveen (1987), *Child Labour: Cause-effect Syndrome,* Janak Publishers, New Delhi.

Nautiyal, K.C. (1995), "Disparities in Public Expenditure in Primary Education and Their Impact & Equality, Quality and Quantity", *Journal of Educational Planning and Administration*, Vol. 9, No. 4, pp. 361-388.

Princy, Packia (1998), "The Profile of Child Population in Some Selected States with Special Emphasis on Education and Child Labour", Seminar Paper, IIPS, Mumbai.

Registrar General and Census Commissioner (2001), *Provisional Population Tables, Series 1.* Census of India, New Delhi, India.

Rodgers, Gerry and Guy Standing (1981), "The Economic Roles of Children in India: Methodological Issues", in Rodgers and Standing (eds.) *Child* Work, Poverty and Underdevelopment, ILO, Geneva.

Sawhney, Nirmal (1979), "Occupational Pattern of Children in Uttar Pradesh" in Srinivasan, K. et al. (eds.), *Demographic and Socio-Economic Aspects of Child in India,* Himalaya Publishing House, Mumbai.

Visaria, Parvin, Anil Gumber and Leela Visaria (1993), "Literacy and Primary Education in India, 1980-81 to 1991: Differential and Determinants", *Journal of Educational Planning and Administration*, Vol. 7, No. 1, pp. 13-62.

UNICEF (1980), *Analysis of Situation of Children in India, Country Programming Exercise* (micro), New Delhi.

PART IV

Enhancing Food Security to Benefit the Child

16

National Programme of Nutritional Support to Primary Education in India

Venita Kaul

I. THE CONTEXT

International research, including research in India, is increasingly bringing out evidence of the synergistic, interdependent and complementary nature of health, nutrition and educational factors in the context of the overall development of the child. While the focus of integrated development had been, till recently more on the younger child, recent research has begun to direct its attention towards the developmental needs of the school-age children as well. It dispels the assumption that the school-age children have "passed the survival of the fittest" test and emphasises the fact that these children may not be healthier than younger children and could benefit from the provision of health care and good nutrition during school years to restore any vitality lost in the early years because of illness and malnutrition. In the Indian context, the school-age children need to be focused on all the more, since education today has moved from education of 'classes' to education of 'masses' and children from all socio-economic and social categories are expected to be in school. Since the majority of children do not go to any pre-school, the school becomes logistically the most feasible agency to reach children.

The synergy among health, nutrition and education becomes important not only from the overall perspective of child development, but also from the point of view of success in schooling. This is particularly significant for brain development (for which the first few years are critical) and for the development of active learning capacity in the child, which are crucial for learning at school, as well as for life-long learning. For example, the capacity for processing, structuring and classifying information, ability to ask and answer appropriate questions, short-term memory, levels of alertness, attention and concentration are some of the capacities which are crucial for success in school. These are known to be adversely affected by nutritional and health deficiencies, which therefore limit the ability of the child to benefit from classroom instruction or later learning opportunities (Levinger, 1994; Rosso and Marek, 1996). Malnutrition, even in its milder form, can dull motivation and curiosity, reduce a child's exploratory play and interaction with caregivers and the environment, thus restricting the child's psycho-social development. Conversely, there is an evidence that children who receive psycho-social stimulation along with nutritional supplementation tend to benefit more in terms of gain in nutritional status as compared to those who receive nutritional intervention alone.

In the Indian context, several policy and programmatic initiatives have been undertaken to promote child development in areas of health, education and nutrition. The Indian Constitution (1950) formulated after independence, made a commitment through Article 45, to provide opportunities for education to children up to 14 years of age. In pursuance of this commitment the government has tried to address issues relating to children through policies such as the National Policy for Children (1974), the National Policy on Education (1986-92) and more recently through ratification of the Convention on the Rights of the Child (1992). Consistent with the Eighth Plan's acknowledgement of malnutrition as a multifaceted problem requiring an inter-sectoral approach to child development, the National Nutrition Policy was formulated in 1993 and a National Plan of Action was initiated in 1995. The current Ninth Plan has put emphasis on food and nutrition security and on reaching children less than two years of age. As a strategy, it has instituted a National Charter for Children which aims at ensuring that "no child remains illiterate, hungry or lacks medical care" by the end of this plan period.

In pursuance of this policy framework, several centrally-sponsored schemes and state-sponsored programmes have been introduced. Prominent among these are the Integrated Child Development Services (ICDS) and other Early Childhood Education (ECE) programmes, the Mid-day Meal Scheme and the formal and non-formal primary education programmes. An evaluation of some of these programmes do indicate that they have a positive, though fragmented impact in terms of child development indicators (Table 1). While over the last few decades, India has made considerable progress compared to the baseline in ensuring child survival and basic education, the situation in comparison to other developing countries is still not very encouraging. The fact that, despite various interventions over the years, the percentage of children with low birth weight is as high as 33 and almost 40 per cent of the children who enrol in grade I do not make it even to the grade V, continues to be a matter of considerable concern.

It is in this context that this paper focuses on the mid-day meal programme as an intervention which is expected to impact upon the nutritional and educational status of school-age children in the country. The paper begins with a

Table 1
Progress on Selected Developmental Indicators

Indicators	India		Developing countries		Developed countries	
	1960	1998	1960	1998	1960	1998
Infant mortality rate	144	69	138	64	31	6
Under five mortality	235	105	216	95	37	6
Percentage of low-birth weight infants	-	33	-	18	-	6
Gross enrolment ratio (primary)	63.5	101	77	100	103	104
Percentage of grade enrolled reaching final primary grade	53 *	59	66*	98	94*	99

Note: * Data collected for the year 1988.
Source: UNICEF, *The State of the World's Children,* 1994, 1996, 1997 and 2000.

discussion about the nature, objectives and coverage of the programme and goes on to critically assess its impact vis-à-vis the objectives, based on information available from secondary sources. It concludes with some recommendations for making the programme more cost-effective.

II. THE MID-DAY MEAL SCHEME

1. Background and Objectives

In India, the mid-day meal programme historically dates back to 1925 when it was introduced for children from the poorer sections of the society in areas administered by the Madras Corporation. Later, similar school-meal programmes were introduced by numerous other states as well, at varying periods of time, often with the assistance of international agencies like UNICEF, FAO, WHO, CRS, CARE, etc. In July 1996, the mid-day meal programme was redesignated as the National Programme for Nutritional Support to Primary Education (NPNSPE) and included in the seven basic minimum services which were identified as essential for ensuring the rapid growth of the economy along with social justice which, therefore, constitute the core of the social sector development plan.

The NPNSPE was formally launched on August 15,1995 by the Government of India as a centrally-sponsored scheme with the twin objectives of (i) enhancing the nutritional status of children and (ii) giving a boost to universalisation of primary education by influencing the decision of economically disadvantaged people to admit children in schools, retain them there till they complete the primary education cycle and ensure that they attend school regularly. Under this central programme, support is extended towards (a) provision of foodgrains, free of cost, to the implementing agencies for which economic cost is reimbursed to the Food Corporation of India; and (b) reimbursement of transportation cost to district authorities for moving foodgrains from Food Corporation of India godowns to schools/villages.

The scheme offers the states three options: (i) cooked meal (100 grams per day for 200 school-days); (ii) pre-cooked meals; or (iii) 3 kgs of wheat/rice per primary school child per month for 10 months. The per child provision has been fixed by the Committee on NPNSPE on the basis of the estimated additional nutritional value required by children in the primary school-age group to meet their nutritional requirements. A higher provision of foodgrains vis-à-vis cooked meals is provided in the expectation that a part of it would be shared by other family members. A minimum school attendance of 80 per cent in the previous month is required to be eligible for receiving the food/foodgrain.

The scheme is proposed to be universalised to cover all the rural blocks and urban slums, and disadvantaged sections during the Ninth Plan. Once universalised, the annual expenditure of the scheme, estimated in 1997-98 at constant prices, would be of the order of Rs. 22.26 billion. This paper evaluates the implementation of this scheme, on the basis of a review of information from secondary sources, in terms of (a) its intended vs. actual coverage; and (b) its impact vis-à-vis its stated objectives, and concludes with the implications for the future.

2. Coverage of NPNSPE

The coverage of the scheme is discussed in terms of (a) its geographical spread across districts and blocks; (b) the percentage of intended beneficiaries regularly covered; and (c) extent of targeting of the socially and economically disadvantaged. The scheme was intended to cover all the government, government-aided and local-body primary schools in the country in a phased manner over a period of three years. Private un-aided schools and NFE centers were not envisaged to be covered under the programme.

Table 2 indicates the overall progress vis-à-vis coverage within the last four years. During 1995-96, that is the first year of the programme, the scheme covered 2499 blocks including 2446 blocks under the Revamped Public Distribution System (RPDS)/Employment Assurance Scheme (EAS), two border blocks in Jammu & Kashmir and 37 low female literacy blocks in Punjab which had no RPDS/EAS blocks. Preference was given to weaker sections in society, which included those living in urban slums in Delhi, Chandigarh, Goa and Pondicherry. During 1996-97, the second year of the programme, 1927 low female literacy blocks were covered, bringing the total coverage to 4426 blocks in 475 districts of the country. In the third year i.e., 1997-98, the programme was further extended to cover 5451 blocks in 510 districts. By December 31, 1998, the programme covered 544 districts in the country.

In respect of the mode of implementation of this scheme, there are state-wise variations. For instance, Gujarat, Kerala, Orissa, Tamil Nadu and Pondicherry provide cooked meals under the scheme, while in Delhi and Chandigarh the items distributed were processed foods and in the rest of the states and union territories only foodgrains were distributed. While states like Haryana, Madhya Pradesh and Jammu started with cooked meals they subsequently shifted to foodgrains due to the difficulties faced in the provision of cooked meals. In

Table 2
Progress in Coverage of NPNSPE Scheme

Year	Number of children (in millions)	Expenditure (in Rs. millions)	Quantity of foodgrains (in metric tonnes)	
			Allocated	Lifted
1995-96	33.4	4412.1	713347	536016
1996-97	55.7	8000.0	1585651	1112489
1997-98	91.0	10703.8	2567634	1808827
1998-99	97.5*	10300.0*	2707307**	182564**

Notes: * Up to November, 1998, **Up to June, 1998.
Source: Annual Report, 1999, Ministry of Human Resource Development, Government of India, New Delhi.

Madhya Pradesh there is a mix, with cooked meals being served in EAS blocks and foodgrains in the other blocks.

In 1998-99 the total number of beneficiaries was estimated to be 97.5 million in nearly 700,000 schools in all the rural blocks and urban areas in the country (GOI, 1999). A recent study undertaken by the Operations Research Group in February 1999 in 10 states, indicates that 59 per cent of the children enrolled in primary classes reported having received mid-day meals. Excluding Jammu and Assam, in which there was a greater disruption of supply, the percentage of beneficiaries increased to 66 per cent. Analysis of the state-wise coverage revealed that the coverage was poor in Haryana and Madhya Pradesh (47 per cent), moderate in Gujarat (65 per cent) and good in Orissa, Rajasthan and Uttar Pradesh with 76-83 per cent of the enrolled children receiving the meals/grains.

The scheme is evidently targeting the socio-economically disadvantaged group, as intended, with self-targeting occurring to some extent, since in many states most children from more privileged backgrounds, are migrating to private schools. Caste-wise, the programme revealed not only a higher coverage of SC/ ST students with 71 per cent of the students being from these two categories, but also that 94 per cent of the ST and 88 per cent of the SC students belonged to families below the poverty line, with a monthly income of Rs. 2000 or less. The coverage of general category students was lowest. In terms of gender, there were no variations.

Regularity in the Provision of Mid-day Meals

A significant dimension of the coverage under the scheme is the regularity maintained in the provision of meals to children. In this context, it is important to clarify that while determining the coverage of the programme, children receiving the benefit at any point of time, (even on only one occasion) during the past six months, were also considered. Thus, the proportions of students receiving mid-day meals regularly was actually much lower as reflected in the wide variations in coverage of students across the various months, as per school records. Among the households covered in the ORG study, which were receiving foodgrains, only 25 per cent reported monthly receipt of foodgrains with delays of three months or more being often cited with wide state-wise differences. The delays can be attributed to a complicated system of delivery in some states involving many departments and agencies at the same level and a tedious process of lifting and transport reimbursement. The transportation cost from district FCI depots to the schools is borne by the lifting agencies across the states and later reimbursed by the MHRD through different agencies according to the norm. In most states there is a delay in reimbursement which affects the timely distribution of foodgrain. Often the transport cost in difficult terrain is more than that reimbursed. The foodgrains are transported to a central point and the subsequent transportation arrangement is left to the teachers which creates its own logistical problems. Provisions for storage in the schools are also highly inadequate resulting in both pilferage and hygienically unsafe practices.

3. Impact of the Scheme

The impact of the scheme is analysed in terms of its two-stated objectives: (i) enhancing the nutritional status of children; and (ii) improving the status of the elementary education parameters i.e., enrolment, retention and attendance. It may, however, be noted that any study of the impact must necessarily take into account both the regularity of distribution and the total period for which the child received food under the scheme as well as the quality.

(i) Enhancing Nutritional Status

There has been no systematic assessment of the impact of the mid-day meal scheme on the nutritional status of children. However, a related study conducted by the National Institute of Nutrition in 1993 on the mid-day meal programme in Andhra Pradesh indicated that, since the extent of energy deficiency in the diets of school children is about 750 kcal per day (while deficits of protein are negligible viz., 3 to 5 gm per child per day), the school-meal should aim at providing at least 750 kcal of energy to every child partaking the meal. The meal supplied under the scheme, however, provided just around 300 kcal, which is less than 50 per cent of the observed gap in dietary energy. The programme was, therefore, more in the nature of a supplement rather than providing a complete meal. Consequently, as expected, the gains as assessed through body measurements, were not significant.

But this is not to disregard some of the larger questions relating to the usefulness of nutritional supplements at primary school-age, given the enormous investments and the existing mechanisms for delivery. Just over half of India's children under four years who are the potential entrants to primary school, tend to be underweight and a similar proportion are stunted, indicating chronic undernutrition. It is in the first half of this period, i.e., 0-24 months that both growth and development (including that of the brain) is most rapid. Plainly, it is at this stage that prevention of growth and development failure is most critical and growth faltering occurs. The nutritional performance of the child, during this period of intense growth and development, sets the stage for his/her later achievements. Accordingly, interventions to address prevention of malnutrition need to be directed toward children below two years of age to be most effective, since the school-going age may prove to be more resource-demanding and therefore less cost-effective.

The next period of accelerated growth occurs in the pre-pubertal age group which corresponds to the upper primary stage of education. Nutritional supplementation is likely to have a significant impact at this stage, although the interventions may not fully offset the earlier injury to the system. Nevertheless, supplementation during this period might be used to kick-start 'catch up growth' and correct important mineral deficiencies e.g., anaemia.

At the primary stage, with a view to maintaining/improving the nutrition and health status of the child, greater priority needs to be given to periodic deworming of the children within a larger programme of school health. Also, if the school-meal programme aims at making the child food-secure it is important to ensure that the child gets a nutritionally balanced meal for himself/herself, and not to be shared with the family. From this perspective, the school-meal programme should emphasise serving of a cooked meal in the school itself, which is cooked and served in a hygienically safe manner on a regular basis.

Any nutrition programme to be effective, must also include a package for community education in personal and environmental hygiene and facilities for the same. In the absence of such a package and keeping in view the way the scheme is being implemented, with the states moving towards a system of supply of grains rather than cooked meals, that too irregular, the chances of the programme impacting on the nutritional status of children are minimal.

To effectively meet the challenge of ensuring the virtuous cycle of health, nutrition and education, the interventions must therefore be conceptualised in a more holistic perspective so that they not only address the entire development continuum vertically with appropriate priorities for each stage, but also horizontally across different sectors in a complementary manner. Convergence and interlinkages between programmes like the Integrated Child Development Services (ICDS), School Health Programme and the NPNSPE both at the stage of planning and implementation, which at present are negligible, thus become crucial. Possibilities of integrating a health component into the mid-day meal programme, as successfully experimented within 19 districts of Gujarat, can also pay back a high dividend and should be considered for expansion to other states. (Gopaldas and Gujral, 1996)

(ii) Improving Educational Status

The mid-day meal scheme is directed towards improvement in enrolment, attendance and retention levels of children at the primary level. The impact of NPNSPE on these indicators as evaluated in the ORG study is discussed below:

(a) Enrolment: The study indicates a comparatively higher growth in enrolment during 1996-97, the year in which the scheme was introduced, compared to the earlier years, and this has been sustained over the next two years.

The growth rates were comparatively higher for girls (9 per cent) as compared to boys (6 per cent) and for the SC and ST categories too from pre-NPNSPE to post-NPNSPE periods. State-wise comparisons indicate higher growth rates in enrolment in Uttar Pradesh, West Bengal, Assam and Haryana in 1996-97. While it is very difficult to isolate the impact of the NPNSPE on enrolment, since several other incentive schemes and projects have been simultaneously floated, the study also reports that 79 per cent of the community members interviewed believed that the mid-day meal scheme had led to higher enrolments. This observation is substantiated by the author's own interactions with the various community groups in the states.

Interestingly, the ORG study also presents a counter-situation wherein of all the households surveyed, about 29 per cent in Karnataka, 16 per cent each in Gujarat and West Bengal and 8 per cent in Haryana, there was a presence of both out-of-school and school-going children in the same household. This indicates that the provision of mid-day meals is not always an adequate incentive for sending all children to school since three-fourths of these households were primarily engaged in farm or farm-related activities. The economic benefits realised by engaging the children in on-farm activities was evidently higher in comparison to sending them to school.

(b) Attendance: This objective is central to the scheme in its very concept, since it is supposed to cover only children who have a school attendance in the previous month of 80 per cent or more. A precondition for ensuring this impact would logically be that the community/parents /children are aware of this criterion and therefore, perceive the meal provision as an incentive to fulfil it. Interestingly, the ORG study indicates that only 20 per cent of parents were aware of this criterion and could relate the provision of foodgrains or cooked meal to an attendance of 80 per cent. A majority believed that all children in primary classes were eligible. The low level of awareness could be attributed to the fact that teachers themselves did not or could not, in most cases, apply this criterion due to social pressures. While in states where a cooked meal is provided, the scheme may still be an incentive for regular attendance, in those where grains are provided, its implementation is likely to be taken for granted by parents, children and the community in general as a right. This is corroborated by the fact that in these states, the study found no significant variation in the attendance patterns of students during the pre- and post-programme period.

(c) Retention: The ORG study made a comparison between the pre- and post-programme trends in dropouts in the sample states which indicated state-wise variations. In Karnataka and Orissa, though the dropout rates continued to remain high there was an improvement of almost 6 per cent in the post-programme period. An improvement in the retention of girls was also observed. In addition, marginal improvements were also observed in some other states such as West Bengal and Uttar Pradesh. In Rajasthan, Jammu & Kashmir, Gujarat and Haryana there was no improvement in this area as a result of the scheme.

A significant issue that emerged from the study was the need to record and maintain data more systematically at the school level on both the educational parameters as well as on monitoring of the mid-day meal provisions.

III. CONCLUSION

Presently, the NPNSPE covers 544 districts in the country and is slated to be universalised across the country by the end of the Ninth Plan period with an expenditure of Rs. 22.26 billion. The evaluation of this scheme suggests that while community perceptions with regard to the scheme are positive, its impact on the nutritional status of children or on the education parameters, excepting enrolment, is not entirely commensurate with the investment. Problems in implementation, largely due to a centralised distribution system and inadequate infrastructure have evidently adversely affected the outcomes of the scheme. Clearly, the scheme needs to be reviewed and this requires to be done from two separate perspectives—as a nutrition supplementation scheme and as an incentive for school participation, which is explained below:

1. NPNSPE as a Nutritional Supplementation Programme

From this perspective there is a need to take more holistic, developmental approach, as discussed earlier, keeping in view the priorities at each stage and by conceptualising the scheme in convergence with the ICDS and the School Health Programme or giving it a more comprehensive form as in Gujarat, for a more definite impact. Convergence becomes logistically more feasible given the current trends in many states towards the decentralised Panchayati Raj system. Also, if the nutritional objective is to be taken seriously, it becomes important to ensure that (a) the meal for the child has adequate calorific value and is supplied regularly; and (b) the meal supplements and not substitutes the child's home meal.

2. NPNSPE as an Incentive for School Participation

As an incentive and input for universalising primary education, the programme needs to be considered in terms of the two practiced modes of implementation-monthly distribution of foodgrains and providing cooked/pre-cooked meals daily.

The monthly distribution of foodgrains is evidently more feasible logistically and in terms of infrastructural requirements. However, linking the provision of foodgrains to 80 per cent attendance is a difficult criterion to apply both from the point of view of administration of the scheme as well as from the evidence of adverse impact on teacher-community dynamics. Therefore, while the scheme may have a positive impact on the enrolment and possibly retention of children, it may not influence the daily attendance or the level of food security provided to the child. If this mode of implementation were to be adopted/continued, there would be a need to streamline coordination between various agencies involved in the supply and distribution of foodgrains and provide necessary facilities to the concerned teachers in order to ensure that it has the desired impact.

The cooked/pre-cooked meal would be a preferred option from the point of improving school participation and making the school-going child food-secure.

This was also the preference indicated by the community and teachers in the ORG study. This mode of implementation is expected to have the following advantages:

(i) It ensures greater food security for the child and can facilitate concentration and learning particularly if served in the morning rather than at mid-day.

(ii) It will provide greater incentive for attending school daily as compared to the monthly rations.

(iii) It can very effectively serve as the practical component of health education which is a part of the primary curriculum, by providing a basis for nutrition education, development of healthy habits as well as of pro-social behavior in children like sharing, waiting for one's turn, etc., which will lead to more sustained benefits. Eating together can also be an exercise in social cohesion if made compulsory for children of all castes and creeds. The linkage with the curriculum can only be possible if the mid-day meal programme is not seen by those who implement it as a separate 'scheme' but as an integral part of the school programme.

(iv) In the case of a cooked meal, the availability of provisions will be less dependent on a wide distribution network which has been seen to cause delays and interruptions, and this would facilitate availability of the meal on a more regular basis.

However, there can be logistical difficulties in implementing this modality on a large scale as is evident from the fact that many states have moved to foodgrain distribution. The issue of involving teachers in the procurement and distribution of food is also important since this often cuts into the teacher's teaching time. In this context, lessons can be learnt from the Tamil Nadu Nutrition Programme for pre-school children (TNNP), where it was effectively implemented through an independent worker and by encouraging community involvement at the local level. This also reinforces the need for more effective communication strategies for the community, which will ensure ownership of the programme as well as help them understand the importance of making the child food-secure and the significance of the scheme for ensuring both participation and success in school.

(The author acknowledges the input received in the preparation of this paper from Suneeta Singh and Kalpana Seethepalli of the World Bank. The author is currently Senior Education Specialist in the World Bank.)

References

GOI (1999), *Annual Report (1998-99)*, Government of India, Ministry of Human Resource Development, Department of Education.

Gopaldas, T. and S. Gujral (1996), *The Pre-post Impact Evaluation of the Improved Mid-Day Meal Programme*, Tata Consultancy Services, Baroda, Gujarat.

Levinger, Beryl (1994), *Nutrition, Health and Education for All,* Mass Education Development Center, Newton.

National Institute of Nutrition (1993), *ICDS: Appraisal in Four States,* Hyderabad.

ORG (1999), *Evaluation Study to Assess the Effectiveness of the National Programme for Nutritional Support to Primary Education,* Operations Research Group, New Delhi.

Rosso, D. and T. Marek (1995), *Class Action, Improving School Performance in the Developing World Through Better Health and Nutrition,* Directions in Development, World Bank, Washington DC.

UNICEF (1994, 1996, 1997 and 2000), *State of the World's Children.*

17

The Role of Food Assistance Programmes in Promoting Education and Reducing Child Work in Rural India

UTE MEIR

I. CHILD WORK AND EDUCATION

1. The Dimensions of Child Work

According to the International Labour Organisation (ILO), there are currently at least 250 million children world wide between the ages of 5 to 14 who are working, of whom some 120 million work full-time. The vast majority of child workers (61 per cent) are to be found in Asia, with 32 per cent in Africa and 7 per cent in Latin America. The ILO defines 'child labour' as "work that deprives children of their childhood and their dignity, which hampers their access to education and the acquisition of skills, and which is performed under deplorable conditions harmful to their health and their development" (ILO/UNICEF, 1997). This definition encompasses the full range of work performed by children, whether gainful employment, work in the informal sector, traditional agriculture or domestic services, and all conditions under which children work, from the most exploitative and hazardous such as in certain industries to more "moderate work which can itself be a positive educational experience which boosts self-esteem and inculcates responsibility" (UNICEF, 1997). In this paper, we will refer to this as 'child work'.

This definition was adopted by the ILO in 1996 when it revised its earlier estimate of the number of child workers, recognising that the problem concerned a far larger age group and was not limited to children in full-time employment but included huge numbers of children who perform invisible, often unpaid work in the informal sector, in agriculture and at home. In many respects, this is the most typical form of child work and one which affects the largest number of children. It is particularly typical of the employment scenario in rural areas and of girls who form the vast majority of the invisible child workers.

To many, such child work and the work performed by girls is not taken seriously and not considered as real work and forming part of the 'child labour' issue. Yet, the research uniformly shows that on an average girls work for more hours than boys, start working at an earlier age and perform the bulk of domestic labour. They are also exposed to the most serious abuses and the greatest risks since their informal work places them beyond the reach of protective legislation and inspection. In India, there are an estimated 11.28 million child workers of whom 45 per cent are girls. More than half of these, namely seven million are domestic labourers of whom 88 per cent are girls. Boys are mostly engaged in farm work, wage labour or help in other household income-generating activities (PROBE, 1999). Girls look after younger siblings, fetch water and fuelwood, pound grain, cook, clean and often run the household, while their mothers work in the field or are engaged in wage labour. In rural India, a girl works for nine hours a day and an average of 315 days a year in the fields and at home, providing her family an annual labour which at a minimum wage would cost Rs 2,200 (or approximately US$63) to hire (UNICEF, 1997). A survey conducted by the MV Foundation amongst farm labourers in India found that girls worked for 29.4 days in a month, compared to 22.2 days and 18.6 days for women and men respectively (Oonk, 1998). In Burkina Faso, girls above seven years of age spend an average of 3.5 hours a day on household chores, compared with 1.5 hours spent by boys (Oxfam International, 2000). Studies from several other African countries have come to similar conclusions (Canagarajah and Coulombe, 1997).

At the same time, latest estimates place the number of children of primary school-age who are not in school at 113 million. Of these, 97 per cent live in less developed regions and nearly two-thirds (approximately 67 million) are girls (UNESCO, 2000). Girls also form the majority of the roughly 150 million children who enrol in primary schools but drop out before completing four years of education, which means they have not acquired even basic literacy and numeracy skills (Oxfam International, 2000). In the developing world in general, just over half of all students complete primary school. South Asia remains the region with the largest educational gender gaps, although the situation there has improved over the last decade. Along with Sub-Saharan Africa, it also accounts for the largest number of out-of-school children and of primary school drop-outs. In India, just over 70 per cent of children in the age group, 6-11 enrol in primary school, of which 40 per cent drop out before completing class V. In the elementary education age group, 6-14 years, some 90 million children are estimated to be out of school. The world community therefore still has a long way to go to reach the goal of Education for All to which it committed itself at the World Education Forum, held in Dakar, Senegal last year.

2. What Causes Child Work?

What are the factors which keep such large numbers of children from exercising their fundamental right to education or force them to work? Child work is a complex issue which has many origins. Most analysts agree that the most powerful force driving children into work is poverty (ILO/UNICEF, 1997). Poor families depend on their children's workforce to ensure their survival and provide supplementary income. Although this may appear to be poor economics, poor families have in fact very limited choices between immediate survival and investment in long-term development. Moreover, there is evidence that children in poor families contribute substantially, up to one third, to household incomes and that their income source cannot be treated as insignificant by poor families (Canagarajah and Coulombe, 1997). At the macro-economic level it has been shown that the proportion of children in the total labour force declines with rising per capita income. The impact is most pronounced when the incomes of the poor, and women in particular, increase (ILO/UNICEF, 1997). A review of nine Latin American countries showed that without the income of working children, the incidence of poverty would rise between 15 and 20 per cent.[1]

At the same time, poverty does not automatically force children to work, and not all children from poor families are working. Child work is also a result of exploitative practices in many industries where children are preferred to adult workers because they are less able to defend themselves, more obedient and work for lower wages. This, in turn, depresses wages paid to adult workers and perpetuates the vicious cycle of poverty and child work. Another factor relates to the negative socio-cultural customs and traditions. For example, the low status of girls in many societies automatically confines them to a life of work and subservience. Thus, girls work not only because the family depends on their labour, but because this is considered to be their main role and duty. In some areas, child work is considered a normal practice and no one realises that there could be anything wrong with it. Child work is also intrinsically linked with the discrimination of certain groups, such as ethnic minorities, migrants or refugees. In many parts of the world, child work is relegated to certain minority groups or disadvantaged lower classes, whereas the dominant culture may not want its own children to work.[2] In India, caste and partly feudal structures are blamed for allowing many forms of child work (Oonk, 1998).

Inadequacies in Education as a Causative Factor

Last but not the least, many children work because of the inadequacies of the education systems in their countries. Schools may be inaccessible because they are too far, or overcrowded or not suitable to the needs of girls or certain minority groups. Many families cannot afford the cost of uniforms, textbooks and stationery or other direct and indirect contributions to education, particularly if they have many children. In cases where parents have to select the children who are to be sent to school, girls are often given the least priority. The rising trend in 'cost-sharing' in education means that in countries such as Zambia, Vietnam or Tanzania households now pay for about half of total spending on elementary education (Oxfam International, 2000). In India, the PROBE (1999) report calculated that an agricultural labourer in Bihar with three children in school, for example, would have to work for 40 days per year just to pay for educational costs. Ninety per cent of parents interviewed by the PROBE team quoted the direct costs of education as the main reason for not sending their children to school. In fact, there is evidence that many children work in order to pay for their own schooling or that of their siblings (ILO/UNICEF, 1997). A World Bank study in Ghana observed the following: "The high costs of schooling increases the probability of child work. This is because as children find that they cannot afford school, they are pushed into working in order to enable them to attend school, or it may just completely prevent them from going to school and participate in household enterprises" (Canagarajah and Coulombe, 1997).

On the other hand, children and their parents are also often discouraged by the poor quality of many schools and of the education provided as also the lack of tangible economic and social benefits which should result from attending school. Many rural schools in particular are housed in buildings, which lack furniture and equipment and are staffed with poorly trained and underpaid teachers who remain frequently absent. Educational contents are ill adapted to local needs and interests, and many school leavers cannot find jobs. As a result, the very state of education often drives children away from school and into work.

Unfortunately, this seems to be very much the case in India. Reports abound about the poor state of primary schools in many parts of India, particularly in rural areas, where classes are overcrowded and teaching methods are not child-centred. Non-availability of teaching aids and chronic teacher absenteeism are the common phenomena in these schools. Many analysts attribute this to a lack of relevant government commitment and action which itself is viewed as a reflection of the underlying factors of the Indian social structure and the lack of political clout of the illiterate masses (Oonk, 1998). Thus, many parents feel discouraged by the current type of primary and elementary education, despite their high interest in education in general.[3] It has also been shown, for example in Kerala, that even poor families can make substantial contributions to education provided they are assured of its quality (ibid). Significantly, there seems to be a growing consensus, including amongst UN agencies, to reject poverty as the main cause of child work in India and emphasise the need to make elementary education more meaningful and accessible as the principal means of eliminating child work (ibid.).[4]

3. Child Work: An Obstacle to Education

At the same time, child work is also a major obstacle to education. The opportunity costs of sending children to school, which result from the loss of their labour, are a key reason for non-enrolment, irregular attendance and early drop-out. This is particularly true of poorer families in rural areas (because of the predominance of labour intensive agricultural work and the need for children to help with this work) and of girls. The PROBE survey in northern India found that girls' preoccupation with domestic labour and sibling care was by far the most important reason for not sending them to school or for their dropping out.[5] Since girls spend a greater amount of time at work, their 'child work benefit' for parents and thus the opportunity costs of their schooling are greater than for boys. Another study from India pointed out that domestic chores account for approximately 15 per cent of rural and urban girls not attending schools as opposed to 2 per cent for boys. A study from Bangladesh concludes: "Normally, a rural Bangladeshi woman works 10-14 hours a day, though most of this work is not visible or reflected in national statistics. The need to perform domestic chores to help their mothers impedes girls' participation in formal education, forcing them into irregular attendance and/or to leave school."[6]

Because of the link between child work and poverty, the negative correlation between economic status, gender and educational opportunity provides additional evidence for the role of opportunity costs as an obstacle to education. A study from Guinea concluded that "Family income or wealth is a key variable that explains differences in educational opportunities and attainment between families. ... Poverty in a family will have a more detrimental effect on the decision to enrol a girl in school than boys (Tembon and Al-Samarrai, 1997)." World Bank research in India showed that, amongst poor girls, less than 10 per cent had completed elementary education (grade 8), compared to 85 per cent of rich boys age group, 15-19. Educational attainment of girls was consistently lower than for boys across all income groups (Filmer, 1999).

At the same time, child work also affects children's learning achievements. Several studies confirm that children carrying the double burden of work and attending school show a poorer performance in class and slower progress and are at greater risk of repeating or dropping out (UNICEF, 1997). A study from Ghana found that "work has a substantial effect on learning achievement in the key areas of reading and mathematics. The directs links could be because of exhaustion or because of a diversion of interests away from academic concerns" (Heady, 2000).

4. The Vicious Circle of Child Work and Under-education

Child work, therefore, denies children not only their right to a childhood but also their right to education. It deprives them of any possibility of escape from the poverty trap, by acquiring the knowledge and skills they need to improve their condition. Child work and under-education mutually condition each other in a vicious circle: just as child work keeps children from attending school, a lack of education breeds and perpetuates poverty and other social evils which underscores the need for child work.

At the same time, the issue does not pose itself in any 'either/or'-dimensions. Most of the time, children are neither in school nor at work but very frequently combine both, even if there is an indication that the workload of children in school is significantly less than of those who are not in school (UNICEF, 1997). "According to available national surveys, between 50 and 70 per cent of all child workers attend school, or intend to do so (ILO/UNICEF, 1997)." Of the child workers surveyed in Ghana, more than two-thirds were also simultaneously attending school (Canagarajah and Coulombe, 1997). A study from Bangladesh concluded that "one cannot assume that the time these children spend working must come at the expense of formal time at school, although there may be displacement of information (after-school) tutorials or homework (Ravallion and Wodon, undated)." A review of the situation in India leads to the conclusion that the current school hours in rural areas (4-5 yours per day for 150 days per year) should not make it impossible for children to also work (Oonk, 1998). This is particularly true of girls who often perform important domestic chores before and after school. Enforcing compulsory education will thus not automatically do away with all child work, just as the elimination of child work will not necessarily result in all children attending school.

The Way Forward—Combining Work with Education

While the abolition of the worst forms of child labour is a non-negotiable, immediate priority, the way forward lies in a strategy which both encourages and enables working children to attend school. On the one hand, this requires the transformation of education systems to make them more accessible, affordable, responsive and relevant to children and their parents and thus more attractive than work. On the other hand, even in places where there is no other immediate option than work, the need for the children's labour must not be accepted as an argument against their schooling. "As an interim measure, a combination of work and school is better than no school at all (UNICEF, 1997)." Schools should, therefore, become more flexible so as to allow children to combine work and education, such as by adapting the school calendar to the agricultural calendar (in view of the seasonal need for child work), adjusting school hours on the basis of children's working hours or locating schools closer to children's workplaces. Girls' education can also be facilitated by setting up of more child care facilities near schools (to ensure that the need for sibling care does not interfere with the girls' schooling) or other measures aimed at reducing the workload of girls (such as provision of potable water supply close to homes, fuel-saving stoves or hand mills).

Lastly, "there is also a growing consensus among governments and civil society that, if poor families are to choose education over work for their children, special measures and incentives will be needed. In the final analysis, simply making schools available and improving their quality will not be sufficient to overcome all the problems faced by the poorest families. For this reason, economic incentives that support or compensate families for the loss of income when children go to school rather than to work will be required (ILO/UNICEF, 1997)." Participants at last year's World Education Forum concluded that "wider social policies, interventions and incentives should be used to mitigate indirect opportunity costs of attending school."[7] Of course, all these measures must form part of a package of interventions to tackle the vast and complex problem of child work, such as changes in negative mindsets and traditions which force children to work or the promotion and enforcement of anti-child work policies and legislation.

II. FOOD ASSISTANCE AND THE EDUCATION OF WORKING CHILDREN

1. Food Assistance Programmes to Offset the Opportunity Costs of Schooling

As mentioned above, if poor, working children are to attend school it is often necessary to compensate their families for the loss of the child's labour—even if the loss is partial and children combine schooling and work. This needs to be addressed through the offer of incentives, which transfer income to families. These take various forms, ranging from cash stipends or the waiver of school fees to in-kind incentives such as the provision of free school uniforms, textbooks or school meals, which seem to be the most common type (Anker and Melkas, 1996). In addition to alleviating opportunity costs, incentives can also be provided to families to help them meet the direct costs of education, either directly (cash incentives) or indirectly through savings generated in the family budget.

Many of these incentive-based programmes have shown encouraging results. For example, cash education grants provided to very low-income families in Brazil reduced drop-out and increased the rate of promotion to the next grade (UNICEF, 1997). A scholarship programme for poor, indigenous girls in Guatemala resulted in higher enrolment, lower drop-out and more girls completing primary school (Prather, 1996). On the other hand, many of the government's incentive schemes for poor and disadvantaged groups (cash scholarships, free textbooks and uniforms) were not successful. These were largely attributed to poor targeting and erratic implementation of the schemes (due to irregularity and insufficiency of supplies, limited coverage, confusion about entitlements or lack of community involvement) (Meir, 2000).

Food-based incentives, whether in the form of school meals or food rations for children to take home are among the most common forms of income substitution and a common feature in many developing countries. Although not systematically targeting working children, many such programmes are directed at poor sections of the population groups and thus directly related to the problem of child work (because of the link of child work and poverty). In recent years, several evaluations of such food assistance programmes have been carried out.

In a comprehensive review of studies on the educational effects of school feeding programmes in developing countries, published in 1986 Bery Levinger referred, amongst others, to a programme in the Dominican Republic where an interruption in feeding resulted in a 25 per cent drop in enrolment, the effect being particularly strong in rural areas and for girls. While pointing out the flaws in many school feeding studies she concluded that such programmes clearly made a difference with respect to school attendance and enrolment. At the same time, she also made several practical recommendations for improving the food incentive programmes. For example, the size of the food ration needs to be sufficient to act as an incentive, particularly for girls. "It seems likely that where the need for child labour and availability of employment opportunities for children coexist, school feeding programmes are likely to act as an incentive for school attendance only when the ration size is large enough so that feeding can be viewed by parents as a significant income-transfer programme. In such circumstances, it might even be desirable for children to take part of the ration home.... If school feeding programmes are to be successful in encouraging girls' participation in the education system, the 'income transfer potential' of food must be fully utilised" (Levinger, 1986). She also pointed out that school feeding was probably not enough to overcome the effects of abject poverty on education.

A survey of 51 NGO programmes in 18 countries conducted by the ILO in 1995 (Anker and Melkas, 1996) found that food assistance figured prominently amongst the different types of economic incentives provided to reduce child work. All programmes provided for them supplied cooked food at school. On the other hand, opinions were divided in regard to the effectiveness of school lunch programmes in attracting working children to school and keeping them there. A little over half of the respondents (55 per cent) thought that their programmes were effective, whereas 39 per cent held the opposite opinion. Many also pointed out certain practical problems in implementing food assistance programmes, such as that of (a) ensuring that children did not come to school only to eat; and (b) sound targeting to contain programme costs. There is also a feeling that school feeding alone was not sufficient to retain working children in school if the quality of the education and its relevance to poor families was not ensured.

In India, the school feeding programme has a long tradition and in some states can be traced to as early as the 1920s. In 1995, the government launched the centrally-sponsored National Programme of Nutritional Support to Primary Education, or Mid-day meal (MDM) scheme. It aims at enhancing the nutritional status of children and promoting enrolment, retention and attendance in elementary education by encouraging poor parents to admit and retain their children in school. Under this programme, children either receive a meal at school or a dry ration to take home (3 kg of grain per month), conditional upon regular attendance. Unfortunately, there are numerous problems with the implementation of the scheme such as irregularity and insufficiency of supplies, a complicated implementation system and lack of community co-operation. Not surprisingly, an evaluation of programme results revealed a mixed pattern. While enrolment seemed to have increased, there were no traceable effects on attendance and little change in the generally high rates of drop-out.[8]

The World Food Programme has initiated several food assistance programmes specifically for girls. These programmes target countries and areas where girls' education is particularly underdeveloped and girls are unable to attend school because of their heavy workload. This constraint is addressed by distributing dry take-home food rations to the families who agree to send their girls to school. The type and size of the food ration and regularity of distribution vary depending on local conditions. In Pakistan, for example, girls attending school for at least 20 days per month receive a 5 litre can of vegetable oil which is a precious commodity for local families. At assisted schools, the enrolment of girls increased by some 200 per cent over a period of four years, while it dropped at control schools. Student attendance and drop-out rates were also positively affected. Moreover, the programme has helped develop a positive attitude among parents with regard to girls' education and their status in the family (Meir, 1999). This was also true of a similar programme in Morocco, which distributes 100 kg of wheat and 10 litres of vegetable oil per year to girls who regularly attend primary school. The programme significantly increased the girls' access to targeted primary schools where they now account for 43 per cent of all students, compared to only 10 per cent in the early 1990s. This has been achieved despite the fact that the ration compensates families only partly for the value of a girls' labour and was even reduced since the beginning of the programme (WFP, 2000).

In 1993, the Government of Bangladesh launched a "Food for Schooling" programme under which a monthly ration of grain is distributed to poor families who send their children to primary schools. The ration size depends on how many children are sent to school from the household (maximum 20 kg), and receipt of the ration is conditional upon regular attendance. A recent evaluation (IFPRI, 2001) showed that the programme had been successful in increasing enrolment and ensuring regular attendance and in reducing drop-out rates. For example, the introduction of the programme resulted in a 35 per cent increase in enrolment, whereas in control schools, number of students increased by only 7 per cent during the same period. Notably, enrolment for girls increased by as much as 44 per cent compared to 28 per cent in the case of boys. The gender-differential effect of the programme is supported by the findings of several other school-feeding studies (e.g., from Morocco, India, Dominican Republic) (WFP, 1999). On the other hand, the success of the programme had a negative effect in terms of overcrowding and thus a reduction in educational quality and student-achievement at assisted schools. Targeting mechanisms were also found to need improvement in identifying poorest households.

However, a World Bank review of the same programme found that the increase in school enrolment and attendance had only partly reduced the incidence of child work, and that the effect was particularly limited for girls. It observed that "the reduction in the incidence of child labour by boys (girls) represents about one quarter (eighth) of the increase in their school enrolment rate. Parents are clearly substituting other uses of their children's time, so as to secure the current income gain from access to the programme with modest impact on earnings from their children's work" (Ravallion and Wodon, undated). The review also pointed out that programme results had been achieved despite the fact that the value of the stipend was considerably less than the mean child wage.

As mentioned above, in-kind incentives and particularly food-assistance programmes are amongst the most common forms of incentives provided for promoting school education. According to an ILO survey, NGO representatives preferred in-kind payments over cash grants because they were felt to be less open to misuse and corruption (Anker and Melkas, 1996). There are also indications that food, rather than other types of in-kind support, is particularly valuable to poor families. For example, reviews of the different types of incentive schemes in

India found that school meals had a relatively greater effect on enrolment and retention and were the preferred option of students and parents (Meir, 2000). A report on a WFP-assisted food assistance programme for girls from Niger observed: "In rural areas, the main characteristic of poverty is hunger. Food aid is probably the only form of aid which is capable of overcoming traditional barriers to girls' education and creating a real motivation for sending girls to school (Hamza, 1998)." This is supported by WFP's own research which points out that "food is a form of assistance which meets one of the most basic needs of poor families, who typically devote 65 to 70 per cent of their income to food."[9]

The main conclusions that emerge from the literature[10] regarding incentive schemes, including food-based incentives are:

(i) Food assistance programmes and other incentives are not a panacea but contribute, amongst others, towards reducing or eliminating child work and promoting education for all. In particular, they will not be effective in bringing all children into school as long as the educational quality remains poor and parents and children are not motivated about educating their children. Moreover, while incentive programmes can facilitate the education of working children they cannot completely prevent children from working.

(ii) Incentives clearly have positive impact on enrolment and retention at schools by transferring income to the families of school children. However, it is unclear whether this works through a direct exchange for children's time or through other factors. In other words: does the value of the income transfer have to be equivalent of the value of the children's labour which is lost by their attending such programmes in school? Several analysts claim that it does (Anker and Melkas, 1996; Levinger, 1986). On the other hand, experience from Bangladesh and Morocco shows that significant results can be achieved even with relatively reduced food rations. Although incentives should probably not fall short of a certain minimum value, this appears to be in line with the previous observations that child work is not the only factor which keeps children out of school and that attending school will not automatically result in children giving up work. In addition to substituting for income lost, incentives also appear to encourage parents to overcome other obstacles to the education of their children.

(iii) Incentive programmes are more likely to be effective if they include a 'critical mass' of programme elements to address the complex web of factors causing child work and under-education. This will not only increase impact but also the sustainability of programme results such as the (risk of children returning to work when incentives stop. Additional elements in such programmes should include, for example, income-generating activities for adults to reduce their dependence on their children's income, raising community and family awareness against child work and in favour of education, raising the educational level of adults, particularly women or, not least, improving school quality, relevance and accessibility.

(iv) Decentralisation, bottom-up approaches and adaptability to local conditions should be the key features of incentive schemes, as in the case of development programmes in general. Meaningful community involvement, in particular, is essential for the success of such programmes. Thus, parents should be partners at all stages of a programme's implementation. This helps ensure that programmes are locally understood, and accepted, which will result in their effective implementation. Programmes need to be sensitive to the local economic and cultural context. Another factor essential to their success is decentralised programme management, by involving local NGOs or other groups.

(v) Programmes should be well targeted to areas and population groups where they are most relevant, i.e., where poverty, food insecurity (in the case of food incentives) and the incidence of child labour are highest and education is underdeveloped. This will not only help contain the potentially high costs but also increase programme effectiveness. Food incentives, for example, may be particularly relevant in areas where girls' education is at an initial stage, as this could help 'kick off' a process of sending girls to school (WFP, 2000).

2. Food Assistance to Make Schools More Attractive

If working children are to attend school, schools need to become a more viable, valuable and interesting option for children and their parents. School feeding and take-home food rations programmes can contribute towards this objective in several ways. Firstly, the distribution of food at school will itself make the school more attractive. At the same time, school feeding programmes can be a formidable vector to stimulate parental support, interest and participation in education. This, in turn, is widely recognised as a key strategy for improving the level of education at the local level (see, for example, the experience with Village Education Committees under the *Lok Jumbish* or *Shiksha Karmi* programmes in India). School feeding programmes are designed to ensure their relevance to the needs of poor families and parents usually go fully motivated to lend them their support. Where parents are in charge of food preparation and distribution they need to form a committee which can be the first step towards a more broad-based parents' committee. Levinger (1986) pointed out that communities often need to achieve a certain degree of organisation in order to become eligible for successfully organising a school feeding programme (e.g., working together for the construction of storage or cooking area). At the same time, success in this area may reinforce parents' belief that community organisation can lead to concrete benefits. Experience from Pakistan shows that parents kept a close watch over the functioning of their local school and the presence of the teacher introducing a take-home rations programme (since this was a condition for programme continuation) (Meir, 1999).

3. School Feeding can Improve Learning Capacity of Working Children

The research on school feeding programmes shows that they have a great potential to improve the learning capacity of students and, eventually, their learning achievements (WFP, 1999). When children come to school on an empty stomach and remain hungry for several hours they experience 'temporary hunger' which has been shown to seriously reduce their cognitive function. The effects of temporary hunger are worst in, but not limited to, already malnourished children. This can be overcome by distributing a snack or meal at school, preferably soon after children arrive in class. For additional benefit, the food can be enriched with essential micronutrients (e.g., iron, iodine, vitamin A) if these are lacking from the children's normal diet. It is safe to assume that working children, who are often from poorest families, are also relatively more affected by hunger and malnutrition. Moreover, those who combine work and school are probably more tired and have less energy to study than their non-working peers. This is supported by the aforementioned observation that working children perform less well in school. For these children, a feeding programme at school can make a significant difference to their health.

III. HOW FOOD ASSISTANCE IN RURAL INDIA CAN HELP PROMOTE EDUCATION AND OVERCOME CHILD WORK

As outlined above food assistance can contribute in a variety of ways to breaking the vicious circle of child work and under-education. In the food distress-prone areas of rural India, this could be translated into a school feeding programme in the following ways:

1. School Feeding as an Incentive and Nutritional Support

A well-designed and implemented school feeding programme can go a long way towards increasing school enrolment, attendance and retention of working children and allow them to gain greater benefit from the teaching provided. Food as an incentive, as compared to other types of income transfer, is particularly appropriate in areas of high food insecurity. Such a programme is also justified by the prevalence of hunger and undernutrition in these areas. However, the current mid-day meal (MDM) scheme of the Government of India is ill-suited to meet these objectives and needs to be improved in several ways (Meir, 2000):

(i) By adjusting the design of school feeding to meet its objectives: While food as an incentive can be distributed either directly at school or in the form of dry rations, if the objective is to relieve temporary hunger, children need to consume the food at school. Accordingly, the programme could be reoriented towards feeding at school.

(ii) By identifying a suitable food ration for on-site school feeding: The type of food which is currently distributed is often difficult to prepare and served too late in the day to relieve temporary hunger. A suitable ration should be one that is easy to prepare and has both sufficient nutritional and incentive value, while using commodities readily available to the government.

(iii) By improving the regularity and adequacy of supplies: School feeding can only work if food is supplied regularly and in sufficient quantities, according to set ration scales. Greater programme regularity will also eliminate the current tensions between parents and teachers who are often accused of misusing the food when deliveries are late. This mostly requires improvements in the current, complicated system of food deliveries and logistics, for example, by delegating management responsibility to local bodies such as Panchayati Raj Institutions.

(iv) By involving communities and parents in the operation of the school feeding programme: As mentioned before, community involvement is the key to the success of any incentive programme. This should not only help ensure that the programme is better understood and accepted but also reduce pressure on the teachers who currently bear the brunt of the workload in implementing the scheme, much to the disadvantage of their teaching tasks.

(v) By targeting school feeding to where it is most needed: While the MDM scheme is generally designed to benefit poor, disadvantaged rural areas and urban slums it is unclear to what extent these criteria are followed in practice. Moreover, there seems to be scope for more refined and narrow targeting of the programme, to further enhance its effectiveness and contain costs. While targeting of individual schools, or of students within schools should be avoided for on-site feeding, the programme could be targeted by block which is a relatively small administrative unit and usually quite homogeneous. Using administrative units for targeting also helps ensure acceptance by the general public.

2. Dry Take-home Food Rations: An Additional Incentive for Girls

Girls in Indian society face particular disadvantages both with regard to work and education. They work at least twice as much as boys and perform a major part of domestic tasks and work as agricultural labourers, starting from a very young age. The country-wide primary net enrolment ratio in 1997 was 64 per cent for girls as compared to 78 per cent for boys, and in many rural areas, female literacy is barely above 10 per cent (1991 Census). Opportunity costs are amongst the most important factors which keep girls out of school. At the same time, as is now widely recognised, girls' education is amongst the most significant strategies to combat poverty and improve living standards in many ways (for example, reduced fertility, maternal and infant mortality rates; better family health and nutrition). It also empowers girls to deal with adverse situations better, defend their interests and break out of traditional moulds. The international community has committed itself to eliminating gender disparities in primary and secondary education by 2005.[11] All this warrants special efforts to help girls set aside their traditional work duties and go to school.

While an on-site feeding programme benefits both boys and girls it is unclear whether these will be sufficient to offset the effects of the particular constraints faced by girls in rural India. Several analyses indicate that food incentives for girls need to be more substantial than for boys (Levinger, 1986; WFP, 1999). It may therefore be necessary to provide additional dry-food rations to girls, particularly in those areas where girls' education is least developed and traditional negative attitudes towards sending girls to school is most prevalent. As mentioned before, WFP experience has shown that take-home ration programmes for girls can be particularly effective under such conditions to create awareness of the importance and benefits of girls' education. At the same time, while implementing such a scheme, it is important to:

(i) discuss it with parents beforehand, to ensure that they accept the programme and understand its purpose as well as the reasons for the 'positive discrimination' of girls (which should not create any prejudice for girls);

(ii) make receipt of a food ration by a girl conditional upon regular attendance (e.g., at least 80 per cent average monthly attendance rate) to ensure that girls don't just enrol but actually attend classes; effective community participation will be important to ensure application of this principle;

(iii) use food incentives to increase the number of girls enrolling in school as to tackle the problem of early drop-out. Depending on the local context and needs, food incentives can thus be provided to students in all grades, or limited to the lower grades (if emphasis is on enrolment) or targeted to girls from grade IV upwards where they often begin to drop out in great numbers.

(iv) identify a sufficient food ration. There is no standard rule to determine the necessary size of the food ration to effectively act as an incentive for girls' education. At the same time, there is a widespread feeling that the current dry rations distributed under the MDM scheme (3 kg of cereal per month per girl) are insufficient. In order to contain costs it may be considered necessary to adapt individual rations to the number of girls per family who are sent to school (e.g., provide full ration for first and reduced rations for additional girls enrolling from the same family).

Many parents are demotivated by the poor state of primary and elementary education in many parts of India, particularly in rural areas. Children, thus, end up working in fields and factories, sometimes almost 'by default'. Education is perceived as a responsibility of the state—a state, however, which doesn't take this responsibility seriously. It is thus crucial to mobilise communities to assume greater responsibility of providing education and put pressure on the school system to perform better. Accordingly, community participation and the formation of village education committees are now recognised as the key elements of the strategy to universalise elementary education in the country.[12] As mentioned before, this can be strengthened by a school-feeding programme.

3. Food-Assistance for Residential Bridge Courses for Child Workers

The problems of the origins of child work and under-education in India have not been completely solved. Facts and arguments exist to support both the importance of poverty as the key factor behind child work and the view that other elements, such as state of inertia in education or long standing discriminatory social practices are more important. This latter view is supported, for example, by the work of the MV Foundation in the State of Andhra Pradesh (Oonk, 1998), which has been successful in reintegrating child workers from the poorest families, including girls, in the normal education system. The MV Foundation deliberately avoids the use of incentives to facilitate schooling, relying instead on intensive community work and social mobilisation and effecting improvements in the quality of schools. One element of the model established by the MV Foundation are bridge courses for older children who cannot start a primary school in the first grade. The courses prepare these children for direct entry into a grade corresponding to their age group through several months of intensive training and counselling. Oftentimes, the courses are residential since the Foundation has observed that working children need to be temporarily taken out of their normal family environment to reduce the possibility of them being 'lured back' into work.

It is noteworthy that the work of the MV Foundation has gained wide recognition in India and bridge courses and 'back to school camps' have become part of the government's strategy for bringing out-of-school children into the mainstream of regular schools.[13] The provision of food assistance is an important element of such courses where they are residential, not as incentive but simply because children need to be provided with food while they attend the courses.

4. Provision of Food-Assistance to Promote Parental Education and Literacy

The educational level of parents, particularly of mothers, has a decisive influence on whether children should go to school or work.[14] In particular, women's education, just like education of girls, has multiple beneficial effects on family income and well being, thus again reducing the risk of child work and improving the likelihood of children being provided education. At the same time, educational gender gaps amongst adults are even more serious than for children. According to the latest Census (2001), the overall literacy rate was 76 per cent for men and 54 per cent for women, but in some states the gap is even wider (e.g., in Rajasthan: it is 76 per cent for men and 44 per cent for women).

Amongst other factors (e.g., non-availability or unsuitability of adult education programmes especially for women), this can be attributed to negative socio-cultural practices as well as the very high workload of women which makes it difficult for them to set aside time to attend training. Many women also question the importance of literacy and skills training for themselves. This problems could be addressed through the distribution of food incentives. Food could either be distributed and consumed during the training period or as dry-rations for women to take home and share with their families. The effectiveness of food-assistance in promoting female literacy has been tested in Jhabua district in Madhya Pradesh with promising results: amongst women who benefited from this assistance, 84 per cent successfully completed the literacy training, whereas amongst non-participating women the success rate was only 56 per cent (Akhtar, 2001).

IV. CONCLUSION

Food assistance can be an important element in the battle against child work and under-education in rural India. At the same time, it can only be a part of a comprehensive package of interventions to tackle these ills. It must also be recognised that, at least in the immediate future, food assistance will only partly solve the issue of child work since most children can be expected to continue with some form of work, even if they attend school. Nevertheless, a greater spread of elementary education, particularly among girls, will have substantial longer-term effects on improving food security and living conditions and reducing child work amongst the poorest people in rural India.

Notes

1. UN Economic Commission for Latin America and the Caribbean, quoted in UNICEF, 1997.
2. Ibid.
3. According to the PROBE (1999) survey, which focused on some of the most backward villages in northern India, 98 per cent of parents wanted their sons to attend school and 89 per cent wished the same for their daughters.
4. The author refers to a Common Position of all UN agencies in India on the issue of child labour, including UNICEF, ILO and UNDP, publicised in October 1998.
5. The PROBE Team, 1999.
6. Ibid.
7. The Dakar Framework for Action; Education for All: Meeting Our Collective Commitments; Adopted at the World Education Forum, (2001), Dakar, Senegal, April 26-28.
8. ORG (1999), *Evaluation Study to Assess the Efficiency and Effectiveness of the National Programme for Nutritional Support to Primary Education in Ten States of India; Final Report,* Operations Research Group: New Delhi, July.
9. *Enabling Development* (1999), WFP, Rome, May.
10. This is based on the following documents: Anker and Melkas, 1996; UNICEF, 1997; ILO/UNICEF, 1997; Prather, 1996.
11. The Dakar Framework for Action, April 2000.
12. *Sarva Shiksha Abhiyan: A Programme for Universal Elementary Education in India,* (undated), Ministry of Human Resource Development, Department of Elementary Education and Literacy, New Delhi.
13. Ministry of Human Resource Development, Department of Elementary Education and Literacy (undated).
14. See, for example, Tembon and Al-Samarrai, 1997; Canagarajah and Coulombe, 1997; Ravallion and Wodon (undated).

References

Akhtar, Wasim (2001), "Role of Food in Rural Development", Paper presented at *Consultation on Towards Hunger Free India,* World Food Programme, New Delhi, April 24-26.

Anker, R. and H. Melkas (1996), *Economic Incentives for Children and Families to Eliminate or Reduce Child Labour,* ILO, Geneva, May.

Canagarajah, S. and H. Coulombe (1997), *Child Labour and Schooling in Ghana,* Policy Research Working Paper No. 1844, The World Bank, Washington DC.

Filmer, Deon (1999), "Educational Attainment and Enrolment Profiles: A Resource Book Based on Analysis of Demographic and Health Survey Data", Development Research Group, The World Bank (mimeo).

Hamza, Halima (1998), *Rapport de Consultation, Project PAM/Niger 2445.04 "assistance alimentaire aux écoles en milieu nomade et transhumant"*, Niamey, June.

Heady, Christopher (2000), *What is the Effect of Child Labour on Learning Achievement? Evidence from Ghana,* Innocenti, Working Papers No. 79, UNICEF, Florence.

IFPRI (2001), *Food for Education: Feeding Minds Reduces Poverty,* International Food Policy Research Institute, Washington (as published on the IFPRI website: www.ifpri.org).

ILO/UNICEF (1997), *Strategies for Eliminating Child Labour: Prevention, Removal and Rehabilitation* (Synthesis Document), International Conference on Child Labour, Oslo, Norway, October .

Levinger, Beryl (1986), *School Feeding Programmes in Developing Countries: An Analysis of Actual and Potential Impact,* Agency for International Development, Washington, January.

Meir, Ute (1999), *End of Term Evaluation of the WFP Country Programme in Pakistan,* Technical Report, Education Sector; UNESCO, Paris, January.

—— (2000), *Review of Possibilities for WFP Support to the Education Sector in India.* UNESCO, Paris, July .

Oonk, Gerard (1998), "Elementary Education and Child Labour in India: India Committee in the Netherlands," July, (as published on the following website: www.india.net.nl/liw_f_e.html).

Oxfam International (2000), *Education Now: Break the Cycle of Poverty*, UK.

Prather, Cynthia (1996), *Exploring Incentives: Promising Strategies for Improving Girls' Participation in School,* U.S. Agency for International Development, Washington.

Ravallion, M. and Q. Wodon (undated), *Does Child Labour Displace Schooling? Evidence on Behavioural Responses to an Enrolment Subsidy*, The World Bank, Washington.

Tembon, M. and S. Al-Samarrai (1997), *Who Gets Primary Schooling and Why? Evidence of Gender Inequalities within Families in Guinea,* IDS Working Paper 85, Institute of Development Studies, Brighton.

The PROBE Team (1999), *Public Report on Basic Education in India,* Oxford University Press, New Delhi.

UNICEF (1997), "Education and Child Labour Background Paper", *International Conference on Child Labour,* Oslo, Norway.

UNESCO (2000), *Education for All Assessment - Statistical Document,* UNESCO, Paris.

WFP (1999), *School Feeding Handbook,* World Food Programme, Rome.

WFP (2000), *Girls on the Frontline: Take-home Rations for Girls' Education*, World Food Programme, Rome.

18

Averting Food Insecurity: The ICDS Programme and Its Implications

D.B. GUPTA, ANIL GUMBER, POUSHALI MAJUMDAR, V.S. SARAVANAN AND DALIP KUMAR

I. INTRODUCTION

The health of a nation is a sum-total of the health of its people, communities and settlements as well as the overall climate within which the people and communities live. In the last five decades, there has been significant progress in various human indicators including the state of health in the country. But sadly, this advancement has been uneven and restricted to a few selected states. A very large part of the Hindi-speaking areas of the country, as well as the states of Orissa and Assam remain poorly developed. Interestingly, even in the better off states such as Kerala, Maharashtra, and Punjab, there are pockets such as the Malabar Coast and the high-ranges of Kerala, where the health status of people has remained stagnant over the years. Further, the progress in this indicator in respect of the health status of the vulnerable population, including women and children also remains sluggish.

In fact, a very large proportion of India's child population under six years still remain moderately and severely malnourished. Besides, a significant number of the newly born are underweight. It is generally agreed that early childhood is a crucial period in one's life when the foundation for cognitive, social, emotional and physical development is laid. A malnourished child is vulnerable to various diseases impacting on his/her cognitive development and nutritional status.

Ever since India's independence, the Government of India has sought to provide at least the minimum health facilities that integrated family welfare with nutrition for women and children. Keeping in mind the large size of our young population, schemes for child development have been given a place is the main frame of India's planning process right from the First Plan itself. While in the initial years, the main responsibility of developing childcare services had rested primarily with voluntary organisations, the Central Social Welfare Board, set up in 1953, assumed the lead role in promoting and assisting voluntary efforts in this area. Subsequently, a number of programmes—Welfare Extension Project, Applied Nutrition Programme and Special Nutrition Programme - were launched. However, these programmes made only a limited impact as resource constraints and a fragmented sectoral approach prevented the development of a co-ordinated strategy.

The Fifth Plan saw a shift in focus from child welfare to child development with integration and convergence of sectoral social inputs for the well being of infants, children, pregnant and lactating women. The National Policy for children enunciated in 1974 provided added impetus to programme implementation and in pursuance of this policy the 'pilot' project, the Integrated Child Development Services (ICDS) Scheme, was launched on an experimental basis in 33 blocks across the country. The scheme was given a boost during the Eighth Plan when it was decided to gradually extend this programme to cover the entire country. Currently, it covers 4200 projects in the country (Annual Report of the Development of Women and Child Development (DWCD), 1999-2000.

This paper attempts to establish a relationship between the ICDS programme, Food Security and Child Work. The underlying rationale behind this effort is that the first six years of a child's life constitute the most critical period in its growth since 80 per cent of the mental growth and 40 per cent of the physical

Figure 1
Poverty Food Insecurity Cycle

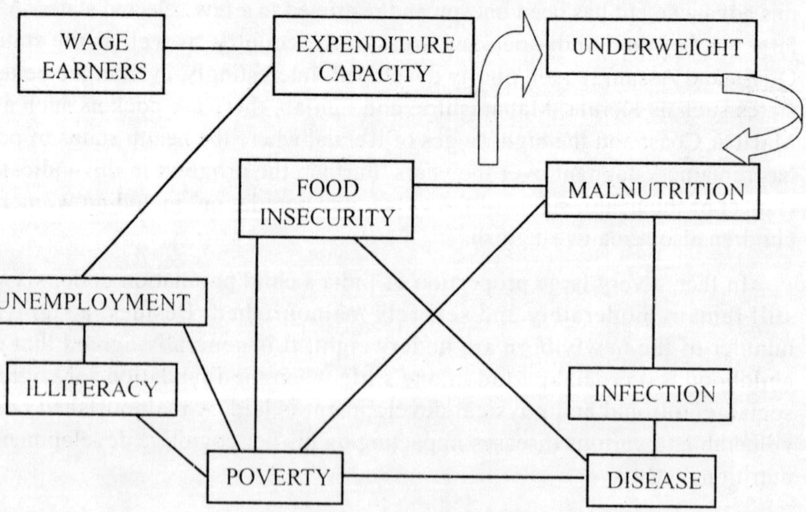

WAGE EARNERS
EXPENDITURE CAPACITY
UNDERWEIGHT
FOOD INSECURITY
MALNUTRITION
UNEMPLOYMENT
ILLITERACY
INFECTION
POVERTY
DISEASE

growth takes place during these years. Dietary inadequacy during pregnancy combined with malnutrition, poor environmental sanitation, and lack of medical services makes the child more vulnerable to disease and infection. Inevitably, such children grow up to be unhealthy and disabled adults with poor productivity, who only become an added burden on the nation. *Women and child welfare should thus form the basis of any strategy aimed promoting at human resource development.* This will help in shaping them into adults capable of contributing to the social and economic development of the country. Significantly, these programmes also have a positive impact on women's empowerment, gender discrimination, education, health, and many related issues, which impact directly or indirectly on food security. (Figure 1)

II. ICDS IN INDIA: A CASE STUDY

The basic objective of the ICDS scheme was to promote the holistic development of children upto six years, through strengthening the capacity of caregivers and communities and ensuring improved access to basic services at the community level. Initially, the programme was targeted at children upto six years. However, it was realised that an improvement in the child's health and nutritional status depended on the mother's health during the pre-pregnancy period, as well as on the type of attention and care that she could provide to the newly born. This resulted in the inclusion of women in the reproductive age group, 15-45 years and adolescent girls (11-18 years) in the programme, with special emphasis on the nutritional and health needs of pregnant and lactating women. In effect, the programme has emerged as a multi-sectoral package offering supplementary nutrition, immunisation, health and nutrition education, growth monitoring and promotion, pre-school education and a first level link to enable poor families to access referral services.

Integrated Child Development Services (ICDS), the only community-based nutritional programme to address the major food security needs, is perhaps the largest programme engaged in a wide range of nutrition-related activities in India. It must be admitted that a major constraint in assessing nutritional improvement in the weaker section of the population is the limited availability of information at the national level, though some indirect results are available from a number of evaluations of the programme. Some surveys have demonstrated that the services provided under the ICDS programme have had some positive impact on both nutritional status and on IMR. The chain envisaged under the programme is that the provision of food would help in improving the nutritional intake, and hence nutritional status of the vulnerable groups, eventually resulting in their reduced morbidity and better living standards. Unfortunately some ICDS evaluations show that in most cases, the food provided under the ICDS is taken home, and thus becomes a part of the household food supply. To avoid this situation, the least we can do is to educate the beneficiary households that the food supplement is needed for the vulnerable groups within the households.

1. Reach of ICDS Scheme

According to the DWCD data pertaining to the Status report of ICDS as on September 30, 2000, on an average children were covered for the Supplementing

Nutrition Programme (SNP) per AWC is 71 for SNP and 32 for Pre-School Education (PSE), with considerable inter-state variation. The gender analysis of the coverage is death with below.

Gender Analysis of Coverage of Children

An important dimension concerning food intake and schooling is the bias generally observed in favour of the male child. This has direct relevance to food security and child work issues, an analysis of which was done by carrying out a special tabulation, with the help of recent NCAER data related to ICDS evaluation.

According to the DWCD data there is a negligible difference between the male and female children registered in an AWC. However, the male bias is observed in the actual utilisation of ICDS, (PSE) services, although it varies from state to state. This male bias emerges in the face of intra-household discrimination, as is the case with SNP. Gender differentials were prominent largely with a male bias, especially in West Bengal, Bihar, Uttar Pradesh, Rajasthan and Assam.

One significant observation is that gender discrimination is more prominent in PSE than SNP. This indicates that the older the girls the greater is the pressure on them to stay back home to look after household activities (including sibling care, and household chores), besides the low priority accorded to the education of girls. Even noted activist, Mina Swaminathan, has very often highlighted the issue of childcare, especially that of girls being burdened with sibling care.

It is observed that as the age of the girl child increases, her attendance at the PSE decreases. This clearly indicates the possibility of her being involved in household activities like fetching water or sibling care, etc. The above table (Table 1) for select states shows that there is a male bias in the utilisation of ICDS (PSE) services, although this varies from state to state. However, the bias in favour of boys is found to be prominent in those states where female literacy is low. This male bias is clearly reflected in the existence of intra-household discrimination.

2. Supplementary Nutrition: Key Component of the Scheme

The component of Supplementary Nutrition, the core of the ICDS programme, is critical for fighting/preventing malnutrition in the crucial years of growth (both before and after birth). This comprises:

a) a food supplement (provided to children up to six years as well as to pregnant and nursing women) to bridge the caloric (and protein) gap in their daily dietary intake, and

b) Vitamin A and/or Iron-Folic Acid doses (administered to children up to six years and pregnant women, respectively) to prevent the deficiency of these two micronutrients.

Some other factors that bear on the timely and adequate provision of supplementary nutrition are discussed below:

Table 1
Gender Analysis of ICDS Beneficiaries across States

State	Percentage of enrolled children attended PSE last week prior to the date of survey	
	Boys	Girls
Andhra Pradesh	83	83
Karnataka	82	80
Kerala	67	66
Tamil Nadu	50	41
Bihar	50	75
Assam	64	86
West Bengal	108	61
Orissa	73	86
Punjab	30	24
Jammu & Kashmir	27	31
Himachal Pradesh	42	42
Haryana	41	52
Delhi	47	56
Rajasthan	71	136
Gujarat	63	64
Maharashtra	56	77
Madhya Pradesh	77	79
Uttar Pradesh	61	146
Sikkim	36	45
Tripura	53	71
Meghalaya	53	59
Manipur	50	40
Nagaland	25	36
Arunachal	87	70
Mizoram	64	70
All India	65	78

Note: The figures include both eligible and non-eligible children and as a result the percentages may exceed 100.

Source: NCAER, ICDS Field Survey, 1999.

(i) Availability of Inventories

The availability of inventories plays an important part in the effective delivery of services. The inventory for supplementary nutrition consists of cooking pots for cooking food supplements, storage vessels for storing raw food materials, and vessels for serving meals (including plates, spoons and other serving utensils). While in most of the states, inventories for SNP were found to be adequate, in many of the southern states, Uttar Pradesh, Bihar, Orissa and in a few Northeastern states, they were inadequate. Of the three main inventories, a higher percentage of AWCs reported availability of cooking pots than serving and storage vessels, which were reported to be inadequate in many of the Northeastern states.

(ii) Duration of Service Provided and Consumption of Food

According to the National Institute of Public Cooperating and Child Development (NIPCCD) report (1992), 27 per cent of the AWCs did not receive any nutrition supplement for over 90 days, i.e. the average disruption in their supply was for 63.7 days. This in turn had its effect on the functioning of the AWC during this period. In some cases the AWCs are closed altogether for weeks due to the non-availability of nutrition supplements. In addition, there are other factors like the poor attendance of children of the working parents belonging to the poorest sections as a result of which these children cannot avail of these services to the fullest extent. Similarly, the provision of a double ration to the severely malnourished children is often ineffective, because such children are often incapable of eating much at one go. Again, often the morning hours appear to be the time when pregnant and lactating women are busy with domestic chores and hence their attendance at AWCs for providing these services, specially for supplementary nutrition, tends to be poor. A flexibility of the AWC timings to account for the pre- occupation of these women during the morning hours would be required in such cases.

It has been reported that in some AWCs, the Iron and Folic Acid (IFA) tablets are not administered at the proper time and as a result they become brittle, powdered and even discoloured, which sometimes make them unfit for human consumption. Also, in dispensing Vitamin A to children, it is reported that the doses are not administered in the required quantities.

Food supplements are mainly provided to children and women at AWCs. To ensure that the benefits reach the target population, it is preferable for the beneficiaries to consume the food supplement within the AWCs. However, due to the prevalence of socio-cultural factors it becomes necessary for them to consume food at home. At the same time, those who do so, as was seen in NCAER's pilot survey, especially in the case of the ready-to-eat foods, do not benefit from the intake of the supplement provided as part of any nutrition programme, because most of those who take food home, especially women, share it with others.

(iii) Malnourishment of Children

The incidence of moderate malnourishment and severe malnourishment among children has also been reported in a majority of the states. Table 2, which classifies children by the grade of malnutrition and by age group across the states, shows that the incidence of moderate malnourishment and severe malnourishment among children is observed in a majority of the states. Among the three age groups, children between 37-72 months reported relatively higher incidence of moderate malnourishment. Except for a few states, the incidence of moderately malnourished children in this age group (37-72 months) was evenly spread. The incidence of severe malnourishment in all the three age groups was less than 2 per cent in most of the states except Bihar.

Table 2
Percentage of Moderately and Severely Malnourished Children across States

State	Normal children			Moderately malnourished (Grade I & Grade II combined)			Severely malnourished (Grade III & Grade IV combined)		
	6-12 Months	13-36 Months	37-72 Months	6-12 Months	13-36 Months	37-72 Months	6-12 Months	13-36 Months	37-72 Months
Andhra Pradesh	77.1	80.3	77.7	17.7	17.8	21.0	5.2	1.9	1.3
Arunachal Pradesh	93.3	98.7	98.0	0.7	1.1	1.8	0.0	0.2	0.2
Assam	85.9	89.2	89.2	12.3	10.8	10.8	1.8	0.0	0.0
Bihar	84.7	68.2	68.9	9.2	3.4	26.4	6.1	28.4	4.7
Delhi	95.5	91.3	84.2	4.1	8.7	15.6	0.4	0.0	0.2
Haryana	95.9	89.2	80.3	4.1	10.7	19.5	0.0	0.1	0.2
Himachal Pradesh	97.6	96.0	86.2	2.2	3.9	13.5	0.2	0.1	0.3
Jammu & Kashmir	99.9	98.9	97.8	0.1	1.1	2.2	0.0	0.0	0.0
Karnataka	82.4	79.4	79.9	14.6	19.2	19.3	3.0	1.4	0.8
Kerala	91.3	88.5	88.5	8.1	11.2	11.2	0.6	0.3	0.3
Madhya Pradesh	97.0	94.9	87.6	2.8	4.8	11.8	0.2	0.3	0.6
Manipur	100.0	100.0	100.0	0.0	0.0	0.0	0.0	0.0	0.0
Meghalaya	100.0	100.0	100.0	0.0	0.0	0.0	0.0	0.0	0.0
Mizoram	96.0	90.3	83.2	3.9	9.4	16.3	0.1	0.3	0.5
Nagaland	100.0	100.0	100.0	0.0	0.0	0.0	0.0	0.0	0.0
Orissa	92.7	89.4	79.5	7.0	9.9	27.2	0.3	0.7	2.3
Punjab	99.1	96.8	92.2	0.9	3.2	7.7	0.0	0.0	0.1
Rajasthan	99.6	97.0	93.7	0.4	2.9	6.1	0.0	0.1	0.2
Sikkim	100.0	98.9	92.9	0.0	1.1	7.1	0.0	0.0	0.0
Tamil Nadu	86.4	84.5	78.1	12.6	12.7	18.4	1.0	2.8	3.5
Tripura	100.0	100.0	95.0	0.0	0.0	3.1	0.0	0.0	1.9
Uttar Pradesh	99.6	98.3	93.5	0.4	1.6	6.3	0.0	0.1	0.2
West Bengal	98.9	93.8	78.2	1.1	6.0	21.2	0.0	0.2	0.6
All states	92.3	80.7	91..9	6.4	7.7	15.7	1.3	3.6	1.4

Source: Same as in Table 1.

The above results suggest that the states that performed well, such as the southern states, have a higher number of moderate malnourishment cases in the age group, 37-72 months. This may be because of certain severely malnourished children moving up the ladder due to the ICDS programme and due to early and accurate identification of malnourishment among children in these states. Another reason for this finding might be the inadequate measures to assess malnourishment among children—one of the commonly used measures in AWCs has been through height and weight of children, which is a crude measure of malnourishment because it does not reflect the anthropometric variations existing across the country.

3. Provision of Health Services

Surveys covering persons below the poverty line reveal that the dietary intake of children and pregnant and lactating women is inadequate. Diets of these women and children are particularly deficient in important nutrients including energy, vitamin A, calcium, iron, and riboflavin (NIN, (Indian Council of Medical Research (ICMR), 1995). This deficiency, along with lack of access to health services by pregnant women and children, is attributed to persistent poverty levels coupled with a large number of dependents. This is also true for children during their crucial period of growth in the first six years, resulting in the vicious cycle of poverty-malnutrition-infection-disease-poverty. Therefore, provision of health services for this vulnerable group assumes a significant role in breaking the vicious cycle of poverty-malnutrition-infection-disease-poverty by reducing Infant Mortality Rate (IMR), Child Mortality Rate (CMR), Maternal Mortality Rate (MMR) and so on. Delivery of health services at AWCs is the second most important component of the ICDS programme, and includes immunisation, health check ups, ante-natal and postnatal care, provision of IFA tablets to pregnant women, treatment of minor illness and referral services. These are discussed below.

(i) Immunisation

On an average immunisation is provided once in a month in the AWCs across the country. Most of the AWCs in the southern states have reported immunisation activity for as many as three times in a month. More than 75 per cent of the children across many states had received immunisation against six major diseases: measles, tuberculosis, diphtheria, pertussis, tetanus and polio myelitis and a marginally lower percentage of children were immunised against these diseases in the northern and northeastern states. Less than 15 per cent of the children were immunised against five diseases, except measles. On an average about 50 children per AWC had availed of vaccinations against all major diseases, subject to variation in the average number of vaccinations between states.

Immunisation of women against these diseases has been comparatively lower, with nearly 30 per cent of the women across the country having received Tetanus Toxoid vaccination. The number of women availing Tetanus Toxoid was above the national average in Himachal Pradesh, Punjab, Orissa, Karnataka and Rajasthan.

(ii) Health Check Up

The number of women who availed of health check ups was lower compared to that of children. On an average, about 30 per cent of beneficiary women have availed of health check up services in the country, of which nearly 70 per cent are from Orissa, Punjab and Mizoram and less than 10 per cent from Gujarat and Goa. A comparatively higher percentage of children were reported to have received these services, especially in a few northeastern and eastern states, while the proportion of those who did so in the rest of the states, ranged between 30-40 per cent.

The coverage of women for antenatal services has been encouraging, with 50 per cent of eligible women availing of the service from AWCs, out of 90 per cent of all women registered at other institutions and more than 50 per cent of them being registered with AWCs. Among the women availing of antenatal services, the percentage of women who availed of supplementary nutrition and received iron and folic acid tablets was higher than those who received Tetanus Toxoid injections.

As far as postnatal services are concerned, Auxiliary Women Worker (AWWs), along with Auxiliary Nurse Midwife (ANM)/Local Health Visitor (LHV) advise lactating mothers on the need for better nutrition, health care, child care practices and also observe the growth of the child through home visits. The percentage of mothers covered through home visits was high with over three-fourth of eligible mothers having been advised on the importance of better nutrition and health care. AWWs in southern, eastern, and northeastern states have carried out more home visits to advise mothers on various requirements of child care after delivery. In most of the states, coverage has remained between 50-75 per cent. They are also involved in advising mothers regarding diet and on an average, they have covered more than 70 per cent of them.

According to Dr. Ramesh Potdar, Secretary, World Congress on Foetal Origins of Adult Diseases Organising Committee (UNI Mumbai, January 10, 2001), an average baby should weigh at least 2.5 kg in accordance with WHO standards and up to 3-3.5 kg. according to scientists. Judged by this norm, around 90 per cent of the babies born in India are underweight, which may be the cause of the rising incidence of adult diseases, especially diabetes and heart trouble. British Paediatrician Caroline Fall explained how the nourishment of a child is important from the foetal stage itself. " The mother is herself undernourished and she gives birth to an undernourished child, and that child grows up to give birth to a generation of undernourished young ones".

The NCAER evaluation shows that 25-50 per cent underweight children are born in as many as seven states and in 13 states less than 40 per cent of the deliveries are institutional. This indicates that although a substantial number of women register themselves for ANC, the component of adequate and appropriate diet might be totally missing. With regard to institutional delivery, the issue needs to be further explored to find out why large numbers of deliveries are taking place at home. All this also has many local, cultural and regional connotations.

Table 3 clearly shows the negative correlation between IMR and Institutional Delivery (ID), which means that if there were a higher number of institutional deliveries then the infant mortality rates would automatically be lower. A similar relation is also observed between mothers mortality rate (MMR) and ID.

(iii) Referral Services

Only a marginal coverage of beneficiaries for referral services has been reported. It was found that a higher percentage of women were provided with referral services compared to children—on an average, about 30 per cent of the women have received referral services in the country. State-wise, the percentage of women beneficiaries who have availed of referral services in Rajasthan, Uttar Pradesh and Delhi is higher than in other states and less than 10 per cent beneficiaries were reported in Goa, Gujarat, Haryana, Nagaland, Orissa and

Table 3
Institutional Delivery and Infant Mortality Rate—A Correlation

State	Institutional delivery	Infant mortality rate	Correlation value
Andhra Pradesh	47	65	
Assam	31	74	
Bihar	11	71	
Delhi	39	NA	
Gujarat	33	61	
Karnataka	65	53	
Kerala	97	14	
Maharashtra	35	48	
Madhya Pradesh	15	97	-0.8975
Orissa	13	96	
Rajasthan	13	85	
Uttar Pradesh	9	85	
West Bengal	49	55	

Sources: 1. *IMR, State Profile, 1991*, Census of India, 1998.
2. *Institutional Delivery*, NCAER Survey, New Delhi, 1999.

Tamil Nadu. In the case of children, referral services have been negligible in the country, except in Madhya Pradesh, Tripura, Uttar Pradesh and Rajasthan, where more than 15 per cent of children were provided with referral services.

The use of medical kits is not popular among the AWCs, of which only about 26 per cent used these kits. In most of the states, between 25-50 per cent of the AWCs used medical kits—in Uttar Pradesh, Maharashtra, West Bengal, and in many of the northeastern states less than 25 per cent of the AWCs were reported using a medical kit. One of the main reasons for non-usage of medical kits could be either their non-availability or these being outdated as was apparent in our visits to some of the AWCs.

4. Monitoring a Child's Growth

Close monitoring of children's growth ensures early identification of malnourishment, so that timely action can be taken. Children upto three years are weighed once a month and those between three and six years, every quarter. Weight for age cards are maintained for all children to enable early detection of faltering growth, or decline in growth since the last measurement. Weighing the child also enables assessment of the child's nutritional status, indicating whether he or she is malnourished and the grade of malnutrition. On the basis of individual growth cards a Community Growth Chart (CGC) is prepared which depicts the current and previous age and genderwise status of all the children.

Growth monitoring depends on the availability of weighing scales and the type of training received by AWCs. Often the growth of the child is being recorded without (a) analysing the implications of growth monitoring and promotion and (b) involving the mothers of the beneficiary child in this service. Detection of patients requiring referrals is also not being pursued in an effective manner. The nutritional status of the child in the early age group of 0-6 years showed a marginal difference over that in the non-ICDS areas, specially in the rural and tribal sectors, according to the NIPCCD report.

5. Pre-school Education

The pre-school education (PSE) component of the ICDS scheme is targeted at children between three and six years. It focuses on the overall development of children up to the age of six years. The programme designed for children in the age group, 3-6 is directed at providing a joyful and stimulating environment, which is conducive for learning. It also prepares the child for primary schooling. A primary stimulus for motivating children is the availability of adequate play and learning materials: posters, toys and a learning kit. PSE is not only beneficial for the all round mental development of the child, but also encourages school enrolment and lessens school dropouts. In order to increase the effectiveness of this component, the daily attendance at each AWC has to be increased further.

The inventories for PSE include toys, posters and learning kit. In most of the states, except some of the southern states, Uttar Pradesh, Bihar and a few northeastern states, these are satisfactory. Of the three main inventories, toys were favoured more than posters and learning kits.

Impact of PSE

Almost one-third of households recognised the fact that sending their children of pre-school going age (between 3-6 years) to AWCs had helped in their smooth enrolment in the school. A higher number of households in Andhra Pradesh, Punjab, Haryana, Assam and Nagaland, who sent their children to AWCs, perceived the smooth enrolment of their children in school. However, a smaller proportion of households in Karnataka and Kerala perceived PSE to be beneficial in this respect.

One way to assess the impact of the PSE is the ability of children to perform PSE-related activities: read simple words, count numbers, write alphabets, distinguish objects, colours and recognise pictures. Of the various PSE activities, many of the children reported the ability to count numbers, read simple words and distinguish objects, but in writing alphabets or words and recognising pictures their performance was not considered satisfactory. A higher percentage of children in the eastern and northeastern states were able to perform these activities compared to other states. Most children in Uttar Pradesh, Tamil Nadu, Rajasthan and Madhya Pradesh were reported to have the ability to perform these activities.

6. Households Perception of ICDS's Benefits

It would be interesting to see how the beneficiaries view the ICDS programme in terms of the benefits accruing to them. The programme can be addressed in terms of (a) the services actually available, and utilised by the households and (b) the nutritional, health and education parameters of the programmes. Thus, the programme is analysed on the basis of: (i) Provision of Services and (ii) Perceived Benefits of Households.

(i) Provision of Services

A majority of the households reported receiving services like SNP, PSE, immunisation, NHE, etc. Average to poor response to these services was indicated from the households of Bihar, Assam, Punjab, and Manipur. The satisfaction and benefits derived from these services or inputs offer an important indicator of the functioning of the ICDS programme. These have been assessed by the beneficiaries themselves who also offer insights into the lacunae and potential of the programme.

However, households' responses have not been satisfactory in terms of suggesting various improvements in the delivery of services in the ICDS programme. A few of the households in the country suggested regular functioning of AWCs, improving the food quality, improved facilities, more time allocation to PSE, and other services.

A majority of the households were satisfied with the delivery of the critical components of the programmes—the SNP, PSE and health services. Supplementary nutrition and pre-school education were considered satisfactory by more than 80 per cent of the households. A comparatively lower percentage of the households reported satisfaction at the health related services (immunisation, health check-up and ante/postnatal care). In regard to referral and counselling services, the households reported growth monitoring and treatment of minor ailments to be below average.

However, variations in satisfaction levels exist across the states. In Mizoram, Orissa and Madhya Pradesh, about 90 per cent of the households reported satisfaction with the SNP, PSE and health-related services, only about 80 per cent of the households reported satisfaction with the rest of the services and about 6 per cent on the counselling services of the ICDS. In Assam and Manipur, 30 and 50 per cent of households reported satisfaction with the SNP component, but more than 70 per cent were satisfied with the PSE component. The rest of the services were not found to be generally satisfactory. In Bihar and Nagaland, about 50 per cent of the households reported satisfaction with the SNP, more than 80 per cent reported satisfaction with the PSE component and there was poor response to the rest of the services.

(ii) Perceived Benefits of the ICDS Programme

Perceived benefits of the ICDS Programme have been minimal. This may be due to non-availability of any yardsticks to measure these benefits. The benefits have been assessed in terms of the households' perception of the decline in infant and maternal death rates, decline in morbidity of children, smooth enrolment of children in school, reduction in malnourishment, consciousness of the family members of nutrition habits and improved childcare (Table 4). It is interesting to note that a higher percentage of households perceived smooth enrolment of their children from pre-school to primary level as important benefits of the ICDS programme, compared to the rest. Decline in maternal mortality and child mortality and morbidity was perceived by about 40 per cent of households.

A higher percentage of households in Punjab, Goa, Andhra Pradesh and Bihar felt pre-school education provided under the ICDS programme had enabled smooth enrolment of their children to primary school. However, regarding decline in mortality rates and other benefits, the household's perception in these states was restricted to between 30 and 40 per cent. However, in Karnataka, Kerala and Rajasthan a higher percentage of households perceived the benefits in terms of a decline in mortality and morbidity rates, compared to smooth enrolment.

Table 4
Percentage of Households Reported AW Services as Beneficial by Type of Benefits

State	Infant deaths declined	Mothers death declined	Morbidity of children declined	Smooth school enroll-ment	Reduced malnut-rition	Created conscious-ness about nutrition	Improved child care practice	Immuni-sation consci-ousness	Other
Andhra Pradesh	44.5	42.5	40.5	62.5	30.7	23.5	26.0	8.0	0.4
Arunachal Pradesh	38.0	33.0	20.0	48.0	39.0	26.0	25.0	16.0	28.0
Assam	33.0	36.0	21.0	60.0	26.0	30.0	37.0	20.0	38.0
Bihar	30.0	26.0	34.0	44.0	16.0	22.0	40.0	29.0	45.0
Delhi	43.0	44.0	45.0	43.0	17.0	30.0	27.0	29.0	5.0
Goa	14.5	18.1	18.1	77.0	33.7	46.8	29.4	28.4	0.0
Gujarat	44.6	31.3	36.1	33.3	26.5	31.0	19.5	11.4	0.7
Haryana	38.0	40.0	36.0	48.0	24.0	19.0	16.0	15.0	1.0
Himachal Pradesh	26.0	27.0	29.0	55.0	20.0	22.0	26.0	16.0	1.0
Jammu & Kashmir	28.0	25.0	15.0	34.0	11.0	17.0	29.0	13.0	8.0
Karnataka	79.6	85.4	53.6	21.3	0.0	0.0	0.0	0.0	0.0
Kerala	96.3	64.4	26.3	4.6	0.0	0.0	0.0	0.0	0.0
Maharashtra	40.4	33.2	34.7	44.0	14.3	27.8	19.1	5.3	0.3
Manipur	36.0	27.0	23.0	37.0	21.0	26.0	39.0	18.0	46.0
Meghalaya	30.0	19.0	17.0	36.0	26.0	30.0	33.0	25.0	55.0
Mizoram	69.0	44.0	33.0	43.0	43.0	23.0	29.0	11.0	58.0
Madhya Pradesh	51.0	43.0	46.0	42.0	19.0	21.0	16.0	15.0	18.0
Nagaland	8.0	3.0	2.0	52.0	11.0	46.0	38.0	74.0	77.0
Orissa	42.0	34.0	30.0	34.0	30.0	34.0	31.0	38.0	53.0
Punjab	30.0	30.0	30.0	65.0	10.0	12.0	17.0	10.0	22.0
Rajasthan	55.0	53.0	56.0	39.0	19.0	30.0	26.0	25.0	12.0
Sikkim	6.0	2.0	2.0	39.0	13.0	52.0	3.0	47.0	86.0
Tamil Nadu	21.5	24.7	24.3	36.1	35.1	31.5	31.2	24.3	1.3
Tripura	11.0	9.0	2.0	14.0	32.0	52.0	60.0	22.0	48.0
Uttar Pradesh	42.0	36.0	49.0	41.0	20.0	29.0	27.0	24.0	5.0
West Bengal	23.0	21.0	20.0	35.0	19.0	18.0	20.0	11.0	45.0
All-India	41.1	36.5	34.5	39.1	20.7	24.2	24.2	18.2	17.9

Source: NCAER, ICDS Survey, 1999.

III. IMPACT OF ICDS PROGRAMME ON SELECT CRITICAL INDICATORS

The impact of the ICDS programme on certain critical indicators is discussed below:

1. Women's Empowerment

One desired outcome of the ICDS programme on women's empowerment has been to enhance the decision-making capabilities of women regarding critical issues of nutrition, health and finances. This has also helped in reducing gender discrimination and ensuring uniform distribution of food and other resources among male and female children. Specifically, women's empowerment, is analysed here with the help of certain indicators on decision-making powers of women on health issues, financial matters, time spent, etc.

Select indicators show a positive impact of the ICDS programme on women's empowerment. As women spend more than 75 per cent of their time on childcare and on domestic activities across the country, most beneficiaries thought that the ICDS programme had contributed towards better health care and child development. Many women across the country 'always have a say' in matters concerning their own health and their child's health. However, when confronted with decisions regarding financial matters, they had a small role in taking independent decisions.

2. Antenatal Care

Table 5 shows state-wise comparisons of women who have received antenatal care based on an NCAER study, the findings of which are compared with those of the NFHS and RHS surveys. The Ante Natal Care (ANC) coverage was expected

Table 5
Percentage of Women Enrolled for Antenatal Care

State	NFHS-II	RHS-RCH I	NCAER: Percentage of mothers reporting ANC	NCAER: Percentage of mothers registered with AWC
Andhra Pradesh	93	95	91	53
Arunachal Pradesh	62	52	70	74
Assam	60	64	89	38
Bihar	36	31	83	67
Delhi	84	90	97	19
Goa	99	98	96	53
Gujarat	86	80	96	54
Haryana	58	70	97	20
Himachal Pradesh	87	86	97	27
Jammu & Kashmir	83	64	71	61
Karnataka	86	89	96	48
Kerala	99	99	96	24
Maharashtra	90	89	96	75
Manipur	80	73	93	53
Meghalaya	54	51	67	74
Mizoram	92	37	85	49
Madhya Pradesh	61	59	80	60
Nagaland	60	56	70	70
Orissa	80	79	99	87
Punjab	74	85	93	56
Rajasthan	48	52	94	79
Sikkim	70	71	89	96
Tamil Nadu	99	98	97	81
Tripura	-	75	76	61
Uttar Pradesh	35	47	80	65
West Bengal	90	88	94	41

to be similar or higher among ICDS beneficiaries as the services are provided at their doorstep through AWCs. It was encouraging to note that, except in Jammu & Kashmir, the hypothesis is true for all the other states—in 18 out of 26 states the percentage of mothers reporting ANC was higher than the findings of the NFHS and RHS-RCH and in the remaining states the percentage of mothers reporting ANC was more or less similar to the secondary data. ANC, therefore, plays a significant role in reducing the IMR and MMR.

3. Institutional Deliveries

Table 6 below presents percentages of institutional deliveries in the different states based on studies carried out by NCAER, NFHS and RHS-RCH. The NCAER results are compared with the findings of the NFHS and RHS surveys.

Table 6
Percentage of Institutional Deliveries Across States

State	NFHS II	RHS-RCH I	NCAER
Andhra Pradesh	50	54	37
Arunachal Pradesh	31	31	20
Assam	18	30	31
Bihar	15	17	11
Delhi	59	70	43
Goa	91	92	82
Gujarat	46	42	23
Haryana	22	25	8
Himachal Pradesh	29	38	21
Jammu & Kashmir	36	40	17
Karnataka	51	53	63
Kerala	93	97	95
Maharashtra	53	53	15
Manipur	35	39	24
Meghalaya	17	27	27
Mizoram	58	16	20
Madhya Pradesh	20	24	65
Nagaland	12	10	6
Orissa	23	21	13
Punjab	38	40	22
Rajasthan	22	22	12
Sikkim	32	37	23
Tamil Nadu	79	76	69
Tripura	-	44	26
Uttar Pradesh	16	17	9
West Bengal	40	37	48

Source: NCAER, ICDS Survey, 1999; NFHS-II 1989-99, RHS-RCH (Unpublished).

The percentage of institutional deliveries was expected to be lower as per NCAER's findings than the other surveys as the ICDS beneficiaries are the poorest of the poor and cannot always afford deliveries at institutions. However, in almost all the states, the figures are comparable with those of the general population. Notably, in Assam, Karnataka, Madhya Pradesh, and West Bengal the percentage of institutional deliveries is higher amongst the ICDS beneficiaries. This explains the strong impact that the ICDS programme has been able to make in the area of health services.

4. Immunisation of Children

Table 7 presents percentages of children in different states who received full immunisation, based on studies carried out by NCAER and RHS-RCH. The immunisation status of ICDS beneficiaries was expected to be higher as the immunisation services are provided at their doorstep.

Table 7
Percentage of Children who Received Full Immunisation

State	RHS-RCH	NCAER Phase I
Andhra Pradesh	72	64
Arunachal Pradesh	34	59
Assam	50	74
Bihar	17	45
Delhi	85	88
Goa	85	91
Gujarat	50	84
Haryana	67	80
Himachal Pradesh	87	76
Jammu & Kashmir	70	54
Karnataka	68	84
Kerala	81	90
Maharashtra	77	79
Manipur	59	83
Meghalaya	30	75
Mizoram	30	77
Madhya Pradesh	53	84
Nagaland	39	50
Orissa	56	99
Punjab	72	77
Rajasthan	30	94
Sikkim	63	88
Tamil Nadu	90	91
Tripura	43	62
Uttar Pradesh	43	80
West Bengal	52	90

Source: NCAER, ICDS Survey, 1999. RHS-RCH (Unpublished).

The percentage of children who received full immunisation as per the state-wise NCAER study should be higher than that according to other surveys. Except in Andhra Pradesh, Himachal Pradesh and Jammu & Kashmir, this hypothesis holds true for all the other states with a higher percentage of children having received immunisation among the ICDS beneficiaries than the general population.

5. Malnourishment Status

The perpetuating effect of malnutrition starts to surface even before the baby is born. Of an estimated 190 million children in the world who are moderately or severely malnourished, 73 million, i.e., 40 per cent are Indian children. In India, approximately 70 per cent of children suffer from moderate and severe forms of malnutrition and a high incidence of IMR due to the poor availability of adequate nutrition and health services at affordable prices. Actually, the IMR and malnourishment depends on many complex factors and therefore even if the data is comparable Table 8a & 8b that used in the other studies, it speaks of the impact of the ICDS programme as its beneficiaries are the poorest of the poor. Interestingly, except for Bihar the IMR of the NCAER findings are lower than those of the other studies in all the states. The results of the Survey on malnourishment status are also comparable to those of other studies on the general population. However, while comparing the data on malnutrition one should remember that the data of NCAER consists of the figures based on the records of *anganwadi* workers (AWW) and, therefore, is dependent on the identification skills of the AWW, rather than the actual malnutrition situation.

Table 8a
State-wise Comparative Data on IMR

(Per 1000 births)

State	Infant mortality rate			
	SRS*	NFHS-I	NFHS-II	NCAER
Andhra Pradesh	65	70.4	65.8	50
Assam	74	88.7	69.5	44
Bihar	71	89.20	72.90	87
Gujarat	61	68.70	62.60	32
Haryana	68	73.30	56.80	37
Himachal Pradesh	NA	55.80	34.40	27
Jammu & Kashmir	NA	NA	65.00	40
Karnataka	53	65.4	51.5	22
Kerala	14	23.80	16.30	15
Madhya Pradesh	97	85.20	86.10	55
Maharashtra	48	50.50	43.70	35
Orissa	96	112.1	81	54
Punjab	51	53.70	57.10	21
Rajasthan	85	72.6	80.4	44
Tamil Nadu	53	67.7	48.2	38
Uttar Pradesh	85	99.9	86.7	86
West Bengal	55	75.3	48.7	20

Note: * Data as per 1988-90.

IV. CONCLUSION

A brief description of the services offered under the ICDS programme and its utilisation shows that the ICDS has made a positive impact on the nutritional and health status of the target population comprising children under six years and pregnant women and lactating mothers. The study also shows that pre-school

Table 8b
State-wise Data on IMR

State	Normal children		Moderately malnourished (Grade 1+2)		Severely malnourished (Grade 3+4)	
	NIN	NCAER	NIN	NCAER	NIN	NCAER
Haryana	52.4	85.7	43.1	14.2	4.5	0.1
Himachal Pradesh	46.0	91.6	50.1	8.2	3.9	0.2
Punjab	52.9	94.9	43.6	5.1	3.5	0.0
Rajasthan	37.8	96.5	46.1	3.4	16.1	0.1
Delhi	63.2	88.9	26.5	11.0	10.3	0.1
Bihar	32.2	71.1	37.1	15.8	30.7	13.1
Sikkim	54.3	96.5	40.0	3.5	5.7	0.0
Arunachal Pradesh	30.7	98.5	63.0	1.3	6.3	0.2
Assam	59.4	88.5	36.3	11.1	4.3	0.4
Manipur	63.7	100.0	30.0	0.0	3.3	0.0
Meghalaya	84.5	100.0	14.3	0.0	1.2	0.0
Mizoram	72.9	88.0	25.8	11.6	1.3	0.4
Nagaland	70.1	100.0	26.6	0.0	3.3	0.0
Tripura	55.3	97.4	39.3	1.6	5.4	1.0
Kerala	65.5	89.0	33.3	10.7	1.2	0.3
Tamil Nadu	46.9	82.0	50.7	15.0	2.4	3.0
Karnataka	36.7	80.0	58.4	18.8	4.8	1.2
Andhra Pradesh	33.0	78.4	60.9	18.8	6.1	2.8
Orissa	31.6	81.3	64.5	17.3	3.8	1.4

Notes: 1. Both NIN (National Institute of Nutrition) and NCAER data followoed IAP classification to estimate the extent of malnutirion. NIN data for the first 14 states refer to the period 1994-94 and for the remaining states these refer to 1996.

2. *Special thanks are due to NNMB, Hyderabad for the analysis of the data for the year 1996 in respect of these states on the basis of IAP classification especially for NCAER to carry out this comparative exercise.

education has been helpful in ensuring the smooth transition of children to the formal school system. Select in-depth studies have also shown that the pre-school education component of the ICDS programme has enabled children to get a headstart in learning and life and has led to an improvement in school retention. Another gain of the ICDS has been to create consciousness amongst women on the role of nutrition in both mother and child health. For the cognitive development of the child, both nutritional consciousness and feeding practices have to be ensured during the first 12 months of the child's growth. Here, the Anganwadi Worker has an important role to play as an educator. The ICDS has also made a significant impact in reducing malnutrition and, consequently, infant and child death. Over all, this programme can be viewed as a positive intervention which has made a vital contribution towards tackling the problem of food security and child work in the long run.

References

Census of India (1991), *State Profile, 1991, India,* Registrar General and Census Commissioner, India, Delhi.

Ghosh, Shanti (1997), "Integrated Child Development Programme: Need for Reappraisal", *Indian Paediatrics*, Vol. 34, India.

GOI (1997), *Convention on the Rights of the Child, Country Report,* Government of India, Department of Women and Child Development (DWCD), Ministry of Human Resource Development, New Delhi.

—— (1997), "Integrated Strategies for Young Children and Families: The India Case Study on the ICDS", Paper presented by Sunil Bhargava, Feb 26-28, Cape Town, Africa.

—— (1999-2000), *Annual Report,* Department of Women and Child Development, New Delhi.

NCAER (2000), *The Integrated Child Development Services: Lessons from a Pilot Study* 1996, National Council of Applied Economic Research, New Delhi.

NIPCCD (1992), *National Evaluation of Integrated Child Development Services,* National Institute of Public Co-operation and Child Development, New Delhi.

19

Food Security for Reducing Child Deprivation: Kerala's Remarkable Record

K.P. KANNAN

Of the many achievements of the State of Kerala in India, in the field of social development, the reduction in child deprivation should stand out as the most remarkable. A number of factors converged, despite slow economic growth and high unemployment for a long period of time, to create a favourable social ambience for child development. Of these, the first and foremost is the premium attached to education of the children, responsive state policies with regard to the spread of education as well as primary health care, and lately, the establishment of a food security system that benefited children the most. The success achieved in these areas gave rise to some unintended but positive social externalities that further benefited the children. The most notable is the demographic transition leading to the attainment of replacement level fertility, i.e., an average of two children per couple-by the end of the eighties. This has further enhanced the value of children in the family leading to greater attention being devoted to their upbringing, especially in regard to food, health care and education. The other is the social and political mobilisation of the poor which made it possible to enhance the average family earnings (first through obtaining minimum wages and then a higher than minimum rate of wages), thereby reducing the family's pressure to send children for work. However, a crucial form of state intervention since the mid-sixties in terms of providing food security might have played a key role in reducing child deprivation in terms of reducing the proportion of out-of-school children. It is on this aspect that we focus in this paper.

I. CHILD DEPRIVATION: THE MAIN PROBLEM IN INDIA

If child labour, as classified in official statistics, is perceived as the main problem in India then one is missing the trees for the wood. It varied from 5.4 in 1991 (as per the Census) to 6.2 in 1993-94 (as per the National Sample Survey) covering the age group, 5-14. While the incidence of child labour is high in a few states, the overall incidence is not so alarming. In the international context, child labour refers to the age group, 10-14. Even then the incidence of child labour in India at 13 per cent cannot be considered high because it is the same as the world average (for 1997). The regional average for South Asia is higher at 16 per cent indicating the higher incidence in the neighbouring countries such as Pakistan (17 per cent), Bangladesh (29 per cent) and Nepal (44 per cent). The incidence in Sri Lanka is the lowest (2 per cent) which compares well with the State of Kerala (one per cent) in India. Only in Sub-Saharan Africa (with 30 per cent) is the incidence higher than in South Asia.

A narrow focus on child labour would miss a sizeable segment of the child population who are neither at school nor at work (to qualify as labour). They are known as 'nowhere' children. In the Indian context, it is not difficult to recognise that there is no such category as 'not working' 'out-of-school' children. As discussed in the Workshop Theme Paper (Ramachandran, 2001), 'a child who does not go to school is a working child'. Such work may not qualify for official classification as 'child labour' but it certainly is not devoid of work that combines household work to manage the home as well as to assist in a variety of ways to contribute to livelihood. Those children who are out of school "stay at home to care for cattle, tend younger children, collect firewood, and work in the fields" (Weiner, 1991). It is, therefore, my contention that the discussion on child labour should be focused on children out-of-school, who are working in one way or another to help themselves and/or their families. It is in this sense, I use the term 'child deprivation' here.

Even when there is a slow decline in the share of out-of-school children in India, the problems continue to be alarming both in terms of share as well as magnitude. As per the 1961 Census the proportion of deprived children was 60 per cent for boys and 80 per cent for girls. This came down to 43 and 54 per cent, respectively in 1991. This wider focus on out-of-school children who are presumed to be working is indeed crucial in the Indian context because the narrower category of child labour hardly captures the magnitude of the problem (Table 1). It is for this reason that attempts to correlate incidence of poverty with that of child labour do not show a convincing relationship (Mahendra Dev, 2001). This seeming puzzle of the lack of a close correspondence between income-poverty and child labour seems to solve itself if one is prepared to look at the problem in a broader framework. This calls for widening the notion of poverty to one of household deprivation and that of child labour to out-of-school children. Viewed in this way, it seems that there is a close correspondence between states with low social development and high incidence of out-of-school children (Table 2).

Table 1
Percentage of Deprived Children Across States, 1961 and 1991
(Child Labour + 'Nowhere' Children)

1961										
		Boys					Girls			
Rank	State	CL	NWC	DC	Rank	State	CL	NWC	DC
1	Kerala	3.4	30.4	33.8	1	Kerala	3.0	39.3	42.3
2	Tamil Nadu	14.5	34.3	48.8	2	Himachal Pradesh	13.8	52.2	66.0
3	Himachal Pradesh	9.3	39.7	49.0	3	Tamil Nadu	10.6	57.5	68.1
4	Maharashtra	13.6	36.7	50.3	4	Punjab	7.1	61.8	68.9
5	Gujarat	11.4	42.4	53.8	5	Maharashtra	14.1	58.7	72.8
6	Karnataka	18.3	38.4	56.7	6	Gujarat	10.6	62.7	73.3
7	Punjab	14.6	42.8	57.4	7	Karnataka	12.6	63.4	76.0
8	West Bengal	7.8	49.6	57.4	8	West Bengal	2.0	74.5	76.5
9	Orissa	18.9	38.7	57.6	9	Haryana	6.0	72.3	78.3
10	Haryana	12.3	45.4	57.7	10	Orissa	10.5	69.1	79.6
11	Andhra Pradesh	24.0	40.1	64.1	11	Andhra Pradesh	17.4	63.3	80.7
12	Bihar	14.0	51.2	65.2	12	Madhya Pradesh	18.3	70.6	88.9
13	Madhya Pradesh	19.3	47.2	66.5	13	Bihar	9.6	81.1	90.7
14	Rajasthan	21.4	48.8	70.2	14	Rajasthan	19.8	71.4	91.2
15	Uttar Pradesh	13.3	58.0	71.3	15	Uttar Pradesh	6.7	85.3	92.0
	India	14.6	45.5	60.1		India	10.6	69.4	80.0

1991										
		Boys					Girls			
Rank	State	CL	NWC	DC	Rank	State	CL	NWC	DC
1	Kerala	0.5	12.9	13.4	1	Kerala	0.4	12.9	13.3
2	Himachal Pradesh	2.2	20.3	22.5	2	Himachal Pradesh	2.8	26.7	29.5
3	Tamil Nadu	4.4	21.3	25.7	3	Tamil Nadu	4.3	27.8	32.1
4	Maharashtra	4.1	24.8	28.9	4	Maharashtra	4.5	32.1	36.6
5	Gujarat	4.7	27.4	32.1	5	Punjab	0.5	39.1	39.6
6	Haryana	3.0	30.2	33.2	6	Gujarat	2.7	38.2	40.9
7	Punjab	4.9	28.9	33.8	7	Haryana	1.0	43.6	44.6
8	Karnataka	8.2	28.5	36.7	8	Karnataka	6.5	39.5	46.0
9	Orissa	5.6	33.9	39.5	9	Orissa	2.8	49.2	52.0
10	Andhra Pradesh	9.1	35.3	44.4	10	West Bengal	1.8	54.3	56.1
11	Madhya Pradesh	6.6	38.2	44.8	11	Andhra Pradesh	9.4	48.0	57.4
12	Rajasthan	4.4	41.5	45.9	12	Madhya Pradesh	5.2	52.6	57.8
13	West Bengal	5.1	43.8	48.9	13	Rajasthan	3.8	66.1	69.9
14	Uttar Pradesh	4.6	49.6	54.2	14	Uttar Pradesh	1.3	68.6	69.9
15	Bihar	4.7	52.0	56.7	15	Bihar	1.9	70.5	72.4
	India	5.2	37.7	42.9		India	3.4	50.7	54.1

Note: CL = Child Labour, NWC = 'Nowhere' Children, DC= Deprived Children.
Source: Chaudhri (2000).

II. KERALA'S ACHIEVEMENTS IN REDUCING CHILD LABOUR AND CHILD DEPRIVATION

What makes Kerala's efforts in reducing child labour and deprivation significant is the fact that it seems to have been ahead of the rest of the country in this area for quite some time. However, the proportion of 'out-of-school' children, even in Kerala, was close to 34 per cent for boys and 42 per cent for girls in 1961,

Table 2
Human Poverty Index and Deprived Children Across States, 1991

State	HPI 1996	Deprived children	
		Boys	Girls
Kerala	1	1	1
Himachal Pradesh	NA	2	2
Tamil Nadu	2	3	3
Punjab	3	7	5
Maharashtra	4	4	4
Haryana	5	6	7
Gujarat	6	5	6
Karnataka	7	8	8
West Bengal	8	13	10
Andhra Pradesh	9	10	11
Orissa	10	9	9
Madhya Pradesh	11	11	12
Rajasthan	12	12	13
Assam	13	NA	NA
Uttar Pradesh	14	14	14
Bihar	15	15	15

Source: For HPI, S.Prabhu (1998), and Deprived Children from Table 1.

whereas the figures for all India were 60 and 80 per cent, respectively. By 1991, the figures for Kerala declined to 13 per cent (for both boys and girls), whereas for all India it was 43 and 54 per cent respectively. The NCAER Survey of 1994 (for rural areas) showed that Kerala reported 9 per cent deprived children as against 38 per cent for all India. Had this rate of decline continued till 2000, then the problem in Kerala might have been reduced to a very insignificant level. Indirect evidence suggests that this might indeed be the case—the percentage of children at school is around 100 per cent of those estimated to be in the school-going age group (Table 3). The latter should, however, take into account some children remaining in school even when they have passed the school-going age group.

Table 3
Children in School-going Age Group and Actual Number of Children at School in Kerala

	1991			1996		
	Boys	Girls	Total	Boys	Girls	Total
Age group, 5-15	29.80	29.15	58.95	28.38	27.25	55.63
Children at school	30.12	28.89	59.01	28.57	27.71	56.28
Per cent	101.10	99.11	99.11	100.66	101.69	101.17

Source: Estimated figures for children (in the age group, 5-15) at school from Government of Kerala, *Economic Review* (1999).

The initial advantages that Kerala enjoyed as in 1961, for example, should be viewed within the context of social change in Kerala and the consequent response of the state in terms of formulating pro-poor state policies particularly on land reform, school education and health (UN/CDS, 1975). Since the mid-sixties, Kerala had built up a fairly comprehensive social security system of which food security formed an important part (Kannan, 2001a). However, the significant point here is that even in 1961, the percentage of boys and girls in Kerala who were deprived in the sense of not being able to attend school was 34 and 42 respectively. It is this gap that has since been filled. One cannot claim that this is entirely due to the food security interventions of the state, especially in a situation where a number of factors could have played a mutually reinforcing role. However, it is quite plausible that those who were out-of-school might have come from poorer families and were not able to go to school even when physical access to schooling was ensured. It is in this context that we highlight the role of food security. Our own interaction with social activists from among the school teachers suggests that food security, especially the introduction of the free School Feeding Programme (known as mid-day meal), helped increase enrolments especially from the coastal as well as the hilly areas-the two regions where poverty is concentrated.

The public food security system in Kerala has four elements. The first one is focused on households providing ration cards for purchasing foodgrains at subsidised prices from the Public Distribution System. The second one involves the provision of free lunch to children at mid-day. The third one is a supplementary nutrition programme for pre-school children and pregnant mothers and the fourth one relates to providing old-aged poor with a monthly pension that could take care of at least one meal a day. Thus, the problem of food deficiency is attacked at the household level (first and fourth) as well as directly for the benefit of pre-school and school-going children (second and third) these arrangements are discussed below.

III. FOOD SECURITY AND ACCESS TO FOOD

Two important factors seemed to have weighed on the Government of Kerala in according a high priority to food security. One is the generalised nature of food shortage, especially that of foodgrains, and its political implications. The other is the priority given to people's needs in social development, including social security, so that successive governments are compelled to accord a high priority to food security as part of a wider system of social security for the people. It is for these reasons that in an otherwise highly contested political terrain in Kerala, the question of food security has enjoyed a remarkable degree of political consensus cutting across the ideological spectrum.

Perhaps the most important form of protective social security in Kerala is the food security system. As mentioned earlier, this consists of four important programmes. The functioning of these is explained below.

1. Public Distribution System

Although the PDS in Kerala does not have the advantage of bringing positive benefits through public policy over such a long period as is the case with health care, its origins go back to the pre-independent days when food rationing was introduced in India at the start of the Second World War. It took almost a quarter of a century to establish a Public Distribution System in India as part of the public policy on food security (Mooij, 1996). In Kerala, the system was expanded during 1965 at a time when the state was undergoing an acute food shortage. Hence the present PDS should be reckoned as having started in 1965. This shortage, as we saw earlier, is structural to the Kerala economy in that a major share of value added in the agricultural sector is through the production of cash crops such as coconut, rubber, tea, coffee and spices, etc., which earned or saved considerable foreign exchange for the national economy. Even at the best of times, Kerala could not produce more than 50 per cent of its foodgrain requirements. This was the case until the early seventies. By the mid-nineties the share of internal production declined to a quarter of its requirements (see Government of Kerala, 1999, Table 2.13). This was recognised by the central government which agreed to supply foodgrains (mainly rice and wheat) to meet the requirements of the PDS. Therefore the introduction of the PDS in Kerala is indicative of the overall concern of the state to take care of its food security. As such, almost all the households have now been brought under the PDS, resulting in the establishment of a large network of ration shops throughout the state (Table 4).

Several studies have underlined that the Kerala PDS is by far the most efficient and egalitarian system under Indian conditions where access of the poor to food remains the single-most important factor in determining their poverty status. The salient features of the Kerala PDS, which has been showing signs of strain since the policy shift at the centre from the early nineties assume much importance in the all-India context of the need for an effective PDS and thus have been summarised below. This indeed has a child dimension since the vulnerability of children in the face of food insecurity is the highest.

Table 4
Public Distribution System in Kerala

Year	Household ration cards (lakhs)	Ration permits to institutions (nos.)	Distribution of Rice (000 m.ts)	Wheat (000 m.ts)	Sugar * (000 m.ts)	Kerosene* (000 kl)
1975	36.16	7634	531	490	97	107
1985	43.73	7922	1412	110	142	235
1995	56.54	13173	1130	423	150	360
2000	62.62	17528	614	62	NA	NA

Note: * Allotment only.
Source: Government of Kerala, *Economic Review,* Various Issues.

(i) Universal Coverage

The coverage is universal in that 97 per cent of the households have ration cards. In addition, a number of institutions have also been issued ration cards, as has been the case for the last three-and-a-half decades. As of last year, there were more than 62 lakh family ration cards and more than 17 thousand ration permits given to institutions. It must be mentioned here that the dual pricing policy implemented by the central government since April 2000 had indeed adversely affected the PDS in Kerala almost immediately. Table 4 shows that the quantity of rice distributed during 2000 declined to around 40 per cent of that distributed during 1997 and 1998. In the case of wheat, it declined to around 15 per cent. Such large declines, as mentioned earlier, were due to the dual pricing policy, under which the price went up for everyone, but that for 'above poverty line' households reached a level equivalent to the open market price. This resulted in moving these households away from the PDS for purchase of foodgrains.

(ii) Physical Access

This is an important consideration in the Indian context. If the time and energy required to purchase the ration is significantly higher than what it would otherwise take (i.e., in the open market), it entails an opportunity cost to the families. The widespread network of ration shops in Kerala numbering more than 14 thousand has ensured physical access in both rural and urban areas. The First Economic Census of India, carried out in 1977, reported that 99 per cent of the villages in Kerala have a fair price shop within a distance of two kms; Maharashtra came second with 67 per cent of the villages covered under the PDS. The all-India average was just 35 per cent. From the perspective of child deprivation, the easy physical access to ration shops should be viewed as a very positive factor. They bring down the time spent on visits to ration shops (located at fairly long distances in several parts of rural India) thus reducing the need to depute children for collecting the rations from the ration shops or keeping them at home when adults go to the shops.

(iii) Absence of Urban Bias

While a major drawback of the Indian PDS is its urban bias, this is something that is not found in Kerala. As Suryanarayana (1996) pointed out, if anything, it is somewhat rural-biased in Kerala for the share of rural areas in the total purchase of rice, wheat, sugar and kerosene is higher than its population share. In the case of edible oil (70 per cent), it is only somewhat lower than its population share (74 per cent).

(iv) Economic Access

One of the most powerful arguments for setting up of a PDS is that it ensures economic access. This is because unequal distribution of income and purchasing power renders the poorer sections vulnerable to food security. Given the fundamental constraints (such as distribution of assets and income), the Kerala PDS seems to have addressed this issue effectively in a relative sense. Studies (e.g., UN/CDS 1975; George, 1979; Suryanarayana, 1996) have revealed that nearly two-thirds of the total purchase of rice for the poor in Kerala come from the PDS. While, for the whole population this is around half (51 per cent for rural and 46 per cent for urban in 1986-87). The picture is similar in the case of sugar, whereas with regard to wheat, more than 90 per cent is purchased by all the population through the PDS. The consumption of wheat in the state is low, but is slowly picking up. It would appear that while the per capita consumption of cereal has increased for the entire population-unlike all India-the increase among the poor is considerably higher than that of the population as a whole. Between 1961-94, the lowest three deciles increased their consumption between 32 and 49 per cent in rural areas and 27 to 59 per cent in urban areas, whereas it increased by only 2 per cent in rural areas and decreased by 6 per cent in urban areas for the population as a whole (Suryanarayana, 1996, pp. 23-24). While the average monthly per capita consumption of cereals of the lowest decile was only 52 per cent of the average consumption of the population in 1961-62, it was 71 per cent in 1993-94 in rural areas and 45 and 76 per cent respectively for urban areas. One of the noteworthy features of the Kerala PDS in terms of facilitating economic access is its flexibility in permitting households to purchase their ration in installments rather than in one lot for a given period as is the practice in many other states.

All these features should have led to a serious consideration for replication of the Kerala's PDS in other parts of India where economic and physical access of the poor to food remains a major problem in ensuring their food security and consequently in alleviating poverty. Instead, the recent policy changes of the central government seem to threaten not only the well-established and institutionalised PDS in food-deficit Kerala but also the even more fragile system in the rest of the country (Suryanarayana, 2000). It would appear that the basis for the change in policy was solely on cost considerations driven by the objective of reducing the fiscal deficit. Larger considerations of human development, not to speak of the need to reduce child deprivation, hardly entered the picture.

2. Free Noon-meal Scheme for School Children

While the PDS in Kerala is the most important component of food security for the people in general and poorer sections in particular, provision of cooked food to the vulnerable among the poor (by self-selection) has come to assume a crucial role in the larger scheme of social security. A notable feature of this scheme is that cooked food is distributed free to the targeted groups (children at school) as against distribution of foodgrains at subsidised prices under the PDS. This scheme is also characterised by its relatively earlier vintage (introduced in 1961) as well as its spread throughout the state. The scheme provides approximately 410 calories and 15 grams of protein to school-going children. Till the mid-eighties it was confined to children in the primary classes (I to IV) and in class V, wherever these are attached to the primary schools. Since then the scheme has been extended to children up to Class VIII, roughly corresponding to children in the age group, 6-12 years. The food (usually cooked rice and a curry) is usually prepared in the schools for which a part-time assistant is provided for. The Head Teacher is responsible for organising the scheme and the teachers help in arranging the children and serving the food. The budget provides for noon-meals during 180 school-days in a year.

As mentioned earlier, the scheme also has a pre-independence history. The CDS study on poverty and public policy traced its origins to the mid-1940s when "the princely states of Travancore and Cochin had established a system of free mid-day meals for poor children in the lower primary schools' (UN/CDS, 1975, p.35). However, the scheme in its present form was introduced in 1961, much earlier than the currently well-known scheme introduced in the state of Tamil Nadu in 1982, covering the entire state. Until the mid-seventies, commodity aid for the programme was received from a consortium of American voluntary organisations known as CARE (Cooperative for American Relief Everywhere). Since then the state government has been providing the commodities required from its stock. Table 5 gives an idea of the coverage of this programme. During the sixties and until the end of the seventies, more than 70 per cent of the children in the age group (since Kerala had already achieved high enrolment at the primary stage) were covered. The declining coverage ratio during the eighties may be interpreted as a sign of the declining incidence of poverty as families pull out their children from the scheme when they no longer consider it as a much-needed relief. When the scheme was extended to children in the upper primary stage, the coverage ratio increased, but the nineties have been registering a declining ratio-again a sign of the continuing decline in the incidence of poverty. At the same time, one should note that the coverage ratio is well above 50 per cent, which is almost double the incidence of head-count poverty estimate for Kerala in 1993-94. While the latter provides a clear cut-off mark for poverty, the coverage ratio may be interpreted as a sign of families at the margin of the poverty line, even if somewhat above it, that consider the free noon-meal for their children as a welcome relief.

The most important feature of the scheme, in terms of its impact is, in our view, the direct nature of food transfer to the targeted group, i.e., the children. Children attending school get a meal at noontime on all school days. This stands in contrast to the system of providing foodgrains (i.e., uncooked food) to children for taking home which they share with other members of the family as cooked food. Such systems were tried out in some states (e.g., Orissa, Bihar and Andhra Pradesh).

Table 5
Free Noon-meal for School Children

(In lakhs)

Year	Number of students in primary level	Number of students at upper primary level	Total eligible students	Students enrolled in the scheme	(5)as % of (4)
1	2	3	4	5	6
1979-80	25.76	-		18.12	70
1984-85	25.01	-		14.81	59
1987-88	25.86	17.90	43.76	32.00	73
1990-91	25.27	19.00	44.27	20.57	46
1991-92	24.72	19.30	44.02	24.10	55
1992-93	24.21	19.33	43.54	23.42	54
1993-94	23.72	19.08	42.80	24.00	56
1994-95	23.25	18.67	41.92	21.21	51
1995-96	22.51	18.39	40.90	20.86	51
1996-97	21.98	18.13	40.11	23.75	59

Note: Children in private unaided schools are not eligible for the scheme. The decline in total eligible students is due to the decline in birthrate in Kerala.

Source: Government of Kerala, *Economic Review,* Various Issues.

3. Supplementary Nutrition for Pre-school Children and Nursing Mothers

A third and equally important component of food security is the various schemes for providing supplementary, but free nutrition to pre-school children and expectant or nursing mothers. This scheme is relatively recent (compared to the above two) in terms of its coverage. The CDS study, while noting the existence of such a programme, stated that "in terms of the quantity involved, this programme is not significant" (UN/CDS, 1975, p. 41). However by the late seventies, the programme assumed a huge dimension covering more than a million pre-school children, i.e., close to 40 per cent of the total number of children up to five years of age. This programme, in fact, was a combination of a number of schemes such as Special Nutrition Programme (SNP), Applied Nutrition Programme (ANP), Composite Programme for Women and Children (CPWP), World Food Programme supported feeding scheme, One-meal-a-day Scheme, Health and Nutrition Programme and the well-known national programme called Integrated Child Development Scheme (ICDS), sponsored by the Government of India but implemented by the state governments. Through a series of reorganisations, the ICDS has now emerged as the most important scheme followed by ANP/CPWP and the SNP in Kerala.

Started in the mid-seventies the ICDS aims at providing 300 calories and 8.15 grams of protein per child and 500 calories and 15 grams of protein per day per person for women. These rates of food intake are roughly equivalent to one-fourth of the requirements of the beneficiary groups, and to be provided for 300 days in a year. In Kerala, approximately 84 per cent of the beneficiaries are children and the rest expectant/nursing mothers. Table 6 shows that close to a million beneficiaries are now covered by the scheme, which is supported by financial assistance from the central government to cover 80 per cent of its cost. The Applied Nutrition Programme and Composite Programme for Women and Children are slightly different in orientation and are also sponsored by the central government. The Special Nutrition Programme, started by the state through commodity aid from various agencies, has progressively been integrated into the ICDS. Its aims are the same as that of the ICDS. Currently SNP is in existence in areas which are not covered by the ICDS.

Table 6
Beneficiaries in Nutritional Programme for Children and Women

(000's)

Year	ICDS	SNP	ANP/ CPWP	WFP	OMD	HNP	Total
1977-78	57	200	-	200	-	-	457
1980-81	117	319	610	230	462	165	1903
1991-92	855	47	200	-	-	99*	1201
1995-96	960	-	123	-	-	-	1083

Note: 1. ICDS refers to beneficiaries under the Feeding Centre Programme. 2. * Closed in April 1985 as part of streamlining the nutrition programmes.

Source: Government of Kerala, *Economic Review,* Various Issues.

The supplementary nutrition programmes are implemented with the help of a large number of women's welfare organisations called *Mahila Samajams* and other organisations in the state, which have helped set up *anganwadis* and *balwadis.* Young educated women in rural areas who face the highest incidence of unemployment in Kerala, are recruited as volunteers and receive only a monthly honorarium. The 1999 rate of honorarium was around Rs. 600 per month, which was equivalent to nine days of the wages of female agricultural labourers. But there is a high social premium attached to a regular job outside the farm and hence this abundant supply at a very low wage. For all these programmes there are about 18,500 centres including 11,268 centres under the ICDS.

As in the case of the mid-day meal programme for school-going children, this one is also a direct food transfer to children outside their homes at a specified time for a specified number of days in a year. This is also the practice supposed to be followed throughout the country.

4. Old Age Pensions to Destitutes, Widows, Disabled and Rural Labourers

Unlike the primary health care system and the Public Distribution System, this scheme is targeted only at the poor based on their social or physical vulnerability or their status as labourers in the unorganised sector. The system of giving old age pension has come to occupy an important place in the social security provisioning in Kerala because its coverage, progressively being extended to most rural labourers, totalled around 60 per cent of the old aged poor in Kerala in 1991 under the two major pension programmes viz., destitutes and agricultural labourers (Table 7). The four most prominent schemes for old age pension for the poor are: (i) Pension to Destitutes and Widows; (ii) Pension for the Disabled; (iii) Pension for old aged agricultural labourers; and (iv) Pension for the old aged fish workers. All these have been in existence for more than 10 years now with the first one dating back 40 years. The number of pension schemes now in vogue in Kerala is around 17.

It is not difficult to relate the old age pension to persons in poor households with that of child deprivation. Given the fact that maintenance of old aged persons is wholly a family responsibility in India, the meagre resources of a poor household would be further stretched when there are old aged members, thus the fact that the pension covers at least the cost of one home-cooked meal per day reduces the family burden. This means that the other members would get a somewhat higher share of the family food basket and children are likely to be the beneficiaries. This is all the more so in the Kerala context where even the poorer households have only two children, on an average per couple. As mentioned before, this has enhanced the value of children and the attention they receive within the household.

IV. A PRELIMINARY ASSESSMENT

We have attempted an estimation of the coverage of these food security schemes for 1991 (Table 7). It is interesting to note that the coverage under the major programmes such as PDS, supplementary nutrition and pension for agricultural

Table 7

Selected Food Security Some Estimates for 1991 Covers for the Poor in Kerala

(Nos. in '000s)

	Total population		Estimated poor[a]	Beneficiaries	(5) as % of (4)	(5) as % of (3)
1	2	3	4	5	6	7
Male	Female	Total		Public distribution		
14289	14810	29099	9602	26696	278	92
	Children (0-4)			Supplementary nutrition		
Boys	Girls	Total				
1410	1349	2759	911	1201	132	44
	Children ([illegible])			Free noon-meal		
Boys	Girls	Total				
1760	1701	3461	1142	2410	211	70
	Old aged (60+)			Old age pension		
Male	Female	Total				
1689	1371	2560	845	505.3	60	20
	Widows			Widow pension		
Male	Female	Total				
137	1298	1435	474	129.3	27	9
Total agricultural labourers(60+) Main workers (Total cultivation + AL 60+) Main workers				Pension for agricultural labourers		
Male	Female	Total				
108	40	148	87	344.3	396	233
(298)	(55)	(353)	(151)		(228)	(96)
	Divorced/ Deserted/Widowed			Pension		
Male	Female	Total				
167	1461	1628	537	51.76	10	3
	Physically disabled			Pension		
Male	Female	Total				
		145	48	8.35	17	6

Note:
1. Except for 'Physically Disabled', columns 1, 2 and 3 are from the 1991 Population Census reports For Physically Disabled, the source is the *Report of the National Family and Health Survey: Kerala for* 1992-93. The information pertain to, on a per 1000 population basis, 11.0 for partial blindness, 3.0 for complete blindness and 6.6 for physical impairment. The number of estimated poor is based on an incidence of 33.3 per cent as the Head Count Ratio for 1991.
2. The number of estimated poor for 1991 is based on the highest estimate of the available figures. The Planning Commission's Expert Committee estimated the percentage of population below the poverty line in Kerala as 25.43 for 1993-94 while the World Bank estimated it at 33.8 for 1990-91 and 31.07 for 1993-94. We have taken the 1990-91 estimate and estimated the number of poor by taking the HCR at one-third of the population (33.33 per cent). For agricultural labourers, it is well known that the HCR is much higher than for the general population For 1993-94 this has been estimated as 58.8 per cent for India. We have applied this for Kerala. The HCR for self-employed in agriculture was 31.1 per cent in 1993-94.
3. The estimate of the number of physically disabled is obtained from the National Family Health Survey for Kerala in 1992-93.

4. The beneficiaries (under children aged 0-4) refer to the various nutritional care programmes such as the Integrated Child Development Service, Special Nutrition Programme, etc. The number of beneficiaries of this category may include women (as mothers) but is likely to form only a small proportion of the total.
5. The beneficiaries (under children aged 5-12 years) refer to the number of children availing of the free noon- meal in schools.
6. The old (60+) beneficiaries, refer to those receiving old age pension from the state. The categories included here are destitute and agricultural labourers.
7. All other beneficiaries refer to those receiving old age or special (as in the case of widows) pension.

workers exceeds the estimated poor below the poverty line. In fact, 92 per cent of the population are covered under PDS, 44 per cent of pre-school children under the supplementary nutrition programme, more than 50 per cent of the children between five and 12 years under the free noon-meal scheme and more than the total main agricultural labourers above 60 years under the old age pension scheme. In the case of agricultural labourers, the much higher coverage is perhaps due to the fact that many of them are only marginal agricultural labourers and have to do a variety of jobs in the casual labour market because of the declining employment opportunities in agriculture. However, they identify themselves as agricultural labourers while applying for old age pensions.

A valid question that could be raised here is: why should there be people below the poverty line in Kerala (the head count varied from 25 per cent according to the Planning Commission to 33 per cent according to World Bank estimates in the early 1990s) when more than the estimated poor are covered by one or more of the social security schemes? The answer lies in the fact that the benefits are still too meagre to pull them out of even the officially determined low poverty line. For instance, the PDS is able to cover only two-thirds of the requirements of rice of the poorer households, while the calories provided for children cover only one-fourth of their daily requirements and the real value of old age and other pensions has steadily declined over the years and now hardly covers one meal a day.

In 1980, the agricultural labourer's pension was Rs. 45 per month; in 1991 its real (deflating it with the CPI-AL) value was only Rs. 25.

There are a few income/employment-generating programmes in Kerala that could come under 'food security'. Those that are implemented are centrally-sponsored poverty alleviation programmes such as the IRDP, JRY, etc. The per capita benefit of these programmes is too meagre to make any perceptible dent on poverty (Kannan, 1995). In terms of employment generation, they hardly give employment for more than a few days per labourer. Here again, funds have been spread too thinly without being able to make significant reductions in poverty on their own.

V. FOOD SECURITY AND CHILD UNDERNUTRITION

The various state interventions for ensuring food security can only give us an idea of the effort being made in this direction, but not their outcome. The latter will have to be examined in the light of the human development indicators that are related to food security. Nutritional status of a population, especially its vulnerable sections, is perhaps the more reliable indicator of the impact of food security measures. However, this will have a bearing on broader and perhaps robust indicators such as life expectancy, infant mortality and, to some extent, on the incidence of absolute poverty. When we examine Kerala's food security in terms of these indicators, its performance is the best (or one among the best achievers). While the state's relatively better record is well known in informed circles, what makes it exceptional is the fact that it scores over states which are economically much more advanced in terms of per capita income, food consumption, urbanisation and industrialisation.

According to a study by the National Nutritional Monitoring Bureau, Kerala ranked first in terms of lowest percentage of undernutrition among children (below four years), in the eight states studied in two-time periods viz., 1974-79 and 1988-90. At the same time, it improved its position by reducing the incidence of severe undernutrition among children by 59 per cent and overall undernutrition by 31 per cent. In 1988-90, Tamil Nadu, Maharashtra and the three other southern states followed Kerala's performance. This performance sharply contrasts with Kerala's position in respect of the average consumption of nutrients at the household level as the second lowest both in terms of energy and protein. Tamil Nadu, interestingly, has the lowest position (Table 8).

Table 8
Nutritional Status and Energy Consumption, NNMB data, 1988-90 and 1974-79, by States

State	Ranking* according to nutritional status	Nutritional status of children below four years <-2SD	<-3SD	Ranking according to energy consumption	Average consumption of nutrients (cu/day) (at household level) Energy (kcal)	Protein (g)
Kerala	1(1)	42.5(61.2)	11.8(28.9)	6(7)	2,140(1,978)	52.9(46.4)
Tamil Nadu	2(3)	56.6(66.3)	22.6(34.7)	7(5)	1,871(2,275)	45.6(54.8)
Maharashtra	3(7)	60.1(72.8)	24.0(40.6)	5(3)	2,211(2,300)	61.7(64.5)
Andhra Pradesh	4(4)	60.7(66.9)	28.4(35.6)	4(2)	2,340(2,447)	55.7(59.8)
Karnataka	5(6)	65.9(71.6)	31.1(36.4)	2(1)	2,431(2,932)	65.4(79.3)
Gujarat	6(8)	67.2(74.4)	36.9(43.4)	3(6)	2,375(2,162)	69.3(64.2)
Madhya Pradesh	7(5)	68.9(70.8)	41.8(41.3)	1(4)	2,614(2,283)	82.5(71.5)
Orissa	8(2)	69.5(62.8)	35.7(33.2)	NA	U	U

Notes: 1. Figures in parentheses correspond to 1974-79 values; 2. *Rank of state with lowest per cent of undernutrition=1; 3. ** Rank of the state with highest level of energy consumption=1; 4. U=Not Available; NA=Not Applicable; 5. <-3SD indicates severe under nutrition, <-2SD indicates overall (mild, moderate and severe) undernutrition.

In 1994, nearly half the children (51 per cent) suffered from malnutrition in India and the picture was reportedly the same for the adult rural population at 46 per cent. The regional pattern was similar to those among children with Kerala recording the lowest (33 per cent) followed by Tamil Nadu (37 per cent) and

Gujarat, Maharashtra and Madhya Pradesh showing relatively higher levels of malnutrition-all above 50 per cent (Radhakrishna, 1999, p. 96). Commenting on the interstate variations in the malnutrition levels of children under five years, Radhakrishna observed: "In 1994, the percentage of moderately and severely malnourished children varied between 34 per cent in Kerala and 57 per cent in Gujarat. Middle-income states such as Kerala, Tamil Nadu and Andhra Pradesh performed better than high-income states like Gujarat and Maharashtra in terms of the nutritional status of children. Not surprisingly, poorer states such as Madhya Pradesh and Orissa performed the worst. Tamil Nadu could perform better. The National Family Health Survey data also reveal more or less similar patterns as the NNMB data".

However, when Radhakrishna compares all states by using another measure of nutritional status viz., Weight-for-Age available from the National Family and Health Survey (1992-93), the 'southern advantage' suggested, disappears. Kerala retains its first place along with such northeastern states as Mizoram and Nagaland (at 28 per cent)—almost half of the national average of 53 per cent. Andhra Pradesh (49 per cent), Karnataka (54 per cent) and Tamil Nadu (47 per cent) rank below the northeastern states (except Tripura) as well as the northwestern states of Punjab, Haryana Rajasthan, Gujarat and Jammu & Kashmir. West Bengal, where a supposedly more pro-poor government is in existence for the last quarter of a century, recorded high overall undernutrition among the children at 49 per cent, which is the same as that of Andhra Pradesh (Table 9).

In terms of life expectancy at birth, in Kerala (more than 70 years in 1991) this is at least 10 years higher than the all-India figure (close to 60 years). As Amartya Sen has argued, this measure has to be reckoned as a robust one, for, all efforts at human improvement are intended to achieve a longer and healthier life. Under-five and infant mortality rates are also one of the lowest in Kerala, outperformed by only two states viz., Mizoram and Nagaland (see Table 9).

The comparatively better performance of some of the northeastern states in respect of a number of human development indicators and being close to Kerala's achievement in many others, warrants a closer study of these societies in terms of their traditional socio-economic organisation and the current dynamics of state and society. While Kerala has received considerable attention and been subjected to close examination through several studies, a similar focus on the northeast is lacking. It is my view that the social science community needs to be alerted to what may promise to be another interesting development within the otherwise depressing Indian scenario in human development.

VI. CONCERNS OVER SUSTAINING FOOD SECURITY: THE IMPACT OF ECONOMIC REFORMS

The process of economic reform has brought in its wake, certain changes in the policy on the PDS. The decision to limit the PDS subsidy to those 'below the poverty line' since 1997 has meant a decline in the availability of foodgrains at a subsidised price to the states for their public distribution systems. Secondly, the differing interpretations of those 'below the poverty line' by the central and state

Table 9
State-wise Comparison of Nutritional Status and Mortality Rates of Children Under Four Years, NFHS, 1992-93

State	Sex of child	Nutritional status (Weight for-age) per cent <-3SD	<-2SD	Mortality rates* Neonatal	Infant	Under five	Death rate** (0-4) years
India	M	20.2	53.3	57.0	88.6	115.4	23.0
	F	21.0	48.1	48.1	83.9	122.4	23.6
	T	20.6	52.7	52.7	86.3	118.8	23.3
Kerala	T	6.1	28.5	15.5	23.8	32.0	3.8
Tamil Nadu	T	13.3	48.2	46.2	67.7	86.5	17.7
Karnataka	T	19.4	54.3	45.3	65.4	87.3	13.7
Andhra Pradesh	T	15.6	49.1	45.3	70.4	91.2	18.5
Haryana	T	9.0	37.9	38.4	73.3	98.7	22.1
Delhi	T	12.0	41.6	34.9	65.4	83.1	18.6
Punjab	T	14.2	45.9	31.2	53.7	68.0	14.9
Rajasthan	T	19.2	41.6	37.2	72.6	102.6	26.3
Gujarat	T	17.6	50.1	42.3	68.7	104.0	20.6
Maharashtra	T	21.3	54.2	36.4	50.5	70.3	12.1
Goa	T	8.9	35.0	20.6	31.9	38.9	4.9
Madhya Pradesh	T	22.3	57.4	53.2	85.2	130.3	27.3
Bihar	T	31.1	62.6	54.8	89.2	127.5	28.0
Uttar Pradesh	T	24.6	59.0	59.9	99.9	141.3	31.6
Himachal Pradesh	T	12.9	47.0	34.2	55.8	69.1	15.5
Jammu & Kashmir	T	13.8	44.5	31.9	45.4	59.1	15.6
Orissa	T	22.7	53.3	64.7	112.1	131.0	27.3
West Bengal	T	18.6	48.8	51.8	75.3	99.3	18.7
Assam	T	18.7	50.4	50.9	88.7	142.2	32.1
Arunachal Pradesh	T	14.5	39.7	17.5	40.0	72.0	U
Manipur	T	7.2	30.1	25.1	42.4	61.7	U
Meghalaya	T	17.2	45.5	37.8	64.2	86.9	U
Mizoram	T	5.3	28.1	8.3	14.6	29.3	U
Nagaland	T	7.6	28.7	10.0	17.2	20.7	U
Tripura	T	18.6	48.8	43.6	75.8	104.6	U

Notes: 1. U=Not available; 2. * Mortality rates for India are calculated for the 10-year period preceding the survey while mortality rates for the states are for a five-year period preceding the survey in 1992-93; 3.** The age- specific death rate is based on the annual number of deaths reported during the two-year period prior to the NFHS, 1992-93.

governments have led to an additional burden on the states. In Kerala, the state government continued its policy on universal coverage of the PDS but introduced a dual pricing system. Under this system, 42 per cent of the family ration cardholders were treated as 'below poverty line' and were identified as part of the exercise for implementation of the Integrated Rural Development Programme (IRDP). This has meant that 17 per cent of the cardholders were supplied with foodgrains at a subsidised price over and above the 25 per cent recognised by the central government. In 1998, these cardholders were given 10 kg of rice per family (as per the central government norm) at a subsidised price of Rs. 3.90 per kg (revised to Rs. 4 from January 1999). Any additional requirement of rice for these families was met at a price of Rs. 8.60 inclusive of a one-rupee subsidy by the state government. All the non-poor cardholders were also given rice at this subsidised price of Rs. 8.60 per kg. The estimated subsidy for rice alone works out to nearly Rs. 188 crores per annum.

The hike in issue prices for the PDS announced by the then Union Finance Minister in his Budget Speech (February 29, 2000) would severely hit the PDS in Kerala threatening its very survival. A rise in these prices will be the end of a PDS hailed as a model for other states. The contours of the emerging economics of Kerala's PDS are only beginning to be realised.

There are a number of issues involved in the changed context of the role of PDS. Let us take the strict application of the official 'poverty line' that will exclude a number of households who are just above but around the poverty line. This calls for a broad band in determining the eligible poor households rather than a strict line. Such an approach is already in existence in regard to the implementation of IRDP. The implication of such a strict 'poverty line' approach is incompatible with the nutritional status of children. We have seen that the incidence of the overall undernutrition of children in the country (53 per cent in 1992-93) is considerably higher than the incidence of head count poverty (at 35 per cent in 1993-94). We have also seen that the enrolment (by self-selection) of school-going children for the mid-day meal programme in Kerala is at least twice that of the incidence of poverty in Kerala. Therefore, the new PDS propounded by the central government is likely to increase the food insecurity of the poor which will have a debilitating effect on children. This, in turn, could undermine the attempts at inducing more children to attend school. Special programmes for children designed to reduce their deprivation cannot work effectively in the absence of adequate food security at the household level. It is, therefore, imperative that food security at the household level is recognised as a crucial element in reducing child deprivation.

If this line of reasoning has any validity, then the targeted PDS to cater to those 'below poverty line' should be linked to the incidence of overall undernutrition among children as a measure of food insecurity.

VII. LONG TERM SOLUTIONS FOR FOOD SECURITY IN KERALA

While children no doubt constitute, one of the most vulnerable sections of the population in the event of food insecurity, the experience of Kerala suggests that the provision of food security to the population as a whole is a necessary condition for reducing child deprivation. At the same time, targeted programmes for children in terms of food security can also go a long way towards eliminating child deprivation. Here again Kerala's experience of both the mid-day meal for school-going children and the supplementary nutrition programme for the pre-school children have made notable contribution. A number of factors contributed to the slow but steady evolution of the state as a 'child friendly' place. At the outset, women's education and the relatively easy availability of health care services initiated a process of demographic transition. State-sponsored programmes in social security in general and food security in particular have contributed to the decline in child deprivation. All these initiatives taken by the state have put the children in Kerala much ahead of the national average in terms of a number of indicators such as average number of children in the family, infant and child mortality, severe and overall undernutrition. Having noted these achievements, one must not jump into the conclusion that the task of child development is complete in Kerala. As we have repeatedly stated, the state support systems including food security are in the nature of 'poor relief' only and not adequate to meet the requirements of the poorer sections. This applies to school education as well as health care. The advantage Kerala now enjoys is in terms of the reduction in the number of children born giving a higher premium to the care of children in the family, thus removing the quantitative burden of child development in the state. For example, the number of children in the primary school stage was around 24 lakhs in 1992, which has declined to around 19 lakhs in 2000. This demographic advantage offers an opportunity for the state to focus on the qualitative improvement of child development programmes.

Measures for bringing about qualitative improvement should start, in our opinion, from the provision of food security. The impact of the mid-day meal scheme for school-going children is minimal. Efforts will have to be made to improve the nutritional quality of this meal. The recent announcement of the government to provide a glass of milk to the children in school is a welcome initiative. The transfer of supervisory and infrastructure development functions of schools to the panchayats is an important step in this direction. The creation of better building, and the provision of drinking water and sanitary facilities in schools are now being taken up by the panchayats, which could also contribute to the food security programmes for the children. The maintenance and developmental functions of child care centres for the pre-school children have also been transferred to the panchayats. Thus, the local level participation of these institutions could be enhanced to improve the quality of public services to the children. Given the average of two children per couple, the necessary social ambience for public support for child development is already in place. In fact, child development programmes have enjoyed a remarkable degree of societal as well as political consensus in an otherwise highly contested political terrain in Kerala.

Clearly, Kerala's experience should be subjected to a close examination by other states in India striving for the reduction and eventual elimination of child deprivation. Given the size and diversity of India, there is considerable scope for the Indian states to learn from the experience of each other in diverse, fields of activity that constitute the Indian Union. And the arena of child development is certainly one such field. One of the lessons of the Kerala experience is the focus on food security in general and child nutrition in particular as an instrument for reducing child deprivation. Certainly, a number of complimentary measures are needed, the most important one being the easy access to schooling as well as health care facilities. Here again, Kerala's experience is nothing less than remarkable when viewed from an Indian perspective.

References

Chaudhri, D.P. (2000), "Sources of Supply of Child Labour and the State: Explorations of Historical and Contemporary Evidence with Focus on States and Districts of India," Paper presented at the *National Seminar on Child Labour: Realities and Policy Dimensions*, Organised by V.V. Giri National Labour Institute, Noida and Institute for Human Development, New Delhi, December 5-7.

George, P.S. (1979), *Public Distribution of Food Grains in Kerala—Income Distribution Implications and Effectiveness*, Research Report 7, International Food Policy Research Institute, Washington.

GOK (1999), *Report of the Expert Committee on Paddy Cultivation in Kerala*, Government of Kerala, July.

Kannan, K.P. (1995), "Public Intervention and Poverty Alleviation: A Study of the Declining Incidence of Rural Poverty in Kerala, India", *Development and Change*, Vol. 26, No. 4, October.

—— (2001a), "State Assisted Social Security for Poverty Alleviation and Human Development: Kerala's Record and Its Lessons", in Mahendra Dev, S., et al. (eds.), *Social and Economic Security in India*, Institute for Human Development, New Delhi.

Mooij, Jos (1996), *Food Policy and the Indian State: The Public Distribution System in South India*, pp. 69-76, Oxford University Press, New Delhi.

Mahendra Dev, S. (2001), "Child Labour in India: Dimensions, Determinants and Policies", in Kannan (ed.), *Child Labour in India*, Deep and Deep Publishers, New Delhi.

Radhakrishna, R. (1999), "Food Security and the Poor", in Chelliah, R.J. and R. Sudarshan, (eds.), *Income Poverty and Beyond: Human Development in India*, Social Science Press, New Delhi.

Ramachandran, Nira (2001), "Food Insecurity and Child Work: A Concept Paper", *Consultative Workshop on Food Insecurity and Child Work in Rural India*, Institute for Human Development, New Delhi and The World Food Programme of the United Nations, Delhi Office, March 15-17.

Suryanarayana, M.H. (1996), "Food Security and PDS in Kerala: Form and Scope for Reform," Paper presented at the *International Conference on Kerala's Development Experience: National and Global Dimensions*, New Delhi, 9-11 December.

—— (2000), "Backdoor Closure of PDS?", *The Hindu*, March.

United Nations (UN/CDS, 1975), *Poverty, Unemployment and Development Policy: A Case Study of Selected Issues with Special Reference to Kerala*, New York.

Weiner, Myron (1991), *The Child and the State in India*, Oxford University Press, Delhi, pp. 3-4.

20

Investing in the Poor: A Food Credit Scheme for Rural Households

PRAVESH SHARMA, AODITTI MEHTTA AND PEDRO MEDRANO

I. INTRODUCTION

The problem of endemic hunger rarely makes news, unlike famines, which in their pictorial misery merit media attention. This phenomenon can be partly explained by the unremarkable appearance of the average poor household, undistinguished from millions of others. Although it may be perched dangerously on the brink of starvation, on the surface, life goes on almost at a normal pace. A World Bank study (1986) estimated that more than 340 million people did not have access to a normal diet which could prevent stunted growth and over 700 million had a food intake less than what is essential to combat serious health risks. Two-thirds of both these categories live in South Asia and a staggering 40 million people die every year from the causes directly related to hunger. Sen and Dreze (1989), quoting from a background paper presented at the Nordic Conference on Environment and Development (1987), have observed that this calamity can be compared with the crash of 300 fully loaded jumbo jets killing all the passengers everyday for a whole year. Nations all over the world have met the challenge of feeding their populations with a variety of policy options, ranging from the provision of incentives for agricultural production, price controls and food stamps to the setting up of soup kitchens and even outright, free distribution of food to the needy. The term "food security" has come to encompass any policy initiative that seeks to ensure the continued availability of food at the national and/or household level.

Chronic food insecurity, which is reflected in endemic hunger, is a stark reality which a large number of poor households in the developing world will continue to face in the medium-term future, notwithstanding the ongoing efforts to spur economic growth and to ensure an equitable distribution of its benefits among all groups in society. In such a dismal scenario, there seem to be few options open for governments but to adopt policies which, in the short term, create, enhance and protect entitlements to food among vulnerable groups. This is now almost an essential prerequisite of any model of economic development, so that the poorest sections of the population do not suffer during the transition to a better economic future. The key question is: will the poorest households have to endure a long, hungry wait before the long-term benefits of economic growth trickle down to them in course of time? Or, is it possible to devise a short-term strategy that eliminates at least the endemic hunger that haunts the lives of the poorest?

This paper proposes a model to achieve household level food security, which questions the mainstream assumptions about the capacity of poor families to service debt. It recognises consumption of food as a primary credit need and suggests a mechanism that caters to this need. The basic premise of such a model is the recognition of the ability to work as the most critical asset of poor households. The proposed mechanism seeks to 'invest' in this asset by extending credit to them on reasonable terms for meeting their food requirements, and offering them the facility to repay the loan from future income over a period of time. While, on the one hand, this approach guarantees medium-term food security, it also protects livelihoods by offering a buffer against high cost debt which food insecure households are forced to access from informal credit sources. For the purpose of our discussion, we call this the Food Credit Scheme or FCS.

II. SOME MAJOR ASSUMPTIONS

Before we discuss the proposed model in detail, some major underlying assumptions which form the essential context of this paper need to be stated:

1. In the medium-term perspective, lack of purchasing power, which arises out of the absence of economic assets and uneven access to regular wage employment, will remain the major cause of endemic hunger among poor rural households. While this traps them in a cycle of debt, low productivity, illiteracy and malnutrition, it also depresses demand for food-potentially the single largest group of wage goods likely to be consumed with the rise in the incomes of the poorest households.

2. Given the present state of government finances, political compulsions and the large number of potential beneficiaries, any scheme resembling the food stamp programme of the United States of America, in which the beneficiary households receive food without any return obligation, is not feasible in India.

3. The Public Distribution Scheme (PDS) in India will continue in its present form in the foreseeable future and only address the issue of macro food security. This approach leaves out a large number of poor rural

households from accessing the limited quantities of subsidised food offered by the system on account of their uneven income earning pattern.

4. Food insecure households are likely to continue to suffer from hunger spells of varying length during different periods in the year unless a specific strategy is devised to address this problem.
5. The open market meets 70-80 per cent of the food needs of poor families, thereby placing considerable pressure on the family's cash flow, which must be even to ensure availability of food to them.
6. Informal credit mechanisms, e.g., the village moneylender, general-store owner, landlord, etc., offering advance against future labour serve the food needs of the poorest households at rates of interest ranging between 25 per cent and 70 per cent per month.
7. The lack of physical assets (land, cattle and tools) in a large number of poor households relegates them as 'credit risks', and inhibits investment by institutional sources in their basic consumption needs.
8. The urgency of meeting the food requirements of poor households are driving them into a debt and/or asset alienation trap.
9. Household level food insecurity constitutes India's "silent emergency", manifested in distressingly high levels of Infant Mortality Rate (IMR), Maternal Mortality Rate (MMR) and Low Birth Weight Children (LBW), stunting, a high morbidity rate and a vicious circle of low productivity and low incomes as well as their adverse impact on basic human development indices such as enrolment and retention in schools.

III. MACRO FOOD SECURITY VS. HOUSEHOLD FOOD SECURITY

The FCS is proposed as a practical policy instrument that emanates from the need to ensure food security at the individual household level. In India, thus far, macro level food security has been sought to be achieved through a state-led programme of encouraging agricultural production, largely consisting of price incentives, subsidised credit and inputs and guaranteed purchase of the surplus arriving in the market at a support price. This strategy has been successful at the macro plane, as is evidenced by a progressive increase of foodgrain production, leading to a situation where the country becomes self-sufficient or even a net exporter of grains in some years. The per capita availability of foodgrains has also steadily improved since 1947. Moreover, sizeable buffer stocks with the government provide an adequate cushion against fluctuation in production, sudden price escalation or special needs arising out of temporary conditions such as droughts, floods, etc.

However, this success has not been replicated at the household level due to a variety of reasons. Among the most apparent ones are the uneven spread of the new agricultural technologies, whereby high yields are limited to certain areas in the country, the absence of a breakthrough in dry farming techniques, on which a majority of Indian cultivators still rely, and finally—what is no less significant—

the varied experience of the states with the PDS as a means of entitlement creation. Since a detailed probe into the causes of the lack of food security at the household level is not the subject of this paper, it should suffice to say that a vast number of poor households are continually threatened with endemic hunger, be it due to the low returns from agriculture or the general lack of access to assets and opportunities of income generation to meet their nutrition needs.

But, it may be argued, that it is precisely this latter problem which poverty alleviation programmes such as the Integrated Rural Development Programme (IRDP) and the rural employment generation programme, the Jawahar Rozgar Yojna (JRY), are trying to address, though of course, with mixed results. What may well be asked is: is there a need to put forward a new approach to entitlement creation in the presence of these existing entitlement strategies?

Limitations of Existing Programmes

Official planners in India assume that (a) the poorest among India's rural population are gainfully employed during the main agricultural season (between July and October), thus ensuring for them adequate food security and (b) supplementary employment generation efforts by official agencies should be concentrated only on the so-called lean season which follows. Though in theory, agricultural labour is most secure against hunger in the main cropping season, in actual practice this is most often not the case. In fact, during this period the poor households' stocks of stored grain are very low and quite often exhausted. While wage opportunities in bigger farms, in which intensive operations like ploughing, seeding, weeding and harvesting are carried out, are available, the returns from them are not immediate and not always in cash. These mostly comprise of deferred payment in kind after the harvest has set in. This is the time when public works are virtually frozen; because the Indian monsoon makes it impossible to execute all but the bare minimum of forestry projects for three months. Also, official planners are of the view, that agricultural labour should be allowed to take advantage of opportunities in the sector which arise in the natural course during this period. This is also the time when open market prices of food are at their highest level, and PDS food supplies at the end point, especially in the remote hinterland, are most likely to be disrupted during these four months. Thus, being under pressure from several directions, the poor households are in fact more vulnerable to hunger at this time than at any other time of the year. However, no existing programme is designed to identify and cover this vulnerable slot.

In the following period, it is not possible to honestly claim that official employment generation programmes step in to take up the slack in the demand for labour. This is due to several reasons; firstly, public works are not triggered off by demand. Depending on the efficiency of local personnel to plan ahead, secure funds and execute projects expeditiously, the pattern of employment availability through public works can vary drastically from region to region and even year to year. Even in the most responsive situations, agricultural labour can at best hope for something between 10-25 days of supplementary employment between

January and June. Secondly, employment generation projects can rarely absorb all the available labour in the area. Most of these works include small rural roads, dikes or village ponds, which may employ anything from 10 to 80 per cent of the labour force of an area for a period as brief as a week and rarely more than a month. Furthermore, wage disbursement is erratic and fitful; it is not uncommon for a project engaging labour for a month to wind up without a single weekly payment of dues being made. Thus, the fact that access to employment opportunities on public works is neither automatic nor perennial, makes them an episodic, and often idiosyncratic, means of entitlement creation. The ground realities, therefore, reveal that the poorest households have to often contend with the threat of hunger, forcing them to scout for wage employment in the neighbourhood or to migrate great distances to look for them in the off season. Alternatively, in case the household has a small buffer stock of grain, it can seek employment avenues at a public work being commissioned nearby, at some point of time between the harvest and the next monsoon. The conclusion that there are seasonal variations in access to food, with periods of hunger in the event of poor rains and reduced employment opportunities, is inescapable.

IV. FOOD CREDIT SCHEME: A VIABLE OPTION

In recommending the adoption of the Food Credit Scheme (FCS) we have approached the problem from another angle. What must be done to ensure the food security of a household that cannot create opportunities for income generation at the time when these are most needed? The low income of a household at one level can simply be attributed to its failure to generate a cash flow by exchange of labour or goods produced by it.

Another view of the same situation can be that the potential of income generation in the household has not been fully harnessed. This latter view spreads the onus of income generation at least partly outside the household into society. In other words, the household always has some assets-goods or the means to produce goods or services such as labour—to offer for exchange, but the opportunity for exchange is not always available. This is especially true of an underdeveloped, labour-surplus economy. A simple linear succession of events has come to be accepted as the lot of the poor: Hunger = Working = Earning = Eating. It is the order in the relationship between these events which needs to be rearranged. Why, for instance, can't the sequence read: Hunger = Eating = Working = Earning? Working does not necessarily have to precede eating, least of all for the poorest groups in society who do not have control over the incidence and timing of employment. But then the question that arises is: how do we propose to make them eat now and pay later? This can happen, if instead of looking for wages earned, we can recognise the potential earning capacity of the household.

Even the poorest rural households have at least one of the following two assets: a piece of agricultural land, however impoverished and lacking in infrastructure, and, two adult members capable of performing manual labour. If we were to recognise the potential income generating capacity of a combination of both, or even one of these factors, then it is possible to devise a feasible scheme under which 'investments' are made in these assets. We can guarantee a minimum level of food security to the target household in advance, as food credit, in lieu of future 'adjustment', or pay back, by the household through its income generating assets. In brief, we can extend an advance entitlement to the household to have access to a certain quantity of food for the most vulnerable slot of the year—at least for two months, but not exceeding three months. To 'adjust', or pay back the advance entitlement credited to it, the adult members of the household can either simply repay a comfortable cash monthly installment, perform labour at a public work site or sell their agricultural produce to an official procurement agency over the next one year. Each time such an 'adjustment' is made the household automatically becomes entitled to another advance installment of food credit. Thus, as long as it is willing to work off the entitlement to food already enjoyed by it on credit, a household can accumulate future entitlements and achieve medium-term food security.

1. Instrument of Investment: SHG Managed Food Bank

The FCS is proposed to be implemented through a self-help group (SHG) run food bank, which would function in different stages:

(i) Stage I

(a) The target group for the FCS is ideally a group of 10-15 landless families, or one where some members hold plots of marginal and little economic value. These families, by definition, are located in rainfed regions, prone to droughts and other natural disasters. The economy of these regions is characterised by subsistence agricultural activities, generating few wage employment opportunities. Indebtedness, malnutrition, illiteracy and lack of opportunities to upgrade income-earning skills aggravate poor resource and entitlement profiles for individual members of the group. The underlying feature unifying the group is their vulnerability to seasonal and/or endemic hunger.

(b) Each such group of 10-15 families with a common resource and entitlement profile is initially motivated to form an informal Self-Help Group (SHG).

(c) Since the focus of the SHG will be on managing a food bank, it would be desirable to involve only women in the formation of the SHGs to the extent that this is feasible. In the pilot scheme, it is proposed that at least 50 per cent of the SHGs should be constituted with all-women membership. This would also make possible a comparative study of the efficacy of the functioning of the SHGs, recovery rates, conflict resolution and management styles of these bodies with different gender profiles.

(d) Each member of the SHG makes an annual 'deposit' of 2 kg of foodgrains into the food bank to be maintained by the SHG to begin its activities. This initial deposit can be made in upto four equal installments over a period of time as decided by the SHG (ideally the SHG allows a period of 2-3 months for this saving). The critical issue is that only the deposit entitles the family to withdraw up to 20 times the quantity deposited. Thus, the total entitlement of each family to draw from the food bank would be 40 kg. However, at any given time, even a one kg deposit would entitle the family to withdraw up to 20 kg of foodgrains.

(e) Once the initial corpus is created, the SHG is linked to a credit agency [ideally a micro-finance institution (MFI) working through a local NGO partner] for a line of credit to buy food and create its full corpus for lending.

(f) Each of the member families of the SHG is entitled to draw a maximum of 40 kgs (or 20 times his/her deposit, whichever is less) of grain from the food bank at any given time. The SHG decides how and where the grain is to be stored, how much is to be lent to each member family at one time, subject to the overall limit of its entitlement etc., and takes all other decisions necessary for the efficient management of the food bank.

(g) All replenishments of the food bank's grain resources are made by the members themselves, and only in cash in Stage I as per a repayment plan worked out with the MFI. This enables the SHG to service its loan and slowly build up its own grain reserves through the savings of its members.

(h) The expectation is that the SHG members will take recourse to the food bank when all other opportunities of wage earning or accessing food have been exhausted. Payback of the food taken on credit from the SHG is spread over a long-term period (at least 12 months and can even be extended to 24 months in case the beneficiary is willing to bear a slightly higher rate of interest).

(i) At the current rates of interest being charged by the Rashtriya Mahila Kosh (RMK)—a Government of India promoted MFI, which extends group loans to women the rate of interest devolving on the beneficiary works out to 20-22 per cent per annum. Compared to the open market rates for food credit being paid by poor households, this is the most reasonable rate which the beneficiaries can expect.

(ii) Stage II

(a) In the second stage, the SHG takes on the task of the distribution of subsidised food being channeled through the PDS, thus becoming a fair price shop that offers food on credit.

(b) For the PDS at the field level, the SHG-run food bank is the ultimate answer to ensure off-take, by solving the problem of purchasing power in the hands of the BPL consumers. If successful, the model can be upscaled to become a fully integrated chain from the FCI onwards, with provision of credit at each level.

(iii) Stage III

(a) After the successful management of the food bank in Stage I and integrating the FCS in Stage II, the SHG is gradually equipped to take on other official food-based programmes operating at the field level such as the Mid-Day Meal scheme, Food for Work, ICDS, etc. Eventually, stronger SHGs can also be linked to the minimum support price (MSP) procurement system in areas where surplus grain is available for sale.

(b) In this stage the SHG allows its members a choice of payback mechanisms for the food borrowed: cash, performance of labour on a Food For Work (FFW) site managed by the SHG, through adjustment against MSP purchase, etc.

(c) The savings/earnings of the SHG (from PDS margins, service charges for running government schemes) are utilised for buying more food to build up the corpus and gradually increase the entitlement of the members.

(d) Once the members of the SHG realise that the food bank stocks food reserves on which they can fall back in times of crisis such as crop failure on their own marginal plot, depletion of the family's food reserves and purchasing power and failure to access wage employment opportunities, they will have a vested interest in ensuring that the food bank is managed successfully. It is entirely feasible that a family may choose to 'deposit' food into the bank in a period of plenty, to increase its own entitlement to draw from the bank in a moment of scarcity.

2. Strengths of the Scheme

There are several strong features, which make the FCS a viable and practical option. Some of these are listed below:

(i) The primary advantage of the scheme is that it guarantees food security created at the household level. Thus far, in India, we have primarily relied upon two methods of entitlement creation for the poorest groups. The first of these aimed at ensuring that expanding employment opportunities accompanying growth in agricultural production would engage rural labour in the main cropping season. Later, in response to growing evidence, which suggests that the labour force was expanding much faster than job opportunities, the government attempted to target the poorest households with supplementary asset creation and income generation schemes, such as IRDP and JRY, to generate purchasing power. We also created the PDS as the mechanism with which to deliver subsidised food to these households. However, both these schemes suffer from certain drawbacks. Although Indian agriculture has grown since 1947 at a slightly higher rate than that of the rate of increase in the population, its growth has not been of a uniform nature throughout the country. IRDP schemes involve varying gestation periods and are dependent on a number of factors such as entrepreneurial, marketing and managerial ability to be successful. As mentioned earlier, JRY does not offer perennial employment opportunities. Empirical studies have shown (Tyagi, 1990; Howes and Jha, 1992) that the uneven performance of PDS in India has led to a major share of its benefits accruing to groups with higher purchasing power, at the cost of the poorer groups.

The inescapable conclusion that emerges from the above analysis is that there are periodic gaps in access to food among the poorest households, which cannot be bridged by any of the existing entitlement creation programmes. The FCS provides for recognizing the potential income earning capacity of the household and accordingly offering it food on credit. By accepting the fact that there are 'lean' and 'full' periods of employment, and extending food credit to bridge the gaps, the scheme aims at breaking the link between the capacity for earning and expenditure on food. In other words, the FCS becomes a method of ironing out the fluctuations in the household's real income, whether this is due to changes in employment availability or prices, and stabilises its purchasing power over a medium-term period. By offering foodgrains and not cash on credit, the scheme guarantees poor households insurance against hunger.

(ii) The other features of the scheme may be listed as:

(a) The food bank manages to circumvent both the problem of erratic deliveries to the FPS and fluctuations in the purchasing power of the card-holders. It also empowers the most likely victims of endemic hunger to manage a small food resource in tune with their changing requirements.

(b) Carrying costs of the food bank are kept at a minimum as the foodgrains are stored and managed by the SHG.

(c) While the most efficient PDS can only ensure availability of foodgrains at the FPS level, the food bank, with its credit approach, can ensure household level food security in the medium term by delinking the period of wage earning with access to food.

(d) Since the SHG consists of families with a common entitlement profile with the primary objective of meeting short-term food, requirements, it is a highly accurate method of targeting subsidised food towards the most vulnerable and needy groups.

V. CONCLUSION

In the medium-term, the low income of poor households will constitute a major cause of endemic hunger among them. While the existing policies of agricultural and industrial development address the problem of employment generation, they are unlikely to create large scale opportunities for employment in the short-term perspective. Though the government has initiated several schemes aimed at employment generation, these have not been adequate to compensate for the lack of job opportunities in the open market. In such a situation, there seems to be no alternative to stepping up of government intervention to protect the food entitlements of the poorest groups in society. This can be done without causing any major changes in the existing food policies of the country or making serious modification of the PDS. The poorest households can be provided food on credit for a minimum period of two to three months as an investment in their potential to pay back through labour and sale of their agricultural produce. The coverage of the scheme can be restricted to households below the poverty line to ensure accurate targeting of food to the most needy. Ultimately, the additional demand for foodgrains will lead to enhanced production, creating more job opportunities and higher productivity. This in turn, will reduce the need for protecting entitlements through official intervention and result in an accompanying decline in the food subsidy burden of the government.

References

Howes, Stephen and Shikha Jha (1992), "Urban Bias in Indian PDS", *Economic and Political Weekly,* Vol. 27, No. 19.

Sen, Amartya and Jean Dreze (1989), *Hunger and Public Action,* Oxford. Clarendon.

Tyagi, D.S. (1990), *Managing India's Food Economy: Problems and Alternatives.* Sage Publications, New Delhi.

World Bank (1986), Poverty and Hunger, *A World Bank Policy Study: Issues and Options for Food Security in Developing Countries,* Washington D.C.

21

Food Insecurity and Child Labour: The Markapur Experience

M.P. Joseph

I. CHILD LABOUR AND ILO'S RESPONSES

1. The Concept of Child Labour

Definitions of child labour vary. The International Labour Organisation (ILO, 1996) has distinguished child work from child labour and offers a specific definition which is "*the type of work performed by children that deprives them of their childhood and their dignity, which hampers their access to education and acquisition of skills and which is performed under conditions harmful to their health and their development.*"

Child labour can be understood as work by children, which interferes with their mental and physical health, normal life or emotions. Any work that interferes with the education of the child would be child labour and any work that is undertaken for long hours that affects the health, safety or the morals of the child constitutes child labour.

2. Why do Children Work?

While poverty is a prime cause of child labour; there are many other factors that contribute to it. These include parental illiteracy, family occupation, non-availability of employment, male unemployment, etc. Poor households tend to send children for work to supplement the family income, but poverty alone does not necessarily cause child labour.

There are many forms of economic insecurity, of which insecurity due to lack of food can be high among the fears of a poor family. The fear that there may not be enough food in the house to feed children, that children may have to remain hungry, can be a powerful determinant in economic decision-making within poor families. The fear of her children remaining without food, drives a mother to take decisions regarding the future of the child, which in the long run, are at odds with and contrary to the best interests of the child. In such a situation, where the choice is between hunger and education, she would prefer that her children work and earn enough for meeting their food requirements rather than make what seems to her the *luxurious* choice of sending them to school, with the prospect of hunger and starvation *attending* on that choice.

3. The ILO and Child Labour

The foundations of the ILO policy on child labour are set out in the Preamble of the Constitution, the declaration of Philadelphia and relevant international labour standards as well as in resolutions adopted by the International Labour Conference and in decisions taken by the ILO governing body. The fundamental objective of the ILO policy in this matter is the abolition of child labour.

Since its inception, the ILO adopted numerous conventions and recommendations on child labour. The most recent and comprehensive conventions on child labour are: (i) Convention No. 182 on the Worst Forms of Child Labour, 1999 and (ii) The Minimum Age Convention No. 138 of 1973.

The Minimum Age Convention 1973 (C.138) lays down the basic principle that the minimum age for admission to employment should not be less than the age for completing compulsory schooling and in no event less than age 15. The Convention also provides that the minimum age should be progressively raised to a level consistent with the physical and mental development of young persons. It also allows an element of flexibility for countries whose economic and educational facilities are insufficiently developed.

The Convention on the Worst Forms of Child Labour, 1999 (C.182) and the Recommendation on the Worst Forms of Child Labour were unanimously adopted at the 87th International Labour Conference in November 1999. The Convention and the accompanying recommendation applies to persons under the age of 18 and calls for immediate and effective measures to secure the prohibition and elimination of the worst forms of child labour as a matter of urgency.

In order to achieve the goals set by its conventions, the ILO has been providing technical assistance to its member countries. Since 1992, this technical cooperation has taken the form of a global programme against child labour called IPEC, which is an acronym for the International Programme on the Elimination of Child Labour. India was the first country to join IPEC as a participating country in 1992. Today, IPEC is a global programme with about 60 participating countries and 30 donor countries. IPEC in India has tried out and tested various approaches and concepts for the elimination of child labour while working with the government and its agencies, with NGOs, trade unions, employers' groups, etc. It has built up capacities of organisations and institutions for taking action against child labour. IPEC has also done some preliminary work in the country on developing strategies for supplementing the incomes of families that have rehabilitated their children from the workplace into schools.

II. FOOD INSECURITY AND CHILD LABOUR IN ANDHRA PRADESH

1. What is Food Security?

The World Bank defines food security as *access by all people at all times to enough food for an active and healthy life.* The essential elements of food security are the availability of food and the ability to acquire it. Food insecurity can be of two types: chronic food insecurity and transitory food insecurity. Chronic food insecurity is a continuously inadequate diet caused by the inability to acquire it, which is often due to lack of ability either to buy or to produce enough food. Transitory food insecurity is a temporary decline in a household's access to enough food which results from instability in food prices, food production or household incomes (NGDO-EC Liaison Committee, 1994).

Food insecurity can lead to a variety of problems, of which one is child labour, whereby the children of families where food insecurity exists, participate in economic activities.

2. Food Insecurity as a Cause of Child Labour

Child labour begins with the high degree of insecurity regarding food in poor households. It is not only poverty *per se*, but food insecurity or the threat of food insecurity or the (at times the less than rational) fear of food insecurity that drives families to take the decision to send children to work. The threat of food insecurity drives even house holds that otherwise have the capacity to educate their children to send them to work instead, fearing future droughts and famines that could lead to food insecurity.

In sum, poverty translates itself into a high degree of food insecurity. The hard reality of poverty to many families is hunger and poverty in the context of child labour translates itself into lack of food at home and the overwhelming need to fill empty stomachs. Child labour is thus seen as an insurance against food insecurity.

3. Child Labour in Andhra Pradesh

Andhra Pradesh has the highest number of child labourers in the country with a child labour workforce of 1.66 million, which is 14.7 per cent of the country's child labour force. Out of these, 91.7 per cent are working in rural areas and the rest (8.3 per cent) are in urban areas. Another interesting dimension of the problem in the state is that girls account for a majority (51.5 per cent) of the total population of child workers. The child labour population in the state accounts for 2.5 per cent of the total population, 7 per cent of the total child population and 5.5 per cent of the total labour force—all above the national average.

A majority (59.4 per cent) of the child labourers are agricultural labourers, followed by 19.6 per cent in cultivation, 4.1 per cent in manufacturing, processing, servicing and repairs in household industry and the rest (16.9 per cent) in other categories (Census of India, 1991).

One of the causes of child labour in rural Andhra Pradesh is poverty, which very often reflects itself in the insecurity over food. Significantly, the intensive pockets of child labour in the state are clearly juxtapositioned with pockets of intensive food insecurity.

Providing food to children occupies prime space within parental concerns, and in cases where their incomes are not sufficient to provide food security to children, they encourage children to contribute to family incomes through work.

Another cause of food insecurity in rural Andhra Pradesh is the lack of security of employment in all sectors. The supply side argument that in conditions marked by under-employment, non-payment of minimum wages and a poor working environment there would be food insecurity leading to child labour is particularly applicable in Andhra Pradesh.

Evidence suggests that where there is food insecurity, the families send children for employment even in dangerous and hazardous conditions. This is exemplified in the presence of child labour in the Markapur slate mines. In Markapur child labour has been an inter-generational phenomenon perceived as a tool to enhance family incomes to overcome food insecurity.

III. THE ILO PROJECT IN THE MARKAPUR SLATE INDUSTRY

1. The Andhra Pradesh State-based Project for the Elimination of Child Labour

As part of its strategy to increase capacities of projects set up in the country to eliminate child labour, IPEC decided to focus on the state as a cohesive cutting edge unit for action to end child labour. Policies and programmes on child labour get ultimately implemented at the state level, and unless the state government is an active participant in the process, initiatives taken by the central government level directly may not lead to action and results in the districts.

The Andhra Pradesh Project seeks to contribute to the progressive elimination of child Labour in India by focusing on building up capacities within the state for its elimination. The immediate objective of the project is to reduce the number of child workers in Andhra Pradesh through the development and implementation of replicable, pilot interventions.

2. Markapur: Its Slate Industry and Child Labour

Markapur is a revenue division of Prakasam district one of the 23 districts of Andhra Pradesh, located about 100 km. to the west of Ongole and away from the coast. It has a population of 543,957, of which 253,372 are workers. Having a very dry and arid climate, it is a drought-prone area with extensive waste lands and poor agriculture.

Markapur town and its surrounding villages are mainly engaged in the manufacture and supply of writing slates used by small children in primary schools in large parts of the country and in Asia. There are 120 main quarries in Markapur and within a radius of 25 km. covering an area of 4,000 hectares. The slate mines are the main source for raw slate slabs, which are split into thin sheets and cut into various required sizes. The raw slates are then sent to the factories located in and around the town for processing and production of final and finished writing slates. There are 92 slate factories and 320 cottage industries that produce writing slates and on which some 12,340 families are completely dependent. In the process of slate manufacturing from the mines to the factories, thousands of children work in the various stages of the slate industry. In recent times the slates are being increasingly sold in international markets where they are used for decorative purposes. The specific problem of Markapur is its large number of child labourers due to poor socio-economic conditions and because work in slate quarries is the main, and at times, the only source of income for the poor in this area.

The industry in Markapur can be divided into four categories: factories, commercial establishments, cottage units and mines. Payment is on a piece-rate basis and an individual can earn about Rs.25 per day. The child workers in the commercial establishments also work for about 8-9 hours a day and are engaged mainly in activities like polishing, colouring and nailing the wooden frame.

Children employed in mines usually work from 6 a.m. to 1 p.m. and are engaged in carrying the quarried stone. The child workers do not appear on the records of the employers, because the latter are aware that the employment of children is illegal. The children do not receive education; they are exposed to the risk of contracting respiratory diseases and other occupation-related diseases and ailments and most of them suffer from malnutrition, lack of physical and psychological care and attention, unhealthy working conditions, etc.

3. ILO-IPEC Project in Markapur

In October 1999 the ILO-IPEC launched a pilot project for the elimination of child labour in the hazardous slate industry in Markapur, funded by the Department for International Development (DFID) of the Royal Government of the United Kingdom of Great Britain and northern Ireland, the project has an integrated set of 14 different strategies all of which combine to focus on the sustainable weaning away and rehabilitation of the child labourers. The Markapur initiative, called the Integrated Area-Specific Approach against hazardous and exploitative forms of child labour in the slate industry, brought together various solutions to the different converging causes that contributed to child labour in that area.

These interventions of the project can broadly be categorised as:

(i) Mobilisation of government agencies in the district to focus on child labour in the area and provide convergence of state services.

(ii) Mobilisation and sensitisation of target communities, civil society groups and their organisations, employer-employee groups, media, etc.

(iii) Provision of education to the children by establishing transitional education centres (TECs).

(iv) Introducing technology changes; and

(v) Addressing concerns of food insecurity within target families.

4. Impact of the Integrated Area Specific Approach at Markapur

The Integrated Area Specific Approach adopted at Markapur has created an observable impact on child labour in the area. The perception of the community about and its attitude towards child labour has changed. The impact that the project has generated can be divided into five broad categories[1], as discussed below:

(i) Better Utilisation of Existing and New Education Opportunities

The improved utilisation of educational facilities consequent to the launching of the project is reflected in the following trends:

(a) The enrolment rate in the 1st standard in the government-run schools has increased substantially compared to the pre-project situation. This is because the project was successful in mobilising parents to admit children in the age group, 5-7 who otherwise might have remained at home and gradually drifted into work, into government schools.

(b) The drop-out rate in Class V has come down significantly to 6 per cent from 17 per cent within one year. Government-run-*anganwadis* set up for children in the age group, 3-5 are running to packed strength, indicating that the school-going habit among children in the early age group is picking up.

(c) The transitional education centres (TECs), of the IPEC project are currently running with more than its targeted strength. The drop-out rate at these centres is one per cent or less, whereas it was 25 to 30 per cent in the government-run special schools earlier.

(ii) Improvements in the Physical, Psychological, Social and Behavioural Patterns of the Targeted Children

The physical condition of the children studying in TECs (in terms of weight, height, ability to participate in games and incidence of diseases, etc.) is far better than that of those of the same age working in quarries. With the provision of nourishing meals, the introduction of facilities for play and games and the inculcation of good healthy habits in the TECs—the physical condition of children in these centres has attained the level of those of other regular school-going children.

(iii) Improvements in the Community's (Particularly Women's) Understanding of Child Labour and Child-care

The impact of the Integrated Area Specific Approach adopted in Markapur has been felt at three levels:

(a) The practices of women engaged in child care have undergone perceptible changes. They now send their children to TECs and *anganwadis* instead of to work. Health care practices adopted by them for the benefit of children, as also their child-feeding habits have improved.

(b) The convergence of services is seen as an opportunity for enhancing family income. The ongoing Micro Entrepreneurship Development

Programme under IPEC is the first of its kind under which mothers of the rehabilitated children have been trained in entrepreneurship development, thus providing them an opportunity to launch ventures for enhancing the family income.

(c) Networking with an apex body consisting of representatives from all the communities is an innovative example in the action programme for effective participatory action within the community, on child labour.

(iv) Attitudinal Change Among Employers and Workers Organisations

Sensitisation of employers under the IPEC action programme is yielding results. There are two sections of employers in Markapur: the factory/industry owners and the mine/pit owners. The response of the factory owners is more positive and they are exposed to frequent meetings with government officers, enforcement officials, trade unions and NGO representatives. This is reflected in a significant reduction in the employment of children in factories, which is now less than 0.5 per cent compared to 9 per cent one year ago. Furthermore, factory and industry owners have taken a decision to work in the campaign against the use of child labour. The influence of the action programme in the area is also evident in the decision that emerged in tripartite meetings to display "Child Labour Free" boards in front of the factory/mines or any workplace where children are not employed. The commitment of trade unions and workers' associations is evidenced in the meetings, seminars and workshops with grassroot-level leaders and parents, that they hold.

(v) Recognition by Local Government Departments that the Problem of Child Labour is a Core Issue for Them as Well

Convergence of government services is seen in the implementation of departmental programmes in the area, which are aimed at reducing or preventing child labour. There is also an indirect influence of the programmes through the transformation of various sectoral services into actions against child labour. The government's sanction to different services in this area shows substantial improvement both in their number as well as quality during the year. The frequency of official meetings on child labour in recent times is also clearly indicative of the increasing priority given to the issue in official circles.

It is important to understand that the impacts explained above could not have been achieved, if the children targeted under the programme had not been enroled and retained in the TECs, both of which (enrolment and retention) were made possible primarily because of the food security-net that the project provided.

IV. ADDRESSING FOOD SECURITY CONCERNS IN THE IPEC MODEL

1. Causes of Food Insecurity in Markapur and Approaches to Address the Problem

The factors contributing to food insecurity in Markapur are:

(i) Low productivity in agriculture due to scarce cultivable land, frequent drought conditions, etc.

(ii) High seasonal year-to-year variability in food supplies often resulting from unreliable rainfall and insufficient water for crop and livestock production.

(iii) Lack of employment opportunities other than in slate quarries.

The approaches taken towards enhancing food security in the project can broadly be categorised into three broad categories:

(i) The direct interventions that have been adopted by and within the project as a bulwark against food insecurity.

(ii) The indirect interventions that have been adopted beyond the frame of the project (but which are direct outcomes of the project) by government, NGOs and the community.

(iii) Close scrutiny of the existing systems like the Public Distribution System (PDS) and the Integrated Child Development Services (ICDS) Scheme.

The first category of *direct interventions* can itself be divided into two key areas:

(i) Providing a hot cooked meal to the children who are being rehabilitated under the project in its transitional education centres (TEC), and

(ii) Addressing the long-term food insecurity concerns in the target families through providing families (mothers) of the rehabilitated children with sustainable income generation activities, which would provide them with the means to access food on a sustainable basis.

Under the second category of *indirect interventions* four different interventions can be identified. The project does not have any direct components in the fields mentioned below. These interventions, which have resulted indirectly and partly from the project and are not part of the project itself, are:

(i) Increasing food production through farm water control, crop intensification, diversification of production systems and constraints analysis and resolution in the existing farmlands in the area.

(ii) Converting wasteland into cultivable land and enhancing the agricultural operations to produce more food in the area.

(iii) Providing opportunities for non-farming employment in the area.

(iv) Dealing adequately with disaster and taking steps to prevent drought conditions and facilitate agricultural operations.

2. Direct Interventions on Food Security within the Project

(i) Mid-day Meal Scheme

Mid-day meal schemes, as a means of retaining children in schools is not a new concept. Perhaps the best example of the successful operation of such a scheme is provided by the mid-day scheme introduced in schools sponsored by the Tamil Nadu Government more than two decades ago, which has led to a perceptible increase in school attendance, retention and the total literacy levels in the state. In Markapur the nature, quality and quantity of the food being provided is quite different from that in the other divisions of the district. The emphasis is on providing a cooked hot meal with plenty of proteins, vitamins, carbohydrates, minerals and fat.

The nutritive value of the meal provided under the project at noon-time (roughly around 1.00 or 1.30 p.m.) is high. Rice being the staple food in the area and more pleasing to the palate than other foods, is the preferred item both within the house and during the noon-meal at Markapur. At the same time, it is a relatively more expensive item and so within the families *jawar* and *sajja roti* would be provided instead of rice. The mid-day meal under the project consists of rice and a child, on an average, consumes 200 to 250 gms. of rice per meal.

The cost of the one full meal provided in the TECs and the quantity is indicated in Table 1.

Table 1
Cost of One Full Meal Per Child

Item	Quantity (in kg.)	Unit rate per kg. (in Rs.)	Total cost per meal per child (in Rs.)
Rice	0.250	14	3.50
Red gram	0.020	32	0.64
Tamarind	0.010	36	0.36
Dry chillies	0.004	35	0.14
Oil	0.008	34	0.27
Onion	0.005	6	0.03
Spices	0.003	40	0.12
Salt	0.010	2	0.02
Vegetables	-	-	0.80
Milk	-	-	0.80
Total			6.66

The mid-day meal programme is one of the factors that are responsible for the high retention in the TECs. Not surprisingly the health and physical well-being of the children covered under the programme has improved in the first month of the project itself and this encouraged the parents to send their children to school. That the attendance in the TECs during the first month of the programme was lower than that from the second month onwards by about 40 per cent to 45 per cent is indicative of the favourable response of the parents to the scheme.

The corresponding programme in government schools aims at providing children with uncooked raw rice to be taken home at the end of the month on the basis of their attendance. Moreover, with the mid-day meal in these schools consisting of neither pulses nor vegetables its nutrient value is low, making it relatively less attractive both for the child and the family.

What would have been the situation in case a meal had not been provided under the IPEC project? Had this been the case, the initial attraction to send the children to the TECs would have been much lower. Also, retention of the children initially enrolled would have been difficult and instead of there being accretion to the strength of the TECs after the first month of it's running, the reverse would have been the case with the children dropping out from the TECs. Worse still, most of the children would have continued to work, because the parents are neither physically nor economically capable of providing food for them. The predominant feeling of the parents that the income derived out of the child's work will not only feed the child, but also prevent the family from starvation would have continued to hold sway. In effect, the child in such a situation, would have continued to be seen as a burden for the family.

(ii) Economic Empowerment of Families Enabling Them to Sustainably Access Food

Women's limited access to resources and poor purchasing power are the products of a series of interrelated social, economic and cultural factors that force them into performing a subordinate role, which is detrimental not only to their own development but also to that of their children. Women's access to income would improve food security within the household because they tend to spend a significantly higher proportion of their income on food for the family.

A long-term solution to the problem of child labour occasioned by food insecurity is to increase the purchasing power of the families at risk. The project in Markapur has piloted such an intervention, focusing on the mothers of the rehabilitated children seeking to increase the purchasing power of the family by providing additional income opportunities to the mother.

A two-tier training system has been implemented in Markapur, where 40 social workers belonging to ASSIST, the NGO that is executing the project, have been trained to train the mothers to work in micro enterprises. A total of 1200 mothers have been targeted for micro enterprise training of whom 440 have been trained during the last four months. The social workers who train the mothers would provide them escort support to enable them to identify appropriate enterprises, set them up and provide all necessary assistance to them till the enterprise becomes self-sustaining.

The results clearly indicate that, where economic empowerment is provided to a family and particularly to a woman, it would lead to an increase in real and felt food security leading to the elimination of child labour and the enrolment and retention of children in schools.

Another-important tool for the economic empowerment of women that would lead to long-term food security in terms of increased purchasing power for the family, is the formation of self-help groups (SHGs) of the mothers whose children are being rehabilitated under the project. As many as 2500 mothers have been formed into 100 SHGs, each comprising 25 and they have been encouraged to save a nominal amount of Rs.10 per month, the project contributed an amount, which is about seven times the amount saved.

3. Contribution of Indirect Interventions to Food Security

While the Markapur project has a set of 14 defined components, the implementation of these components has led to a series of important outcomes that can in the long term contribute to food security in the area. Four of these are described below:

(i) Increasing Food Production

With the convergence of services from different government departments in Markapur, development of irrigation and drainage systems along with irrigation bore wells and other simple lifting devices are being planned to multiply the farming activities and to increase the yields. Improved methods of agricultural operations including mechanisation, tillage systems, etc. are also being demonstrated and farmers are being educated on their successful application by the agriculture and other departments.

Sustainable intensification of crop production systems such as introduction of new technologies, effective use of high-yielding varieties, improved cultural practices, integrated pest management, credit schemes, etc are under way for better production of food in the area.

(ii) Converting Wasteland to Cultivable Land and Enhancing the Agricultural Operations

Markapur has extensive wastelands. Due to inadequate provisions and poor practices, the lands remained idle for the past many years. With the introduction of minor irrigation techniques and groundwater lifting through bore or tube wells, conversion of these lands to cultivation is under process. Even if all those converted cultivable lands cannot be used for intensive cropping, they can be used to grow fodder or pasture for grazing the animals.

(iii) Providing Opportunities for Non-farm Employment

Activities other than quarrying for writing-slates are gradually improving in the area with the coming up of design slate industries, and the partial mechanisation of quarrying in the Mines. The IPEC action programme also spells the need for more diversified industrial occupations. The convergence of state services aimed at increasing the non-farm employment by exploring avenues for non-hazardous occupations, other than the writing slate industry. Steps are being taken to provide greater opportunities to improve their economic conditions as well as the accessibility to food.

(iv) Taking Adequate Steps to Prevent Disaster and Drought Condition

Most of the area under the project is drought-prone, on which watershed development programmes are being implemented for the last two years, leading to an improvement in the groundwater table and vegetation. Tadivaripalli and Vemulakota villages in the IPEC action programme are the best examples of villages that have witnessed a dramatic improvement in the agricultural operations as well as food production.

4. Analysis of Existing Systems: PDS and ICDS

The Integrated Child Development Services (ICDS) scheme and the PDS in Markapur can be important instruments for enhancing food security provided to the target families in the area.

i) Integrated Child Development Services Network

There is a widespread network of the ICDS scheme in Markapur area. The provision of food to pre-school children up to the age of five through the ICDS network is an essential requirement of food security. In one of the villages under the Markapur project area where there are five TECs with a total of 125 children, it was noticed that one of the outcomes of the enrolment of the older children in schools was a 100 per cent increase in the enrolment of pre-school children in the *anganwadis*.

(ii) Public Distribution and Rationing System Network

The PDS in Andhra Pradesh occupies an important place in the state's economy due to the government's policy of providing the basic food items, particularly rice, at highly subsidised prices. It needs to be mentioned here that the price of rice was increased from 1995 to Rs. 3.50 per kg. The state government had provided rice, the basic food item in the state at a very low price of Rs. 2 per kg. from 1984 to 1989. In Markapur, rice, oil and sugar are being distributed through the PDS network. Due to the absence of fresh enrolment of families into the PDS network for many years, deserving families who are below the poverty line do not get a subsidised ration. As a result, a high percentage of children from these families are working as child labour.

Presently, only about 70 per cent of the target families are covered by the ration system in Markapur, under which there is a maximum limit of 20 kg. of rice per family per month. This leaves a large percentage of families who have to go in for purchases of rice (or other foodgrains) from the open market. Except for rice, oil and sugar, no other food items are supplied by the PDS. Thus, while there is a PDS system in place in Markapur, it is not adequate even for small families, leave alone the larger ones.

V. ELIMINATING CHILD LABOUR THROUGH FOOD SECURITY: LESSONS FROM MARKAPUR

1. Provision of Cooked Meal Even at High Cost Essential for Rehabilitation of Children

The criticality of providing a mid-day meal as an essential element of any programme to rehabilitate child labour in rural areas is clearly borne out from the Markapur approach. The enrolment of children in the TECs and more importantly their retention there, could not, perhaps, have been possible without the attraction of the mid-day meal provided under the project. The meal was an important factor in breaking the practice of using child labour, prevalent among families for generations. The food security that the project provided was the key factor that enabled it to find any acceptance in the local community.

In Markapur, the project provides a hot cooked meal, which is a much greater attraction for the families than a snack or a dry uncooked meal. This is possibly why, the provision of snacks or a dry uncooked meal would not have drawn a similar positive response to the TECs—snacks are cheaper and many similar initiatives elsewhere in the country have provided snacks at Rs. 1-2 a day. A dry uncooked meal would be more expensive than snacks but less expensive than the cooked meal that is provided by the project. It is significant that the cost of the food items in the cooked meal provided under the project is Rs. 6.66 per day per child, which is much higher than what the NCLP project or other similar initiatives provide. There could be a lesson here, namely that in areas where child labour is deeply entrenched, provision of a cooked meal even at a greater cost might be a necessary condition for the rehabilitation of children to be successful and sustainable.

A crucial period for sustaining the rehabilitation of children into the education stream is about the first one year, which is the period when the child, his family and the community are in the process of changing their entrenched thinking on child labour and of understanding the value of education. Without the provision of a cooked meal during this phase, the acceptance by families of education as an alternative to working would be extremely difficult.

It would be interesting to mention here that the experience of children who have been inducted into the mainstream of the school system from the TECs and the confidence of those who have initiated this process that children can be successfully brought into the formal education system indicate that once families are weaned away from the concept that child labour is essential, they tend to accept the continuance of their child in the school, even without the provision of food.

Is there a contradiction here? Apparently two different processes have to be understood to answer this question. Firstly, during the period in which the children are in the TECs there is a conscious and an unconscious adjustment that take place within the family to the situation arising from the drop in incomes when the children stop working. The family, thus, readjusts itself economically and otherwise to survive without the income that was earlier being provided by that child. This can take many forms including cutting down of non-essentials in expenditure. It can also take the form of the family trying to source additional income to make good the decline in the child's income. In the process, the family also learns to live without even small luxuries, like cigarettes, *beedis*, films, expenditure on ceremonies, etc.

The second perception is more interesting as a concept. This is the possibility that food insecurity in many families may be much more a perception of a threat, than a real threat itself. In the socio-economic context within which families live in rural areas the threat of food insecurity is much more frightening than the food insecurity as it actually exists. This means that families send their children to work more out of trying to prevent what they perceive as future food insecurity than to meet a real food need. If this premise is accepted, then it follows that what the mid-day meal programme in the TECs does, is to help the families understand that the present food insecurity can be overcome by adjustments and that the food insecurity in the future can be much better met (particularly for the child) if the child is provided education. Therefore, what the noon-meal is really doing is to break the fear of future food insecurity by providing security of food to the child over the immediate period.

2. Need to Address Long-term Food Insecurity: Concerns of the Family

The second lesson that the project throws up is the need to address the real long-term food insecurity concerns of the family.

The project has attempted to provide long-term purchasing power to the women in the family. The approach has been taken on the premise that the mother in the family when provided with increased purchasing power would spend it on food security needs of the family, rather than on other luxuries or trivialities. Training of mothers on setting up, running and sustaining micro enterprises that would ensure an additional income to the families has been an important aspect of the project. The results seen in the few cases where the mothers have actually set up their own businesses after their training indicate that this strategy could develop into a long-term family focused intervention to increase food security. The mothers who have set up businesses are sending not only the child targeted under the IPEC programme to schools, but also all their other children.

However, the project aimed at providing long-term food security through increasing the purchasing power of mothers has certain drawbacks. Firstly, providing micro enterprise training to mothers on a large scale is a difficult process, as it necessitated thorough planning and execution. It presupposes a strong organisation capable of working in the community, whose social workers can first be trained on micro enterprises as trainers to train the mothers. Since the first results of the micro enterprise training can take some time to materialise, its immediate demonstration value is weak even though its long-term demonstration value can be very high.

It is also not easy to get the consent of the male head of the household in many cases for the mother to attend such training programmes and for her to be running a business in which he might play either a marginal role or no role at all. In Markapur this husband-block was overcome by inviting the husbands also to participate in the training programme on the first one or two days when the purpose behind the training was explained. This first common interaction in the training largely eliminated the fear that the husband might have had of his wife attending a programme outside the home. This early interactivity with the husband also facilitated his full participation in the selection of the business and his full support in its setting up and management.

Thirdly and undoubtedly, the biggest difficulty in this approach is to find the necessary capital for the trained mother to set up her business. Even in a situation as in Markapur where the district administration is fully behind the programme, the credit flow from the government has been cosmetically nominal. There is a need to tap large sources of rural credit for such activities at reasonable interest rates. One emerging source in rural India that can be tapped for this purpose are the micro-credit financing institutions, which can provide the required finance. Andhra Pradesh has at least a couple of excellent micro-credit institutions. The possibility of a non-government micro-credit financing agency being the source of funding, would depend on the relationship between it and the NGO in Markapur, which is now executing the project.

3. Importance of Efficient Public Distribution System

The improvement of the public distribution system is a key factor in any scheme introduced in rural area to provide food security as a means of ending child labour. The Markapur experience shows that a nominal and weak PDS system is one of the factors that contribute to the perpetuation of food security and child labour. The lesson from Markapur is that while the distribution of items like sugar and oil through the PDS may not be particularly important for the target families of child labourers, it essential that the PDS undertakes the distribution of rice in adequate quantities to take care of the full rice requirement of even larger families at prices affordable to them. The imposition of a maximum limit of 20 kg. per family on rice is an effective means of generating food insecurity in the area.

The experience of Markapur, which represents rural India in many ways, therefore, brings home the key lesson of the need to have an efficient public distribution system that can provide the appropriate foodgrains (rice in the case of south India and perhaps wheat in north India) to target families at affordable prices. In the context of the present situation in the country where there is large food surplus with burgeoning food stocks, what would be a constraint is not the domestic availability of foodgrains, but the designing and setting up of an efficient PDS network that can distribute foodgrains at affordable prices across the country.

4. Need to Tap Potential for Community Action to Meet Basic Needs

Markapur has shown that an initiative directed against child labour can lead to indirect outcomes on the use of land and agriculture practices. In this context, the community mobilisation process that the project set in motion empowered the community to identify its needs and, thereafter, make the district administration responsible for meeting them. The visits of *Mandal* and District officials of different departments to the villages under the project provided an opportunity to the community to persuade the government to meet these needs through its schemes. The project generated strengths within the community to be able to identify its basic needs and thereafter enabled them to approach government representatives and urge them to meet their requirements in areas such as crop intensification, water control, diversification of protection systems, all of which lead to increase in food production. The digging of bore wells, tube wells, simple lifting devices, etc. which also have been the outcomes of such community action, would also lead to long-term food production increases in the area. Similarly, pressure was brought to bear on the administration to convert wasteland into cultivable land and to increase the efficiency of agricultural operations to produce more food.

The long-term focus on dealing with disasters in a drought-prone area like Markapur (particularly watershed management) has resulted in improvement in the ground water table and a slow greening of an otherwise arid landscape. Watershed management has led to a dramatic improvement in agricultural operations and food production during the last two years in at least two villages in the target area.

The Integrated Child Development Services (ICDS), also called the *anganwadi* system, is perhaps the largest such network in the country. The *anganwadi* worker is in constant touch with families of young children and mothers. She is a part of the community and it would be interesting to consider whether it would be possible to supply food to families of children at risk of working through the ICDS network. The ICDS network has a greater strength in reaching the target families as compared to the PDS system, which caters to a much broader target group. There is scope for initiatives towards extending food security to child labour families using the *anganwadi* network.

5. Adoption of Holistic Strategy Essential

The Government of Andhra Pradesh is presently implementing a scheme for providing uncooked rice to school-children based on their attendance. The Markapur experience shows that when it is not integrated with other elements as part of a holistic strategy on child labour, the food for education scheme would not, by itself, lead to the ending of child labour.

Finally, the Markapur experience shows that provision of food security itself does not guarantee the elimination of child labour. While food security is an important and necessary condition for ending child labour, it is not a sufficient condition for achieving this objective. The success of Markapur lies as much in the importance that it gives to providing food security directly and to the indirect outcomes that the project has brought about in increasing future supply of foodgrains in the area, as in the integrated set of interventions described above. Any provision of food security as part of a strategy directed at eliminating child labour should be coordinated with a set of other interventions, including community mobilisation, sensitisation, quality education, etc.

VI. ELIMINATING CHILD LABOUR IN RURAL INDIA: SOME RECOMMENDATIONS

Some key recommendations for eradicating child labour in rural India are detailed below:

1. Any scheme for providing food security as a means of ending child labour, cannot be an isolated intervention. The key lesson that emerged from the Markapur experience is that food insecurity is a prime concern amongst families that induces them to send children to work. But providing for food security would not by itself end child labour. Food security would have to be a part of an integrated set of inputs that provide solutions to the

complex variety of problems that necessitate the use of child labour in rural India. It has to be part of a basket of initiatives that address all other causal factors. Accordingly, it would be best to identify the ongoing rehabilitation efforts on child labour and supplement them with inputs on food security. Many such rehabilitation initiatives in the country are supported by the government, international agencies, private and voluntary agencies and it would not be difficult for any initiative towards ensuring food security to work together with them.

2. One of the factors that attract children to education centres is the provision of cooked mid-day meal as in Markapur. The ongoing schemes for rehabilitation of children in the country and particularly the large network of government funded national child labour societies (NCLPs) only provide for a snack. Markapur shows that it is the availability of cooked meal (particularly, rice) that is the chief initial attraction for enrolling and retaining the child in the TECs. Emerging from this lesson, an initiative on food security that could be undertaken is to support the ongoing child labour rehabilitation efforts with supplementary food items in the form of a cooked meal. This provision could be supplemented with the ongoing child labour projects through the NCLPs with requisite support in the form of funding and technical inputs.

   The funding could bridge the gap between what the government scheme now provides for their mid-day snacks and what a cooked meal would cost. Though costs are likely to vary across the country, the IPEC model would be a rough guide to actuals. A cooked meal in Markapur is found to cost Rs. 6.66, while what the government provides for the snack in the NCLPs is Re. 1 per day per child. ILO also has set different meal costs in different projects. The initiative on food insecurity could meet this differential.

   The technical inputs required would include advice on the type of food to be provided, considering the differing availability of food across the country and the eating habits of the people across such areas, the nutritive content of the food, methods of cooking the food economically and without losing its nutritive value. It is important that the technical inputs also include a healthy system of monitoring to ensure that the cooked food reaches the needy children. This latter input is particularly important because in any scheme of this kind and particularly in respect of one for the distribution of cooked food, leakages are likely. A well-developed system of monitoring is imperative, if the cooked meal scheme is to be replicated on any wide scale.

   A pilot programme covering a large number of NCLPs in a contiguous area would be the best entry point in a matter like this. The contiguity of the area would help in testing out monitoring systems over a focused geographical area.

3. The provision of foodgrains in sufficient quantities for families to meet their needs is another area where initiatives on a moderately large scale could be introduced. Such initiatives should be linked to the conditionality that the beneficiary family admits and retains all its children in schools. This would succeed only in areas where there are ongoing rehabilitation efforts by government or other agencies which could be supplemented by this initiative. The input here (sufficient quantities of rice or wheat to the family) would be an additional incentive to the families to what is being already provided by the existing rehabilitation efforts.
4. The key requirement would be to identify areas where an NCLP (or other rehabilitation schemes) is running moderately well and provide the rice or wheat to target families as an insurance against food insecurity. A pilot project conducted after well run pre-intervention status survey would provide results on how the additional foodgrain supplements are impacting on family attitudes, the children's attendance, health, the family's resolve to continue with education and the response of other families in the community. In this case too it would be important for a good monitoring system to be put in place and tested out.
5. In Markapur, the PDS was found to be weak and unable both to reach all the target families and to fully meet the needs of the families. This is almost certain to be the case in most other parts of the country where child labour is endemic. There is a need to strengthen the PDS system in such areas, vis-a-vis families of child labour and families at risk of sending their children to work. Focus areas in the country could be chosen to put in place an add-on element to the PDS where additional foodgrains at ration costs are distributed to meet gaps in the actual requirement of the families and what is being provided by the PDS. This system should also identify eligible child labour families that are now not covered under the rationing system and provide them with the ration foodgrains that they would have got had they been so covered. The system should be highly flexible and capable of working with and through the government channels for foodgrain distribution but without being affected by its present shortcomings.
6. There is also a need to enter into a policy dialogue with the government on foodgrain distribution in child labour endemic areas. This could relate to improving the present PDS in the country and at developing more efficient alternatives for distributing food in rural India. In the context of the ongoing government efforts to end child labour and the articulated policy of the Government of India and many state governments (e.g., Andhra Pradesh) on ending child labour within specific time-frames, such an offer of policy support is likely to be welcomed by the government.
7. Collaboration with the private sector and particularly the corporate sector on aspects of food security is an untested area that could be tried out.

Many corporate houses in the country now have a social agenda and set apart fairly large sums of money for work on their social objectives. It should not be difficult to identify willing corporate partners for the tasks that lie ahead on food security, who may have both ideas and funds for the effort.

8. The Integrated Child Development Services (ICDS) scheme would be a useful network through which information on the issues centring on child labour could be communicated across the country. The ICDS network now covers most parts of the country and reaches out to the communities in a way that is unlike any other network in the country. As such, providing food security as an instrument against child labour could use this wide network for achieving the desired objective.

   The *anganwadi* network can be used as a distribution network for foodgrains, including ration. The ICDS has the capacity to focus exclusively on the target group families to the exclusion of other families. This carries an advantage in providing supplemental food grain support to families of child labour or families at such risk rather than to a very large general target group (as would be the case with general rationing). The Anganwadi worker would also serve as the most effective monitor of whether the children in the target families are in school as they have the additional advantage of being in touch with the child from an early age, when s/he was in the pre-schools of the ICDS. The worker is also in close touch with the mother of the child, having escorted her through her confinement, pregnancy and lactation. An initiative in this direction, on a pilot basis would lead to valuable lessons for replicable interventions.

   The ICDS is now providing nutritional support to children up to the age of five only. But a network like the *anganwadi* can be used, where necessary, to provide nutritional support to children up to the age of 14. Thus, the cooked meal programme in the ongoing rehabilitation schemes for child labour discussed earlier can be delivered through the ICDS system as well, perhaps with greater efficiency and effectiveness.

9. It is true that the *anganwadi* system is over-stretched. But this has to be seen in relation to the personnel provided in an *anganwadi* and the salaries paid to them. Without augmenting its strength and paying a reasonably fair salary to the *anganwadi* worker, the ICDS system that was developed for a particular set of interventions is now being used for many others. However, the system itself is reliable, its network across the country works well, and there is some good infrastructure in place. When an initiative like the present one is added on to the system, it could be done together with additional (wo) manpower and sufficient increases in the compensation package of the *anganwadi* worker, commensurate with the additional responsibilities and work. Clearly, these additionalities should be a part of the package that a pilot project puts in.

10. There is also a need to look at long-term measures for increasing food security in rural India—measures aimed at improving agricultural production such as watershed management, conversion of wastelands, improvement of irrigation facilities, improvement in soil fertility, crop intensification are important to increase local food supplies and augment food security. Efforts in this direction could lead to long-term solutions for food insecurity in rural India, which would be welcomed by state and district administrators.

11. Finally, providing additional income to target families and particularly to the women in the house, to enhance their food purchasing power has emerged as an important lesson from the Markapur experience on child labour,—one that needs to be followed up in all earnestness. In tandem with NCLPs in the country, an initiative could be put in place for training the mothers of the children being rehabilitated in the NCLPs on setting up, running and sustaining micro-enterprises. There are many good entrepreneurship development agencies in the country that focus on women and on micro-enterprise development for such difficult target groups that can collaborate in this endeavour. The Manual that the IPEC programme in India has developed for training mothers of rehabilitated child workers on micro-enterprise development and for training social workers as trainers of such mothers would also be a useful tool in this exercise.

(The views expressed in this paper are those of the writer and need not always be representative of the views of the ILO).

Note

1. These are largely based on observations made by a group of Canadian interns from the CODY University after informal assessments made by them on the project.

References

Census of India (1991), *Economic Tables*, Series-2 Andhra Pradesh, Part III - B Series, Directorate of Census Operations, Andhra Pradesh.

Joseph, M.P. (1998), *IPEC in India 1992-97: Looking Back*, ILO, New Delhi

ILO (1996), *Child Labour: Targeting the Intolerable*, ILO, Geneva.

ILO-IPEC (1999), *Finding Out About Child Labour*, Geneva.

NGDO-EC Liaison Committee (1994), *Food Security Beyond 2000*, European Commission Liaison Committee, Brussels.

World Bank (ND), Quoted in NGDO-EC Liaison Committee (1994), *Food Security Beyond 2000*, European Commission Liaison Committee, Brussels.

United Nations (1998), *UN System in India: Position Paper on Child Labour*, ILO, New Delhi.

22

Coming to Conclusions

LIONEL MASSÜN

The contributors to this volume, have dealt with the linkage between food insecurity and child work from different viewpoints based on their professional background and experience and many of them have arrived at interesting conclusions and made some recommendations for future action. This final section is an attempt at synthesising their most significant inputs, as well as the key points that emerged in the rich discussions that took place during the three day WFP/IHD workshop on the abovementioned subject.

Significant evidence has been accumulated and presented by the contributors to enable them to confirm that in rural India today, food insecurity is a key explanatory factor, even if it is not the sole one, behind the persistent presence of millions of deprived children, be they out-of-school and working, or prone to work.

Indeed, recent statistical data show remarkably similar patterns and trends in the spatial distribution of the incidence of child-work and food insecurity and econometric analysis generally confirms the hypothesis of an interaction between nutritional poverty and child-work with positive and significant elasticities.

All the estimates of child work show a highly positive and significant correlation with negative nutritional indicators like infant mortality rate, underweight babies, wasting and stunting among under five children and chronic energy deficiencies among adults.

I. SOCIAL AND GEOGRAPHICAL COINCIDENCE OF HIGH INCIDENCE OF CHILD WORK

In addition to the above general observation, the analysis of the geographical location of child-work reveals the existence of depressed pockets, where the phenomenon of child work coincides with recurrent periods of food distress and inter-relates with drought, seasonal migrations, environmental degradation, nutritional poverty and adult illiteracy. These are also areas where the percentage distribution of the scheduled caste and scheduled tribe population as well as the percentage of out-of-school children and drop out rates among children, particularly at the upper primary levels, is significantly high.

All the state-level surveys confirm that food insecurity is concentrated largely among the lower caste and class groups and that most households that are food insecure report a higher incidence of child work. The manifold, and mostly unpaid, activities of the children of the poorest rural households are essential to ensure the provision of supplementary food or cash income, which is vital for their survival. As a result, the rural vulnerable households are less prone than others to send their children to school and more likely to put them to work early. Moreover, the children of these households are less likely to develop a positive attitude towards education and less able to concentrate on their studies due to the effects of malnutrition—temporary or permanent. Because of the persistent socio-cultural gender bias, girl-children are disadvantaged in the intra-household distribution of work, food and educational opportunities. As child workers at home or outside, girl-children are often engaged in more tedious work and, when paid, receive lower wages than the boy-children.

II. SEASONALITY, NATURAL DISASTERS AND COPING MECHANISMS

Many landless labourers and marginal farmers are adversely affected by their occupational instability and the uncertainty of their income flows. In addition, while on the one hand, seasonality determines variations in their labour opportunities, as well as price fluctuations, resulting in food shortage or food insecurity for these households, at regular periods of the year, on the other hand, in specific areas, climatic or geological disasters (drought, cyclone, flood and earthquake) not infrequently occur at any time of the year, disrupting agricultural work and reducing or eliminating rural household incomes, thereby occasioning temporarily food-distress situations. These hazards of nature aggravate the food insecurity of these farmers and trigger a feeling of vulnerability among them, which, over time, becomes a permanent attitudinal feature among households affected by these phenomena and a permanent component of the culture of poverty. Faced with an actual situation of food distress or by the recurrent threat of it, most vulnerable households are likely to opt, consciously or by cultural reflex, for several coping mechanisms. Of these, one is seasonal migration and another is the non-enrolment or withdrawal from school of their children, with a view to ensure that they are available for working on domestic or agricultural chores, or in wage labour. One major reason for child work is the household's need for diversifying its sources of income as a strategy to minimize the risk of interruption of the income stream. Lack of parental education and literacy, and the large number of children in the household, generally aggravate this trend.

III. RELEVANCE AND QUALITY OF EDUCATION

Negative judgments by the poorest rural households regarding the quality and relevance of education would seem to be another cause for the existence of large numbers of working and out-of-school children among those categories The analysis by P. Nangia and N. Khan of the data collected in Madhya Pradesh, Orissa and Andhra Pradesh during the last National Health Sample Survey (2001) (Chapter 15) shows that more than 30 percent of the poorest households interviewed, cited the poor quality of the schooling facilities and the irrelevance of the teaching as one of the main reasons for not sending children to school. In many cases, this negative response to schooling can explain the fatalistic acceptance by these households of the impossibility of upgrading the socio-economic status of their children through education. As F. Leclercq (2001) points out in his analysis of the impact of school quality:" school quality is likely to affect education production more than initial enrolment, especially for households who never educated members and lack information on the nature of the schooling process".

IV. THE MIND-SET FACTOR AND CHILD WORK

The approach of UNDP and the MV Foundation (NGO) to the phenomenon of child labour is based on the perception that it results from exploitation, social exclusion and discrimination, and from the false consciousness and wrong mindset of the poor (Burra, 2001). Since the obstacle to the elimination of child work is this wrong mindset, UNDP's "strategy is focussed on social mobilization and community empowerment programmes for getting children out of work and into school". The paper states that although the provision of food, in the form of a mid-day meal, is a component of UNDP's school-bridging projects, it should not be used as an incentive to attract participation and that programmes designed for the elimination of child work should not be based on incentives, as "food and stipends can only reach very few families."

Ignorance and wrong mind-sets being important obstacles in combating child work, the appropriate strategy for eradicating this scourge is to supplement strong action by central and state governments with media campaigns and social mobilization by NGO's, which can contribute effectively towards bringing about the necessary attitudinal change in the poor and the elite regarding child work. But these changes generally occur slowly given the fact that poverty is a painful reality that cannot be eliminated overnight.

Meanwhile, an essential, immediate, objective must be to a) devise and test institutional models of food-based projects, such as NPSNE, which could contribute to the government's efforts in improving the nutritional status of school-age children and b) re-affirm and fulfill, the right of as many rural children as possible to be hunger-free at school as well as the right to food security and education. Notably, two UN agencies (ILO and UNICEF) that have a clear mandate and wide experience in the area of child labour and child protection have adopted a similar approach: "there is also a growing consensus among governments and civil society that if poor families are to choose education over work for their children, special measures and incentives will be needed, and economic incentives that support or compensate families for the loss of income when children go to school rather than work will be required." (ILO/UNICEF 1997)

Moreover, it is noteworthy here that the world leaders assembled at the World Food Summit of 1996 in Rome pledged to "develop within available resources well targeted social welfare and nutrition safety nets to meet the needs of the food insecure, needy people, the children, and the infirm". They further made a commitment to "promote access to, and support for, complete primary education, including, where appropriate, school feeding programmes, with particular attention to children in rural areas and to girls." (World Food Summit, 1996)

V. RELEVANCE AND EFFECTIVENESS OF FOOD ASSISTANCE TO REDUCE CHILD WORK

Properly designed and well implemented school feeding programmes, and particularly, the provision of a balanced cooked mid-day meal, exercise a positive and direct influence on the level of school enrolment, regularity of attendance and retention rate of school age children. Furthermore, school feeding programmes also have a positive impact on the learning capacity and the school performance of children, even though this is difficult to measure. Consequently, they help to minimize, directly and indirectly, the incidence of child work in the rural areas, as it has been widely recognized that, in rural India, out of school children are prone to become, sooner or later, working children. Thus, by increasing school enrolment and ensuring regular attendance of the children, school feeding programmes are effective in preventing some portion of children from falling into the trap of child labour. This is best exemplified in Kerala's success story in eliminating child work and achieving high literacy levels as has been highlighted by K.P. Kannan in his paper (see Chapter 19). He states that the root causes of the remarkable success achieved by the state in eradicating child work were "the premium attached to education of the children, responsive state policies with regard to the spread of education as well as primary health care, and lately, the establishment of a food security system that benefited the children most" and further points out that "a crucial state intervention since the mid-sixties in the form of food security might have played a crucial role in reducing child deprivation in the sense of reducing the proportion of out-of-school children." He adds that "it is quite plausible that those who were out-of-school might have come from poorer families not being able to go to school even when physical access to schooling was ensured."

Indeed, the absorption of food in sufficient quantity and variety should be accepted as a necessity and a right for any child. As they are an invaluable asset for the future of any society, all children should be given priority in the provision of health care and adequate nutrition.

However, notwithstanding the crucial importance of food security at the household level, this does not necessarily guarantee the elimination of all child work. This is because the decision not to send or withdraw children from school, and put them to work, can be attributed to the shortsightedness of their parents. The reason for such a decision may be adverse opinions as to the relevance of education and the quality of schooling, illiteracy of the parents, or the age-old conviction that children must contribute to the household's income, even if hunger is not perceived as an actual threat. As was borne out from the Markapur Experience (Chapter 21), awareness-raising programmes, supplemented by food assistance, contribute in modifying these negative attitudes toward schooling.

VI. CHANNELING FOOD THROUGH SCHOOL

Since current statistical data reveal that the percentage of children enrolled in primary and secondary levels is in excess of 80 per cent, it would seem logical and advisable that school children be the first beneficiaries of the food-assisted programmes or components and that, with a view to maximizing retention rates and ensuring regularity of school attendance, such programmes be implemented in the school premises. The mid-day meal system should be extended to the largest possible extent and its nutritive qualities should be enhanced and checked continuously by the school or village committees and parents associations. For the remaining 20 per cent children not enrolled or not attending school, it would seem necessary to investigate the reason as to why this was the case at the household level and to devise a specific course of action to influence parents to take a positive decision.

Guidelines Suggested for Designing School Feeding Programmes

The various guidelines suggested for designing school feeding programmes are:

- School-feeding programmes can be a valuable instrument for encouraging enrolment and regular attendance, and to a lesser extent, for preventing dropouts. What is important here is the income transfer effect, which needs to be sufficiently high to offset the opportunity costs of child labour.
- The impact is particularly significant in the case of girls as evidenced from studies based in India and elsewhere.
- SFPs work best in borderline communities where poverty is high, but not too high and enrolment levels are low.
- SFPs should be coordinated with other efforts to facilitate access to schooling and improve its quality.
- School feeding can enhance the cognitive function of children by offsetting the effects of short-term hunger.
- SFPs are particularly effective amongst already undernourished children.
- In order to enhance the impact of SFPs, they should be made part of a larger school health and nutrition programme.

VII. SHOULD FOOD-BASED INTERVENTIONS BE AT SCHOOL OR AT THE HOUSEHOLD LEVEL?

The question should not be formulated in terms of either-or. As has been clearly established, in the case of Kerala, interventions against food deficiencies must be targeted simultaneously at the household level (in terms of giving ration cards for below poverty line adults and adequate pension for old age poor) and at the pre-school and school age children.

In view of the importance of the goal of attaining an adequate nutritional status for all school age children and of maximizing their school participation, food assisted programmes should be designed to make use of all possible means and forms of interventions: such as the availability of a morning snack, a hot mid-day meal at school, as well as a take-home dry ration, and special food ration in order to exercise a "positive discrimination" to facilitate and enhance girl-child school enrolment. Unfortunately, because of the costs involved, as also the logistic difficulties in some states, it is not possible to provide all these benefits simultaneously, to all school age children of India.

Due to these limitations, and in order to suit local preferences along caste and ethnic lines, food interventions must be designed with a specific objective in mind and accordingly the choice of approach adopted in each case could vary from region to region and group to group. Clearly, therefore, both the objectives and type of interventions must be determined on the basis of a case by case assessment of needs in each region. A morning snack can offset short-term hunger and impact positively on the child's learning performance, but financially it is not a sufficient incentive to enhance school enrolment and attendance. The provision of a hot mid-day meal on the other hand is considered to be an important initial factor in breaking the practice of child work in families generationally accustomed to it (M.P. Joseph, Chapter 21). In order to be effective, food assistance, in the form of take-home food rations must compensate for the opportunity cost of child work (F. Leclercq and Ute Meir, Chapters 8 and 17). It must also necessarily be linked with bringing the child to school and, if required, out of the work pool necessitating the setting up of an effective implementation and monitoring system.

Food assistance programmes cannot be isolated from the other forms of intervention in favour of the families and the village community, as well from policy measures designed to improve the schooling system K.P. Kannan, Ute Meir and M.P. Joseph (Chapter 19, 17 and 8) have emphasized the need for and the effectiveness of a package of interventions, as against any one intervention, however significant it may be. This is because addressing the overall economic situation of the poor and the long and short-term food insecurity need of the families is a prerequisite for the sustainability of any child labour elimination programme.

VIII. NEED FOR TARGETING SPECIAL FOOD INTERVENTIONS AT THE GIRL CHILD

By adopting the "Time Use Survey" methodology, Indira Hirway (Chapter 5) has been able to show that child work was more important than revealed by official statistics and that, combining activities covered under national income accounts with those not included under it, but covered under General Production Boundary like household maintenance, care of siblings and others and community services, girls contributed much more than boys to the total work in the society, which clearly hampered girls' attendance in school.

On the other hand, several contributors observed that the bias against the girl-child adversely affects her situation in terms of food distribution, household chores, work participation and school participation (S. Deshpande and S. Mahendra Dev & C. Ravi, Chapters 4 and 9). Chaudhri (Chapter 6), remarks that the "proportion of rural girls found in full-time labour is higher than boys for virtually all expenditure classes, from the poorest to the richest." And that "girls from the poorest households drop out at rates at least 50 percent higher than that of boys." At the same time, it is widely accepted that a clear correlation can be established between female literacy and the education of women, and a lower percentage of child work among vulnerable rural households. Ute Meir (Chapter 17) recalls that "girls education is among the most significant strategies to combat poverty and improve living standards in many ways (for example, reduced fertility, maternal and infantile mortality rates, better family health and nutrition)".

Inasmuch as the involvement of the girl child in household chores facilitates the possibility of women earning incomes outside the home, it is generally more important to compensate the household for the opportunity cost of girl child work than that of boys. The scheme of intervention proposed to enhance girls school enrolment and avoid early drop-out carries a special incentive, in the form of an individual and sufficient dry food ration per girl enrolled and regularly attending school. In addition, alternative measures are proposed (S. Deshpande and Mahendra Dev & C. Ravi, Chapters 4 and 9) as a substitute for the time-consuming services which the girl-child is urgently required to perform, such as the provision of water and fuel in the immediate proximity of each rural household and alternative arrangements for the care of the siblings (*anganwadis* and mobile creches).

The need to focus on the girl child commands unanimous support, because of the fact that in order to break the inter-generational cycle of hunger, in which young uneducated rural mothers are the weakest link, special programs have to be designed for the girl child. However, a caveat was expressed concerning the excessive use of positive discrimination" mechanisms in favour of the girl child: international experience has shown that occasionally, successes achieved with policies aimed at retaining girls in school have proved to be detrimental for boys school attendance.

IX. FOOD DISTRESS SITUATION AND SEASONALITY

The section on the profiles of vulnerable states reveals the importance of the incidence of seasonal food distress rather than food insecurity that prevails during the whole year. One conclusion that emerges is that it is of the utmost importance to adjust the school calendar at the district level, to the seasonal rhythm of agricultural tasks in order to ensure that children: (a) could be assured of a cooked meal during the lean season and (b) be less prone to drop out of school during the peak period of agricultural work

Even if all the family-oriented food assistance programmes are not equally successful, or even conclusive, it is essential that they are continued with an improved design and better mechanisms of distribution. This underscores the need for mapping, with much greater precision, the areas or pockets (at district or even block level) of highly vulnerable rural households. Another conclusion is that food-based interventions should be designed by using micro-planning techniques on the basis of the answers to the following questions: (a) Does the selected population need food interventions in the first place ? (b) What do they need? (c) Who should deliver it? (d) How should it be delivered?

Further, the programme should be designed and implemented with the involvement and active participation of the stakeholders themselves and continued for a minimum period of four to five years to ensure that the vicious cycle of food insecurity-child work is broken.

X. FOOD CREDIT SCHEMES AND CHILD WORK

Besides the government's mainstream employment and income-generation programmes and the PDS and ICDS and food for work schemes, an additional step towards meeting the food requirements of the vulnerable rural households in the food insecure districts of the country could be to devise and launch appropriate and sustainable food credit programmes in order to ensure food security for them all the year round. Food credit programmes can be seen as a potential supplementary strategy in combating child work, as food insecurity of the poorest households is mostly seasonal and children are pushed into the labour force during distress periods or when there is a perceived threat of food insecurity. Hence there is a need for food off take on a credit basis for a short period, during the lean agricultural season. P. Sharma, Aodiiti Mehta and Pedro Medrano (Chapter 20) have proposed that a sound programme of food credit could be operationalised by mobilising food insecure families into self-help groups preferably of women, that would have to be endowed with the capital and know-how to form a food bank. In order to improve the working of the food credit scheme, adequate safeguards must be devised to respond to the contingencies of crop failure, pest attack, etc. through group insurance and crop insurance, so as to avoid their falling into the debt trap.

XI. SUGGESTIONS FOR ACTION-ORIENTED RESEARCH

In the near future, in order to fine tune the targeting of food assistance programmes against child work, a fair amount of research needs to be done on the relationship between food insecurity, child work and schooling, and a full-fledged database on the issue is still to be developed. In particular, as observed by several contributors, further research is required on the evaluation of the food-assisted programmes, their impact and their sustainability, with special emphasis on the regional variations in respect of the social, cultural and geographical contexts. The following aspects deserve special attention:

(i) More detailed research of a sociological and psychological nature to verify parental motivations for non-enrolment, school dropout and irregularity of attendance and anti-school attitude in general;

(ii) More detailed information on the mechanisms required by the poorest rural population to cope with problems arising from food insecurity and food distress situations;

(iii) Research information at the village level on the structure of power and vested interest groups which can constitute stumbling blocks with conservative position towards schooling for the poor, and issues of child-work in the poorest families;

(iv) Research on the handicaps and types of discrimination suffered at school level by children of lowest castes and classes that explain higher rates of out-of-school children and dropouts among these categories;

(v) As food distress is often seasonal, seasonality has a very important bearing on rural child work, so that any food assisted programme designed to combat child work will have to be carefully "season-tailored" and adjusted in each region/district/taluka to the agricultural calendar;

(vi) As school enrolment, retention and drop- out phenomena follow a caste-based pattern, information on local caste distribution will be crucial to efficient implementation of school feeding programmes for the benefit of all the targeted families, without exclusion.

References

Burra, N. (2001), "Child Labour, Poverty and Development: UNDP's Approach to Child Labour Elimination", Paper presented at the *IHD-WFP Workshop on Food Insecurity and Child Work,* New Delhi, March 15-17.

ILO/UNICEF (1997), *Strategies for Eliminating Child Labour: Removal and Rehabilitation,* Synthesis Document presented at the International Conference on Child Labour, Oslo, Norway, Oct 1997

Leclercq, F. (2001), "Patterns and Determinants of Elementary School Enrolment and Child Work in Rural North India," Paper presented at the *IHD-WFP Workshop on Food Insecurity and Child Work,* New Delhi, March 15-17.

World Food Summit (1996), *Plan of Action,* Objective 2.2C.

Notes on Contributors

Antony, Piush is currently a Visiting Fellow at the Institute for Human Development, New Delhi. She holds an M.Phil in Applied Economics from the Centre for Development Studies, Thiruvananthapuram. She has earlier worked as Research Associate at the Gender Studies Unit of the National Institute of Advanced Studies, Bangalore. Her areas of interest include decentralisation, women and development, food economy, child labour, informal sector workers and migration. She has conducted studies and published articles on the above themes. She has co-edited a book on Social and Economic Security in India.

Bhattacharyya, Dipayan is currently with the Technical Support Unit in the UN World Food Programme, India Country Office at New Delhi. He is working in the development sector for the last one decade. Prior to joining UNWFP, he worked in NRDMS (Department of Science and Technology, GOI), Indo-Dutch Rural Water Supply and Sanitation Programme and ORG Centre for Social Research. He has been associated with food security analysis, natural resource management, geographic information systems and water-sanitation with special thrust on quantitative and qualitative analyses.

Chaudhri, D.P. has been with the University of Wollongong since 1990. Prior to this, he was Professorial Fellow and Director, Agricultural Economics Research Centre, University of Delhi (1987-90). He has done contract research work for FAO & ILO, UNICEF and the World Bank and has been a consultant to various national and international organisations. His earlier academic appointments were at the Australian National University (Senior Research Fellow and Programme Director, Graduate Studies in Development Economics 1979-86), University of New England (Senior Lecturer, 1971-78), Lecturer, Delhi University 1960-71) and University of Chicago (Post-Doctoral Research Fellow 1968-69). His special interest, reflected in published research papers, research reports, monographs and books, has been in Development Economics & Policy with special reference to the Economics of Education, Labour Productivity and

Rural Development. His major books include *Indian Agricultural Policy at The Cross- Roads* (co-editor); *A Dynamic Profile of Child Labour in India (1996); Agricultural and the Development Process* (1985) (co-author); *Rural Development and the State* (1983) (co-author); *Education, Innovations and Agricultural Development* (1979). His current work is focussed on: *The Sources of Modern Economic Growth in Contemporary Asia, with special reference to Gender Bias in Education*; *Economics of Child Labour and Equity Driven Trade Policy Strategies for Agricultural Development.*

Daly, Gerald is currently working as Programme Advisor in the UN World Food Programme, at New Delhi. He is a Masters graduate from the Fletcher School of Law and Diplomacy in Boston, USA and holds a BA degree from Trinity College, Dublin, Ireland. In 1986, he started his professional career in Sudan with an Irish NGO (GOAL) that specializes in refugee health care. Prior to joining UNWFP, he worked in UNHCR with Ethiopian and Mozambican refugees. Mr. Daly has published articles ranging from emergency management, to the impact of anthropology research. Currently, his main area of interest is finding the wisest way to move from analysis to action.

Dash, Bal Paritosh is currently with the Technical Support Unit of the UN World Food Programme, India Country Office at New Delhi. He is also a doctoral fellow in the Department of Economics, Center for the Study of Regional Development, Jawaharlal Nehru University, New Delhi. As a professional, he has been working for projects on poverty, food security, social security in slums and child work and on contemporary developments in the development sector. Prior to joining UNWFP, he worked for the IDPAD project on the Integrated Development of Delhi and its Periphery and an ICCSR project on *Journal of Abstracts and Reviews*. In WFP, he has been associated with projects on food security analysis, vulnerability analysis and mapping and disaster management.

Deshpande, Sudha is currently a Senior Visiting Fellow at the Institute for Human Development. Retired as a Reader in Demography from the Department of Economics, University of Mumbai, she has a Diploma in Demography from the International Institute for Population Sciences, Mumbai and a Doctorate in Economics from the University of Bombay. She collaborated with her husband and colleague on projects relating to labour markets and urban issues sponsored by the International Labour Office, Geneva and its affiliates in Delhi, the ARTEP and SAAT. She has carried out two studies of slums in Mumbai for the Ministry of Human Resource Development and the University of Derby, U. K., held the Wibau Chair in Urban Economics at the Amsterdam Study Centre for Metropolitan Environment, University of Amsterdam. She has published, jointly two working papers, and many articles in the *Indian Journal of Labour Economics* and *the Economic and Political Weekly*. Her special areas of interest are migration, employment and unemployment, particularly of women, gender discrimination and child labour.

Gumber, Anil is a Senior Economist at the National Council of Applied Economic Research, New Delhi. He was awarded a Ph.D. from Gujarat University, Ahmedabad and Post-Doctoral Takemi Fellowship from Harvard

School of Public Health, Boston. Dr. Gumber's research papers have focused on issues relating to human development including migration, resettlement, poverty, employment, education, health and nutrition. He is the author of *Displaced by Development: Oustees of an Irrigation Project* and co-author of *Inter-Village Differences in Social Overheads and Their Correlates in Matar Taluka.*.

Gupta, D.B. is currently Senior Consultant at the National Council of Applied Economic Research (NCAER), New Delhi and Visiting Professor, Institute for Human Development. Prior to this assignment he was Director, Population Research Centre at the Institute of Economic Growth, Delhi. He has worked extensively in several areas including population, health and nutrition.

Hirway, Indira is currently Director and Professor of Economics at the Centre for Development Alternatives, Ahmedabad. Earlier, she was at the Mahatma Gandhi Labour Institute, Ahmedabad. As a development economist she has done extensive research work in the areas of poverty and employment, labour market structures, environment and development, environmental accounting, gender and development. She has been associated with several national and international committees and expert groups in these areas. She has a number of books and research articles published in Indian and foreign journals to her credit. In the field of child labour she has contributed several papers on the constraints and problems of child labour and has co-edited a book entitled *Towards Eradicating Child Labour in the World.* Prof. Hirway headed the Technical Committee on the Pilot Time Use Survey, which was set up by the Dept. of Statistics, Government of India to develop a conceptual framework and methodology of conducting time use surveys.

Joseph, M.P. has been working in the area of child labour for about 15 years. He has been with the International Labour Organisation (ILO) since 1992, and has been piloting their International Programme on the Elimination of Child Labour (IPEC) in India. From November 2000, he has been managing the IPEC project against child labour in Andhra Pradesh. Working closely with the government and other partners, he has developed and piloted a host of strategies for ending child labour in the country. His work has influenced government policies and programmes on child labour across the country. He holds a postgraduate degree both in Physics from the University of Cochin, India and in Human Resources Development from the Victoria University of Manchester, UK. A former member of the civil service in India, he has worked as Commissioner of Labour in Kerala, District Executive Magistrate of Ernakulam district, Kerala and Mayor of Cochin.

Kannan, K.P. is Fellow and Indian Planning Commission Chair Professor of Development Economics at the Centre for Development Studies, Thiruvananthapuram, Kerala, India. He is the author of several books including of *Rural Proletarian Struggles: Mobilization and Organization of Rural Workers in South West India* (OUP, 1988, 1989) and is co-author of *Urban Labour Market Structure and Job Access in India: A Study of Coimbatore* (International Institute for Labour Studies, Geneva, 1990). Currently he, along with S Mahendra Dev and Nira Ramachandran is editing a volume on *Food Security in India* (forthcoming). His research contributions cover a wide range of topics related to development, including agriculture, poverty and human development, labour studies, social security, health and political economy of development. He was Professor of Development Studies and Research Co-ordinator at the Cambodia Development Resource Institute, Phnom Penh, Cambodies during 1995-97. He is closely associated with national and international development organisations including the ILO, UNESCAP and the UNDP as an external expert.

Karan, Anup K. is currently working as a Fellow in the Institute for Human Development (IHD), New Delhi. His primary area of interest includes poverty, employment, human development and their interlinkages and he has worked intensively on these issues in rural Bihar and Jharkhand. Presently he is associated with the preparation of the Bihar Development Report for the Planning Commission, Government of India. He has also been closely associated with several other research projects sponsored by the Government of India as well as other national and international agencies. The important research reports authored by him include *Dynamics of Employment, Poverty and Human Development in Rural Bihar; Levels of Livelihoods in Jharkhand*, and *Labour Market Flexibility in India*. He has also published a number of research papers in various journals and books of repute.

Kaul, Venita is Senior Education Specialist at the World Bank since 1998. Prior to joining the Bank she was Professor and Head of Department of Preschool and Elementary Education at the NCERT, which is a premier institution at the national level set up by the Government of India to advise the ministry on all stages of education. She was also a National Coordinator of an Early Childhood Education project in 12 states of the country. A doctorate in Psychology from the Indian Institute of Technology, Delhi, she has written extensively on various themes in the areas of early childhood development and early primary education in the Indian context and has several books and papers to her credit. Her primary interest lies in advocating the promotion of a child-centered, pressure-free and active learning approach to the education of young children. She has been an active spokesperson for the adoption of such an approach in various fora, both at national and international levels.

Khan, Nizamuddin is a Research Officer in the National Family Health Survey (NFHS-2), a project undertaken by the International Institute for Population Sciences, Mumbai, in technical collaboration with ORC Macro, Maryland, USA and East-West Center, Hawaii, USA, and sponsored by the United States Agency for International Development (USAID). After completing his Master of Population Studies (MPS) Mr. Khan has been working in different areas of demographic research. His work is mainly related to on fertility, family planning, urbanization, reproductive health, domestic violence, and child labour.

Kumar, Dalip holds a Ph.D. in Economics from Patna University and is working as a Consultant in the National Council of Applied Economic Research (NCAER), New Delhi. He is currently working on diverse issues related to health, labour and other social issues. Earlier, he has worked in several institutions such as V V Giri National Labour Institute, Institute for Human Development, etc.

Leclercq, François is a Ph.D student at the Université de Paris I (Sorbonne) which is affiliated with the Centre for Human Sciences (CSH), Delhi. His work focuses on the determinants of schooling and the quality of elementary school system.

Mahendra Dev, S. is currently the Director of the Centre for Economic and Social Studies, Hyderabad. He holds a Ph.D from the Delhi School of Economics and post-doctoral degree from Yale University, USA. He was a faculty member at the Indira Gandhi Institute of Development Research, Mumbai for 11 years and has written extensively on themes such as agricultural development, poverty and public policy, food security, employment guarantee schemes, social security and farm and non-farm employment. He has been a consultant to many international organisations like the UNDP, World Bank, International Food Policy Research Institute, ESCAP and has also worked as a member in various committees set up by the Government of India.

Majumdar, Poushali, a Ph.D. from the University of Rajasthan, is presently working in the in the National Council of Applied Economic Research, (NCAER), New Delhi and is associated with its Human Resource Development Division. A socio-medical anthropologist, she has been working in the area of reproductive health as well as on women and child- related issues for the past several years.

Massun, Lionel is currently a Consultant with the World Food Programme (WFP). After obtaining a Law Doctorate and a Master's Degree in Social Development at the U.C.L, Louvain, Belgium in 1965, he spent a year teaching in a secondary school in Buta, Democratic Republic of Congo. This was followed by a four year period teaching sociology and conducting in research activities on the peasant movement in Colombia, for the National University of Colombia (Bogota). Later, he joined the UN and worked with the International Labour Organisation (ILO). In the context of his management functions at the ILO Office for Central America, and later, as the Director of the ILO Office in Mexico, he has been constantly involved in the formulation, implementation and evaluation of ILO's programmes for the poorest segments of the rural population in several Latin American countries. In Mexico, in particular, he launched an important UNDP funded programme, for the benefit of the indigenous populations of the drought-prone areas of the State of Oaxaca, by enhancing livelihoods and promoting community empowerment, through the self-construction of water harvesting infrastructure and income generating activities. As the ILO Representative for India and Bhutan until November 1999, his first priority was the supervision of the ILO International Programme for Elimination of Child Labour (IPEC) in India. He also started research and technical co-operation activities in the informal sector, with a focus on rural women in Gujarat.

Mathur, Ritu is currently with the Programme Coordination Unit in UN World Food Programme, India Country Office at New Delhi. She has been associated with the WFP for the last one decade in different capacities and has worked in the fields of monitoring and evaluation, food security analysis and mapping.

Medrano, Pedro has been the WFP Representative and Country Director of the WFP in India, since January 1999. Prior to this assignment, he was Chile's Ambassador to FAO, IFAD and WFP, based in Rome. He also served as Chairman of the Committee on World Food Security, which was responsible for preparing the World Food Summit that took place in Rome in 1996.

Mehtta, Aodiiti is currently the Executive Director of the Rashtriya Mahila Kosh, an agency under the control of the Department of Women and Child Development of the Government of India that offers micro-credit to women's self help groups. She belongs to the Indian Administrative Service and has over two decades of field experience in Rajasthan, especially in the areas of poverty alleviation, health, nutrition and literacy. She was a Mason Fellow at Harvard University, USA during 1993-94 and was awarded the Litteaur Prize during her stay there for her work on female literacy.

Meir, Ute is Chief of the UNESCO/WFP Co-operative Programme at UNESCO in Paris. For the last 10 years she has worked on issues relating to the use of food assistance in education, through work on operational field projects and policy development. Her main areas of interest have been school feeding, particularly the monitoring and evaluation of such programmes and their contribution to the decentralisation of education, as well as the rehabilitation of education systems in post-emergency situations. Very recently, she has been engaged in the study on the role of food assistance in promoting girl's and women's education. She is co-author of the WFP/UNESCO/WHO School Feeding Handbook and has contributed several other reports and articles in her field of work.

Nangia, Parveen is a Reader at the International Institute for Population Sciences, Mumbai. He is also the Coordinator of the National Family Health Survey (NFHS-2), which is designed to provide national and state level estimates of demographic, health and social parameters. During the past two decades Dr. Nangia has been engaged in considerable research on child labour. After completing his Ph.D. on this topic he did a study for UNICEF on working and street children in Delhi. He has also worked in many other areas of social research, mainly international migration, fertility and family planning, child nutrition, population and environment, and gender issues. He has several publications to his credit which include two books on child labour entitled *Child Labour: Cause-Effect Syndrome* (1987) and *Working and Street Children in Delhi* (1992).

Prakash, Aseem is a Visiting Fellow at the Institute for Human Development, New Delhi. He has earlier worked on issues related to gender and development for the Unit for Women's Studies, Tata Institute of Social Sciences, Mumbai. He was also involved in research on various aspects of child labour in his capacity as Research Consultant to the ILO. Presently, he is working as Principal Resource

Person on Governance for the Bihar Development Report being prepared by the Institute for Human Development, New Delhi, for the Planning Commission.

Raj, Nikhil is presently an Associate Fellow and Co-ordinator of the National Resource Center on Child Labour at the V.V. Giri National Labour Institute, Noida. He is also the Associate Editor of the *Indian Journal of Labour Economics*. He holds an M.Phil in Economics from the Jawaharlal Nehru University, New Delhi and has completed a number of projects for UNICEF, ILO and the World Bank. He has written extensively on child labour, food security, and farm and non-farm employment. His areas of research include natural resources management, child labour, food security and areas pertaining to investment and business decisions.

Ramachandran, Nira is a Development Consultant and Senior Visiting Fellow at the Institute for Human Development, New Delhi. Prior to this, she was engaged in post-doctoral research on sustainable development as an ICSSR Senior Fellow at the Lal Bahadur Shastri National Academy of Administration, Mussoorie, where she also spent two years as the Co-ordinator, Centre for Sustainable Development. Her previous appointments were as CSIR Senior Fellow, Delhi University; Assistant Professor, Department of Geography, Bangalore University and Research Fellow, Indian Institute of Management, Bangalore. She holds a Ph.D in regional development from the Jawaharlal Nehru University, New Delhi and has received training at the Institute for International Studies and Training, Fujinomiya, Japan. She has lectured extensively and conducted training programmes in the areas of food security, environmental sustainability, primary education and project management. She has several publications to her credit including a book entitled *Monitoring Sustainability: Indices and Techniques of Analysis* (2000) and *Carrying Capacity of Mussoorie* (co-author) forthcoming. She has also worked as Consultant for International Organisations like the FAO and is EDI Fellow of the World Bank.

Ravi, C. works with the Government of Andhra Pradesh and is presently a Visiting Fellow at the Centre for Social and Economic Studies, Hyderabad. He has worked extensively in the areas of food security, nutrition, etc., and has several publications to his credit on these themes.

Saravanan, V.S., currently with the National Council of Applied Economic Research (NCAER), New Delhi, has received interdisciplinary training from universities both within and outside India. He specialises in community-based management of irrigation systems, and watershed management and women and child development in India.

Satpathy, Anoop K. is a Senior Research Scholar at Jawaharlal Nehru University, New Delhi. He holds a M.Phil in Economics from JNU, New Delhi and has earlier worked in the V.V. Giri National Labour Institute, NOIDA. His areas of research pertain to agricultural and rural development, food security and nutrition, child labour and employment issues.

Sharma, Pravesh is on deputation with the UN World Food Programme Country Office at New Delhi from the Indian Administrative Service since July 2001. He has worked on various assignments with the State Government of Madhya Pradesh for the last two decades and in the Prime Minister's Office in New Delhi for the last two years. He has been associated with poverty alleviation, food and agricultural programmes for several years and has written extensively on these subjects. He has been a Visiting Fellow at Princeton University, USA where he has worked on food policy issues.

Spitz, Pierre graduated from the National Institute of Agriculture (INA, Paris) in Agricultural Economics. He was Research Fellow at the Indian Statistical Institute, Calcutta from 1962-63, and thereafter, Adviser to the Ministry of Planning in Tunisia, and Research Fellow at MIT and Harvard University. After co-directing the Food Systems and Society Programme at UNRISD (Geneva), he was Research Coordinator of the Independent Commission on International Humanitarian Issues (Geneva), and from 1989 to 1998, Director of the Office of Evaluation and Studies, IFAD (Rome). As Director of Research (Economics), National Institute of Agricultural Research (INRA, Paris), his areas of teaching and research related to development issues, the right to food and evaluation methodology. A Harkness Fellow, he received an FAO Andre Mayer Award in 1974, and is presently a Fellow of the World Academy of Art and Science. His numerous writings include *The Roots of Catastrophe.* with R. Garcia (Pergamon Press, 1986).

Wilson, E.J. is Senior Lecturer in the Department of Economics, University of Wollongong, Australia and Co-ordinator of the Honours Programs in Economics and Econometrics. His recent research work includes economic modelling and empirically estimating the determinants of productivity and economic growth. He has been working closely with national and international planning and policy agencies including the Australian Council for International Research (ACIAR), Canberra, the Indian Council for Agricultural Research (ICAR), the National Centre for Agricultural Economic Policy Research (NCAP), the Institute of Development Studies - Jaipur (IDSJ) and the Indian Council for Social Science Research (ICSSR), in India. He has several papers and a book entitled *Economics Web Based Resources and Instructors Manual* to his credit.

Abbreviations

ALC	:	Active Learning Capacity
ANM	:	Auxiliary Nurse Midwife
ANP	:	Applied Nutrition Programme
ASWPRs	:	Age Specific Work Participation Rates
AWCs	:	Anganwadi Centres
AWW	:	Auxiliary Women Worker/Anganwadi Worker
BIMARU	:	Bihar, Madhya Pradesh, Rajasthan, Uttar Pradesh (including Chattisgarh, Jharkhand, Uttarakhand)
BPL	:	Below Poverty Line
CARE	:	Co-operative for American Relief Everywhere
CBOs	:	Community Based Organisations
CDS	:	Current Daily Status
CGC	:	Community Growth Chart
CMIE	:	Centre for Monitoring Indian Economy
CMR	:	Child Mortality Rate
CPWC	:	Composite Programme for Women and Children
CRS	:	Catholic Relief Services
CSO	:	Central Statistical Organisation
DEVEX	:	Development Expenditure
DFID	:	Department for International Development
DNP	:	District Nutrition Profile
DPAP	:	Drought Prone Areas Programme
DPIP	:	District Poverty Initiative Project
FAO	:	Food and Agriculture Organisation
FCI	:	Food Corporation of India
FCS	:	Food Credit Scheme
FFW	:	Food for Work

FIARI	:	Food Insecurity Atlas of Rural India
FISM	:	Food Insecurity with Hunger Moderate
FISS	:	Food Insecurity with Hunger Severe
FISWH	:	Food Insecurity Without Hunger
FYP	:	Five Year Plan
GCA	:	Gross Cropped Area
GCUD	:	Gram per Consumption Unit per Day
HYVP	:	High Yielding Varieties Programme
ICDS	:	Integrated Child Development Scheme
ICMR	:	Indian Council of Medical Research
ICRISAT	:	International Centre for Research in Semi Arid Tropic
IFA	:	Iron and Folic Acid
IFPRI	:	International Food Policy Research Institute
IIPS	:	International Institute for Population Sciences
ILO	:	International Labour Organisation
IMR	:	Infant Mortality Rate
IPEC	:	International Programme on the Elimination of Child Labour
IRD	:	Integrated Rural Development
IRDP	:	Integrated Rural Development Programme
ITDP	:	Integrated Tribal Development Project
LBW	:	Low Birth Weight
MDMS	:	Mid-day Meal Scheme
MMR	:	Maternal Mortality Rate
MPCE	:	Monthly Per Capita Consumer Expenditure
MPHDR	:	Madhya Pradesh Human Development Report
MSP	:	Minimum Support Price
MSSRF	:	MS Swaminathan Research Foundation
NCAER	:	National Council of Applied Economic Research
NCERT	:	National Council of Educational Research and Training
NCLPs	:	National Child Labour Projects
NFE	:	Non Formal Education
NFHS	:	National Family Health Survey
NGDO		Non-Government Development Organisation
NGOs		Non-Government Organisations
NIN	:	National Institute of Nutrition
NIPCCD	:	National Institute of Public Cooperation and Child Development
NNMB	:	National Nutritional Monitoring Bureau
NPNSPE	:	National Programme for Nutritional Support to Primary Education
NPSNE	:	National Programme of Nutrition Supply to Primary Education

NSA	:	Net Sown Area
NSDP	:	Net State Domestic Product
NSS	:	National Sample Survey
NSSO	:	National Sample Survey Organisation
OLS	:	Ordinary Least Square
ORG	:	Operation Research Group
PCA	:	Primary Census Abstract/Principal Component Analysis
PDS	:	Public Distribution System
PILER	:	Pakistan Institute for Labour Education & Research
PPE	:	Poverty Population Growth and Environment Degradation
PRA	:	Participatory Rural Appraisal
PROBE	:	Public Report on Basic Education
PSE	:	Pre-school Education
PSU	:	Primary Sampling Unit
RDA	:	Recommended Dietary Allowances
RGMWD	:	Rajiv Gandhi Mission for Watershed Development
RHCP	:	Rural Head Count Poverty
RMK	:	Rashtriya Mahila Kosh
RPDS	:	Revamped Public Distribution System
RWAGE	:	Rural Wage Rate
SCF	:	Save the Children Fund
SDP	:	State Domestic Product
SEBCOM	:	Socio-economic & Business Consultancy
SEWA	:	Self Employed Women's Association
SFPs	:	School Feeding Programmes
SHGs	:	Self-help Groups
SLI	:	Standard of Living Index
SNA	:	System of National Accounts
SNP	:	Supplementary/Special Nutrition Programme
TECs	:	Transitional Education Centres
TFP	:	Total Factory Productivity
TNNP	:	Tamil Nadu Nutrition Programme for Pre-school Children
TPDS	:	Targeted Public Distribution System
TUS	:	Time Use Survey
UNDP	:	United Nations Development Programme
UNESCO	:	United Nations Educational, Scientific and Cultural Organisation
UNICEF	:	United Nations International Children's Emergency Fund
VVGNLI	:	V V Giri National Labour Institute
WFP	:	World Food Programme
WPRs	:	Work Participation Rates

Index